The
Secret
History
of
Gender

Women,
Men, and Power
in Late Colonial
Mexico

Steve J. Stern

THE UNIVERSITY OF NORTH CAROLINA PRESS

Chapel Hill & London

The
Secret
History
of
Gender

© 1995

The University of

North Carolina Press

All rights reserved

Manufactured in the

United States of America

The paper in this book meets the guidelines for

permanence and durability of the Committee on

Production Guidelines for Book Longevity of the

Council on Library Resources.

Library of Congress

Cataloging-in-Publication Data

Stern, Steve J., 1951–

The secret history of gender : women, men, and

power in late colonial Mexico / Steve J. Stern.

  p. cm.

Includes bibliographical references and index.

ISBN 0-8078-2217-5 (alk. paper)

1. Sex role — Mexico — History. 2. Power (Social

sciences) — Mexico — History. 3. Rural women —

Mexico — Social conditions. 4. Peasantry —

Mexico — History. 5. Mexico — Social conditions.

I. Title.

HQ1075.5.M6S74   1995

305.3′0972 — dc20   94-39349

CIP

99 98 97 96 95   5 4 3 2 1

For Florencia, Ramón Joseph, and Ralph Isaiah

Contents

MAPS

Preface and Acknowledgments

This book is a historical study of the relationships between gender and power in Mexican popular culture. The historical research is anchored in the late colonial period (ca. 1760–1821), and I present a portrait of an era rather than a study of change over time. Especially in the concluding section, however, I also pursue a dialogue with more recent Mexican history, with long-term questions of continuity and change, and with theory.

In this book I pursue three main themes. First, I study social relations of gender, in the vast bottoms of the color-class pyramid, as a conflictual arena of power, ambivalence, and mediation. I argue that subaltern women and men engaged in bitter, sometimes violent struggles over gender right and obligation, and developed distinctive and contending models of legitimate gender authority. In their conflicts and mediations, subaltern women and men created a world of contested patriarchal pacts. Second, I study the gendered dynamics of political culture in subaltern life. Here I argue that deep interplay and parallelism marked the languages of legitimate and illegitimate authority associated with "gender culture" (arenas of domestic and familial power) and the languages of legitimate and illegitimate authority associated with "political culture" (arenas of community and state power). The gendered foundations of political life also illuminate the strategies of mediation peasants used to bridge their own political contradictions. Third, I study the problem of regionalism and ethnocultural variation. Here I argue that comparative regional analysis enables us to apply our main findings on gender and power at a supraregional level while taking into account regional idiosyncrasies. This is in part because local twists that serve to differentiate between regions also occurred at the microregional level within regions.

Taken as a whole, these arguments add up to a picture of gendered life in Mexico as an arena of cultural argument that laid a certain foundation for understandings of authority and power in general, not simply at the familial, domestic, and neighborhood levels of society. In the conclusion I also consider the ways that findings originally formulated in a Mexican context may have a certain paradigmatic value for the historical study of gender and politics in other societies, including Western societies.

This book has four parts. Part 1 introduces the central issues and questions at stake, provides a feel for the human dramas that animate the book, and offers contextual and theoretical background. Part 2, the monographic heart of the book, explores the politics of gender and the gendering of politics in late colonial Morelos, the region that gave rise to *zapatismo* in the Mexican Revolution. Part 3 sets the case of Morelos in a comparative regional perspective that includes a specific analysis of Oaxaca and Mexico City and a final twist in the analysis of Morelos. Part 4 is an extended reflection on the main findings of the book. A chapter of conclusions (Chapter 13) provides both a summation of the main arguments and an exploration of implications for history, historiography, and theory. A postscript (Chapter 14) provides an opportunity to insert the preceding portrait of an era within a reflection on long-term continuity and change since late colonial times.

The central metaphor of this book is that of a journey into a land of historical secrets. I do not wish to imply, of course, that the entire history presented here has been a remarkably well guarded secret that will sound totally unfamiliar — shocking — to readers. On the contrary, this book is but one effort within a wider intellectual effort to achieve gendered readings of historical experience. As will be clear from the text, notes, and acknowledgments, I have benefited enormously from the research, insights, and generosity of many other scholars. Moreover, at an anecdotal level, some of the stories of gender conflict told in the following pages may have a certain ring of familiarity to students of gender, including students of gender in other societies. The sense of recognition is only in part deceptive. If there is a "secret history of gender" in the pages that follow, it resides in the way that the entire package of gender stories and political stories, analysis, and theorization fit together and yield implications. The fitting together and the implications that together yield "secrets" come out into the open most explicitly in the conclusion.

Some particulars of presentation require mention here. This book does not provide a formal glossary for Spanish-language terms. Foreign words are defined upon first usage, and the index will point the reader to the placement of definitions. Tables are grouped together after the main text to facilitate cross-reference checks; key statistics important to the argument are incorporated within the main narrative. For spelling of proper names of persons, I use the orthography of the documents (although I supply accent marks if needed), even when the spelling diverges a bit from contemporary practice. Quotations within Spanish follow the orthography and punctuation of the documents, but some punctuation is supplied for English translations. The somewhat awkward terms "female youth" and "male youth" are used from time to time. I ask for indulgence: I have not found a more graceful gender-specific English equivalent for the cultural in-between category of "junior-woman-in-the-making" and "junior-man-in-the-making." Spanish-language glosses (*jóven, mozo, moza*) are readily available, but contemporary English social categories (teenagers, adolescents, young adults, girls, boys) create more problems than they solve. Finally, "subaltern" is a term I have found descriptively convenient. A word sufficiently elastic to embrace the subordinated peoples of popular culture, it captures a meaningful social category, a certain porousness of boundaries and social patterning in common that happens, notwithstanding distinctions (peasant versus plebeian, Indian versus mulatto versus mestizo versus *castizo* versus "white"/español, woman versus man, elder versus youth, and so on) that also happen within popular culture and that for some purposes also have analytical importance in this book. I am aware that historical uses of the term—pioneered by Gramsci and more recently put forward as a historical category by the *Subaltern Studies* scholars—have generated significant debate. Although I have sidestepped explicitly theorized or historiographical discussion of the term in this book, readers who wish an orientation may find useful the forum on the *Subaltern Studies* scholars in *American Historical Review* (scheduled for December 1994).

Any originality this book may achieve cannot be fairly described as an individual contribution by the author, and it is a pleasure to acknowledge my intellectual, personal, and financial debts. As will be clear from the text and notes, I am greatly indebted to many people I have not personally met—to a community of scholars and pioneers who have promoted gendered rethinkings of history and society and whose writings have taught and provoked me. I also have a number of more individualized personal and intellectual debts. At relatively early stages of this project, Asunción Lavrin and William B. Taylor, scholarly pioneers in the study of Latin American women and colonial violence, respectively, were models of scholarly generosity. They kindly read and commented on early versions of the project and supplied references, ideas, and support. Friedrich Katz also provided gracious support at a crucial early moment. During my core research year in Mexico in 1984–85, I benefited from the advice, ideas, prodding, and support of Josefina Alcázar, Carlos Sempat Assadourian, Roger Bartra, Marjorie Becker, Francie Chassen-López, Manuel Esparza, Juan Carlos Garavaglia, Soledad González Montes, Rodolfo Pastor, Carmen Ramos Escandón, Leticia Reina, María de los Angeles Romero Frizzi, and on a brief return trip, Pilar Gonzalbo Aizpuru and Alicia Hernández Chávez. I am also grateful to the staffs and directors of the archival repositories listed in the bibliography. Upon my return to the United States, several student research assistants helped me sift, organize, and reflect. Kath Pintar transcribed with incredible care and skill Spanish-language notes from Oaxaca that I had dictated into a cassette machine. Luís Figueroa was my dedicated teacher and partner during the computer coding and processing phase of the project. Jim Krippner-Martínez and Sinclair Thomson skillfully helped me digest extensive literatures in allied fields such as criminality, family violence, feminist theory, and contemporary Mexican ethnography and social studies. During the years of sifting, reflection, and writing, graduate students at the University of Wisconsin at Madison, both within and outside the Latin American history program, prodded my thinking and made learning about gender and about Mexico a community endeavor. My colleagues at Wisconsin, particularly Florencia Mallon, Francisco Scarano, and Thomas Skidmore (now at Brown University) in Latin American history and Gerda Lerner, Linda Gordon, Jeanne Boydston, and Judith Walzer Leavitt in women's history, helped create a supportive and stimulating intellectual milieu for this project. My colleagues Suzanne Desan and Steven Feierman (now at the University of Florida at Gainesville), perhaps in ways unknown to them, also helped me to learn.

When the time to begin drafting the manuscript arrived, in 1990–91, I was fortunate to live and write for a year at the Center for Advanced Study in the Behavioral Sciences (CASBS). The remarkable intellectual environment, infrastructural support, and freedom from university routine organized by Bob Scott and Phil Converse and the staff enabled me to draft a large chunk of the manuscript and to stretch my intellectual horizons in the process. Without the CASBS community and environment, this book could not have "happened."

This book took shape originally as a much longer manuscript. Persons who read the original manuscript in its entirety and who offered astute advice on matters ranging from authorial strategy and interpretive framework to specific details and bibliographical suggestions include Barbara Hanrahan, Gil Joseph, Gerda Lerner, Eileen McWilliam, Ben Orlove, and several anonymous readers. Their critiques were wonderfully frank and constructive and helped me sharpen and trim the manuscript. Persons who read portions of the manuscript and who offered important support and advice included my colleagues at the state and society seminar — especially Wendy Griswold, Jacquelyn Hall, Bill Sewell, and Arnold Zwicky — during my CASBS year and my Wisconsin colleague Linda Gordon. Colleagues and students at oral presentations given at CASBS/Stanford University, Universidad de Puerto Rico–Recinto Río Piedras, Trinity College, the University of Kentucky, Princeton University, the University of Wisconsin at Madison, and the "Familia y vida privada" conference organized by El Colegio de México and Universidad Nacional Autónoma de México also provided feedback and insight. I also benefited from excellent advice and hard work by a wonderful team of colleagues at the University of North Carolina Press — particularly Barbara Hanrahan, Kathleen Ketterman, Pamela Upton, and the manuscript's copyeditor, Stephanie Wenzel.

For financial support of research and writing, I owe heartfelt thanks to CASBS, the Fulbright-Hays Faculty Research Abroad Fellowship Program, the John Simon Guggenheim Memorial Foundation, the National Endowment for the Humanities, the University of Wisconsin Graduate School, and the Tinker-Nave Summer Field Research Program administered by the Latin American and Iberian Studies Program at the University of Wisconsin. I am grateful for both the financial support and the votes of confidence.

Last but definitely not least I owe deep thanks to my colleague and partner in life, Florencia E. Mallon, and to my children Raji and Raffi. Keeping up with Florencia intellectually is no easy task! Her remarkable creativity and insight, her dynamism in intellectual give-and-take, and her personal generosity and support all inspired me as I wrestled with the project, and helped me to learn, grow, and refine ideas along the way. My children Raji and Raffi drew me again and again into a multidimensional life despite my obsession with a book. They also helped me select a book title and offered instruction in the wonders of power and authority. I hope their student has learned a thing or two.

PART ONE

The Journey

CHAPTER 1

An Invitation to Readers

Enter the conflicted world of José Marcelino and María Teresa that fateful Wednesday, October 23, 1806.[1] Young, Indian, and poor, the couple belonged to the stratum of land-poor villagers, common in the Morelos region, whose male household heads worked the lands of richer peasants or found jobs on the region's sugar haciendas to keep the household economy afloat.[2] From Texalpa, where Nahuatl speakers such as José Marcelino and María Teresa had been born, raised, and married, work on haciendas such as Atlacomulco lay within an easy day's walk.[3] That Wednesday José Marcelino found no work in Texalpa, possibly because of the rains, and passed the time drinking and (presumably) talking with the other men. As the day slipped by, he did not bother to return home for a midday meal and exchange of words, nor did he venture farther afield looking for work.

To José Marcelino this sort of response to slack time seemed normal. To María Teresa, however, such liberties embodied her husband's irresponsibility and laziness. When José Marcelino returned home that night, the tension mounted quickly. Asked where he had passed the day drinking and scolded that he smelled foully of cheap rum (*chinguirito*), José Marcelino retorted "that none of it was her matter." In María Teresa's eyes the assertion itself underscored José Marcelino's failure to meet his obligations. María Teresa, who had not prepared the customary meal for her returning husband and was not about to do so, stormed out and took refuge in the house of her mother, Micaela María. José Marcelino tried to drag her back; but the two women resisted him, and he was forced to return home empty-handed—without wife, food, or authority. Alone, frustrated, and angry, José Marcelino vented his wrath by breaking up María Teresa's kitchen belongings.

3

The target had its logic. The kitchen was a symbolic and practical seat of female identity. It served as burial site for the umbilical cords of newborn girls (the cords of boys were buried outdoors, in forest, field, or mountain).[4] It constituted both an arena within which even poor women might exert a modicum of property rights and social control and a principal locus of female labor obligation in the economic pacts that, along with sexual and other pacts, sealed patriarchal arrangements between peasant husbands and wives. The target also had its irony, for José Marcelino's anger and frustration would be compounded by hunger. Men depended on women for food preparation, an arduous task that required considerable labor, skills, and advance preparation to transform corn into the tortillas that made up the bulk of the diet of poor peasants. Particularly critical was the back-straining work of grinding soaked corn (*nixtamal*) on the woman's grindstone (*metate*) to produce wet flour suitable for tortillas; depending on the size of the family, this part alone of the daily tortilla work normally took between one and a half and three woman-hours a day. A like amount of labor was needed for the rest of the process — the initial shelling and soaking of dry corn in water and lime and the final patting out and cooking of freshly ground tortillas on the woman's griddle (*comal*).[5] When a wife withdrew her labor in food preparation and a female relative did not discreetly step in, alternative means of acquiring food brought new complications. Poverty restricted discretionary income, and a married villager who acquired his meals by calling on credit, friendship, or kinship invited talk about the state of his marriage and household authority. That fateful Wednesday, José Marcelino returned home alone to face this dilemma.

Thursday morning José Marcelino left the house to find day work in fields that needed to be prepared for the next planting cycle, and María Teresa returned home to discover the kitchen breakage. As matters turned out, Wednesday's drenching rains had left the fields too mucky to work, and José Marcelino, whose breakfast had been limited to a bit of raw rum (*aguardiente*) on his way to the fields and who had begun to feel dizzy and faint (*algo trastornado*) from the effects of drink and hunger, decided to return home to eat. At this point the outlines of the story diverge sharply according to the narrator. In José Marcelino's version, almost certainly apocryphal,[6] a niece warned him on the way home that the infuriated María Teresa wanted the community officials and elders to punish her father-in-law in the absent José Marcelino's place. This led to an angry confrontation when José Marcelino returned home. To José Marcelino's demand that his innocent father be left out of the dispute, María Teresa replied that she would press the community governor (*gobernador*) to whip both father and son. At bottom, a father who indulged his youthful son's failings was responsible for the son's abuse and negligence: "He was guilty of turning out a drunkard by not punishing him. . . . He was a lenient indulger of a father [*un viejo consentidor*]." Provoked by the threat and the slander of his father, José Marcelino picked up a rock, hurled it on María Teresa's head, and fled to a *milpa* (cornfield) to sleep off the incident.

The wounded María Teresa was discovered by Micaela María soon thereafter. Micaela María arrived about midday with some squash, a symbolic and material gesture that might help reestablish the peace between daughter and son-in-law. In María Teresa's version of the wounding, as told to her mother, María Teresa had not threatened to have her father-in-law whipped. The dispute — and José Marcelino's wrath — focused instead on María Teresa's insistence the night before on the right to abandon her home (and thereby her customary duties) in view of her judgment of José Marcelino's behavior. This alone sufficed to provoke the violence notwithstanding María Teresa's peaceable willingness to leave the earlier dispute behind: "Even though he had broken her kitchen things she had his food ready . . . [and] without any other cause he had broken her head with a rock." That afternoon the community officials found and arrested the sleeping José Marcelino, who proceeded to escape — "considering," he would later explain, "that the crime did not merit so much punishment."

In fact, José Marcelino escaped with the hope that he might achieve a reconciliation by informal means. He found day work at Hacienda Atlacomulco, where he sought to redeem his standing as a responsible breadwinner. After collecting two days' wages on Sunday, he returned to Texalpa hoping that the money would "remove his wife's anger." By this point, however, María Teresa had slipped into a coma and died. José Marcelino was again taken prisoner.

The drama of José Marcelino and María Teresa, although revealing and compelling, followed a fairly routine path through the second arrest of José Marcelino on October 27, 1806. As we shall see throughout this book, it resonates with multitudes of similar minidramas that punctuated peasant and plebeian life in late colonial Mexico and therefore forms part of a larger pattern. Like many such dramas, however, it also had its more idiosyncratic — and equally revealing — quirks. In this instance the peculiar twist did not come until June 1807, after José Marcelino had languished in jail nearly eight months. On June 18 Micaela María came forward to pardon José Marcelino and to desist her criminal complaint.[7] She claimed too much, however, when she added that she had pardoned her son-in-law "from the very moment her daughter Tereza Maria [*sic*] died." The historical record of the case proves this assertion patently false. What had happened during the intervening two-thirds of a year? What pressures had driven Micaela María — after the kind of prolonged delay and bitter accusation that indicated determination to carry through the prosecution — finally to declare not only a pardon but also that she had forgiven her daughter's assailant all along?[8]

The answer is community pressure — more specifically, a decision by the community's male elders, who bolstered Micaela María's belated pardon with testimonies designed to rewrite José Marcelino's personal history. In testimonies by the current and former *gobernadores* of the village José Marcelino was said to have lived the life of a model peasant. He had generally treated his wife well, he was orderly and hard working, he was not prone to drinking, and he had a peaceable manner with everyone. This discourse transmuted the homicide incident into an anomaly, an accident in the heat of provocations for which José Marcelino was not responsible, rather than an expression of his character or of the social relations he had established with his wife. The community elders had decided that the time had arrived to lift José Marcelino off the criminal hook and to reintegrate him into the structure of community life and labor. Like other land-poor peasants, José Marcelino was customarily advised by the elders where he could find day work in agriculture[9] and was counted on to contribute to the community's tributary obligations to state and church. Few peasants of modest means, let alone an apparent widow like Micaela María,[10] could withstand for long pressure to reestablish the facade of harmony that would draw an able-bodied man back into community service and life after a respectable interval of punishment.[11] We do not know when the campaign to release José Marcelino began in earnest and therefore cannot calculate how long, if at all, Micaela María resisted such pressures. We know only that eight months after she lost her daughter, Micaela María submitted to the wisdom of the elders and that her pardon and their testimonies, in turn, paved the way for a royal pardon of José Marcelino.[12]

ON THE MEANING OF A STORY

The story of María Teresa's killing by José Marcelino invites us to reflect on the historical connections between power and patriarchy, politics and gender, in the lives of the Mexican poor. We shall have occasion to develop these concepts and connections with greater precision and formality later in this book. For now, let us reflect on the richness of the invitation. The details of such a minidrama bring into focus social dynamics and arenas normally clouded by personal discretion and cultural mythology. In this instance the view afforded by a single episode of gender dispute raises challenging questions about the received wisdoms, historical and theoretical, that shape our understanding of gender and its intersection with more well known issues of politics, community, and class in Mexico.

Let us begin with our understanding of gender relations and violence in the patriarchal culture of Mexico. The standard portrait blends the themes of women's victimization and complicity. On the one hand, wives and daughters are the long-suffering victims of patriarchal dominance by husbands and fathers. On the other hand, "culture" consists of a body of values commanding a near-consensus among members of the participant society, and Mexican women subscribe to the honor codes and patriarchal values deemed to infuse Mexican culture in particular and Latin American and Mediterranean cultures more generally.[13] The story of María Teresa and José Marcelino guides us past the mythological fog that protects the shadowy forms of an imagined picture. As we draw closer to the scene of action, the invented image of the submissive Mexican wife, ever the victim of gratuitous violence despite her obedience to an uncontested code of patriarchal values, seems either to disappear or to resurface ironically as a discourse mobilized in a sharply contested field of action. (Recall María Teresa's assertion that she suffered the violence of her husband despite her submissive preparation of food and her peaceable willingness to forget the earlier dispute.) We begin to see a bitterly contested world of gender right and obligation. In this world women like María Teresa and Micaela María did not challenge the principles of patriarchal dominance as such but reinterpreted their operational meaning so markedly that conflict ensued on the practical issues that defined the meaning and limits of patriarchal authority in everyday life.[14]

In the tragedy of María Teresa, Micaela María, and José Marcelino we witness the emergence of three such conflicts in rapid succession. The first was the dispute over a man's accountability for his physical whereabouts and activities. María Teresa asserted a right to monitor and evaluate her husband's physical mobility and activities, an arena José Marcelino considered his absolute domain. The second arena of contestation extended the argument from men's to women's physical mobility. Did a woman have the right to abandon her home and to suspend meal preparations for her husband? The practical answer given by the two women asserted the right of a wife to abandon — at least temporarily — her dutiful place in a husband's home if the husband-patriarch failed to fulfill his obligations or if he became abusive. The practical answer given by José Marcelino asserted a more unconditional domain of husbands over their wives' physical mobility and labor. Finally there arose the question of rights of punishment. What was considered sufficient provocation to justify physical punishment of wives by husbands, what types of private patriarchal punishment were considered within the range of the permissible and the proportionate, and to what extent should a husband's mistreatment or excess lead to his own punishment (or punishment of his relatives) by a higher authority? María Teresa, Micaela María, José Marcelino, and the male elders of Texalpa did not easily reach a consensus on these questions, although all might have conceded, in principle, the right of a husband-patriarch to discipline his wayward dependents.

If we shift the focus from gender relations as such to the intersection of gender and the more public and familiar arenas of politics, the story of María Teresa's homicide again challenges a received wisdom. Until relatively recently one of the most widespread theoretical premises concerning gender and women's social experience has been the bifurcation of society into public and private arenas of experience and interest divided largely by gender. In this bifurcation men's important experiences connect primarily to the domain of public life and activity, the visible world of politics and power wherein the great issues of war and peace, order and disorder, and justice and injustice are experienced, contested, and perhaps compromised or resolved. This is a world of dynamism, consequence, and historical change. It is the arena that determines social winners and losers. On the other side of the great bifurcation women's important experiences connect primarily to the domain of private life and activity, the shielded world of family and domestic arrangements wherein the natural functions of child rearing, sex, and familial reproduction hold sway. This is a world of little social consequence and comparatively gradual historical change. Its conflicts and tyrannies assume petty dimensions and are in any event rather isolated from the great political issues of the day. This is an arena closer to nature than culture.

The assumption of a sharp and gendered line of demarcation between public and private spheres of experience has exerted a pervasive and recurring influence in Western thought. One may find the dichotomy in Aristotle as well as nineteenth-century Victorians. As recently as the 1970s and early 1980s the power of this assumption was evident in the way it could mark otherwise antagonistic frameworks. Notwithstanding the agenda embodied in the important slogan "The personal is political," some of the most valuable and influential early contributions to modern feminist social science and history built their critical frameworks on the analysis of public/private and culture/nature splits and on the study of male control of the articulation between public and private domains.[15] On the other side of the spectrum antifeminist diatribes ridiculed historical analysis of private matters as trivial and prurient. Women's history became an example par excellence of the ways an explosion of interest in the everyday lives and social history of marginalized groups with little power had diverted historians from the great issues and men traditionally examined in political history.[16] Insofar as social history remained conceptually apart from political history (a claim of only partial accuracy), the conservative critique raised a valid point, albeit in caricatured form. But it did so by reaffirming a public/private split and labeling one side of the divide trivial, rather than asking the more profound critical question, to what extent was the great divide itself an obsolete intellectual artifice? Even Michel Foucault, who did so much to extend our perception of power to virtually all arenas of human activity and speech, saw the invasion of interior life by totalizing power—a kind of dissolution of historical boundaries between public and private as regimes of public power and expertise invaded and objectified human body and soul—as a relatively recent historical creation, the very measure of modern tyranny.[17] Only recently, since the mid-1980s, has there emerged a thick cluster of feminist works calling into serious question, on a theoretical as well as historical level, the very premises of the public/private demarcation.[18]

The story of María Teresa's homicide melts the public and private spheres of experience into a single whole: the separation of public and private becomes contingent, a temporary condition subject to reversal depending on circumstances, a historically constructed and reversible moment in a process of oscillation that includes both fusion and separation. In this respect it echoes in concrete form the conceptual thrust of the newer wave of feminist history and theory. Recall the fusions of public politics and private domains that occurred in Texalpa despite José Marcelino's initial efforts to keep his domestic quarrel private and despite María Micaela's personal interest in prosecuting the murder of her daughter. The community's male elders and officials assumed a right and responsibility to take on an adjudicating role in family quarrels, schisms, and violence precisely because matters intensely personal might affect the well-being of the community as a whole. Contributing tributaries might be lost, the necessary facade of community harmony might be broken, and community cohesion in the face of external intrusion might founder. When such circumstances arose, the connections between public and private well-being gave the community's leaders a platform for initiative and intervention; they had a duty to render judgments about a person's character, family life, and private quarrels and to proffer advice and counsel as a matter of public necessity. The same public/private connections provided a platform for individuals seeking to transfer private grievances to a more public terrain. Thus María Teresa could threaten to punish her husband, and thus the allegation that she threatened to defame and punish her father-in-law had at least an air of plausibility. In Texalpa as in other peasant villages, community politics and domestic relations sometimes merged in a single, contested drama.

María Teresa, José Marcelino, Micaela María: the violent climax of their joined lives pulls us away from the received wisdoms. The stereotyped imagery of Mexican women as long-suffering objects of gratuitous violence — both victimized and complicitous in an aggressive patriarchal culture — begins to look like a stereotype whose grain of truth must be inserted and reinterpreted in a new context. An important corollary, the notion that gender harmony and balance prevailed among Indians, as contrasted with the power-seeking and violence of gender relations among mestizos, also begins to look like a stereotype. The facile assumption that the history of public life, a political arena of broad import populated mainly by male historical actors, is sharply demarcated from the history of private life, a social arena of narrower concerns populated mainly by women, families, and male losers, begins to look like an artifice whose foundations require critical reexamination. A single story or case study, however, cannot by itself carry the weight of major historical and theoretical revision. Does our story challenge received wisdoms because it is filled with idiosyncrasy—because it is the proverbial exception that proves the rule—or does it challenge received wisdoms because the conventional wisdoms are themselves profoundly, perhaps fatally, flawed?

One cannot answer the crucial question by circular self-reference to the initial anecdote or case study. The story of María Teresa's killing by José Marcelino can only constitute an invitation to readers, a provocation at the beginning of a journey of discovery and inquiry. One is free, of course, to refuse or to accept the invitation, and requirements of analytical precision, evidence, or formality may on occasion burden the traveler. But those sufficiently piqued to embark will discover the general inside the particular. Buried at the Texalpa churchyard with María Teresa were not only details of a life intensely personal, but also patterns of living more broadly social.

CHAPTER 2

Power, Patriarchy, and the Mexican Poor

An Inquiry

Historians and contemporary observers of Latin America have long discerned a powerful patriarchalism, presumably rooted in the Iberian colonial past (ca. 1520–1820) and its legacies, yet vital to understanding contemporary history and life. The figure of the domineering patriarch has repeatedly captured the imagination of the great writers of Latin American literature, and for good reason.[1] The annals of power in twentieth-century Latin America seem filled with men who fused the exercise of highly visible public power, a domination of subaltern groups and even entire nations rooted in the control of economic and political resources, with a more personal and interior drive to dominate, a controlling will exerted in direct face-to-face relations with individual women, dependents, relatives, and clients. The variations on the theme abound. The writer might cast the spotlight at the apex of national power in the presidential palace or at the rustic setting of a provincial hacienda; the writer's purpose might be to denounce capricious power cruelly exercised or to capture the human vulnerabilities and solitude of the patriarch. Whatever the variations, however, they should not obscure an underlying unity of perception. The fascination with the patriarch derived from a sense that he embodied something quintessential, yet problematic and transitory: an entrenched historical legacy very much alive, yet necessarily doomed to extinction, suppression, or denunciation in the interests of political struggle, social modernization, or simple justice.[2] The patriarch's melding of benevolent pretense and gesture with cruel violence and subjugation, his insistence on exerting power personally and sexually as well as in more socially distant and indifferent ways, his drive to possess people and retinues as a husband-father possesses wife and children and to possess wife and children as a master possesses a slave, his impulse to build legitimacy on a mystique of fear and adulation appropriate to metaphorical fathers—these sometimes paradoxical fusions of extreme exploitation and social indifference with more organic human dependencies and pretenses seemed to capture something fundamental and distinctive about the human contours of domination, struggle, and culture in Latin America.

In the mid-twentieth century, celebrated works by cultural critics and historians exhibited a similar fascination with the patriarchal bases of culture and power in Latin American civilization.[3] The Black Legend debate and the related controversies over the feudal or capitalist character of the colonial experience drew attention to the paradoxical combinations of professed paternalism and calculated exploitation that pervaded colonial decrees, statecraft, and social policy in Spanish and Portuguese America.[4] Researchers encountered in Spanish political philosophers and officials the assumption that well-ordered families and lineages, ruled wisely by father-patriarchs commanding obedience, constituted the foundation of a healthy body politic whose kings, viceroys, and archbishops were metaphorical fathers.[5] Social observers wondered if the historic patriarchs of civil society—the conquerors of Indians, the rulers of the great landed estates, the masters of slaves and peons—had embedded a paternalistic value system and psychology of dominance/emasculation so deep that it would outlast the political and social storms of the twentieth century.[6] At a time when the politics of agrarian reform and social modernization constituted a fresh and embattled agenda, such musings seemed especially relevant.

The awareness of patriarchalism as a potent force in Latin American history and life, then, is hardly new. It preceded the explosion of interest in social history and women's history that reshaped historiography in the 1970s and 1980s. But awareness is paradoxically founded on negation; one form of awareness is constructed on the suppression of another. The form taken by this particular awareness of patriarchalism exacted an important price.[7] The obsession with the legacy, psychology, and exploits of Latin America's domineering patriarchs constructed awareness of patriarchalism and gender in ways that relegated women and poor men to comparatively one-dimensional roles, as foils and objects useful to develop the characters of the main drama. Women came out from the shadows fleetingly, as objects and symbols of male manipulation, domination, desire, and honor codes, only to retreat when the necessary point had been made. Men in the vast bottoms of the social pyramid came forth to play out the gender roles defined by the patriarchalism of their superiors—as emasculated pawns and victims or more rarely as macho rebels, the explosive Pancho Villas who inverted the dominance/emasculation roles of the old order. The ironic result was that works rich and perceptive in their awareness of patriarchalism as a force in Latin American life and in their understanding that the roles and pretenses of gender and color-class power merged at the male apex of the social pyramid offered a mix of silences and half-empty symbols when the focus shifted downward. Fascination with patriarchalism and a certain recognition of the politics of manhood had not yielded much analysis of women or of the gender dynamics in the lives of most men as well as women.[8]

Historians of Latin American women sought to fill the void and replace the stereotypes. Their research questions and findings, part of the broad trend to elucidate the history of previously invisible social groups, have laid the groundwork for a substantially distinct picture. One may discern four principal contributions that changed the shape of historical knowledge in the 1970s and 1980s.[9] First, a series of works provided a more precise view of the laws, prescriptive codes, and institutions directly pertinent to female life in Spanish and Portuguese America. These studies sharpened understanding of the institutional baseline against which the female experience might be measured, and brought into view institutions such as convents and legal openings such as dowry and inheritance rights that created spaces for greater female initiative and autonomy than that envisioned in stereotypes and prescriptive tracts.[10]

A second major contribution has been analysis of women as key participants in society, notwithstanding — and in relation to — their gender subordination and the cultural biases limiting their visibility. These studies have collectively recast social understanding from the vantage point of female participation. They have illuminated the crucial yet often devalued roles of women in the economic activities and social organization of humble households and elite clans; their contributions to collective acts such as riots, rituals, and political uprisings; and the difficult, ambivalent dilemmas women have faced as persons ensnared by the twin effects of gender and color class imperatives.[11] By focusing tightly on the interplays, ironies, paradoxes, and cultural denials that issue from women's combined participation and subordination in society, these studies have deepened our appreciation of the spaces that have continually opened between formal prescriptive codes and women's actual behavior, and the social ideologies and institutions that work to close such spaces, or at least render them less visible.[12]

A third and widely influential advance has focused the study of normative institutions and women's participation more specifically on the social relations and values of honor and the connections among honor, family, and sexuality. In practice these contributions have taken two main (and overlapping) forms: analysis of the social implications of male honor codes or, more precisely, the complex of honor/shame values familiar to students of Mediterranean and

Latin American cultures, and study of the disparity or tension between the stringency of formal prescriptive norms of honorable conduct and the more permissive variability of everyday family and sexual life.

The honor codes require discussion in some detail precisely because the norms and appearances they promote have proved so important in Latin America, both as cultural ideals and as a source of misleading stereotypes that recur in the lived culture as well as the scholarship about the culture.[13] The honor/shame complex prescribed codes of proper manhood and womanhood that invoked honor's double meaning: honor as personal virtue or merit and honor as social precedence. In the colonial and neocolonial societies of Latin America the key link joining the two meanings of honor derived from the ways that social precedence, group-derived superiority in relations with others, usually implied enhanced virtue, a superior individual and familial ability to sustain appearances of worthy masculinity or femininity.

At bottom personal honor depended, at least in part, on social advantages that demeaned the virtue of others. For men, honor as virtue implied a cluster of visible accomplishments and postures: personal forcefulness, a valor embodied in strength of will and sexual possessiveness; success as a ruler of households; and respect for social rank and decorum. In the colonial cultures of Latin America personal forcefulness accrued most readily to men whose material advantages lifted them to positions of command over the labors, sexual services, and property of inferiors whose duties included the presentation of meek demeanors. Success as a ruler of households implied cultural display of the combined roles of family provider, protector, and authority. These measures of manhood were almost synonymous with the trappings of wealth. The socially privileged could sustain a luxurious home and lifestyle, could protect and restrict daughters and wives by cloistering them in homes or convents and by surrounding them with servants and companions when they ventured out to street and church, and could enlarge the aura of socially accepted patriarchal authority by taking in clients, servants, visitors, and hangers-on who expanded the household head's retinue of dependents. Respect for social rank and etiquette did not undercut a posture of forceful strength and household authority so long as the sense of decorum came from on high, in a context of respectable social intercourse among the strong and well mannered that proved perfectly compatible with contempt for less respectable inferiors.

Similarly the code of proper womanhood esteemed in the honor/shame complex was, in the Latin American context, most accessible to the socially advantaged. A woman's duty to cultivate a well-developed sense of shame, a sensitivity to moral duty and reputation that screened her from social circumstances inviting opprobrium, called upon her to adopt social appearances that contrasted with those prescribed for honored adult men. These appearances included a submissive posture of obedience, support, and acceptance in household relations with husbands, fathers, and elders; a fierce regard for sexual propriety — virginity by daughters, fidelity by wives, abstinence by widows; and a respect for social place and decorum whose female version emphasized a sense of self-enclosure and discretion that shielded women and their families from dangerous gossip, quarrels, and sexual entanglements. It is important to note, of course, the dubiousness of assuming that most women of most social strata subscribed fully to the idealized honor/shame codes well elucidated in the scholarly literature. It is also important to note that the most idealized version of these norms elevated femininity to a pedestal of submissive self-control and saintly endurance that few living, flesh-and-blood women could consistently and fully sustain. These were standards of perfection that encouraged misogyny while proclaiming worship: all living women, regardless of color-class standing, might be suspected of falling short of the ideal unless strictly monitored by a vigilant patriarch.[14] Precisely for these reasons, to those who subscribed to the honor/shame complex of values, external appearances mattered as much or more than well-hidden facts of dutiful or deviant behavior.

Notwithstanding these qualifications, the point remains that for women as for men social circumstances distributed virtue — the ability to project and sustain the outer manifestations of honored womanhood — unequally. Submissive appearances that rendered familial tension and conflict less visible could and did break down at all social levels. But for poor women, keeping up such appearances posed added dangers: tolerance of male negligence and sexual improprieties implied the risk of destitution. The presumption of sexual propriety was strengthened by access to servants and resources that shielded women from exposure and suspicion in arenas outside the home: domestic service in the homes of other families; the selling of produce, cloth, food, and drink on market days in the village and city plazas; and the hauling of food, water, and laundry between home, river, and *milpa*.[15] Respect for decorum required the suppression of activities and attributes demeaned as gossip, scandal mongering, and unfeminine resort to physical force. For poor women such suppressions made little sense if the conflicts and self-defenses of everyday life required a network of conversation and potential allies, a disposition that counterbalanced discretion with an implied threat to bring family quarrels into the open, and a readiness to intervene physically to defend families, neighbors, and communities in moments of personal or collective crisis.

For women as for men, in short, honor as social precedence set in motion an initial predistribution of honor as personal virtue. Racial subordination and ideology underpinned much of this predistribution by wealth and power. Racial subjugation, the foundation upon which labor, politics, and culture were built in a colonial context, made most Indians, Africans, and *castas* (persons of mixed racial descent) unlikely to demonstrate the material requisites of elite honor and respectability.[16] Racial-ethnic ideology, which originally evolved in close relation with the discourses of Christian/pagan conflict and encounter, tainted the honor of the colored descendants of "pagan" and "barbarian" bloodlines, even for social climbers whose wealth and acquired culture lifted them to an otherwise honorable status.[17]

In the colonial societies of Latin America, therefore, the ultimate beneficiaries of the honor/shame complex were the male patriarchs who headed the major families, the leading aristocrat-entrepreneurs of a multiracial order founded on the fusion of dependent labor with a social dialectic of honor-degradation. (Women of the leading families also enjoyed privileged access to honor, of course, but the privilege was also encumbered by subordination: social vigilance and constriction and a placement of ideal femininity atop a pedestal that highlighted the weaknesses and shortcomings of living women. The lesser males and dependent male youth of the leading families, although less encumbered in their physical and social movements and less subject to judgment by a larger-than-life ideal, still owed deference to family elders and patriarchs.[18]) To these men accrued the most lustrous concentrations of honor, and for these men and their families the values enshrined in the honor/shame code facilitated efforts to develop the marriage and family alliances integral to strategies of inheritance, economic diversification, and political influence.[19] A major contribution of the students of the honor/shame complex in Latin America has been analysis that enables us to perceive the way gendered codes of honor and the social control of women and sexuality proved fundamental to the construction, perpetuation, and self-legitimation of the color-class order.

Equally important for historians of women and youth, however, has been the investigation of loopholes and spaces for maneuver within the honor/shame complex of values. The premium placed on protecting the virginity of unmarried female dependents and the canon law tradition of supporting free will in choice of marriage partner so long as major social status boundaries were not transgressed enabled some women and youth to resort to elopement and church protection to gain leverage against parents in conflicts over marriage choice. In cases where race or color was at issue, a cultural flexibility that recognized gradations of race mixture and that enabled some individuals to elevate their "social race" on the basis of their economic standing, cultural trappings, and personal virtue added another useful loophole. Only a minority of individuals from comparatively middling and privileged social strata could successfully manipulate the institutional and cultural loopholes.[20] Moreover, the colonial state sought to close such openings in the late eighteenth and early nineteenth centuries. Nonetheless, the honor/shame studies have elucidated spaces for individual maneuver that belied the posture of submissive obedience by females and youths prescribed in normative tracts and stereotypes. The spaces between outer acquiescence and interior choice, the institutional contradictions and forbearances that allowed for individual manipulation and sexual deviation, the rise of large numbers of female-headed households in societies whose norm prescribed rule by father-patriarchs — wherever one looks closely, it seems, one finds slack rather than taut connections between socially tolerated behavior and normative codes of honor, family, and sexuality.[21]

The combined weight of these three scholarly advances is formidable: more precise analysis of the laws, prescriptive codes, and institutions that purported to govern gender right and obligation in general and female behavior in particular; deepened cognizance and analysis of women's wide-ranging participation in society and the roles, responsibilities, initiatives, and dilemmas implied in their subordinate participation; more searching elucidation of the structure and myriad interstices of the honor/shame complex and its connection to the color-class order. All these advances have contributed to a heightened awareness of the manifold ways that Latin American women, as living social participants, engaged in activities and maneuvers that deviated in small or large ways from the stereotypes — formally esteemed prescriptions — enshrined in the ideal code of female comportment: submissive obedience to family superiors, sexual purity and fidelity, and discreet self-enclosure. The new scholarship has moved us considerably from the female icons, archetypes, and symbols evinced in a literature on patriarchalism fascinated by the social psychology and drama of the great power-seeking patriarchs.

We have, then, a new awareness: a gendered code of honor and degradation and a dialectic of women's active conformity to and deviance from the code. This dialectic, in turn, has heightened our sensitivity to institutional loopholes and tensions between church and state, to cultural and ecclesiastical expectations that man sinned (a consequence of Eve's temptation of Adam) and that women by nature fell from the pedestal of duty and morality unless vigilantly controlled, and to the manifold ways that women, men, and institutions sought to cover up, dismiss, or otherwise mediate deviances made more tolerable by cultural screening.

The fourth major scholarly advance underscores this particular awareness, a dialectic of women's active conformity/deviance, by focusing on deviants as such. A growing literature has made visible the collection of mystical heretics, magical practitioners, and defiant rebels and feminists who challenged social codes and gender conventions more squarely. The scale or notoriety of these women's deviance from the norms of the honor/shame complex marked them as dangerous, powerful, or subversive figures at the fringes or margins of the accepted social body and therefore subject to repression, stigma, or controversy.[22] If we may extend the logic of Mary Douglas's and Michel Foucault's studies of the marginal and the deviant to scholarship as well as social life, we may observe that—in scholarship as in life—the demarcation of marginals and deviants, misfits beyond the boundaries of social tolerance, convention, and acceptance, may also serve to demarcate an implicit norm within the social body.[23] Social and historical analysis becomes, once more, the study of a norm—in this instance a code of gendered behavior—and the small and large deviations from the norm. One may place the emphasis closer to the norm and the loopholes, tolerances, and half-screened deviations that allowed for a measure of maneuver and flexibility that belies stereotypes, or one may place the emphasis closer to the more extreme and threatening deviations that implied a deeper dissent and the risk of stigma or repression. One may even interpret society as a whole in terms of the tension between declared norm and tolerated practice.[24]

The new awareness of the dialectic of women's conformity/deviance is an enormously important accomplishment built on solid foundations of historical research, analysis, and insight. Yet if every awareness exacts a cost, suppresses a distinct type of awareness, we may ask at what cost has this new advance been achieved.

The new awareness has exacted a double price. First, framing women's historical experience as a history of conformity/deviance tends to sidestep the critical question of whether the code of gender right, obligation, and honor was itself fundamentally contested within the social body. To put it another way, the framework presumes the absence of alternative and competing gender codes before the advent of modern feminism. One sees only deviance and deviants, the latter socially isolated and stigmatized if their deviation was too notorious or great. The conformity/deviance framework tends to solidify the assumption that the honor/shame complex constituted "a" culture of gender values to which most Hispanized social participants—women and men alike—subscribed.[25] Before the era of modern feminism and social movements associated with the development of modern capitalism, alternatives to the accepted code become visible mainly at the margins of the culture, in the subculture of female outcasts and mystics at the fringes of social convention or in cultural worlds beyond the Hispanized framework, ethnic frontiers where Indians, for example, might have preserved a culture of gender values distinctive from the familiar Hispanic norm.[26] Within the Hispanized social body one sees loopholes, maneuvers, and initiatives through the lens of a normative code but not the patterning of those deviations into a distinctive code or framework. The framework of conformity/deviance becomes all the more curious and limiting since the literature recognizes that the idealized honor/shame code was not entirely realistic for the poor and the colored, who may therefore have deviated more strongly than privileged folk from some of its tenets.[27] As long as historical research on women remains comparatively stronger on the middling and privileged rather than the poorer strata of society, however, such deviations may be acknowledged without examining more seriously whether they are symptoms of a distinctively patterned culture of gender right, obligation, and honor among the poor. The poor simply deviate from a norm.

Left comparatively unexamined in the formulation of conformity/deviance is the possibility that well within the margins of the social body (whether the Hispanized social body or an Indian or Afro-Latin ethnic frontier) women and men developed multiple codes of gender right, obligation, and honor within patriarchy; that they developed these codes in a process of contestation between women and men that makes the notion of "a" culture of common gender values a half-fiction; and that within this context of multiple codes forged in a process marked by contestation as well as solidarity the culture of gender practices and meanings among the poor requires analysis as a complex of social practices and values in its own right.

The second cost exacted by the new awareness of women's active conformity/deviance has been one of omission rather than commission: comparative negligence of the broad analytical connections between political culture, understood as concepts and languages of legitimate and illegitimate authority forged in the social relations of publicly recognized powers of governance, and gender culture, understood as concepts and languages of manhood, womanhood, and authority forged in social relations, including power relations, between and among the sexes. As we have seen, the earlier fascination with Latin American patriarchalism perceptively linked the politics of color-class power with a politics of manhood and gender dominance. But it reduced the connection of gender and political culture to the drives, social psychology, and legacies of powerful men at the heights of power, rather than exploring the relationship of political culture and gender culture from the bottom up as well as from the top down. In addition, it relegated women to a role as stereotyped female symbols and archetypes at the margins of analysis, rather than scrutinizing them as complex and consequential social participants worthy of analysis in their own right. The surge of important research and scholarship in women's history addressed the second weakness better than the first. As historians of Latin American women took on the immense and urgent task of replacing stereotypes with the once concealed history of women's active interventions in conformity and at odds with the formal codes of female behavior and subordination, the challenge of exploring the broad analytical connections between political culture and gender culture was by and large postponed. Although the theme of women and politics drew significant attention, the contributions to the topic generally fell within the conformity/deviance mold. Historical studies showed how women contributed to political mobilization and insurrection, in conformity or at odds with traditional roles, symbols, and values, rather than asking in what ways gendered social relations of power between and among the sexes may have contributed to the entire gestalt of politics.[28]

The new awareness of women's conformity/deviance, then, has exacted a double cost we may summarize as a negation of multiple and contested gender codes in the social body and a negation of the interplay between gender culture and political culture at all levels of the body politic. The truism that real knowledge leads to awareness of the depths of our ignorance is exaggerated but aptly captures the point of constructive and respectful critique: when all works well, the advance of knowledge and critical reflection unleashes a spiral of new questions. Despite and because of notable scholarly achievements in the historical study of gender and the social relations between the sexes, we know enough to perceive how little we know about the crucial questions. How were patriarchal gender ideals and values actually experienced in daily life? To what degree were such ideals contested in practice, and with what material consequences for women and men? How widespread were such ideals and their contestation among the poor, and indeed, what particular form did patriarchal concepts, practices, and conflicts take among poor people of color? In societies profoundly divided by color and class and whose elites characteristically sought legitimacy by presenting themselves as paternal patrons, in what ways and to what extent did popular experiences of and struggles over patriarchal authority facilitate elite efforts to build a paternalist political culture? Until we develop convincing answers to such questions, our ability to discern the roots, inner dynamics and contradictions, and wider significance of patriarchal traditions in Latin America will remain severely handicapped.

DESIGN OF AN INQUIRY (I): THEORY, TIME, AND PLACE

This book represents one effort among multiple efforts by scholars to approach such questions.[29] It does so by studying the history of peasants and plebeians in Mexico, the Latin American country where archetypes of masculinity and femininity are most intensely interwoven with mythologies of national self-definition. The inquiry pursues two main arenas of analysis suggested by the double negation discussed earlier: (1) the significance of gender relations and tensions in the everyday life of Mexican peasants and plebeians and in the construction of authority at the household and community/barrio levels of society, and (2) the interplay and convergences between gendered understandings and organization of authority at the household and community levels of society and popular understandings and experiences of legitimate and illegitimate authority in general. An important leitmotif of this book, therefore, will be the relationship in Mexican society, culture, and history between patriarchal power specifically and power more generally—the relations of class power, ethnic dominance, village politics, village-state interplay, and the like that comprise the structure of color-class power. This is a book, in short, about the politics of gender and the gendering of politics.

Because terms like *patriarchy* have received varied meanings and uses, some theoretical specification may be useful. For my purposes, patriarchy refers to a system of social relations and cultural values whereby (1) males exert superior power over female sexuality, reproductive roles, and labor power; (2) such dominance confers both specific services and superior status upon males in their relationships with females; (3) authority in family networks is commonly vested in elders and fathers, thereby imparting a generational as well as a sex-based dynamic to social relations; and (4) authority in familial cells serves as a fundamental metaphorical model for social authority more generally. In such a social system the gendered rewards of service and status not only differentiate men from women but also serve as a basis for alliance, subordination, and ranking among men and among women.[30]

Three specific features of this working concept of patriarchy have proved especially helpful in studying Mexico. First, this concept of patriarchy acknowledges gendered ranking and tension, as well as alliance, among men and among women, rather than limiting gender status to an alliance of men to subordinate women. The divisive as well as unifying dynamics of gender among men and among women are especially pertinent in societies where gender dominance has intersected with color-class hierarchies and polarization. In the Mexican research materials as in our earlier discussion of the honor/shame complex such intersections are fundamental: they granted a higher, superior masculinity to elite men in their relations with subaltern men, and a superior femininity to elite women in their relations with subaltern women.[31] Second, this definition builds generational as well as sex-based dynamics into the very core of the concept. These dynamics are closely and pervasively bound together in the Mexican research materials—in the youth of newlywed wives relative to their husbands; in the fusion of age rank and life cycle stage with the politics of familial deference and assertion; in the flexibility that allowed females to acquire a measure of elder authority as mothers-in-law, widows, and family heads vis-à-vis youth while severely circumscribing female independence of action vis-à-vis men; and in the language of community authority that lent highest symbolic prestige to the village *viejo* or *pasado*, words that fused patriarchal position, maturity of years, and community service into an indissoluble category. To relegate generational dynamics to the margins of the concept would be to misconstrue how patriarchal power actually operated in families and communities and, indeed, how a measure of female elder power over youth was not only compatible with patriarchal social arrangements but integral to them.[32] Third, by focusing attention on specific services, duties, and privileges in the arenas of sexuality, human reproduction, and labor, this working concept of patriarchy allows for a material (or practical) as well as cultural (or ideological) analysis of patriarchal social relations and conflicts. This is important precisely because so many of the conflicts between women and men focused on the practical meanings of gender right and obligation.[33]

The chronological focus of this book is on the last half-century (ca. 1760–1821) of colonial Mexican history, a unit of analysis justifiable on pragmatic and conceptual grounds. The late colonial period is attractive because it generated the thickest corpus of revealing archival records for the colonial period and because it also enjoys a rich secondary literature for the regions under study. In addition, a relatively mature colonial era has certain advantages over early colonial times. The dislocations, epidemics, and experimental quality of social relations in the sixteenth century make it too fluid and unsettled to provide a reliable picture of enduring gender patterns. Moreover, the indigenous/Spanish cultural divide was so fresh and pressing that the multiplicity, nuances, and tensions of gender codes and relations within the social body (whether the Hispanic or the Indian social body) would be largely suppressed in the documentary record. At the level of peasant and plebeian culture the documentary record would be absorbed, rather, with the evangelical duty to discern differences between the gender codes of the distinct ethnocultural worlds, Spanish and Indian, that impeded the creation of a more unified Christian social body.[34]

The last half-century of Spanish colonial rule in Mexico is also a conceptually appealing period in its own right. Not only had the social formation matured sufficiently to open a documentary record of gender tensions and conflicts within a more amalgamated, or colonial, social body. In addition, the extreme pauperization and sharpening social tensions of the period created an environment in which the latent gender tensions of everyday life perhaps became more forcefully manifest — more frequent or violent or subject to state surveillance and intervention, and therefore more visible to historians. The indices of economic immiseration, in some regions a crisis that seems near-Malthusian, are pervasive and convincing.[35] In the regions of central New Spain that surrounded Mexico City this was an era of intensified pressure on the land and water base of a growing and internally differentiated peasant population that competed for resources with large landowners (*hacendados*) and independent medium- and smallholders (*rancheros*). It was an era when land concentration and price speculation intensified the magnitude of grain harvest crises and unleashed waves of migration to the cities. In the southern as well as central agrarian regions it was an era when a tightening alliance of mercantile and political power ensnared even landholding village peasantries in a web of forced and unforced purchases of money and products exchanged for grain, cotton and textiles, cochineal dye, and day labor. In the mining regions of the center-north as well as the agrarian regions and Mexico City, this was an era of downward pressure on real wages in day labor and a concomitant squeeze on artisanal incomes. The immiseration of peasants and plebeians did not imply a lack of prosperity, since the logic of colonial political economy often conjoined economic boom and economic deterioration in a single, polarized process.[36] In the eighteenth century the immiseration of labor was accompanied by a spectacular mining, commercial, and tax revenue boom that made Mexico the crown jewel of the Spanish empire. In Mexico City the process of polarized economic growth reached its visual peak in the graphic contrast between the palatial splendor of the leading families and the utter destitution and near nakedness of the folk who slept in the street. All of this contributed to the unmistakable signs of social tension that pervaded the late colonial era: an attempted crackdown on the alleged plebeian spree of crime and drunkenness, the proposals of agrarian reform by dissident elites, the heightened concern with family and racial order by the state, the increased presence of militias and professional troops in the provinces, the fear that injudicious repression of village riots might spark wider uprisings, the tensions among elites provoked by the Bourbon kings' efforts to reform imperial administration and finance, and the reality of popular insurrection and guerrilla war once the independence crisis exploded in 1810.[37]

Whether we believe that economic immiseration intensified conflict and violence over the practical issues of gendered life among the poor[38] or that a sense of social flux and disorder provoked a heightened effort by state officials and social elites (not to mention subaltern men and village notables) to reassert the "fixity" of family and gender order, the late colonial crucible is a promising period to explore gender relationships, tensions, and values often latent or otherwise screened in the records available to historians.[39]

Although this book focuses on gender and power in late colonial times, it allows a longer historical span to creep in on occasion. Such moments, most obvious in the conclusion and postscript (Chapters 13 and 14), occur for two reasons. First, the ghosts of the colonial past seem strikingly evident to the observer of gender and politics in twentieth-century Mexico and suggest at least the appearance of important long-term continuities. Second, this book marshals its evidence on late colonial times to present a portrait of an era rather than a study of change over time. The brief moments of past-present dialogue, especially in the concluding section of this book, enable us to take cognizance of these issues and thereby insert a reflection on late colonial times within a long-term reflection on Mexican history and civilization.

Yet in what sense may we speak of "Mexico"? The regional heterogeneity of Mexico is dramatic, even notorious. The variety of languages, ethnic and cultural contexts, regional economies, and regional political cultures dazzles both the superficial tourist and the assiduous scholar. The ever growing mountain of superb regional histories corroborates the sense that "Mexico" is a half-fiction, a patchquilt of "many Mexicos" stitched together as much by political fiat and cultural proclamation as by unity of experience, memory, and identity. The problem of place cannot be easily resolved. In the absence of a plenitude of painstaking regional studies that capture the history of gender and power on a peasant or plebeian level, a national-level narrative slides easily into a vision through the prism of elites and overarching normative institutions.[40] It is not clear that such a narrative would tell us much about peasant or plebeian versions of gender culture and political culture or about the problem of national unity and regional variety. Yet to coordinate dozens of laborious research projects on gender in specific regions would be tedious, if not utopian.

In this book I adopt an imperfect solution to the problem of place. I compare a modest number of regions. The regions selected are Morelos, Oaxaca, and Mexico City. (See Map 1.) To facilitate vividness and depth, in Part 2 I focus on Morelos alone. This is the monographic heart of the book. In Part 3 I use Morelos as a baseline for comparative discussion. This is my effort to discern whether there is a Mexico in "many Mexicos."

The three regions varied significantly in their political economies and ethno-cultural dynamics. The Morelos basin, nestled just south of the volcanic plateau that bounds the cooler Valley of Mexico, has long offered a subtropical complement to rulers and emissaries from Tenochtitlán–Mexico City.[41] As one descends from the cool-to-temperate mountains and forests of northern Morelos toward the valleys and plains, one encounters at the base of the escarpment, about 1,500 meters above sea level, a confluence of warmth, water, and fertile volcanic soil—all within hours of adjacent mountain and forest resources and all within a two- or three-day walk to Mexico City itself. This nearby confluence has long induced strong economic integration and ethno-cultural mingling between peoples and migrants sponsored by Mexica (Aztec) and Spanish colonial elites rooted in Tenochtitlán and Mexico City, and the rural peoples of Morelos. Hernán Cortés himself quickly laid claim to enormous holdings in Morelos, and his counterparts were not far behind. Sugar replaced cotton, the strategic regional commodity of the Mexica, and there began the slow development of coexistence and struggle between large capitalized sugar estates, owned by or allied with leading mercantile families in Mexico City, and peasant villages, zealous defenders of an independent land and water base. Indeed, villagers sought not only to produce corn and other subsistence foods for themselves but also to provision Mexico City and the hacienda economy—with the corn and beans, fruit and vegetables, drink and chilies, wood and charcoal, animals and fowl, textiles and crafts, and peddling and transport services of a small-scale truck garden economy. As Cheryl English Martin has shown, hacienda/village tensions intensified sharply with

MAP 1. *The Study Regions in New Spain, Late Colonial Times*

the resurgence of the sugar economy in the late eighteenth century. The resurgence, moreover, increased the influx of non-Indian populations: the blacks, racially mixed *castas* (mulattoes, mestizos, and additional permutations), and poor and middling whites brought in to work and manage the expansive sugar hacienda economy and the mines at the southern fringes of Morelos, or seeking a modest prosperity as independent small producers, craftsmen, muleteers, and traders.

Significantly the peasants responded to this challenge not by building refuge communities premised on ethnocultural distance from other peoples but by forging an aggressively integrative strategy that drew non-Indians into the village side of a bristling village/hacienda struggle. In the warm zones (*tierra caliente*) of central and southern Morelos, peasants rented village lands to non-Indians whose interest in small-scale agricultural commodity production would lead them to join Indian *comuneros* in defending the legal land rights of Indian villages. By the eighteenth century, non-Indian majorities had emerged in many of the larger and more influential *cabeceras* (head villages that enjoyed administrative superiority and in some instances tributary rights over their *sujeto* villages).

MAP 2. *The Morelos Region. (Adapted from C. Martin 1985)*

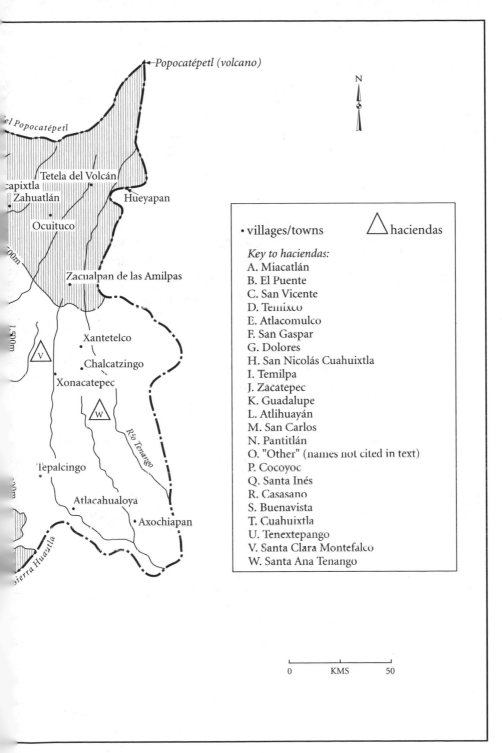

Popocatépetl (volcano)

N

el Popocatépetl

Tetela del Volcán

capixtla
Zahuatlán
Hueyapan

Ocuituco

Zacualpan de las Amilpas

Xantetelco

V

Chalcatzingo

Xonacatepec

W

Río Tenango

Tepalcingo

Atlacahualoya

Axochiapan

Sierra Huaztla

• villages/towns   △ haciendas

Key to haciendas:
A. Miacatlán
B. El Puente
C. San Vicente
D. Temixco
E. Atlacomulco
F. San Gaspar
G. Dolores
H. San Nicolás Cuahuixtla
I. Temilpa
J. Zacatepec
K. Guadalupe
L. Atlihuayán
M. San Carlos
N. Pantitlán
O. "Other" (names not cited in text)
P. Cocoyoc
Q. Santa Inés
R. Casasano
S. Buenavista
T. Cuahuixtla
U. Tenextepango
V. Santa Clara Montefalco
W. Santa Ana Tenango

0   KMS   50

Other social forces also encouraged ethnocultural mixing and proximity. The reality of growing and internally differentiated populations on a limited land base impelled temporary labor migration to haciendas, notwithstanding hacienda/village tensions. The poorer strata of Indian villagers supplied a stream of male day laborers and female servants (often *molenderas*, grinders of corn for tortillas) to haciendas, middling landowners, and prosperous villagers. Even in the northern villages in the temperate-to-cool sierra lands (*tierra fría*), more emphatically Indian in population and superficially more shielded from the core hacienda zone, peasant strategies drew villagers frequently into interethnic spaces. The peasants supplied day laborers and servants to haciendas, made the rounds to the weekly markets (*tianguis*) of villages and haciendas, and organized their own transport services and commodity shipments to Mexico City. In short, the villagers integrated the *tierra caliente* and *tierra fría* zones into a single arena of resources and experience rather than demarcating the *tierra fría* as a zone of ethnic refuge or withdrawal.[42]

Given such integrative strategies of resistance and adaptation, ethnic blurring was common. Although one may estimate the late colonial population of Morelos as about three-fifths Indian, one-third *castas* and blacks (mainly *castas*, with mulattoes perhaps as important as mestizos), and less than a tenth white (see Table 2.1), such estimates are somewhat beside the point. Except for small populations at the very top and bottom of the social pyramid — the "pure" Spaniards who dominated the haciendas and mercantile economy and the black slaves who remained a significant work force on the sugar estates — the density of interethnic encounter and networking sparked irony and confusion. It was in Morelos that non-Indian majorities filled out selected Indian villages. It was in Morelos that multiple labels like "mestizo" and "mulatto" and even "Indian" were attached to single individuals and seemed to hide extensive black and mulatto mixture with Indians. It was in Morelos that even the more emphatically Indian villages — the mountain villages of the *tierra fría* and selected *sujeto* villages of the hacienda zone or *tierra caliente* — developed a way of life premised on peripatetic marketing, labor, and social networking in the interethnic spaces of haciendas and villages alike. It was in Morelos that a person might invoke ethnic rank and epithet as a weapon, even as the circumstances and shared social spaces of the quarrel belied the social distance proclaimed in insult. It was in Morelos that inclusionary reconstructions of village rights and ethnocommunal identity and repeated crossovers between more Hispanized hacienda arenas and more Indianized village arenas yielded a relatively "mestizo" style of regional Indian.[43]

All in all, the peasants' economic and ethnocultural strategies achieved an impressive, albeit limited success. The peasants fortified and reconstructed the peasant village tradition with resources and social alignments sufficient to withstand the sugar utopia of the *hacendados* in the late eighteenth century.

The result was a complex standoff that blended economic conflict with symbiosis and coexistence, and ethnoracial ranking and epithet with interethnic fusion and networking. The climactic explosion of the hacienda/community struggle would be postponed for a later day. An Emiliano Zapata would not lead an agrarian revolution in Morelos until 1910.

Rural Oaxaca seemed a world set apart from the dense juxtapositions of haciendas and villages, and Spaniards, *castas*, and Nahua peoples, that marked the human ecology of Morelos.[44] In Oaxaca dispersal and variety ruled. The physical variety of Oaxaca was evident in the core subregions examined in this study — the eroded and in dry years parched sierras of the Mixteca Alta to the west, the comparatively broad and fertile Zapotec valleys that spread out south of Antequera (the region's capital city) in the center, and the steep and often rain-drenched Villa Alta sierras that suggested isolation and physical immobility toward the east.[45] The physical variety was matched by ethnolinguistic diversity. The Spanish and Nahuatl that dominated the linguistic environment of Morelos gave way to a multiplicity of indigenous languages: Mixtec in the Mixteca Alta; Zapotec in the central valleys; Zapotec, Mixe, and Chinantec in the Villa Alta mountains; and a series of lesser indigenous languages and linguistic localisms in all three subregions.

The human diversity of Oaxaca derived from a historical process whereby communities "reconstituted" (to use Marcello Carmagnani's apt term) an emphatically indigenous ethnicity in the seventeenth and eighteenth centuries.[46] Carmagnani has convincingly demonstrated that a given indigenous community might incorporate more than one indigenous ethnolinguistic group within the communal social body. This flexibility did not preclude, however, the building of a kind of psychologically insular militance that set village insider, identity, and customary right against ethnocommunal outsiders (and against persons considered internal traitors and tyrants). The core of Oaxaca was not only a rural world that remained about 90 percent Indian (see Table 2.1), not only a rural world whose indigenous communities retained a strong land base of their own, and not only a world where hacienda development was somewhat stifled and where the largest private haciendas belonged to Indian owners. It was also a world whose Indians separated into a plethora of strongly bounded — in the cognitive rather than literally physical sense — ethnic communities scattered across distinctive subregions. The barriers to dense interaction across the ethnic boundaries of Indian/non-Indian seemed compounded by barriers to dense interaction across the ethnic boundaries of Indian/Indian.

In truth, the active insularity built up by communities implied not an absence of interethnic contact or points of integration but the more subtle process of holding such contacts and networks at arm's length. The logic of insularity as a countervailing force to multiethnic arenas of coexistence and

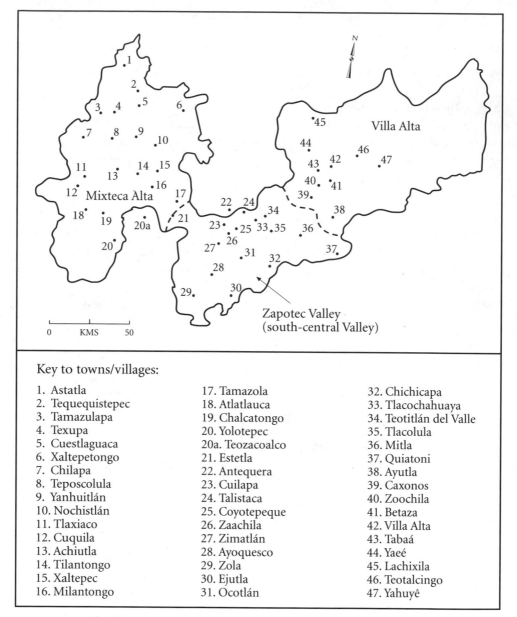

Key to towns/villages:

1. Astatla
2. Tequequistepec
3. Tamazulapa
4. Texupa
5. Cuestlaguaca
6. Xaltepetongo
7. Chilapa
8. Teposcolula
9. Yanhuitlán
10. Nochistlán
11. Tlaxiaco
12. Cuquila
13. Achiutla
14. Tilantongo
15. Xaltepec
16. Milantongo

17. Tamazola
18. Atlatlauca
19. Chalcatongo
20. Yolotepec
20a. Teozacoalco
21. Estetla
22. Antequera
23. Cuilapa
24. Talistaca
25. Coyotepeque
26. Zaachila
27. Zimatlán
28. Ayoquesco
29. Zola
30. Ejutla
31. Ocotlán

32. Chichicapa
33. Tlacochahuaya
34. Teotitlán del Valle
35. Tlacolula
36. Mitla
37. Quiatoni
38. Ayutla
39. Caxonos
40. Zoochila
41. Betaza
42. Villa Alta
43. Tabaá
44. Yaeé
45. Lachixila
46. Teotalcingo
47. Yahuyê

MAP 3. *The Oaxaca Region (core study area). (Adapted from Gerhard 1972)*

collaboration becomes clearer if we examine the political economy of rural Oaxaca. Oaxaca's indigenous peoples, like peasant smallholders and villagers in Morelos, sought to produce and market commodities independently in the trade circuits of a commercially active region. The Mixteca Alta, for example, exported cochineal insects and dye (the latter made from the laborious cultivation, collection, and processing of dried female cactus insects) to the regional capital city of Antequera, the Zapotec valleys, and ultimately to Europe; traded swine and sheep in all directions; and sent wheat and some sugar to Antequera. The Zapotec valleys south of Antequera shipped considerable maize to Antequera and to adjoining subregions with maize deficits and also exported cochineal and *pulque* (the fermented drink derived from the maguey century plant). The Villa Alta district produced not only cochineal and some silver but, most especially, tens of thousands of cotton mantles (*mantas*) destined each year for popular consumption in the cities and mining camps of the Mexican center-north. For humble peasants as well as wealthy Indians in Oaxaca, an important strategy of subsistence and well-being lay in the effort to insert themselves directly and independently into the corresponding trade circuits.

The problem was that the same trading circuits attracted the attentions of colonials who used the state's coercive power to dominate, if not monopolize, trade in key commodities. Spanish hacienda development was comparatively stifled in Oaxaca, in part because of the tenacity of indigenous resistance to land appropriations since early colonial times.[47] Moreover, the region's most lucrative commodities — cochineal, cotton textiles, and to a lesser extent maize — were produced in an Indian-owned economy by Indian-managed labor processes rather than in more capitalized Spanish-owned and Spanish-managed haciendas, plantations, workshops, and mines. All this implied not only the relatively weak growth of the non-Indian population but also a path to colonial prosperity founded on graphic ethnic coercion: the imposition of heavy tributes and forced commodity exchanges (the *repartimiento de mercancías*) by right of Spanish conquest and privilege over Indians. The object of this forced tribute and commodity exchange system was to channel the bulk of Indian-produced cochineal and cotton into Spanish-controlled mercantile circuits at a lesser price and in larger quantities than might accrue from voluntary market transactions. The principal players in the colonial alliance were a handful of colonial district magistrates (*alcaldes mayores* and, after administrative reform in the late 1780s, the *subdelegados* of regional intendants) and their merchant backers in Antequera, Mexico City, and Veracruz. In this system of tributary coercion, imposed by ethnic outsiders by right of ethnic domination upon an Indian-owned economy, interethnic collaboration took place mainly within a world of multiple indigenous ethnicities and was limited mainly to trading contexts.[48]

Power, Patriarchy, and the Mexican Poor : 31

The coercive integration of Oaxaca in an economy of ethnic tributary right placed a premium on the kind of insular militance that held interethnic contact at arm's length: a temporary device easily renounced, a social etiquette counterbalanced by the notorious "ungovernability" of communities that readily substituted riots and rocks for more peaceable languages of interethnic relations. If one may discern a limited peasant success in their struggles with colonials in Oaxaca, it lay in the effective assertion by communities of a right to guard zealously their land bases and to resist fiercely intrusions on their sense of community autonomy, self-governance, and identity in exchange for a grudging, partial acquiescence to the tribute-commodity system of the colonial magistrates.

In sum, late colonial Oaxaca presented an ethno-economy that contrasted sharply with that in Morelos. In Morelos the main axis of peasant struggle vis-à-vis powerful colonizers was defined by a sharpening contestation over land and water rights; in Oaxaca the main axis was defined by contestation over political coercion used to impose exploitative terms of trade and tribute upon a subjugated but Indian-owned economy. In Morelos the struggle over the appropriation of lands and waters took place in a densely heterogeneous racial context that placed a premium on peasant efforts to construct multiethnic and inclusionary networks of trade, reciprocity, work, and community in villages and haciendas. In Oaxaca the struggle over the coercion of low-cost commodities out of an Indian-owned economy took place in an overwhelmingly indigenous context and placed a premium on peasant efforts to construct communities of insular and exclusionary militance (notwithstanding the reality of interethnic contact and collaboration in indigenous market plazas, the colonial courts and markets of Antequera, and the like) that made governance, intrusiveness, and economic knowledge by outsiders all the more difficult.

One need not exaggerate the contrast of Morelos and Oaxaca or reify abstractions into the contrasting quintessential realities of two regions. The diversity of Oaxaca's subregions, for example, qualifies the contrast. Among the three subregions under consideration, Villa Alta stands closest to the construction of an emphatically indigenous and exclusionary ethnicity, an active ethnic insularity constructed in relation to a forced tribute and commodity distribution system. The Mixteca Alta, on the other hand, stands closest to more dense and ongoing multiethnic arrangements and understandings that partly redrew the map of community and property. Here non-Indian traders, peddlers, and smallholders made their greatest mark; land rental and tenantry rights ceded by Indians to non-Indians were not uncommon; and wheat and sugar production by non-Indian producers found a modest presence. In Morelos, too, one discerns patterns that qualify the contrast. On the one hand, the sheer productivity of the Indian-owned sector of a well-located

commercial economy invited, in a colonial context, the imposition of substantial tributes and fees and forced commodity exchanges, backed by the
alliance of political magistrate and merchant financier more notorious in
Oaxaca. If exploitative terms of tribute and trade did not define the main axis
of peasant struggle and constructions of ethnicity in Morelos, they were
nonetheless a significant feature of local life.[49] On the other hand, selected
cabecera communities of the northern *tierra fría*, and *sujeto* communities in
the *tierra caliente*, could assert a more emphatically Indian and exclusionary
construction of ethnicity that held the inevitable interethnic contacts and collaboration at greater distance from the ethnic community.[50]

Finally, in both Oaxaca and Morelos, constructions of ethnicity and peasant defense and well-being were complicated by internal differentiations between village elite and Indian commoner. In Oaxaca, for example, the assertion of community right vis-à-vis outsiders implied something different for
the land-poor Indian woman who wove cotton *mantas* or collected thousands
of cochineal insects off cactus than it did for the Indian governor who served
as prosperous broker in the political chain of tributary command or who held
access to good maize *milpas*. In Morelos, multiethnic reconstructions of community and collaboration implied something different for the land-poor Indian man who depended on supplemental day labor to stay afloat than it did
for the village leader — mestizo, Indian, or white — who coordinated the
village pool of day laborers, held good lands, and defended village land and
water rights. In both Oaxaca and Morelos, tension between elites and commoners could spill into factionalism, accusation of political abuse, and even
riots asserting community right against abusive community leadership. Folded
within the construction of community, whether more multiethnic or insular
in texture, was a sometimes subtle, more interior struggle over the social
meaning and power balances of community.[51]

These qualifications refine but do not erase the broad contrast of regional
ethno-economies. Compared to the peasants of Morelos, those of late colonial Oaxaca constructed lives more emphatically Indian in language and culture; more emphatically insular in ethnocommunal networks of work, property, reciprocity, and social identification; and more coercively and indirectly
integrated into the major markets and cities of the colonial Hispanic world.

In addition, the contrast in the regional ethno-economies that framed
peasant life is buttressed by a contrast of cultural foundations specifically pertinent for the study of gender in Mexico. In Morelos the main foundations in
play at the popular level derived from the Spanish and Nahua cultures at the
heart of imperial power in central Mexico.[52] These Spanish and Nahua cultural foundations are generally conceded by scholars to have been patriarchal
in gender orientation, whatever the specific differences between them and
however limited such terms are as a guide to social and cultural practice. In

Oaxaca the main foundations in play derived from the plurality of indigenous cultures — Mixtec, valley Zapotec, mountain Zapotec, Mixe, and the like — at the southern fringes of imperial power in Mexica (Aztec) and Spanish colonial times. The gender orientations of southern Mesoamerican cultures are more ambiguous and less well known to scholars than those of the Spanish and Nahua cultures nearer the imperial power center of Mesoamerica. But the assumption often is that Indian cultures in general and southern Mesoamerican cultures in particular manifested a more egalitarian approach to gender — or at a minimum a less pronounced and violent male dominance — than that presumed to prevail in the Spanish-mestizo cultures of central Mexico. Indian peasants, even Nahuas in central Mexico, are commonly considered to manifest a more relaxed approach to gender dominance and sexualized expressions of power than mestizos and plebeians considered more vulnerable to aggressive assertions of masculinity — an exaggerated negation of emasculation — within a Hispanized honor/shame culture. When the focus shifts to the Mesoamerican south a contrast perhaps subtle and even questionable in the central Mexican context gives way to more full-blown distinctions. The more relaxed approach to gender is evident in the weight given to complementarity rather than hierarchy in the scholarly and cultural discourses of gender; in the historical and contemporary observations of women's confidence, visibility, and occasional leadership in public arenas; and in historical findings that women within the Mesoamerican south were sometimes publicly recognized *cacicas* (village or ethnic lords by right of descent from the local nobility or ruling stratum).[53]

Missing from the Morelos/Oaxaca comparison, of course, is consideration of the racially fluid plebeian cultures in New Spain's cities and mining camps. In these settings popular culture rested on a plebeian rather than peasant foundation. In the peasant-based regions the economic foundation of everyday life and social networks among poor and laboring folk lay either in the landholding communities whose families produced food and agrarian commodities directly and perhaps supplemented their production and marketing activities with seasonal or day labor on landed estates; with the landed estates and their communities of resident peons and slaves and temporary laborers; or in *ranchero* zones where independent landowners of more middling fortune forged an existence in the interstices between community and hacienda possession. In such regions, opportunities for plebeian lifestyles such as muleteering, artisanal services, or the peddling of food, drink, or other wares at the local *tianguis* rested largely on the commercial health of the agrarian economy and might represent for many families and individuals a part-time supplementary activity and source of income. In the plebeian-based cities, on the other hand, the economic foundation of everyday life and social networks among poor and laboring folk lay in the sale of labor power, domestic service, or more specialized services and crafts in the urban marketplace. Opportunities for direct production of food or truck gardening commodities rested on the ability to accumulate land through successful participation in the specialized or lucrative sectors of the urban market.

The racial dynamics of the large cities and mining camps also varied significantly from regions such as Morelos and Oaxaca. In the urban plebeian milieu, one found the most thoroughly Hispanized or mestizo folk cultures — the most preponderant concentrations of self-defined Spaniards and racially ambiguous *castas* or mestizos; the greatest densities of interethnic networks in work, living quarters, family relations, and cultural diversion; and the widest use of Spanish rather than Indian language and the most acculturated Indian populations.

Mexico City, the richest city in Spanish America in late colonial times, also contained the biggest urban plebeian population.[54] This was the largest city in the Americas, with an estimated 137,000 persons in 1803. This was a social world where white racial labeling and a more or less Hispanic cultural milieu spilled well beyond elite and socially respectable middling ranks. Alexander von Humboldt, the celebrated German scientist, estimated the 1803 population as half white (49.3 percent); a fourth mestizos, mulattoes, or other *castas* (26.6 percent); and a fourth Indian (24.1 percent). The phenotype boundaries were blurred and confusing, since "a great number of the Mestizoes are almost as white as the Europeans and Spanish Creoles!"[55] Yet the comparative whiteness of Mexico City hardly signified a wide middling stratum of property owners who sustained a modestly comfortable living standard. On the contrary, poor persons predominated in the capital city. The city was inundated in the late eighteenth century with migrants who sought refuge from the grain crises and land concentrations that bedeviled the late colonial countryside. They joined a plebeian population already stressed by depressed wages and volatile grain prices, underemployment and crowded living quarters, and outbreaks of smallpox, typhus, and pneumonia. The economic hazards of plebeian life weakened the meaning of occupational backgrounds and labeling: a baker might have to look for work in a tobacco factory; a weaver might have to find work as a mason in a public works project; a tortilla vendor might switch to trading fruit; a domestic servant might take to food vending in the streets; and a mason might become a human carrier or a street hustler.

In a city half white and a fourth *casta*, contemporary observers estimated the plebeian population at four-fifths.[56] Historical research confirms the picture of extreme concentrations of wealth and a narrow middling sector. Even among private homeowners, a privileged group (in 1813 they constituted 1.7 percent of the city population, or perhaps 10 percent of families) in a city where most persons had to rent a cramped room or apartment, a mere sixth (16 percent) of the group accounted for three-fourths (75 percent) of the property value.[57] Humboldt considered the contrast between the European-like fortunes, architectural grandeur, and cultural glitter of Mexico City's leading families and the graphic destitution that cast twenty or thirty thousand persons into lives of near nakedness and street sleeping more extreme than the contrasts of rich and poor elsewhere in Spanish America. "Mexico," he proclaimed, "is the country of inequality."[58]

In this world of extremes, verticality and enclosure ordered urban space. Fantastic wealth was situated literally above plebeian destitution and exposure. At the street level of society circulated plebeian bustle and smells: the persons who walked to work, church, or diversion in old, often tattered clothes; the vendors, laborers, and passersby who prepared, sold, and consumed food and drink in public; the criers who hawked a commodity or service with a loud sing-song chant amidst the noise and distractions; the traders and food vendors who set up flimsy marketing stalls near popular taverns and plazas; the fun seekers who played games, joked, and flirted in public; and the desperate who found spots to relieve themselves or to sleep on the street. The street level mixed those who managed to sustain an honorable plebeian life one or two steps removed from sheer destitution, those who had fallen into the economic abyss, and those who fended off disaster through streetwise hustling and petty thievery. As we shall see (Chapter 11), elite fears of moral and social decay would inspire stereotypes of the street subculture and an effort to crack down on its alleged excesses. Above the noise and smells and bodily exposure at the street level circulated the privileged: those whose wealth enabled them to ride in carriages or on horses that elevated them to a plane above the smelly, the degraded, and the merely tainted; those whose servants, companions, and clothes allowed for symbolic enclosure and segregation when they descended to the street. Even the architecture of the city echoed the symbols of verticality and protective enclosure within a shared urban space: the apartments, workplaces, and storefronts of plebeians clustered toward the street level; the living quarters and offices of the honorable and the wealthy were lifted above the street level or were at least symbolically separated by exterior walls and interior gardens.[59]

The ordering of urban well-being and degradation, moreover, failed to line up clearly with ethnoracial rank or labeling. Notwithstanding the presence of two Indian districts (*parcialidades*) with their own corporate structures of rule, Indians amounted to only a fourth of the urban population, worked and lived and moved about in all areas of city, and were not always easily demarcated from their non-Indian counterparts by language, clothes, friendships, living quarters, or social styles.[60] The racial, cultural, and linguistic mixing and self-presentation of Mexico City's poor and laboring populations had yielded a popular culture of comparatively Hispanized or mestizo appearance. In addition the economic foundation of popular culture was plebeian and impoverished rather than middle class and modestly prosperous. In smaller regional capitals a city's modest size and tributary or commercial exploitation of a surrounding Indian countryside might allow the majority of a whitened population to forge a sense of middling rank and respectability sustained by relatively wide ownership of property.[61] In Mexico City the middling ranks probably failed to extend beyond the upper fifth of the urban population, and relatively prosperous plebeians competed in their work with a large mass of more desperate counterparts.[62]

The main differences of political economy and ethnocultural dynamics for comparative purposes are now evident. Morelos, a region of peasant villages and sugar estates strategically located near Mexico City, presents us with rural folk, a narrow majority of whom remained Indian but who were drawn into a life strategy marked by considerable ethnocultural mixing and by direct participation as laborers and vendors in Hispanized arenas such as haciendas and in major urban marketplaces. In addition this was a region where both Spanish and indigenous cultural roots encouraged patriarchal social mores. Oaxaca, a region of landholding villages in the Mesoamerican south, presents us with rural folk overwhelmingly indigenous and drawn into a life strategy marked by the building of strong ethnocommunal barriers and by greater colonial dependence on indirect or coercive forms of tributary or commercial exploitation. In addition the indigenous cultural roots of the region imparted a more ambiguous or flexible tone to gender relationships. Mexico City, the epicenter of colonial Hispanic culture and economy in New Spain, presents us with a vast, racially mixed plebeian population relatively Hispanized in language, appearance, and cultural mores, yet marked off, in daily life strategies and in cultural symbolism, as an urban subculture noxious to elite and middling sensibilities. If one were to situate popular culture in the three regions on spectra of apparent Hispanization and patriarchalism, Oaxaca would appear the least Hispanized and the least patriarchal, Morelos would occupy a middling position, and Mexico City would stand in the most Hispanized and patriarchal positions.

DESIGN OF AN INQUIRY (II): SOURCES AND METHODS

Some preliminary observations on sources and methods will provide orientation for the narratives and analysis in this book. Although this project incorporated a wide range of archival sources and supplemented archival research with readings of published works on Mexico and on themes of comparative or theoretical interest, the heart of the research is the study of late colonial criminal proceedings in some 800 incidents involving either violent assault (homicide, physically injurious assault, rape, kidnapping) or transgressions of sexual or family morality (adultery or incontinence, domestic maltreatment or neglect, seduction under pretense of false marriage promises, and the like). For purposes of qualitative analysis I reviewed all these cases carefully (as well as many criminal cases involving other matters). For statistical purposes somewhat smaller case sets of net incidents applied. For example, all morality incidents had to be jettisoned, for statistical purposes, from the Morelos and Oaxaca case sets because relatively small numbers weakened their reliability for regional analysis. After such pruning, the net number of criminal cases used for statistical purposes amounted to 708: 613 violence incidents and 108 morality incidents (of which 13 constituted overlapping violence and morality cases).

These criminal proceedings, of course, did not include all such violence and morality incidents but, rather, those where levels of injury, complaint, or judicial interest led to actual proceedings and investigations deposited in a court archive. Informal incidents outside the gaze of the authorities and incidents handled through quick verbal resolution or summary action by the authorities drop out of this core case set. For this very reason wide-ranging archival research and immersion, with an eye open for more informal or summary handling of similar disputes, has been an important part of the research process.

Nonetheless, for historical study of often hidden or elusive gender dynamics of everyday life among the multiracial poor the criminal records hold enormous research appeal. Their ability to generate sociologically meaningful data for statistical analysis, while useful, is only a secondary part of their appeal. Indeed, the size of the regional case sets, although adequate for basic social profiles and findings within the "portrait of an era" approach taken here, would not provide a convincing statistical platform for study of change over time.[63] The main attraction of these records lies in the extremely rich quality of the depositions and testimonies given by poor women and men, including Indians and *castas*. (One advantage of criminal violence records, compared with Inquisition records, is that Indians were not exempt from charges.) Although witnesses and interested parties certainly had the rules and expectations of the local judicial authorities in mind, their initial testimonies failed to fall into set legal formulas but often either followed the logic of local and domestic grievances, alliances, and networks or took on the character of rather rambling, sometimes quite intimate, social commentaries, character descriptions, and exposures of half-hidden vignettes. In murder cases or in assault cases where the injured person might yet die and where guilt and sentencing determinations required detailed understanding of context and circumstance, the range of witnesses drawn into the process was often quite extensive. Moreover, the records emphasize to an unusual degree the experience and perceptions of peasant and plebeian commoners—the friends, relatives, lovers, neighbors, and enemies of the interested parties rather than the more high-status leaders or cultural brokers of a community or barrio.

In short, both the characteristics of the persons involved and the testimonies they provided offer a rare opportunity to study gender relations and authority at the level of popular culture. The gossipy, personal character of the initial testimonies draws the researcher into the world of everyday behavior, expectations, and resentments among the poor and the colored, thereby exposing gender relations, tensions, and values difficult to discern in other historical records. In the initial stages of a case, at least, notaries provided near-verbatim recordings of testimonies (in addition to the legal consideration, their fee structures militated against formulaic summaries). As the case proceeded into its middle and latter legal stages, institutional mediation and stylization thickened notably. Fresh and sometimes rambling testimonies about immediate events became retrospective ratifications of earlier testimony through set legal formulas, responses to the leading questions of a formal legal interrogation or confession, summaries of confrontations between witnesses now committed to the essential and hardened outlines of discrepant stories, or summary descriptions of a case and its testimonies by lawyers providing a defense or a recommendation of legal findings and sentencing.[64] By focusing intensively on the rawer (less institutionally "cooked") early testimonies and by attending to the full range of witnesses and social commentaries, to the uncontested matter-of-fact observations or details declared in passing, and to the cultural plausibility of more directly relevant statements whose literal truth might have been contested, the researcher is able to achieve culturally realistic insight into everyday social dynamics and disputes that erupted in violent assault or in accusations of moral transgression.

In short, intensive qualitative readings of testimonies and social contexts enable us to see and to analyze in greater depth—with more feel for the humanity of the individuals and their cultural milieu—the ways in which gender relations and tensions worked themselves out in daily life, and the ways issues of gendered authority were connected to issues of political authority and culture more generally.

These preliminary remarks on sources and method have not yet addressed the most obvious objection to the use of criminal records as a window on society or popular culture as a whole (rather than as a means to study criminality or deviance as such). To the extent that criminal records privilege peculiar or deviant sociological slices of society, or at least abnormal moments or behaviors by otherwise "normal" individuals, how applicable to a wider sociocultural arena are findings drawn from criminal incidents and proceedings?

The question is a fair one, and I have sought to deal with it in two ways. First, I have examined the problem of deviant social profiles and behaviors rather extensively in Chapter 3, from statistical, qualitative, and theoretical points of view. As we shall see, the result is to diminish greatly the force of the deviance objection. Second, I have relied on a consistency-of-findings method as a check against bias or unwarranted extrapolation from criminal records. That is, I supplemented the research in criminal violence and morality records with simultaneous research in a wide array of additional sources that might yield patterns or clues about gender relationships and political culture. When supplementary research on such matters as church litigation of marriage, inquisitional proceedings, political riots or uprisings, community politics and' factionalism, civil litigation and property transmission, and discourses of expectation and disappointment in authority provided patterns or hints consistent with the findings on gender and political culture in the criminal records, I have gained all the more confidence in the wider applicability of criminal evidence for the particular themes of this study. In addition to this specific benefit, the supplementary sources allowed for a more diversified immersion in the social dynamics and cultural expectations that defined the late colonial milieu. As every historian knows, the immersion effect provides an important check in a more diffuse sense: it allows historical data and personalities to "talk back" in more diverse or unexpected ways.

FROM DESIGN TO INSPIRATION

We have devoted considerable space to questions of research design: the questions of historiography and theory, time and place, and sources and method that define the historian's craft in the technical sense. But in truth it is human inspiration, not research design, that motivates this study. History is at once art and science, vision and technique. Let us return to the call of persons such as those visited at the outset: María Teresa, José Marcelino, Micaela María. The drama and agony of their lives and the lives of many other peasants and plebeians is compelling — far more compelling than technical aspects of historical research and far more compelling, even, than the sometimes graphic physical depictions of injury, blood, and violence in the documents they bequeathed to us. The larger drama and agony lie in the way human kin and friends and families who developed bonds of solidarity, common interest, and at times affection with which to face the hardships and injustices of subaltern life could end up drawn nonetheless into bitterly divisive, poisoning struggles with one another. Sometimes these struggles over power and dignity among the powerless culminated in destructive violence; sometimes they did not. Either way, the process soured relationships among those who could ill afford such souring. The souring could render problematic and ambivalent and in some instances damage beyond repair the bonds of affect, collaborative adaptation, and destiny in common that may once have held force. Lives could be destroyed spiritually or physically.

This painful drama is the inspiration that motivates this study.

PART TWO

Before Zapata

Culture as Argument

CHAPTER 3

Counting Surprises

The Art of Cultural

Exaggeration

INTRODUCTION: DISCOURSES OF GENDER AND VIOLENCE

Between 1943 and 1963 Oscar Lewis returned again and again to talk with Pedro Martínez, a dirt-poor peasant of Tepoztlán who had fought with the Zapatistas, took on a certain prominence in the turbulent politics of his community after the war years, and survived to lament the declining interest of the young in the village needs and politics so important to their elders. For several reasons these interviews ended up providing raw material for a powerfully compelling book, perhaps the best biography of a peasant ever written.[1] Because Pedro Martínez's voice was supplemented by those of other family members—Pedro's wife, Esperanza, and their eldest surviving son, Felipe—the biography gained depth by constant movement between self-presentation and the more discordant orchestration of plural discourses. The structure of the narrative moved the reader back and forth between empathy and distance, understanding and critique. Because the family endured such graphic poverty and suffering—six of twelve children died young—and recounted hardship, illness, and violence in their own matter-of-fact voices, their history acquired a terrible authenticity. Theirs was neither the sanitized nostalgia of the well off nor the exaggerated melodrama of the shocked outside observer. Because Oscar Lewis had directed a superb historical and ethnographic field project in Tepoztlán, he and Ruth Lewis could shape, edit, and contextualize the interviews in a manner that convincingly integrated one family's history with a larger history of community and society.[2] In the biography of Pedro Martínez there emerged an almost equally tangible biography of Tepoztlán. The prominence of Tepoztlán in Mexican history—Tepoztlán had drawn into its local stage the major figures and social forces of Mexico from Cortés to Zapata—added to the sense of unity between a family history and a history of society. Finally, because Oscar Lewis defined almost all aspects of individual, family, and community life as pertinent, he pressed for knowledge and comment on topics normally shielded by a sense of privacy or politeness. This determination bore fruit in the holistic texture of Lewis's books on Tepoztlán and Pedro Martínez. It also meant, in a Tepoztlán where wife beating and family violence were commonplace although said to be declining,[3] that Oscar Lewis elicited Pedro Martínez's comments on violence against women.

The subject of violence and women was not a new one for Pedro Martínez. One could hardly expect otherwise, given the pervasiveness of physical punishment of wives and children, the commonplace escalation of familial tension or conflict into more serious beatings or injury, and the need to socialize the young. One of Pedro Martínez's responses drew on an oral tradition he had heard in his youth, when he elicited comment from the elders and his grandmother on the same subject. This chilling discourse is worth reproducing at length.[4]

My grandmother used to say that the people here were more cruel in the past. For example, the way they treated their mistresses, the loose women who went with many men. According to the old people, these same men would get together and say, "Well, how is it that she is going with me and with you and with him? She is just causing trouble. Why should we fight and kill each other while she has a good time? So, now let's do something to her."

One of them would take her out and then they would all get together and carry her off into the fields. And the things they would do to her! They drove a sharpened stake into the ground and greased it with a lot of lard. Then they all made use of her and had fun with her. They didn't kill her first but stuck her onto the point and there she sat until she died. Then they would undo her braids and put a *sombrero* on her head and a red kerchief around her neck, like a man. They would put a cigar in her mouth and cross her shawl on her chest the way a vagabond does, to show that she tried to revel and make merry like a man. When she was found the next morning, people would say only, "Well, now, who could have killed her? I wonder." They could only guess, but nobody really knew.

That's what the old folks told us they used to do. We would say sometimes, "Why do some people beat their women so much, their wives as well as their mistresses?" The old people would say, "What you see is nothing. It was worse before."

At least four related messages are encoded in the tale of the elders. First, the women who suffered truly harsh and cruel violence — gang rape, torture, and homicide — were deviants. Their insistence on sexual autonomy and gratification reversed gender roles, marked them as abnormal, and spelled trouble for their multiple lovers. Second, the women's deviance was indistinguishable from their status as loners. Unattached to a supervising patriarch (a father, a husband, an older brother or uncle, or a dominant lover), such women could pursue a delinquent sexual morality. Unprotected by family or lover, they could also be assaulted, tortured, and killed without provoking revenge. Third, such deviant loners were dangerous and brought violence upon themselves. Their role reversals subverted the social peace by provoking violence and mayhem among men. The dangers provoked by their deviance and their social isolation as unprotected and insubordinate female loners justified a violent male response and the impunity with which such a response was greeted. Fourth, the extremes of gender violence — the torture, rape, and homicide reserved for female delinquents and more commonplace in an earlier era of greater cruelty placed "normal" domestic beatings in a moderate light and underscored the benefits of family attachment and protection. Compared with the violence that befell female delinquents and compared with the violence of an earlier time, everyday domestic violence was rather trifling. A woman's subordination to patriarchal authority and sexual morality might subject her to beatings. But such violence did not contradict the notion that the same attachments protected her from the far more dangerous fate that befell isolated delinquents who strayed from morality and protection.

Something of the contrast, in this discourse, between "loose" women properly subjected to serious violence and "honest" women spared from it, is echoed in Esperanza's moral contrast between the Zapatista armies deserving of the villagers' loyalty and the Constitutionalist troops who invaded Morelos during the revolutionary wars of 1911–17. Soldiers on both sides, she observed, carried off women and female youth who had not managed to hide. But the Constitutionalists were indiscriminate kidnappers and rapists, while the Zapatistas respected the demarcation between loose and honest women. "The *zapatistas* were well liked in the village, because although it is true they sometimes carried off young girls, they left the majority of women in peace. And after all, everyone knew what kind of girls they took. The ones who liked that sort of thing!"[5]

The oral tradition recounted by Pedro Martínez demarcated serious male-on-female violence as a phenomenon directed mainly at deviant loners and more commonplace in the past. By way of contrast it defined domestic male-on-female violence as a lesser phenomenon, comparatively insignificant and lighter in injury. What trivialized more commonplace male-on-female violence even further was a related discourse on its motivation. In this discourse domestic violence often lacked a motivating cause within the social relations between men and women. As Pedro Martínez explained, the source of domestic violence was usually external to the domestic realm. "Occasionally, I would come home . . . and scold [Esperanza], unjustly sometimes, like any man can do. Then I regret those things of the moment and I try to console her. . . . I say to her, 'Look, *hija*, forgive me. Really, it's not in your nature to ask me why. You know how it is, how a man can be going along and something enters his heart or his spirit and makes him feel violent, on account of poverty or because of one of his friends, or maybe it's a debt. . . . Well, you know . . . the main mortifications of this life of ours.'"[6]

In this discourse "normal" male-on-female violence was a *descarga*, an unleashing of male tension motivated not by the social relationship between assailant and target but by a transference and venting of anger and frustration upon an available target. Motivations derived from the external realm of male-male social relations that generated cumulative frustration and passing fits of tyrannical temper. The fits would pass as frustration was released, and the bouts of violent temper were not to be traced to the specific conflicts of a power-laden domestic relationship. Even when Pedro Martínez connected domestic violence to male-female social dynamics, he rooted the connection less in the specific struggles of a power-laden relationship than in a more diffuse misogyny: the assumption that men had to assert their authority decisively, physically, even capriciously to keep women in line — even in the absence of specific conflicts over gender right and obligation. "[Village] men do get drunk sometimes and they do beat their wives, but not very much any more. Before, it was done in every house. . . . It is a matter of village custom and the ways of the women. Here, if a man is easy on his wife and then hits her later, she will raise her hand to him."[7] Husbands therefore trained wives to submit to their authority, and such submission included acceptance of passing fits of *descarga* anger and violence rooted in external frustrations. These fits had the added advantage of keeping women in their properly subordinate place, and thereby preventing domestic struggle and contestation over specific issues of gender right and obligation. *Descarga* violence against women was not seriously injurious, and it had no specific motivation.

We have introduced Pedro Martínez not to argue for continuity of gender relations since late colonial times but to expose, in the language of a Morelos commoner from our own times, the swirl of cultural mythology, exaggeration, and stereotypes that surrounds any attempt to study gender and violence in Mexico. The crux of the problem is not truth or falsehood in a simple sense, but the "art of cultural exaggeration." Even if the specific tale of cruel vengeance inflicted on deviant female loners were literally true, to what extent was it a misleading magnification of a small truth to place violent ritual vengeance against deviant loners on center stage as *the* representation of willful and truly serious violence against women? Even if *descarga* violence vented upon wives and lovers without apparent motivation literally happened, to what extent was it a misleading magnification of a modest truth to define such ventings against female dependents as *the* representation of domestic violence? Even if *descarga* moods and incidents whose injurious consequence were slight actually occurred, to what extent was it a misleading magnification to imply that most or all domestic violence was less than seriously injurious? When stereotypes and clichés represent not fictional invention in a purist sense but the magnification of real phenomena into archetypal statements, their power becomes all the harder to resist. One can always find true anecdotes to match the archetypal statement. In the circular process of corroboration, the archetypal statement then swells the anecdote into an imposing, quintessential representation of reality.

In the case of gender and violence in Mexico the discourses of Pedro Martínez open the door to a much larger realm of stereotypes, understood as the art of exaggeration rather than pure invention. Particularly important are four sets of stereotypes: (1) the equation of assailants with deviants and loners; (2) the association of gender violence with Hispanic-mestizo folk rather than Indians, and with plebeians rather than peasants; (3) the attribution of most violence to property or class issues on the one hand and *descarga* ventings on the other; and (4) the attribution of violence against females to a combination of willful violence against deviant women and less serious *descargas* against more "normal" female dependents. Confronting cultural exaggeration requires that we go beyond countering anecdote with anecdote. Instead we must construct social profiles designed to test the hypotheses implicit in each set of stereotypes.

SOCIAL PROFILES (I): OF DEVIANTS AND LONERS

Let us begin with the problem of deviance.[8] For the Morelos region the net case set from which we may construct social profiles consists of 206 incidents of violence leading to criminal prosecution during the years 1760–1821.[9] These cases clustered in the closing decades of colonial rule: fully three-fourths (75.7 percent) of the incidents occurred during 1790–1821. The Morelos cases tended toward seriously injurious violence. Homicide alone accounted for about half (53.9 percent) the incidents. Major assaults excluding rape and kidnapping (that is, violence causing wounds or internal injury sufficiently serious to make ongoing medical treatment and supervision important) accounted for about another quarter (23.3 percent) of the pool. When sexual assault (6.3 percent) is taken into account, the aggregated total of homicidal and major bodily violence accounts for fully four-fifths (83.5 percent) of the incidents. The assailants were mainly individuals (93.0 percent) rather than bands of four or more persons and were about nine-tenths (89.7 percent) male.[10]

The problem of deviance may be summarized as the supposition that these records privilege especially deviant individuals or social groups — that is, pathological behaviors by loners and criminals at the fringes of social norms and conventions and perpetually in trouble. A more subtle version of the problem supposes that the records privilege deviant moments or situations in the lives of otherwise normal individuals. Such people may have deviated from their usual patterns of behavior in fields of time-space — drunkenness, late-night hours, isolated roads and spots, relations with loners or strangers — that temporarily suspended normal social convention.

On every count the profiles of assailants and surrounding circumstances fail to support these suppositions. (See Table 3.1.) For the cases in which we can confirm the marital or family status of assailants, we may conservatively estimate that family-attached assailants — that is, married individuals and unmarried individuals living as dependent minors — represented nearly three-fourths (72.4 percent) of the offenders.[11] Loners — widowers and widows, unmarried individuals living as adult household-head equivalents, and abandoned spouses — constituted the remainder (27.6 percent). These proportions echo those in society at large. Moreover, a Chi-square test for statistically significant nonrandom distributions of variables fails to establish correlations between loners and gender-rooted violence.[12] The statistical insignificance of loners in the assailant group is consistent with the profile of previous criminal arrest. Four-fifths (80.7 percent) had no formal arrest record prior to the incident. Only one in twenty (5.5 percent) had been previously arrested for crimes of violence. In addition, examination of circumstances where the normal rules of social convention may have been suspended — extreme late-night hours, isolated roads and spots, scenes of heavy drinking, situations where victims were loners or strangers to their assailants — also fails to support the suspicion that violence records privilege moments of deviance in otherwise normal lives. (Again, see Table 3.1.)

Even on the sometimes vexing issue of drinking, the data corroborate social science studies that undermine the presumption that the physiological effects of drinking lead to deviant outbursts by individuals uncontrolled by social convention. These studies suggest that drinking behavior varies widely by culture, that it conforms with predictable cultural expectations, and that it has little causal relevance in explaining acts of violence or deviance. In some cultural contexts the discourse of drinking behavior becomes an acceptable convention whereby assailants — and their targets — may lessen an assailant's personal responsibility for acts of violence whose causes have little to do with drinking.[13] In about two-thirds (64.9 percent) of the Morelos incidents, drinking by assailants was either nonexistent or unmentioned despite a context in which drinking, if present, would have been mentioned to diminish legal or cultural culpability. The irrelevance of drink accounted for an even stronger majority (78.2 percent) among the targets of violence. Equally revealing, the minority of cases where drinking was clearly or ambiguously mentioned as relevant clustered toward more seriously injurious incidents. A (somewhat weakened) surrogate measure of this clustering effect is visible if one examines the association between alcohol as a mentioned relevant factor and homicidal rather than nonhomicidal violence. For assailants depicted as alcohol-influenced, the odds that a case was homicidal were nearly three times (2.8) the odds for other assailants; for victims of homicide, who could not provide a competing discourse if they died soon after the wounding, the corresponding odds rose to over five (5.5). (See Table 3.2.) These nonrandom distributions suggest that alcoholic consumption was not so much a cause of deviant outbursts or loss of control as it was a discursive strategy that gained urgency when homicide or grave wounds placed the accused in jeopardy. Assailants needed to convince judges that drink-related loss of control was a mitigating factor. As with loners, a Chi-square test to probe whether alcohol-influenced assailants were more likely than other assailants to have committed gender-rooted violence yields negative results.[14]

In short, the data undermine the deviance stereotype. Assailants were generally neither loners nor previously arrested; incidents of violence did not generally occur in fields of time-space when normal rules were suspended; and these variables bore no significant association with the distribution of gender-rooted violence. The quantitative findings match up well with more qualitative and theoretical insights. In reading the records, especially the gender violence records, one is struck by how normal and matter-of-fact most of the people and situations seem to have been. The testimonies of witnesses show that often a criminal transgression involved not so much pathological peculiarity as an extension of normal rules and practices to an unacceptable conclusion or accident. In male-on-female violence, for example, the culturally commonplace practice of physical punishment of wives by husbands who considered their patriarchal authority challenged could, in the heat of bitter and escalating dispute, cross over almost imperceptibly into deadly criminal violence. In male-on-male violence the commonplace practice of threatening or initiating a fight if one's manly honor was publicly challenged, while relying on bystanders to restrain the escalation and prevent serious injury, could easily slide into episodes of serious violence. Restraint might prove inefficacious, verbal escalation might spark added volatility, or reflexes dulled by drink might turn offensive or defensive feints into serious injury.[15] The pertinent theoretical and sociological literatures support the impressions given by the testimonies. Sociological studies of violent crime underscore the normality of assailants within their cultural (or subcultural) contexts.[16] Studies of family violence in particular underscore a pervasiveness of violence that transforms criminal instances of family violence into episodes, within a much broader class of similar phenomena, when the normal dynamics of conflict, threats, and violence cross a certain threshold of injury, bitterness, escalation, or repetition that leads to formal proceedings.[17] Feminist sociologists and criminologists argue convincingly that as offenders and victims, women enter criminal records and proceedings as striking extensions of normal rules and practices of gender comportment.[18] Tempting and comfortable as it may be to assume that criminal violence records capture pathological loners and deviants or temporarily abnormal behavior by otherwise normal individuals, the stereotypes built on this assumption do not hold up under scrutiny. The term *exceso*, so ubiquitous in the criminal documents of late colonial Mexico, captures the point nicely. Often, episodes of criminal violence represented not so much a rupture that stood apart from normal social dynamics but an excess committed within a recognizable logic of behavior.

SOCIAL PROFILES (II): OF MESTIZOS AND PLEBEIANS

The normality of assailants does not address the question of sociocultural differentiation within a multiethnic world. A second realm of entrenched stereotypes suggests that records of violence, above all violent episodes used to examine gender, will better capture the sociocultural segments of popular society more inclined to violent and sexually charged expressions of personal dominance.

The key axis of distinction is between relatively Hispanized and racially mixed popular sectors (mestizos, mulattoes and other *castas*, and poor whites), and Indians.[19] The latter group presumably exhibited greater flexibility, if not egalitarianism, on issues of gender subordination and leaned toward a view of the world that emphasized complementarity and harmony. The non-Indians, especially low-status non-Indians such as mestizos and poor whites, presumably tolerated challenges to gender dominance and honor more poorly and moved toward violence and sexually charged conflicts more readily. A corollary draws a parallel distinction. Plebeians, presumably more Hispanized or mestizo in culture and racial composition and less rooted in an alternate culture of indigenous values, were relatively vulnerable to the volatile interplay of emasculation and compensatory violence within a Hispanic framework of honor and degradation. Peasants, on the other hand, tended toward a more Indian way of life, a cultural foundation more resistant to gendered outbursts of compensatory violence by the dispossessed in a Hispanic/mestizo cultural framework. Yet another variant on the sociocultural differentiation problem asks whether the records of gender-rooted conflicts and violence might highlight comparatively well off strata within popular society: the upper peasants, upper plebeians, and middling strata for whom Hispanic honor/shame notions and the control of women and virginity were more viable and bore greater connection to property transmission and inheritance. To explore violence and gender in a manner that focuses on the more mestizo, plebeian, or middling sectors of rural popular society, of course, would be illuminating and revealing in its own right. This would be different, however, from a study of the Indian and peasant sectors that comprised a majority in the bottom of the color-class pyramid.

We may summarize the problem of sociocultural differentiation as the supposition that the records of criminal violence privilege non-Indians rather than Indians, plebeians rather than peasants, and high-status or middling strata of popular society rather than low-status commoners. A more subtle version of the problem supposes that within the set of violence records the episodes of gender-rooted violence are more closely associated with non-Indians, plebeians, or high-status popular sectors.

Let us begin with ethnicity. The overall distributions of assailants and targets represent a broad cross-section of the region's ethnic populations, and the Indian shares in particular are of the same order of magnitude as those in Morelos as a whole. (See Table 3.3.) This broad representativeness holds despite a somewhat greater tilt toward lower ethnic status among targets rather than assailants (65.3 percent and 55.5 percent Indian, respectively). In addition, the distinction between Indian and non-Indian fails to yield statistically significant associations with the distribution of gender rooted violence.[20]

Since we lack reliable estimates of the shares of the Morelos regional population who may be plausibly identified as peasant or plebeian, we cannot compare their order of magnitude with those found among assailants and targets in the criminal records. Nonetheless, the peasant dimension of the region comes through strongly in the records. (Again, see Table 3.3.) Better than three-fifths of assailants and targets were peasants. Moreover, as in the case of Indians versus non-Indians, the distinction between peasant and plebeian fails to yield statistically significant nonrandom associations with the distribution of gender-rooted violence.[21]

The expectations suggested by stereotypes surrounding the distinctions between Indian/non-Indian and peasant/plebeian fail, therefore, to show up in the violence records or in the distribution of gender-rooted violence within the records. A similar finding occurs when we distinguish between low-status and upper-status groups within the peasant/plebeian milieu. (See Table 3.3.) The low-status commoners account for about three-quarters of the total pool (72.6 percent of assailants and 77.9 percent of targets), while the more intermediate sectors account for less than a fifth (18.5 percent of assailants and 17.2 percent of targets). Only small minorities of assailants (19.5 percent) and targets (12.3 percent) could sign their names.[22] Moreover, the distinction between low-status commoners and their more prosperous counterparts fails to yield statistically significant associations with the distribution of gender-rooted violence. The main significant finding is the moderately greater vulnerability of low-status commoners to homicidal violence, whatever the motivation of the incidents.[23] This finding is consistent with the indications that the targets of violence in these records tended toward slightly lower status than the assailants, but that both groups were of predominantly poor extraction.

We may lay to rest, then, not only the stereotyped exaggerations linked to deviance but also those linked to sociocultural differentiation. The violence records as a whole and their gendered dimension in particular do not focus mainly on a particular sociocultural segment or subculture predominantly non-Indian or plebeian or middling. The records touch a broad spectrum of popular society—it is the elite groups who are sparsely represented in the criminal records—and include sufficient numbers of Indians and non-Indians, peasants and plebeians, and low-status commoners and their more high-status or middling counterparts to allow for meaningful statistical comparison.

Ironically the biases of the records line up not with sociocultural segments or subcultures but with age and sex distinctions *within* popular culture. (See Table 3.4.) Although the population of assailants and targets touches a wide spectrum of age groups, the assailants, especially, lean toward youth (near-adults approaching marriage age, approximately fifteen to nineteen years old) and relatively young adults (less than thirty-five years old). In general, the age spread of the targets of violence is less compressed, but even so, violence against younger children is poorly represented in the criminal records.[24] The sex distribution of assailants and targets also exhibits greater compression among assailants, about nine-tenths of whom were male,[25] than among targets, about one-third of whom were female. Women are obviously underrepresented in the records as a whole and are poorly visible as assailants subjected to criminal violence charges. As we shall see, however, women's visibility as targets of violence is sufficient to generate meaningful statistical comparison of violence against women and men as well as a reasonably thick set of materials for qualitative analysis.

The age and sex biases of the records are noteworthy, but they do not alter our conclusions about the stereotypes linked to sociocultural differentiations between Indians and non-Indians, peasants and plebeians, and low-status commoners and comparatively middling popular groups. Particularly on the questions of age and sex, moreover, one should bear in mind that offenders and victims constituted but a portion of the people directly involved in the social relations recorded in the criminal violence documents. Most assailants were family-attached rather than loners, and most had relatives of both genders and varied ages directly affected by or engaged in the swirl of events, relationships, and disputes that led to violence. As is clear in a qualitative reading of the records themselves, the community of participants, witnesses, and directly affected individuals spread well beyond the age and sex map of the assailants and targets. In short, the criminal violence records open an entire sociocultural world. That world was predominantly poor and illiterate, and its gender-rooted violence was as closely associated with Indians and peasants as with non-Indians and plebeians.

SOCIAL PROFILES (III): OF VIOLENCE, GENDER, AND MOTIVATION

Even if the records of criminal violence do not privilege deviants and loners, and even if they do not privilege mestizo or plebeian sociocultural slices of popular society, there is always the possibility that gender-rooted disputes constitute a very modest share of the overall pattern. If violent incidents were most often either willful acts motivated by class and property-rooted disputes or were more casual *descarga* ventings that lacked specific motivation, then analysis of gender relations and conflicts through the prism of violence shrinks somewhat in its significance. The cultural imagery surrounding the motivations of male violence underscores the importance of property/class issues on the one hand and *descarga* ventings on the other. The poverty and subjugations of peasant life and the associated land struggles that loom so large in the history of Morelos lead us to connect willful male violence to issues of class and property. Land disputes, robbery, labor relations, tributary extortions, and debt and credit — these are the issues that spring to mind when we think about the motivations of willful violence by peasants, above all Morelos peasants locked in a kind of death struggle with an expansive sugar hacienda economy.[26] To the extent, moreover, that *descarga* ventings are themselves viewed as diffuse effects of color-class frustration, the implications of studying gender through the medium of violence shrink further before the ever expanding mass of violence rooted in color-class and property issues. Even if *descarga* ventings acquire a gendered social expression, the latter becomes something of an epiphenomenon: an exaggerated and compensatory masculinity that protests the symbolic emasculations derived from the injustices, legacies, and psychologies of the color-class order.[27]

The attribution of most violence to property/class issues and to *descarga* ventings calls upon us to construct a profile of the motivations of disputes culminating in criminal violence proceedings. But to construct such a profile first requires that we deconstruct the meaning of motivation. The problem of motivation has some complicated wrinkles, especially in the context of homicide. On the one hand, at least since Freud, Western analysis of human motivation extends into the realm of the human unconscious. Although this extension has not particularly troubled historians when analysis focuses on the experiences or relations of social groups as groups, it brings forth knottier issues in more intensely personal historical analysis such as biographies or individual acts of violence. For the latter, if one seeks to understand the etiology of motivation at a deeply psychological level, the results are inevitably speculative and problematic. On the other hand, if one chooses to take assailants' statements of motivation and institutional glosses at face value, one accepts a certain amount of obfuscation. In the Western legal and cultural tradition and particularly in the context of homicidal violence, "crimes of passion" or spontaneous outburst have been more excusable than those of premeditation or calculated, rational pursuit of interest.[28] Moreover, elite prejudice and mythology regarding casual outbursts of violence by subordinated groups tends to ratify the obfuscation. The net result, if one does not scratch beneath the surface to scrutinize more closely the social context, dynamics, and discourses — including the assailants' own more extended explanations — of a violent act is that one accepts rather meaningless and obfuscating categories of motivation: passionate outbursts, drunken fits, inexplicably escalating altercations over trivia, and the like. These categories, of course, resonate strongly with the mythology of *descarga* ventings.[29]

Fortunately the problem of motivation is not nearly as intractable as these considerations might at first sight suggest. The quest for a deeply psychological level of explanation was most urgent in an early era of criminology, when crimes of violence were more readily assumed to be the expression of deep-seated psychopathologies among offenders. Once one shifts the question of criminal violence to more normal or culturally patterned populations, however, this level of explanation loses much of its urgency. Psychoanalytical and similar probings, while insightful about the deeper dimensions of human motivation in general, no longer seem indispensable to discerning the issues, arguments, and contexts that animate conflicts and violence among "normal" people.[30] Similarly, the obfuscations of assailants and related institutional glosses such as police blotters pose a less serious problem than appears to be the case at first sight. When the focus of analysis is the attempt to establish the degree of culpability and the sentencing of an alleged assailant, the role of the assailant's deeper motivations or "uncontrolled passions" may take on urgency. But once one shifts the focus from the culpability of accused offenders to the causes of the disputes that culminated in violence, the problem of motivation also shifts. The shift may be summarized as that between asking whether an assailant killed a potential burglar out of deep-seated fears leading to an overreactive self-defense, or whether the reason the assailant and target got embroiled in a dispute in the first place was an attempted robbery.[31] When one scrutinizes closely the discourses of assailants, targets, and witnesses; sets these discourses in dynamic social context; and inquires about the causes of the dispute rather than the culpability of the individual offender, it does not become difficult to discern how individuals become entangled in arguments and situations culminating in violence.[32]

In short, once one addresses the question of motivation less as a question of interior psychology (whether the psychopathology of presumed deviants or the unconscious motivations and volcanic passions of otherwise "normal" individuals) and more as a question of social relations—provocations, contestations, and assertions recognizable as such in a given cultural milieu—the motivations of disputes leading to violence are in most instances reasonably clear. For depth and corroboration one needs to examine the documentary discourses closely, critically, and sometimes laboriously. But the basic motivations of dispute turn out to be accessible. As two leading criminologists put it (in the rather clinical language of their field), "In general, the less clearly motivated a murder is (in the sense that it is impossible to comprehend the motives) the higher is the probability that the homicidal subject is very abnormal."[33]

Let us turn, then, to the motivations of disputes leading to criminal violence incidents in Morelos. The initial coding of motivations followed a logic of disaggregated categories that allowed for more precise subcategories that might subsequently be aggregated into major categories such as gender-rooted violence, property/class violence, and *descarga* ventings. Even if one glances at the disaggregated list of frequencies (Table 3.5), however, what leaps to the eye is the prominence of gender-rooted disputes in the overall pattern of violence. Male-female disputes over gender right and obligation by itself accounted for about a fourth (24.1 percent) of all the incidents. Yet this was only one item within a considerably larger set of gender-rooted incidents. Violence rooted in property/class conflicts and casual or inexplicable ventings, on the other hand, accounted for comparatively modest shares in the overall pattern.

Indeed, once one constructs the major categories of motivation (Table 3.6), gender-rooted violence accounts for by far the largest share of incidents. Gender-rooted violence accounted for about half (56.2 percent) the incidents, property/class violence for about a quarter (24.1 percent), and *descarga* ventings for about a seventh (14.1 percent). (The percentage estimates in the preceding sentence represent midway points between the restricted and amplified models presented in Table 3.6.) If one excludes incidents attributed to female assailants and mixed-gender assailant groups, the structure of motivation in the remaining violence incidents—that is, those attributed exclusively to male assailants—remains much the same. Indeed, gender-rooted violence increases slightly (to 60.3 percent).[34]

These figures help us to understand stereotypes as cultural exaggeration. On the one hand, they demonstrate that one may discover considerable anecdotal material to convey a sense for the reality of *descarga* ventings of casual violence as well as more willful violence rooted in property/class motivations (robberies, money and land disputes, work conflicts, and the like). On the other hand they demonstrate that cultural stereotypes expand the reality of phenomena deemed quintessential into magnified representations that crowd out phenomena of greater frequency in everyday life. In the process the weight assigned to diverse phenomena may become culturally inverted. *Descarga* ventings that accounted for about a seventh of violent incidents leading to criminal prosecution crowd out the specific gender-rooted conflicts that animated about half the incidents.

We may lay to rest, therefore, the attribution of most violence to property and class issues on the one hand and *descarga* ventings on the other. On the contrary, gender-rooted disputes accounted for the emphatically largest share of violent incidents. Moreover, gender-rooted violence was as seriously injurious as incidents sparked by other motivations; the distributions of gender-rooted violence fail to yield statistically significant associations with non-homicidal rather than homicidal violence.[35] Under these circumstances and in view of the normalcy of the populations and social dynamics illuminated in the records, it seems entirely appropriate to study violent incidents and the documentary materials they generated for the way such incidents open a world of gendered social life, conflicts, and accommodations.

Of course, one may yet ask whether gender-rooted disputes accounted for a minor share of male-on-male violence, even if they accounted for large shares of male-on-female and total violence. It is possible that the imagery that attributes violence mainly to *descarga* ventings and to property/class conflicts corresponds well to a world of male-male interaction in which gender-rooted disputes (as distinct from less conflictual forms of gendered bonding and as distinct from disputes where a gendered behavior was present but not specifically at the center of the dispute) played a slight role in stimulating violence. The issues raised by this possibility are really twofold. First, did the structure of motivations leading to violent dispute vary significantly according to the gender of the participants? Second, once one takes cognizance of the variance by gender, does gender-rooted violence decline into a minor category of male-on-male violence?

The short answers to these questions are yes and no. Yes, the structure of motivation varied importantly by the gender of the participants. But no, this variance did not imply that gender-rooted violence declined into a minor category of motivation in all-male settings. Let us begin the longer answers by comparing the predominance of gender-rooted violence according to the gender of the participants. The variance in the structure of motivation is indeed quite striking when the focus is on the gender of targets rather than assailants. If we use conservative (that is, restricted model) criteria, the share of violence attributable to gender-rooted disputes varies dramatically. By these criteria gender-rooted violence accounted for about a third (32.3 percent) of violence directed at male targets but about six-sevenths (86.7 percent) of that directed at females. The odds that violence directed at females was gender-rooted amounted to 13.6 times the odds in violence directed at males. (See Table 3.7.) But does this contrast in the structure of motivation imply that gender-rooted violence was a rather minor motivation in male-on-male violence? Not at all. Even when we isolate male-on-male violence, gender-rooted violence accounts for the largest share of cases (44.5 percent, if one selects the midway point between restricted and amplified models; see Table 3.8). The structure of major motivations is far more diversified in male-on-male violence than in mixed-gender situations. Nonetheless, even in a male-on-male context, the exaggerated images of *descarga* and property/class violence crowd out the most frequent motive of dispute: the claims of gender.

Gender-rooted disputes constituted the predominant share of criminal violence episodes. Their weight enlarges the sense of implication one may draw from the study of gender through the medium of violence records. To put it another way, whether one studies the case set as a whole or male-on-male violence in particular, the structure of motivation demonstrates that a focus on gender-rooted violence does not turn a molehill into a mountain.

SOCIAL PROFILES (IV): OF WOMEN AND DEVIANCE,
MEN AND FRUSTRATION

These findings bring us face to face, finally, with our fourth set of stereotypes: the attribution of violence against females to willful violence against female deviants and to less serious or injurious *descarga* ventings against more normal female dependents. The normality of assailants, the sociocultural breadth (at the level of popular culture) of the individuals who appear in the records, and the weight of gender in the motivation of disputes do not by themselves dispense with the imagery and stereotypes voiced in the words of Pedro Martínez. Perhaps in the end the targets of the most dangerous and willful (that is, clearly motivated) violence against females were indeed loners and deviants. Perhaps, too, instances of more normal domestic and family violence were both less injurious and attributable to the ventings and diffuse misogyny associated with male-on-female *descarga* violence. Upon closer examination, will the entrenched ideas we have thus far called stereotypes turn out not to be so exaggerated after all?

Let us begin with the problem of female deviants and loners. As we have seen, in the discourse of legitimate cruelty and violence directed at female deviants, women's deviance was indistinguishable from their status as independent loners. The woman who freed herself from the moral vigilance of a supervising patriarch (a father, a husband, a lover exerting quasi-marital rights, or a surrogate such as a supervising relative) was freer to pursue a delinquent sexual independence or to subvert gender roles, and the woman who had been loosened from the protective disciplinary vigilance of supervising patriarchs and kin was presumably most vulnerable to seriously injurious violence. The discourse demonstrates, of course, a desire to socialize female youth, married and unmarried, to accept the necessity of patriarchal supervision as a protection against violence. It expresses as well a resentment of female loners who did not submit to the symbols of gender convention. Particularly important in this regard were those widows or other older women who had outlived a life cycle phase of direct subordination to a father or husband (or a family elder such as a mother-in-law or an uncle), who chose not to submit to quasi-marital subordination to a dominant male partner, and who adopted a social style too assertive or extraverted to conform to the stance of moral discretion and social reserve prescribed for more respectable, morally upright widows.[36]

But the socializing and expressive dimensions of the discourse, important as they are, do not necessarily disprove the possibility that criminal violence targeted female loners. Nonetheless, female targets of violence were overwhelmingly family-attached individuals. Married women accounted for about two-thirds (64.9 percent) of targets, and female dependents living under the supervision of household heads for another fifth (19.3 percent). Female loners, usually widows, accounted for less than a sixth (15.8 percent) of the targets. These figures compare well with estimates of loners in the female tributary adult population of Morelos. (See Table 3.9.) Moreover a statistical test of variance according to the gender of the victim shows that female targets of violence were no more likely than male targets to be loners rather than family-attached.[37] These figures, if they are at all reliable, belie the myth of patriarchal protection. Contrary to the expectations embedded in patriarchal discourses stigmatizing female loners as individuals both morally suspect and especially targeted for violence, women's vulnerability to incidents of criminal violence bears no significant statistical correlation with their isolation from familial vigilance and protection by a patriarch or patriarchal surrogate.

Yet who assaulted the women? That family-attached status afforded little or no extra protection against criminal violence tells us little, by itself, about the human sources of violence against women. One might hypothesize, for example, that women suffered violence *despite* the protection of patriarchs, family, and quasi-kin. At moments of vulnerability, when protective vigilance by a woman's primary social group weakened, she might suffer violence by acquaintances or strangers beyond the primary group of kin and fictive kin with whom she engaged in dense relations of mutual obligation, loyalty, interest, and reciprocity—a protective solidarity that was not mutually exclusive with an internal hierarchy of duty and authority. In this line of reasoning, when a husband, father, or protective lover assuming the husband role left the village for day work on a sugar estate or was en route to a market, or when a wife or daughter or otherwise attached female walked alone to a river to fetch water or to a *milpa* to provide tortillas or to the *tianguis* of a nearby village or hacienda, effective male vigilance weakened. Even a protected female might prove vulnerable to assault. Alternatively one might hypothesize that women suffered violence not despite patriarchal vigilance and protection but because of it. In other words, precisely because patriarchal vigilance implied the problem of authority, discipline, and accommodation in an unequal and often conflictual web of relationships, the greatest danger of violence actually came from within the primary group of real and fictive kin who theoretically shielded their female dependents from external dangers. Each hypothesis is consistent with the finding that family-attached females were as vulnerable as loners as well as the hypothesis that women faced a cruel trade-off: protection against the harm that male acquaintances and strangers felt free to inflict on female loners required commitment to primary relations of familial subordination that, in turn, exposed women to domestic violence.

The crux of the matter, if we are to sort out and evaluate such hypotheses, is the assailant/target relationship, and on this point the evidence is unequivocal. The most frequent assailants in violence against females were the relatives and quasi-relatives who formed a group of primary solidarity, authority, mutuality, and obligation. Even a casual glance at the disaggregated distribution of assailant/target relations is quite clear: husbands account for about a third (33.3 percent) of the incidents, and quasi-husbands (that is, sex partners adopting a husbandlike authority) account for about another fifth (18.3 percent). When one adds other kin and quasi-kin to the count, the cumulative share of primary relations rises to nearly two-thirds (63.3 percent). More secondary relations—friends, acquaintances, sex rivals, and enemies who constituted a known world of social intercourse beyond the primary group— figure in perhaps a third (31.7 percent) of the incidents, and the tertiary realm of interaction among strangers amounts to a marginal share (5.0 percent). Even a casual comparison of these shares with those in all incidents, regardless of the target's gender, draws attention to the specificity of assailant/target relations in the case of female targets of violence. (See Table 3.10.)

Indeed, the vulnerability of women and female youth to violence at the hands of would-be protectors—the husbands, sexual partners, and other kin who exerted claims in and authority over female relations and dependents and who presumably shielded their women and female youth from aggressions by others—captures a strong gender contrast. This contrast comes out strongly even in a crude model that distinguishes simply between primary, secondary, and tertiary relationships. In this model the odds that female victims of violence were targeted by primary relations were ten (10.4) times the odds for male victims. One may refine the model by subdividing primary relations into an "inner primary" category composed of partners with direct sexual claims (spouses, sex partner/concubine relations outside formal marriage, and *novio* relations that implied intent to pursue marriage and the possibility of sexual contact within the framework of marriage intentions) and an "outer primary" category constituted of primary relations whose sexual claims were either less relevant or more mediated and custodial (parent-child relations, sibling relations, fictive kinship such as co-godparenthood, and the like).[38] Once this refinement is introduced, the gender contrast leaps out even more strongly. (See Table 3.11.) The odds that female targets were injured or killed by inner primary relations soars to over twenty times the odds for male targets.[39]

These findings underscore the extreme exaggerations of discourses that associate serious violence against women and female youth with aggression against deviant female loners at once unprotected and unsupervised. Most female targets of violence serious enough to lead to formal criminal proceedings were family-attached rather than loners. Their assailants tended mainly to derive from the web of male kin and quasi-kin embedded in primary relations with female dependents and sexual partners.[40] Finally, the types of social relations that generated violence sufficiently serious or intimidating to spark criminal proceedings constituted an emphatic point of contrast between male and female targets of violence. Indeed, if one constructs a spectrum of social relations ranging from primary bonds to stranger relations, one may summarize the gender contrast among targets as follows: *the more closely bonded the relationship, the more likely the danger of violence for women compared with men; the more loosely bonded the relationship, the more likely the danger of violence for men compared with women.* (See Table 3.11.) When one recalls, in addition, that domestic violence, even seriously injurious violence that might plausibly lead to criminal prosecution, is notoriously underreported,[41] the implications of this gender contrast assume even starker dimensions. The formal data may actually understate the social pattern.[42]

These correlations expose, at the level of the frequency of criminal violence incidents, the myth of patriarchal protection against the cruel fate bestowed upon deviant loners. But this level of analysis does not by itself address the related stereotypes concerning the distinctive severity and motivations of violence. As we have seen, the idea here is that men direct truly severe and willful violence at loose women — at once deviant, unprotected, and subversive of the gender order and its appearances. In more normal domestic relations, male-on-female violence is presumably less severely injurious and less specifically willful or motivated. Normal domestic violence is attributable more vaguely to the ventings and diffuse misogyny associated with male-on-female *descargas.*

Let us begin with the question of the severity of violence. In general the cases of violence against females lean strongly to severe violence. About a third (35.5 percent) of the incidents were homicidal, another third (32.3 percent) was comprised of major assaults excluding rape, and another fifth (21.0 percent) of sexual assaults. Given the general severity of the violence cases targeted at women and female youth and the preponderance of family-attached targets and primary bonds in assailant/target relations, the distinction between cruel violence directed at loners and deviants and a lesser violence directed at family-attached and conventional targets begins to take on an air of unreality. Indeed, if one uses the homicidal/nonhomicidal distinction as a marker of severity, the statistical distributions suggest the emphatic exaggeration of the comparative severity of violence stereotype. Tests for nonrandom distributions between homicidal violence and female loners or extramarital lovers or women judged sexually insubordinate all proved inconclusive. Similarly, sexually rooted disputes proved no more linked with homicidal violence against females than disputes rooted in more mundane (that is, nonsexual) aspects of gender subordination and resistance: labor, physical mobility, verbal deference and affronts, and the like.[43]

As we shall see (Chapter 5), these findings do not suggest that female loners escaped special resentment and suspicion, nor do they deny that on occasion especially notorious female delinquents might be singled out for particularly cruel and symbolic violence. They do suggest, however, that the discourse of distinction between severe violence targeted at female loners and deviants and a lesser violence of domestic relations magnifies the "truth" of exceptionally notorious and cruel incidents into a profoundly misleading "Truth" about violence against women.[44] The conventional targets of male-on-female violence not only outnumbered the deviant targets, and their assailants were not only their presumed protectors in primary relations. In addition, the severity of violence inflicted upon conventional female targets matched that meted out to "deviants."

Let us turn, finally, to the question of *descarga* ventings. As we have seen, the discourse of patriarchal protection suggested not only that loose female loners were the chief targets of severe and willful violence and not only that normal domestic violence against family-attached females was by contrast less than seriously injurious. It also interpreted normal domestic violence as acts not specifically or directly motivated or willful but as epiphenomena of forces largely external to the dynamic social relationships between assailants and targets and transferred rather arbitrarily upon domestic victims. Domestic violence attributable mainly to the ventings and diffuse misogyny of male-on-female *descargas* and not all that injurious became an accepted and acceptable phenomenon even to its targets. In this discourse wives presumably learned to submit to passing fits of violent temper and aggressions that they themselves interpreted less as a problem of abuse or struggle within power-laden domestic relationships than as an acceptable transfer of external frustrations to family settings.[45] The venting almost expressed a kind of ultimate family solidarity: "If my grandmother wasn't beaten, she wouldn't eat. She even liked it!"[46] Given the preponderant proportion of family-attached women and female youth subjected to normal domestic violence in primary relations in the Morelos sample of incidents, the *descarga* claim — if it is not grossly exaggerated — should find a strong echo in the structure of motivation in violent incidents against women.

The echo, however, turns out to be quite faint. As we have seen, an important contrast between incidents with male and female targets lay precisely in the more diversified structure of major motivations in disputes leading to violence against male targets. Among incidents with female targets, even by the criteria of the restricted model of gender-rooted motivations, the latter accounted for about six-sevenths (86.7 percent) of the cases. (Let us recall that qualification for this category required specific disputes animated directly by claims of gender right and obligation or by social expressions of masculinity or femininity. It does not include more vaguely gendered behaviors or *descargas*. For a review of criteria, see Table 3.6 above.) *Descarga* ventings amounted to only a small fraction of the incidents (6.7 percent) even by the criteria of the amplified model of *descarga* motivation. By contrast, the amplified *descarga* share for male targets amounted to about a fourth (27.7 percent).[47]

The faintness of the *descarga* echo makes it hard to escape a sobering conclusion: the discourse of *descarga* ventings is a discourse that trivializes domestic violence against women. The trivialization occurs not only because the discourse of less injurious *descarga* violence denies the severity of domestic violence against normal family-attached women and female youth compared with violence against their more "deviant" counterparts. The trivialization also occurs because the discourse of externally motivated fits or *descarga* ventings denies that specific contestations and assertions of gender right and obligation — over sexual rights and property, labor and economic claims, physical mobility and abuse, verbal deference and insubordination, intervention in disputes, and the like — stimulated the overwhelming majority of disputes culminating in serious acts of violence against women.

Let us avoid the either/or trap of pretending that alternate explanations are mutually exclusive. Notwithstanding the trivializing implications of the *descarga* discourse and the way such trivialization serves male gender interests, the social basis of the discourse is obscured if we treat it simply as falsehood propagated by self-interested men. Lesser incidents of *descarga*-like violence that did not lead to criminal proceedings undoubtedly happened.[48] Even in more injurious acts of violence animated by specific contestations, a backdrop of stress linked to external issues such as poverty, color-class relations, or community politics undoubtedly figured in the ill temper men and women brought to some disputes.[49] The discourse of *descarga*, therefore, constituted a discourse of conflation and exaggeration rather than one of inventing falsehoods. The truth of lesser *descarga* ventings mingled with, expanded, and finally subsumed the truth of more severely injurious assaults; the remembered backgrounds of external stress or frustration mingled with, expanded, and finally subsumed the once vivid foregrounds of specific gender contestations. Moreover, since families were units of social solidarity as well as conflict (a point to which we shall return in some detail in Chapter 6), women as well as men might engage in the conflations and exaggerations of *descarga* discourse. The reconstruction of gender dispute and violence as a not very injurious venting vaguely motivated by external frustration might smooth the road — at least temporarily — to a restored semblance of familial harmony and collaboration.[50]

The attribution of violence against females to a combination of willful and serious violence against deviants and vaguely motivated and less injurious ventings against more normal dependents does not stand up under scrutiny. Women and female youth suffered serious acts of violence not because they were notorious loners and deviants loosened from patriarchal vigilance or because momentary weakenings of vigilance left otherwise protected females vulnerable or even because would-be protectors sometimes exploded in fits of volcanic violence vaguely rooted in external frustrations. The greatest dangers derived from the commonplace webs of closely bonded primary relations. The situations that culminated in violence were usually animated by the specific contestations and tensions of power-laden familial and gender relationships.

Even the trade-off hypothesis presented earlier as a possible explanation of the finding that family attached females were as vulnerable as loners to serious violence requires subtle modification. To the extent that poor women in Morelos faced a cruel trade-off, the dilemma constituted not a choice between the exposure to severe violence that came with loner status on the one hand, and the exposure to domestic violence that came with patriarchal protection against worse violence on the other. The more likely trade-off was more complex: the increased economic vulnerability and cultural stigmatization that accompanied greater personal autonomy and freedom from domestic violence in a loner adaptation was pitted against the increased exposure to violence and personal surveillance that accompanied a wider net of economic claims and cultural acceptance in a family-attached adaptation. Not all women, of course, had the freedom to choose between these destinies. For female youth who wished to escape the vigilance of parents, the only realistic alternative might be to substitute the vigilance of a husband or lover.[51] The dilemma posed by the trade-off connected more strongly to realistic powers to choose in the case of older women, especially widows and abandoned wives, who had outlived a life cycle phase of direct subordination to fathers and husbands. These women entered a murky arena of difficult and varied adaptations: quasi-marital subordinations to dominant male partners, stances of discretion and reserve that etched the image of the morally upright widow, more emphatically independent social and sexual styles that asserted a life beyond patriarchal vigilance, and adaptations that shifted ambiguously, depending on circumstance and necessity, among these major poles. For such women the trade-off between heightened economic vulnerability and comparative freedom from domestic surveillance and violence on the one hand, and quasi-familial economic claims and comparative exposure to violence on the other, might indeed become cruel and contradictory.[52] Moreover, as in more conventional family-attached adaptations, the trade-offs brought no guarantees. Inside and outside marriage, attachments to patriarchs brought no guarantees of freedom from economic neglect, even within the modest terms of care available to those who lived in poverty. Yet as the words of Pedro Martínez made clear, a life beyond direct patriarchal attachment brought cultural suspicion that might quickly turn freedom from surveillance and violence into an illusion.

FIVE SURPRISES: A RETURN TO PEDRO MARTINEZ

This chapter began with the words of Pedro Martínez, a peasant who had endured a hard life of poverty, suffering, and political disappointment and whose comments on gender and violence introduced us to the swirl of cultural mythology, exaggeration, and stereotypes that bedevil the analysis of gender and violence in Mexico. As we analyzed, deconstructed, and reconstructed the problem of stereotypes, violence records, and gender, we proceeded to discover four surprises. (How surprising these findings are depends partly, of course, on how attached one is to the cultural exaggerations I have called stereotypes.) The length and necessary detours of this journey of analytical deconstruction and reconstruction warrant a brief restatement of the four surprises before we proceed to a fifth surprise.

First, the criminal violence records do not focus on an assailant population comprised of loners and deviants or upon deviant moments or time-spaces in the lives of otherwise normal people, nor do markers of deviance correlate with distributions of gender-rooted violence. The records bring into view normal social dynamics among normal people: their misfortune was to have crossed thresholds of escalation, accident, and bad luck within rather commonplace logics of personal conflict and risk. As a result, normal contestations, threats, and physical aggressions became transformed into criminal violence incidents.

Second, the violence records in general and their distribution of gender-rooted violence in particular do not privilege particular sociocultural segments, deemed to be more disposed to a charged mix of gender rigidity, sexualized expressions of power, and power-seeking or compensatory violence, within a multiethnic popular culture. The violence records capture a broad spread of popular society—peasants as well as plebeians, Indians as well as non-Indians, and low-status commoners as well as more intermediate strata—in proportions that match up reasonably well with regional popular culture as a whole. Equally important, the plebeian, non-Indian, and intermediate sociocultural segments within the records were no more correlated with gender-rooted violence than their peasant, Indian, and low-status commoner counterparts.

Third, the structure of motivation demonstrated that study of gender-rooted violence does not steer us away from more important or fundamental causes of violence. Studying gender through the medium of violence records introduces the possibility of an implicit and rather subtle bias: the association of gender dynamics and violence dynamics as a matter of methodological convenience may create the presumption of a substantive association that overlooks the minor place of gender in the total structure of criminal violence. The bias of such a presumption would not undermine the value of the study of gender through the medium of violence, but it would shrink somewhat the sense of legitimate implication that might be inferred from such a method. Upon closer scrutiny, however, the association is substantive as well as methodological. Criminal violence incidents were sparked far more often by specific and directly gender-rooted disputes than by diffuse *descarga* ventings bearing little direct motivation, or by property- and class-rooted disputes. The strong presence of gendered life and disputes in patterns of popular violence prevailed even in the world of male-on-male violence.

Fourth, the women most commonly subjected to criminal violence of all kinds and to dangerously injurious violence in particular were not female loners and deviants unprotected by patriarchs and conventional family attachment. On the contrary, family-attached females turned out to be every bit as vulnerable as their loner counterparts, and an inverse logic of danger and social relations prevailed for female and male targets: the more closely bonded the social relationship, the greater the danger for women and female youth compared with men and male youth; the more loosely bonded the relationship, the greater the danger for men and male youth compared with women and female youth. Furthermore, violence against females serious enough to lead to criminal proceedings was not motivated very often by the diffuse frustrations of *descarga* ventings. Whatever the role of external stress in the background of some violent incidents, and however much fragile family reconciliations might enhance the appeal of ex post facto emphasis on *descarga* discourses, most incidents of male-on-female violence were specifically motivated and precipitated by gender-rooted disputes between individuals in power-laden and contested relationships. The vulnerability of family-attached women to violence by their would-be protectors and the preponderance of motivations rooted specifically in disputes over gender rights, obligations, and assertions contrast sharply with the cultural messages Pedro Martínez learned from the elders and reproduced in his own way for Oscar Lewis.

Our return to Pedro Martínez brings us face to face with a fifth surprise: the context and meaning of Pedro Martínez's own words. Taken out of the specific context of Pedro Martínez's life history and that of his family, and separated from the longer passages in which these observations arise, his comments on gender and violence seem simply like general commentary — an oral tradition or a general observation about village life, produced in the perspective of a slightly detached informant, when Oscar Lewis probed for comment on the problem of violence against women. Placed in the context of a specific personal and family history, however, Pedro Martínez's words acquire a new meaning. He uttered them in relation to a particular episode of violent humiliation that left a traumatic mark on the family.[53] Sometime in the early 1940s Pedro Martínez befriended and struck up a sexual liaison with Eulalia, a perhaps poverty-stricken village widow (she was actually an abandoned wife). The affair was not his first, but it occurred in a phase of growing imperiousness by Pedro, who had become a village judge, had taken to working his dependent sons in the field more harshly, and was developing a more rigidly authoritarian demeanor at home. Despite Pedro's prominence in the village the family remained poor. They relied on *tlacolol* agriculture, hoe culture on communally owned and rocky hillsides left available as a last resort for land-poor families, and the problem of securing sufficient money allowances to purchase family food remained a chronic source of anxiety for Esperanza.[54] When Pedro ordered his two elder sons to make some ropes for the widow Eulalia and openly intended to take Eulalia rather than his wife, Esperanza, to sell the ropes at the fair in the *tierra caliente* village of Tepalcingo, the conflict broke open. There followed in quick succession a hard beating of Esperanza, an ugly humiliation wherein Esperanza was forced to scrape up and eat beans off the dirt floor, and a flight from home by the two elder sons.[55]

The Eulalia episode left deep, festering wounds in the family and was closely associated in the family lore with a hard beating Pedro administered when Esperanza — who relied on improvised petty sales and networks of credit, reciprocity, and sociability to mitigate food or income deficits — visited her cousin Agata to "borrow" some corn. Pedro feared that Agata might convince Esperanza to use her cousin's magical and medicinal powers to tame, sicken, or otherwise harm Pedro, and he had ordered Esperanza "not to mix with people like that." He believed that Agata had indeed turned her own husband into a dominated "fool."[56] Years later, at the wake when Esperanza died, her cousin Agata bitterly recounted for all the story of Pedro's violence, proclaimed that Esperanza was better off dead, and reduced Pedro Martínez to tears.

The episode with Eulalia left a searing mark on the family and perhaps constituted a decisive watershed in Pedro Martínez's transition to a more harshly abusive stance vis-à-vis Esperanza and their eldest surviving son, Felipe. Yet at the same time Pedro and Esperanza shared a deep solidarity and a certain affective bond, forged in a life of tremendous suffering and necessity in common.[57] When Esperanza died, Pedro Martínez had to make his peace with their past in common and with the wounds — never quite healed — of that earlier episode of conflict, humiliation, and violence. It was in that context of peacemaking with the past that Pedro Martínez shared with Oscar Lewis a retrospective discourse about his life with Esperanza. The discourse blended fond remembrance with a sense of mourning and loss and presented an idealized summary of Pedro's life with Esperanza that had somehow to acknowledge yet neutralize the problem of violence. Oscar Lewis and Pedro Martínez both knew that Pedro's violence and the Eulalia episode in particular had wounded the family and Pedro's relationship with Esperanza. Pedro Martínez's solution was to invoke the exaggerated stereotype of a real phenomenon: *descarga* violence. By magnifying *descarga* ventings into the apotheosis and explanation of domestic violence, Pedro Martínez could crowd out the specific disputes and motivations of the most traumatic episode of violence and humiliation in his relationship with Esperanza.[58] Since *descarga* violence was in any event not very injurious — so long as wives knew better than to provoke their husbands when external mortifications threw them into bad temper — Pedro Martínez's sanitized retrospective could at once make peace with the past, acknowledge violence, and idealize a life together. Esperanza had understood Pedro's fits of *descarga* temper and knew not to provoke serious violence. In Pedro's words, "We lived together very peacefully for all the forty-five years we were married." Notwithstanding a solidarity with family and husband that sometimes led her to emphasize a *descarga* discourse with her children, Esperanza could not pass so lightly over the Eulalia conflict: "Pedro beat me very hard and . . . he almost drove me out of the house."[59]

Pedro Martínez's vision of *descarga* violence, supplemented by the refrain that earlier times were more cruel and that unattached women were almost by definition immoral delinquents legitimately subject to severe violence, turns out to have been a power-laden discourse of denial. This, then, is our fifth surprise.

CHAPTER 4

Woman, Man, and Authority

The Contested Boundaries of Gender

Right and Obligation

THE MARIAS

The first María, the murdered one, minced no words while defending her marital rights.[1] Strong words and force of will held a man to his obligations and protected a woman's rights even as they stirred resentment. From time to time in nearly four years of marriage María Gertrudis Martínez's husband, Francisco Gerónimo, tried to fend off her challenges by violence and intimidation. He had bought a knife and occasionally threatened to kill her with it. But he had always limited his violence to beatings with a stick, and she had protected herself from worse by complaining about beatings and death threats to Don Clemente, the second manager (*segundo administrador*) of Hacienda San Gaspar. In addition she and her husband, although Indians, were among the better off laboring families on the hacienda. Francisco Gerónimo was a hacienda mason (*albañil*), not a fieldworker or cane cutter, and during María Gertrudis's recent illness they had had the means to hire a *molendera*, an Indian servant to grind corn on the *metate* and to prepare tortillas. In addition, although María Gertrudis, like her husband, had migrated from another community, she at least had a sister nearby. If this was a life of adversity, it was not unbearable either. If her husband oscillated between economic negligence and duty, between physical violence and companionship, María Gertrudis had at least managed to assert her will and to survive the difficult scrapes. Strong words and force of will had always pulled her through. All of that changed, however, shortly before the bells tolled for evening prayer on Sunday, October 23, 1803.

The day had begun auspiciously. That morning María Gertrudis had convinced her husband to pass this Sunday with his wife and sister-in-law instead of drinking with the other men. "Francisco, let's go wash up today," she had told him. "You're filthy as a pig. Don't be that way, going away . . . to drink without washing yourself." Francisco acceded, and around noon they made their way to a washing stream with María Gertrudis's older sister, who had also settled with a husband on the hacienda. The afternoon went pleasantly enough. María Gertrudis's stomach was tender, but María Torivia Guadalupe spared her younger sister by washing the clothes. The afternoon sun beat down strongly, but Francisco Gerónimo agreed to fetch his wife a hat. On his way back to the women, he bought a jug of cheap rum (*aguardiente*) to share with his wife and sister-in-law. As the afternoon of washing and conviviality drew to a close, María Gertrudis and Francisco Gerónimo bade María Torivia goodbye and returned home. In view of the tension and violence that sometimes marred their marriage — María Gertrudis's assertive outspokenness and Francisco Gerónimo's sense of manly authority did not always mix well — this had been a particularly pleasant and easygoing afternoon. To their Indian servant, María Francisca, who was married but needed work as a *molendera*,[2] the couple seemed "very contented" upon their return home.

Then the trouble began. When Francisco Gerónimo discovered that the *molendera* had not finished preparing the tortillas, his mood took a foul and imperious turn, and he began to scold the servant. María Gertrudis, however, intervened. Her rebuke — by her own account — was scathing. She told her husband to stop the scolding because it would drive María Francisca to leave at a time when María Gertrudis's stomach troubles made it impossible for her to grind corn. She added, moreover, "that it seemed that he was always looking for trouble, that whenever he gave [María Gertrudis] some rag, he would either hit her or scold her, and . . . if his fit was because of the skirts he had given her, he could have them." It was understandable that María Gertrudis set the incident against a background of economic contestations linked to violence. Twice before, Francisco Gerónimo admitted, he and his wife had quarreled when she claimed that he had fallen short two reales, the equivalent of one day's wage for a common laborer,[3] in the allowance he turned over from the Sunday *raya* (the hacienda's weekly net wage payment, often calculated at the hacienda store and in relation to goods advances or debits).

What stood out, however, was not simply María Gertrudis's fear that her husband might force out domestic help at a time when she especially needed assistance, or María Gertrudis's determination to deflect her husband's alienation of their servant. What stood out, as well, was a verbal defiance that openly taunted his authority. All three key witnesses recalled the sharpness of her tongue. María Gertrudis's own account recalled her challenge that Francisco Gerónimo take back his skirts. María Francisca recalled María Gertrudis's rebuke when Francisco Gerónimo told the women "that the two of them should go to shit." María Gertrudis retorted "that they wouldn't be going while he wasn't paying for it." Francisco Gerónimo at first claimed that his wife had told him "to go to shit," then withdrew the claim when confronted with María Francisca and her testimony. But the sense of insolence remained: Francisco Gerónimo never withdrew the claim that his wife taunted him by pulling his hair, and it was immediately after a verbal retort that he stabbed María Gertrudis in the belly. It was a deep wound that reached the lower intestines, and the local barber-surgeon (*cirujano*) judged it fatal from the start. María Gertrudis Martínez would agonize two weeks before she died.

The second María, the exiled one, had struggled vainly to return to a peaceable life.[4] Originally from the community of Totolapa in the cooler upcountry (*tierra fría*) of northern Morelos, María Lucía and her husband José Luciano had descended to the warmer climes of Oaxtepec. Oaxtepec was something of a minor mecca. Its fertility had long drawn sugar planters as well as small-scale fruit and vegetable farmers to compete for land and with the local Indians, and its health-giving mineral springs had attracted missionaries and a hospital in early colonial times. María Lucía and José Luciano had managed to gain access to land in Oaxtepec, possibly through rental. Like other Indians and peasants in the area María Lucía and José Luciano lived a life of travel. Oaxtepec exported fruit to *tierra fría* villages like Totolapa and to Mexico City as well. Perhaps it was during one of her innumerable trips back and forth between Oaxtepec and the Totolapa *tianguis* that María Lucía's sexual liaison with Eugenio Esquicio Ponciano had begun. In 1814 María Lucía had been only eighteen years old. Probably rather inexperienced in marriage, she was nearly ten years the junior of her own husband as well as Esquicio Ponciano, a married Oaxtepec Indian who also plied the Oaxtepec-Totolapa trade circuit. In 1814 the young María Lucía perhaps failed to appreciate fully that under certain circumstances older wives might contest fiercely the sexual liaisons of their husbands. If so, she paid dearly for her ignorance. Esquicio Ponciano's wife "wounded me and broke my head," and the scandal brought the liaison to the attention of María Lucía's husband José Luciano.

Since that time the return to a peaceable life was fragile, if not beyond hope. José Luciano agreed to reconcile with María Lucía, but the price of domestic peace was heightened vigilance and suspicion by José Luciano and heightened fear by María Lucía that another scandal would bring violent retribution by her husband. Moreover, the troubles with other men did not cease. Esquicio Ponciano did not accept María Lucía's termination of their liaison but presumed instead that her earlier consent to his sexual entreaties granted him a permanent right to hound her. To protect the fragile peace, she had had to rebuff his insistent possessiveness repeatedly, and she had even had to run to the village *gobernador*, Don Rafael Hilario, to have Esquicio Ponciano thrown out of her house. But Esquicio Ponciano was not the only man to pursue her. Perhaps emboldened by a sense that the earlier scandal marked María Lucía as a less than honorable woman, José Esmeregildo, another married Indian from Oaxtepec, had also sought a sexual liaison. He pressed less insistently than Esquicio Ponciano, and María Lucía fended off both men. If she wished to live in peace with her husband, however, she needed to wage such battles as silently as possible: "Although both of them persecuted her, she got too mortified, since for the very reason that her husband knew about the antecedents with Ponciano she did not want to tell him any of it." Within these limits María Lucía constructed a more or less peaceable domestic life for nearly three years following the scandal and wounding of 1814.

The peace broke when José Esmeregildo killed Esquicio Ponciano. On December 19, 1817, José Esmeregildo went to the Totolapa *tianguis* to sell fruit. Like María Lucía he regularly traded in Totolapa, and his day followed the familiar rhythm — still evident in rural Mexico — of *tianguis* days. After selling his fruit to one of his regular buyers, José Esmeregildo joined the stream of peasants who stopped at the village church to hear mass, light candles or incense, or otherwise take care of their supernatural obligations. There followed a visit with a *comadre* to pass the afternoon with some drink and conversation. (*Comadre* literally means "cogodmother," but this fictive kin term could also be extended to other important reciprocity relationships and friendships.) When José Esmeregildo headed back in the late afternoon and checked for companions from Oaxtepec who might join him on the road home, the one person who remained turned out to be María Lucía, whom he accompanied, for sake of propriety, "not side by side, but at a distance of some twelve or fourteen steps." Near Oaxtepec, the fatal encounter took place. Esquicio Ponciano, on return from a trading trip of his own, met up with the pair and reacted as a sexual possessor. When he approached María Lucía (who was walking in front) to demand an accounting of her whereabouts, José Esmeregildo moved forward to deflect the confrontation. The social dynamics shifted quickly to those of male rivals asserting competing claims in or protections of a female dependent. The conflict ended with a fatal stab to Esquicio Ponciano's stomach as the men relegated María Lucía to the sidelines of a male-on-male encounter. In María Lucía's view Esquicio Ponciano's uncontrolled and illegitimate possessiveness made his death self-inflicted: "He himself sought out death because of his ill founded jealousies. Why even though I left him, he never stopped bothering me with his jealousy and his insistence that I resume." In this discourse María Lucía was an innocent bystander in a homicide caused by male excess and caprice, a sexual possessiveness that failed to respect boundaries of right and obligation.

The problem was that María Lucía's language of explanation was not the only one that circulated in the village. Esquicio Ponciano's wife, who had three years earlier wounded María Lucía to break up the initial liaison, asserted that María Lucía was the real culprit in her husband's murder. In this discourse Esquicio Ponciano was the victim of uncontrollable passions provoked by female immorality. The competition amongst competing discourses, and the networks and force of will of Esquicio Ponciano's wife (who remained unnamed in the documents), spelled trouble for María Lucía. As the discourse that assigned responsibility to María Lucía circulated in Oaxtepec and apparently garnered some approval, the facade of peaceable reconciliation after a youthful mistake disintegrated and gave way to uncertainty and danger. The risk of ostracism and retribution loomed menacingly. María Lucía's husband, José Luciano, had been in Mexico City on the day of the violence, but María Lucía feared that village talk assigning her responsibility for homicide would inevitably reach his ears upon his return. Even if social ostracism did not make life unbearable, even if Esquicio Ponciano's wife did not attempt direct or supernatural retribution, and even if the community authorities did not punish María Lucía in an effort to restore community peace, there was always the possibility that José Luciano would — on the strength of the earlier scandal — believe that she had pursued sexual encounters that sparked the murder. Under the circumstances, she could not know "if perhaps the Devil might tempt him."

These dangers and fears drove María Lucía into exile. She fled to Cuautla, where she worked as a domestic servant for at least three months. Although María Lucía consistently professed a desire to return to a peaceable marriage in Oaxtepec, she also professed fear. Her anxiety was not exaggerated: José Luciano would testify that although his vigilance had satisfied him that María Lucía remained sexually faithful during the years following the initial scandal, her flight indeed renewed his suspicions. We do not know if the community authorities arranged a peaceable reintegration of María Lucía into the local social fabric. What is clear is that unless they did so, María Lucía faced grim prospects: a life of indefinite exile from her customary networks of community and property and a transition from the partial autonomy of a mobile peasant woman engaged in petty marketing and travel to the more vulnerable lot of an isolated female servant subjected to a harsh trinity of poverty, surveillance, and servility.

The three Marías we have met — María Gertrudis of Hacienda San Gaspar, whose strong words and sociable Sunday afternoon suddenly turned murderous; María Lucía of Oaxtepec and Totolapa, whose efforts to put a youthful sexual scandal behind her dissolved in a nightmare of fear and exile; and María Teresa of Texalpa, whose fatal withdrawal of self and service from her husband José Marcelino opened this book — introduce us to the range of issues at stake in a world of contested gender right and obligation. The stories of the three Marías are revealing, moreover, precisely because of their normality. Until the moment when an unpremeditated act of murderous violence shattered previous life trajectories, the three Marías led lives fairly commonplace in the world of the rural poor in Morelos. All three were Indians, all three were married, and all three adapted to family lives where dynamics of power and violence as well as unity of purpose and reconciliation filled a woman's primary social relationships. All three struggled to carve out boundaries of gender right and obligation that allowed a woman to assert rights and to contest power in her relations with men even as she avoided open defiance of patriarchal first principles. Like many women, all three sought social alliances and connections to bolster their efforts or to ward off retribution. Until violence and misfortune crossed a terrible and not precisely predictable threshold, at least two of the three Marías could claim a measure of success in the practical struggles of everyday gendered life. María Gertrudis of Hacienda San Gaspar laid claim to economic rights — a regular weekly allowance from the Sunday *raya*, a *molendera* during her illness, and new clothes — notwithstanding the fact that these claims required a certain vigilance and contentiousness. María Lucía of Oaxtepec and Totolapa laid claim to independent physical mobility and market activity in a reconciled marriage and blocked Esquicio Ponciano's sexual possessiveness despite the earlier liaison and scandal.[5]

The range of contested gender issues in the stories of the three Marías and the contingencies that surrounded such contestations defy one-dimensional depictions of gender conflict and subordination. In the story of María Gertrudis of Hacienda San Gaspar, verbal deference and economic obligation come to the fore. María Gertrudis challenged her husband's expectation of a verbal deference that symbolized a wife's duty to concede authority to her husband. The challenge was all the more serious when it took place before a third person, let alone a servant. María Gertrudis undoubtedly understood the seriousness of taunting her husband in view of Francisco Gerónimo's earlier violence and threats. But in the practical life adaptation she had worked out, when a husband neglected his economic duties, a woman was well advised to speak up forcefully to claim what was hers. A man's right to symbolic deference was contingent: the right eroded if a man neglected his economic obligations, or inflicted physical abuse and threats that were excessive or without cause, or provided for his family under duress and mixed such provisions with implied or real threats.

In the story of María Lucía of Oaxtepec and Totolapa, sexuality comes to the fore. Esquicio Ponciano's wife (whose name eluded mention in the historical record) challenged her husband's right to extramarital sexual liaisons by attacking María Lucía and creating a public scandal. The youthful María Lucía challenged her husband's expectation that a wife avoided sexual impropriety at all costs. The older María Lucía challenged her former lover's claim that sexual property in a woman, once conceded, granted permanent rights. Esquicio Ponciano's wife undoubtedly understood that if a woman sought to disrupt her husband's sexual liaison, she risked domestic abuse and conflict. But in the practical life adaptation she had worked out, a woman also risked troubles — economic negligence, loss of kin to violence, cultural humiliation, domestic violence — if she allowed her husband to pursue a sexual liaison beyond the most discreet and fleeting contacts. A man's right to pursue extramarital sexual liaisons was contingent: the right eroded if, in his wife's view, an ongoing liaison placed at risk her well-being or that of her children, her other kin, or even the offending husband. María Lucía learned the hard way that once a suitor successfully exerted a sexual claim in a woman, he often assumed a quasi-marital right of permanent sexual possession. But in the practical life adaptation she eventually worked out, a woman could best protect herself from violence and from curtailed physical mobility in marriage if she asserted a right to terminate liaisons and to block sexual predators. In extramarital sexual arrangements a man's right to continuing sexual access depended on a woman's consent, and his right to demand her consent eroded if he neglected the implications of a continuing liaison for her well-being.

In the story of María Teresa of Texalpa physical mobility comes to the fore. María Teresa challenged her husband's expectation that a man owed no accounting of his physical whereabouts and activities to his wife. Whatever María Teresa thought of the matter in principle and whatever the risk of provoking violence, in the practical life adaptation she had worked out, a woman who failed to demand such an accounting indulged a lazy or negligent husband's vices to her own detriment. When María Teresa responded to José Marcelino's neglect by abandoning their home, a husband's right to control his wife's physical movements and to draw upon her labor also entered a contested arena. A man's right to move about freely and to hold his wife to her *metate* and other domestic duties was contingent: it eroded if he failed to own up to his economic obligations.

Verbal deference, economic obligation, sexuality, physical mobility — the diversity of gender rights and claims that sparked conflict is impressive. Equally important in the three lives we have glimpsed are the interconnections among the diverse domains of gendered life. María Gertrudis's verbal taunts sparked violence. But as we have seen, her challenge to domestic authority was closely related to a background of ongoing contestations over economic resources and rights. The tangled conflict between Esquicio Ponciano, his wife, María Lucía, and her husband over an extramarital sexual liaison nourished ongoing conflict between Esquicio Ponciano and María Lucía over her right to end the liaison. But as we have seen, the conflict took its disastrous turn to male-on-male rivalry and homicide when Esquicio Ponciano asserted a corollary to his sexual claims: the right to exercise vigilance over a woman's physical mobility (and by implication her male company). If we ask, moreover, why Esquicio Ponciano's wife was so determined to break up her husband's sexual connection with María Lucía, the answer may have just as much to do with the connections between men's sexual freedom and their economic negligence of wives and children as with sexual rights and desires.[6] María Teresa's assertion of a right to monitor and influence her husband's physical mobility and to withdraw her own physical presence by fleeing to her mother's house culminated in violent tragedy. But as we have seen, the dispute over physical mobility was closely related to economic contestations as well: María Teresa's frustrations with her husband as an economic provider nourished her determination to monitor his physical movement and activity, and José Marcelino's dependence on the labors of his wife for food compounded his anger when she asserted a right to abandon him.

Finally, because patriarchs, would-be patriarchs, and women assumed that men held rights of punishment in a world of contested gender right and obligation, conflicts over gender claims inevitably sparked connected tensions over the rightful boundaries of violence. María Gertrudis of Hacienda San Gaspar judged Francisco Gerónimo's threats and beatings, found them disproportionate and arbitrary, and drew them to the attention of the hacienda manager. María Lucía of Oaxtepec and Totolapa conceded the right of her husband as well as a female sexual rival to punish her for sexual infractions, but she also constructed a discourse of unjustified violence based on ill-founded rumor and gossip. María Teresa's wounding and death led to extended, shifting, and pressure-packed dialogues between her mother, her husband, and the Texalpa elders over the meaning, legitimacy, and culpabilities of provoked violence.

The three Marías were humble folk, individually insignificant by the standards of traditional historical biography. They entered the historical record as individuals almost by accident, by virtue of tragedies that might well have ended up among the countless near misses or lesser episodes of everyday life and violence that elude historical documentation. Yet the range, variation, and quirks—in a word, the individuality—of three episodes in the lives of three Marías are not insignificant at all. The individuality of three lives—the range of contested issues in play, the interconnections among distinct dimensions of gender right, the contingencies surrounding contested definitions of right, and the varied social alignments and contexts—open a vast social panorama. Taken together as well as separately, as a range of experience and as individual stories, the lives and tragedies of María Gertrudis of Hacienda San Gaspar, María Lucía of Oaxtepec and Totolapa, María Teresa of Texalpa, and the persons who populated their worlds resonated strongly with larger patterns of life experience. Their stories would have seemed familiar and recognizable to the women, men, and youth of late colonial Morelos. If it was almost by accident that these three Marías entered the historical record, it was not by accident at all that Marías such as these fill the historical annals.

GENDER RIGHT:
CONTESTATIONS, CONNECTIONS, AND ENTANGLEMENTS

Let us begin the exploration of this lack of accident by identifying the issues that sparked violence against women and female youth. As already observed in Chapter 3, gender-rooted motives accounted for the overwhelming majority (88.7 percent, about seven-eighths, by the midway calculation in Table 4.1) of criminal violence episodes directed at female targets. What is obscured by the aggregated category of gender-rooted violence are the particular issues of gender right and obligation that gave rise to violence disputes.

From both quantitative and qualitative points of view the violence incidents expose a wide range of contested issues. As one might expect, sexuality looms large in the overall pattern of criminal violence against women and female youth. Disputes that focused on sexual claims and assertions accounted for about half (49.0 percent) the conflicts culminating in criminal violence incidents directed at female targets. At the same time, however, disputes that focused on nonsexual aspects of gender right and subordination — labor and economic obligations, physical mobility and abuse, and verbal or other challenges to gender domain or right — accounted for nearly a third (32.0 percent) of the incidents. (See the restricted model figures in Table 4.1.) If one uses amplified criteria of classification that allow for overlap and for proxy motives by recording near-prime as well as prime motives, the findings are similar. Sexual claims and assertions were important in a clear majority (58.4 percent) of cases, yet nonsexual contestations of gender right were also important in a large share (39.5 percent) of incidents. (See the amplified model figures in Table 4.1.)

One may summarize and begin to elaborate the larger meaning of these findings with an apparent paradox: sexuality was central yet less than subsumptive in the gender-rooted contestations that culminated in criminal violence against women and female youth. In other words, gender subordination and conflict entailed such multiple dimensions of right and obligation that sexual claims and contestations, while fundamental, did not subsume or eclipse nonsexual gender claims and contestations.

Let us examine sexuality further, then proceed to other gender claims and contestations. At first sight the enormous weight of sexuality is fully consistent with expectations that in a patriarchal culture men considered wives, lovers, female dependents, and vulnerable or unprotected women as sexual property. In this context one might expect not only that a great deal of male-female gender conflict focused on sexual behaviors but also that such disputes were mainly sparked by male assertions of right in female sexuality. In this line of reasoning, disputes might be expected to fall into two major categories: sexual assaults, an extreme taking of sexual property that in some social circumstances transgressed conventional understandings of patriarchal property and propriety;[7] and male jealousies (*celos*) or claims sparked by real and imagined female sexual infractions. Explicit female jealousies or assertions in male sexuality were dangerous to women and presumably anomalous, at most a topic for offstage discussion, largely latent or stifled in a patriarchal culture whose norms validated a double standard of sexual freedom. Female jealousies might be expected, therefore, to account for a modest fraction of violent sexual conflicts in general and *celos* disputes in particular. These expectations reverberate strongly with the familiar stereotypes of Latin American women as believers — participating carriers — in the dictates of a Latin culture of values about appropriate and expected sexual behavior for men and women.[8]

The expectations, however, are only partly corroborated by the evidence. (See Table 4.2, midway column, for the figures cited below.) On the one hand, male assertions of right in female sexuality did account for a large share of Morelos cases. Sexual assault accounted for over a third (36.1 percent) of the violence incidents where sexual claims or motives were present, and *celos* (54.7 percent) accounted for most of the other such incidents. But significantly, and at odds with the expectation that open sexual contestation in patriarchal Latin American cultures centered nearly exclusively on male control and repression of female sexual property, female *celos* were quite prominent among the *celos* cases. Indeed, female *celos* were present in about half (51.5 percent) the *celos* cases. These figures do not belie, of course, the importance of male assertion and aggression: sexual assault and male *celos* together figured in a large majority (69.3 percent) of the sexual conflict cases. Nonetheless, the normality and seriousness of female *celos* is also apparent and important.

The normality of female *celos* invites us to explore disputes focused on sexual claims and assertions not simply as a one-way process of male assertion of sexual property in females but as a larger contestation over rights in sexuality. This larger contestation belies simple notions of female acceptance of a double sexual standard: the right of a male to exert absolute and exclusive sexual possession in a female while pursuing additional sexual liaisons or claims, and the duty of a female to submit to exclusive sexual possession while tolerating male sexual freedom. At bottom the normality of female *celos* helps explain why Juan Sebastián of Tepoztlán thought it culturally plausible to fend off charges that he sexually persecuted María Antonia de Tapia, another village Indian, by claiming that he had spied on María Antonia's house not to persecute her but to prove to his wife that María Antonia had a different *amasio* (lover).[9]

The social and cultural logic of this larger contestation over sexual property and behavior — female *celos* and claims in males as well as male *celos* and claims in females — are not immediately apparent. After all, the political culture and legal practice of colonial Mexican society were premised not on an egalitarian form of contract theory — not even among men or among male property holders — but rather on an organic vision of divinely sanctioned human hierarchy. This vision distinguished between higher and lesser forms of human intelligence, responsibility, and service within the social body. This was a political culture that drew hierarchical distinctions of right, restriction, and social standing according to race and lineage descent, gender and age, corporate group and community attachment, and cultural and religious descent. The notions that men and women were fundamentally different; that such differences implied natural (and socially beneficial) distinctions of right, restriction, and social standing; and that such distinctions granted men superior freedom while consigning women to greater restriction resonated deeply with the wider political and religious culture of a colonial order. Even at the community or village level of political culture (a complex topic to be explored in greater detail in Chapter 8), the poor and predominantly peasant women of late colonial Morelos participated in a culture of rank that drew hierarchical distinctions according to age, gender, lineage, and barrio/village attachment, and that was not immune to the color-class distinctions of the wider society.

All of this made poor women unlikely to have contested male sexual behavior on the basis of an equality or equivalence principle resonant with post-Enlightenment feminisms. Nor is it clear that the dynamics of women's contestations of male sexual behavior constituted female analogues to male imperatives that linked sexual prowess and possessiveness to dynamics of power and humiliation, honor and degradation, and alliance and enmity among men. How, then, are we to understand female contestations of male sexuality on terms other than a familiar protofeminism or an assertion of male-female parallelism?

To answer this question we must return to our earlier paradox: sexuality was both central and less than subsumptive in gender-rooted conflicts culminating in violence. At stake in male sexual behavior and in female rights to monitor and contest it was not sexual right and property alone, but a series of interconnected rights and practices.

Precisely because the consequences of sexual behavior could not be sealed off from other arenas of gender right and obligation, women — even those who accepted in principle the idea that men were by nature sexually predatory and even those who preferred sexual distance from their partners — might be driven to evaluate and contest the boundaries of male sexual right and freedom. The close interconnection of sexual and economic issues, in particular, gave wives vital reason to assert claims in their husbands' sexual behavior, even at the risk of violence. As Yndoza Gertrudis, a mestiza married to a peon on Hacienda Miacatlán, put it in 1815, she had asked her husband Antonio Sosa "what he had done with the *raya, and because of that she had become jealous* of the said Aleja [Antonio Sosa's *amasia*]." The conflict over the liaison was serious: Antonio Sosa beat Yndoza Gertrudis, threatened to kill Gregorio Roa, an Indian peon whom he accused of spreading sexual gossip to his wife, and was himself killed by Roa in a confrontation shortly thereafter.[10]

In extreme instances the evaluation of a husband's economic commitment and competence could spark wives or their relatives to assert a right to withdraw sexual property from a husband by abandoning him and reinforcing the separation, if necessary, through a sexual liaison with another man. Juana Trinidad, a widowed cook on Hacienda de Dolores, thought poorly of her son-in-law José María Jaymes. She therefore resisted her son-in-law's efforts to end his separation from her daughter Marcela Josefa and apparently tolerated or encouraged a sexual liaison between Marcela Josefa and a high-status hacienda resident (a skilled purger in the sugar mill) that might seal the separation. The impoverished José María Jaymes had lived for a time with Marcela Josefa among the poorer strata of Xiutepec villagers but had gotten into trouble for rustling some mules and horses and failed to establish himself as a reliable provider. When he sought to reclaim his right to Marcela Josefa, Juana Trinidad interposed herself, "telling him that she would not turn her over because he would take her to die of hunger." It was the first of several confrontations that finally ended, in 1808, when José María Jaymes killed his wife, his mother-in-law, and a newborn child of unclear paternity.[11]

The presence of the child reminds us to consider that for women who were mothers, conflicts over men's economic obligations to wives and sexual partners probably constituted, in addition, a marker of conflicts over the duties of fathers to children. The mother considered the children to be hers, and accusations of economic negligence implied negligence of children as well as wives and sexual partners. The masking effect of this marker or partial proxy may explain why, in the coded data on the motives of violent dispute, conflicts over children constituted a negligible share. Even when children figured in the dispute, the language of conflict focused on male negligence of economic obligations to women. The last moments of Juana Trinidad's life capture this fusion poignantly. When Juana Trinidad, whose contempt for her son-in-law focused on his economic incompetence, emerged from her house fatally wounded, her last thoughts turned to the protection of the newborn grandchild she carried in her arms. She came out "screaming that someone should catch the said little one [*criatura*], because her son-in-law José María had killed her."[12]

The linkage of sexual property and access on the one hand and economic right and obligation on the other recurs again and again in a variety of social contexts: in hacienda as well as village life, and in mulatto and mestizo networks as well as more Indian circles. The linkage is evident both in the assumption that husbands and fathers who had female lovers (*amasias*) channeled gifts and resources to their *amasias* and extra children, and in the refrain that justified women's extramarital liaisons as a consequence of poverty and negligence by husbands.[13] The linkage is also evident in a reverse direction. Not only did wives contest their husbands' sexual liberties in part to reclaim for their households resources and attentiveness channeled to *amasias*. In addition, a wife's evaluation of the impact of a husband's sexual liaisons on his role as a provider affected her own sense of economic obligation. Andrea María, a Tlayacapan Indian caught in a bitter struggle with her husband over his domestic violence and his persistent and rather public visits to an *amasia*, neatly formulated the connection when she told her husband to go to his *amasia*'s house if he wished to eat.[14]

The linkage of sexual and economic rights in what may be called a contested patriarchal pact enmeshed male visions of male gender right and female obligation within female evaluations of female gender right and male obligation. It rendered male sexual rights and freedoms contingent rather than innate, conditional rather than absolute. As one might expect, men resented and resisted such linkages. A man placed on the defensive in such a struggle saw his sexual ownership of his wife in rather absolute terms, unconditioned by the question of economic negligence; saw his rights to her labor in rather absolute terms, unconditioned by the question of his sexual freedoms; and saw his extramarital liaisons as a matter that belonged absolutely to the domain of men (that is, sex rivals), unconditioned by female accusations of familial negligence.

The entangling linkages of sexual and economic rights, although fundamental, constituted but one of several such linkages. Precisely because gender right and subordination embraced varied arenas considered important in their own right, and precisely because women and female youth sometimes conditioned the extent of male right in one domain on the fulfillment of male obligation in another, the tension between contingent and absolute notions of male right pervaded a wide array of contested gender issues. Precisely because of these interconnections, moreover, men on the defensive feared that weakness or laxity in one domain might imply weakness or laxity in another. They might therefore respond to specific female challenges with an insistence and violence that seemed out of proportion to the specific issue at hand.

Three examples suffice to illustrate the ways a logic of disproportionate male reaction sometimes surfaced. The first concerns the question of economic rights. In general, men held greater access than women to discretionary income spent on personal relaxation or diversion, while women held greater responsibility to treat resources ceded to their control—goods in kind such as maize, weekly allowances, and incomes from petty marketing — as a household allowance to be devoted nearly completely to household needs rather than discretionary or diversionary spending. When José Antonio Terrón and María del Carmen went to the Tepalcingo fair in 1807, María del Carmen controlled at least a portion of the Indian couple's money. After they had passed some time drinking, María del Carmen judged that they had had enough. She acceded — grudgingly, one surmises — to her husband's first two requests for extra money to drink on his own. When she refused to acquiesce to his third request, José Antonio stabbed her four times. María del Carmen died seven hours later.[15] Even though José Antonio later vindicated his wife's judgment by acknowledging that he had indeed had too much to drink, even though his wife had acceded to his first two requests, and even though the final conflict by itself said little about the larger balance of power governing the couple's household allowances and discretionary spending practices, José Antonio reacted *as if* María del Carmen's refusal to accede to his third request signified a larger challenge to his authority.

A second example concerns the question of physical mobility. In general, men had a greater right to monitor or demand an accounting of women's physical movements and activities outside the home; women's surveillance of men's physical movements was comparatively weak, and efforts to monitor men's movements outside the home might spark domestic violence. When Vicente Xocototo and María Carpia of Tlayacapan, land-poor peasants who depended on a better-off mestizo peasant family for work and sustenance, went out in search of music and drink one evening in 1809, they were joined by a mestizo friend in the landowning family. (In village life certain homes were known to sell drink, and part-time musicians could be hired or convinced to play a violin or guitar. Hence it was normal to expect that one might be able to visit a small *fandango* [party] in progress, or to arrange one.) After a great deal of walking and some drinking, the trio ended up at the mestizo family's *milpa* to pass the night. Vicente Xocototo ordered María Carpia to return home. When she refused to comply — pointing out that he should not have taken her along in the first place had he wanted her at home — Vicente Xocototo threatened his wife with some rocks. Since María Carpia was still recovering from a recent head wound inflicted by her husband, and everyone knew that the complications of stone-inflicted head wounds sometimes yielded death, the threat was serious. The Indian couple's mestizo friend, José Apolinario Vega, stepped in to calm Vicente and deflect the violence. Even though María Carpia's refusal did not in this context imply her assertion of a right to unmonitored female movement or a right to monitor male movement, Vicente Xocototo reacted *as if* her refusal to respect his order signified a larger challenge to his authority. Indeed, even though José Apolinario was a friend about whom there had been no earlier hint of sexual impropriety or rivalry and who advised María Carpio to defuse the confrontation by going home, Vicente Xocototo responded as if José Apolinario's intervention implied a sexual rivalry. José Apolinario "was defending her for a reason," exclaimed Vicente as he began to beat his rival, "and now we'll see who is a man." The battle ended when José Apolinario cut Vicente Xocototo's jugular vein.[16]

A third example of a logic of disproportion concerns the question of sexual property. In general, men asserted a right to monopolize sexual ownership of wives (as well as daughters before marriage, unmarried *amasias*, and common-law wives) without comparable restriction on the sexual freedom of men. As we have seen, this meant that male *celos* and sexual claims sparked important conflicts between women and men. Within this context a wife who sought to limit her husband's right of sexual access to her could do so without directly challenging his sexual ownership. She might avow reasons of illness, the recent birth of a child, religious imperative, or an episode of spiritual fright (*susto*). But a man on the defensive might choose to define the evidence of female sexual impropriety liberally: withdrawal of sexual access, an unsupervised or otherwise suspicious exchange of words with a man or male youth, or a delay in returning home from a walk to fetch water might be taken as provocation of *celos*.[17] In 1801 the newly married Luciana Francisca Placiencia of Hacienda Mapaztlán, trapped by a physically abusive husband whose roughness and violence extended to genitalia and sexual encounters, sought relief by claiming a right to sexual abstinence during Lent. Her efforts to establish sexual distance, however, met not only with increased physical abuse by her husband José Leandro but also with claims of sexual jealousy directed at an elderly uncle.[18] Indeed, if one distinguishes between *celos* incidents that yielded plausible evidence of an inflammatory sexual liaison and incidents that seem constructed on a more imaginary basis, the contrast between female and male *celos* is striking. About three-fifths (58.8 percent) of male *celos* incidents but less than a fifth (16.7 percent) of female *celos* incidents relied on imaginary rather than plausible constructions. (See Table 4.3.)

The world of female-male tension was a world of entangling linkages, an interconnected multiplicity of gender right, obligation, and authority that sometimes heightened the sense of implication drawn from specific contestations. The arenas of such contestations went beyond the domains heretofore mentioned. If disputes over sexual rights, economic and labor rights, and physical mobility and abuse figured as prime causes in a large majority (72.6 percent) of incidents, it remains nonetheless the case that a wider array of issues — verbal affronts, female rights to defend children and relatives, nearly total insubordination, and miscellaneous assertions of gender right — figured explicitly, as prime or near-prime causes, in about a fifth (22.3 percent) of violent incidents.[19] At bottom, moreover, the sexual and nonsexual arenas of gender right and practice were not neatly sealed off from each other. If a man's extramarital sexual liaisons implied economic negligence, domestic violence or abuse, or open cultural humiliation, then a woman had to assert boundaries of permissible male sexual behavior even when male sexuality as such was not the main point of concern. Conversely, when a man professed sexual *celos* on a rather imaginary basis, at times the sexualized claim drew upon tensions built up in other domains of gender right. Anger over a woman's unmonitored physical movements and conversations or her irregular fidelity to timely tortilla preparation or her verbal and symbolic assertiveness might find a sexualized expression that legitimated violence.

The contradictory tangle of this pattern is captured by the paradox of sexuality as both central and less than subsumptive in conflicts leading to violence against women. On the one hand, sexual claims and contestations were pervasive; they explicitly accounted for about half the cases and figured significantly in about three-fifths of cases. It is evident that male appropriation of wives, *amasias*, female dependents, and vulnerable or unprotected females as sexual property, and female responses to that appropriation, constituted a central touchstone of gender right, subordination, and conflict in male-female relations. On the other hand it is equally evident that sexual claims and contestations, however fundamental, were not so overriding that they subsumed or eclipsed nonsexual claims and contestations in male-female relations. The variety of contested gender issues that culminated in serious violence, the efforts of women to draw conditional boundaries of male gender right through linkage and contextual judgments of right, and the entanglements among different domains of gender right and obligation that developed in the course of gender disputes and violence all served to render sexuality less than overriding. The arenas of gender right, subordination, and conflict in female-male relations were too varied to be reduced to a single dimension, above all since female strategies of linkage built upon this multiplicity. Women connected the sense of priority men attached to their sexual property in women to the sense of priority women attached to economic survival for themselves and their children, to female latitude of movement and conversation, and to freedom from undue domestic violence.

In a world of contested patriarchal pacts women and female youth — however foundational their status as sexual property in the organization of male-female gender relations — did not consent passively to the implications of that status. For that very reason, their contestations simultaneously included and went beyond the fundamental arena of sexuality.

OF WIVES, *AMASIAS*, AND DAUGHTERS

Thus far the elucidation of contested patriarchal pacts and female emphasis on contingent — that is, conditionally and contextually defined — gender rights in male-female relations has focused largely on the experiences and contestations of wives. This has been the case despite general reference to women and female youth as a group. In addition, most of the female individuals depicted in other social roles, such as servants, sisters, and mothers, have appeared as allies of wives in struggles with husbands. The discussion has thus far avoided, therefore, two complicating dimensions. First, we have not yet examined seriously the ways female-female enmity and division might figure in female-male relations and in the tension between contingent and absolute approaches to gender right. This topic requires a broader discussion of the problem of solidarity and conflict, from both a color-class perspective and a gender-kinship perspective, in poor people's lives and shall therefore be postponed (see Chapter 6). Second, we have not yet examined the particular ways tensions between contingent and absolute approaches to gender right figured in the experiences of *amasias* and daughters as distinguished from wives. The potential contrast or variation matters not only because the experiences of wives cannot be assumed to be prototypical for all women and female youth, but also because a single woman could hold multiple social roles vis-à-vis multiple patriarchs. She could be a wife, an *amasia*, and a daughter all at once.[20]

Let us begin with wives, the chief female protagonists in the foregoing discussion. In effect, wives treated marriage as a formal pact that coordinated several arenas of right and obligation and that implied a certain mutuality of obligation between husbands and wives. As we have seen, this approach imparted a conditional quality to gender right in male-female relations, as well as the possibility of complicating linkages. If a husband had a right to exert a sexual monopoly on his wife and to pursue extra liaisons of his own, a wife had a right to expect that his sexual freedoms would be sufficiently fleeting, discreet, or unencumbered to free his wife and children from economic negligence, physical abuse, or cultural humiliation. If this was an unequal reciprocity, its conditional tonality nonetheless allowed for some fluidity, a drawing and redrawing of male and female right and obligation in accord with condition and circumstance. It might be possible to imagine circumstances wherein extramarital liaisons by wives and loud efforts to destroy the liaisons of husbands were justifiable. Similarly, if a husband had a right to expect a wife to devote intensive labor to preparing tortillas and food for ready consumption at the times he desired them, and if he had a right to withhold some of his physical energies and economic resources for male diversion, a wife had a right to expect a husband to channel most of his energies and resources into household support or allowances. It might be possible to imagine circumstances wherein wives had a right to withhold their services or to monitor the labors and activities of husbands. Finally, if a husband had a right to demand an accounting of a wife's physical movements outside the home, to expect her to avoid appearances of sexual impropriety, and to prohibit her abandonment of kin, a wife had a right to a certain latitude of everyday movement and conversation compatible with propriety and household responsibility. She had a right, moreover, to expect that the comparative freedom of movement of her husband would not lead to prolonged abandonments of a wife and children or to irresponsible dissipation. It might be possible to imagine circumstances wherein a husband lost his moral claim to monitor and control a woman's movements, or circumstances wherein a wife gained a right to abandon her husband.

Finally, insofar as these or other issues yielded conflict and violence, if a husband had a right to punish a wayward wife, a wife had a right to evaluate whether domestic violence was justifiable and proportionate. It might be possible to imagine circumstances wherein wives might gain a right to seek physical punishment or even retribution of husbands.

In short, wives tended to treat marriage as a virtually indissoluble pact, an ongoing relationship of unequal mutuality that imposed permanent moral responsibilities on men. Wives might define right and obligation within marriage conditionally, but this did not make the pact itself conditional. Wives broke the pact only under the duress of extreme irresponsibility of husbands — dangerous violence, economic negligence akin to abandonment, or outright physical or sexual abandonment. If an abusive or negligent husband forced his wife to flee or disown him, the woman might still believe that "her husband had abandoned her."[21] Whatever the narrow facts of who had left whom, it was men, not women, who abandoned the permanent responsibilities of the state of marriage.

For *amasias*, especially older women or widows who had outlived life cycle phases of more direct and continuous subordination to the patriarchal authority of fathers and husbands, the terms of female-male relations worked themselves out somewhat differently. If wives tended to view marriage as a pact that imposed permanent moral obligations on men, and thereby conditioned wives' responsibilities, *amasias* tended to insist on a looser and more consensual pact that made them more the owners of their own sexuality and person. The informality and irregularity of male economic contributions and commitments to *amasias* went hand in hand with the right of an *amasia* to withhold consent to a continuing liaison. In the dialectic of *amasia-amasio* relations and conflicts, men tended to try to tighten the pact, to impose a quasi-marital right of indissoluble male sexual possession. As in marriage, the permanence and obligatory character of female duty was not necessarily conditioned by the regularity or quality of male fulfillment of obligations to *amasias*. The key contingency was whether the man chose to continue or abandon the relationship. Women, on the other hand, strove to carve out a more consensual female space, a looser pact that implied a right to withhold consent from time to time or to discontinue the relationship altogether. Under these circumstances, repeated manifestations of male obligation — a kind of continuous courtship reaffirmed in gifts and solicitousness — might become a necessary but insufficient precondition of an *amasia*'s willingness to continue the relationship. In short, *amasias* sought to enlarge the conditional dimensions of female strategies in marriage to the point where the sexual pact itself took on a more voluntary, contingent, or consensual aspect for women.

An *amasia* might use such an enlargement in varied ways. On the one hand, the looseness of her pacts might facilitate a measure of sexual freedom and personal independence formally proscribed in more directly patriarchal social arrangements. On the other hand, the looseness of her pacts might facilitate a heightened leverage with which a poor woman might press for male economic assistance in the form of gifts and contributions to offspring, especially children of the *amasio*.

The tension between an enlarged right of female consent and a male quest for permanent, quasi-marital possession recurs repeatedly in *amasia-amasio* conflicts. We have already seen the tension, of course, in the struggle between María Lucía of Oaxtepec and Totolapa and Esquicio Ponciano. But examples abound.[22] The quasi-marital possessiveness and dynamics of some *amasio-amasia* relations could even foster legal ambiguity and confusion. Francisco Doroteo, a married free mulatto who worked at the sugar mill (*trapiche*) on Hacienda Chiconguaque, had more or less abandoned his wife, who lived on Hacienda San Nicolás. He visited his wife and contributed money to her upkeep only once every two or three weeks. Meanwhile, on Hacienda Chiconguaque, Francisco Doroteo had established a second household with María Dolores, probably a free mulatta. By 1813 the couple had been together about ten years and had raised a nine-year-old daughter. Yet despite the quasi-marital continuity and open visibility of their relationship, María Dolores held a less than exclusive view of her *amasio*'s right of possession. On February 28, when Francisco Doroteo went out on his customary Sunday diversion — Sunday was a day to collect wages, visit the hacienda *tianguis*, and drink and play cards — Lucas Plácido visited María Dolores. The interaction was comfortable rather than secretive and took place before the eyes of an Indian *molendera* who helped out in the kitchen. Lucas Plácido approached, spoke a bit with María Dolores on the patio, received a plate of food, and thanked María Dolores with a caress and a kiss. The only problem was that Francisco Doroteo had just returned from his diversions and witnessed the encounter. He reacted as an infuriated husband and asked María Dolores "upon what right [Lucas Plácido] treated her with such familiarity [*confianza*]," particularly when Francisco Doroteo "had already warned her not to speak with Lucas."

The angered *amasio* had in effect become a common-law husband who questioned the invasion without right of an *amasio* and who held a right to destroy his adulterous wife. He stabbed María Dolores in the stomach, and as she fell dead while stumbling her way out of the kitchen, he proclaimed a right of ultimate — and wounded — possession: "Dolores now you've died, know then that Francisco Doroteo has killed you and will pay with his life." (The words are taken from Francisco Doroteo's own testimony.) He then turned himself over to the master of the hacienda.[23]

The quasi-marital features of this *amasio-amasia* relationship and of Francisco Doroteo's sexual jealousy were so strong that they introduced moral and legal confusion. A husband had a right to expect light legal and moral recrimination if he caught an adulterous wife in the act of treason and killed her in a burst of uncontrollable jealousy. Indeed, María Dolores's only adult relative on the hacienda, her uncle Pasqual de la Trinidad, pardoned Francisco Doroteo the day after the murder. Just as important, the legal authorities evinced an unusual ambivalence about the proper legal trajectory. The lawyer who pleaded Francisco Doroteo's case, of course, pressed for recognition of a burst of jealousy so uncontrollably furious and so legitimate that it called for a near-pardon. This was a case of nearly justifiable homicide. The educated counselor (*licenciado*) who advised the subintendant objected that such jealousies had no legitimate legal standing in the absence of a formal marriage granting property in a wife to a husband but nonetheless recognized in the case a quasi-marital love so strong "that it could not do less than excite wrath in his chest." The subdelegate followed the *licenciado*'s advice by recommending a sentence of ten years of military service in Veracruz. The prosecutor (*fiscal*) who advised the criminal judges of the viceregal high court (*audiencia*) in Mexico City objected to such concessions and asked for the death penalty. Once all the legal ambivalences and see-sawing were worked out, the prosecutor reversed his recommendation and asked instead for a sentence of eight years of military service. The *audiencia* judges — over the *fiscal*'s objections and after the imprisoned Francisco Doroteo had languished during two years of legal wrangling — granted a royal pardon.[24]

In most instances of disputes leading to serious violence in *amasio-amasia* relations, one associates males with the effort to impose a quasi-marital pact or right of possession, and females with the effort to enlarge the consensual space within a looser pact. But *amasio-amasia* relations constituted an ambiguous cultural terrain — only half-acknowledged and considered as much an arena of ad hoc negotiation by individuals as an arena of predictable cultural sanction — and the needs and intents of the individual *amasias* and *amasios* who negotiated this cultural terrain varied considerably. These ambiguities and variations meant that the gender alignments could sometimes run in the reverse direction. The looseness of an *amasia*'s pact might provide leverage to defend a heightened personal and sexual freedom, but it might also provide leverage to press for a heightened sense of male economic obligation to an *amasia* and her children. For an economically vulnerable widow or female loner, the latter imperative might loom quite large and the point of tension might focus on her effort to impose a sense of permanent obligation on an *amasio*. In the most extreme expressions of reversal dynamics, an *amasia* might treat her *amasio* as a husband bound to an ironclad pact. María Florencia Zambrano, for example, an Indian widow of Tlayacapan who sustained four children by raising chickens and selling *pulque*, developed a quasi-marital liaison with Gregorio Abila, a married Indian villager. By 1793 *amasio* and *amasia* had been together some eleven or twelve years, and María Florencia forcefully asserted rights in Gregorio Abila that rivaled those of a wife. In January Gregorio Abila emerged from María Florencia's house with a "broken head" (*rompido de caveza*); they had quarreled over *celos*. In October María Florencia confronted Gregorio Abila in his wife's house despite his warning not to intrude on his proper familial home to press her claims. As *amasio* and *amasia* began beating each other loudly and furiously, a neighbor ran for help to keep Abila from "beating to death his *amasia* Florencia Zambrano."

The role reversals had in effect transformed María Florencia Zambrano into a common-law wife, and the legal wife, Francisca María, into the equivalent of a neglected *amasia*. Small wonder that Francisca María demanded not only the punishment of her husband and his *amasia* but also the permanent exile of María Florencia Zambrano from Tlayacapan.[25]

Notwithstanding such reversals, however, the tensions that exploded in serious violence most often pitted an *amasia*'s assertion of a freer right of female consent against an *amasio*'s determination to enforce a more absolute right of male possession. This pattern could prevail even if a female loner had dire economic need to secure continuing informal help from an *amasio*. Consider, for example, a 1765 petition by María Antonia de Tapia, an Indian *soltera* (an unmarried and nonvirginal woman or female youth) of Tepoztlán. María Antonia complained of persecution by Juan Sebastián, a married Indian and peasant of the same village.

> I say that a short time after my father died my mother went blind, and we went on using up the little we had to sustain ourselves. We reached such extremes of necessity that I had to throw myself into weaving ropes and sashes which provided only a scarce and limited support, and while I was in such straits, three years ago Juan . . . came to my doors, and greeted me with tender words, afterwards dealing with me in an evil and malicious manner, [stating] that he would continue to help with my needs if I would be with him . . . because he would support me and my mother. . . . To that I answered that there was no need of that and that he should not talk with me about that because it was not something I wanted. But he put so much effort in pursuing me that by his insistence as well as his threats, I fell in

with him . . . [and] I ended up with a child (who died) for which reason we lived in sin for two years. And during this period of time it was no longer niceties that he offered but quarrels and bad treatments, such that . . . I no longer had a life.

Whatever her ambivalences, however, María Antonia de Tapia did not break with Juan Sebastián until an aunt with whom she had also quarreled forced the issue by pressing a legal complaint. When legal problems converged with her disgust at Juan Sebastián's negligence and abuse, María Antonia decided to break definitively with her *amasio* and accept that divine will intended that "I find myself poor with my blind mother."

The problem was that for a full year Juan Sebastián refused to accept María Antonia's right to withdraw consent. The tension exploded on Christmas Eve with a loud and drunken scene: Juan Sebastián broke down the door to her house and dragged out and ruined her bedding and clothing. In her petition María Antonia de Tapia concluded with a chilling illustration of the multiple reasons that even an *amasia* in the most dire economic straits might insist on a right to withdraw her consent. She not only demanded that Juan Sebastián be punished for his abusive behavior and that his sexual persecution stop. She also demanded that he be forced to pay her the six pesos she had had to spend for a proper church burial of their child.[26]

For daughters the issues and tensions in play in female-male gender relations took on tonalities distinctive from those of wives and *amasias*. As we have seen (Chapter 3), the criminal violence documents illuminate far less successfully the gender experiences and tensions of children and youths than those of adults. (For practical purposes the rough definition of youths is unmarried minors about fifteen to nineteen years old, while that of adults includes persons married or previously married and unmarried persons whose age approached or surpassed about twenty-five years. These working definitions accord well with those of popular culture.) The gendered dynamics of parent-child relations comprise a field of life largely beyond the horizons of records focused on criminal violence incidents. Despite their adult bias, however, the materials allow for glimpses and informed speculation on female-male relations and patriarchal authority in the lives of youthful daughters, and they serve to remind us that a woman's role as daughter did not entirely disappear upon her transition to marriage and adult status.

In general as boys and girls made the transition from young childhood (say, the period when they were less than six or seven years old) toward household service as contributing youths, they were expected to assist parents in their respective duties. In the early stages of this transition, youngsters (say, children about nine or ten years old) might cross the boundaries that defined a household's sexual division of labor. A young boy might assist with a "female" task such as fetching water or feeding chickens, and a young girl might be asked to perform a "male" task such as going out to the *monte*, a hillside thick with trees or brush, to collect firewood. Heavy woodcutting and charcoal making were male tasks and going out alone to the *monte* was presumably dangerous for women and female youth. But the practical assumption apparently was that prepubescent girls could engage in lighter forms of wood gathering without as much risk of sexual assault, particularly if they went in groups of two or three.[27] As boys and girls grew older, their labor and social rounds lined up more closely with the adult household's sexual division of labor and its gendered pattern of physical movement. An older daughter was to assist with women's work such as tortilla preparation or supervision of young children and was to take greater care to refrain from unmonitored physical movement or appearances of sexual impropriety. An older son was to assist with men's work in the cornfields, could move about in the less monitored style of males, and could adopt a more predatory sexual stance.[28]

The apprenticeship and service roles of daughters extended into marriage. Newly married sons and their wives commonly lived with the sons' parents until an even younger son married and brought a new daughter-in-law into the household or until the couple managed to establish a more independent household — a separate room and kitchen — on the family compound or elsewhere in a village, hacienda, or interstitial zone of *ranchero* settlements.[29] The physical and social arrangements implied that mothers-in-law trained young daughters-in-law in the household service and deference expected of wives. In effect young daughters-in-law became quasi-servants who assisted their husbands' mothers with the myriad female tasks of tortilla and food preparation, provision of water and household supplies, laundering, child care, weaving and mending, and petty marketing and commodity production.[30] The daughter role, therefore, was not so much terminated upon marriage as extended and diversified. On the one hand, daughters might maintain links, reciprocities, and a sense of mutual obligation with their original parents, siblings, and other kin. In a successful postmarriage relationship a married daughter and her parents exchanged visits that reproduced a sense of mutual obligation and familial solidarity through conversation and drink, small gifts, and "loans" of money, goods, or labor. Even a daughter's move to a different barrio, village, or hacienda did not necessarily impede such visitations.[31] On the other hand, daughter roles were extended and modified in the context of her husband's family. The mother-daughter apprenticeship was remolded into an apprenticeship with a mother-in-law. The daughter's deference to the ultimate authority of the father-patriarch of her parental family was remolded into deference to a father-in-law, the ultimate authority of her young husband's household.

As girls made the transition toward the labor and service roles and the restrictions of physical movement of the adult female world, they did so in a particular context: as "junior" females whose sexual futures were yet to be transacted. It is clear from the complaints and remarks in passing of female youth and the recently married that the apprenticeship and servant roles of daughters in some instances subjected them to conditions of work they considered excessive and abusive. It is also clear that economic dependence and physical confinements sometimes subjected female youth to physical abuse by elders—punishments and beatings and in some instances even sexual advances—they considered cruel and unwarranted.[32] Such tensions became all the more explosive when they conjoined with tensions over the transaction of a daughter's sexual and marital future. For daughters the pact between parents and children balanced a daughter's obligation to contribute to female household work, to defer to parental discipline and monitoring, and to honor parental authority and judgment in the negotiation of her sexual-marital destiny against her parents' obligation to demonstrate a concern for the daughter's well-being and future.

The specific manner in which family elders exercised their authority demonstrated whether the relationship resembled one of transitional apprenticeship and familial collaboration premised on a mix of mutuality, authority, and attentiveness to the adult destiny of the daughter, or whether the relationship more nearly resembled a tyrannical servility with little prospect for emancipation. Parents (or surrogate parents such as uncles or aunts) who exercised elder authority with a sense of self-restraint or moderation and an eye on the youth's growth into an adult role bolstered the legitimacy of their ongoing claims to a daughter's labor, surveillance, and deferential solidarity. Parents who exercised a more absolute or untrammeled dominion risked an erosion of legitimacy as daughters came to view themselves as servants or slaves condemned to perpetual abuse and confinement. When parents or elders compounded such control with a callous disregard of the daughter's sexual future—either by blocking her acquisition of an adult marital and sexual identity, the better to retain the laboring daughter-servant, or by transacting a marriage she detested, in the interests of familial politics or convenience—the sense of oppression could become overpowering. Add to such factors the pull of sexual curiosity, desire, and experimentation; the appeal of solicitous interest and wooing by a male suitor; and the cultural assumption that equated marriage with adulthood and one can understand the ways a sense of confinement and a yearning for escape could take hold even when parents seemed less than tyrannical.

Between the poles of a pact softened by a sense of parent-child mutuality and parental attentiveness to the daughter's future and a pact hardened by insistence on a right of parental authority resembling perpetual and unbounded servitude lay considerable room for ambiguity and accommodation as well as tension and open conflict. What is clear, however, is that as a daughter passed into the age of potential marriage and adult sexual activity (as she approached, say, eighteen or twenty years), her assessment of the quality of her pact with elders conditioned her assessment of their more specific right to influence her marital-sexual destiny.[33] But if a daughter considered her parents negligent or oppressive, how might she act on a desire for emancipation from parental control without destroying irrevocably — perhaps dangerously — her family ties?

The diversity of cultural metaphors that governed a female youth's sexual-marital transfer from father to husband provided cultural tools for such efforts. On the one hand, there was the metaphor of masculine transaction and alliance. In this approach a male suitor pursued a transaction whose etiquette of wooing was directed as much at the daughter's father as at his intended partner (*novia*). As one male suitor put it, he visited the house of Hilario José, an Indian of Santa María, "in search of a closer friendship in order to [promote] his pretension" to marry Hilario José's daughter.[34] If the alliance with the father merged with a successful etiquette of wooing, symbolic gift exchanges, and declaration of intent between *novio* and *novia*, the transaction could proceed smoothly as an arrangement that coordinated horizontal (*novio/novia*) and vertical (*novio*/father-in-law) axes of agreement. Under these circumstances poor families and youth might even tolerate common-law unions among *novios* and *novias* who openly declared an intention to marry but refrained from doing so because of economic circumstances, strained relations with a priest, or latent uncertainties that called for a transitional or trial arrangement.[35] On the other hand, there was the competing metaphor of male robbery and enmity. Transaction competed with *rapto*, literally the abduction of a female to transfer her by force from one patriarch to another. Indeed, the historical intermingling of metaphors was so strong that among pre-Columbian Nahua groups in northern Morelos, family transactions culminated with ritual *raptos*: "The father and relatives of the groom went to [the bride's] house . . . and they brought her to [the groom's] house on their shoulders, where they tied or joined the manta [cloak] of the groom and the huipil [blouse] of the bride. . . . The feast for the bride was very great."[36] In the popular culture of late colonial Morelos, where males tended to view females as sexual property, "robbery" was pervasive as both metaphor and reality — bandits sometimes stole women as well as money and goods — and distinctions between coercive and consensual abductions could sometimes blur.[37]

The blurring effect meant that *novios* and *novias* might prod the transition from a state of unmarried youth to a state of married adulthood by wielding the threat of theft alongside the plea for transaction. Prearranged theft and arranged familial transaction each had its ritual etiquette. The rites of male transaction followed the symbolic etiquette of a deferential pursuit of friendship, assisted by gifts or service to the *novia* or her family, as senior and junior patriarchs moved toward agreement on their intentions to pursue an orderly transfer of the daughter-*novia*. The process ideally reaffirmed elder authority, patriarchal authority, and familial mutuality at the same time. The father, presumably counseled by the mother, secured or at least took cognizance of the consent of *novio* and *novia*; youths reaffirmed respectful deference to elders; and patriarchs and aspiring patriarchs formally transacted the agreement. Within this context, if all went well, the process might even include a ritualized *rapto*, the symbolic etiquette of a prearranged theft whose protagonists were mainly men. When serious tension developed between elder and youth, however, a daughter might use the rites of *rapto* to challenge her father's right of transaction—without severing familial ties irrevocably, since the symbolism of abduction implied that she had not openly defied her father. A junior patriarch, assisted by his accomplices, overrode the will of the senior patriarch by forcibly removing the *novia* from her father's home. Ideally the group quickly secluded or "locked up" the *novia* to assure sexual consummation of the "theft."

Of course the rites of *rapto* did not always dissolve the struggle of wills or induce a grudging familial rapprochement. In 1778, for example, Eusebio José, an Indian youth who worked in the house of another Indian, Bartolo de la Cruz, proved unable to work out a transacted arrangement to marry his employer's daughter. (The daughter's name is unmentioned in the documentation.) Eusebio José's prospective mother-in-law, however, favored the intentions of daughter and *novio* and advised Eusebio José to organize a kidnapping. The suitor had five other male Indian youths serve as accomplices in a ritual kidnapping that enjoyed the "full good will" (*plena voluntad*) of the mother. The accomplices played out their roles "with total sincerity and without second thoughts" (*con toda sinceridad y ninguna refleja*). They tied up the father in his own house, transferred the daughter to Eusebio José, enclosed the couple in a house to assure sexual consummation of the transfer, then marched the couple to the priest in an effort to secure an immediate marriage of the youths. In this instance, however, the father remained unbending. The priest—who held the responsibility to balance the church's theological interest in the free will of *novio* and *novia* in marriage choices against the church's interest in the duty of youths and subordinates to respect the authority and wisdom of superiors— ended up backing the father.[38]

Wives, *amasias*, and daughters: these social positions surely do not exhaust the full range of subordinate female roles in the female-male relations of popular culture. Women and female youth also lived out subordinate gender roles as sisters, nieces, cousins, *novias*, and servants of the men and male youth of popular culture. Moreover, our field of vision has thus far largely excluded more superordinate and horizontal female gender roles vis-à-vis males, as

mothers, elders, curers, neighbors, and voices of community morality and rebellion. Our field of vision has also excluded thus far the wider arena of color-
class relations that placed the women and female youth of subaltern groups in
subordinate and highly gendered roles as servants and sexual objects. Nor
have we systematically analyzed female-female relations and their impact on
female-male relations. Thus far we have glimpsed the dynamics of these
largely excluded roles and relationships only intermittently. The full implications of the more horizontal and superordinate roles of women and female
youth, their color-class position and dilemmas, and their female-female relations will emerge cumulatively, sometimes interstitially, in the course of this
book (see especially Chapters 5, 6, 8). This catalogue of the excluded reminds
us not to mistake the triple vision of women and female youth as wives,
amasias, and daughters with the totality of female gendered roles within popular culture. The reminder matters even if we remember that the struggles
and contestations of wives and sometimes of *amasias* may often be usefully
conceptualized as the struggles of wife-mothers and *amasia*-mothers. Wives
and *amasias* who were also mothers often equated their own interests in
struggles with negligent or abusive husbands and *amasios* with the defense of
their children's well-being.

Notwithstanding the exclusions, however, the wife-*amasia*-daughter triad
captures a fundamental dimension of female gendered life and struggle in
Morelos popular culture. The wife-*amasia*-daughter triad constituted the core
foundation of roles that defined a woman's primary relations with superordinate males in a cultural world where serious male-on-female violence generally emerged out of primary rather than secondary or tertiary social relations.
In many respects the relationships of younger sister to older brother, niece to
uncle, daughter-in-law to father-in-law, godchild to godfather, young *novia* to
older *novio*, and the like may be viewed as shadings, variations, and blends
built on this core foundation.

In addition and perhaps more important, comparative elucidation of the
experiences and contestations of gender right among wives, *amasias*, and
daughters illuminates both the common denominator and the variations that
ran through male-female tensions over gender right. In each of women's three
foundational roles a conflictual and sometimes violent encounter between
contingent and absolute approaches to gender right came to the fore and provided a unifying leitmotif within the diversity of female roles and relationships. At the same time, the tension between contingent and absolute models
of gender right took on distinct tonalities adapted to the specific needs and aspirations, life cycle conjunctures, and social relationships that comprised a
particular context of dispute. For wives marriage constituted a virtually indissoluble moral pact, a relationship of unequal mutuality that imposed permanent moral responsibilities on men. The multiple and linked dimensions of

mutual obligation allowed for conditional and contextual definitions of male right and female obligation within marriage; opened spaces for change, individual idiosyncrasy, and the assertion of female right; but also met with husbands' assertions of a more unconditional right and authority. For *amasias*, especially those well beyond youth and of reasonably independent economic means, a sexual liaison outside marriage implied a looser and more consensual pact that enlarged a woman's ownership of her own sexuality and person. The enlargement of the conditional into a right to withhold consent provided leverage for both a more independent ownership of the female body and a more assertive expectation of male obligation or solicitude. It also met, however, with *amasios'* assertions of a more ironclad right of possession. For daughters approaching adulthood the burdens of youth merged with those of gender. Yet even in this instance maturing daughters tended to view their apprenticeship to the mother and their deference to the father as a transitional pact conditioned by a sense of parent-child mutuality and parental attentiveness to the daughter's future. This view opened a space for daughters to decide to what degree their familial role resembled that of protected daughter or abused servant, and legitimized efforts to curtail a father's right of sexual transaction. But it also met with fathers' assertions of a more innate, less conditioned right to transact their daughters' sexual-marital futures. In all of their unfolding variation, then, the dialectics of contingent and absolute assertions of gender right suffused the female-male relations of popular culture.

The wives, *amasias*, and daughters whose lives fill the foregoing pages have not stepped forth as protofeminist characters in the contemporary sense. They did not challenge a right of patriarchal authority as such, and the logic of their practice did not rest on a premise of fundamental equality of ability or likeness of rights across the genders. (They refrained, too, from asserting a vision of woman-centered superiority.) As we shall see (Chapter 6), moreover, their pervasive and sometimes bitter disputes with husbands, *amasios*, and fathers did not necessarily preclude a deeply felt familial solidarity, a condition of ambivalence and contradiction that led women to defend as well as attack male kin.

Nonetheless, wives, *amasias*, and daughters succeeded in constructing a world of contested patriarchal pacts. If they did not challenge patriarchal first principles of male dominance and female subordination as such, they nonetheless surrounded them with pressure. The social conventions of gender that gave life and shape to patriarchal right were surrounded with conditionality and context: obligations, contingencies, and linkages that mapped out a vision of female gender right and imposed a logic of social practice whereby respect for female gender right was made to interact with and shift the boundaries of legitimate male gender right. If this was a prefeminist world of gender contestation, its gender wars could nonetheless shake everyday life with danger and violence and turn calm into a passing illusion. If men brought to gender skirmishes the advantage of superior power in families and social institutions, women could nonetheless establish a destiny other than that of the consistently helpless victim of a consistently one-sided battle. For as we are about to see, women forged a variety of social weapons to irritate, curb, wear down, outflank, and — occasionally — besiege their patriarchal adversaries.

FEMALE WEAPONS

The weapons women used to advance their well-being or to curb abuse are to some extent familiar. We have seen many of them in play in the episodes of conflict and violence already recounted. Nonetheless we have not yet reviewed in more analytical and systematic terms the panoply of resources that women (and to some extent female youth) coordinated in gender struggles with men.

Let us begin with an obvious polarity or continuum in the kinds of acts that expressed resistance. On the one hand, a woman or female youth's individual acts to block harm or affirm well-being could include subtle shadings in behavior that shifted the tone of deference, command, and legitimacy in a relationship but resist scrutiny in historical documents.[39] An extra hint of indifference in the timely preparation of fresh tortillas and food; an added touch of avoidance in verbal or sexual encounters; an inclination to tarry a bit longer on trips to fetch water, purchase chilies, or visit relatives; a cool or grudging response to offers of drink and conviviality — all had the capacity to signal disquiet, to irritate patriarchs, and to induce a silent tension that husbands, *amasios*, and fathers could choose to ignore, escalate, or defuse. Subtle and borderline maneuvers such as these avoided explicit challenges to authority. Yet to the extent that they called forth not loud escalations and violence but more muted, indifferent, or even constructive responses from patriarchs, they could induce small adjustments in the dynamics of domestic power and female self-legitimation. In short, documentary invisibility ought not lead us to underestimate the degree to which women and female youth might mobilize shadings of behavior to resist negligence or abuse or to affirm to themselves a sense of female right.[40]

On the other end of the continuum, individual acts of female resistance could include exertions of sheer physical force that openly defied the will of men. Women intervened physically and forcefully at moments of personal, familial, or community danger and crisis. (Interventions in the interest of familial and community solidarity will be explored in Chapters 6 and 8.) These interventions sometimes required dramatic strength of will and body. Andrés Antonio, an Indian of Tlayacapan, returned home the evening of January 1, 1783, and found that his wife (unnamed in the document) had not prepared tortillas, the supper of the poor. He rebuked and slapped her for shirking her duties. Two versions of events, both culturally plausible, describe her response. In one version she ran to her brother's house for refuge and help. In the other Andrés Antonio's wife dragged him outside. "My wife and I fought about [the fact] that I arrived [home] hungry, and she hadn't made me tortillas to eat supper, and after we had argued about it, I gave her two or three slaps, and angry, she pulled me out of my house by force to take and accuse me before our priest. And as we were going along the street fighting, upon passing the house of Manuel de la cruz, [the] brother of my wife, he recognized the sound [*conosio el eco*] of his sister, and immediately stepped outside and . . . grabbed me by the [hair] braids, and threw me on the ground." The two versions of events are not quite as incompatible as first meets the eye. Even if Andrés Antonio's wife initially fled to seek refuge and did not literally drag her husband out of the house, it is clear that Andrés Antonio would have wanted to keep the dispute private by pulling her off the street. But this he could not do. The net effect of the ensuing scuffle was that Andrés Antonio's wife "dragged" him along in the direction of brother and priest. What made such stories plausible was their resonance with many other physical interventions by women in moments of crisis or conflict.[41]

If individual acts of resistant assertion ranged from subtle shadings to more defiant exertions of will, this continuum describes only one dimension of a much more complex configuration of female acts, tactics, and strategies in conflicts with men. Women and female youth also developed a variety of *social* strategies and weapons that might even out the balance of power and block individual isolation and vulnerability.

One such strategy pluralized the number of active patriarchs, the would-be protectors with claims in the destiny and well-being of a given woman or female youth. In effect this strategy set up male-male rivalries and hierarchies as a check on the power of the patriarch with the most immediate claim of authority. We have already glimpsed such a strategy: when daughters saw in their *novios* or *amasios* a means to curb the power of fathers, and when young wives and daughters-in-law saw in their parental families a means to curb the power of their "political" families.[42] By pluralizing the patriarchs and would-be patriarchs within her web of active primary relations, by appealing to a proprietary sense of male honor and responsibility that blended with a sense of familial solidarity and *afecto*, a woman could seek protection in times of trouble, mobilize intervention if she convinced a rival patriarch that she had been mistreated, or rely on the latent threat of intervention to temper the domestic balance of power. (The Spanish term *afecto* signifies an emotive bond or warm feeling that may stretch to include outright affection but is somewhat weaker, more elastic in implication than the English *affection*. *Cariño* is closer to the English *affection*.)

The pluralization of patriarchs could at times extend to sexual partners. A wife might establish a connection with an *amasio,* or a woman might develop sequential liaisons, partly to block the possessive claims of a previous lover or husband. (The wife of a negligent or often absent husband might view him as having abandoned his wife and claims as a husband even if he claimed a right of continuing possession and service whenever he returned. The cultural euphemism of calling her a widow might enable the woman or her acquaintances to smooth over appearances unless outright conflict erupted.) In an extreme case María Antonia Quevedo, a free mulatta in Tlaltizapán, endured a troubled marriage for twenty years and developed a cycle of escape and reconciliation. Eleven times she fled her husband Nicolás Lorenzo, but after a time she would return, impoverished and "naked," only to escape again when the abuse worsened. At one point Nicolás Lorenzo cut off the fingers on one of her hands, presumably to destroy her ability to live, work, and love independently. By 1765, however, María Antonia had developed a connection with a male suitor or lover on Hacienda San Nicolás and proceeded to marry him to seal the end of her abusive marriage in Tlaltizapán.[43] A woman whose troubles were less notorious among the local priests and who had not compounded the ecclesiastical issues by pursuing a double marriage instead of an informal sexual union would have been less vulnerable to the Inquisition proceedings that render María Antonia Quevedo visible to historians. She may well have known that a second marriage entailed risks. Was the preference for marriage a last quest, against the odds, for cultural dignity by a woman determined to overcome a history of abuse, mutilation, and economic insecurity? Or did she simply presume, in accord with female popular logic, that her first husband had by his actions abandoned and nullified their state of marriage?

Spinning multiple webs of active primary relations implicated more than one patriarch in a woman's life, but it constituted only a first step in the strategy of pluralization. If necessary a woman moved beyond the circle of primary relations with kin and quasi-kin to mobilize the local infrastructure of male authorities and patriarchs — Indian village councilmen (*alcaldes*), governors (*gobernadores*), and elders (*viejos, pasados*) and more whitened brokers such as priests, hacienda administrators and supervisors, and local deputies (*tenientes, encargados*) of colonial magistrates. These figures held authority as superior patriarchs, men whose responsibility to look after local social peace and morals and to serve as informal judges of the first instance gave them a right to review and to punish the excesses of lesser patriarchs. If this secondary net of additional patriarchs and judges proved insufficient and a dispute resisted verbal or informal resolution, a woman might even move beyond the local infrastructure to mobilize the institutional authorities of the colonial legal system proper — the magistrates and judges (*alcaldes mayores, subintendentes,* and occasionally, *jueces de la Acordada* and ecclesiastical judges) who oversaw formal prosecution and litigation in the rural provinces, the appellate judges (*oidores*) and Indian defenders linked to the *audiencia* and viceroy in Mexico City, and the clusters of lawyers, prosecutors, scribes, and other functionaries (*licenciados, fiscales, procuradores de indios, escribanos*, and the like) who made the system workable.[44]

To extend the pluralization-of-patriarchs strategy beyond the immediate circle of primary relations to the larger local infrastructure of male authorities and beyond the local infrastructure to the wider legal system was no simple decision. Given the color-class position of peasant and plebeian women in colonial Morelos, appeals for intervention could expose their households to fees, extortions, and interference by predatory authorities. (The dilemmas posed by this contradiction are explored in Chapter 6.) The gendered aspects of law and culture further complicated such decisions. The status of marriage as a sacrament, the tendency of the legal and church system to push for reconciliation in husband-wife disputes, the inferior legal and cultural standing of female testimony (particularly when the woman was also a poor Indian, mulatta, or mestiza), and the tainted moral standing and legal vulnerability of *amasias* and suspected *amasias* all introduced barriers to a woman's decision to extend the range of patriarchal authorities whose intervention she sought.[45] These color-class and gender considerations imparted a double edge to a strategy that pluralized patriarchs beyond primary relations.

Nonetheless women did not shrink from moving beyond the relatives and quasi-relatives who constituted a first net in the pluralization of male authority. Again and again the documents tell us in passing of the numerous instances when women mobilized the patriarchs of the local infrastructure — village authorities, priests, local elders, and occasionally hacienda authorities or Spanish notables who often doubled as *tenientes* and *encargados* of the legal system. A particularly revealing aspect of such mobilizations is that they were not limited to incidents of serious violence that led women to pursue formal written prosecution or that forced local authorities to take institutional cognizance of homicide and near-homicide. Incidents of serious violence more often yielded extensive written documentation in the formal legal system, but read closely they also recount and expose female mobilization of competing patriarchs even in the absence of major violent assaults. In short, a plethora of more informal, irregular, and infrastructural interventions — the stream of everyday complaints, disputes, and resolutions familiar to every local judge, community leader, and priest in rural Mexico and often labeled verbal complaints and verbal suits (*quejas verbales* and *juicios verbales*) — provided a background murmur to the more formal and dramatic interventions of higher authorities.[46] It was against the backdrop of this murmur that José Marcelino of Texalpa, whose troubled life with María Teresa opened this book, thought it plausible to say that his wife had threatened to have his father punished for raising a lazy and negligent son. The threat meant nothing in the system of formal law. It could only spell trouble in the more informal system of women's appeals for relief and adjudication.

Female mobilizations of the local network of male community authority invoked channels of assistance that seem informal and irregular in the perspective of the wider colonial polity and its formal criminal procedures. But these mechanisms were not at all devoid of authority and solemnity at the community level and in the lives of the individuals in conflict. Village officials and elders, hacienda supervisors, and priests stepped forth as weighty figures of authority on the local stages of human life, and their formal and informal rights of judgment included rights to put in stocks, tie up, imprison, and whip miscreants; to place mistreated or vulnerable persons in protective custody; and to initiate more formal criminal proceedings.

A woman's ability to extend her pluralization of patriarchs beyond kin and quasi-kin, therefore, might bring into play formidable weapons in her struggle to alter the domestic balance of power. Consider, for example, the maneuvers of Victoriana Tomasa, an Indian of Xalostoque, in 1796. Caught in a troubled and violent marriage with Augustín Mariano, who subjected her to economic negligence, sexual license, unjustified jealousy, and repeated violence, she also found that earlier complaints to the local judge — Don Antonio Montoto, the *teniente* of the *alcalde mayor*— had only yielded more trouble. Victoriana Tomasa wanted her Indian husband subjected to a whipping, a standard village punishment for delinquents. (The customary practice of whipping might seem harsh to outsiders, to the comparatively prosperous, or to a twentieth-century eye. Unless carried out to the point of inflicting injury so severe that it impaired work, however, whipping made a point without straining the household economy. From a peasant perspective, prolonged imprisonment or mounting fines might seem harsher, at least to the relatives who depended on the work or income of the punished.) Montoto had failed to whip Victoriana Tomasa's husband, however, and the fines he had imposed added yet another strain to a household economy perpetually in crisis. The cure was worse than the disease: it added hardship but failed to deter further diversionary spending, violence, and humiliation. Victoriana Tomasa adapted by pluralizing further her net of would-be protectors. On the one hand, she apparently struck up a friendship with another man; whether they ended up *amasia* and *amasio*, as charged by her husband, is unclear. On the other hand, when embroiled in the *amasia* accusation by her husband, Victoriana Tomasa stepped outside the authority system of the village and state and mobilized a priest caught up in a factional dispute with the political authorities aligned against her. The maneuver enabled her to abandon her husband for the protective custody of the priest, Bachiller Don Juan Bustamante, until her husband agreed to submit to the kind of punishment she considered a deterrent to further abuse. Only after Augustín Mariano acceded to twelve lashes by Bustamante did Victoriana Tomasa agree to reconcile with her husband.[47]

The pluralization of patriarchal authority within familial networks and beyond them constituted but one social strategy. Another major strategy forged a network of female-female relations: webs of shared knowledge and assessments, constructions of local reputation and rumor, and possibilities of mutual aid and intervention. In effect this strategy cultivated a sense of female solidarity, knowledge, and troubles with men that lessened women's vulnerability and isolation before male power and authority. Such networks of solidarity, conversation, and aid rarely coincided, of course, with a peasant or plebeian woman's total map of female acquaintances in a given village, barrio, hacienda, or cluster of ranchos. One may even discern competing female networks of judgment and solidarity, or a fracturing of networks, and cases of female-female enmity (see Chapter 6).

As in the pluralization-of-patriarchs strategy a woman's first line of defense — her densest network of shared female knowledge and expectations of mutual assistance — usually drew on selected familial and quasi-familial relationships. Not surprisingly, therefore, a husband embroiled in a struggle with his wife sometimes saw her female relatives as his principal enemies. In 1789, for example, an Indian of Atlacahualoya (near Xonacatepec) complained that his mother-in-law, Pasquala María, "has forcefully taken away from me my wife," Juana Josefa, who had returned to her parents' house. Francisco Xavier focused the complaint precisely on target, for Pasquala María had led the effort to intimidate him. Two days earlier Pasquala María, flanked by another daughter and son-in-law, confronted Francisco Xavier's suspected *amasia*, Lorenza Juana, as she emerged from Sunday Mass. The trio proceeded to beat up Lorenza Juana, rip her clothes, and haul her and a sister by the hairbraids to the village *gobernador* for punishment. They then fortified the group with Pasquala María's husband and marched off to Francisco Xavier's house. Notwithstanding the presence of her husband, a prominent figure in local peasant politics and an enemy of his son-in-law, Pasquala María again assumed a central role in the fray, giving and receiving the slaps that were exchanged.[48]

For purposes of female solidarity and mutual aid in troubles with men, however, a woman's network could also extend well beyond familial relations. Neighbors in the barrio who heard or discussed domestic strife, companions at the streams where women fetched water and washed clothes, old-time trading and vending partners at the local *tianguis*, peasant mistresses and *molendera* servants who labored together in humble hearths, female curers and magical specialists, and even female bystanders at a *fandango*: all might figure, at moments of crisis, in a woman's or female youth's expanded net of female allies.

A brief catalogue of examples illustrates the wide range of relationships and contexts that mobilized female-female alliances in quarrels with men.

Magdalena Francisca, an Indian on Hacienda San Gaspar with a reputation as a folk healer (*curandera*), intervened to defend her mulatta neighbor Simona Quitería when the latter's Indian husband wounded his wife and then sought to drag her to the estate's master to complain of a suspicious encounter with a man. Magdalena Francisca had been a close friend of Simona Quitería and her husband, who addressed her by the fictive kin term *comadre*.

Several women at a plebeian *fandango* in Cuernavaca intervened to defend Juana Manuela Cirila de Vargas, probably white (that is, *española*) but of plebeian or intermediate social standing, when Juana Manuela's older brother took umbrage at her singing and dancing. He called her a whore and threw her to the floor. The women, who pulled the brother away by the hair, appeared to have had no particular friendship with Juana Manuela. But they agreed with those who held that her brother had been abusive and exaggerated, that the atmosphere of the *fandango* had been honorable rather than predatory, and that Juana Manuela had been proper rather than licentious.

Ana la Ramírez, of unknown racial-ethnic status, provided a house of refuge to Andrea Antonia, a married mulatta of Cuautla Amilpas who tried to terminate a relationship with an insistent *amasio* of somewhat higher status. (He was the son of a white literate trader or merchant, but his father was insufficiently successful to use the honorific "Don.") Given the prolonged absences of Andrea Antonia's husband, who worked as a mason on Hacienda Tenextepango, Ana la Ramírez was probably Andrea Antonia's most important everyday friend and companion.

María Josefa, a married mestiza originally from Hacienda San Carlos, developed a close friendship with María Gertrudis, a monolingual Nahua peasant in Zamatitlán. Their friendship had had an opportunity to take deep root when María Josefa lived and worked in María Gertrudis's house. The friendship elicited a defensive reaction from María Gertrudis's husband, who dismissed María Josefa. But the friendship continued anyway. A year later, when María Gertrudis's husband suspected his wife of adultery, he was certain that María Josefa served as the go-between (*alcahueta*), the person who tended to the arrangements, communications, and discretion that made such liaisons possible.

María de Guadalupe several times provided refuge to Andrea María, her Indian neighbor in Tlayacapan, when Andrea María feared her Indian husband would kill her. Andrea María's marriage was notoriously troubled and violent: her husband left on long trips to sell cloth, had pursued a rather public and quasi-marital liaison with a married Indian woman, and sought to control his wife's labor and physical movements with beatings. He had developed a habitual violence that sometimes took a homicidal turn. The evidence does not suggest an especially close friendship between María de Guadalupe and her neighbor but rather a sense of neighborly responsibility when homicide was imminent.[49]

This range of examples illustrates the myriad ways women and female youth might move beyond the female kin and quasi-kin who constituted a first line of defense and mobilization in female networks of shared knowledge and expectations of mutual assistance. On the one hand, women might expand their network of effective primary relations with selected female friendships whose density of reciprocity and commitment approached that of kinship. If the women chose to acknowledge their friendliness with a fictive kin metaphor, they might regularly call one another *comadre*, or perhaps *comadrita* to add a slightly more tender touch. As metaphor, *comadre* (co-godmother) signified a sense of connection, obligation, and reciprocity achieved voluntarily rather than by birth. The willful-yet-obligatory aspect of the bond resonated with the social bonding and obligations undertaken in a relation of spiritual kinship.[50] On the other hand, the world of female secondary relations — the networks of neighbors and acquaintances who saw and spoke with one another with some regularity near their homes, at the waters where women gathered to wash or to provision households, at the *tianguis* or in the church, at community assemblies and celebrations of saints, and at more private ritual occasions such as wakes or weddings — nurtured a more diffuse sense of female solidarity and endurance in the face of male abuse or negligence.

One detects in the strategy of female solidarity and intervention a foundation and a potential extension outward in some ways analogous to the escalations evident in the pluralization-of-patriarchs strategy. Women built the strategy of female discussion and solidarity on a foundation of selected relationships among kin and quasi-kin: mothers, sisters, and aunts; more occasionally, cousins, close friends and kindred spirits, and fictive kin such as godmothers or co-godmothers; and still more rarely, in-laws. When necessary or desirable, however, they extended their mobilization of assistance to a broader grid of potential allies, a local infrastructure of female discussion, evaluation, and occasionally intervention.

Despite the parallels of a foundation in family and a progression from primary to secondary arenas of assistance, however, the mobilization of female alliances should not be construed simply as a female replica of the pluralization-of-patriarchs strategy. Three points of difference are as salient as the points in common. First, the institutional and cultural legitimacy of patriarchs who intervened to protect a woman or female youth from abuse by her immediate patriarch contrasted sharply with the legitimacy accorded to female defenders. Fathers, village officials and elders, local priests, hacienda managers, and judges and their lieutenants and deputies all had a recognized standing in customary or formal law or in hegemonic cultural constructions of community[31] to evaluate and if necessary rebuke or punish a rival or lesser patriarch's treatment of a female dependent. Female relatives and allies stood on softer legal and cultural ground. A mother held comparatively weak legal claim to prosecute an assailant who raped, wounded, or killed her daughter unless the father was dead or absent;[52] a female elder held comparatively tenuous cultural claim to the rights of informal counsel and judgment that accrued to a male village elder, a priest, or a hacienda administrator; women held none of the formal rights of judgment conferred upon village officials, colonial judges, and their male deputies and representatives. When women mobilized to defend another woman, therefore, they did so from a more marginal or tenuous position of institutional legitimation.

Second, the basis of appeal for aid differed notably. When a woman appealed successfully to a rival or superior patriarch, she mobilized not simply a sense of familial solidarity or *afecto* or an abstract set of rules governing social behavior, but a man's proprietary sensibilities as a paternal patriarch. A father, an older brother, a husband, or a *novio* each ideally adopted a protective role vis-à-vis the female kin or dependents who needed him and whose treatment reflected on his honor, manliness, and proprietary claims in dependents. A village official or elder, a hacienda supervisor, a priest, or a judge each ideally adopted the protective role of a metaphorical father, a paternal authority whose ability to protect the weak and to rebuke scoundrels reflected on his proprietary guardianship of social peace and morality among the metaphorical children of his community.[53] In short, the pluralization-of-patriarchs strategy appealed to men as men, as gendered persons who exercised culturally recognized rights of authority distinctive to their sex and whose interventions often reflected upon their personal valor and responsibilities as real and metaphorical fathers.

By contrast, the mobilization-of-female-alliances strategy appealed to women as women, as gendered persons whose culturally recognized rights of authority were tenuous or marginal because of their sex but whose knowledge of the troubles, negligence, and excesses that men inflicted on women justified interventions to help or rescue an abused woman or youth. In the female culture of alliance and mobilization the real and metaphorical role of the intervenor was not that of the protective father who righted wrongs or warded off threats by lesser and irresponsible would-be patriarchs. The real and metaphorical relationships were a mix of vertical and horizontal roles of specifically female inspiration: the role of a mother or surrogate mother, a female elder who risked harm by men to defend the well-being of abused or neglected children, and the role of a sister or *comadre*, a female of roughly equivalent age or life cycle standing who volunteered refuge or assistance out of a sense of solidarity or shared destiny with an abused counterpart.[54]

The third point of difference between the pluralization-of-patriarchs strategy and that of female alliance and mobilization rests in their cultural premises. A woman who pluralized patriarchs told a rival or superior patriarch of troubles with her immediate patriarch at crisis moments, when she sought redress. A background of continuing conversation and complaint invited trouble—violence and feuds among kin, extortions by authorities, and foul temper and retribution by the immediate patriarch—if a woman did not seek specific intervention. We may interpret the dynamics of female mobilization of specific patriarchs within a pluralized network of patriarchs as an oscillation between silence and conversation. The cultural premises of female networks and solidarities, by contrast, rested on greater continuity of conversation. In the ongoing conversations often feared by men and denigrated as gossip,[55] women spun webs of shared knowledge and assessments, local reputation and rumor, and a more general sensibility of women's troubles with men. This background of conversation nurtured a larger sense of female grievance and endurance as well as knowledge of specific relationships and troubles—in short, a foundation for mutual aid and intervention in times of trouble. The culture of female conversation and knowledge helped to define the contours of the permissible and the unacceptable, the necessary and the optional, the moral and the immoral, in female lives with male kin and partners.

This background of ongoing conversation illuminates several features of the data. It helps to explain why female witnesses in documents seemed to know a great deal about the lives and troubles of other women, even though, as women, they were not among the institutionally favored receivers of informal and formal complaints. As María Manuela Rodríguez confidently put it, when her friend María Juana of Tepoztlán died under mysterious circumstances, she was certain that the authorities' suspicion that Guillermo Desiderio Rendón had quarreled with and kicked the pregnant María Juana was false. She would have known of any such troubles because the two women were "tight friends and always [walking] together."[56] The culture of female knowledge and conversation also helps to explain how women might build a reservoir of discreet knowledge ("rumor," or *chismes*) that circulated underground but came out into the open only selectively, when needed to serve a particular purpose.[57] Finally, the construction of reputation and truth through informal conversation and repetition helps to explain why words and gossip could be held to have dangerous consequences. When Esquicio Ponciano's widow met a resonant response to her claim that it was really María Lucía of Oaxtepec and Totolapa who had caused Esquicio Ponciano's death, María Lucía had good reason to flee to Cuautla for her safety. When a man complained that "it is said" (*se dice*) he engaged in wrongdoing, he acknowledged that under some circumstances the ongoing murmur of words and gossip could become a threat.[58]

Two ultimate weapons took the strategies heretofore mentioned an extra step. One was the weapon of scandal, and the other was the weapon of magic. The weapon of scandal took the pluralization-of-patriarchs strategy an extra step by creating such a loud, divisive, and potentially threatening ruckus that male authorities had to intervene whether they liked it or not. This was not a weapon to be used lightly: it deepened enmities and made personal reconciliation more difficult; it brought no guarantees that local male authorities who intervened would sympathize with the woman rather than consider her a troublemaker; and it ran up against color-class considerations that rendered intervention by authorities higher up the institutional ladder problematic, a potential source of interference, fines, or extortions that might backfire against a woman, her family, or her community.[59] Nonetheless, the threat and reality of scandal that destroyed the social peace and thereby forced intervention by higher authorities recurred in subtle and obvious ways in women's actions. When Andrea Antonia ran off to live with her friend Ana la Ramírez, she put her former *amasio* on notice that to continue the relationship would require that he break into another woman's house—in other words, that he cause a minor scandal witnessed by an aggrieved party untainted by a prior sexual relationship. When Gertrudis, the mother of Bartolomé Baptista, got caught up in a factional quarrel with Don Manuel Torres, an important village lord (*cacique*), she used scandal to corner Don Manuel and to force intervention by a higher authority. She went about proclaiming in a "loud voice . . . with wrathful and insulting words" that the *cacique* had ordered her son killed. Don Manuel Torres could not ignore the fuss and indeed sued to have his honor and reputation restored. When Esquicio Ponciano's wife wounded her husband's *amasia* with a rock, she used scandal to force an intervention that would undermine her husband's freedom of action. The same strategy was evident when Pasquala María had her son-in-law's suspected *amasia* beaten up in public and—at a somewhat higher social level—when Doña María Josefa Lira confronted her husband's *amasia* in church, "and with the greatest audacity and disrespect, screamed at me that I was a despicable miserable whore, a wrecker, . . . a melona."[60] (*Melona*, literally a female melon, is slang for a juicy, ripe temptress.)

The weapon of scandal was an ultimate weapon, not to be used lightly. But it mattered. Our documents make clear that communities could tolerate, for substantial lengths of time, individual idiosyncrasies, half-acknowledged sexual liaisons and liberties, and considerable domestic tensions and abuse. In the absence of scandal such matters belonged to the realm of background murmur and conversation. It was at moments when idiosyncrasies and ten-

sions threatened, in the eyes of local authorities, to tear apart the facade of social peace — to burst onto the stage as a drama of open conflict, violence, and
retribution — that conflicts once consigned to more or less private and offstage spheres, fit for public discussion mainly as background murmur among
women, came to acquire a more emphatically public character. They became
scandals that required community intervention and resolution.[61]

The other ultimate weapon, magic, takes us into a realm of female strategy,
networks, and culture more difficult to trace in the historical documents of
late colonial Morelos. The weapon of magic (or perhaps better, *hechicería*,
witchcraft) took the mobilization-of-female-alliances strategy a step further
by invoking supernatural and secret powers, a host of remedies and options
learned or bought from female magical specialists who knew how to tame, tie,
weaken, harm, attract, or otherwise influence the men in a woman's life.
Frowned upon by the formal Catholic Church as superstition and, occasionally, heresy, these practices had an underground quality and have eluded most
historical documentation. They are most visible in church records, especially
Inquisition cases that scrutinized, on charges of witchcraft or heresy, female
mystics and magical specialists and the women who consulted them. Unfortu
nately the Inquisition records and cases (so marvelously studied by Solange
Alberro, Ruth Behar, and Jean Franco, among others) excluded Indian practitioners from their jurisdiction and seem to have focused on the center-
north and north regions of Mexico rather than center-south regions such as
Morelos.[62]

The elusive features of this magical culture, however, should not obfuscate
two points. First, women's occasional mobilization of magical remedies for
problems with men emerged out of a larger female cultural construction, a
distinctively female sensibility and connection to spiritual, supernatural, and
healing forces pertinent to female life and troubles and beyond the realm of
the forces controlled by men and the church. It would claim too much to say
that men did not participate in the practices of a magical culture or that they
were immune to a sense of spiritual connection to forces beyond the control
of the colonial church.[63] But it also claims too much to deny the gendered sensibilities and networks within popular religious and magical culture, a sense of
female recourse to spirits, powers, and practitioners who spoke especially to
female needs. A female art used powders, herbs, pubic hairs, human blood,
small animals, and other organic materials to affect the physical well-being
and mental and sexual inclinations of targets and proclaimed a sometimes
dangerous female connection to powers and "frights" beyond the realm of
male control. At its most extreme this sense of connection to powers and
forces pertinent to women could yield a mystical sense of unity and interior
conversation with spirits and could yield female individualists and specialists — deviants in the classic sense — sharply at odds with the gender order.[64]

Second, historical and ethnographic evidence corroborates the participation of the peoples of Morelos in the construction of a magical culture of female supernatural power, danger, and recourse. The historical evidence comes largely in hints and traces: women whose susceptibility to spiritual fright induced abortion, illness, or death; a wife afflicted by a troubled marriage and charges of adultery and found in possession of a suspicious "handkerchief with powders"; women who developed local niches and reputations as curers; an *amasia* whose strangling of chickens conjoined, in the mind of her *amasio*, with a threat of retribution; a mother-and-son team, led by the mother, who made a living wandering about "curing with superstitions, and witchcraft, feigning to be soothsayers who talk with the Christ saint of Totolapa, fooling [people] with herbs, and powders."[65] More recent ethnographic study underscores the historical construction in Morelos of a magical culture, a network of practitioners and knowledge that allowed for female supernatural recourse. In the village culture of the mid-twentieth century, female specialists held to have powers to tame, render ill, or induce foolishness in men provoked anxiety in peasant husbands who feared vengeance by their wives.[66]

We have reviewed a vast panoply of female weapons. These included individual acts of resistance; social strategies of mobilization, alliance, and escalation; and at times, dangerous weapons of scandal and magic. The actions and strategies under review were too pervasive, too socially patterned, and too informed by cultural networking and preparation to be dismissed as isolated ad hoc episodes within a largely harmonious popular culture. They expressed, rather, the reality of deep frictions and conflict of interest alongside, within, and in dialogue with the most primary and solidary bonds of popular culture. If it is clear that familial metaphor served as a powerful language of cohesion and legitimacy in popular culture (see Chapter 8), it is also clear that the conflicts of gender multiplied the meaning of family into a cluster of sometimes contending meanings. On the question of gender right in female-male relations, one finds not a single normative code and deviation from the code, but contending normative codes and interests within the social body: a persistent conflictual dialogue between contingent and absolute orientations to gender right, a cultural argument sufficiently flexible to provide a language of right adapted to women's specific struggles as wives, *amasias*, and daughters. Notwithstanding the important solidarities of affect and interest that bound women and men to one another, the peasant world of late colonial Morelos was a world suffused with contested patriarchal pacts. To these contestations women brought a considerable arsenal of resources and tactics, a will and an ability to resist male fiat and desire. Their weapons entangled male right and authority in a web of contingency, restriction, and complication. Small wonder, then, that peasant men viewed the question of gender authority as no trifling matter and that they sometimes lashed out with the ultimate weapon of violence. Violence in primary relations, whether an outburst of uncontrolled anger or a more coolly calculated instrument of repression, is the ultimate expression of a failed possession in persons. Small wonder, then, that so many Marías fill the historical annals of Morelos.

CHAPTER 5

Cultural Legitimacy, Cultural Stigma

An Interpretation of Widows

THE PROBLEM OF LEGITIMACY

Women and men in late colonial Morelos clashed sharply, sometimes bitterly, over gender right and obligation. The women and female youth we have visited in the foregoing pages rarely challenged patriarchal first principles as such. But as we have seen, they often reinterpreted the operational meaning of such principles so markedly that conflict and violence ensued. As we have also seen, such conflicts mobilized at least two competing popular models of gender right and obligation in the female-male relations of a patriarchal culture. One model emphasized the mutually contingent qualities of gender right and obligation. This orientation to gender right enabled women and their allies to challenge specific patriarchal claims and practices and to assert female rights and linkages among distinct realms of gender right without challenging gender hierarchy as such. Another model emphasized a more absolute or innate conception of patriarchal right and privilege. This orientation to gender right enabled men to insist on enforcing patriarchal claims and authority and to resist female contingencies and linkages regardless of how well or poorly they fulfilled patriarchal obligations.[1]

The conflictual dialogue between these models has emerged rather explicitly in the foregoing narrative and analysis, but the underlying foundations of legitimacy have remained more implicit. Yet cultural conversation about power and conflict rarely takes place in the absence of a sense of legitimacy.[2] We need to specify more clearly, therefore, the moral underpinnings that informed cultural conversation and contestation. Such specification of the culturally implicit requires a certain will to rely partly on informed speculation and intuition as one considers evidence and builds an interpretation.[3] The question of legitimacy, however, is too important to set aside. It enables us to see gendered acts and struggle not only as an instrumental pursuit of practical gender interests but also as a process of moral evaluation of self and other. It enables us to appreciate more fully the ways that patriarchal hegemony, both as coercive dominance and moral dominance, did not preclude power struggle and moral struggle, an articulation of the hegemonic and the counterhegemonic within a larger framework that simultaneously incorporated and blunted challenges to dominance.[4] It will enable us later (Chapter 6) to explore the ways women and men might at times cross over to the other side of a cultural dialogue without fully abandoning their distinctively gendered moral perspective.

Each model of gender right and obligation in female-male relations is perhaps best interpreted not as a singular discourse or understanding about gender but as a cluster of related discourses and suppositions, some of them implicit. The clustering effect made the arguments mobilized by male and female at moments of crisis something more than a set of capricious claims, ad hoc statements that provided transparent cover for self-interest. Arguments of the moment, some of them transparent, certainly "happened." But the clustering effect transformed many arguments of the moment into expressions of larger truths embedded in cultural sediments built up over years and generations of knowledge, experience, and conversation by men and by women. For analytical purposes one may think of a three-way clustering: the orientation to gender right itself (contingent versus absolute), the general characterizations of women and men as flawed human types, and the evaluations of a particular woman or man against the backdrop of the more general characterization. Let us begin with the first two points in this triadic cluster. The orientations to gender right and obligation we have called contingent and absolute each drew legitimacy from judgments about the character flaws of men and women as human types. If men as a group were prone to excess, negligence, violence, and irresponsibility, they could not be entrusted to act as responsible patriarchs. Whatever the ideal relations between men and women, a woman who granted a man absolute authority was something of a fool, and a man who acted as a good patriarch of his own volition was a rarity. Conversely, if women as a group were morally weak and fickle, easily swayed by emotion or the lure of the forbidden, and prone to treachery and sexual deviance, they could not be entrusted to challenge the practices or dictates of their patriarchs. Whatever the ideal relations between men and women, a man who failed to rule his wife and daughters with a strong hand was something of a fool, and a woman who lived a life of fidelity and moral constancy by virtue of her own interior strength was a rarity. In this vision of women as human type, something of the deviant or dangerous resided in most every woman.[5]

The cultural and practical roots of these views of men and particularly women as flawed human types are too complex to reduce to a single stream of historical and cultural experience. One may find in Western and biblical lore and historical experience as well as the more indigenous culture history of Mesoamerica ample streams of thought to nourish a view of women as dangerously prone to depravity and treachery and a view of men as prone to excess and dissipation. In "male-stream" popular consciousness, of course, the degree of flaw and its social implications could run differently by gender. The permanent potential for female depravity might require strict and permanent vigilance by patriarchs who trained and, if necessary, disciplined their female dependents. The potential for violent excess and hot temper by men might require, by contrast, a comparatively benign and transitory prescription: that they learn self-control from their elders as they make the transition from youth to mature adulthood.[6] This contrast pervades the male-stream side of folk culture evident in the criminal violence records of late colonial Morelos.

Such folk truths were anchored in practical experience and struggle and the everyday conversations they inspired. Comparison with more formal "high culture" thinking, however, underscores a resonant interplay up and down the cultural ladder that widened the legitimacy of folk characterizations. Colonial Catholic teaching, for example, nourished the view that human beings were sinful after the Fall. Men evinced a tendency to excess, and women evinced an attraction to the forbidden and the treacherous. Women were especially suspect as moral beings: in the biblical explanation of the Fall, Eve served as the human initiator of forbidden acts; Adam's flaw resided in his openness to her suasion. Church thinking juxtaposed a proclaimed ideal of female purity and male-female reciprocity in families with a profoundly misogynist judgment: in real life few women had the strength to resist a slide toward moral depravity unless monitored by the patriarchs and elders of family and church. The net effect of these views of human sin and limitation was not unqualified endorsement of either the contingent or absolute orientation to gender right in popular culture. To women the church often preached endurance rather than contestation of patriarchal authority, even if the excesses of men violated the ideal of a hierarchical reciprocity between men and women and even if the church sometimes intervened to achieve a reconciliation. To men the church often preached mercy and reconciliation rather than rule through iron authority and discipline, even if women strayed from the path of moral constancy and patriarchal vigilance and even if the church was no stranger to the idea of female depravity.[7]

Despite these church admonitions, it is easy to discern resonance with popular culture, appropriations within a larger cultural conversation. The church's view of men as prone to sinful excess might resonate with the conclusion that women ought to curb their men's freedom of action and authority. The church's sometimes stark misogyny and its view of women as prone to treachery and moral inconstancy easily resonated with the conclusion that men ought to control and discipline women harshly.

In truth, depictions of men and women as flawed human types may be found in almost every stream of formal high culture that converged in colonial Mexico: Catholic discourses about the pervasiveness of sin, the responsibility of men to moderate their impulses, and the moral evils that especially tempted women; Nahua discourses about devouring females, dissipate males, and acquired self-control in a fragile world perched on the edge of destruction; Hispanic discourses about honor, shame, and the moral attributes of men and women; pre-Enlightenment political discourses that endowed superiors with higher moral and mental faculties than their comparatively degraded and protected subordinates and infused the political body with metaphors of father and family, yet acknowledged the potential for excess, tyranny, and contravention of natural law within the chain of divinely sanctioned hierarchy.[8] Of course, these streams of thought were not without internal contradiction and were not simply identical with one another. Indeed they might even conflict sharply on specific gender practices: the Nahua convention of formal polygamy by elite men contrasted with the Hispanic convention of legal monogamy and informal concubinage. High culture ideas, moreover, were not immune to recasting in accord with popular experience and necessity. Notwithstanding such variations and recasting, however, these gendered depictions of human flaw, excess, and treachery resonated with one another and with popular characterization.[9]

The folk characterizations and the sense of legitimacy attached to them mattered. They allowed one to strike the cultural chord of plausibility in one's own mind and ideally in the minds of others, even in the absence of confirmation and agreement on the facts of individual cases. When José Marcelino of Texalpa initially shrugged off the stoning of his wife as a minor event unworthy of punishment and when María Lucía's husband took his wife's flight from Oaxtepec to Cuautla as grounds for sexual suspicion notwithstanding the contrary results of his own surveillance, their judgments drew strength from a larger sense of women as human type. Knowledge of women as human type rendered such acts and judgments understandable — legitimate — even in the absence of confirmed and flagrant insubordination by the two women as individuals. Similarly, when María Teresa of Texalpa presumed that her husband's inactivity reflected irresponsibility and dissipation rather than the vagaries of work in the rainy season and when María Lucía of Oaxtepec and Totolapa saw the killing of Esquicio Ponciano as the self-inflicted denouement to male excess, an unbounded and violent possessiveness, their judgments drew strength from a larger sense of men as human type.[10]

Interestingly, the view of women as prone to moral treachery might serve as a cultural resource even in instances where the immediate objective lay outside the realm of male-female gender conflicts as such. The mobilization of a gendered imagery of legitimation and delegitimation could suit a variety of purposes. In Yautepec in 1809, for example, Máxima Micaela Ramírez claimed that the wife of her *amasio* launched an adultery accusation not because the liaison had done any tangible harm to the family of her *amasio* or because Máxima Micaela held the moral responsibility of initiating the sexual relationship. In Máxima Micaela's eyes, her *amasio* had been the seducer who pressed the affair, and he had provided only negligible help — "scant favors and gifts" — despite the birth of a child. The discourse of adulterous evil served instead as the legitimating cover and instrument for a scheme by the *amasio* and his wife to take over the house and land plot (*solar*) of Máxima Micaela and her mother. By clothing Máxima Micaela in the image of the evil female destroyer of family and moral order, the conspirators could demand economic compensation for family income allegedly lost to the legitimate wife. They could thereby confiscate the coveted *solar* and exile the adulteress, while refraining from the customary prosecution of both husband and *amasia* as adulterers.[11]

The first two points in our triadic cluster — the orientation to gender right as contingent or absolute and the connected characterizations of men and women as flawed human types — have yielded a certain dialogue of legitimacy. Evaluation of particular individuals — and male and female subtypes — constituted a vital third point within a triadic cluster of legitimation whose dynamic whole exceeded the sum of its parts. The entire edifice of female legitimacy, for example, gained strength if particular individuals graphically illustrated the worst excesses of men and if certain male social types — habitual drinkers, headstrong egotists who defied parents and elders, and young men who escaped taming by firm parents and wives — appeared to demonstrate the danger of uncontrolled versions of the immanent male tendency to excess. When, in a specific conflict over gender right with a man, a woman not only developed a language of contingent patriarchal right, not only buttressed it with a diffuse sense of male excess and female grievance, but also identified a particular patriarch as a particularly pernicious and unmanageable example of the problem, she built an especially strong foundation of legitimacy. Even the Indian men of Xalostoque agreed, in 1796, that Victoriana Tomasa had a right to complain that her husband Augustín Mariano was excessive and abusive. The extremes of domestic violence and abuse fit in with a larger pattern. As one male witness put it, "Well, when he gets drunk he lashes out, even against the *viejos*, . . . [and] on one occasion he hurled himself at his father, and on another he struck his mother for defending [his] wife . . . , [and] when he drinks he's like a bull." [12]

The example of extreme individuals gave vivid expression to the truth of more general gender characterizations. The process, however, did not escape ambiguity and interpretation. For men, the example of an Augustín Mariano might be taken to demonstrate the relative moderation and moral legitimacy of most men. By comparison the majority exercised greater self-control. As one Indian put it, although "blinded by wrath" (*ciego de colera*), he had "repressed his impulses, and did not kill his wife as he might have done." [13] For women, notorious examples might illustrate a distinct moral truth. Something of Augustín Mariano possibly resided in most every man. This explained why men contended with quick impulses to excess and why they might readily commit violence yet excuse their own culpabilities. In the endless process of cultural conversation and argument spiced with anecdote, the evaluation of particular — and particularly notorious — individuals buttressed the sense of legitimacy that informed contending notions of gender right and obligation in female-male relations.

WIDOWS, LEGITIMACY, AND STIGMA

Within the triadic cluster of male self-legitimation the evaluation of particular individuals and female subtypes clarifies the special stigma men reserved for widows and female loners with demonstrably independent social styles and personalities. A characterization of women as inherently suspect — prone to moral treachery and sexual evil unless monitored and ruled with a strong hand — bolstered an absolute approach to patriarchal gender right in female-male obligations. But this process of legitimation gained all the more strength if particular individuals or subtypes graphically illustrated the troubles and dangers inflicted by women who escaped supervision. As we have seen (Chapter 3), the cultural stereotyping that equated female loners with female deviants, that attributed serious male-on-female violence to vengeance against delinquent loners, that reduced the rest of male-on-female violence to more inconsequential *descarga* ventings, and that considered attached female dependents protected from both immorality and serious violence is profoundly misleading. Such ideas tell us less about the sociology of violence than about culture: there was a sharp resentment of widows and female loners as symbols of female independence.

The concept of a triadic cluster of gender legitimation in male-female conflicts illuminates why such ideas were far from gratuitous. Symbolic anecdote, the conversion of extreme case into archetype, and the tendency to buttress the larger point through stereotyped example held vital importance in the larger culture of argument and legitimation. Female subtypes — widows and female loners who had outlived or escaped life cycle phases of patriarchal vigilance, loners whose magical or curative knowledge granted them a certain power or leverage vis-à-vis the rest of society, and wives and daughters given too much slack by husbands, fathers, and elders — were especially prone to uncontrolled mischief, a fuller development of immanent female tendencies. Particular individuals — those widows, loners, or poorly supervised dependents libertine enough in personality to flout discretion and propriety — graphically depicted the troublemaking potential of unsupervised women and female youth.

When, in a specific conflict with a woman, a man not only developed a language of absolute authority, not only buttressed it with a diffuse sense of female treachery and provocation, but also identified a particular woman as a specifically pernicious and unmanageable example of the problem, he built an especially strong foundation of legitimacy. In the larger process of cultural conversation and argument, insubordinate mature women — particularly widows and *solteras* whose economic, curative, or magical resources buttressed their independent power — stood out as especially potent symbols of the danger to moral order posed by women who escaped deference and vigilance. When a forceful loner escaped the normal constrictions on female behavior, even her relatives might agree that whatever the source and the particulars, she had brought violence upon herself.

Consider, for example, the ambivalent discourses that surrounded the killing of Magdalena Francisca Morales on Hacienda San Gaspar in 1809. An Indian with a reputation as a folk healer, a woman old enough to have a son listed as a tributary and resident field hand (*gañán*) and authoritative enough to have son and daughter-in-law live on her housing compound, and a loner who was for all practical purposes a "widow" (it remains unclear, however, if a husband had actually died), Magdalena Francisca apparently established a strong and often welcome presence among her neighbors. She had been accepted as a close and constructive friend in the lives of her neighbors José del Carmen, an Indian overseer of field laborers (*capitán de gañanes*), and his mulatta wife, Simona Quitería. The couple addressed her by the fictive kin term *comadre*, Magdalena Francisca at one point proffered a small rosary for one of Simona Quitería's children, and she worked free of charge to cure a leg that afflicted José del Carmen. Partly out of friendship, one suspects, Magdalena Francisca intervened to defend Simona Quitería when José wounded Simona with a small rock, then sought to drag her to the estate's master (*amo*) to complain of his wife's suspicious encounter with another man.

The problem was that precisely because Magdalena Francisca was an independent woman who no longer deferred to an immediate patriarch on a daily basis, she had developed a certain latitude of behavior — a modified habitus, in Pierre Bourdieu's terms — that sometimes transformed her into the most immoral, disorderly, and provocative sort of defiant female loner. At least this was the view of many kin and neighbors. Every several weeks or so, they observed, Magdalena Francisca would go on a drinking binge. Unrestrained by an immediate patriarch, authoritative in her own right as a curer and as head of a peasant household that included a field laborer (her son) and domestic help (her daughter-in-law), Magdalena Francisca would continue on the binge for a week or a week and a half and take on a swaggeringly defiant and insulting verbal style. Her neighbors and relatives generally responded not with the disciplinary action of a patriarch but with a tactic often applied to drunk and hostile men: verbal avoidance until the binge passed. Magdalena Francisca's interventions in the quarrel of José del Carmen and Simona Quitería occurred during the course of a binge that had proceeded for about a week.

This context enabled José del Carmen to depict himself, easily and credibly, as the victim of an unsupervised female loner dangerously out of control. His wife was "giving loud screams, to which his neighbor named Magdalena Francisca came out, [and] as she was drunk, she soon began yanking the hair of the declarant, telling him to leave his wife at home . . . that he was a miserable *carajo* [a curse whose referent is male genitalia], that evil be the one who had given birth to such a despicable type. . . . As best he could he took her off of him without giving offense but rather in a soft voice he told her not to mix in . . . and to retire to her house, but she paid no attention." Magdalena Francisca's intervention stiffened Simona Quitería's resistance to her husband's effort to drag her to the hacienda administrator for punishment. When José del Carmen finally threw a stick ("only to threaten her") at his wife, the uncontrollable Magdalena Francisca stepped in its path, received the blow behind the left ear, quickly lost speech, and lapsed into unconsciousness. She died three days later.

In José del Carmen's discourse an unsupervised woman with whom he at times pursued a neighborly and almost familial friendship had developed a dangerous latitude of behavior. This freedom sometimes turned her into a meddling, provocative, and thoroughly uncontrolled instigator of moral disorder. In his discourse she had cursed his manhood and his mother, blocked his effort to discipline a wife's moral treachery, and forced an escalation of violence. She had brought death upon herself. The symbolism of danger to moral order by women who escaped deference and vigilance and developed more aggressive and even manlike social styles struck a responsive chord. Magdalena Francisca's son, who had not witnessed the violent confrontation but knew his mother's personality and the circumstances of her death, pardoned his neighbor: "Well, . . . she was very insolent and provocative when she drank." Perhaps more remarkably, Magdalena Francisca's brother, ill in Yautepec and therefore unable to travel and only vaguely aware of the circumstances of the violence and the identity of the assailant, sent his wife to Cuernavaca with the instruction "that if she found his sister dead, she ought not claim anything against the aggressors, and on the contrary ought pardon them in his name since he well understood the provocations [she engaged in] when she was drunk." The judges of the *audiencia* in Mexico City responded sympathetically and released José del Carmen from prison eleven months after the initial incident — a fairly speedy resolution by the standards and rhythms of colonial criminal bureaucracy.[14]

The legitimizing symbolism of the dangers posed by women beyond the bounds of effective patriarchal vigilance was potent. One may choose among several possible paths — the paths of psychology, symbolic logic, and practical experience — to explain such potency. These paths, of course, are not mutually exclusive, although they each imply distinct risks. The path of psychology asks us to speculate about the legacy of ambivalence toward older women rooted in the subordination of young sons to their mothers. In this line of reasoning the contradictions between familial elder rank and gender rank in a patriarchal culture presumably fostered in sons an ambivalent and sometimes volatile package of psychological orientations: sentiments of deference-to-worship in unreconciled contention with sentiments of resentment-to-anger. This perspective gains some historical strength if we recognize that in late colonial times men had comparatively higher mortality rates than women; they migrated with some regularity to work or trade on sugar haciendas in major towns or Mexico City and in the mines at the southern fringes of Morelos; and they sometimes abandoned indefinitely the families they had fathered with wives and *amasias*. All this implied that it was not all that uncommon an experience for male youths to depend on mothers who held a magnified authority as parental loners, real and metaphorical widows.[15] The cutting remark remembered by several youths in a play of verbal insult that sparked a murder in Totolapa in 1787 was the comment that a village girl should prefer a destitute *carbonero* (charcoal maker) in his stead. Why? Because the youth was not much of a man, since "he was made for his mother to support him."[16]

The path of psychology asks us to recall, in addition, that parental discipline of younger children implied the psychological processing of hitting by mothers as well as fathers. Although this sort of hitting escapes the purview of criminal violence records, and although the violence of fathers toward children probably exceeded in severity and frequency that of mothers, hitting by mothers happened and was sometimes serious. As one boy of nine years put it, he preferred one day to linger at a friend's house because he was "fearful that his mother might come [home] more drunk, and might beat him."[17] It is not difficult to find possibilities of psychological ambivalence toward authoritative older women in the absorption of such hitting by boys who also contended with the mores of a patriarchal culture.

The path of psychology is suggestive but also easily overstated. The popularity and misuses of a rhetoric of psychological pathology in discussions of Mexican men and violence in the mid-twentieth century warn against facile reductions of social and cultural patterning to alleged psychological complexes. They also warn against the facile assumption that universalizing psychological models apply well across the pluralizing boundaries of time, space, and culture. Used with a sense of cautious reserve, however, and set in the time-space context of the specific familial, generational, and gender tensions of a particular patriarchal culture, the path of psychology may usefully complement the paths of symbolic logic and practical experience.[18]

The path of symbolic logic offers a distinct and well-established line of reasoning to explain the potency of the symbolism that concentrated stigma, resentment, and danger in the figure of mature female loners, especially widows. In symbolic constructions of moral order and constraint, anthropologists such as Mary Douglas have observed, matter at the margins of the social body serves as a powerful and necessary marker, a representation of the dangerous presence of evil, a dirt that threatens to pollute the clean and to impose moral disorder.[19] To these symbols and markers accrue an enormous concentration of cultural devices—a sense of taboo and danger and a proliferation of rules and cleansing procedures—to defend and reaffirm symbolic and moral order. By this symbolic logic widows and established female loners who had escaped or outlasted phases of patriarchal vigilance stood out in the male mind as the ultimate cultural provocateurs, the most powerful expressions of the female potentiality for moral evil and disorder in a world where order implied patriarchal vigilance within the social body. This path of explanation, like the path of psychology, offers suggestive insight. But like the path of psychology, it too easily takes on an air of serene overstatement, a theory comfortably distant from the human conflicts and turmoil of the moment. One needs to complement awareness of the psychological legacy of childhood and youth, and of cultural assignment of danger to matter at the symbolic margins, with attention to practical life struggles that sparked stigma and resentment.

The potent symbolism of widows and other women who had outlasted phases of patriarchal vigilance was refreshed time and time again at the well of practical experience. As we have seen (Chapter 4), female-female alliance and mobilization served as an important strategy of female resistance and defense in conflicts with males. Often it was women in older or relatively authoritative life cycle positions—mothers, surrogate mothers, and established loners— who played central roles in the drama of female mobilization. In addition, *amasias*—frequently widows or loners—tended to press for more emphatically consensual pacts that challenged male assertions of permanent, quasi-marital possession of their lovers. The ultimate example of a troublemaking female — sufficiently experienced and self-standing to endanger male authority — was that of the mature widow or established female loner, an independent *soltera* who acted as proprietor of her own sexual life.

A concluding tragedy, the murder of María Nicolasa Contreras, underscores the practical conditions of life and leverage that promoted sharp male resentment of widows and established female loners. María Nicolasa Contreras, thirty years old in 1806, lived in Cuautla Amilpas, the major *cabecera* and colonial administrative center in the eastern sugar zone of Morelos. The economic circumstances of peasant and plebeian widows left with little property easily turned precarious, even by poor people's standards, especially if the widow had to support not only herself but children or other dependents. Around April 1806 María Nicolasa and her child began to live with Josef Timoteo Rivera, a married confectioner variously identified as mulatto and mestizo and too poor to have any property confiscated upon his arrest later. Josef Timoteo had already run up against challenges to his authority: his wife had abandoned him and would later spurn his efforts to reconcile. The terms of the pact with his new *amasia* were clear enough: *amasio* and *amasia* agreed that central to the building of a life together was Josef Timoteo's provision of food and clothing money to María Nicolasa. The trouble, from Josef Timoteo's standpoint, was that his possession of María Nicolasa ended up as precarious as that of his wife. A legal complaint landed the pair in jail, and after their release in July María Nicolasa decided to establish an independent life.

María Nicolasa got her new start by turning to a much older widow, Ana Salinas. A mestiza fifty-eight years old, Ana Salinas made a living selling sweets and *atole* (the popular corn-based drink). María Nicolasa moved in with Ana Salinas and joined her in provisioning the local food and drink market. The blending of the solidary and the protective, the horizontal and the vertical, in María Nicolasa's turn for help to an older, more well established and independent widow found its way into the women's informal terms of address. Ana Salinas variously referred to María Nicolasa as *comadre* and as *sobrina* (niece). Just as important, she strengthened María Nicolasa's ability to fend off her erstwhile *amasio*. When Josef Timoteo tried to reinitiate his pact by insistently offering María Nicolasa some money, Ana Salinas responded by calling him a vulgar bum (*un grosero*), warning him to stay away from her house, and slapping him in the face.

The two women had effectively suffocated his claims. As widows with an independent livelihood, they could withstand economic pressure to equate the sexual rights of an *amasio* with those of a jealous husband. Josef Timoteo could not exert indirect pressure by compromising either woman before an immediate husband-patriarch or father-patriarch. As a female elder who looked after her own respectability, moreover, the honorable Ana Salinas had turned the tables by denouncing the *amasio*'s immorality and vulgarity and by humiliating him with a slap. The only remaining recourses were retreat or violence. In a final confrontation, Josef Timoteo caught up with the fleeing María Nicolasa and stabbed her in the back.[20]

The murder had nothing to do with female defiance of the formal proprieties of male gender right or female sexual morality. It had everything to do with social independence. Two women had outlasted their legal patriarchs and had learned to outfox the more informal traps of patriarchal possession.

CHAPTER 6

The Crossfires of
Gender and Family,
Color and Class

Solidarity, Conflict, and

Ambivalence

CONTRADICTIONS AND CROSSFIRES

The rights of gender set poor, predominantly peasant women and men into a perpetual, sometimes bitter and violent dance of conflict in late colonial Morelos. Yet the fact of the dance is not the whole story. However pervasive the tensions of male-female gender relations, however commonplace the violence, and however punctured the mythology of a unified culture of gender values, to focus exclusively on points of conflict in relations between women and men of popular culture is to isolate one very important dimension of social life from the wider stage on which it appeared. The premise of the dance was often a certain bonding, now at risk, among its partners. The interior choreography of the dance often blurred the main plot, a drama of male-female conflict, with a dizzying array of crossover alliances and same-gender skirmishes. Indeed, the dance of gender conflict, far from consuming the entire stage of life, developed alongside and in relation to other dances in progress, particularly dances of family solidarity and dances of community and color-class solidarity and conflict. In short, in the gendered relationships of male and female in popular culture there were points of unity as well as division, ambivalence as well as polarization. Women experienced a crossfire between competing imperatives.

124

Families were units of solidarity as well as conflict, for reasons that embraced both gender and color-class considerations. However troubling to our sensibilities and wishes, moreover, dynamics of power, conflict, and even violence in densely joined human relations are not mutually exclusive with dynamics of affect, bonding, and desire. One need not be an expert student of human psychology and emotions to understand that there are possessive and controlling loves, resentful and rebellious loves, indeed a vast array of loves beyond the historically constructed and in many ways misleading ideal of middle class romance and domestic harmony.[1] One need only recall the wounded words of Francisco Doroteo as he proclaimed to his dead wife both his ruin and his jealous right of ultimate possession: "Dolores now you've died, know then that Francisco Doroteo has killed you and will pay with his life." One need only visualize the drama of María Florencia Zambrano as she first inflicted a "broken head" on her married *amasio* and later intruded on his home to proclaim with her fists a right of possession higher than that of his wife. One need only ponder the history of imperious violence and shared suffering that fed Pedro Martínez's sorrow and self-denials upon the death of his wife Esperanza.[2]

The challenge of this chapter is to explore the points of contradiction that yield such troubling paradoxes and associations — not in an effort to smooth the edge of the gender conflicts and violence extensively discussed in the preceding chapters, but to understand better the protagonists of conflict and the depth of female dilemmas.

Let us begin with the crossfires of gender and family. The paradoxical experience of gendered family life as an arena of bitter dispute and deeply felt solidarities may be viewed on two levels: from the perspective of women's gender conflicts with men and from the perspective of women's positive self-legitimation. On both levels the crossfires of gender and family become apparent if we reconsider the previous analysis (Chapters 4–5) with an eye for contradiction and counterpoint. The dynamics of gender conflict itself promoted a simultaneous appeal to familial solidarity. Let us recall two key social weapons mobilized by women and female youth in their gendered struggles with men: a pluralization-of-patriarchs strategy and a mobilization-of-female-alliances strategy. In each instance we witnessed a progression of scale: a woman's first line of defense was either to pluralize the patriarchs and would-be patriarchs within her web of primary relations or to mobilize a primary circle of female relatives and close friends to intervene, offer refuge, or otherwise help her resist maltreatment. From this foundation or in its absence a woman might proceed to mobilize allies within a wider grid of patriarchal counselors and authorities or female allies and sympathizers. Nonetheless, what is obvious in these strategies is the familial foundation of resistance and defense, even in cases of familial conflict. The contradictions of a gendered kinship system facilitated such mobilizations of familial solidarity. Female relatives supplied the bulk of intervenors, male or female, in the female lives we have reviewed thus far. A background of shared female knowledge, conversation, and contention with the specific patriarchs of their familial circle could add depth to the sense of mutuality and solidarity, of grievance and destiny in common. Moreover, because legitimate adult manhood in popular culture was closely tied to patriarchal oversight of family and dependents, male relatives were not immune to female appeals for familial solidarity and assistance. The group interest of men in the subordination of women and female youth as a group ran up against the internally diversified structure of patriarchal attachment—a welter of kin, conjugal, and (at times) consort relations that could transform men as a group into men as individual rivals, potential contenders for protective authority over the well-being and life course of the same woman or female youth. To the consternation of a husband, a wife's brother might even intervene reflexively—"without informing himself of the motive of our quarrel"—to protect his sister.[3]

Given male proprietary sensibilities and female pluralization of relevant patriarchs, therefore, the practical realities of kinship divided male kin into potential rivals as well as allies. At the level of familial clusters, the patriarchs of the parental family cluster and those of the political (that is, in-law) cluster might view one another with latent and sometimes explicit suspicion. In some instances an unofficial (that is, *amasio*) family cluster might introduce yet a third fault line. The paradox of male-female gender conflict in familial and quasi-familial settings is that the process of familial conflict itself induced familial solidarity.

Perhaps equally important but more elusive to historical research are the more positive reasons of self-legitimation that nurtured commitment to familial solidarity alongside an awareness of familial oppression. Within a patriarchal context of subordination, the authority and self-legitimacy of women were closely linked to their age, measured not by a simple chronology of years lived or by the ladder of political service and social placement that transformed mature male heads of family into esteemed community elders and fathers, but rather by a life cycle calendar bound up with women's roles in familial contexts. It was the daughter who married a *novio* who stepped into culturally recognized adulthood beyond the direct jurisdiction of her father and occasionally against his wishes. It was the wife who became a mother who established a wider foundation of moral legitimacy, an affective bond and an identity of survival interests with her young children that deepened her right to criticize negligence or abuse by a husband. It was the mother who became a mother-in-law who acquired a daughter-servant to help with domestic labor and to be trained in the rigors of being a young wife. It was the woman who outlasted her husband, while establishing an effective claim to familial prop-

erty and reciprocities vis-à-vis her children, who became a successful widow—
a female elder whose property, social networks, and freedom from direct patriarchal supervision enhanced personal autonomy and authority.

None of this implies that all women and female youth sought the bonds of
family or contested patriarchal pacts rather than an alternative destiny as loners, or that women who developed deep solidary commitments to their families did so free of ambivalence, grievance, and contradiction. Above all, none
of this implies that women and youth failed to recognize in their husbands
and fathers sources of trouble, abuse, and even danger. The evidence of pervasive and sometimes bitter contestations of patriarchal pacts, the familial
bonds that broke down completely or exploded in homicidal violence, the
sometimes arduous efforts of *amasias* to establish more consensual rights of
withdrawal, and the prevalence of an adult female loner population whose
proportion (21.9 percent) resembled strikingly that of the male loners (23.7
percent) all belie an overly benign, sanitized vision of familial solidarity.[4] But
the connection between aging in the familial life cycle and female legitimation
and authority, in a patriarchal context that tended to subordinate women and
to taint their legitimacy, helps us to understand further why to live a female
life in families was to experience a gendered crossfire: an intensity of divisive
male-female conflicts that could induce both familial embitterment and familial collaboration.

To such microlevel crossfires of gender and family we must add the macrolevel crossfires between the imperatives of gender conflict and the imperatives
of color-class solidarity and survival. As we have seen (Chapter 2), a sharpening village-hacienda struggle and a more intensified rhythm of capitalization
and labor exploitation within the sugar hacienda economy defined the basic
contours of political economy in late colonial Morelos. In addition, although
ethnically inclusionary reconstitutions of village and peasant identity often
blurred ethnic labeling, ethnic distance and distinction lost its blur at the very
top of the class order. (Ethnicity also lost a good deal of blur at the very bottom, in the case of black slaves.) Whites (*españoles*) constituted less than a
tenth of the regional population, and among whites, an even smaller group
of *gachupines* (the popular and often derogatory term for peninsular-born
Spaniards) dominated the overlapping mercantile, landowning, and bureaucratic networks at the apex of the regional economy and social order.[5] The
bulk of the peasants were either Indians or persons dark by comparison with
the rich and the *gachupines*, categories that merged readily in the popular political culture of late colonial Morelos. As the Indians of Tlaltenango put it
in 1764, in a dispute over maize scarcity, commodity prices, and mercantile-
tributary practices, their enemies were "storeowning *gachupín* wolves who
want to eat us, and our children [the] little chickens." As a sugar worker on
Hacienda Temisco was alleged to have said in 1811, when the independence in-

surgency stirred talk of revolt on the haciendas, "The sugar master . . . has to die with the *gachupines*, because he goes around beating the *peones*." The *gachupines* under discussion were the owners of the major sugar haciendas.[6] Indeed, during the independence wars, rebels and patriot insurgents, including the guerrillas led by the radical priest José María Morelos, were active in the Morelos region. By December 1810 the insurgents had invaded at least a half-dozen haciendas in the Cuernavaca district. A year later Padre Morelos began to establish a base of support and operations in the Cuautla and Cuernavaca districts; by the spring of 1812 he was under siege in Cuautla Amilpas by the royalist commander Felix María Calleja. The political and military mobilizations in Morelos during 1810–13 constitute a vast and as yet underexplored area that would take us far afield. Recent research and archival evidence demonstrate, however, that in the region whose name would later commemorate him, Padre Morelos and the insurgents received a more sympathetic popular response than is traditionally acknowledged.[7]

For their part, elites and bureaucrats displayed a certain homogenizing disdain when referring to poor, dark laboring folk. Although colonial censuses drew ethnic distinctions between Indians, blacks, mixed groups, and the like, a census judge in Cuernavaca could also think of all the tributary and colored populations as variations on a theme: "the vile class" (*la clase ínfima*). Parish priests drew ethnic distinctions in the registers of births and deaths and knew from experience that not all villagers were really Indian, but a village priest could nevertheless refer to a mass of insolent and predominantly Indian villagers as "my Indian horde" (*mi Yndiada*).[8]

What must not be underestimated, then, is the depth of color-class polarization, the pressures it brought to everyday life, and the consequent appeal of solidary alliance against external authorities and internal traitors. Not only did the last half-century of Spanish colonial rule witness a sharpening struggle between villages and haciendas and a more intensified exploitation of labor on haciendas. In addition, the commercial buoyancy of the region's villages encouraged colonial elites to use their positions as a platform for mercantile and tributary extortion (hence the reference to "storeowning *gachupín* wolves"). One such extortion mechanism relied on the coercive commodity distribution networks (the *repartimiento de mercancías*) more well known and notorious in Oaxaca.[9] Another such mechanism used the fees and jailings imposed by the official guardians of colonial morality and justice. Time and time again the voices of women and men complain to us that too many officials and priests used roundups of alleged *amasios* and *amasias*, adjudication of domestic quarrels and altercations, and prosecution of immorality and other criminal infractions not as a device to establish moral order or to offer relief to the aggrieved, but as a means to extort fines, fees, and payoff settlements from hard-pressed households or to take vengeance against troublemakers. Given the color-class dynamics of a colonial society, invitations to authorities to intervene in gender conflicts could backfire. As María Josefa de Porras of Yautepec put it in 1792, she had complained to the priest about her husband, "asking only a moderate punishment for his having beaten me." But once the subdelegate of the intendant caught wind of the matter, he ordered a "cruel whipping such that [my husband] found himself in danger of losing his life" and, in addition, extorted seven and a half pesos. María Josefa denounced the abuse and demanded the return of the money.[10]

The force of solidarities rooted in shared color-class experience and community struggle does not imply, of course, an absence of loud factional splits within village or peasant life.[11] Neither does it imply an unwillingness of women and female youth to pursue quarrels with patriarchs and to consider, if necessary, airing such quarrels before local authorities and outsiders. It docs, however, imply something about ambivalence and the zigzag effect it yielded. The same women and men who experienced conflict and bitterness in gendered relations with one another could also experience shared suffering and sympathies rooted in their subaltern relations with others. Just as María Josefa de Porras could first denounce her husband's abuse and violence, then switch to defending him from excessive punishment by colonial authorities, so it was that Juan Joseph Torres of Xochitepec (variously identified as Indian and free mulatto) could first denounce his wife María Vicenta Pacheco for adultery, then plead for her release from abusive treatment. Juan Joseph's initial denunciation of his wife had come in May 1772. His anger had been so great that María Vicenta, a mulatta slave who worked in the *trapiche* on Hacienda San Antonio del Puente, had fled to the priest of Xochitepec, "saying how her husband wanted to kill her." By July, however, Juan Joseph's position had shifted to defense. He and María Vicenta had fled to the viceregal court of Mexico City. There Juan Joseph argued that the hacienda managers had lifted his wife's skirt and administered a cruel whipping as she lay humiliated on the ground, that María Vicenta had fallen ill as a consequence of the whipping, that he had had to pay for her medicines and hire a male peon to replace her labor on the hacienda, and that she ought to be granted the right to find a new owner. By this point, Juan Joseph had backed away from his earlier denunciation, claiming that another man had accused his wife of adultery. He inverted the target of moral accusation. The administrator of Hacienda San Antonio was "exceedingly wicked and cruel with the entire lot of slave women [*toda la esclabonia*] in his care," and his assistant, "proceeding in bad faith with the good looking slave women, pressures them to satisfy his crude lusts, because otherwise he forces them into boundless work . . . [and] scarcity of food."[12]

Indeed, precisely because the dances of gender subordination and color-class subordination sometimes merged dramatically, the contested rights of gender could run along vertical as well as horizontal social axes and might unify subaltern men and women vis-à-vis their oppressors. Powerful men buttressed their virility or enlarged their domain of patriarchal right by targeting subalterns, women and female youth whose vulnerability as low-status laboring folk made it all the more difficult to challenge demands for sexual possession or domestic service. When colonial elites demeaned the poor and the colored through degradation of their womanhood and manhood, the highest expression of color-class outrage might be a gendered grievance. When José Manuel, a leader of Totolapa's struggle to retain water rights in 1801–3, presented a litany of color-class abuses suffered by his village, his rhetoric of indignation moved from ironic understatement ("the worst of it isn't that") to fulsome moral outrage ("the worst of it is that"). As the refrain moved toward its moral climax, what demonstrated the worst of the subdelegate's venality was "that he shows off his power against the poor innocent women, who like mine are not at all to blame." The women, for their part, were outraged that officials forced economic hardships upon them without legitimate cause by manipulating charges of male immorality to extort funds and by requiring unpaid domestic service of the women or their daughters.[13]

It may be wise to consider not only the negative but also the positive foundations upon which peasant men and women constructed a sense of solidarity and shared destiny. Except in extreme instances approaching near total dependence on landed estate owners, domestic service employers, or day labor providers, peasant economic life rested on a familial base: inheritance and claims to vital resources usually depended on membership in families, and within families the sexual division of labor implied mutual dependence of male and female for sustenance.[14] Moreover, the bundle of elements that made "family property" workable in peasant life — defensible claims to land and water, right of access to *monte* resources, small reciprocities and redeployments of labor that smoothed out uneven land-labor ratios and seasonal work rhythms, and protection from external bandits and intruders — generally depended on recognition of rights within a larger community grid.[15] Mutual dependence and collaboration between female and male and between family and community implied arenas of sociability and cultural constructions in common. Even if harvesting corn in the field was deemed men's work, women shared an interest in a bountiful harvest, and men depended on women for their meals. During the harvest, women awoke well before dawn to grind corn for the men's first meal. They brought their tortillas, beans, and chilies to distant *milpas* to assure that the work might proceed unimpeded, and they experienced with men the quickening and excitement of a good harvest and the letdown and anxiety of a bad harvest.[16] Even if women were deemed more devoted to church concerns, more inclined to turn to priests for assistance in gender conflicts, and more in need of moral vigilance, men shared an interest in appealing to the gods and patron saints for protection, health, and bounty. Women depended on men's participation as contributing sponsors (*mayordomos*) in the annual round of religious fiestas, and both depended on the money reserves of lay sodalities (*cofradías*) to meet individual or familial needs such as loans in hard times or proper burials of relatives.[17] Women and men assumed joint responsibility for preparing the lavish propitiations of saints, a responsibility that joined families to a wider sense of barrio or community, and women were sometimes recognized as fiesta sponsors (*mayordomas*) in their own right.[18] Even if tensions between parental and political family patriarchs were common, and even if husbands often sought male diversion apart from their wives on Sundays, husbands also found it necessary to revitalize solidary connections and reciprocities. Some Sundays were times of sociability—conversations, drink, small gift exchanges, and visits to fairs—with wives and in-laws.[19]

One need not romanticize, of course, the more positive material and cultural foundations of the communal and familial solidarities associated with color-class subordination and affirmation in a colonial society. The gendered tensions and violence discussed earlier provide graphic counterpoints to sanitized versions of family or community. The entire approach to culture we have adopted in this book has stressed contestation, culture as a language of argument rather than culture as a unified and unifying body of values. One may even recognize the underside of male-female collaboration in the construction of a more positive sense of cultural or community identity: the absence of decent economic alternatives for young and poor women. For a young woman of intermediate or higher class standing, entry into a convent or the income provided by individually held property—a home with rooms to rent, a slave who brought in an income, or landed property that generated a livelihood— might offer a palatable alternative to marriage and possessive sex partners. One might imagine a life course of survival, self-legitimation, and defense against abuse that followed a somewhat more individualized path, less fully embedded in directly patriarchal familial or communal webs.[20] An older woman of humble background who had managed to outlast directly patriarchal life phases and emerge with a means of livelihood and effective claims on her juniors might also follow a somewhat more individualized path. The path was difficult and precarious, in view of many widows' poverty, vulnerability to communal tributary and land pressures, and conflicts with possessive *amasios*. But it was at least plausible. A widow might hold effective claim to a home and a bit of land, sell some *pulque* out of her home, raise a few chickens, sell food or drink at *fandangos* and *tianguis* gatherings, call on junior relatives for labor or other help, and more or less get by without submitting to a stifling patriarchal dominance. For a woman young and poor, however, the economic alternatives were exceedingly bleak. The likely alternative to a patriarchal familial and communal track was the life of a socially isolated loner-servant, vulnerable to extreme usurpations of her labor and sexuality, exposed to violence if she became too troublesome, and restricted to the recourse of flight to a new home for lack of social allies and defenders.[21] This economic underside to familial and communal sensibilities places in perspective but does not negate the ways women and men built up more positive, affirmative sociabilities and cultural expressions of collective need and mutual dependence.

The bonds of family and community were both unifying and divisive. A sense of male-female collaboration, destiny, and struggle in common was impelled in part by shared color-class experience within a regional world that was sharply polarized, in part by the process of gender conflict itself. Women's strategies of resistance and survival mobilized alliances and solidarities that reaffirmed male-female collaboration and familial and communal identities as integral weapons within the conflictual social relations of gender. The linkage between female legitimation and female aging within the life cycle fostered a similarly contrapuntal logic: a joining of solidary attachment to family and women's gendered roles within families, with embittered grievance about family and women's gendered lot within families.

The crossfire generated by such competing pressures illuminates women's practical life dilemmas. Even peasant women whose gender grievances were profound, violent, and embittered could not afford to ignore lightly color-class imperatives, appeals to community, and participation in affirmative cultural construction. Even the most vehement expressions of solidarity by women with their communities and their men failed to preclude equally vehement disagreement on the practices, values, and assumptions that constituted the social relations of gender. The ultimate paradox for women of popular culture was that the very relationships that offered a measure of protection from the dangers of poverty and social isolation also exposed women to the dangers of physical violence and bitter gender dispute.

ENIGMAS AND CROSSOVERS: THE ART OF FAMILIAL POLITICS (I)

The crossfires and ambivalences we have examined render several patterns of female behavior less mysterious, illogical, or enigmatic than they might seem to an observer limited to the prism of male-female conflict. As we shall see, the potential enigmas are closely linked to the notion of crossovers that appear to contradict the imperatives of female-male conflict: women crossing over to denunciations of female immorality strongly resonant with a male logic of absolute gender right, men crossing over to denunciations of male excess and irresponsibility strongly resonant with a female logic of contingent gender right, and relatives crossing over to stances of enmity that appeared to contradict the logic of kinship alliances.

Such crossovers deepen the notion of culture as a language of argument.

They illuminate the specific circumstances of male-female dispute that might encourage some men to echo a female language of gender right and some women to echo a male language, and they highlight the cultural tools that mediated the contradictions of such stances. In this perspective a language of argument on gender right in male-female relations not only set female against male at moments of dispute but also became a more universal cultural resource: a set of ideas and languages about legitimate right and authority invoked by the whole of popular culture, an ongoing process of discussion and argument among men and among women as well as between them.

Let us begin with women crossing over to denunciations of female immorality resonant with a male logic of absolute gender right. Female placement of moral blame on the "other woman," seen as an immoral provocateur in terms resonant with male notions of female evil, recurs too often to be dismissed lightly in male-female conflicts with a sexual angle.[22] Most commonly a wife might blame her husband's *amasia* for an adulterous liaison, but the theme could reach a more ludicrous extreme. Angela María, an Indian of Totolapa, defended her husband Anastacio José against a charge in 1801 that he raped María, an Indian girl some twelve years old, then carried her off to Hacienda Huacalco. Her defense followed culturally standard depictions of female cunning and duplicity in cases of sexual assault. In Angela María's discourse, María went from victimized youngster to manipulative evildoer: she had invented the rape story to extort a financial settlement; the crime was not rape but the "adulterous concubinage" to which María had consented; and the youngster was not a virginal and inexperienced child but a sexually knowing youth who had "earlier sustained illicit correspondence" with Hipólito Graciano, another Totolapa Indian. The targeting of María did not imply an absence of tension between Angela María and Anastacio José. It was Angela María who had first tracked down her husband and María and who had had them imprisoned. But the targeting of María allowed Angela María to pardon and secure the release of her husband — that is, to achieve a reconciliation that alleviated her household economy's loss of labor and its loss of income to fines, jailing costs, and a financial settlement with María's parents. The targeting of María perhaps assisted, too, in the sociopsychological challenge of reconstructing a life in common with her husband and with other villager families.[23]

As this and other examples make clear, assignment of major responsibility for misfortune to female evil, especially that of *amasias*, did not preclude conflicts with husbands over sexual and economic abandonment of wives. The choice of *amasias* as a preferred target was not uniform or even a dominant tendency, since many wives and their allies focused their efforts mainly on wayward husbands, or on husbands and *amasias* with roughly equal ferocity. But even if husbands did not usually escape moral critique and practical rebuke or disruption, the logic behind the occasional decision of a woman or a female network of supporters to lay most of the blame on an *amasia* is not self-evident. Attacking an *amasia* failed to insure wives against domestic reprisal and violence by their husbands,[24] and channeling public attention and punishment toward the *amasia* did little to restrict a husband's future sexual behavior. In addition, in a face-to-face world where reputation mattered, scandalous verbal or physical attack on an immoral *amasia* added cultural humiliation to the wife's injury. The wife (or her surrogate attackers) admitted publicly that she had proved unable to manage her husband's version of the male tendency to excess and negligence; dueling with rather than disdaining her sex rival conceded a certain symbolic equivalence with the *amasia* denounced as evil.[25] Crossing over to attribute disorder and evil to female sexual sin, in short, exacted serious cultural and personal costs.

When we take into account, however, the contradictory crossfires of female life, the logic behind occasional crossovers becomes more compelling. To the extent that a wife, the female relatives of her parental family, her husband's parental family relatives, and a network of supporters could agree to assign major responsibility to the other woman, they could more readily forgive the wayward husband, blur the distinction between his role as victim or predator, unite in the condemnation of a common enemy, and construct a fragile reconciliation. An early pardon and reconciliation had the further effect of limiting fees, jail costs, and loss of labor to peasant families whose household economies strained under attrition or suffered when colonial justice proceedings blended into elite extortion. To the extent that the *amasia* had her own network of female relatives and sympathizers, a rival network of moral discussion might insist on assigning major responsibility to male excess and moral caprice.

A parallel set of contradictory imperatives impelled the reverse pattern of crossover, that of men issuing denunciations of male excess and irresponsibility resonant with a female logic of contingent gender right. The male crossover pattern was in many respects the mirror image of the process we have just examined and therefore requires less than detailed treatment at this juncture. (For a more extended analysis of male-male enmity and male ideologies of gender, see Chapter 7.) To the extent that a husband and his network of relatives and supporters assigned major responsibility to an "other man" who embodied the worst of male excess, an insistent and even violent disregard of moral restraint, they could more readily blur the distinction between the wayward wife as victim or as traitor and construct a fragile, if face-saving, new start. When Dionicio José of Hacienda del Puente first "stole" and hid away Laureana Filomena, her husband's willingness to assign prime moral responsibility to the violent male swaggerer who had robbed him of his wife eased the path to a speedy marital reconciliation. José del Carmen's forgiveness of his wife neatly sidestepped Laureana Filomena's agency in the early stages of a liaison marked by ambiguity. It was a blend of force, consent, and two-way initiative that did not fit neatly into the rhetoric of robbery or kidnap.[26] But without reconciliation José del Carmen would have lost his wife longer — to colonial judges and jails, or to a "house of honor" to which she would be assigned for moral safekeeping and work as a domestic servant. A peasant who lost his wife for an extended period lost a vital contributor to a precarious household economy, had no coterie of additional female dependents who offered alternate roads to sexual virility, and could ill afford to absorb continuing legal costs with equanimity.

Male and female crossovers, although understandable, complicated the dynamics of legitimacy that anchored the conflictual dialogue between contingent and absolute gender right in male-female relations. Let us recall that group characterization of women as beings prone to treachery and evil legitimized absolutist orientations in male-female conflicts, while group characterization of men as beings prone to excess and negligence legitimized contingent orientations. When men crossed over to denounce male evil in male-female gender relations and women crossed over to denounce female evil in similar contexts, how did they manage to deflect a more complete unraveling of the cluster of ideas and suppositions that legitimated their own positions as men and as women in a world of contested patriarchal pacts? What cultural resources might they mobilize to mediate the contradictions implied by their crossovers?

The answers are several rather than one. One path that bounded the implication of crossover was the path of individual deviance. When responsibility for disorder was assigned to individuals interpreted as flagrant violators of conventional practice and morality — troublemakers sharply different from orderly and morally inoffensive men or women — crossover denunciations did not necessarily unravel gender legitimacy. An individual considered especially extreme or notorious allowed social actors to unite on a target and thereby paper over more serious differences over gender right in male-female obligations. From this point of view, the traditional scholarly notion that cultural specification of deviance simultaneously defines the cultural norm within the social body is somewhat misleading. The unity achieved by deviance may serve as much to evade or mediate the multiplicity of contending norms within the social body as to define the code of legitimate moral behavior.[27]

A second path — or set of paths — that bounded the implications of crossover was the path of ranking within the genders, hierarchical subdivisions of the larger categories of men and women. Let us call one version of this mediation "elder ranking" within a roughly horizontal color-class context. When male responsibility for disorder was assigned to a particular subcategory — youths and new husbands poorly raised, prone to violent excess, or as yet irresponsible — the rebuke of junior or lesser men by fathers and male elders need not imply that men as a group were irresponsible or that men's patriarchal authority over wives and daughters should be entangled by conditioning contingencies. Indeed, intrusive rebuke of youthful husbands and fathers underscored the higher, more absolute authority of mature patriarchs. Similarly when female responsibility for disorder was assigned to a particular subcategory — youths and new wives poorly raised, sexually aroused, or as yet morally fickle — the rebuke of junior or lesser women by mothers, mothers-in-law, and female elders need not imply that women as a group were irresponsible or that all women should submit absolutely to male authority. Indeed, moral rebuke of youthful women by their elders underscored the capacity of mature and experienced women to evaluate gender right in contentious contexts.[28]

Elder ranking within a roughly horizontal color-class context was but one among several cultural means to subdivide the larger categories of men and women. Within more vertical contexts of color-class relations and community hierarchy, social ranking allowed for crossovers that left the larger structure of male and female legitimacy intact. If the male elders, officials, and notables who defined an upper stratum of lineages within a largely peasant community viewed the male commoner stratum as somewhat prone to excess and negligence, the notables might cross over to defend abused women and to surround the patriarchal rights of commoners with contingencies. But these were contingencies ratified from above. They implied little about men or women as social types or about the more respectable patriarchs' right of unquestioned respect and deference.[29] Vertical rankings such as these developed within the milieu of popular culture: between commoners and the intermediate or social broker strata, an upper group of notables very much present in the face-to-face practices and relationships of everyday life. At higher levels of vertical crossover the social distances and ideologies of the larger color-class structure came into play. A more full blown sentiment of honor and degradation shackled the implications of crossover for gender legitimacy. Judges, priests, landowners, merchants, and other elites intervened to protect female commoners against the excesses of specific subcategories of men. But the crossovers expanded rather than diminished the elites' right of patriarchal judgment and implied little about the right of women to entangle the authority of honorable men with contingency. The men of degraded color-class strata, in short, were not to be confused with the normative concept of Man, men as a human type. The social distances were too great, and the subalterns were too much an inherently delinquent rabble in the elite mind. As the subdelegate in charge of Totolapa put it in 1802, the village was "a roguery mill" (*un taller de picardías*) whose judge could contain only somewhat the rush of "squabbles, stabs, prohibited games and gambling, sexual debauchery, lack of respect to the Church, and other excesses."[30]

The contradictory crossfires of gender and family and of color and class illuminate the forces that drew poor women and poor men into both sides of gendered moral argument and supposition in male-female conflict. Up to this point in the discussion, however, those crossovers that developed within a network of primary relations have been assumed to follow a certain logic of kinship alliance. Parental family, political family (spouse and in-laws), and offstage family (that of an *amasio* or *amasia*) defined rival clusters of family solidarity and interest within the larger kinship web, the social contours for male and female crossovers in male-female conflicts. We have not yet addressed a third enigma: relatives crossing over, on occasion, to stances of enmity that appeared to contradict the logic of their kinship alliances. How might the crossfire metaphor illuminate these more counterintuitive crossovers?

ENIGMAS AND CROSSOVERS: THE ART OF FAMILIAL POLITICS (II)

We may approach an answer by considering the story of Ysidro Vicente and Augustina María of Xoxocotla. In the late 1790s Ysidro Vicente, a married landowning Indian, developed a sexual liaison with Augustina María, an Indian widow and mother of a nine-year-old boy. A familial relationship had crept into the relationship with the boy, who called the *amasio* "*tata*" (Dad) and was in turn called "*hijo*" (son). Although both adults were monolingual Nahuatl speakers, they enjoyed reasonably good fortune by village standards. Notwithstanding the absence of the honorific "Don," Ysidro Vicente ranked among those who comprised an upper stratum within peasant society: he held lands and resources sufficient to hire Indian laborers to help work the *milpa*, and his father had once served as village *gobernador*. Augustina María, estimated to be about thirty years old, could not claim rank among peasant notables. But as peasant widows went, she fared reasonably well and managed to sustain herself and her son by running a substantial chicken yard (*gallinero*). Her comparatively healthy economic base and her age relative to that of her *amasio* (who was estimated to be in his mid-twenties) provided a certain foundation for a rather independent stance toward Ysidro Vicente. For about a year before the murder of Augustina María in 1799 the relationship had moved toward a more quarrelsome terrain, and Augustina had asserted a rather independent, self-possessing personhood. In this context Ysidro Vicente stole away to Augustina María's house — only four blocks from his own — late one November Wednesday night, slipped into her bedding, and rebuked her for passing the day drinking and neglecting her son. Augustina

María's reply reminded the *amasio* of her independence: "None of that is your account, since I don't spend anything of yours." Ysidro Vicente countered with an ultimate right of possession: "Now you will see, if I kill you and it is my account." The violence of Ysidro Vicente's words paled by comparison to his physical repossession of the *amasia*. Ysidro Vicente stabbed Augustina María thirty-six times. At first Augustina's shouts of "ay, ay, ay" provided a gruesome syncopation, but the stabbings proceeded even as Augustina María fell into deathly silence. Then Ysidro Vicente set her house on fire.[31]

The counterintuitive dimension of the unfolding tragedy is in the kin alignments. One might expect Ysidro Vicente's wife Marcelina Francisca and her parental family (his political or in-law family) to have pressed hard for an end to the liaison. One might also have expected the *amasia* Augustina María or her relatives to have imposed pressures on the relationship. These expectations are affirmed in the case evidence. But among the triad of Ysidro Vicente's family clusters (the parental, political, and offstage clusters), one would expect his parental family cluster to have remained comparatively indifferent, at most mildly critical, of a married adult son's sexual peccadillos. Yet Ysidro Vicente's parents not only supported their daughter-in-law in her remonstrances. They also took the most vehement action to break up the extramarital liaison. In the earlier stages of the relationship, noted Ysidro Vicente's mother, her husband, Gaspar Melchor, had whipped their son to put an end to the relationship. When Ysidro Vicente took Augustina María to Cuernavaca during Holy Week festivities in 1799, his father "even hanged him" (presumably by the hands from a tree or beam) to administer the kind of severe whipping that might induce their son to forgo the relationship. A month before the murder Ysidro Vicente's mother tracked down her son and Augustina María at a local tavern. She came wielding a cudgel (*garrote*), but Ysidro Vicente fled before she could beat him.[32] Why, on the issue of Ysidro Vicente's sexual freedom, did his parents cross over to a stance of extreme enmity, a punitive violence at odds with the apparent logic of their kinship alliances?

The enigma of this counterintuitive crossover recedes when we integrate a sense of crossfire into the analysis. To reduce social alignments and decisions in male-female gender disputes to a single axis of determination is to make a misleading assumption. On the one hand, the combined effect of tension between female and male orientations to gender right and the contradictory structures of kinship clusters yielded an important axis of determination. A wife, often backed by her mother or other female kin or close friends and occasionally supported as well by male kin such as a father or brother, had an interest in constraining her husband's commitment to an *amasia* who could be expected to assert her own expectations. On the other hand, the color-class structure of colonial society and a conjuncture of sharpening social conflict, polarization, and pressure on peasant well-being yielded another important axis of determination. The various interested parties had to assess the implications of open conflict and contestation over gender right in a color-class context that imposed extortionary burdens on subaltern households, especially peasant and Indian households. As vitally interested participants in the politics of peasant community and factionalism — a politics that framed life chances in an oppressive color-class order — the protagonists of gender dispute and their relatives had to integrate local and sometimes supralocal political assessments into their decisions and alignments.

If the multiple axes of determination (each imbued with its own contradictions) sometimes moved decision making and social alignments in similar directions, they might also move at cross-purposes. As we have already seen, the combined effect of such contradictory pressures could impel a zigzag movement between acrimony and alliance in a specific episode of contested gender behavior. A wife could push hard for punishment of an abusive husband and then experience the cumulative pressure of a husband's lost labor or wages, an official's economic extortions, or excessively violent and indefinite imprisonment of the husband. She then might switch to a stance that defended husband and family against abusive authorities. Less dramatic but impelled by similar considerations were instances when a wife threatened or initiated proceedings to intimidate her partner but moved rapidly to secure a reconciliation and promise of reform that removed the necessity of continuing punishment. The point was to pressure the partner into accepting an altered balance of power, not to destroy him or to remove him indefinitely from the household. At times similar considerations impelled husbands to adopt zigzag tactics of institutional intimidation followed by grudging reconciliation.[33]

In the case of Ysidro Vicente and his parents the politics of community and factionalism provoked them to cross over to a counterintuitive alignment with their daughter in-law against their son. Political assessments ended up surrounding the son's patriarchal and sexual rights with contingencies. These were not so much the contingencies associated with female orientation to gender right in male-female relations, but rather the contingencies associated with elder power: an assertion by fathers and family elders of a superior wisdom and right of intervention, even counterintuitive intervention, in the family interest. Ysidro Vicente's father, Gaspar Melchor, had gotten entangled in a quarrel with the hegemonic power group of the village — the *gobernador, alcaldes*, and at least a portion of the village elders. Beyond the evident personal animosities and political rivalries the local issues in contention are somewhat unclear. A fleeting hint suggests, however, that the distribution of irrigation water rights figured in the split and that Gaspar Melchor's enemies had been coopted into a scheme that left poorer peasant claimants short on water.[34]

However tentative our understanding of the issues in contention, what is

clear is the seriousness — the depth of acrimony and the spiral of escalation —
of Xoxocotla's political split. On the day of Ysidro Vicente's murder of Augustina María, his father Gaspar Melchor had marched off to Cuernavaca
town to pursue his case against the village power group before the *alcalde
mayor* who oversaw justice in the rural Cuernavaca district. The mutual para-
noia and sense of high stakes were evident on both sides. The *gobernador* Juan
García accompanied his enemy to Cuernavaca town to insure that the judge
would hear more than one version of events. Gaspar Melchor, for his part, believed that the power group would seek vengeance on his family "because I
don't cooperate with them in their evil doings [*maldades*]." Gaspar Melchor's
most glaring point of vulnerability in this equation was his son's sexual behavior. Adultery provided an opening for legal harassment if the power group
decided to crack down on sexual immorality. The well-known potential for
violence among wife, *amasia*, and husband-*amasio* added the threat, moreover, that Ysidro Vicente might actually commit an act of criminal violence
that would invite severe punishment, maltreatment, or extortion. Even worse,
should any harm befall the widow Augustina María — even harm perpetrated
by Gaspar Melchor's enemies — the power group would jump at the opportunity to make the culturally plausible argument that the *amasio* should be considered the perpetrator unless someone brought forth convincing evidence to
the contrary.[35]

These political and factional considerations were part of the broad, shifting, and often contentious process whereby peasants continuously constructed and reconstructed the meaning and power alignments of community
in the color-class order of late colonial Morelos. The political context of family and community life impelled Gaspar Melchor and Angela María to take a
severely intolerant stance toward their son's sexual freedoms. Under other circumstances they might have tolerated the sexual liaison as perhaps regrettable
but unimportant, a symptom of fairly standard and usually benign male behavior and a matter mainly of concern to their daughter-in-law and son. But
crosscutting circumstances of village life dictated otherwise. They joined their
daughter-in-law in counseling their son "to separate from the widow's [illicit]
friendship, because if any harm were done to her, it would be pinned on
him."[36] And they backed their counsel with a punitive violence they considered protective.

The crossover to enmity with the son and alliance with the daughter-in-law
in a contest over marital right and obligation represented not a breakdown of
family solidarity with the son. The crossover represented not a stance by Gaspar Melchor against the male presumption that men had both a propensity
and a right to pursue sexual liaisons outside of marriage, that wives normally
ought to endure such episodes without undermining their husbands' authority, and that husbands held monopoly rights in the honor and sexuality of

wives.[37] The crossover did not represent an effort to shield the parents from legal and moral culpability while conceding the son's guilt. Indeed, when the village *alcalde* Domingo Julián showed up at the family compound to arrest Ysidro Vicente for murder, his mother and sisters sprang to his defense, blocked the arrest, and forced the *alcalde* to retreat. On a second try the *gobernador* and two village *alcaldes* mobilized a greater show of force and managed to arrest Ysidro Vicente, but they had to overcome a verbal barrage and physical scuffle led by Ysidro's mother.[38] The crossover signified, rather, the way multiple and sometimes crosscutting axes of assessment might redefine the context within which kin judged, fought over, and redrew the boundaries of permissible gender behavior compatible with family interest.

Women crossing over to denunciations of female immorality, men crossing over to denunciations of male excess, relatives crossing over to stances of enmity that inverted the usual kinship alignments — these crossovers required skill in the art of gender and family politics. They implicated men and women on both sides of the broad language of argument that divided women and men in their gender conflicts, and required cultural mediations that hemmed in the unraveling implications of crossover and contradiction. The crossfires of gender and family and of color and class made crossovers necessary but not necessarily irreversible or inscrutable. Oscillating blends of acrimony and interdependence, of enmity and mutuality, were almost inescapable in a world where peasant households relied on familial claims in property and community and a sexual division of family labor for their well-being, and where peasant women could ill afford in struggles with their men to ignore their subaltern color-class standing. The same peasant woman inclined to interpret her husband's foul and imperious domestic temper sympathetically, as a product of troubles in the difficult and frustrating world of subaltern men, might move toward a decision, nonetheless, to abandon her husband because gendered violence had become habitual and life-threatening. The same woman whose gender troubles led her to abandon her husband and who managed to stay afloat economically by moving from locale to locale in a hard life of domestic service might after a year or two confess her marital troubles to a priest and ask him to secure a reconciliation. These examples of the twists and turns of female life, pushed along by the combined and shifting weights of gender and color-class imperatives, are not at all hypothetical. They summarize the saga of Dominga María, a monolingual Nahua peasant of Xoxocotla.[39]

Sometimes, of course, the tensions and conflicts of gendered life passed an irreversible breaking point. They exploded in homicidal or near-homicidal violence or crossed more subtle points of no return. One readily discerns the former in the criminal cases of late colonial Morelos. To discern the latter sometimes requires an eye attentive to passing detail: the refusal, for example, of Ermenegilda Francisca to plead for mercy when her husband Vicente Ferrer was charged with assault and robbery in 1804. An Indian woman could walk down one or more well-known paths to help a husband threatened with serious punishment. She could offer an alibi to deny his guilt; she could present mitigating circumstances of familial necessity that explained his motivation and lessened his culpability; or she could plead for a paternal understanding and mercy that softened the sentence in view of the disastrous implications of a severe sentence for her household economy. She might even use her defense of her husband as a point of leverage or moral legitimacy in the pursuit of an altered balance of domestic power. Ermenegilda Francisca turned away from all these paths and instead sealed the legal fate of her husband. If her husband was caught in the act of robbery, she observed bitterly, "it was not in order to assist her, even less to fulfill the obligations of his [married] condition, but rather to sustain a concubine named Matiana Maria, [an] Indian widow." Vicente Ferrer was sentenced to fifty lashes and five years of labor in a presidio.[40] The sentence was as close to a legal divorce as a woman like Ermenegilda Francisca could hope for.

The crossfires of gender and family and of color and class encouraged but did not absolutely guarantee ambivalence by women toward the men in their lives. Sometimes the intense wars of gendered life obliterated ambivalence, destroyed the will to pursue the art of crossover and zigzag.

THE POLITICS OF GOSSIP

In the predominantly peasant world of late colonial Morelos the decision to air or to withhold discreet information was an intensely political decision. This was the case even for matters such as individual morality or family quarrels, matters apparently private and narrow in political implication. The airing of discreet information could under certain conditions mobilize clusters of family and kin, even entire factions or communities. It could unleash processes of social alignment and estrangement, local conflict and vendetta, even colonial intervention and extortion. In short, words, information, rumor, and reputation were potentially powerful and dangerous. Knowing when, when not, and before whom to use discreet information was an important cultural skill.

For reasons related to the themes of crossfire as well as gender conflict, the face-to-face world of popular culture was suffused with discreet information. On the one hand, one of the chief strategies of women and female youth in their troubled relations with men and male youth was to forge networks of ongoing female conversation — webs of discussion and observation, grievance and sympathy, suggestion and evaluation. Indeed, "talk" was closely related to one of the most powerful of female weapons: the weapon of scandal, the loud venting of information and accusation in a manner that forced public resolution of a matter heretofore private or discreet. On the other hand, the crossfires of gender and family and of color and class implied that not all damaging rumor and information should be used at all times and that not all the potential receivers in a network of information were fully to be trusted. Accusations could backfire if crossovers inspired by kinship, sexual rivalries, property conflicts, or other influences split networks of sociability into rival factions; if men responded to talk and complaints by women with violence; or if elites and authorities used accusations against subalterns to promote expropriations or extortions. One needed to consider with care questions of audience, timing, and accusatory tone when sharing information. Too indiscreet an airing of information, beyond a network of trust (*confianza*), might provoke trouble, recrimination, or violence. (The trust of *confianza* refers to a confidence that the receiver of discreet information will not circulate or otherwise misuse it.)

In short, there is a sense in which popular culture was both a culture of talk and a culture of discretion. The contradiction almost guaranteed vast cultural reservoirs of half-acknowledged discreet information on personal, sexual, and family life — the sense of secrets, held in reserve for another day, familiar to peasants as well as their students.[41]

In a society where the revelation of secrets could yield harm or provoke conflict and where women's strategies of survival and well-being required that they learn the skill of background talk, the male accusation that females engaged in frivolous and sometimes damaging gossip could serve as a powerful metaphor. The metaphor might refer to any illegitimate use of information and attached to it a sense of personal treason or malice. To call someone a *chismoso* or *chismosa* (gossip) or a *soplón* or *soplona* (informer) was to use words that carried a powerful charge. They accused the target of acting in the manner of women who provoked trouble by spreading false rumor or circulating information better kept secret. Delivered to the wrong ears even trifling talk could cause damage. As an Indian of Tlayacapa put it, a judge had extorted thirteen pesos each (a large sum for peasants) from his mother and brother "because of [a bit of] frivolous gossip and [a] false idea."[42]

The metaphorical stretch of the gossip epithet is evident in the way it applied not simply to betrayal through leakage of information but to betrayal more generally. In 1765, for example, the *teniente* for the Yautepec district of Cuernavaca sent to Tlaltizapán an inspection team led by a deputy constable. The purpose of such visitations was usually to review morality and public order in the village and thereby revitalize a sense of orderly subordination to the representatives of the colonial state and church. A collateral purpose might be more extortionary: to use roundups of delinquents to impose legal fees and costs or to secure extralegal bribes and settlements.[43] At the time Tlaltizapán was tense. Its Indian *gobernador*, Juan Nicolás Zapotitlán, had first agreed to divert water to serve the needs of the whiter stratum of Spanish citizens (*españoles vecinos*) resident in the village, then had reversed himself and supported the Indian commoners opposed to the project. The Tlaltizapán peasants had garnered a particularly tumultuous and hostile reputation among the area's colonial authorities. When the visiting constable ordered Julián Ramos, a villager who served as local minister of the court, to summon Indian officials to mount an inspection (*ronda*) to identify and stop concubinage, the *gobernador* fled to avoid compliance. Julián Ramos told an Indian boy in the *gobernador*'s house to deliver the message that Juan Nicolás had a duty to collaborate rather than flee visiting judges. The next day Juan Nicolás, accompanied by a large crowd of Indian officials and commoners, showed up to intimidate not only the deputy constable but also Julián Ramos. The crowd marched to Ramos's house and threatened to burn it if he did not flee the village, "because they didn't want *soplones* [living] there." Significantly the *soplón* epithet seemed to refer not to any specific secret or damaging item of information but to the larger betrayal of acting as a collaborator, a voice to and for colonials at a time when they were hated.[44]

Peasants who feared, denigrated, or denounced gossip understood its aspect as a political instrument, a use of the power of words at select moments and in select social contexts to alter the destiny of individuals, families, and communities. As we have seen, the metaphorical stretch of the epithet extended well beyond its gendered foundation — male deprecation of female talk as irresponsible, frivolous, and sometimes malicious invention of falsehoods that provoked trouble. The epithet could apply to illegitimate talk by men or by women. It could apply to betrayal in general, to service as a treasonous voice or go-between, and not merely to leakage of a specific secret. It could even apply to illegitimate sharings of truthful information. When gossip carried a strong and harmful political edge, the truth or falsehood of the information no longer mattered.

Consider, for example, the fusions of political and personal accusation that threw Atlacahualoya into turmoil in 1789.[45] For the Indians of Atlacahualoya, a *sujeto* community subordinate to the district head town of Xonacatepec, the lines of power seemed to run not so much to Xonacatepec as to the neighboring sugar hacienda Santa Ana Tenango and its owner, Don Nicolás Ycazbalceta. Hacienda Tenango's permanent resident population of slaves, free mulattoes and *castas*, and Indians surpassed 600: the slaves alone probably numbered over 100. Its annual sugar production capacity had climbed to about 400 tons, easily among New Spain's tonnage leaders, and its appetite for land had become rather voracious. Swept into the powerful sugar vortex of the late eighteenth century, Atlacahualoya not only lost much of its land to Hacienda Tenango but also ended up renting land from the estate to meet the agricultural needs of villagers. The pressures that forced the new arrangement had climaxed in the 1780s and put Indian functionaries, especially *gobernadores* and former *gobernadores*, in a tight political spot. Impelled to cede land at a time of rising populations in need of land, *gobernadores* and former *gobernadores* were also well positioned to become Hacienda Tenango's *repartidores de tierras*, the distributors of the now rented land among village agriculturalists. The new arrangements blurred social alignments and loyalties. Was a *repartidor* an esteemed village *viejo* or a hacienda agent? Did he use control of rented lands to favor a network of allies and clients who comprised a village faction, or did he distribute the lands equitably? Had he been forced to give up village lands provisionally and under protest, or had he sold them definitively and for private gain?

The tensions boiled over in 1789. On August 25 Don Francisco de Villena, the *teniente del alcalde mayor* for the Xonacatepec district, received word of a plot to kill the *hacendado* Ycazbalceta, the former Indian *gobernador* Don Felipe de Santiago, and Villena himself unless the lawsuit between the Indians and Ycazbalceta ended with restitution of the disputed property to Atlacahualoya. Don Felipe de Santiago, the former *gobernador*, held a post on Hacienda Tenango as head *repartidor* (*capitán repartidor*) of the disputed lands, and the rebels accused him of having sold the lands surreptitiously when he served as village *gobernador*. The multitudinous *juntas* that met at the house of the current *gobernador*, Don Marcos Antonio, organized a land invasion to be backed, if necessary, by killing the Indians' internal and external enemies. Villena ordered a secret investigation and had the persons singled out as prominent leaders and promoters — Don Marcos Antonio, Pedro Luís, and the latter's son Domingo José — brought to the Xonacatepec jail. The arrest failed to dampen the rebelliousness. That night the Atlacahualoya Indians rang the church bells to summon a crowd, held a junta, and resolved to march on Xonacatepec to free their *gobernador* and the other prisoners. If necessary they would kill Villena. Villena organized a defense by Xonacatepec's Indians and its whiter *gente de razón* (literally, "people of reason," the standard phrase for the respectable social stratum made up of whites, *castizos* [the offspring of a Spanish parent and a mestizo parent], and people of mixed blood whose lifestyle and cultural mannerisms "whitened" them). The whiter stratum, it appears, was to guard the jail, while the Xonacatepec Indians were to guard the paths of entry into Xonacatepec. A crowd of seventy to one hundred Indian men and women from Atlacahualoya made their way into Xonacatepec anyway, and Villena and his informers escaped by seeking refuge on Ycazbalceta's other sugar hacienda, Santa Clara Montefalco. Villena's superior, the *alcalde mayor* in Cuernavaca, intervened to deflect the dangerous march of events and achieved a semblance of peace by September. The details of the negotiation remain discreet in the recorded documentation of the case, but we may speculate that Don Marcos Antonio was freed and that the land question was ambiguously resolved or postponed to another day.[46]

For our purposes, what matters is the way the metaphor of gossip and fusions of political and personal accusation energized the political drama. The chief targets of the Atlacahualoya commoners and their rebel *gobernador* were two former *gobernadores*, Don Felipe de Santiago and Don Matías Pérez. The hostility toward Don Felipe de Santiago was direct and easy to understand: villagers believed that he had illegitimately ceded their land to Hacienda Tenango. The hostility toward Don Matías Pérez had more indirect inspiration. The sense of internal unity against outside threats had been shaken when informers exposed two community secrets to colonial authorities. An Indian notable, Diego Cortés, was accused of raping his natural (illegitimate) niece María de los Santos, and another notable, Salvador Antonio, was publicly whipped for committing incest with his stepdaughter. At a time when social polarization and tension ran high, exposure of moral misdeeds — especially misdeeds among leading families — to outside authorities provoked censure and distrust. Such exposures jeopardized the politics of internal unity and hegemony and could only add to the difficulty of establishing Atlacahualoya's legal and moral standing before colonial authorities. Villagers believed that Don Matías Pérez had denounced the rape of María de los Santos to the authorities and thought the indiscretion reason enough to consider him "against the pueblo on the lands [question], and for the *Teniente* [Deputy Judge Villena]." The night the villagers gathered to plan their rescue of the *gobernador*, they chased Don Matías Pérez away, "calling him *chismoso*" and did the same to several others "whom they blame as *chismosos* with the *Teniente* and [Don] Nicolás [Ycazbalceta]."[47] Gossip and accusation of sexual or familial immorality were political instruments. In some contexts what mattered was not the truth or falsehood of accusation — there is no reason to believe that the rape and incest accusations were invented — but the political consequences of accusation.[48]

The political use of discreet information on gendered social relations and the sometimes modest relevance of truth suffused the unfolding social struggle in Atlacahualoya. Not only did the exposure of sexual violence and incest by community notables inflame those loyal to Atlacahualoya's leadership at a time of community crisis. In addition, the community leadership used discreet information to increase the pressure on Don Felipe de Santiago's family to cooperate with the effort to win back the lands purchased illegitimately by Hacienda Tenango. On the evening of August 6, in the immediate aftermath of the community festival and procession feting Nuestra Señora de Agosto, Francisco Xavier, the son of the ostracized Don Felipe de Santiago and the son-in-law of Don Marcos Antonio's ally Pedro Luís, had gone to the house of Micaela Gertrudis, the *mayordoma* of the fiesta. The community jailers (*alguaciles*) and their assistants seized him and took him to the *gobernador* for punishment. The community officials claimed that he had visited Micaela Gertrudis's house in continuance of an adulterous relationship with her married daughter, Lorenza Juana. Francisco Xavier claimed that he had visited Micaela Gertrudis in accord with the custom that aspiring fiesta *mayordomos* "asked" the outgoing sponsor to cede the *mayordomía* for the coming year. The truth of the adultery accusation—the two versions of the purpose of Francisco Xavier's visit were not mutually exclusive—is difficult to evaluate. On the one hand, Francisco Xavier's wife and mother-in-law took the accusation seriously, and his mother-in-law assaulted the alleged *amasia*. On the other hand, Francisco Xavier's father-in-law was a key leader of the group that attacked village traitors. Perhaps most important, it mattered little to the community's male leadership whether they had taken advantage of discreet but truthful information or had relied on an invented but plausible story. Everyone understood the politics of gossip, and everyone knew the purpose of the arrest. In Francisco Xavier's version of events, after he passed a night in the community stocks with his right hand painfully tied, the *gobernador* ordered his hand untied and explained the situation. "Hombre, this isn't anything, I also know how to take off [my] pants for women, but come now, as long as you don't testify that your father . . . sold our land to [Hacienda Tenango], I'm not going to have to release you."[49]

In the joined lives of family and community, gossip and silence, talk and discretion, were opposite and complementary faces of the same coin, the coin of language as politics. Female efforts to transform private or offstage gender quarrels into public conflicts requiring resolution contributed to the periodic fusions of public and private life that marked popular culture and to the sense that gossip about matters personal, gendered, and familial often carried a political edge. But as women and men well understood, the crossfires of gender and family and color and class made words both dangerous and powerful. One drank at the fountain of discreet information with care, simultaneously attentive to the power of words and information in specific contexts and to the danger of unleashing forces of vengeance and extortion beyond anyone's control.

For women and female youth especially, such attentiveness could exact a terrible price. The social struggle for Atlacahualoya's lands was urgent, compelling, and legitimate—for women as well as men. But consider the grim implications of a code of silence, observed in the interests of family or community, as defined by the patriarchal custodians of family and community. Before Atlacahualoya broke apart, the rape of María de los Santos by her uncle and the sexual persecution of an anonymous youngster by her stepfather had been assigned to the realm of public silence. Men mistrusted gossip and women's talk not simply because they feared invented falsehood. They also feared broken silences.

WOMEN AS FORCE

The crossfires of gender and family and of color and class enable us to reconcile two images of women at first sight paradoxical. On the one hand, we have viewed women as a formidable force in pervasive, often bitter, and sometimes violent gender conflicts between men and women. In the everyday practice of male-female relations, women and female youth forged a world of contested patriarchal pacts, a continuous and conflictual cultural dialogue between more contingent and absolute orientations to gender right. As we have also seen, women brought considerable resourcefulness and will to small and large struggles over gender right and power. They pluralized the relevant patriarchs in their lives and learned tactics of institutional escalation. They forged primary and secondary networks of female alliance, conversation, and assistance. They learned to engage the dangerous forces of scandal and supernatural power. They resorted to subtle expressions of disquiet that exerted a quiet pressure. They sometimes mobilized dramatic displays of strength, a force of will and body that shattered expectations of female deference and resignation. In the gender struggles of daily life, women were a force to be reckoned with.

On the other hand, every close student of Mexican history and culture will recognize that women have also mobilized formidable force in solidary defense of their children, their families, and their men.[50] As we have noted, the gender wars sometimes crossed an irreversible breaking point that obliterated ambivalence. Not all women defended their men; some wounds festered undiminished; and some relationships broke down altogether. But the crossfire effect and the ambivalence of shared lives and destinies could also dampen the will of women and men to cross such a point irretrievably. However pervasive and often bitter the sense of female grievance and conflict with men, however bruising and damaging the real and metaphorical wounds that nurtured this sense of female grievance, many women nonetheless took physical risks and summoned a powerful resolve to defend their kin, including their male kin.

The examples abound in the documents. Women took physical risks to shield their relatives during episodes of violence. Ysidra María of Tlalnepantla was beaten with a stick on the wrist when she went to rescue her forty-year-old son from a village official who had locked him up. María Magdalena of Tepoztlán was struck on the head with a stick while fighting to extricate her husband from a scuffle.

Women summoned the force of will to confront directly those who threatened their men. Sometimes this force of will was mainly verbal. The mother of Manuel de la Trinidad cursed the village *alcalde* of Amatlán when he tried to arrest her son for stoning another Indian. Sometimes the force of will was more physical. Juana Rodríguez of Cuautla Amilpas joined her husband in assaulting the officials who had come to arrest their son (heretofore considered by his own father a youthful renegade in need of violent punishment) for attempted rape of a mulatta.

Women mobilized powers of determination less directly confrontational yet equally stubborn and audacious. Juliana Antonia and Joaquina Josefa of Xalostoque summoned the resolve to wind their way over the mountains from the eastern hot country of Morelos to the Viceregal Indian Court (*Juzgado General de Naturales*) in Mexico City in order to plead for the release of their husbands from the jail in Xonacatepec. Their priest had ordered the jailing because he resented the Xalostoque villagers' determination to proceed independently with the customary distribution of interest revenues to *cofradía* members who had contributed funds to the confraternity's lending bank.[51]

The paradox of women-as-force in bitter gender struggles against men and women-as-force in vehemently solidary struggles with men is historical rather than intellectual. The crossfires of gender and family and of color and class render the paradox intellectually comprehensible and, indeed, illuminate the depth of the dilemmas faced by the women of popular culture. On the one hand, only a foolish woman ignored the jeopardies of female gendered life and the necessity of defending her needs and interests — and lending aid or sympathy to female relatives, allies, and confidantes — in the inevitable conflicts of women's lives with men. On the other hand, only a foolish woman ignored the jeopardies of social isolation in subaltern and female life and the necessity of establishing her presence as a vital contributor and claimant in solidary relations that included men. The multiple imperatives implied not only ambivalence and crossfire. They also put a premium on a woman's flexibility, her ability to evaluate rapidly shifting social contexts and scenarios and to move between acrimony and solidarity and between deference and confrontation without losing sight of her own needs or eroding her own force of will. The same Yndoza Gertrudis who monitored her husband's weekly wages on Hacienda Miacatlán, questioned his liaison with an *amasia*, and suffered a beating when she challenged him also sought to save him by intervening in a homicidal fight. The same María Francisca who fit the image of female deference when her brother brought home two drinking partners and had her serve them lunch metamorphosed quickly when one of the men stabbed her brother in the chest. She chased the assailant and struck him to the ground by "hitting him with a stone throw." She then turned over her prisoner to the Tlaltizapán *gobernador*.[52]

Women wrestled with the dilemmas of crossfire by resisting entrapment in a once-and-for-all choice between competing imperatives: between the imperat̃ ̃e of gender conflict and that of familial solidarity, between gender contestation and subaltern unity. In their struggles against men and in defense of them, in proximity to patriarchs and apart from them, women developed an attentiveness to the various axes of struggle, necessity, and affirmation that conjoined and contended in their everyday lives: arenas of work, money, and property often assigned to "class" experience; arenas of sociocultural ritual, bonding, and differentiation often assigned to "ethnic" or "community" experience; and arenas of familial, sexual, and sex-based relationships often assigned to "gender" experience. After all, the dance of color-class struggle and survival belonged to women too. When two officials went to an Indian home in Tlayacapan in 1805 to enforce an unfavorable land boundary ruling, María Andrea Carrillo and her two daughters fought their case "with hits, sticks, slaps, and scratches." Like many a peasant defending many a piece of land and like many an Indian resisting many a colonial official, María Andrea Carrillo and her daughters were labeled criminal and were dragged off to the nearest jail.[53]

CHAPTER 7

Battles of Patriarchs

The World of Male Peasant
Violence

AN INTRODUCTORY DETOUR: STEREOTYPES REVISITED

Luis Buñuel, the great Spanish film director, moved to Mexico in 1946. The cultural self-image of Mexican men as casual killers quickly caught his surrealist eye. Soon after he arrived, the newspapers reported a curious episode. A man went looking for a Señor Sánchez at number 39 of a given street. The doorman who greeted him said that he knew no Sánchez. Sánchez surely lived next door, at number 41. The man went to number 41 in search of Sánchez. The doorman at 41 replied that Señor Sánchez certainly did live at 39 and that the first doorman had been mistaken. So the man returned to 39 to ask for Sánchez again. When he told the first doorman what had happened, the doorman politely asked the visitor to wait a bit, retreated to an interior room, returned with a pistol, and shot the visitor. "What most amazed me in this story," recalled Buñuel, "was the tone with which the journalist told it, as if the doorman was right." As the headline to the story put it, the visitor was "killed for asking too many questions" (*lo mata por preguntón*).[1]

To analyze the world of male-on-male violence in late colonial Morelos forces us to return to the problem of cultural stereotyping. The image of male bravado and self-destruction has exerted such a powerful pull in contemporary Mexican culture and cultural commentary that silence is dangerous. It amounts to tacit assent. In the absence of critical reflection that places such imagery in context, historical analysis of male-on-male violence yields silently to the pull of entrenched assumption. The pull is all the greater because one easily discovers historical antecedents to Buñuel's story. One night in 1805

151

Onofre Bautista, a mestizo muleteer (*arriero*) in Tlayacapan, heard a laugh from Deciderio Sarmiento, an Indian baker, as the latter drew near on his horse. Onofre Bautista took the laugh as a challenge. As one witness put it, "Onofre told him it seems that you're laughing and poking fun at me, get off your horse and you'll see if I'm a man." Deciderio Sarmiento, who had continued to laugh, obliged his challenger and paid with his life.[2] As Buñuel's journalist might have put it, the horseman was "killed for laughing too long."

The Mexico of the mid-twentieth century abounded with the imagery of such incidents. In the wake of the Mexican Revolution and in dialogue with the building of a revolutionary state, Mexican artists and intellectuals scoured the long sweep of Mexican history and civilization for meaning and national identity. Two ultimate questions stirred their search. What explained the overpowering torrents of rage and blood that consumed Mexico, like the fires of a cosmic volcano, during the war years (ca. 1910–17) of the revolution? And, in what ways did the traumatic bonding induced by the catastrophic violence express and emerge out of a deeper bonding and trauma, a silent rage at the heart of a national psychology and experience? In short, Mexican intellectuals constructed an imagined community of Mexican national culture and related it to the overpowering cataclysm of their times. The legitimating politics of that construction, so well analyzed and critiqued by Roger Bartra, Carlos Monsiváis, and Ilene V. O'Malley, need not detain us here. The wounding rage could cast the historic task of the revolutionary state and its pantheon of male heroes in a heroic mold. The revolutionary state would constructively acknowledge and engage the rage, attempt to ameliorate it, yet also use all means necessary to hold the propensity to violence and self-destruction in check. Or, the tragicomic outbursts of violence and self-destructive bravado might foster a more resigned and cynical legitimation. The Mexican people got the kind of government they deserved. For our purposes the cultural carriers identified in the discourse matter as much as the message itself. The bearers of the national culture constructed in the twentieth century were the touchy Mexican men — easily offended, quick to explode, dramatic and even swaggering in their masculinity, and dismissive of death — who might kill an annoying visitor or a laughing bystander.[3]

In Mexican intellectual circles, incidents such as the killing of Mr. Sánchez's visitor took on an archetypal quality. They captured the quintessential psychology of Mexican men and Mexican culture (categories that merged readily in such discussions). They distilled in a vignette the tragic imprint of centuries of historical experience, a blend of rage and masculinity that exploded publicly in the Mexican Revolution and more privately in the everyday outbursts that found their way into newspapers and street conversations, memoirs and literature, film and cultural essays. Because the vignettes of self-recognition were so often comic, at times hilarious, they allowed the teller to laugh in the telling of the pain, to brush off blood and death in "typically Mexican" fashion, to mask rage with mirth.

Buñuel, brilliantly alert to the surreal and the archetypal, soaked up the atmosphere. Three images stood out especially. First, Mexican men took offense over trivialities and imagined slights. This was why Sánchez's visitor had died, and this was why to turn down a drink brought danger if the host invoked that "always fearsome phrase: 'You're offending me.'" Under the circumstances, Buñuel noted, "it's better to drink the tenth glass." Second, Mexican men treated murderous altercations casually, as a normal and perhaps gratifying life activity that could occur on a whim. This explained the normalcy that pervaded the newspaper report on the killing of Sánchez's visitor. This explained the words of the mayor of a pueblo who advised Buñuel that one did not make much of a fuss over murders: "Every Sunday has its little cadaver." Third, Mexican men adhered fiercely to their sense of masculine honor, bonded with other men on the basis of it, and if necessary, faced death squarely and dramatically to protect it. This explained the meaning of a wartime anecdote the great muralist David Alfaro Siqueiros shared with Buñuel. Toward the end of the revolutionary fighting, two old friends — army officers who had gone to military school together — meet in battle on opposite sides. One is captured, and captured officers are to be shot. At dusk the victorious officer invites his friend to drink at his table. They embrace and pass the time recalling their youth, their friendship, and the turns of fate that will force one friend to execute the other. Sentiment runs thick. When the victorious friend laments the role forced upon him, his prisoner comforts him: "Do your duty. You have no alternative." But the prisoner's friend procrastinates, the two go on drinking and bonding, and the prisoner must continue to contemplate the terror of his death. Finally he forces his friend to face up to the issue. "Listen, amigo, grant me one last favor. I'd like for you yourself to kill me." The victorious friend, still seated, his eyes moistening with tears, takes out his pistol and grants the favor.[4]

The construction of national culture as a diagnosis of Mexican men's maladies took shape as an enormously influential paradigm around mid-century. The paradigm found dignified, highbrow expression in the celebrated essays of Samuel Ramos and Octavio Paz, and raucous lowbrow expression in the comedy of Cantínflas. Ramos's *El perfil del hombre y la cultura en México* (*Profile of Man and Culture in Mexico*), whose somewhat crude formulations built a foundation for Paz's more sophisticated interpretation, first appeared in 1934. Cantínflas made the transition from popular tent shows to the movies in the late 1930s. He captivated audiences by portraying the improvised verbal barrages and bodily contortions and the nearly incomprehensible play of moods and thoughts they represented as a tragicomic art of poor men's afflicted survival. By far the most perceptive intellectual treatment of national culture as male malady and psychology came in Octavio Paz's *El laberinto de la soledad* (*The Labyrinth of Solitude*), first published in 1950 and revised and expanded in 1959. Mexican men lashed out for no good reason or, more precisely, for the reasons of history and psychology they carried within. They carried the psychic burden of resentment and suppressed rage imprinted in the emasculating experience of the Spanish conquest, the presumed betrayal of the original Mexican peoples by La Malinche (the Indian mistress and go-between of the Spanish conqueror Hernán Cortés), and the knowledge that they had inherited a history of colonial rape and subjugation that somehow seemed endlessly reproduced rather than transcended in the march of historical time. The purest heirs of this psychohistory of resentment and national identity were not the Indians and the peasants, who had been more spiritually broken and culturally resigned to the fact of subjugation, but the mestizos and the urban poor. The mestizos were the literal heirs of betrayal, the resentful sons of La Malinche; the urban *pelados* (literally, the peeled, plucked, or bare ones) were the migrants, proletarians, and street survivors condemned to a precarious plebeian existence, cut off from the psychological security and resignation of rural communities. The mestizos and the *pelados* dropped their placid masks when they drank and when they lashed out with compensatory violence and masculine swagger. Their acts of nearly random violence had little to do with the targets of their violence, who bore little direct connection with the specific social and power relations of their assailants' contemporary lives. The violence had little to do, too, with the defense of a meaningful and positive sense of masculine honor that brought dignity and self-affirmation to daily life. The violence was more in the nature of a *descarga* venting.[5]

Ramos, Cantínflas, and Paz, although important in their own right, participated in a larger cultural movement.[6] This movement contended with several streams of cultural commentary and debate.[7] In the interpretation of Mexican experience and identity, the paradigm of psychological rage and affliction continually competed with that of social trauma and denunciation. One could detect the uneasy competition and coexistence even within single works, authors, and cultural icons. Was the legend of Pancho Villa mainly a story of the bloody conflict between rich and poor? Was it mainly a story of manly rage and valor finally bursting forth, perhaps overpowering the story of rich and poor? Should the two story lines be integrated tightly, connected vaguely, or held apart?[8]

With the shift toward a more conservative and resigned political climate in the 1940s and 1950s — the era when the "institutionalized revolution" took hold and channeled the revolution toward socially regressive models of economic growth backed by tight political control — Paz's brilliant essay struck an exceptionally responsive cultural chord. The deep introspection it encouraged coincided with and contributed to a subtle shift of cultural focus: from

emphasis on the recent and contemporary as well as historical social grievances that sparked violence, rage, and political conflict to emphasis on more
interior legacies, the imprints of earlier times, as much psychological as social,
that were not yet resolved and healed. This interior legacy inspired the cultural pathology of male self-destruction and violence. The shift acknowledged
the social but diminished its edge and urgency. The historic maladies of Mexico had rooted themselves in the interior psyche and spirit, beneath and beyond the more external realm of social relations and grievances. Social relations masked the deeper truth of individual solitude and interior pathology.
This formulation not only had the advantage of diminishing the import of
political critique of the revolutionary state, the "family" of party men who ran
it, and the conservative turn of public policy. It also enabled refined folk to
criticize lower class men for their violence, their hypersensitivity to slights,
and their exaggerated machismo, but to do so in a context of paternal sympathy and cultural self-recognition that at once softened the blow and averted
a more thorough critique of gender subordination and relationships among
the rich as well as the poor. The familiar image of the Mexican man who
lashes out for no particular reason began to congeal into an entrenched cultural icon, a paradigmatic quintessence of Mexican men and Mexican culture
still enormously influential.[9]

In elite culture, at least, the imagery drew on long historical roots. In late
colonial times as in the twentieth century, elites and members of the intelligentsia saw poor men as people inclined to nearly incomprehensible outbursts of anger and perceived slights, to a murderous quarreling over incon-
sequentials. (In late colonial times the characterization extended readily to
peasants as well as plebeians and to Indians as well as non-Indians.) As a legal
defender put it in 1799 when pleading for a merciful sentence in a rather casual killing among two hacienda laborers, such quarrels (riñas) reflected the
pathology of the poor. "As for the death inflicted upon Aparicio Antonio, it is
true that humanity is horrified upon viewing the coldness and the foolishness
with which the homicide was committed. Two friends . . . who had gone about
together to entertain themselves began with those dreadful word games [chan-
zas] that are common among the peoples of their class, and in an instant . . .
the one murders the other."[10] Among the poor and the degraded such events
were too commonplace to warrant draconian punishment. The play of joking
insult and double meanings (chanzas and albures), a repartee amidst drink
that ambiguously blended male competition with male conviviality, sometimes spun out of control. Friends killed one another over nothing. The wise
recourse was not to overreact but to remember, with Buñuel's mayor, that
"every Sunday has its little cadaver."

Buñuel's delightful anecdotes and Paz's brilliant reflections on the psychological weight of history and suppressed rage are not so much wrong as mis-

leading. Enlarged into quintessential statements, they nourish cultural stereo-typing. The stereotyping, precisely because it taps revealingly into experience, elicits a recognition value that deflects attention from three crucial questions. First, to what extent does the process of enlargement misrepresent the motives of male violence as a whole? Second, to what extent does a discourse that attaches the rage of wounded male honor to plebeians and non-Indians underestimate the significance of a jealously defended sense of masculine honor among peasants and among Indians? Third, and perhaps most important, to what extent does emphasis on interior psychological imprinting, near-pathological outbursts over "nothing" induced by a wounded state of mind, oddly move us away from a social analysis of masculinity itself? That is, to what extent might we elucidate, through analysis of ongoing social and power relations in poor people's lives, the shape and meaning of a positive sense of masculine honor, a gendered form of social affirmation in tense dialogue with equally gendered forms of social degradation?

The first two questions ask us to engage in a sociological scaling that places entrenched cultural stereotyping in perspective. The third question asks us to dig more deeply, beneath the sometimes illuminating discussions of psychology and interior imprinting, to discern the social logic of masculinity.

SOCIOLOGICAL SCALING: MASCULINITY AND VIOLENCE

Let us begin with sociological scaling. How strongly did either *descarga* ventings or a certain touchiness about masculine honor in men's social relations with other men shape the overall structure of motivation in male violence? An initial approach notes that among male assailants the evidence on major motivations in criminal violence incidents reduces *descarga* ventings to modest proportions. Gender-rooted disputes accounted for over half (60.3 percent) the incidents, property/class violence for about a fifth (20.0 percent), and *descarga* ventings for perhaps a sixth (15.6 percent). (See Table 7.1, midway point between the restricted and amplifed models.) If one homes in specifically on male-on-male violence, the weight of *descarga* ventings increases substantially, but the rank order among major motivations remains the same. Gender-rooted disputes still accounted for nearly half (44.5 percent) the incidents, property/class disputes for about a fourth (27.8 percent), and *descarga* ventings for about a fifth (22.2 percent).

These figures only constitute a first step. They scale down the daunting mythological presence of *descarga* explosions, but they fail to specify the distinct social expressions of masculinity embedded within the broad categories of gender-rooted and *descarga* violence. The category of gender-rooted violence, for example, included not only male-centered disputes over masculine valor — explicit challenges to or assertions of male honor among men that connected only vaguely, if at all, to specific male-female social relations. The category also included incidents directly related to men's social claims in particular women or female youth. Such incidents might include, for example, cases where a wife entangled in a quarrel over gender right with her husband mobilized a rival patriarch — a father, brother, family friend, or village elder or priest — to intervene as her ally and protector. They might include sexual rivalries between men exerting claims in the same woman or youth. How did the weight of gender-rooted contestations animated by direct, tangible claims in women and female youth compare with that of conflicts driven by a prickly sense of masculine swagger and honor among men?

Similarly, the aggregate *descargas* category included not only incidents whose motives, intentionality, and social antecedents were virtually incomprehensible even to assailants and targets (accidents and nearly pure *descargas*) and in which social expressions of masculinity were either invisible or irrelevant. The amplified *descarga* category added to this core set more clearly gendered behavior among men, incidents wherein a background of masculine social bonding, honor, status, or duty framed the dynamics or context of male interaction and violence even though masculine valor as such did not figure explicitly as the issue in dispute. For example, if two men playing cards in a masculine social context of Sunday drink, conversation, and diversion fought to the point of serious injury or homicide over an aspect of the card game, but did not fight over masculinity as such, a background environment of gendered bonding, challenge, and status among men figured as a frame for the incident. A masculine setting of bonding-enmity had established the logic of social interaction, and the preservation or assertion of one's status as a man among men loomed large, even if latently or indirectly, in the confrontation. Similarly, a man who intervened to defend a brother, father, or friend in perceived danger acted on a background sense of bonding, duty, or obligation, a gendered sensibility that came into play and defined an honorable course of action even if masculine valor as such did not arise as the explicit cause of dispute. Consider a last example: a father who beat a son, or a village elder who beat a son or a commoner for "lack of respect," defended a ranked sense of gendered status. Even if masculine valor as such failed to emerge as the express issue in contention, a social background of ranked masculinity defined the meaning of order, challenge, and confrontation, the logic of respect and insubordination. How did these more indirect, background influences of male bonding, rank, and honor compare in importance to expressions of masculinity rooted in claims over specific women and female youth or in explicit challenges to masculine honor and valor among men?

Once one deconstructs the distinctive social expressions of masculinity that figured in male violence, disputes directly expressive of a touchiness about masculine honor among men cut a substantial yet less than dominant presence. In cases of violence with male assailants, fully two-thirds (66.1 percent) of the incidents expressive of masculine right or status arose in direct connection to claims in specific women or female youth. Only a seventh (14.8 percent) of the incidents focused explicitly on male honor as such in male-centered social contexts. (When such incidents invoked connections to females, they did so rhetorically, as in verbal insult of a man's absent mother in order to challenge his manhood.) Finally, the more indirect or background influences of male honor, bonding, or duty in social dynamics of violence accounted for only another fifth (19.1 percent) of masculinity incidents. Even when one homes in more narrowly on the world of male-on-male violence — a setting where assertions of manly valor as such should reach their maximum expression — male-centered disputes focused explicitly on male honor remained less than dominant. Two-fifths (39.0 percent) of the incidents expressive of masculine right or status arose in direct connection to tangible claims in specific women or female youth. Incidents tied to explicit male-centered challenges to masculine honor or valor rose in importance but nonetheless accounted for only a fourth (23.7 percent) of the incidents expressive of masculinity. Indeed, the more indirect background influence of male bonding, honor, or duty rose more sharply and accounted for nearly two-fifths (37.3 percent) of masculinity incidents. (See Table 7.2.)

Taken together, these findings illuminate the mix of truth and falsehood in cultural imagery and stereotypes of masculine violence. First, the significant presence of *descarga* ventings and male-centered altercations over masculine honor and valor, especially in male-on-male violence, clarifies how easily one may find telling anecdotes. Nearly pure *descargas* — improvised outbursts of violence, virtually random in the selection of individual targets and virtually incomprehensible within a framework of tangible motive — figured in about an eighth (12.0 percent) of all male-on-male violence incidents. (See Table 7.1; note that even the pure *descarga* figures are inflated by some accidents in the strict sense.) Explicit challenges to masculine honor and valor, within a male-centered context free of contestations with or about specific women or female youth, accounted for about another eighth (13.0 percent). (See Table 7.2.) In short, the *descarga* phenomenon and a touchiness about male honor as such did indeed prove important in men's version of popular culture. Anecdotes illustrating a violent masculine theater of *descarga* and honor abound for the student who seeks them.

Second, however, the overall pattern suggests the necessity of sociological downscaling to counteract the magnification effect of cultural commentary and stereotype. *Descargas* by strict definition and explicit male-centered challenges to manly valor together accounted for only a fourth (25.0 percent) of male-on-male incidents of violence. By contrast, violence rooted in contestation over tangible claims — gender-rooted disputes directly linked to claims in specific women or female youth (21.3 percent), and property/class disputes (25.0 percent) — accounted for nearly half (46.3 percent) of male-on-male incidents. One may, of course, construct a more amplified version of honor/ *descarga* episodes by including the altercations (20.4 percent) where social backgrounds and settings of masculine bonding and enmity framed or indirectly influenced the altercation. In these cases a sense of male honor could come into play more implicitly or indirectly; frequently, but not always, the object in dispute (for example, cheating in a card game) may also seem trivial to the outside observer, if not the participants. But even by these rather elastic criteria, the maximum plausible combined share of *descarga* and honor episodes accounted for perhaps half (45.4 percent) the male-on-male incidents and only a third (31.2 percent) of all incidents with male assailants. By contrast, dispute over tangibles — claims in females and property/class conflicts — accounted for three-fifths (61.8 percent) of incidents with male assailants. (See Table 7.3.)

Finally, and most important, these findings urge us to probe more deeply for the social logic of the masculinity expressed in violence. The standard cultural imagery and stereotypes promote a rather undifferentiated and epiphenomenal sense of violent masculinity. The explosions become outer manifestations of interior hypersensitivity and rage, a bursting forth in exaggerated swaggers of manhood and inexplicable ventings that bear little specific or rational connection to the target. Masculine violence and the sense of masculine honor violently asserted or defended become symptoms at the surface. As such they bear little meaning in their own right and require curiously little social analysis. They warrant a more psychological probing of inner wounds and solitude.

The pattern of male violence in late colonial Morelos suggests not the irrelevance of masculine honor and swagger nor the irrelevance of interior rage, but an altered context for their analysis and interpretation. The pattern suggests the necessity of a more differentiated view that sets the honor and rage episodes within a wider range of masculine expression and that opens the door to more social or relational understandings of masculinity, honor, and violence. As we have seen, expressions of violent masculinity developed in three major contexts: conflicts over tangible claims in specific women or female youth, explicit challenges to or affirmations of a male-centered sense of honor and valor, and background settings of male bonding, rank, and honor that framed the dance of masculine alliance, enmity, and violence. The first and third contexts tied the masculinities asserted in violence directly to social or relational logics: to disputes and competitions over gendered resources, that is, tangible rights in women and female youth, and to participation in networks of masculine bonding, rank, and sociability that established one's standing and voice as a man among men, but at the risk of exposure to violent confrontations. Only the second context — explicitly male-centered challenges to manly honor and valor as such — arguably tied masculinity to a more interior will or impulse to escalate disputes and irritations into all-out confrontations of manhood. For the sake of argument, let us agree to interpret *descarga* ventings as a fourth expression of violent masculinity.[11] The assumption has mainly heuristic value as a device that yields an extremely conservative (that is, understated) assessment of social or relational logics within violent masculinities. In truth, the very nature of the *descarga* incidents rendered their masculinity problematic. They were either irrelevant to the incident or relevant but invisible. But even if we interpret the *descargas* as interior masculine rage bursting forth in violence, the masculinities directly tied to social or relational logics far outweighed those arguably driven by a more interior will to challenge manhood or to otherwise vent masculine rage. Among all cases expressive of masculinity by male assailants, the socially driven share amounted to three-fourths (76.0 percent) of the group. Even in the more narrowly focused set of male-on-male violence, the socially driven share accounted for three-fifths (62.5 percent) of the cases. (See Table 7.4.)

The deeper implication is a questioning of the very premise of this finding. To accept a neat division between masculinities driven by a logic of social contestation and bonding and those driven by a logic of interior affliction and pathology is to concede too much. Given the overall preponderance of socially driven logics of masculinity in violence, is it not appropriate to ask whether explicitly male-centered honor challenges themselves constituted something more than epiphenomena of psychic affliction and hypersensitivity? In short, we must ask whether social analysis enables us to discover the shape and meaning of a positive sense of masculine honor, a socially constructed logic of gendered affirmation within a field of power relations between subaltern men and women, between subaltern men and their male counterparts, and between subaltern men and their color-class superiors. To make such a discovery would be to dissolve somewhat the distinction between social and interior logics of masculinity, to scale down the pathological interpretation of popular masculinity to still more modest proportions, and to render more understandable a certain touchiness about masculinity that sometimes escalated into violence.

The importance of the task grows when we observe that the cultural discourse that attaches the rage of wounded male honor to plebeians and non-Indians is overstated. On the one hand, *descarga* ventings figured rather modestly in violence by non-Indians and plebeians as well as Indians and peasants and proved statistically no more associated with one group than another. On the other hand, a jealously defended sense of masculine honor and status stirred violence by Indians and peasants as well as non-Indians and plebeians. Variation within that larger context underscores, moreover, that cultural commentary has tended to magnify tenuous or subtle associations into hard and fast distinctions. Among cases sparked explicitly or implicitly by male-centered notions of honor, rank, or bonding, for example, non-Indian assailants leaned more strongly toward explicit challenges to manly valor, while Indians leaned more strongly toward more implicit or background influences of masculine honor, bonding, and authority.[12]

Sociological downscaling has thrown into disarray the discourse that conflates popular masculinity with interior affliction and pathology, male violence with uncontrolled outbursts of bravado that drop the mask shielding a wounded masculinity. To be sure, near-random ventings and a will to escalate irritation and dispute into explicit challenges of manhood figured in male-on-male violence. But they figured modestly compared with disputes over tangibles and compared with more relational or socially driven expressions of masculinity. Within this context the language, theater, and obligations of masculine honor and bravado embraced Indians as well as non-Indians and peasants as well as plebeians, even if subtle differences of emphasis distinguished different characters in the larger drama. Let us turn, therefore, to the social relationships and experiences that lent meaning to popular masculinity as sociocultural resource, as something more than epiphenomenon and interior disease. For the men of late colonial Morelos, the resource mattered. One sometimes had to claim or defend it by force.

MASCULINITY AND POWER (I)

Men constructed their sense of masculinity on a field of power relations. As practice and as idea, manhood signified rights to power and citizenship within a subaltern context.[13] The cultivation and defense of manhood drew individuals into a socially constructed logic of gendered affirmation within a larger process of affirmation and degradation. This larger field of social forces established close connections between masculinity and power on several planes at once: in relations between subaltern men and their social superiors, in relations between subaltern men (or male youth) and male counterparts of similar color-class standing, and in relations between subaltern men and their wives, *amasias*, and familial dependents. Let us, for the sake of convenience, call these vertical, horizontal, and familial dimensions of the interplay between masculinity and power.

In vertical social relations the power that defined relations between subaltern men and their color-class superiors often took the form of a ranking among masculinities. On the one hand, the honor/shame codes of the colonial elite established a cultural backdrop that tended to equate masculine honor with color-class privilege. As we have seen (Chapter 2), elite codes of male honor rested on cultural displays of forcefulness, household authority, and social decorum. These displays were predicated, at least in part, on the de-meaning of inferiors. Personal forcefulness, a strength of will and sexual pos-sessiveness, accrued more readily to the man who commanded the labors, sexual services, and property of inferiors and whose demeanor of command contrasted with the deference demanded of subordinates. The aura of success-ful household rule accrued more readily to the man whose color-class privi-leges enabled him to sustain a luxurious home, to cloister daughters and wives physically and symbolically, and to establish a retinue of clients, servants, and visitors. Elite etiquette contrasted the presumed moderation and dignity of the well bred and the well mannered with the crude excesses of the poor and the barbaric.

Elite culture, in short, established a diffuse cultural claim to superior mas-culinity, a backdrop that defined poor men as inferior men. Indeed, the elite construction of a hegemonic masculinity contrasted the anarchic *descargas* of poor men — the impulsive outbursts of violence over nothing — with a more dignified elite code of masculine honor and violence. As social degenerates, poor men presumably imagined various affronts and launched into violent quarrels (*riñas*) on the spot. Honorable men of reputable color-class standing lived by a different logic. One succumbed less readily to outbursts over noth-ing, and one rarely lashed out in hot anger — only after repeated forbearance, in response to truly unacceptable provocation.[14] Moreover, a man of superior social standing did not demean himself by fighting a subordinate and thereby granting him the implied equality of a competitor. A man of high social posi-tion used his power to punish a subordinate. Punishment, not rivalry, was a response to insolence. Finally, the sense of enlightened culture by which eighteenth-century elites set themselves apart from the lower orders con-demned as outmoded and backward even dueling, the traditional method by which a socially respectable man might reclaim his honor from an adversary of similar social standing.[15]

The associations between ranked masculinities and color-class power, however, went beyond diffuse background claims. They also included more pointed, specific denigrations of subaltern manhood. The symbolism of rela-tionships between powerful men and their subaltern counterparts could place the latter in structurally female positions of personal deference and depen-dence. Such positioning included a range of situations, from deferential ap-peals for protection to the dynamics of male domestic labor. When the slave Manuel José complained in 1775 that his owner had unfairly imprisoned him in the sugar mill and generally mistreated him, a legal counselor prescribed the institutional handling accorded to wives and daughters who complained of domestic tyranny. During the legal investigation Manuel José would be given over to an honorable household entrusted with "holding him in de-posit" (*manteniendolo en calidad de depocito*). The institutional language and practice of the deposit usually referred to wives and daughters. As females and possessed persons, they required not only protection from abusive masters but ongoing supervision that sharply restricted their freedom of physical movement. The deposit assured physical surveillance and economic maintenance in a morally honorable setting. If the deposited woman or youth was poor, her temporary guardians could also demand that she contribute domestic service to the household.[16]

Domestic labor elicited similar resonances. The dynamics of male domestic labor placed subaltern men in arenas of face-to-face power whose dynamics of deference and insubordination and humiliation and punishment could easily slide into analogues of domestic relations between husbands and wives. Leading figures in the mercantile and landowning circles of Morelos, of course, had male as well as female servants and slaves staff their households and serve their tables. Colonial authorities such as judges, priests, and military commanders demanded quotas of servants and assistants (*topiles*) from the Indians and villagers in their districts, and the duties of assistants included domestic service. When a male domestic seemed insolent or otherwise neglected his duties, his superior assumed a right to rebuke, humiliate, and punish him similar to that held by a husband who faced insubordination by a wife. In 1817, for example, José Francisco of Tlayacapan, the Indian villager who served as chief assistant (*topile mayor*) to Don José María Torres Torija, the local priest, got embroiled in a controversy over the male domestic servant quota owed the priest. When José Francisco declined to clean plates and serve food to the priest and his guests — it was not his duty, he argued — Don José María reacted in a manner recognizable to many husbands and wives. According to José Francisco, the priest threw food at him, jumped on him threateningly, pulled his hair, whipped him, and "mistreated me in front of all the Ladies who were eating." To the priest and his defenders, who disputed the details but not the fact of a conflict followed by a whipping, the punishment was a rightful and moderate response to José Francisco's "lack of respect."[17] The languages of accusation and justification strikingly evoke those found in more obviously gendered disputes between husbands and wives and between family elders and youth.

Beyond such symbolic parallels and resonances, men of color-class superiority used explicit verbal taunting and ritual humiliation to proclaim the poor and the colonized closer to feminine violation and the privileged closer to masculine dominance. Don Rafael Ortíz de Valladares, deputy judge of Totolapa and probably an *hacendado*, confronted Don Asencio de la Cruz Techalco, the Indian *gobernador* of Totolapa, over the two men's conflicting claims in Paulino Antonio Tepeatlaco, a Totolapa villager in the employ of Ortíz. According to an Indian witness, Ortíz reminded his rival of their respective places by conjoining power with the threat of humiliated manhood.

Unless the Indian *gobernador* relented, Ortíz would not only to strip him of his post as *gobernador*. In addition, "his pants would be taken off and he'd carry them in his hand so that he'd be given fifty lashes."[18] Whether the warning was apocryphal matters less than its cultural plausibility or resonance. Indian villagers understood full well that stripping grown men and whipping them on their posteriors not only inflicted physical pain. It also reduced them to the equivalents of weak and exposed dependents: children and women, naked and helpless before the punishing father-patriarch.[19] Indeed, village punishment of miscreants by Indian officials and elders sometimes blended gendered humiliation and whippings in similar fashion.[20]

A less elaborately ritualized form of insult hurled slurs upon the manhood of a subordinate — epithets that might be considered "fighting words" among equals but to which effective reply was difficult among unequals. To force the subordinate man to submit silently to the taunt gave it greater force. In 1780 an apparent legal resolution of a water dispute between Don Miguel Ascarte of Hacienda Nuestra Señora de Guadalupe and the villagers of Tetelpan broke down. When two of Don Miguel's water guards confronted Manuel Antonio, a villager watering his *milpa*, they affirmed their superior masculinity: "Hey, son of a cuckold, stop this water." An effective reply to the taunt was unrealistic. The two men were on horseback and had the power of the hacienda behind them. Manuel Antonio ignored the slur, proceeded with the watering, and suffered a beating anyway.[21] Among equals, to fail to respond to sexualized insults — *cabrón, pendejo, cornudo, carajo,* or *hijo de puta* — could have deleterious consequences. (The insults, familiar to any Spanish speaker, generally equated the man with a cuckold, referred to genitalia, or insulted his mother's honor.) Among social equals the failure of nerve signified weakness and disadvantage as a man among men. Among social unequals, however, responding in kind or with a physical attack could invite disaster.[22]

The ultimate equation of color-class weakness and masculine weakness occurred, however, when powerful men managed to "take" women and daughters, the gendered property of subaltern men, without fear of punishment or vengeance. Such takings took several forms. When a peasant or Indian man escaped before a superior could confront or imprison him, for example, a standard device to force his return was to humiliate the fugitive's wife by hitting or jailing her.[23]

The most graphic takings of women were sexual. When social distances were great, the taking might be achieved through powers of intimidation or persuasion directly linked to color-class power. In effect, a man of power dared the subaltern woman he cornered to resist him and dared her subaltern mate (if she had one) to resist him, in full knowledge that the power advantage discouraged open defiance. Consider, for example, Guillermo Bilbao's plea for mercy after he killed Don Miguel López and took refuge in a church in 1783. López, the administrator of Hacienda Nuestra Señora de Guadalupe, had indebted Guillermo Bilbao, who worked on the hacienda, and had secretly begun an affair with Guillermo's wife (whose name remained unmentioned in the document). When the liaison soured and she resisted him, López took vengeance by entangling his *amasia* in legal accusations that led to her imprisonment. She was seized while serving her husband supper. Guillermo, now apprised of the background to his wife's troubles, sought to mobilize legal assistance on her behalf, but the effort made no practical difference. When his wife escaped and managed to rejoin him, Guillermo himself was beaten and arrested.[24]

Subaltern men and women would have understood Guillermo Bilbao's predicament. A man of high rank who set his eyes on cornering a woman of inferior color-class standing held an enormous arsenal of resources. He might entangle opponents in legal troubles, manipulate labor corvées that exposed women as domestics or sent away their men, create wedges by bribing or intimidating relatives and acquaintances, and proceed with the knowledge that the superior honor and reputation conferred on men of high rank implied a certain shielding from criminal prosecution for rape or other violence charged by degraded subaltern accusers. A man of humble means who dared to compete on a sexual terrain with clear color-class superiors faced enormous disadvantage and might even contend with bands of men hired to beat or kill him.[25]

For sexually assaulted women, of course, the question of violence was more direct and immediately painful, unavoidably built into the confrontation with her assailant. A preponderant power advantage did not always obviate open resistance, fighting, beating, or life-threatening intimidation before or during the act of sexual violence. Yet assaulted women also understood the ways a preponderant power advantage could wear down the will to resist openly and could elicit a tacit yet false consent. A cynical game of sexualized power, when it conjoined bribes, gifts, and empty promises with intimidation and threat, could coerce false appearances and provoke painful ambiguity even in the mind of the assaulted. Consider the unsure words of María Nicolasa Alles, when she complained in 1779 that Don Martín Gil had raped her: "Perhaps what motivated me to do it, was not so much what [had been] promised, as the fear I had of the said gentleman."[26] Perhaps indeed!

When social distances were smaller, the taking of women operated less as an implicit dare to resist, a knowledge that overwhelming superiority allowed for almost silent intimidation effects, and more as explicit social ridicule. The violence of rape merged with the theater of power and emasculation within popular culture; sexual assault reaffirmed and widened color-class distinctions among relatively humble and powerless folk. In 1799, for example, three young single men from Yecapixtla were relaxing at the home of an Indian widow who sold *aguardiente* when four Indian peasants from Guasulco walked in. The Indians — three men and a woman — were on their return trip to Guasulco after selling fruit in Totolapa. The Indians wanted to buy some *aguardiente*. The widow refused the request, presumably because the visitors seemed fairly intoxicated already, and the Indians left. The three men from Yecapixtla belonged to a stratum of folk superior to Indian peasant villagers, yet not all that superior. The trio was of white to mestizo coloration (one was white, another *castizo*, the third mestizo) and engaged in fairly humble work (one was a cowboy, another a muleteer, the third a laborer on local haciendas). After the Indians left, one of the men said, "Hombres, let's go take away from these indios [that is, the men] that india they're taking along, and we'll make fun of her." (The *burlar* verb they used literally refers to making fun of someone by acts of ridicule or scoffery. When used with reference to women, *burlar* was often both a euphemism for rape and a signifier that rape demonstrated the power of men to "have fun" at someone else's expense.) Rape outside of family circles — let us recall that about half the rapes within our case set occurred among primary relations — affirmed not only the power of men over women but a ranked social positioning among men and their respective color-class groups. The latter aspect comes through in the comment by two of the assaulting men that the decision came immediately after the Indians had uttered a curse or indecency (*desvergüenza*) when refused a drink. It was as if the trio had to remind the Indians that their subordinate position precluded such insolence. The trio attacked the Indians on the road, possibly to rob them as well as rape the woman, but mainly to reaffirm their superior power. When one Indian suffered a serious wound by a rock thrown at the head, the trio had had enough. The three young men retreated without consummating the rape and without having taken much money or goods. The "fun" had gotten too serious, even in their own eyes.[27]

The ethnic and class coloration of the incident is significant. A relatively whiter stratum of agriculturalists, livestock owners, respectable plebeians (artisans, muleteers, and petty traders), and low-level supervisors or managers developed a complex relationship with the darker and more Indian commoners who comprised the majority of the laboring population on the haciendas and in the villages. On the one hand, the whiter group bore the markings of superiority: their ethnic coloration leaned toward a white-*castizo*-mestizo blend, a *gente de razón* stratum that contrasted with the more Indian and dark mestizo (that is, more black) groups; their political presence tended to concentrate in the more important *cabecera* villages and in the interstitial *ranchero* zones between villages and haciendas, rather than the *sujeto* villages; and they held advantages as middle-level employees on haciendas, as proprietors of independent ranchos, or as an upper group of landed peasants within an internally differentiated peasantry. On the other hand, the necessities of survival and the inclusionary construction of peasant community in Morelos induced social alliances, political collaborations, and proximities of lifestyle that closed social distances. The whiter stratum held access to land and waters by acquiring practical membership in communities that claimed historic land rights as Indian villages, by renting land and water rights from villagers, and by joining darker and more Indian villages in struggles against expansive haciendas. All of this implied collaboration, the construction of a multiethnic peasantry capable of withstanding the haciendas. The networks of kinship, reciprocity, and landholding; of community service, ritual, and sociability; and of political alliance and conflict did not always line up neatly with hierarchical distinctions between whiter *gente de razón* groups and darker, more Indian and mulatto groups.[28]

Social rank within a context of social proximity, color-class distinction within a context of common subordination to a whiter land-owning elite, and social rivalry within a context of mutual dependence—the mix could turn volatile. Sometimes the explosions took the form of political factionalism or land disputes. Sometimes, however, the explosions took the form of a graphic display of superior masculinity by youthful males of the *castizo* stratum. (*Castizo* is used here as a metaphor for a group considered near-white when compared with Indians, blacks, mulattoes, and dark mestizos, yet considered tainted or dark white when compared with whites of wealth and pure Spanish descent.) The taking of women as open ridicule, an almost theatrical reaffirmation of modest distinctions within popular culture, contrasted with the taking of women as color-class privilege, a manifestation of preponderant power and unquestioned superiority.

MASCULINITY AND POWER (II)

The foregoing discussion underscores the seriousness of gendered ranking among men within a vastly unequal and polarized color-class order. A process of social affirmation and degradation buttressed the power, honor, and masculinity of elite men by defining superior masculinity in terms most accessible to elites, by placing subaltern men in structural positions of femininity vis-à-vis their superiors, and by subjecting subaltern men to open taunts of their manhood. Most graphically and tangibly, privileged men affirmed a superior masculinity by taking or abusing the women of men too weak to protect female relatives and property. What gave such insults added force was precisely the preponderance of power that made effective reply difficult, that encouraged silent swallowings of humiliation. We ought not to underestimate or trivialize the importance of these vertical dynamics of masculine rank and humiliation. They mattered to subaltern men, and they were experienced not only in relationships of great social distance, as impositions upon popular culture, but also in relationships of smaller social distance, as impositions more proximate to and even within popular culture.

To assume that subaltern men simply received, endured, or internalized vertical ideologies of masculine rank—an equation of social superiority and masculine superiority—however, is to slip into a trap. It is to slip into the discourse of humiliated psyches and profoundly wounded manhood that erupt in aimless, nearly random outbursts of violence and bravado. It is to slip into the interpretation of elite pretense and appropriation as social action unbounded by social response, as social design drawn upon a blank slate. It is to slip into a vision that equates relative powerlessness with nearly total victimization. To demonstrate the seriousness of gendered ranking and humiliation does not, after all, demonstrate their uncontested acceptance and does not demonstrate that response took mainly the form of explosive ventings at near-random targets during moments of disinhibition.

Although it is true that subaltern men experienced vertical dynamics of gendered humiliation in relations with men of superior color-class power, it is also true that subaltern men constructed powerful counterpoints and challenges to humiliation. They forged a positive sense of manhood that belied the degradations imposed by power; they cultivated a sense of masculine right, power, and dignity within a subaltern context. One discerns these counterpoints on all three planes of daily life—the vertical, the horizontal, and the familial—where masculinity and power connected.

Even in vertical social contexts marked by sharp inequalities of power, subaltern men constructed a sense of manly courage or valor (*valentía* or *hombría*) in the face of social disadvantage. Subaltern men could not compete with elite men on a terrain of manliness defined by society's privileged men. A habit of command that merged into an expansive sexual possessiveness; an aura of household authority tied to lavish economic consumption, enclosure of female dependents (through architecture, dress, and human accompaniment), and support of a retinue of dependents; and a respect for station and decorum tied to a sense of high rank and descent—these constructions of manly honor would always place subaltern men in a comparatively degraded light. What subaltern men could do in vertical contexts, however, was redefine manliness on the terrain of personal courage. Manly courage signified not the ability to mimic superiors or to overturn obvious power advantages. It signified, rather, the physical and psychological will to stand up to abuse rather than cower before it. Avoiding a demeanor of visible fear or intimidation when taunted or otherwise abused by a superior; responding to humiliation not by swallowing it once and for all but by challenging the violators' right to abuse, either on the spot or in subsequent legal and institutional entanglements; developing a reputation for standing up that shaded into the suspicion that one *might* prove capable of angry vengeance, even against a superior, if provoked too far — these actions defined a terrain of manliness that constituted a counterpoint to humiliation. Indeed, on the terrain of personal courage in the face of adversity and challenge, subaltern men could prove superior to those whose color-class advantages left their mettle untested.[29]

It is a striking aspect of the historical records of vertical ranking among men that even the episodes of humiliation bore witness to the counterpoint of standing up. Consider the examples of explicit humiliation cited earlier. José Francisco, the Indian church assistant rebuked and punished like a wife or female domestic servant, had first refused — before guests — his priest's demand for table service. Attacked for his insolence, José Francisco responded with a lawsuit. Don Asencio de la Cruz Techalco, the Indian *gobernador* warned to concede in a conflict with an *hacendado*, lest the latter strip and whip him, refused to back down. He responded with a lawsuit, claimed that his opponent failed to treat him with the honor and regard befitting an Indian *gobernador*, and petitioned for the *hacendado*'s exile from village environs. Manuel Antonio, the villager cursed, threatened, and beaten in a dispute with the water supervisors of a neighboring hacienda, failed to let the initial curse and threat stop him from proceeding with his work. After the beating, he mobilized a criminal complaint sponsored by the Indian *gobernador* and political officials of his village. Guillermo Bilbao, whose wife was first taken from him by the silent persuasion or intimidation of a hacienda administrator, then vengefully imprisoned for resisting the liaison, first sought legal recourse, then murdered his tormentor.[30]

To put the matter more theoretically, the dynamics of hegemonic masculinity often seemed to elicit dynamics of counterhegemonic masculinity.[31] To stand up courageously by refusing to manifest visible fear, by refusing to concede a superior's right to abuse, or by refusing to concede even one's own right to anger upon provocation did not do away with intimidation, abuse, or provocation backed by power. But such stances did build self-legitimating counterpoints to masculine humiliation. We need not idealize such counterpoints to appreciate their significance as a reply to vertical ideologies of empowerment and emasculation. At the extreme, counterpoints and inversions could mobilize a gendered violence as raw and abusive as that heaped on subalterns. In 1791, for example, a political uproar over labor quotas and fees demanded by Tepoztlán's priest split the local power group. One group of Indian notables and authorities allied with the priest; this group merged into the multiracial power groups of a colonial society. Another, more dissident faction championed the movement to roll back the service and tributary quotas imposed on commoners and to force Indians such as Pedro Alcántara Velasco, a literate Indian notable (*indio principal*), to back off from alliances with the priest. When a band of dissidents, including Indian officials and *viejos*, showed up at Pedro Alcántara's home on November 7, presumably to arrest or threaten him, he had already escaped. The dissidents demonstrated their determination to invert the local power pyramid by using the time-honored technique of humiliating the unprotected female property of powerless men. They beat Pedro Alcántara's wife, María Teresa de Rojas, dragged her to the Tepoztlán jail, and probably had José Ortíz Tlanepantla, a former *gobernador*, rape her.[32]

Subaltern men also constructed their positive sense of masculine right, power, and dignity in what we have called familial and horizontal social contexts. In vertical social contexts the contrapuntal interplays of masculinity and power at best yielded a standoff, a preservation of dignity and self-esteem within a structure of power that assigned subaltern men positions of powerlessness and degradation. In familial and horizontal arenas, subaltern masculinity could signify a fuller sense of empowerment or citizenship as a man among men (albeit a man who was poor and relatively powerless in the larger field of power).

The familial plane upon which masculinity and power intersected has largely been elucidated (see Chapters 3–6). Subaltern men constructed a vision and practice of manhood bound up with the right of men to rule women and youth: the right to impose upon a wife absolute conceptions of male prerogative, particularly if she judged the husband-patriarch negligent or abusive; the right to treat an *amasia* as a quasi-wife and permanent sexual possession, should the *amasio* so desire, even if she withheld her consent; the right to oversee and transact a daughter's marital-sexual destiny, even if she judged herself an abused familial servant in need of escape; the right to demand that a male youth defer, before the age of manly independence, to the counsel and labor needs of his elders. As we have seen, these claims met with resistance, sometimes subtle, sometimes open, in the practice of everyday life. The world of male-female relations was in truth a world of contested patriarchal pacts. Notwithstanding the skirmishes and battles, however, husbands, *amasios*, and fathers could look to familial and quasi-familial arenas of male life to build a sense of masculine legitimacy and competence. The strategies might vary. A man might largely comply with female expectations of him and thereby acquire the consent that buttressed his legitimacy as a domestic ruler. He might choose not to take open notice of most female assertions and initiatives, so long as they did not violate appearances, and thereby secure a formal, somewhat deceptive, deference to male rule. He might adopt a belligerent style that punished alleged infractions severely and violently and thereby affirm who controlled whom. He might even focus struggles for manly empowerment selectively — on the labor of sons or the sexual destinies of daughters, or on the all-around duties of a wife or the sexualized possession of an *amasia*. Whatever the strategy or blend of strategies, a man could look to his relationship of rule with female and youthful Others to build a sense of masculine legitimacy.[33]

We need not overstate the point. Given the pervasiveness of gender conflicts in male-female relations, the assertion of manly power in a familial arena yielded both tarnish and legitimacy. The aura of male rule might require a certain dose of self-deception. Beyond a certain point, moreover, the regularity and intensity of gender conflicts not only tarnished the aura of male rule but destroyed it. Short of this extreme, however, even a tarnished legitimacy mattered, and women evinced a certain awareness that it mattered. Even in instances of bitter gender dispute, women often avoided blunt verbal challenges to manhood as such. They understood that the weapon was both strong and dangerous, sometimes more effective and safe if deployed obliquely.[34] Gender struggle could prove compatible with a positive, if blemished, sense of masculine empowerment and legitimacy.

It was in the company of men of similar color-class standing that subaltern males built up their strongest affirmations of masculinity. In this horizontal arena men created cultural spaces to affirm their valor and competence, their honor and importance as men, and they could do so without running up against the degradations imposed by color-class domination or the tarnish imposed by female and familial resistance.[35] To be sure, the horizontal arena was not pure, not sealed off entirely from vertical or familial dynamics of masculinity and power. Differences of wealth and color, age and local influence, or personal reputation and history injected vertical elements into the equation of male sociability. In addition, subaltern men developed their gendered consciousness and solidarities in part by allusion to the troubles inflicted on them by women and the rich. Most important, and as we shall explore, the horizontal arena of male interactions yielded its own complicating impositions. It brought forth among men a certain dialectic of risk: dynamics of bonding and enmity, challenge and response, honor and humiliation. Sociability could give way to violence; political citizenship could spill into severe factionalism. Nonetheless, it was with counterparts of similar color-class standing that a man experienced socially ratified empowerment, a sense of citizenship and weight as a man among men.

Several pathways ratified subaltern masculinity and empowerment in these horizontal contexts. The path of formal politics constructed community voice and stewardship as an arena of male leadership, discussion, and apprenticeship. The connections between gender culture and political culture constitute a vast and complex topic that would take us far afield. We must therefore postpone a thorough analysis of gender and community politics (see Chapter 8). Suffice it to say, at this juncture, that except at moments of outright crisis and riot, subaltern men defined community voice and politics as a male terrain and that they employed thoroughly patriarchal metaphors to describe the formal institutions of local politics: relations of leadership and authority, service and apprenticeship, and assembly and approval. The net result was an affirmation of citizenship, albeit a subordinate form of citizenship within the larger society, that empowered men. Subaltern patriarchs acted as the formal, institutionalized custodians of family and community.

A second path, the path of gendered spectacle, constructed metaphorical dramas of masculine conquest and revindication. In part because the colonial authorities officially disdained subaltern versions of these spectacles (even if some unofficially attended or enjoyed them), in part because the festivals led to comparatively few homicides or other criminal violence cases, the evidence on these spectacles is too thin to permit a "thick description" of them. But we do know that they mattered: cockfights and an Indian brand of bullfighting had become popular in a number of Morelos pueblos by the late colonial period.[36] The symbolism of both dramas ratified masculinity and power. The man whose rooster won the cockfight, the man whose bird risked all and lost, and the spectators and bettors who surrounded surrogate struggle to the death with comment, joke, debate, and significance all bore witness to the sense that men led embattled lives and that they knew how to face up to the gamble and challenge of this hard destiny. The bulls who constituted symbols of virility and Spanish power yet succumbed to the Indians who rode, taunted, or killed them served as symbolic vehicles of masculine empowerment. The men who mounted or challenged a bull risked their manhood and took on a position that brought them closer to symbolic femininity. Whatever their initial swagger or the desired outcome, the men were vulnerable to danger and humiliation by a virile bull. (Tlayacapan villagers in the twentieth century referred to the rider as the bull's *novia* and provoked the bull by taunting its masculinity.) By the end, if all went well, the challengers had refortified their manhood. They had summoned the physical and mental will to dominate and feminize the bull, to incorporate its masculinity—its virility and power— into themselves.[37]

Of course spectacles such as subaltern cockfights and bullfights often drew together men of somewhat different strata — *castizo* peasants and plebeians as well as their darker counterparts, relatively privileged local notables and intermediaries as well as poor peasants and commoners. But the arena of male spectacle could exert a certain equalizing influence. Even at the more glamorous versions of cockfight spectacles — staged with fanfare as a major social event, attended by both genders, and complete with special boxes and viewing sections for the rich and powerful — one could sometimes observe a bit of this equalizing influence. In 1840 Frances Calderón witnessed an early republican version of the phenomenon when the president of Mexico attended a major cockfight: "The gratifying spectacle may not infrequently be seen, of the president leaning from his box in the *plaza de gallos* [cockfight arena], and betting upon a cock, with a coatless, bootless, hatless, and probably worthless ragamuffin in the pit."[38] The social lines between commoner and high elite were probably more rigidly demarcated, even at major cockfight spectacles, in the late colonial period. But in subaltern versions of masculine spectacle, where social distances were smaller to begin with, the equalizing effect was more pronounced, the style of interaction and bonding more horizontal.[39]

A third path toward horizontal ratifications of subaltern masculinity and power drew men into the practice of informal male sociability. This was the culture of masculine play—gatherings of men for a camaraderie laced by competition or innuendo, a game of masculine bonding that acknowledged the reality of rivalry and insult. Cockfights, in this sense, constituted but one instance of a larger theater of masculine bonding and competition. Gatherings of men for drink and comment, games and sport, and friendship and quarrel patterned much of the rhythm of daily life. One saw such clusterings of men even within large and relatively formal events with a mixed-gender flavor: the major *fandangos* and parties given to celebrate key moments (weddings, for instance) in a family's life cycle, or the annual round of fiestas, fairs, and processions that marked the cycle of community life. A virtually all-male ambiance often prevailed in many informal spaces: at small *fandangos* and parties organized among friends on the spur of the moment, in popular drinking spots (whether an informal bar run out of a widow's home or a more established tavern) where men gathered to pass the time and share some drink, or in the customary practice of men meeting their counterparts for Sunday diversions. Sunday was usually payday (*día de raya*) and market day (*día de tianguis*) on the larger haciendas, and it was also a day when people clustered for mass, *tianguis,* and diversion in many villages.[40]

Masculine sociability followed a course different from the female pattern of background conversations pursued amidst female work such as washing, water gathering, or petty vending. For men the context of sociability was more often a diversionary release, a time-out from work and drudgery. The process of gendered bonding resembled not so much a running commentary on gendered life as an enactment of it. To be sure, verbal comment on male life and troubles—whether with women, local rivals, the rich, or other villages or haciendas—spiced masculine encounters. But the emphasis lay elsewhere, on the contrapuntal play of a masculine solidarity tinged by rivalry, a somewhat competitive bonding that seemed to capture the meaning of masculine life and challenge. On the one hand, the entire gathering amounted to a kind of declaration of masculine solidarity. Reciprocal invitations to drink together; the joining together in song or card games; the comments about people, enemies, and events; and the premise that men needed to seek diversion from the troubles of work and family all promoted a shared sense of masculine right and experience. On the other hand, men often expressed this sense of solidarity through the medium of competition and challenge. To refuse an invitation to drink could amount to an insulting declaration of superiority or hostility; if

The World of Male Peasant Violence : 173

one avoided an initial affront, deciding when and how to stop the cycle of reciprocal invitations could pose similar issues of diplomacy. (Recall Buñuel's injunction: "It's better to drink the tenth glass.") Joining together in song and music could turn into contests over who controlled the guitar. Card games had winners and losers; monetary stakes of two or three reales risked a day's wage for a field laborer. Verbal commentary on masculine life and prowess often took the form of *chanzas* and *albures*, a spiral of competitive jokes, playful double meanings, and (often sexualized) innuendo that questioned the competence of one's counterpart.

Finally, when men gathered in informal spaces of sociability and diversion, they took up the challenge of the unknown. Strangers and travelers from rival communities or haciendas as well as local friends and acquaintances might stop in a bar for a drink, join a Sunday card game at a hacienda's *tianguis*, or step into a bout of verbal sparring at a noisy *fandango*. Under these circumstances the play of masculine camaraderie and competition could sometimes take a volatile turn, a confrontational insult of manhood. Even if strangers or external enemies did not mix in, local hierarchies and animosities might affect the atmosphere. The mingling of *castizo* peasants and plebeians with more Indian or mulatto strata, for example, could inject vertical dynamics of power and resentment into a socially equalizing atmosphere of release and jousting masculinities. The mix could turn volatile, and the diversion of jousting masculinities among peers could become a drama of social domination and ranked masculinities. The appearance of local sexual rivals or other personal enemies brought similar dangers. Finally, even if strangers and external enemies and local hierarchies and animosities did not intrude, friends could get carried away or careless or become confused about the seriousness or frivolity of a challenge. In an atmosphere that blended masculine camaraderie, jousting, and escalations assisted and justified by drink and fun, friends might inadvertently cross the line between the somewhat controlled play of solidarity and provocation among friends and a more serious confrontation of masculine prowess.[41]

This was a recipe for ambiguity, a culture of sociability tinged by challenge and risk. The records of criminal violence by definition lean toward the moments when the play of masculine bonding and competition crossed thresholds of accident, misunderstanding, or deadly escalation. They therefore exaggerate and dramatize the physical risk embedded in informal sociability. Nonetheless, they illustrate usefully the ambiguities that crept into masculine play and sociability. Of course, when masculine play and sociability mixed with established hostilities (the entry of men from a rival village, hacienda, or political faction; men of somewhat distinct socioethnic standing; or local sex rivals or family enemies), the script could turn readily to more aggressive and violent assaults.[42] But even among friends the ambiguities of male play and sociability are striking. Examples abound and extend from hacienda settings with a clear mulatto flavor, to village scenarios with a more Indian flavor, to more interstitial and mixed settings marked by the presence of plebeians as well as peasants, *rancheros* as well as villagers and hacienda laborers, light as well as dark ethnic strata.[43]

Consider several examples. Somewhat playful *chanzas* and challenges might take a turn toward serious insult and provocation. On Hacienda San Gabriel in 1799 José Eusebio Serna, a mulatto servant from a neighboring hacienda, joined his friend Aparicio Antonio, a field laborer, at a local *fandango*. Verbal play and a loosening justified by drink blended into outright hostility and hitting. The confrontation took a deadly turn when José Eusebio took out a knife — simply to fend off with light pricks and cuts, he claimed later, the blows of an aggressive friend who failed to stop his own forward physical movement. José Eusebio obviously reconstructed the ambiguities in the manner that best diminished his culpability. But the ambiguities of male play rendered this reconstruction plausible, and none of the witnesses presented an alternate scenario.

Similar accidents of misunderstanding and escalation could mar parties among Indian villagers. An evening in Cuentepec that began with a friendly invitation to a *fandango* in honor of a wedding ended with tussles over a guitar, verbal insults, and a homicidal chase of the guests with words ("stop, *carajos*"), stones, and knives.

Declarations of masculine valor sometimes dismissed as harmless venting and fun might turn unexpectedly into a serious invitation to risk one's manhood in a fight. The content of such declarations were not terribly ambiguous: "If they're men they should step outside," boasted an Indian peasant from Cuernavaca; "Tonight we've got to spurt blood," spouted a mulatto tenant on Hacienda del Puente. The comments were made at parties, in the company of friends who might be presumed to deflect the challenge and to understand that the intentions of verbal provocations amidst fun and drink were more ambiguous than their literal content. The social contexts differed notably from those of cases where a man clearly itched for a fight and would stop at nothing until he got it. "You're an *alcahuete* [cuckold, go-between]"; "I'll be shitting on you"; "You stick your neck out for this *alcahuete*, I've got to shit on the both of you"; "The small switch is for women, the big stick for men," went one string of determined provocations. The problem was that even among friends the distinctions of context did not always end up as clearly as they had begun. Something could go wrong, the ambiguities of manly boasting could take friends, even, down the path toward homicide.

The ambiguities that turned play into quarrel and quarrel into violence made it possible for men and youth to declare that they had long been friends and that a violent episode between them neither destroyed the friendship nor left behind a lingering rancor.[44]

The ambiguities of male verbal play and boasting, in short, could at times breed cultural confusion. A certain similarity of style marked both argument leading to serious violence and a more controlled play at masculine insult and challenge tempered by tacit restraint. The similarity of style enabled men to incorporate and neutralize a sense of intramasculine rivalry by transmuting it into more playful teasing, competition, and challenge — that is, masculine sociability and bonding. But similarity might also induce a mistaken reading of cultural signals. On Hacienda Casasano in 1803 Miguel Carrales, a resident mestizo peddler, quarreled with Miguel Gerónimo Treque, a mulatto laborer in the sugar mill, over a debt of six reales. As the quarrel escalated, Miguel Gerónimo hurled insulting words at Miguel Carrales, and the latter exposed his knife. But Miguel Carrales then put away the knife, as if signaling a de-escalation. When he subsequently approached Miguel Gerónimo to say that he would disembowel him, his "smiling good cheer" convinced one Indian that the threat "would of course be in jest."[45] But jest it was not. Did Miguel Gerónimo also misread his adversary just before the fatal assault?

The paths toward horizontal ratifications of subaltern masculinity and power were multiple. They included not only the construction of formal politics and community voice as a male arena and not only the staging of metaphorical spectacles of masculine valor, but also the bonding derived from a culture of masculine play. This was a culture of play tinged by jousting and risk, a solidarity achieved in part through competition. The entire process of informal masculine gathering amounted to a dramatic enactment, albeit one refracted by the context of diversion and companionship, of the meaning of subaltern masculinity. The act of coming together with some regularity for diversionary drink and music, songs and games, and jokes and comments expressed the sense that male life was hard and embattled, filled with provocations, frustrations, and challenges. Diversionary release, a time-out from the worlds of work, family, and social dominance, was both a masculine necessity and a right. The content of song, joke, innuendo, and comment served as a reminder of the adversities to which men returned after their time-outs. The enactment of camaraderie through the medium of competition, a kind of jousting of masculinities, signified that the afflictions of male life included not only humiliations by the rich and the powerful and not only resistance or betrayal by women and relatives, but also rivalry — including sexual rivalry — with one's counterparts and friends. At the same time the transmutation of intramasculine rivalry into a playful format converted the challenges of life into laughter and shared experience and signified that men could face up to the gambles and hardships of masculine life, including its undercurrent of violence. Indeed, the will to enter and survive social spaces tinged by some risk—the possibility that camaraderie among friends might take an ugly turn, that outsiders or enemies might inject hostility and danger, or that local drunkards and antisocial braggarts might show up itching for a fight—reinforced the sense of manly competence. In horizontal arenas, challenge and complication did not necessarily tarnish manhood. On the contrary, skilled handling of the dialectic of risk enhanced one's empowerment, one's status as a man among men.[46]

THE SOCIAL LOGIC OF SUBALTERN MASCULINITY: AN INTERPRETATION

As we have seen, in each of the arenas where masculinity and power intersected—the vertical, the familial, and the horizontal—subaltern men constructed affirmative visions of their manhood, declarations of masculine valor, right, and citizenship within a subaltern context. How might we interpret a social logic of popular masculinity evident in all these arenas?

For subaltern men successful manhood implied competence and courage amidst adversity. Adversity, more than the truism that life has its setbacks, constituted a defining condition: the embattled life confronted by subaltern men in almost every social arena. The vertical lines of power subjected them to economic hardships and extortions and to a string of provocations. The familial arena of power presented them with contestations of patriarchal authority that tarnished, challenged, and sometimes even destroyed the facade and privileges of domestic authority. Relations with male counterparts of similar color-class standing brought its own set of challenges. (1) The horizontal arena of male popular culture was relatively rather than purely horizontal. It intersected with dynamics of dominance, deference, and ranked masculinities within popular culture, between communities, between barrios within a community, between social networks of distinct ethnic coloration or economic resources, between social notables and commoners, and between elders and juniors. (2) Even within the equalizing atmosphere of informal sociability, male play and diversion often developed a competitive idiom, and sometimes its dialectic of risk turned serious and violent. (3) Disputes over tangible resources sparked conflicts between men of similar color-class standing. These resources included not only economic matters such as property, labor, and debt but also gender holdings—wives, amasias, and daughters. The latter mattered. Gender holdings conferred property and privilege—rights of sexual possession and transaction, claims in the labor of women and family juniors, and respectable standing in the world of male politics and community—even upon poor men of dark ethnic coloration. In male-on-male violence sparked by disputes over tangibles, conflicts connected to male-female rights and claims accounted for a share nearly as large (21.3 percent of all male-on-male cases) as conflicts rooted in property/class claims (25.0 percent). The sexualized undercurrent to male verbal play was in this sense far from gratuitous. (See Table 7.3.)

Men of similar color-class standing — not only relatives embroiled in a familial power struggle and not only strangers and outsiders who made ready targets, but also the friends and acquaintances who made up a man's circle of secondary relations — had good reason to consider themselves potential rivals as well as allies. Let us recall the striking gender contrast in the social bonds between assailants and targets of violence. (See Chapter 3 and Table 3.11.) For women, compared with men, primary relations presented more danger than secondary or tertiary relations; the overwhelming bulk (63.3 percent) of assaults derived from primary relations. For men, compared with women, the world of secondary and tertiary relations presented more physical risk; the overwhelming bulk of assaults (66.2 percent) derived from secondary relations. In secondary relations cases, moreover, the odds that male targets suffered homicidal rather than nonhomicidal violence amounted to fourteen (14.2) times the odds for women. (See Table 7.5.) Primary relations cases, by contrast, failed to yield statistically significant variations between the risk of homicide and the gender of the target.

The premise of adversity, then, was not delusionary. The vertical, familial, and horizontal arenas of subaltern male life all posed their challenges. What constituted successful manhood was not simple resignation to adversity or suppressed rage followed by inexplicable outbursts, but the competence and courage with which a man faced his challenges. As a subaltern subjected to superiors, a man sought to summon the physical and psychological will to stand up to abuse by avoiding manifest fear and by challenging the right to abuse during or after the fact. As a ruler of women (a wife, the occasional *amasia*, and daughters) and of sons, a man sought to contain the potential for resistance and insubordination. He might even seek a measure of legitimacy as an economic provider by demonstrating resourcefulness and determination despite the vagaries of poverty and agriculture. As a man among men, a man sought to negotiate the formal maze of community responsibility, rank, and politics as well as the more informal pathways of male spectacle and sociability with a skill that demonstrated his right to a place among subaltern citizens and their politics.

Subaltern men could not live up to these attributes with perfection. Life and people presented too many obstacles. Precisely for this reason the sense of *valentía* — courage and forcefulness in the face of challenge — was the inescapable corollary of manly competence (*habilidad, aptitud*). But these attributes, even if imperfectly attained, mattered. They defined a positive standard of honorable manhood, the means by which a sense of competence and empowerment might be achieved, and a gender contrast that served to legitimate privilege and subordination among the poor and the relatively powerless. Men, as human types, presumably held the competence and courage to face life's adversities and to do what was necessary. Left to their own devices, women presumably tended toward weakness and moral betrayal — in a word, incompetence — when challenged.

Competence, courage, adversity: their convergence goes far in defining the social logic and content of honorable manhood for subaltern men. Men could not achieve this convergence except by entering into relational practices: logics of power, challenge, and alliance they could not fully control. The wives, *amasias*, and family juniors who made up a circle of familial and quasi-familial subordinates; the high elites, local notables and intermediaries, and family and community elders who constituted a world of superiors in a system of ranked masculinities; and the acquaintances, rivals, and strangers who comprised an arena of peers, at once potential allies and competitors — these figures brought their own needs and agendas to relations with subaltern men and supplied the social logics that both challenged and affirmed masculine competence, courage, and right.

Precisely because an affirmative vision of masculinity justified power, privilege, and respectability within the gendered world of the subaltern, moreover, the social content of honorable masculinity was not at all trivial, not quite intangible.[4] Earlier (Tables 7.3, 7.4) we contrasted violent conflicts over male-centered honor as such with conflicts driven by tangibles and with conflicts driven by a social rather than interior logic of masculinity. For the sake of argument we proceeded conservatively by treating disputes over male-centered honor as indicators of an interior impulse to self-destructive escalation — an outburst detached from specific tangible claims or assailant/target relationships and similar to the invisible rage associated with *descarga* ventings. By this point in our analysis, however, violence over male-centered honor as such begins to look far more complex (whatever the psychological dimensions of the conflicts). Given the connections between the prestige of one's manhood and effective citizenship and privilege in subaltern life, such conflicts amounted to more than a defense of intangibles and more than an outburst of interior rage and compulsion. Similarly, we have heretofore excluded from disputes over tangibles those incidents driven indirectly by masculine bonding or honor. (In these cases, let us recall, backgrounds of masculine bonding or honor framed the dynamics that led to violence, but the disputes did not focus explicitly on masculine honor or valor as such. The specific focus of violence centered on matters such as cheating in card games, disrespect by juniors or commoners toward elders or community authorities, or the duty of a man to intervene to protect a brother, father, or friend in perceived danger.) Although we have recognized the social logic of such incidents, we have treated them as outbursts closer to the intangibles of *descarga* ventings than to tangible claims such as women and property. Yet here, too, the connections between the prestige of one's manhood and effective empowerment in subaltern life argues for a more complex view.

In this modified perspective the roles of tangibles and of social logics of masculinity in violence assume even greater statistical prominence. Disputes over tangibles rise to better than seven-tenths (73.3 percent) of all cases with male assailants and three-fifths (63.0 percent) of male-on-male incidents. Among cases where we may discern expressions of masculinity in violence, incidents driven by a social logic rise to four-fifths (82.6 percent) of violence with male assailants and seven-tenths (72.2 percent) of male-on-male violence. (See Table 7.6, midway shares between conservative and elastic criteria.) The main point is clear. The famed outbursts of cultural mythology—the inexplicable ventings symptomatic of interior rage and impulse, at best vaguely connected to tangible claims or to social relations between assailants and targets—offer a colorful but misleading detour from the principal meanings of masculinity, even violent masculinity, in subaltern life. In most violent incidents involving men, even male-on-male incidents, the disputes connected their protagonists to tangible issues of power and well-being—resources, privilege, and citizenship—or to the relational logics that ratified masculine empowerment.

In short, a certain touchiness about masculinity, even escalation to violence in defense of it, was more often a social necessity than a symptom of interior psychopathology. This social necessity flowed out of the intersections of masculinity and power within popular culture, and within the wider color-class order of late colonial Morelos. Against the backdrop of these intersections we have interpreted subaltern versions of honorable masculinity as socially recognized affirmations of competence and courage amidst adversity. The argument developed thus far, however, has largely sidestepped two complicating features: the problem of variation and the dialectic of vengeance and survival.

THE PROBLEM OF VARIATION IN THE CULTURE OF POPULAR MASCULINITY

The problem of variation may be formulated as the argumentative questions of a skeptic. Let us grant that statistical analysis suggests overstated stereotyping in the cultural discourse that attaches the rage of wounded male honor mainly to plebeians and non-Indians. A jealously defended sense of masculine honor and status stirred violence by Indians and peasants as well as non-Indians and plebeians. A qualitative reading of the evidence corroborates the quantitative findings. Again and again, Indian peasants proved they were not strangers to the language of masculine honor, challenge, and affront: "Now we'll see who's a man"; "This is nothing, I too know how to take my pants off for women"; "It's painful to me that they've taken away my wife's reputation [*crédito*]"; "offending God and my honor [by adultery]"; "having taken . . . the precious Jewel of her virginity."[48] Let us grant, too, that the bulk and breadth of the evidence suggest widespread participation by Indians and peasants in the specific patterning of popular culture we have studied: the intersections of masculinity and power in vertical, familial, and horizontal contexts, and an understanding of masculine valor as competence and courage amidst adversity. Even if we grant the inclusion of Indians and peasants in the masculine version of popular culture we have studied, however, were not individual, generational, or sociocultural variations also significant? Is our model of subaltern masculinity so socially overdetermined that it loses sight of individual initiative and differences of personality, culture, and social position? On matters as intensely personal as manhood, valor, and honor, is it not especially dangerous to overlook such differences? Just as we granted that women selected from a panoply of weapons and needs to build their social strategies of resistance, alliance, and crossovers within subaltern life, should we not grant greater latitude for variation and individual decisions among men?

The answers to such questions do not require that we abandon the sense of social patterning and inclusion developed earlier. They do require that we recognize the spaces left for varying emphasis within the culture of popular masculinity, the spaces for cultural argument between individuals, generations, and sociocultural strata. They also require that we recognize the ways the culture of masculinity demanded individual initiative and therefore variation in response to challenge and uncertainty.[49]

Let us begin with variations of emphasis. The culture of popular masculinity bundled various pathways to affirmation. For this very reason men and youth of distinct personality, generation, or sociocultural rank could place the accent on somewhat distinct parts of the bundle even as they participated in the more general intersections of masculinity and power we have described. We have already analyzed at length the various elements of a deconstructed bundle: within society at large, the familial, vertical, and horizontal arenas of masculine affirmation; within the familial arena, affirmation through containment of insubordination or treachery, through acquisition of legitimacy from subordinates, or through success as an economic provider; within the vertical arena, affirmation by avoiding manifest fear, by contesting abuse via institutional appeal after the fact, or by challenging abuse personally during the fact; within the horizontal arena, affirmation by negotiating the maze of community responsibility, rank, and politics, or affirmation by negotiating the informal routes of male spectacle and sociability; within each arena, the multiple persons and relations among which a man might select to develop such affirmations; between the various arenas, a certain interplay and porousness in relations of masculine honor and degradation. Even this spare listing suggests the possibilities for different individual accenting, spaces for different micrologics within a larger logic.

To some extent the different accenting within popular culture corresponds to socioethnic imagery. Let us recall some of our quantitative findings. The overall structure of motivation in violence did not vary significantly between Indian and non-Indian assailants or between peasants and plebeians. The incidence of *descarga* ventings also failed to line up with standard imagery. Within the overall pattern, however, we discerned more subtle associations. Disputes that focused explicitly on male honor as such — suggesting a readiness to escalate irritations and quarrels into straightforward challenges of manhood that overshadowed originating issues and contexts — tilted somewhat more strongly to non-Indian assailants. Conversely, disputes governed by a more emphatically relational logic — a background of masculine honor or bonding that framed the dynamics of challenge, response, and assistance but left male honor as such more implicit or embedded — tilted moderately more strongly to Indian assailants.[50]

These findings accord well with a qualitative reading of the evidence. The case materials suggest that for Indians and peasants in village settings, men and male youth could more easily accentuate communal pathways to masculine rank and respectability. Keeping up appearances as rulers of households and as economic providers through avoiding scandal and complying with tributary obligations; garnering a measure of approval through service in the community's ranked ladder of political posts; standing up to abusive superiors by securing community backing during or after the fact — these pathways allowed some men to emphasize a communal ratification of honorable manhood that sidestepped one-to-one confrontations of manhood as such. In this ranked system, when disputes broke out in male-centered contexts, they often focused not on pointed challenges to manhood as such but on more implicit or socially embedded concepts of manhood. The language of dispute often focused on "respect" — the violation of appropriate demeanors of authority or deference that paid due regard for elder rank within families, political rank within communities, or the adult citizenship that accrued to male heads of household. For non-Indians, plebeians, and hacienda dwellers the formally institutionalized pathways to community affirmation of manhood were more tenuous, and the reliance on ad hoc encounters between individuals and the informal culture of male play was a bit more pronounced.[51]

Such patterns illuminate the grains of truth encoded in stereotypes but are sufficiently subtle and modest to warn against their exaggeration and reification. They illuminate not so much the presence of several subcultures among the poor of late colonial Morelos as the spaces for variation — the different emphases and strategies that allowed room for argument within masculine popular culture. The dangers of exaggeration emerge both quantitatively and qualitatively. The statistically significant variations tend toward the fleeting. For example, plebeian assailants leaned somewhat more strongly to homicide, the ultimate act of escalation, than peasant assailants. This association tends to confirm the sense that Indians and peasants ratified and challenged masculinity within frameworks of community life that deflected all-out confrontations between individuals. But the data also warn against making too much of such distinctions. The statistical lean fades out when the focus shifts from plebeian assailants to plebeian targets. For non-Indians compared with Indians, moreover, the statistical tilt toward homicidal violence is so weak for both assailants and targets that it is virtually meaningless. (See Table 7.7.)

A qualitative reading of the evidence similarly suggests variation and argument within a shared arena of cultural experience. Within Indian community settings, after all, it was mature male heads of household and local notables who reaped the greatest immediate benefits from formal channels of respectable masculinity. The younger generation might lean more strongly toward informal and confrontational assertions of masculine prowess, including not only male-on-male confrontations but also the hounding of women or female youth.[52] If a youthful tendency toward confrontational manhood hardened in adult life, it could draw even reluctant elders onto a terrain of confrontational masculinity. Marcelino de Jesús, a monolingual Nahua villager in Tepoztlán, earned a reputation as a "youngster of very bad habits, slow and moody, so much so that he has struck his own father." The reputation for irresponsibility and a confrontational style stuck into adulthood. He remained unmarried; he was accused of thievery and an adulterous liaison; and in 1802 he killed an older Indian. The elder man had impugned the younger man's honor, refused to serve him *pulque*, and chased him from his home. This sort of play between distinctive generational and personal styles lent authority to Juan Domingo's explanation that Juan de Santiago, a younger unmarried Indian with a reputation for thievery and excessive confrontation, stabbed him simply "because as an elder [*viejo*] he gave him advice." The unspoken side of such discourses was that on occasion personality or situation channeled belligerence and temperament in a reverse generational direction.[53] Subtly varied emphases within the popular culture of masculinity failed to line up with distinctions between subcultures or ethnic strata or even generations.

The culture of popular masculinity not only left spaces for somewhat distinct emphases and pathways to manly affirmation. It also demanded individual initiatives, personal responses to challenge and uncertainty that of necessity implied variation within and occasionally beyond the boundaries of acceptable behavior. The demand for individualized response within a larger cultural pattern comes through most forcefully if we consider the most dangerous challenges of all: aggressions that required vengeance. Let us turn finally, therefore, to the dialectic of vengeance and survival.

VENGEANCE AND THE ART OF SURVIVAL

The problem of vengeance is that an apparently iron code of revenge runs up against issues of personality and survival. Honorable manhood occasionally dictates a confrontation with death, but individuals may want to avoid the kill-or-be-killed trap. Gabriel García Márquez brought the problem into focus in the novella *Crónica de una muerte anunciada* (*Chronicle of a Death Foretold*). When a wedding is ruined because the bride turns out not to be a virgin, her two brothers must avenge the loss by killing the person their sister identifies as the taker of her virginity. Vengeance will restore moral order to the town and honor to the family and its men. We need not dwell here upon the many ambiguities García Márquez offers us — including doubts about the bride's intentions in the making of the scandal and doubts, too, about the identity of the seducer. For our purpose the response of the brothers to their obligation is crucial. In an ingenious twist García Márquez depicts them as thoroughly evasive. The reluctant avengers take every step to have the murder stopped. They go about the vengeance plot conspicuously, announcing timing and destination, brandishing the intended murder weapon before townsfolk, and offering opportunity after opportunity to be thwarted. It seems that the brothers believe that they do not really have to murder anyone. So long as they go through the effort to avenge the dishonor and so long as others "force" them to back away for the sake of social peace, the chain of challenge/response may be broken without reflecting poorly on their manhood.[54]

The dilemma of the brothers — their earnest effort to abort the vengeance while appearing to proceed with it — sums up the cultural problem beautifully. In the masculine popular culture of late colonial Morelos, certain types of extreme aggressions by men not only justified serious and even homicidal assaults. They virtually demanded it. These challenges were those that explicitly violated one's manhood, personal reputation, or protection of family — categories that merged readily in male-on-male challenges. Verbal sparring that escalated into explicit attacks on manly valor or honor, sexual liaisons in progress that came to the explicit attention of aggrieved husbands, and unjustified killings or other violence against male or female kin all demanded retribution, an effort to destroy or punish the transgressor and thereby redeem the masculinity of the avenger.[55] Failure to respond aggressively to extreme challenges such as these had an emasculating effect on the man who lost his nerve. But to respond risked death. Not all individuals, moreover, were equally strong and confident or equally adept at fighting, equally committed to violence or equally tranquil in the face of death.

The problem could not simply be wished away. Even in the absence of sexual rivalries or blood vengeance conflicts, to participate in the informal culture of masculine play implied at least some risk that the jousting of manhood would spiral out of control. How to affirm manhood while deflecting severe affront or challenge, how to face up to the occasional severe challenge yet escape disaster, and how to keep up appearances in arenas of varied temperaments and experience all demanded individual initiatives and responses to a more general cultural dilemma.

The brother-avengers of García Márquez's novella worked out their own comic version of a response: companionship and avoidance. The brothers went about their task together rather than alone, they occasionally tried to expand the web of involved persons, and they played an elaborate game of avoidance while keeping up appearances. The tools of companionship and avoidance were well understood in the popular culture of late colonial Morelos. Men commonly entered the arena of informal masculine sociability in the company of a friend or two. If joustings of manhood began to spin out of control, a man relied on his companions to help him escape the trap. They might deflect verbal sparring and innuendo in another direction. If challenge/response dynamics nonetheless escalated toward direct attacks on manhood, friends could "force" their companion to retreat from violence without losing face, or they could provide an excuse for the outnumbered adversary to back down. If physical fighting broke out anyway, friends and bystanders might intervene to prevent serious injury or to protect a man in an uneven fight.[56]

Companionship, in short, enabled a man to affirm masculine valor while avoiding the kind of one-on-one confrontations that proved most dangerous. The cultural assumptions came into the open when Antonio de la Cruz, a Tlayacapan Indian working on his *milpas* in the warm country, complained to a bypasser, Augustín Ruíz, that his mules were eating corn from the *milpa*. (Augustín Ruíz, variously identified as a mestizo and a mulatto, worked on Hacienda San Carlos and was transporting wood on the mules. It is unclear if Antonio de la Cruz's *milpa* possessions derived from a tenantry relationship with the same hacienda, from village-based land claims, or both.) The adversaries were not alone. Antonio de la Cruz was accompanied by his wife and daughter, and Augustín Ruíz by a mulatto companion from the hacienda. When the intruder responded heatedly, Antonio de la Cruz's warning made plain the assumptions about companionship. "Go on, dog . . . we'll see one another alone another day. Don't think that I'm acting valiant because I'm here with my wife, and you because you're with your friend [*compañero*]."[57]

The entire encounter illustrated the cultural importance of companionship as well as the fact that accidents could take the protagonists farther down the road of criminal violence than they might have wished. Augustín Ruíz's companion apparently tried to calm his friend in the early stages of the confrontation, but to little avail. Augustín Ruíz considered the taunts (at least some of them delivered in Nahuatl) too much an affront for him to back down. When some of the rocks thrown by Augustín Ruíz struck their target, Antonio de la Cruz's wife yelled for help to Joseph Espinoza, a mestizo villager at work on a nearby *milpa*. Espinoza intervened to stop the violence: "Let him be, man, look how you've already injured him." The verbal exchange escalated. Augustín Ruíz told Espinoza it was not his affair and threatened to kill him with a machete. When Espinoza refused to back down and said he would tie up the assailant and have him prosecuted, Augustín Ruíz finally allowed his friend to drag him away. During the retreat, however, he symbolically affirmed that it was his friend who forced the retreat. Augustín Ruíz continued to fling rocks and protested, "I still have to take out this Indian's tongue." Companions and acquaintances had played their prescribed roles.[58]

When companionship did not suffice to reconcile the arts of manly affirmation and physical survival, outright avoidance could prove important. Companionship was a preventive tool a man could bring to known spaces of male jousting. It might hold in check the dangers that lurked in informal arenas of masculine sociability or in predictable meetings with adversaries. But in some instances an extreme aggression against manhood yielded a more powerful vengeance drama. The sense of rancor and sullied honor festered, the aggression had been left unatoned, and the desire or duty to exact retribution might follow its target continuously and catch it unawares.

When this happened, avoidance, whether discreet or formally arranged, might offer a way out. Antonio Sosa, a peon on Hacienda Miacatlán, beat his mestiza wife, Yndoza Gertrudis, in 1815 because she had caught wind of a sexual liaison and challenged it. Antonio Sosa angrily proclaimed that the problem was one of gossip by Gregorio Roa, an Indian canecutter (*machetero*) who would pay for his loose talk and interference. Yndoza Gertrudis discreetly warned Gregorio Roa to avoid an encounter with her husband. Gregorio Roa's mistake was that he only half-heeded the advice. He simultaneously tried to clear the air and to avoid a confrontation. He sent his wife to Antonio Sosa's house to talk the matter over and to assuage Sosa's fear of gossip — while Gregorio Roa lurked outside. The effort failed, the two men soon challenged each other directly, and Gregorio Roa ended up killing Antonio Sosa. Gregorio Roa received a royal pardon soon thereafter, but it was conditioned on his compliance with Yndoza Gertrudis's desire to break the chain of masculine injury-vengeance. Gregorio Roa agreed to leave the hacienda to avoid vengeance by Yndoza Gertrudis's eldest son. The flight or exile of an aggressor constituted a social death that might serve as a symbolic equivalent of physical death, a retribution that restored masculine standing. Yndoza Gertrudis's son would be allowed to escape the necessity of vengeance.[59]

Some versions of avoidance operated more subtly than flight or obvious efforts not to cross paths. One method of indirection was to avoid a decisive physical endgame while appearing to be unafraid of it and to appeal simultaneously to local authorities to punish the culprit. Institutional retribution would spare the aggressor (and the avenger) the volatile unknowns of personal fury and retribution among men. The most subtle versions of such avoidance through indirection are by their nature unprovable. But avoidance maneuvers illuminate cases where husbands found wives in compromising encounters with other men; "tried" to seize, injure, or kill the fleeing aggressor; proved unable to accomplish the task; and were therefore left to vent physical anger on the wife and institutionally mediated punishment on the other man. At times the husbands appear to have given up rather readily in their hot pursuit of male-on-male retribution.[60]

Sometimes, of course, even the most elaborate companionship and avoidance tools failed to work their magic. Accidents happened; events strayed from intentions; one or another person failed to agree tacitly on avoidance.[61] The reluctant brother-avengers of García Márquez's novella would have understood. Stuck by their creator in a somewhat overdetermined vision of the code of vengeance, they discovered that all the townsfolk deferred to the iron law of the code. In García Márquez's tale, no one intervened appropriately to stop the murder; everyone became an accomplice to vengeance.[62]

KILLED FOR LAUGHING? AN AFTERWORD

We have traveled far from Buñuel's captivating images of casual killers who explode for no reason, of hypermacho sensibilities that breed indifference to death. We have recognized the grains of truth embedded in stereotyped cultural imagery and the availability of anecdotes to confirm the imagery. But we have inserted the grains of truth in a new framework of analysis. This framework asks us not only to count anecdotes and incidents but also to explore the profound intersections of masculinity and power in subaltern life. In this new context interior rage and wounded masculinities that explode almost at random take on lesser proportions, and the social logics and the tangibles that drove masculine affirmation and conflict become clearer and more important. The motives of male-on-male violence lose some of their psychopathological texture, and the sometimes secret routes to individual survival amidst competitive affirmation become more visible. Archetypes fade, and the spaces for variation and argument within a shared arena of masculine popular culture come into focus.

The net effect unsettles not only our vision of masculinity as a whole but that of incidents that once seemed to accord well with ready-made cultural imagery. When we first described Onofre Bautista's killing of Deciderio Sarmiento, the laughing horseman of Tlayacapan, it seemed fine to assimilate

the sense of affront, the urge to confront and kill the offender, and the sud-
denness and randomness of the whole sequence to a Buñuel-like surrealism.
Deciderio Sarmiento was "killed for laughing." But was the whole affair quite
as socially random and casual, quite as purely an interior drama, as it seemed?
When Onofre Bautista was given, in accord with legal procedure, a chance to
ratify, amplify, or modify his initial testimony, he tried to explain why he felt
compelled to challenge a bystander's private laughter. "Knowing the insulting
character of Deciderio Sarmiento, and that he was a man who ridiculed everyone, . . . [he] knew that he was doing it to him."[63] The excuse looked lame to
the authorities, who sentenced Onofre Bautista to five years of hard labor, and
it has continued to look lame to this historian, who notes that Onofre Bautista
and other witnesses failed to mention this aspect of the case in their more
spontaneous initial testimonies. Yet we cannot dispel completely a tiny seed of
doubt. Was Deciderio Sarmiento really killed for laughing? Or did both men
know, given the specific Tlayacapan personalities and social relationships in
play, that the laughter had a target, that it would mark the beginning of power
positionings between two villagers? Our new framework of analysis offers no
final answer. But it makes it possible to ask the question.

CHAPTER 8

Gender Culture and Political Culture

Languages of Community, Politics, and Riot

In 1763 the peoples of Morelos witnessed a strange inversion of conventional social alignments. Don José Jiménez de Cisneros, the *alcalde mayor* of Cuernavaca, came under fire for committing one excess after another during his first year in office. He and his lieutenants participated in debauchery and violence at *fandangos*, protected friends and accepted bribes in criminal violence cases, harassed and imprisoned women, and demanded their domestic labor. Charges that an *alcalde mayor* abused his authority or that he stood at the center of a privileged power group whom he enriched and protected were not unusual in late colonial Mexico. What made this case striking was the identity of the accusers and defenders. Those who denounced Jiménez de Cisneros included Cuernavaca's storeowners and merchants, its citizens and respectable folk (*tenderos, vecinos, gente de razón*). Those who defended the *alcalde mayor* included the Indians of fourteen pueblos scattered throughout the Cuernavaca district. For whatever reason, Jiménez had offended the privileged and interfered with their perceived prerogatives. They complained that Jiménez gave "free rein to the Indians and their constables."[1]

The complaints emerged at a moment of hardship in the rural economy of Morelos. The outbreak of a smallpox epidemic in 1762 converged with a poor maize harvest that made 1763 a year of scarcity and fragile health. Normally, grain scarcity signaled an opportunity for *hacendados*, merchants, and their political allies to gain windfall profits. By hoarding grain and encouraging prices to soar even higher, then slowly releasing grain onto the market, the power group secured unusual revenues, placed poor folk in their debt, and made up for years when plentiful harvests and competition by small producers placed large estates on the defensive. This well-known windfall profit mechanism, however, exacted a political cost. By exacerbating scarcity crises and provoking the moral wrath of the poor, it heightened the risk of disorder. The famous corn riot of Mexico City in 1692 exploded against the backdrop of rumors that the viceroy encouraged rather than blunted profiteering. In the Morelos of 1763 tension was palpable, and riot broke out in Tlayacapan.

During such crises the complex role of an *alcalde mayor* was to take visible action to relieve the crisis by enlarging the supply of grain and selling some of it at moderate public granary prices but not to press such action and symbolism so hard that they undermined the mercantile mechanisms of his elite allies. Jiménez de Cisneros broke the conventional rules. His motives elude us. Perhaps he sympathized with the poor and the diseased; perhaps he feared a contagion of riot and disorder; or perhaps he saw an opportunity to achieve personal enrichment and social peace at the same time. For whatever reason or combination of reasons, Jiménez de Cisneros appears to have pursued aggressively the detection and seizure of hoarded grain, the distribution and sale of the maize at prices below those demanded by regional traders and storeowners, and the granting of personal credit to Indians who would repay the functionary at the next harvest. Jiménez, in short, enlarged his role to the point of displacing the usual merchant-allies of an *alcalde mayor*. This was why respectable folk complained that he had abused his powers and given free rein to Indians; this was why Indians defended the beleaguered colonial official from his Spanish accusers.[2]

The denouement of the controversy was not pretty. In January 1764 the *audiencia* ordered Jiménez de Cisneros into temporary exile from Cuernavaca during the continuing investigation of complaints. His physical presence would be too provocative. By March the fourteen pueblos, led by their elders, current and former *gobernadores* and municipal officials, and the notables and assistants who filled out the ranks of prestige and political service in the villages, had convened assemblies and fashioned statements defending the *alcalde mayor*. In April Jiménez de Cisneros died in mysterious circumstances that suggested foul play.[3]

The strange inversion of social alignments allows a rare glimpse at popular languages of legitimacy as applied to political authority beyond the community level. The statements of the fourteen pueblos bear the trademarks of the rough literacy that developed within popular culture: the shaky handwriting, the tenuous grammar, the guesswork in spelling, the occasional resort to Nahuatl word and concept. These markers signaled reliance on the elderly and the unpolished when organizing written declarations. In eleven of the fourteen cases the language of praise and legitimacy was strikingly patriarchal. Jiménez de Cisneros was a good political authority because he acted as a responsible father who fulfilled obligations to his dependents and thereby garnered prestige, authority, and affection. Let us sample this language.[4]

> He looks with mercy upon the poor, our *hijos del pueblo*, [and] so that they don't go hungry he looks for maize and lends it from his own account, so that [they may eat] . . . and that the storeowners don't take from us more money than it's worth. . . . He says we are his children, and defends [us] from storeowning *gachupín* hawks and wolves who want to eat us, and our children the little chickens. [Tlaltenango]

> We've experienced and known more the love of a father than a judge. [Texalpa]

> He's attended to us with love and kindness overlooking our defects. . . . He has ordered us not to allow concubinage nor those who go around selling [gossip] because if we don't tell him he'll punish us very well. [Xiuchtepec]

> He's a good *clatoane* [*sic*; that is, *tlatoani*, a Nahua dynastic ruler] who looks at us with much love [and] does justice well without mistreating poor Indians. [Caquequeye]

> looking after the poor not allowing that the rich hurt my children [that is, the *alcalde mayor*'s metaphorical children] [Tetecala]

> He gives to each *hijo* [*del pueblo*] what belongs to him in the lands he has planted and doesn't allow there to be things lacking, since when we lack maize he gets it from the bins where it is hidden and sells it to us and has even loaned it to us from what he has had in his house and later we pay at the harvest [and] he doesn't allow the rich to take the mules nor the *gachupín* storeowners when the *hijos* [*del pueblo*] don't pay their debts right away. . . . Treating us like *hijos* he embraces us. [Quantetelco]

It would be misleading to suggest that Indians and peasants saw most colonial officials as benevolent patriarchs. The idealized imagery, after all, focused on a man whose legitimacy among Indians aroused wrath among his natural allies and compatriots. Few Indians expected that an *alcalde mayor* would act as the good patriarch attending to the needs of metaphorical children to whom the father owed vigilance and sustenance. The problem of interpretation, therefore, is not whether Indians and peasants expected most colonial officials to act as responsible patriarchs enmeshed in webs of mutual obligation with social unequals. The problem is more subtle. Notwithstanding the authenticity of the pueblo declarations defending Jiménez de Cisneros, was the language of legitimacy mainly a calculated appeal to colonial pretense, fundamentally a misrepresentation of popular understandings of rightful authority? Although colonial Mexico was a society profoundly divided by color and class, and social polarization ran particularly strong in Morelos, colonial elites sometimes sought to forge a positive aura of legitimacy among themselves and in relation to their subordinates. The posture of self-presentation that accompanied such efforts was that of paternal patrons who looked mercifully upon the needs, foibles, and well-being of their inferiors. Was the language of metaphorical father and child more a ploy directed outward than a representation from within popular culture?

To answer this question convincingly requires that we complement incidents that directed languages of legitimacy upward and outward with more interior struggles over legitimate and illegitimate authority. One such incident convulsed Tlayacapan in 1784.[5] When on March 1 Don Nicolás de Santa María, the *gobernador* of Tlayacapan's Atecpan district (*parcialidad*) went on his rounds to collect tributes not yet paid, he ran into trouble in the house of Andrés Antonio, a forty-year-old Indian peasant. Andrés Antonio had a reputation for defiant character and associations. His father had been a key leader of the 1755 riot that cost "such loss of life" (*tanta ruina de vidas*). His ally Tomás Zolís, a local notable who would become an upstart *gobernador* with a substantial social following, had led an uprising against the local power group in 1783. That same year Andrés Antonio himself had allegedly resisted tribute collection, forced a *gobernador* to flee to a Spaniard's house for refuge, threatened to mobilize a revolt, and collected monetary contributions from commoners who backed his legal efforts to expel the *gente de razón* from the theoretically Indian village of Tlayacapan. The foundation for such tensions was the internal reconstitution of Tlayacapan in the late eighteenth century: the demographic growth of the village and the influx of a non-Indian stratum of prosperous peasants, *rancheros*, and traders; the increasing internal differentiation of Tlayacapan into prosperous and land-poor strata and the attendant disputes over land rights and animal damages to *milpa* agriculture; and the consolidation of an Indian power group allied to the *gente de razón* and implicated in self-aggrandizing tributary schemes disguised as collections for public works such as bridge or church repair. By 1784 the figure of the local *semillero*, the vendor of seed grain to Indian women and men too poor to save seed for the next maize planting cycle, was an important local fixture. The ethnic and economic reconstitution of Tlayacapan had widened political spaces and followings for discontented Indian notables.

The language of factionalism, discredit, and legitimacy mobilized images of authority resonant with those evident in our earlier analyses of gender conflicts (Chapter 4) and in the 1763 controversy over the *alcalde mayor* of

Cuernavaca. Critics of the Indian power group depicted them as parasites, as irresponsible, egotistical, self-aggrandizing schemers who neglected community obligation and well-being and who insisted on rights to deference, resources, and privilege unencumbered by reciprocity and unconditioned by the evaluations of subordinates. Andrés Antonio summed up the matter pointedly when he declared he would not pay *gobernadores* who collected money "in order to fatten themselves." Don Nicolás's response underscored the irrelevance of such charges and contingencies to the wielders of power who insisted on a more absolute law of social rank and deference. What mattered was not the truth or falsehood of the charge of parasitism and irresponsibility but "the impudence" (*el atrevimiento*) of the person who dared make the charge. Andrés Antonio had dared to insult Don Nicolás by asserting that tribute collections "were to fatten me." The verbal disrespect had been accompanied by "two slaps, that put me on the floor." We cannot discern who actually initiated the physical scuffle, but as authority crumbled and gave way to physical confrontation, Don Nicolás found himself in jeopardy. When the apparently stronger Andrés Antonio wielded a rock, Don Nicolás de Santa María made one last attempt to invoke a respect for rank and deference that transcended evaluations of negligence and parasitism. "Do you know," he demanded, "whom you are striking?" The devastating and ironic response was "more than if it were my father." The exchange is revealing. In play were not only tensions between conditional and absolute models of rightful authority but associations between community authority and familial authority.[6]

This would not be the last time such associations came to the fore. The intervention of third parties aborted the danger to Don Nicolás and led to the arrest and transfer of Andrés Antonio to Tlalmanalco. Precisely because Andrés Antonio's defiance represented more than an individual quarrel, however, his case became a cause célèbre. Tomás Zolís had by this time taken over the leading *gobernador* post in Tlayacapan. He and other allies of the prisoner mobilized a social following, displaced the previous Indian power group, collected monies for Andrés Antonio's legal defense, and — in just three weeks — secured a viceregal decree ordering the prisoner's release. Andrés Antonio and his allies had garnered considerable prestige and legitimacy among Indian peasants who tilted toward a more fluid and conditional model of community authority. As responsible leaders who followed a more duty-bound and reciprocally obligated political trajectory, they had acted as good patriarchs. Andrés Antonio acquired a striking sobriquet: "Father of the Pueblo."[7] Word spread quickly that release of the Father of the Pueblo would take the form of a triumphal procession out of Tlalmanalco accompanied by music and festive celebration, to be followed by a revolt and settling of scores in Tlayacapan. The local authorities set aside the viceregal decree in view of the imminent danger of rebellion.

What matters in the Tlayacapan affair, for our purposes, is not how universal a following Andrés Antonio and his allies secured among Indian commoners in Tlayacapan. The turmoil split a complex community already splintered not only into the comparatively rich and poor and the comparatively *castizo* or Indian, but divided, too, by rival barrios and rival contenders for Indian leadership. It would be naive to believe that the once hegemonic power group had lost its entire social base among commoner clients, dependents, and kin. The same upstart leader viewed as a responsible good patriarch by one faction might be viewed as a capricious tyrant by another. Since the same leader could pursue varied social practices and coercions with distinct groups, experience might lend truth to both claims at once.[8] The larger point, for our purposes, is the language of political legitimacy and illegitimacy: the patriarchal metaphors that contrasted good fathers who ruled by prestige earned through service, risk, and reciprocity in the common good with self-aggrandizing parasites who ruled by absolute right and sheer power; and the resonance between competing models of rightful authority that developed in the realm of gender and familial relations ("gender culture") and those that developed in the realm of community rule or governance ("political culture"). The political turbulence of the Cuernavaca district in 1763 and the political wars of Tlayacapan in 1784 ask us to probe seriously the familial metaphors and gendered foundations of peasant politics in late colonial Morelos.

THE GENDERED POLITICS OF COMMUNITY AUTHORITY (I): CONTRADICTIONS

Peasant political culture was marked by a deep contradiction between egalitarian or democratic values that stressed reciprocities and likenesses among families and citizens who shared a rough similarity of economic condition and a readiness to subordinate individual interest to community well-being, and more hierarchical values that stressed obedience to constituted authority and legitimate differentiation of circumstance and privilege according to barrio or lineage, economic base, or political status. Taken as a whole the scholarly literature on peasant history and life in Mexico has recognized both axes of peasant political life. On the one hand, one finds a vision of egalitarianism and commitment to community service as the quintessential bedrock of peasant communities and their political vision. "In times of defeat the leaders shared the poverty and hunger. . . . The distance . . . never became a class gulf."[9] On the other hand, a vast literature also documents the *caciquismo*, a political and economic bossism backed by sometimes ruthless violence, that constituted the pervasive and defining weave of the political fabric in rural communities. "Many [peasant leaders] became true despots. . . . When one commissary refused to give him a payoff, [the local *cacique*] attempted to kill him." [10]

Both dimensions of peasant political culture come through, then, in the scholarly literature, but in a curiously dichotomized fashion that rarely brings them together. One may find the contradiction, for example, presented in the form of contrasting regional patterns within a world of "many Mexicos." The egalitarian, communal vision propagated by Zapata suffused peasant political culture in a Morelos, while the more hierarchical, militarized vision of peasant *caciques* prevailed in a San Luís Potosí. [11] The regional contrasts sometimes carry an ethnic subtext: the south, more influenced by an Indian background that placed the accent on communal well-being, gave rise to a more horizontal and egalitarian political culture of reciprocity and service, while the north and west, more influenced by a Spanish-mestizo colonization movement that placed the accent on social superiority and external connections, gave rise to a more vertical and authoritarian political culture of command and intimidation. A similar contrast emerges in the contrapuntal imagery of community culture versus hacienda-rancho culture. These imageries reformulate contradiction as contrast—between regions or microregions, between Indian culture and Spanish-mestizo culture, between community culture and hacienda culture. The other dichotomized form in which the contradiction appears is that of scholarly debate on a specific community or region. One votes with Robert Redfield, whose idealizations of peasant folk culture yielded a vision of community harmony, or one votes with Oscar Lewis, whose restudy of Redfield's Tepoztlán yielded a sobering world of mistrust and abuse of power. [12]

The historical materials suggest a more profound and subtle problem: the coexistence of contradictory and competing political styles and visions within single regions and communities, even in Morelos. Just as important, one detects this volatile coexistence even in communities whose struggles and sense of values encouraged sharp antagonism with the vertical milieu of haciendas. On the one hand, one may readily find in late colonial Morelos a vision of community reciprocity and commitment for which the region would later become famous. This was a vision that accented a fundamental likeness of condition, rights, and destiny among a community's constituent families and citizens. The sense of likeness perhaps drew on indigenous cultural roots: the Nahua tendency to modular social organization—the building of the whole out of self-contained social units marked by rotational cycles of duty to the whole yet potentially able to split off—emphasized in James Lockhart's analysis of the ethnic state (*alteptel*). [13] Whatever its roots, examples of a likeness sensibility abound. One finds it in the claim by a land-poor Indian that a *gobernador* authorized him to open up a *milpa* on "a piece of hilly land" in the community's *monte*, the woodlands reserved for "common benefit"; in the gathering of community officials and commoners to hunt down together, then stone and whip, rustlers who stole village pigs and mules; in the semi-clandestine network of peasants who enabled the leader of a water struggle to slip in and out of the village undetected by authorities eager to arrest him; in the mobilization to protect a peasant commoner from a visiting official intent on arresting, fining, and whipping him on a morals charge; in the assumption that regardless of formal title or customary possession, peasants held land on sufferance and protection of the community and therefore owed contributions to community tribute and labor, and festivals and struggles; and in the ire aroused by a *gobernador* who refused to follow "the custom . . . of his predecessors" by accepting drinks that signified an obligation to reciprocate, a symbolic acknowledgment of fellowship in common.[14]

Perhaps most important is the repeated practice of disobedience — *faltando respeto* (lacking respect) to community officials, or even mobilizing factions, legal claims, and tumults against them if they became devouring parasites who abused commoner rights or community needs. Commoners, in alliance with elders who acted as prestigious guardians of community values or with upstart notables who challenged the established power group, asserted a right to judge their authorities and to suspend deference in view of "the evil with which these [power abusers] proceed against the commoners and the poor." [15]

These examples and practices emerged out of the more egalitarian impulse within peasant political culture and sustained a rather conditional — fluid and democratic — vision of community authority. Earned prestige and respect counted for more than institutional coercion or inherited station. The ethos of community service and evaluation counted for more than sheer wealth or power in the acquisition of prestige and authority. All families held a right to resources, respect, and citizenship. This was the Morelos that would produce a Zapata.

On the other hand, the fact that commoners and allied notables repeatedly challenged community officials and notables and accused them of self-aggrandizing and imperious behavior testifies to a competition of political claims and visions. In a deep sense the more egalitarian impulse is not comprehensible except in relation to its contrasting counterpoint. One was the justifying premise of the other. The division of political units into ranked constituent parts (*alteptel* or *calpolli* in Nahua cultural contexts, head towns and subject towns [*cabeceras* and *sujetos*] in Spanish colonial contexts); the division of communities into barrios of varied size, prestige, and resources; and the division of families into dynasties and lineages of distinct political privileges and economic endowments: these more vertical features of community life had a long history in Mesoamerican culture and had been reorganized rather than obliterated by the Spanish colonial experience. Distinctions between notables and commoners and between the prosperous and the poor still prevailed among the peasants of late colonial Morelos. For key political posts the machinery of local elections often restricted voting and officeholding to a minority of local notables.[16] As we have seen (Chapters 2, 6), the vertical dynamics of Indian village life could intersect with the multiethnic dynamics of colonial life. Major head towns in late colonial Morelos often took on more racially mixed and *castizo* ethnic textures, while subject towns often remained more heavily Indian. Within a *cabecera* or *sujeto* community, moreover, internal differentiation might yield a relatively prosperous power group and a poorer, less politically advantaged stratum. The latter group sometimes ended up viewing the former as suspect, of a piece with the larger provincial power group comprised of colonial officials and priests, hacienda owners and administrators, and merchants and store managers, and assisted by the abusive elements within a *castizo* stratum of traders and muleteers, agriculturalists and ranchers, artisans, and petty functionaries and brokers who blended into the community or clustered in the neighboring *ranchero* zones. The suspect group, for its part, might view the commoners as lesser folk who owed obedience to constituted authority and superiors, who held little right to question social prerogatives and privilege. Under pressure the power group laid claim to a social superiority beyond rightful challenge by inferiors inclined to vice and ignorance, treachery and falsehood.[17]

In many respects both the horizontal and the vertical dimensions of peasant political culture were anchored in gendered understandings of power and rightful authority. As Florencia Mallon has argued for nineteenth-century Mexico, the egalitarian impulse of rural popular culture may be viewed as an assertion of "democratic patriarchy." Political citizenship within this vision devolved upon the citizen-patriarchs who ruled the families that constituted a peasant community and who attended to their needs as a community. Particularly at moments of community crisis this brand of politics could foster generational challenges of established local authorities by younger citizen-patriarchs—disgust that "nobody had known how to be [*gobernador*]".[18] As we have also seen (Chapter 7), the acquisition and maintenance of one's standing as a man among men—a person fit for political voice and empowerment within the community—drew peasant men into spaces of horizontal bonding and rivalry. The rites of manly valor and assembly—the drink and games accompanied by verbal sparring, the spectacles of masculinity such as cockfights, and the political assemblies of men to administer justice, elect officials, and voice or ratify community decision—imparted a thoroughly gendered understanding of the political community.

This gendered sensibility had important practical consequences for women. First, it rendered widows politically vulnerable. The same community that took care to find lands for growing populations of married male tributaries might stigmatize widows and redistribute their "excess" lands. Second, it confined women to ad hoc brands of politics. Women pushed their way into public political space as persons of consequence in a crisis, not as formally empowered citizens. Third, it drew a boundary on conditional models of authority. The peasant men who might assert horizontal and conditional approaches to public authority and relationships among men could also resist extension of the approach to male relationships with women and familial dependents.[19]

Gendered understandings also suffused more vertical visions of politics and rightful authority. The great offense of subordinates, in this vision, was their lack of respect (*falta de respeto*) for authority. To evaluate a superior's behaviors and demands and to judge them unworthy or to rebuke verbally or even raise one's hand against a superior constituted acts of impudence by persons who owed a more unconditional deference. To tolerate such insubordination was to invite disorder and treachery. What is striking in the language of accusation against impudent inferiors is its utter familiarity to the student of gender struggle in late colonial Morelos. As the *gobernador* of Totolapa put it, the Indians who challenged him were "absolutely mindless . . . of their obligations, and duties, buoyed by haughtiness and arrogance." They needed the strong hand of authority "so that . . . they will be made to recognize their duties, and be subjected to the fulfillment of their obligation." Manuel de la Trinidad of Amatlán, an Indian accused of assaulting a respected older man who had served as a local *fiscal de iglesia* (in effect, the folk enforcer of church activity and obligation), was considered by local notables a youth "much too shameless who respects no person, whether a [community] elder or former official or his mother."[20] The language of respect and shamelessness, duty and haughtiness, youth and elder, suffused both public and familial politics. Peasant life gave rise not only to the ethos of democratic patriarchy but also to vertically ranked patriarchy, assertions that placed inferior men in structurally female or junior positions of deference to male superiors and elders.

Even in Morelos, then, horizontal and vertical visions of the masculine political community competed for legitimacy within popular culture. This was the case even in the peasant villages, whose social ethos contrasted sharply with the vertically ordered world of the sugar haciendas. These contradictory visions were not only suffused with gendered understandings of citizenship and authority. They also sustained an interplay between contingent and absolute orientations to rightful authority that bear a resemblance to those we examined earlier (Chapter 4) in the realm of gender power and conflict. How, then, did peasants bridge or mediate the gap between a political vision that accented privilege, subordination, and a near-absolute duty to defer and a vision that accented service, reciprocity, and the conditional basis of authority?

How might they even forge a myth of community harmony that partly disguised the practical experience of conflict?

THE GENDERED POLITICS OF COMMUNITY
AUTHORITY (II): MEDIATIONS

Answers to such questions come into view if we juxtapose knowledge that gendered understandings of citizenship and authority suffused peasant political culture, with knowledge that patriarchal authority in family networks was vested in elders and fathers, thereby imparting a generational as well as a sex-based dynamic to social relations. It is in the institution of the community *viejos*, the male elders who assumed a special role as collective fathers of the *hijos del pueblo*, that peasants mediated the contradictions of their political lives.

Ideally the *viejos* were to act as guardians of community wisdom, values, and necessity. They acquired a special prestige and right of moral authority not by chronological age alone but by a background of service as responsible community leaders and officials (as *gobernadores, alcaldes, regidores* [councilmen], and *escribanos* [notaries] in the community's municipal structure, and perhaps as officers and sponsors in local church and *cofradía* affairs).[21] Ideally a history of prior service conformed to an image of earned or conditional authority and thereby laid the groundwork for a more inalienable, less easily defied brand of moral leadership. At moments of crisis or trouble the elders were to step forth to counsel their juniors, help lead the community toward a decision, and if necessary discredit traitors and parasites. When the tensions between horizontal and vertical axes of authority reached the breaking point, it was up to the elders to denounce the powerholders as abusive or the restive as malcontents and somehow strike a new balance. Precisely because the elders had earned their prestige through service and had passed beyond the life cycle stage of power seeking and political climbing, they were likely to use the power of their moral authority sparingly and benevolently. To the *viejos*, in short, was entrusted the role of the good patriarchs who were granted a special authority but who were too wise and community-minded to channel it toward self-aggrandizement and parasitism.

This, at least, was the cultural theory of the wisdom and mediation roles of the elders.[22] The practice was more complicated. On the one hand, a great deal of evidence does testify to the special status attained by the *viejos* and to their readiness to use that status to restrain power groups they considered abusive. In the sugar zone of Miacatlán, for example, *viejos* of the pueblo Santo Tomás Miacatlán stepped forward in 1775 to denounce their current *gobernador*, Martín León, for diverting waters and turning over pastureland to Hacienda Miacatlán. They demanded the right to hold a new election to select a *gobernador* "to our satisfaction." Speaking as the community voice, they declared that León "tears us to pieces" and had been appointed by colonial elites rather than elected by the community. In the *tierra fría* zone of Totolapa in 1801 *viejos* intervened to stop a water sale scheme by a discredited *gobernador* and his ally, the local lieutenant (*subdelegado*) of the colonial intendant. They backed a campaign of disobedience and temporary flight that thwarted local tribute collection and suffered a repressive fury that included whippings. In these and other instances elders claimed a right to speak in a higher community voice, as collective guardians against "despotic rule" imposed by the self-aggrandizing and the capricious on the *hijos del pueblo*.[23]

Viejos intervened not only at moments of crisis but in preemptive anticipation of them. When internally delicate political decisions loomed and augured potential controversy, the *viejos* could supply counsel and prestige. In 1806, for example, Miguel Gregorio, the Indian *gobernador* of Xoxocotla, suspected that a missing youth had been killed by an uncle who coveted the boy's modest inheritance. (The youth was an orphan.) The matter was delicate since the *gobernador* lacked hard evidence or witnesses, the uncle had not caused any trouble before, and an accusation would transfer control of the boy's property from the uncle to the community leadership. Miguel Gregorio met the elders for guidance and legitimacy. The *viejos* decided that Miguel Gregorio had good reason to suspect the uncle, and they helped organize a confrontation that yielded a confession (and later the body). Similarly, if informal advice or onetime punishments failed to reform community troublemakers — for example, individuals whose open and indiscriminate sexual aggressiveness threatened to plunge families into unending violence and discord — the *viejos* lent moral weight to extreme decisions such as expulsion.[24]

The cultural theory of the wisdom and mediation roles of *viejos*, then, found significant confirmation in practice. From time to time *viejos* intervened as guardians of community necessity and experience. They denounced abusive authorities or disruptive malcontents; they proffered advice at moments of uncertainty and crisis; they steered families and communities toward paths that averted crisis. When all worked tolerably well, their prestige as authoritative and responsible patriarchs who looked after community sons and children allowed them to mediate tensions between the more conditional, consensual, and egalitarian dimensions of peasant political culture and the more unbending, coercive, and authoritarian dimensions of peasant politics. In effect well-regarded *viejos* could be expected to favor the kinds of responsible interventions associated with mutually contingent visions of authority, even as their moral esteem granted them the latitude and expectations of deference associated with more absolute visions of authority.

The problem is that all did not always work tolerably well. Many *viejos* did not quite enjoy the prestige they asserted. Given the pressures on local power groups to accommodate the desires of colonial authorities and elites, given the opportunities for gain by community officials who merged into multiracial power groups or tilted toward a more authoritarian and privilege-oriented style of politics, and given the factionalism and internal differentiation that marred peasant life, these basic conditions of local politics could taint the record of prior service and claims of prestige by many *viejos*. Local critics might remembers a *viejo*'s earlier periods of officeholding not as community-oriented service but as times of self-aggrandizement, ambiguity of loyalties, or community strife and harm. Moreover, the active interventions of the *viejos* in community decision making drew them into contemporary controversy and blurred the distinction between prestigious elder and current officeholder. Three categories of historical service and prestige defined the upper reaches of community political structures. The *oficiales de república* were the current officeholders of major municipal and barrio posts such as *gobernador, alcalde, regidor, fiscal de iglesia* (church officer), or *escribano*. The *pasados* were ex-officeholders whose opinions counted but who might or might not have achieved the age, length of service, and esteem associated with a *viejo*. The *viejos* were those former officials whose experience, age, and prior service had garnered them a special moral prestige. In actual practice and language, however, these categories signified not hard and fast distinctions but a blurry spectrum marked by overlapping roles, temporary movement back and forth, and collective responsibility. The categories could blend into one. *Pasados* moved in and out of office, and *pasados* and *viejos* joined *oficiales*—the frequency probably varied by individual and by community but the practice was commonplace enough not to stir a fuss—in presiding over community decisions, courts, assemblies, and elections. The practice of joint responsibility encouraged a language that assigned decision, voice, and authorship not to the current *oficiales de república* alone but to the *oficiales, pasados y viejos de república*.[25]

In short, a less than ideal history of prior service could call the esteem of *viejos* and *pasados* into question, and ongoing interventions in contemporary political affairs could target them for controversy and resentment. Consider, for example, the case of the Tepoztlán *viejos* who in 1769 denounced Don Miguel Gerónimo, the current *gobernador*, for concocting self-enriching schemes—tributes theoretically assigned to church repair and community ritual—that ignored commoner poverty and ran roughshod over *viejo* rights to consultation. Among Don Miguel's abuses was treatment of *viejos* as enemies—"without attending to the posts we have obtained . . . or to the advanced age, of many of us, as the *viejos*." The *viejos*' self-styled role as protective guardians of the *hijos del pueblo* did not go unchallenged. Don Miguel Gerónimo and his allies countered that the real problem lay not with Don Miguel's alleged misrule but with the *viejos* themselves. *They* had been corrupt during their tenures in office, and they now refused to turn over community monies once entrusted to their care. Their claim to a wisdom beyond the fray of everyday ambition was further compromised by their alliance with the current *alcalde ordinario*, an officeholding rival of the *gobernador*. The *viejos'* assertions, in this view, simply provided cover for enrichment and power-seeking by a faction that had lost hegemony and wanted to reinstall its own *gobernador* candidate.[26]

The contradictory underside to *viejo* mediation will not sound unfamiliar to students of political brokers and state structures. Brokers, like the state itself, serve not only to mediate social tensions and contradictions. Precisely because they provide a leading arena for negotiation and contending pressure, they may also concentrate the contradictions of political life.[27] As responsible community patriarchs whose proven service and experience garnered them moral esteem, the *viejos* could foster unity and mediate tensions between visions of authority rooted in more absolute or proprietary claims and visions rooted in more conditional or reciprocal claims. But as political authorities and claimants of deference in their own right, *viejos* themselves could come under fire as irresponsible and self-aggrandizing patriarchs, as tyrants who abused their privileged place in a hegemonic power group or power seekers who parlayed their tainted esteem into political factionalism. Small wonder, then, that the same cultures that produced idealized images of *viejos*, cherished for their wisdom and community service, also yielded sharp and tumultuous accusations against particular *viejos*. The ideal *viejo* was a good father. The real *viejo* sometimes turned out to be a bad one.

The profoundly gendered constructions of community authority—the tensions between democratic patriarchy and vertical patriarchy and the mediation of such tensions in the higher wisdom of *viejos*— underscore the aptness of the familial metaphors that suffused political language. When the collaboration of *viejos*, *pasados*, and current *oficiales* worked smoothly, the patriarchal texture of community counsel and politics thickened. Familial metaphor acquired a certain symbolic and social depth, and the *hijos del pueblo* reference moved beyond casual analogue, closer to an affirmation of near-equivalence with family dynamics. This depth imparted a matter-of-fact tone, a kind of familial proprietorship, to the defense of a youthful peasant commoner by Tetelpan's *gobernador* and allied officials and notables. The water guard of a neighboring hacienda, complained Juan Joseph in 1780, had beaten "an *hijo* of this my pueblo."[28]

The depth behind familial metaphor might emerge not only in matters of protective solidarity but in cases of internal discipline. Miguel de Santiago, the *alcalde* of Barrio Huispalca of Tlaltizapán, explained a sequence of disciplinary events in 1809 in terms that placed a premium on "advice" by elders and authorities to the pueblo's sometimes obstinate *hijos*. Vicente Alejandro, an

Indian peasant widower, had persistently pursued a sexual liaison with María Ygnacia, a married Indian, and their relationship had provoked repeated discord in the community. "For once and twice and three times we have rebuked Bisente Alexandro that he should leave off the evil state with a married woman, and he has been plenty punished and he has been given plenty of advice, but he has not wanted to learn a lesson, until now the husband of the woman caught them again. . . . And we ordered him brought, and all the *viejos* met and they ordered that he be whipped." The *alcalde*'s assistant (*topile*) then proceeded to administer a particularly harsh whipping. Significantly, in the minds of Vicente Alejandro and María Ygnacia, it was the *viejos* who punished them in the early confrontations, regardless of who actually performed the physical acts of bodily seizure and punishment. In the final confrontation Vicente Alejandro's son intervened to plead or demand a halt to the whipping. He first removed his hat to greet the *alcalde* and the *viejos* respectfully, according to father and son, who also viewed the intervention as beseeching. Whatever the tone of the challenge — a deferential plea for mercy, a hostile questioning of right, or an ambiguous call for explanation — it seemed to inspire a sense of personal affront and determination. The *alcalde* took the whip from his assistant and proceeded to administer a resolute lashing himself.[29]

The initial admonitions and punishments; the disappointment that a wayward subject had failed to heed advice and discipline; the personal determination to carry through a lashing sufficiently severe and humiliating to drive home the lesson and to remain unswayed by objection or pleading; the presiding role of *viejos* from beginning to end: the entire sequence echoed the sounds of familial authority and politics.

We first encountered patriarchal metaphors in the languages of praise and denunciation inspired by two striking upheavals. Indian pueblos of the Cuernavaca district defended a controversial *alcalde mayor* who proved to be an exception to the colonial rule: a good patriarch who offered paternal love rather than parasitism to Indian *hijos*. Tumultuous dissidents in Tlayacapan displaced a power group discredited as self-fattening parasites and transformed a hero-prisoner into the redeeming father of the pueblo. Our subsequent analysis of the gendered politics of community authority clarifies the depth of such metaphors. They constituted more than cynical ploys directed upward and outward and more than exceptional metaphors within an otherwise horizontal or egalitarian political milieu. The contrapuntal language of good patriarch and parasitic tyrant evident in each upheaval pointed, rather, to the gendered and contradictory foundations of popular political culture. This was a political culture marked by contending visions of legitimate authority among its citizen-patriarchs and families. This was a culture whose language of argument about political right and obligation resonated strongly with its language of argument about gender right and obligation. This was a culture whose political contradictions were mediated—imperfectly—in the image of the wise patriarchal elder who looks after the needs of respectful community sons and children.

IN DEFENSE OF FAMILY AND COMMUNITY: WOMEN, POLITICS, AND RIOT

Did women forge a political space within a masculinized political culture? Subaltern political communities conflated the images of man and citizen. Citizen-patriarchs held an institutionally advantaged voice in public deliberation, decision, and justice by communities subject to poverty and social domination. Yet formal institutional constructions are one thing, and everyday practice and assertion are another. Notwithstanding the masculinized quality of subaltern citizenship, women pushed their way into public political space, often with men's complicity, and they forged important roles and influence in popular political culture. Women practiced with particular skill and visibility the ad hoc politics associated with emergencies. They garnered their political influence not from institutional standing as citizens but from cultural reputation as persons of consequence in a crisis.

In a sense, women extended into public arenas the practices, reputations, and moral sensibilities they forged in familial and quasi-familial contexts. As we have seen (Chapter 4), subaltern women were particularly practiced in the denunciation of excess and abuse by the men in their lives and in the promotion of a contingent model of reciprocal right, obligation, and authority. This background of female struggle imparted a certain moral consistency when women denounced excess and caprice by political officials who violated duty, reciprocity, and restraint. As we have also seen (Chapter 6), subaltern women mobilized formidable force not only in conflicts with their men but also in solidary defense of their children, families, and men. This background of female defense of kin imparted a certain moral credibility when subaltern women ferociously attacked elites or officials who threatened immediate harm to kin or community. When crisis required action and loosened social convention, women rushed into public space to assert their own moral sensibilities, their own versions of community voice and citizenship.[30]

The crossfires of gender and family and of color and class set the context for women's political activism. We have already observed the ways such crossfires impelled a certain zigzag in relations with male kin. On the one hand, only a foolish woman ignored the jeopardies of female gendered life. This implied the necessity to assert her needs and interests—and to help female kin, allies, and confidantes—even at the cost of bitter conflict with men. On the other hand, only a foolish woman ignored the jeopardies of social isolation in subaltern and female life. This implied the necessity to establish herself as a vital contributor and claimant in solidary relations that included men. What matters for the purposes of the present chapter is women's extension of solidary roles and claims to wider networks of barrio and community well-being. At moments of violence, for example, women might intervene to stop local men from their tendency to excess and escalation — even if the male assailants and targets who spiraled toward disaster did not include the women's own kin. In 1798 Juan de Santiago of Ocotepec stabbed an older Indian who advised the young cane cutter to mend his irresponsible ways. At that point, recalled Juan de Santiago, "the women seized him." They then transferred custody of the prisoner to village officials.[31]

The most dramatic public interventions occurred at moments of emergency mobilization and riot. William B. Taylor has observed, in a pioneering study of 142 rebellions in mid-to-late colonial Mexico, the highly visible and sometimes leading roles of women. "In at least one-fourth of the cases," he writes, "women led the attacks and were visibly more aggressive, insulting, and rebellious."[32] The Morelos materials corroborate this salience. Consider, for example, the case of Tetelzingo in 1778. The pueblo, considered both rich and tumultuous, drew the ire of Cuautla Amilpas's *alcalde mayor*, who sent a team headed by his deputy chief constable to crack down on the sale of popular drink (*mezcal, tepache, chinguirito*). The prime target of arrest was José Vizcarra, a Spanish schoolteacher married to an Indian woman, well regarded by villagers, and known to have assisted Tetelzingo in its legal battles in Mexico City. Vizcarra's home apparently served as an informal local tavern. As a precaution Don Francisco García del Barrio, the head of the inspection team, ordered Tetelzingo's *gobernador* and other local officials to accompany his party on the search for Vizcarra. Church bells rang out and called forth a "crowd of Indian men and women — something like over five hundred persons with sticks and stones." The *gobernador* refused to order the crowd to disperse (to do so would probably have been futile and self-defeating anyway), and Don Francisco and his group retreated before a hail of insults, threats, and stones. The verbal volleys reestablished community boundaries by threatening immediate violence: "Stop, Dog, we have to kill you and drink the blood." But the stone throws signified tacit agreement to allow the official to escape: all the stones missed their ostensible target. It was the Indian wife of José Vizcarra who pushed the volatile sequence to its very edge. Don Francisco's hat fell off in the confusion of the initial retreat. As he leaned down from his horse to nab it, she ran up, grabbed the hat and the horse halter, and urged the crowd to rush forward to seize Don Francisco himself. The terrified official broke loose and retreated quickly on his horse.[33]

The prominence of women, both as rioters in the crowd and as vehement leaders of confrontation, comes through repeatedly in the records of community riot. This prominence is all the more striking if one recalls the tendency of the documentary record to hide women and female youth within masculinized and generic categories (*indios, hijos,* or *padres de familia,* for example).[34]

There was more to women's prominence in riot, however, than female participation or leadership. Women played key roles in a gendered etiquette of revolt. The rites of gendered anger not only promoted a brand of female citizenship and influence; they also buttressed the legitimacy—and necessity—of male revolt. The sequence ran as follows: A community's outraged wives, mothers, and widows risked physical attack in order to defend their children, men, or families from abuse or extortion. The ferocity and insolence of the women dared the authorities to hit, injure, or seize them. If the authorities proceeded with repression, the attack against female property and kin provoked subaltern citizen-patriarchs to defend their masculinity.

These dynamics were sufficiently well understood to induce caution by authorities. A land judge, sent in 1793 to Zahuatlán (a tiny pueblito considered a barrio of Yecapixtla) to execute a ruling in favor of Hacienda Cuahuixtla, encountered an angry, insulting crowd of Indians. He explained how he avoided entrapment in a riot. "I dissimulated . . . despite having seen a woman among them pick up rocks, and of that I feigned ignorance precisely not to give them occasion for a tumultuous outburst that they had already been preparing." The inspection team retired prudently. In January 1794 the authorities got their revenge: they returned in force and burned to the ground the pueblito's twenty-four households.[35]

Sometimes, however, angry women did not leave much room for retreat. Such was the case in Tepoztlán in 1777.[36] Late in the morning on Friday, October 17, *arrieros* showed up to transport eighty loads of lime to Tlayacapan for church repair and construction. Tepoztlán's Indians had produced the lime for use on their own municipal and church facilities, but Don Manuel de Gamboa, a recently arrived priest, had decided that Tepoztlán did not need the lime and could therefore ship it to the church in Tlayacapan. Although the shipment was theoretically a loan, the terms of repayment were at best vague. Gamboa had secured the approval of Tepoztlán's *gobernador* and perhaps some other current officials, but he knew that the project sparked dissidence, particularly by "the *viejos* [and] some other Indians." When the *arrieros* began to load up and transport the lime, three men dashed off to the local *tianguis* "to summon the women." The women then took their lead role. "The Indian men, and many Indian women, went to tumble over [the lime], from behind the church, where the loads were already passing by, and the said Indian women in tumultuous fashion unloaded the lime . . . and threw out the mules and *arrieros* from the pueblo with stones." The women not only led the ambush of the caravan; they also led the confrontation with Padre Gamboa, who sought vainly to stop popular seizure of the shipment. The women roughed up their new priest: they scratched him and pulled and hung on to his clothes.

Gamboa, for his part, struck the clawing women with his staff. Gamboa called on the Indian *gobernador*, Juan Pedro, to help him out of his scrape. Juan Pedro's efforts came to nothing. He whipped one Nicolás Guaracha for "inciting the Indian women not to respect their *gobernador* or their priest" and set about trying to reorganize the lime shipment. But his presence and punishment failed to intimidate the women and other rebels, who turned on the *gobernador*. To achieve an uneasy — and temporary — peace, Gamboa had to settle for a distasteful quid pro quo. The women and other rebels would back away from physical confrontation with the priest and *gobernador*, but Gamboa and Juan Pedro would concede the women their victory in halting the lime project.[37]

Poor Nicolás Guaracha! The women had needed no special incitement to resent Gamboa and his associates. As members of the community, of course, they had good reason to thwart diversion of local resources by outside authorities who presumed a right to commandeer local labor and commodities. In addition, since his arrival in July, Gamboa's efforts to stamp out immorality had trod on gendered sensibilities, practices, and privileges that directly affected women. He opposed, for example, several customary practices associated with courtship and marriage: the brideprice service required of *novios* who brought water and wood to the households of *novias* before formal marriage, the social tolerance of sexual contact between *novias* and *novios* when poor families postponed marriage or encouraged a prolonged courtship phase, and the residence of newlyweds with the young man's parents and the accompanying apprenticeship of the young wife-servant to her mother-in-law. Practices such as these directly affected the organization of family economy and female labor, and Gamboa's attack on the prerogatives of mothers-in-law sparked heated exchanges of words. Finally, there was the question of humiliation. Indians asserted that for reasons they found frivolous, Gamboa had stripped and whipped several women. Given this background of tension and the fact that Indian women had dared to lift their hands against Gamboa and gotten away with it, the priest knew that Friday afternoon's peace was temporary. The women who clawed him had left his authority in tatters. Gamboa sent an urgent message for help; the *alcalde mayor*'s lieutenant in Yautepec commissioned Don Manuel Vicente Acosta to lead an armed band of eight men to Tepoztlán. Acosta understood his duty as that of providing "relief against some Indian women who had scratched [Gamboa], and lost respect."[38]

The repression backfired. It simply reignited the gendered etiquette of revolt. When the Yautepec group arrived in the early evening, they received directions to the homes of María Xolapa and María Tepoxpisca, two women judged particularly incendiary in the midday events. Acosta and his associates arrested the two Marías and brought them to Gamboa. But the bells began to ring — first from Barrio Santo Domingo Atenco, then around the several barrios of Tepoztlán, until finally someone slipped in to ring the bells of the principal church on the main plaza. Streets and plaza filled with Indian men, women, and youths (Gamboa estimated the crowd at 2,000), and the rebels proceeded to rescue the women and to invert the social roles. They knocked down Gamboa's door, seized Acosta and two other men in his Yautepec band, confiscated Acosta's wooden staff of authority and some weapons, and placed their three prisoners in stocks. (Gamboa, the other auxiliaries from Acosta's band, and the *gobernador* of Tepoztlán managed to escape during the melee.) When a relief force arrived from Yautepec the next morning, a crowd of Indian men and women forced them to retreat under a hail of stones. Finally, on Sunday morning, the rebels decided to comply with an order, issued by the *alcalde mayor* of Cuernavaca, to release the prisoners. First, however, two *pasados*— Pedro Marcos and Juan Lorenzo, former *gobernador* and former *alcalde*, respectively — showed up "dressed as judges and they took testimony." [39]

The details of the denouement need not concern us here. Rebellion continued to flare up, Viceroy Bucareli issued orders to put down the insubordination, and local officials and *hacendados* organized an ad hoc military force. It all came to naught, however, since most everyone in Tepoztlán fled to the nearby hills when the military expedition showed up. Bucareli retreated to a more diplomatic route to the restoration of authority — the pardons, couched in paternalistic language, common in Spanish colonial statecraft. "Contemplating that soft and benign measures are the most appropriate in the present case, . . . expressing to them that I make use of [my] widely known compassion, and attending to [the fact] that their rusticity and misery would lead to such heinous disorder, . . . I pardon the *común* [commoners, community] of their error." Key leaders of the revolt, continued the face-saving retreat, would not qualify for the pardon, and Tepoztlán's residents should return to their homes within eight days. [40]

For our purposes, women's leadership in a gendered etiquette of revolt is as important as the achievement of impasse and viceregal retreat. Padre Gamboa understood quite well that his principal obstacle was the alliance between *viejos* opposed to the lime project they considered an abuse imposed without their advice and consent, and women deeply angered by this and other intrusions on local right and willing to force the issue by physical action. As everyone knew, women responded fiercely in crises that threatened — in the women's view — the well-being of community families. As everyone also knew, the leading positions of women could place men in a bind. The ferocity of rebel women made it more difficult for authorities to find a face-saving retreat from physical confrontation, yet the status of women as gendered property also made it difficult to repress them without inciting proprietary outrage by men. Francisco Metla, a Tepoztlán Indian who served as a church singer, put the matter well in his summary of the uprising. "The priest was the cause of the tumult for wanting to take their lime, and . . . because their women had wanted to defend it the priest beat them with his staff. . . . At night, seeing that they wanted to seize their women, everyone rose up to defend them." Small wonder that when the muleteers arrived to load up and ship the lime, dissident men sent immediate word to the women. The critical moment had arrived.[41]

CULTURE AS ARGUMENT:
THE ECHOES OF GENDER CULTURE AND POLITICAL CULTURE

The echoes of gender culture and political culture bounded in both directions and sometimes merged into one. The language of argument about legitimate authority within subaltern political arenas bore striking kinship with arguments about right within arenas of gender and family. Although subaltern men constructed a masculinized sense of political prerogative and citizenship, and might seek to limit the tension between contingent and absolute right of authority to the arena of politics among citizen-patriarchs, life experience and struggle undermined such neat divisions. Women pressed contingent and reciprocal visions of right within familial and even sexual arenas; men brought familial languages of rank and dominion to their political relations with other men and with male youths. Women's pluralization-of-patriarchs strategy undermined private patriarchal domains and drew men in on the female side of specific arguments; men's reliance on women's forcefulness at moments of community crisis opened spaces for female brands of political voice and citizenship.

As we have seen, interpretation of culture as a practical language of argument about experience and social relations in common need not preclude recognition of mediation and unity of purpose.[42] The culture-as-argument approach frames mediation and unity as achievements—sometimes fragile and temporary—within a larger process that includes plural and often conflicting cultural precepts and practices. Even our study of mediation, however, underscored the two-way echoes of gender culture and political culture. Viejos, the metaphorical father-elders of the community, presumably supplied the wisdom and loyalty to the common good that restored balance when the group or its leaders lost their way. The gendered foundations of political argument and mediation encourage us to see familial metaphor not as casual analogue or charming folkloric idiom but as a capturing of deep and ubiquitous interplays of the political and the familial within subaltern life.

This depth of interplay emerged not only in verbal expressions and metaphors but also in more unspoken or subtle practices. The peremptory voice of senior rank, the beseeching intonation that mediated or camouflaged resistance, the obligatory hand-kiss to male parent and visiting priest (both "fathers"), the eyes averted then suddenly direct and confrontational, the hand lifted to a striking position — the extraverbal habits of domination, deference, and challenge learned in a familial arena of face-to-face relations might pass, with some transposition, into a community arena. The profile of sons walking ahead of their father on the way to the family *milpa*, their shoulders bearing the *coas* (digging sticks), seed, and other appurtenances of field labor, might be difficult to distinguish from the profile of a prosperous peasant marching along behind the land-poor peons sent his way by the community's *viejos* and *oficiales*. Unfortunately, however, nonverbalized connections such as these tend to elude the historian of times long past. The ethnographer of the living is more likely to catch a glimpse.[43]

The extraverbal dimensions of interplay between gender culture and political culture, however, do not entirely escape historical documentation. We have noted, for example, an etiquette of revolt that played on female and male sensibilities of right forged in familial and sexual contexts. An equally striking example of two-way echoes is the practice of whipping. Flogging constituted a commonplace device of both community and family punishment.[44] (Let us note before proceeding further, however, that we should avoid assumptions of cruelty, or simple conflations of political and familial flogging, even as we explore echo. The instruments of flogging varied considerably, from small, readily available sticks and switches [*varillas*], to more painful fiber whips ranging from simple maguey ropes [*mecates*] to cat-o'-nine tails [*disciplinas*], to leather and riding whips [*cuartas*, *látigos*] still more wounding and potentially dangerous. The degree of physical injury ranged enormously according to the instrument of flogging; the strength, number, and bodily location of lashes; and the age, health, and bodily attributes of the target. This variability warns us not to assume that all instances of switching or flogging led to major injury and thereby descend into middle-class stereotypes of barbarous Others.)

On the one hand, *oficiales*, *pasados*, and *viejos* occasionally used whipping not simply as community ritual and punishment but as an instrument of the humiliation associated with familial minors. In a confrontation over adultery charges and troublemaking in Xochitlán in 1789, the *amasio* suffered not only a shackling and whipping performed as spectacle before the assembled crowd of *gobernador*, authorities, and Indian commoners. His punishers dared "even to reach the point of lowering my pants." The *amasia* fared no better. After she removed her *huipil* (shift-blouse) to receive the lashes, the *gobernador* "ordered the underskirts [*naguas*] entirely removed, leaving [her] naked" to receive a lashing on the buttocks. The point of such episodes was to strip the miscreants of adult standing and respectability by transposing the imagery and practice of familial dominance and humiliation. Adults became symbolic minors, perhaps even cowering "children."[45]

On the other hand, the echo effect sometimes moved in the reverse direction. Husbands, *amasios*, and fathers sometimes resorted to switches or whips not simply as handy devices of spontaneous anger and punishment but as symbols within a more elaborate ritual of power. The targets were usually female, principally wives and *amasias*, but they occasionally included sons. In these rituals the patriarch did not strike right away at his insubordinate dependent. He followed the more demanding three-step process that prevailed in community rituals of punishment: the transport of the prisoner to the place of punishment, the binding of hands and the shackling or suspension of the body (via stocks, a tree, or a post), and the methodical humiliation and whipping of the offender. Augustín Mariano of Xalostoque, challenged in 1796 by his wife Victoriana Tomasa to stop his liaison with an *amasia*, and suspicious that *she* perhaps had an *amasio*, dragged her to a ravine, hoisted her on a tree or post, cut her braids and stripped her, then finally proceeded with the whipping.[46] I freely confess that during archival research my first encounter or two with such elaborate rites of family punishment and cruelty struck me mainly as the kind of pathological extreme or bizarre curiosity that invites psychological probings of particularly deviant or warped personalities. Why would patriarchs bother to drag away, bind, and hoist their targets rather than proceed immediately to a flogging or other violence? Only after I encountered repeated and varied instances of the phenomenon and reflected more seriously on the way most males had opportunities to participate—as municipal officials, rotating *topiles* (assistants), or witnesses—in community punishment did I come to appreciate social and cultural patterning.[47] These were rites of familial power and authority that borrowed and refracted symbols of governance, legitimacy, and delinquency from the arena of community ritual and power. Husbands, *amasios*, and fathers were enlarged into symbolic *alcaldes* and *gobernadores*.

Given the rotations of men and their kin into the community political structure of officials and assistants, the mental distance from one role to the other was not always large. Juan Pablo, an Indian tributary of Tepetlixpa, recruited his brother to help break the stubborn insubordination of Rita Desideria, his young Indian wife. Rita Desideria, only fourteen years old, had run away repeatedly to escape her husband's abuse and violence. Juan Pablo's brother also happened to be the *alcalde* of Tepetlixpa. When the two of them proceeded to haul, tie up, hoist, and whip Rita Desideria, did the presence of a brother-*alcalde* enlarge the sense of righteous governance Juan Pablo drew from ritualized violence?[48]

We have argued that processes of echo, resonance, and temporary fusion promoted deep interplay between the domains of gender politics in civil society and public politics in formal governance. Peasants did not demarcate rigidly between public and private arenas of jurisdiction but extended and adapted ideas of right from one arena to the other.[49] We have set this argument in a theoretical context that asks us to discern the conflictual as well as the unifying and mediating dimensions of culture. The sense of echo and the notion of a conflictual culture of argument are brought together powerfully in a single word: *respeto*. The language of respect, like familial metaphor, facilitated transposition and occasional fusion between familial and political domains of everyday life. As we have already seen, the great offense of political subordinates was their *falta de respeto*, and the language of such accusations bore striking resemblance to the language of affronted familial authority. Yet the meaning of *respeto* could cut in several directions. From the point of view of an affronted superior, *falta de respeto* signified a failure to defer to the inherent prerogative and status of the superior. One owed respectful deference to a family elder, a patriarch, or a community official or *viejo* even if the inner self questioned the rightness of specific acts, demands, or excesses of the superior. To lose the fear of disorder or punishment, to dare to question bluntly or to lift the hand, to lose the restraint that kept the sense of quarrel more or less inside the self and weakened its outer expression — this was to lose respect. This turned subordinates into "shameless" people, "mindless . . . of their obligations, and duties, buoyed by haughtiness and arrogance."[50]

But the vantage points of the relatively empowered did not exhaust the cultural meaning of *respeto*. From the vantage point of abused inferiors, *falta de respeto* signified failure to defer to the duty of reciprocity and restraint in the exercise of power. This failure trampled on the dignity and rightful claims of subordinates and unleashed its own brand of disorder. Superiors became tyrants or parasites whose excesses wrecked social balance, divided families and communities, and provoked challenges that rendered authority all the more contingent and uncertain. In 1805 José Silverio Barreto, an Indian tributary of Cuautla Amilpas, lagged in his contribution to community water works and was thrown in jail by the *gobernador*, Anastasio Antonio Gutiérrez. To José Silverio the problem was that the *gobernador* had given free rein to his power and "intrepid temper." José Silverio had simply lagged a bit in work rendered dangerous by the rains, and Anastasio Antonio reacted as if a terrible offense had been committed. He arrested, slapped, and insulted José Silverio and threatened to destroy his house and seize his goods. All of this signified a man who had lost respect for the proper order of things and had thereby become a tyrant. Without a trace of irony the subordinate man accused his *gobernador* "of an undeniable insubordination, and lack of respect, about which there are not a few complaints." The *gobernador*, of course, saw the matter differently. He had arrested José Silverio because the malingerer was an "insurgent against the authority, and respect of his *gobernador* and his territorial judge."[51]

The contested meaning of *respeto* condenses the conflictual dynamics of culture and the two-way echoes of familial and public politics into a single loaded word. There was more to this multivocal word, of course, than conflict over its meaning. All twists on the word's meaning incorporated a core idea of restraint, a deference to order, place, and legitimacy that restrained destructive inner impulses — whether the impulse to challenge authority or to abuse it. The core idea itself bears echoes of earlier times and places and several cultural influences: the emphasis, in the Nahua cultures of Mexica (Aztec) times, on control of inner energies that could burst forth to destroy or dissipate the order of life; the insistence, in early colonial Spanish culture, on constructing a firm sense of conquistador rank and respect for seniority out of the turbulence of a conquest society; the condemnation of blacks and mulattoes in colonial racial stereotyping as symbols of licentiousness, people who lacked family lineage and respect for social order.[52] But at the core of the term was not only an idea of restraint, deep and varied in its cultural and historical roots, adaptable to varied uses and contexts, a potential resource for mediation and shared understanding. At the core, too, was culture as a language of argument in the exercise of power.

The boundaries between distinct arenas of subaltern power and argument blurred, and the arenas could end up overlapping in more ways than one. For these very reasons the languages of familial and political argument threw up striking echoes. This was a society whose politics of gender and whose gendering of politics sometimes merged into one.

PART THREE

Many Mexicos?

Culture as Variation

CHAPTER 9

Regionalism and *Mexicanidad*

Toward a Framework

No single region can stand for the abstraction we call Mexico. More than a half-century ago Lesley Byrd Simpson wrote a classic work whose title, *Many Mexicos,* evoked the diversity of Mexican life. In Simpson's usage the plurality of Mexico referred more to differences of physical geography and climate, ethnolinguistic group, and historical moment than to contrasts between regional worlds as such. Indeed, south of the arid northern zone (Simpson's "Gran Chichimeca"), heir of nomadic rather than sedentary indigenous cultures and marked by thin population, eventual spread of Spanish ranching and missions, and occasional mining strikes in colonial times, Simpson saw a certain cultural unity, the "heart and kernel of Mexico." His synoptic treatment of Mexican history as a whole implied belief in a certain *mexicanidad* (Mexicanness) within the diversity of "many Mexicos."[1]

During the last twenty-five years the idea of many Mexicos not only gained great currency among students of Mexico; it also acquired a more regionalist meaning. Some of this new meaning derives from currents in historiography beyond as well as within Mexico. The U.S. history profession, which generates a large corpus of historical writing on Mexico, experienced the social history revolution — the movement to recover the histories of social groups and experiences neglected or trivialized in elite-centered histories of high politics and high culture. The social history movement promoted a turn toward regional and microregional units of analysis. Methodologically, it seemed to require an on-the-ground approach built on gleaning and synthesizing huge volumes of documentation within local or regional contexts. Conceptually, exploration of regional or microregional worlds far removed from the centers of official power also seemed to offer an important counterpoint to standardized views from the top. This shift in perspective, along with the prior turn toward regional and local perspectives encouraged by the outstanding *Annales* school historians, lent greater international prestige to subnational approaches to historical writing. The Mexican intelligentsia and U.S. historians of Mexico participated in this shift in international historiography.[2]

In the Mexican context the turn toward regional study gained ground for additional reasons as well.[3] It built on a tradition of local intellectuals who promoted microhistorical visions of identity and meaning, a sometimes dissenting counterpoint to official histories from the national center. It also reflected new developments in Mexico. First, the center of economic and political gravity shifted north in Mexico in the twentieth century. The faction that emerged dominant from the revolutionary wars; the Pancho Villa who became an icon of popular anger, foible, and aspiration; and the dynamic new centers of industry and "green revolution" agriculture that propelled economic growth and development after World War II all were rooted in the Mexican north. Given these developments, the northern regions could not as easily be dismissed as a frontier outside the heart of "Mexico." Even a history centered on elites and power at the top would have to step outside a Mexico City frame and take account of regional diversity.

Second, and probably more important, the trauma of 1968 — the massacre of demonstrators by army and police forces at Tlatelolco — dealt a death blow to the prestige of official history and its more centered sensibility of "Mexico." The Tlatelolco affair climaxed the Mexican version of the political restlessness of the 1960s: the juxtaposition of the Cuban Revolution with Mexico's continuing social misery and polarized distribution of an economic "miracle" strained political legitimacy. The shock of lethal violence against a mass of unarmed Mexicans made all the more unreal the picture of a revolutionary state organizing a democratic march of economic development and social justice. The crisis not only widened cracks within the state's hegemonic party; it also turned out to be a formative event in the making of the intelligentsia of the 1970s and 1980s. The official version of state history acknowledged diversity but incorporated it into the making of oneness out of diversity. The state celebrated *mestizaje* (racial fusion and mixing) as the building of a people from several races. The state acquired, moreover, a heroic vitality precisely because it forged oneness out of plurality. A historical background of regional, ethnic, and linguistic diversity, preserved not only in history books and anthropological museums but in living Indian tourist sites for national and international visitors, turned the creation of effective national identity and nation-state formation into a formidable revolutionary accomplishment of integration and cultural appreciation. Tlatelolco undermined this picture. It fostered an intellectual milieu more concerned with exploring regional worlds and socially marginalized people in their own right.

For reasons both Mexican and international, therefore, historians of Mexico participated strongly in the turn to regional and microregional framings of history. One result is that a plethora of fine monographic studies, both historical and ethnographic, has served to draw out the particularities of many Mexican regions, locales, and experiences. There is, in this sense, an undeniable authenticity to the discourse of regional plurality and difference.

Yet if each region's experience contributes to our understanding of the Mexican mosaic, the new dominance of regionalism can also exact a price. The most searching students of regionalism in Mexican history have observed at least two dangers. First, definition of the region under study may reflect convenience — the way documentation lines up administratively — rather than conceptual criteria or variables for comparison. Second, focus on a regional world as such can breed a self-defeating insularity — a failure to recognize the center/periphery dynamics that integrate a given region or locale into wider structures of power and historical process, a willingness to settle for analysis of idiosyncrasies that leave national story lines and periodizations curiously intact, either accepted as given or hopelessly in tatters.[4] In short, when regionalism becomes professorial common sense, the concept may lose some of its intellectual edge. Comparison across regions and reconsiderations of the whole may fall by the wayside. National essentialism may give way to regional essentialism. The question of whether there is a Mexico in many Mexicos fades from view.

For the purposes of this book the challenge of many Mexicos is to forge an analytical framework that enables us to explore the many and the Mexicos simultaneously. On the one hand, the framework must succeed in cutting down to more modest, less fetishized size the vaunted regional and microregional heterogeneity of Mexico. It must present and interpret data that suggest dimensions of culture and power in common. On the other hand, the framework must interpret and contextualize rather than suppress authentic heterogeneity, and it must reconcile the emphasis on similarity, resonance, or points in common with our theoretical approach to culture as argument, a process that implies plurality and conflict.

Substantively we shall argue that regional difference often resides in somewhat distinctive, even subtle reconfigurations of recognizable cultural practice and argument. Qualitative and quantitative analysis of gender and power in the Indian peasant world of Oaxaca and in the racially mixed plebeian world of Mexico City will suggest both striking resemblance with the general patterns in Morelos and regionally distinct shadings and emphases within the overall pattern. Once magnified, these sometimes subtle variations may obliterate one's vision of dynamics in common and may serve as a platform for a discourse of quintessentially distinct regional worlds. Yet as students of Mexican locales have observed in other contexts, the uniqueness of a region may reside in particular twists placed on a recognizable theme, in particular syntheses of social practices or forces that reverberate more widely. The challenge of comparative regional analysis is to draw out consistency and variation simultaneously.[5]

Theoretically we shall argue that culture itself is not only a language of argument but also one of variation. That is, cultural practice and discourse not only mobilize the shifting processes of conflict, mediation, and unity that constitute argument. Cultural practice and discourse also mobilize processes of identifying self and group in relation to variant Others. In a deep sense, social solidarities and understandings have as their premise a discourse of variation. Simone de Beauvoir made the point long ago, within an existentialist framework and with specific reference to gender: the cultural history of Man as Self, in Western culture, is incomprehensible except in relation to a cultural history of Woman as Other.[6] More recent writers have studied the problem of Othering in crosscultural, imperial, and ethnic as well as gendered contexts.[7] The key theoretical point, for our purposes, is that the cultural language of the self, whether applied to an individual, a social group, or a regional world, implies a cultural language of the Other. Moreover, the discourse of variation commonly focuses not only on cultural strangers beyond the self's social world but also on variance within the known world of the cultural insider. The individuals, genders, and generations; the families and lineages, ethnic strata and social classes; and the barrios, communities, and microregions all introduce a potential for culture as a language of variation as well as argument within a given regional world.

In this theoretical context the problem of many Mexicos becomes not only a problem between regions but within them. An argument of resemblance in patterns across regions need not preclude pluralized approaches to culture — as argument and variation. Once we explore the many Mexicos of *every* Mexican region, moreover, we discover that languages of gross difference applied between regions may also have characterized variation within them. This perspective will not only suggest a fresh reconsideration of the Morelos materials (Chapter 12). It also establishes a basis for reconciling the findings of triregional resemblance, in the contending visions of gender right that suffused subaltern conflict and politics, with a contextualized sense of regional heterogeneity. For as we shall see (Chapters 10–12), even as they mobilized sometimes violent argument about gender right recognizable across several Mexican regions, the peoples of distinct Mexican regions, microregions, and social groupings brought distinctive accents, shadings, and social conventions to gendered cultural argument.

CONSISTENCY AND VARIATION (I): REGIONAL PROFILES

Let us turn briefly to triregional profiles that will set a context for later discussion of specific regions. For the regions of Morelos, Oaxaca, and Mexico City the net total of criminal violence cases analyzed statistically amounted to 613 incidents. The net total of violence and morality cases analyzed statistically was 708. (See Table 9.1. As observed in Chapter 2, for Morelos and Oaxaca the family or sexual morality cases proved too few for useful statistical analysis; only for Mexico City did such cases survive into the net case set.) The comparatively small size of the Mexico City violence case set (156 incidents) is ameliorated by two considerations. First, the number of cases is more than sufficient for reliable comparative analysis of variance between the three regions. Second, the comparatively large number (108) of sexual and family morality cases in the Mexico City materials allows us to examine the Mexico City violence incidents within a larger Mexico City pattern and thereby to introduce another avenue to check for potential bias in the social profiles of the violence cases. After elimination of potential double counts caused by 13 overlapping cases, the fuller Mexico City case set amounts to 251 net incidents of criminal violence and morality proceedings. All in all, the regional samples of criminal violence yielded low-to-moderate error margins for simple analysis of statistical distributions. The error margins of regions considered individually hover in the 6–7 percent range (by a conservative 95 percent confidence level calculation); the margin amounts to only 4 percent for the triregional set as a whole.

The types of incidents and their chronological spread compare reasonably well across the three regions. In all three regions seriously injurious violence dominated the case sets. Homicides, major assaults, rapes, and kidnappings accounted for about five- to six-sevenths of the cases in each region. Although the balance among these incidents tilted more sharply toward homicide in the case of Morelos, the homicide/nonhomicide distinction failed to yield statistically significant nonrandom associations in the motivations of disputes culminating in violence.[8] The chronological consistency was spottier. The incidents studied for Morelos and Mexico City clustered toward the latter half of the 1760–1821 period under study (three-fourths of the cases in both regions occurred in the 1790–1821 period). The Oaxaca incidents exhibited a more even spread (about four-ninths occurred in the 1790–1821 period). Fortunately, however, the distinctive chronology of the Oaxaca materials appears to be inconsequential as a marker of historical changes in the social dynamics of violence within the 1760–1821 period and is more important as an expression of institutional record keeping and sampling choices.[9]

In Oaxaca and Mexico City, as in Morelos, the sociocultural normalcy that appeared in the criminal violence records is striking. On the one hand, markers of deviance — whether deviant persons such as loners or repeat offenders, or time-out situations such as drunkenness, late night outings, or confrontation in isolated spots — failed to weigh heavily or disproportionately in the case set as a whole and failed to yield statistically significant nonrandom associations with gender-rooted violence in particular.[10] On the other hand, the color-class markings of the case set were consistent with those of regional popular culture. As in Morelos, assailants and targets were comprised mainly of poor and illiterate commoners, in ethnic proportions roughly comparable to that of the local society, and the targets of violence bore somewhat closer connection to the bottom of the social pyramid. In addition, color-class markers failed to yield statistically significant associations between middling or lighter strata and gender-rooted violence.[11] The main imbalances in the Oaxaca and Mexico City violence records were those already encountered in the Morelos case set. The distribution of assailants and targets touched a wide spectrum of ages but leaned somewhat toward youth and young adults. This tilt is only moderate: if, in view of early modern life expectancies, one defines middle age as beginning at about thirty-five years, even middle-aged adults were present in reasonable numbers. As in Morelos, it was violence against younger children (under sixteen years) that especially eluded the proceedings and testimonies recorded in our documents. As in Morelos, the sex distributions of assailants and targets were also notably uneven. The distribution emphasized males, but the tilt was especially one-sided in the case of assailants. Males comprised about nine-tenths of assailants, but females accounted for roughly a third of targets. (See Table 9.2.)

Regional comparison yielded two major surprises. The first was the degree of interregional consistency in the general structure of motivation and social bonding in disputes culminating in criminal violence. Let us recall that the analysis of Morelos yielded a tripartite structure of major motivations: gender-rooted disputes linked directly to claims of gender right and obligation or to social expressions of masculinity or femininity; property/class disputes linked to theft or contestations over money, property, debts, work in public spaces, tributary obligations, and the like; and *descarga* ventings that unleashed anger, hostility, or frustration on an available target, in contexts suggesting casual or hypersensitive outbursts bearing little specific motivation or relationship to the target.

The discourse of ethnoregional contrast might lead one to expect substantial differences in the structure of motivation. In particular one might expect sharp contrasts in the dynamics of gender, power seeking, and violence that have infused the regional worlds of mestizo and Indian Mexico. Presumably, gender-rooted violence weighed more heavily in relatively Hispanized arenas such as Mexico City and Morelos than in more thoroughly Indian settings such as Oaxaca. The contrast between Nahua indigenous roots in central Mexico and the indigenous cultures of the Mexican south presumably exerted a similar effect. *Descarga* ventings ought to have been a greater affliction in the insecure world of plebeians, poor Spaniards, and *castas* in Mexico City than in Morelos or Oaxaca, where a sense of community order and responsibility would have discouraged casual and self-destructive ventings. Property/class disputes over tangibles such as land and labor, money and commodities, and debt and tribute might have accounted for a greater share of violent assaults in Oaxaca. The modest weight of gender-rooted violence and *descarga* ventings and the vulnerability of isolated rural travelers to assault contrasted with a city world where sparks to violence were more diverse and even casual, where individuals with goods or money could avoid the isolation of rural roads, and where opportunities for relatively anonymous and nonviolent forms of theft and burglary were more abundant.[12]

The expectation of contrast, however, was borne out only weakly, if at all, in the statistical distributions. The relative weight of motivations varied somewhat, and the heavier accents on gender-rooted disputes in Mexico City and property/class disputes in Oaxaca accorded with the expectations discussed above. But these distinctions represented subtle shadings that shrink to statistical insignificance when one examines the larger picture. In all three regions, gender-rooted disputes accounted for about half the violence incidents, by far the largest share, and *descarga* ventings — even by amplified criteria — accounted for about a fifth. (See Table 9.3.) Testing for nonrandom associations between regions and major motivations of dispute failed to yield statistically significant variations.[13] Even if one focuses exclusively on motivations of violence against women and female youth and the relative weights of specifically sexual claims and rights within such cases, a pattern of modest shadings within broad interregional consistency emerges. As in Morelos, contestations over sexual matters proved central yet less than subsumptive. In each region, conflict over sexual claims accounted for a majority or near-majority (three- to four-sevenths) of the total cases, by far the largest share. Within this context, the spectrum defined by Mexico City's four-sevenths (58.2 percent), Morelos's half (48.4 percent), and Oaxaca's three-sevenths (43.9 percent) conformed to expectations. Conflicts over nonsexual gender rights such as labor obligations, physical mobility, and verbal affronts, however, proved important in their own right and accounted for roughly three-tenths of the incidents in each region (30.6 percent, 28.8 percent, and 27.3 percent for Morelos, Oaxaca, and Mexico City, respectively).[14]

Not only did the general structure of motivation compare well across regions. In addition, a broad interregional consistency emerged in measures of the association between the gender of the assaulted and their social bonding with assailants. Let us recall that for the case of Morelos, an emphatic gender contrast among violence targets called into question the myth of patriarchal protection. We summarized the contrast as follows: the more closely bonded the relationship, the more likely the danger of violence for women compared with men; the more loosely bonded the relationship, the more likely the danger of violence for men compared with women. One might expect the pattern to have varied sharply by region. In the plebeian setting of Mexico City, presumably, women moved about with greater anonymity and freedom from male surveillance, forged a somewhat freer sexual style, and faced husbands and *amasios* more inclined to imagine sexual betrayal. In addition, they fought with plebeian husbands and *amasios* over insecure urban household economies and negligent dissipation of resources in masculine diversion. All of this might lead to heightened conflict within the arena of primary, especially inner primary, relations. The connection between closeness of social bonding and specifically female targets of violence might overshadow even that of Morelos. In Oaxaca, women presumably exerted a bolder, more independent and defiant presence in economic transactions and disputes with friends, acquaintances, and strangers (secondary and tertiary relations). They presumably intervened — with even less inhibition than their Morelos counterparts — to protect husbands, kin, or community citizens in physical confrontations with nonkin and strangers, and they proved vulnerable to assaults by ethnic enemies who attacked female as well as male members of the enemy group. All of this might lead to heightened conflicts and violence within the arena of secondary and tertiary relations and thereby yield a weaker gender contrast than that found for Morelos.

These expectations are logical and plausible by-products of our understanding of Mexico's regional and cultural heterogeneity. For this very reason the interregional consistency in the association of female targets with closer social bonds, and male targets with looser bonds, is striking. Not only was the connection of specifically female danger with comparatively closer social bonding impressively strong in all three regions. The degree of strength was also remarkably consistent. (See Table 9.4.)

In short, roughly parallel structures of motivation in criminal violence incidents prevailed in all three regions. Within this context, gender-rooted incidents overshadowed by far property/class incidents and *descarga* incidents, and a dramatically tight association of close social bonding and the danger of violent assault distinguished women from men.

The second major surprise in the data was the consistency of motivation for violence within Oaxaca. Let us recall that we selected for study three distinctive districts in the heart of the region: the Mixteca Alta to the west, the southern portion of the Zapotec Valley in the center, and the Villa Alta zone of the Sierra Zapoteca to the east. Let us recall, too, that the Oaxaca region is celebrated as an area whose ethnolinguistic, ecological, and economic diversity serves as an extreme microcosm of Mexican diversity. Implicitly or explicitly, study of the Mixteca Alta, Zapotec Valley, or Villa Alta zones would appear to confirm this framework of contrast. If one seeks to highlight bold women, a tradition of relative equilibrium of power and respect among the genders, and cohesive indigenous communities able to adapt well to the market and to resist cultural and economic inroads by Hispanized social sectors, one points to the southern portion of the Zapotec Valley. (For the themes of powerful women and militant ethnic radicalism, the Isthmus Zapotec area beyond the core districts of this study has drawn even greater attention.) If one seeks to highlight indigenous poverty and decline and a level of Hispanic economic and cultural penetration considered strong within a Oaxacan context, one points to the Mixteca Alta. If one seeks to discover more remote indigenous worlds whose internal class dynamics were comparatively muted and whose ideologies stressed community harmony and balance, one points to the Villa Alta region.[15] The cultural differences might lead one to expect relatively greater emphasis on gender-rooted and *descarga* violence in the Mixteca Alta (an expectation further reinforced by the somewhat greater presence of plebeians and non-Indians in the Mixteca Alta documents) and a greater share of property/class disputes in the Zapotec Valley.[16] A parallel contrast between the Zapotec Valley and Villa Alta might complete a spectrum of variation. One may detect certain shadings in conformity with these expectations: in Villa Alta, property/class disputes indeed weighed more heavily and *descargas* less heavily than in the Mixteca Alta or the Valley. But such shadings emerge only spottily, within a context of surprising intraregional consistency. In all three microregions, gender-rooted disputes accounted for nearly half the violence incidents, by far the largest share. In two of the three zones, property/class disputes and *descarga* ventings filled out the balance of remaining cases in roughly equal measure. (See Table 9.5.) Testing for nonrandom associations between microregions and the relative weight of major motivations failed to yield statistically significant variance.[17] As in the comparison of Morelos, Oaxaca, and Mexico City, what stands out are the predominance and remarkably similar shares of gender-rooted violence, the broad similarities in the overall distribution of violence motives, and the subtlety of variation within or alongside consistency.

CONSISTENCY AND VARIATION (II): CAUTIONS

This chapter has not attempted to argue for the absence of regional heterogeneity in the history of Mexico. It has sought, rather, to lay the groundwork for a more considered reflection of plurality—an assessment of contrast in relation to countervailing currents of similarity and resonance. Specifically, our framework asks us to formulate an understanding of many Mexicos on terms that avoid essentialism, an assumption of quintessential character or idiosyncrasy that contrasts one regional world with another. Our analysis asks us to consider, too, that the interplays of gender and power constitute a domain of experience that may cut across boundaries discerned in other domains of experience. Notwithstanding regional differences that may (or may not) have prevailed in the realms of political economy, ethnocultural dynamics and social composition, and strategies of elite control and popular resistance, the conflictual constructions of gender and power examined for Morelos resonated deeply with popular experience elsewhere in Mexico.

Finally, the foregoing analysis invites us to theorize culture in terms that transcend treatment of variation and consistency as mutually exclusive. Once one explores culture not as a unified and unifying "body of values and understandings," but as languages of argument and variation within shared social arenas, the mental grip of the dichotomous opposition between similarity and contrast weakens. Within and across regions our task becomes one of excavating subtle variations within contexts of consistency, underlying consistencies within contexts of variation.

Let us illustrate with a brief example the contrapuntal patterning of variation within consistency, consistency within variation. The structure of motivation in violence disputes was broadly similar in Morelos, Oaxaca, and Mexico City. Even so, this finding does not address the comparative frequency or severity of violence. Gender-rooted and other disputes may have followed recognizable contours of argument and relative importance in violence across several regions. But how, for example, did regions compare in the frequency with which such disputes unleashed homicidal violence? Homicides constituted half (53.9 percent) of the violence cases in the Morelos sample, two-fifths (39.7 percent) of those in Mexico City, and only a fourth (24.7 percent) of those in Oaxaca. The spectrum suggests contrasting comparative tendencies of dispute to metamorphose into dangerous violence. It is possible, of course, that idiosyncrasies of institutional record keeping and sampling choices account for most of the difference. The homicide rate per 100,000 population is a more meaningful statistic, but its calculation is elusive, given the sources and sampling methods used in this study. (My best guesstimate is a rate of about 10 per 100,000 for Oaxaca, 11 per 100,000 in Mexico City, and 20 per 100,000 in Morelos in late colonial times, but these calculations are tenuous and may serve only to suggest orders of magnitude.) If we assume, however, that the samples for Morelos and Oaxaca captured roughly equal proportions of total homicides (whatever the differences in their recording of assaults short of homicide), we may calculate the ratio of their respective rates. By this method the homicide rate in late colonial Morelos appears to have been double or more that which prevailed in the Oaxaca districts.[18]

Consistency, in short, fails to exclude variation. Both sides of the counterpoint are necessary to a contextualized assessment of transregional resonance and regional diversity. The similar weight of gender-rooted disputes in the overall patterns of criminal violence, and the distinctive readiness to resort to deadly violence to resolve disputes, are *both* pertinent to a comparative assessment of gender, power, and violence in popular culture. Indeed, as we explore more closely in Part 3 the specific regional content of gendered argument culminating in violence, we will find distinctive emphases and shadings within struggles that had a familiar ring in more than one region.

In short, the approach advocated here argues not for one Mexico but for scrutiny, from the angle of gender and power, of the tension embedded in an oxymoron: many Mexicos. The dramas of gender and power we encountered in Morelos would have been recognizable to many an ear in Oaxaca and Mexico City. But from time to time, specificities of plot and choreographic style might also have seemed a bit odd or idiosyncratic. In the chapters that follow, we journey toward the mingling of similarity, resonance, and difference that comprised a world of many Mexicos.

CHAPTER 10

The Indian South

Gender, Power, and Ethnicity

in Oaxaca

MEMORIES OF MORELOS

One need not probe long before encountering in Oaxaca gendered dramas familiar to the student of Morelos. In Oaxaca as in Morelos the dialectics of cultural argument brought forth contending visions of gender right: an orientation to male-female relations that emphasized the mutually contingent character of right and its corollary, a large space for female critique and initiative; and an orientation that stressed the innate or absolute character of male right and its corollary, an insistent demand for female obedience notwithstanding inner grievances. In Oaxaca as in Morelos we may read this conflictual cultural dialogue in part as an argument between women and men and in part as an argument that ran through popular culture as a whole. On the one hand, it was women or female youth who usually had the most pressing reasons to initiate and to defend contingent visions of gender right in male-female relations and to seek allies and supporters. When mediation or deflection disintegrated, the tension could escalate into a drama of violence and ruin that brought forth starkly polarized conflict between female and male visions of right. On the other hand, the crossover phenomenon we witnessed in Morelos blurred neat gender alignments and could implicate the same individuals, at different moments, on both sides of cultural argument about male-female relations. As we have seen, the social dynamics that induced ambivalence and crossovers—male support of the female position and female support of the male position—were numerous. They included the connections of adults, mainly through marriage but also through fictive kin relations and extramarital sexual relations, to competing kin clusters; the forging of pluralization-of-patriarchs strategies by women; the generational powers women mobilized as family elders, mothers, and mothers-in-law; the cross-fires of women who experienced imperatives of color-class and familial solidarities alongside the imperatives of gender conflict; the interests of men as well as women in avoiding subaltern ruptures that might break the facade of community harmony or invite abusive interventions and extortions; the rankings among men who distinguished between elder and youth, notable and commoner, and worthy patriarch and deviant troublemaker.

In short, one may discover in Oaxaca women and men whose stories conjure up memories of the Marías of Morelos. On Wednesday morning, June 28, 1775, Mariana López, an Indian of Cuquila (Mixteca Alta), woke up to good news. Caught in a marriage of perpetual fights with a husband she considered lazy and abusive, Mariana had gotten some support from Cuquila's Indian authorities. The *oficiales* had pressured her husband, Baltasar, to tend to the clearing and planting cycle in the family *milpa*, and the pressure was apparently producing the desired effect. That morning Baltasar told Mariana to wake up and get busy grinding corn for tortillas. He was leaving with their young sons to work the *milpa* and to cut wood; she would need to bring freshly ground tortillas to the *milpa*, about an hour's walk from Cuquila.

The news was welcome, but the rancor of the marriage did not magically dissipate upon Baltasar's departure for the *milpa*. During planting season a wife would normally have roused herself at dawn or earlier to begin the arduous work in time for a mid-to-late morning meal. Mariana's more casual rhythm in early morning tortilla matters signaled an unpleasant fact of life: a negligent and abusive husband could not expect timely labor from his wife — not without reminders and wake-ups, harassments, or even quarrels. The signal did not sit well with Mariana's husband. When Mariana arrived late (perhaps around eleven o'clock) with her tortillas, did Baltasar's irritability merely signify a passing anger induced by a morning of hunger and slack attention from his wife? Or did it signal a deeper fury called up by the symbolism of the day's events? On this day, as on other days, Mariana had failed to defer internally to her husband's authority. Instead she ensnared it in a web of foot dragging, remonstrance, and appeal that curtailed his authority within and beyond the household arena. Indeed, Baltasar had come to feel the sting of community pressure to overcome his laziness. Given the moral pressure roused against him, work in the *milpa* conveyed no particular legitimacy to his tainted standing as a community son and patriarch. It simply implied that the community had managed to coerce one of its lazy *hijos* to work.

Because family life and economic sustenance implied the necessity of collaboration, notwithstanding conflictual assertions of right that also proved pervasive, it is not surprising that Baltasar and Mariana reached for a means to deflect or ease the tension. When three women bearing *pulque* approached on the path alongside the *milpa*, the Indian couple found an opportunity to signal to each other a readiness to back away from confrontation. Mariana stopped the women and used her own money to buy a jug of *pulque* to share with her husband. After the refreshment Baltasar bought another jug, and the women left. He promised to pay the women with maize he would deliver later in Tlaxiaco. Baltasar then proceeded to invite Mariana to drink with him.

When Mariana declined the invitation to conviviality — she could drink no more, she said, because her stomach ached and she was still nursing a child — Baltasar's fury erupted. He began the beating with a *mecapal* (a leather and maguey rope band for carrying loads on one's back), proceeded to knock his wife to the ground and beat her on the back with the handle of his machete, and finally turned the machete around to beat and prick Mariana on the head and face. The torture stopped when Mariana could lift her head no more. Baltasar then left for the *monte* with his machete, his *mecapal*, a basket of tortillas, and the jar of *pulque*. The couple's twelve-year-old son Marcelo returned to Cuquila to advise the Indian authorities of the horrible events he had witnessed. The village authorities had an official and some assistants spy on the *milpa*. Later that afternoon they caught their prey when Baltasar sneaked back to view the body and told his dead wife, "Now you're done dying, now yes." He would later concede, after retracting a "provocation" story that proved transparent, that his wife's refusal to drink sufficed to drive him over the edge because he had never let go of his anger — anger about late tortillas, anger about a wife who quarreled more readily than she deferred.[1]

The conflict in Cuquila is but one of many examples that in Oaxaca, too, women and men forged tense, sometimes violent dialogues over the contingent or absolute quality of gender right in male-female relations. The examples embrace all three microregions under study,[2] and they abound for the indigenous peoples who comprised the overwhelming majority. (During the remainder of this chapter, all individuals cited will be indigenous unless otherwise noted.) In Oaxaca as in Morelos subaltern women and men fought over a wide array of specific gender rights — sexual ownership and latitude, labor and economic obligation, physical mobility and punishment, and verbal propriety and symbolic acquiescence. In these struggles it was the female disputants who tended to press for conditional, interdependent approaches to gender right: "If I have to be good for working, why ought he be bad wandering around getting drunk?" Male disputants tended to press for a more unconditional, innate sense of male right and ownership, sometimes by sexualizing the conflict with the familiar imagery of female betrayal. Even in an extreme case such as attempted rape, the accusatory assumption might burst forth: a husband might demand that his wife explain why the assailant had "taken the action of seizing her by the hair. . . . What dealings had she been having with him?"[3]

In short, the student of male-female relations in Morelos may encounter in Oaxaca surprisingly familiar social dynamics. Let us review briefly several striking resemblances: (1) contestations of gender right that usually side-stepped the principle of male superiority while entangling the specifics of male practice in rancorous assertions of contingent right; (2) the paradox of sexual contestations as central yet less than subsumptive in the pattern of male-female disputes; (3) the mobilization of delegitimating gender stereo-types — the character flaws of male excess and irresponsibility and of female moral weakness and betrayal; (4) the availability of allies of the opposite gen-der (crossovers) to those who learned to untie and reknot the complex tangles of family interest, elder and status rank, intragender rivalry, and color-class vulnerability that pervaded subaltern life and community. As we shall see, too, the actions and strategies of Oaxaca's subaltern women yield a profile that stirs memories of Morelos. In Oaxaca as in Morelos one is struck by women's forceful physical interventions, their pluralization-of-patriarchs strategies, their networks of female allies and advisers built up and sustained through background conversation, and their resort to community scandal and super-natural retribution as weapons of intimidation.

SPECIFICITIES: FEMALE POWER AND
FEMALE SUBORDINATION IN OAXACA (I)

However strong the resonances, they do not quite erase Oaxaca's speci-ficity. Resemblance does not imply isomorphic duplication. Even when the broad outlines of a gendered drama in Oaxaca converge with memories of Morelos, the twists and turns of the story sometimes resist mental transplant and bear witness to a more complex blend of interregional consistency and variation. The interplay between female power and female subordination comes through more strongly — more evenly matched and more culturally sanctioned — in male-female struggles over gender right in Oaxaca. In Oa-xaca the cultural affirmation of contingent gender right seems broader and deeper, less confined to aggrieved females and specific allied kin and friends, more widely legitimated within subaltern indigenous culture as a whole. Con-versely, the cultural affirmation of absolute gender right seems more narrow and shallow, more clearly an argument whose burden rests on the aggrieved male and specific allied kin and friends, an argument less widely ratified by the subaltern community as a whole.

The familiar struggles, in short, seem to unfold in a somewhat different ter-rain — a distinctive configuration of gender power and cultural assumption.

In Morelos the interplay of female power and female subordination seems more emphatically an extrainstitutional female achievement against daunting odds. The formal institutions of subaltern community and power and the leading cultural assumptions about gender right in the masculine political community seem to offer precious little collective backing for assertions of female power and contingent views of gender prerogative. Opening such spaces seems more fully a practical achievement by women and female youth despite their formal marginalization from power. In Oaxaca the interplay of female power and female subordinations seems to find a more substantial institutional and masculine support and to rest less exclusively on the shoulders of women facing a stacked cultural deck. The formal institutions of subaltern community and power and the leading cultural assumptions about gender right in the masculine political community offer a wider platform for assertions of female power and contingent views of gender prerogative. The task of women and female youth in Oaxaca was to build upon, appropriate, and defend this cultural platform. As we shall see (Chapter 12), this formulation may, if left untempered by a sense of intraregional variation and the plurality of human choice and arrangement, encourage too overdrawn and rigid a depiction of regional contrast. Nonetheless, it serves as a rough approximation of the regional specificity that comes through in the Oaxaca cases.

Let us illustrate with three arenas of evidence—cultural practice and expectation concerning physical mobility and separation in marriage, the nuances of rhetoric by crossover allies who supported the female position in specific male-female disputes, and the open recognition by men of female powers to play leading or directing roles in masculine life. We shall draw our examples from all three microregions of Oaxaca and shall specifically identify the microregional settings in the examples cited. (The protagonists are Indians unless otherwise identified.)

Consider first the problem of physical mobility and separation in marriage. Around 1773 Margarita Morales of Tamazola (Nochistlán, Mixteca Alta) married Marcial López and followed the customary practice of relocating to her husband's nearby pueblo, Estetla. In Estetla there began a saga of abuse and quarrel that culminated eleven years and three children later with a dramatic escalation of the stakes. Margarita and her father followed the winding descent past the *nopalera* cactus fields, *milpas*, and eroded hillsides of the Mixteca Alta down to Antequera, the Oaxaca region's capital city. When she arrived, Margarita requested that she be deposited in an honorable house at the expense of her husband, Marcial, and that Marcial be remanded to Antequera—"if necessary, by force"—while she sued for ecclesiastical divorce. For eleven years Margarita and Marcial had fought bitterly about work and economic support and rights of marital punishment and violence. "I have to work alone," she complained, "while he lives a lazy life." The family seemed to live off peddling and petty commodity production—movement from *tianguis* to *tianguis*, probably with items of female peasant labor such as spun cotton, *mantas*, and *nixtamal* (soaked maize for grinding). Margarita not only considered her husband an economic parasite; she also resented the extremes of labor exploitation and physical abuse to which he subjected her. On marketing trips across broken and sometimes steep terrain, Marcial literally prodded his wife into the role of a load-bearing mule—"hurting me with hits from sticks." Once, after a ritual binding, undressing, and whipping in the *monte*, Marcial followed the ordeal with an insistent demand that the wounded Margarita get to work spinning cotton.

Up to this point the history of conflict between Marcial and Margarita broadly conforms to a conflict one might have observed in Morelos. A husband neglected his economic duties, exploited the labor of his wife, and sought to impose discipline and break resistance with violence and ritualized humiliation. Margarita responded to the abuse, moreover, with a strategy well known in Morelos. She pluralized the relevant patriarchs who might assume a proprietary and intervening role in her life. At various times Margarita's father, the local priest, and the community officials and elders all intervened to ameliorate Margarita's indigence or to rebuke and even punish Marcial.

The idiosyncrasy of the case lies not in its broad outlines but in the details of its resolution. After forcing her husband to languish in jail for over ten months, Margarita agreed to drop the suit under the following conditions. First, if Marcial failed to provide for his wife and children in Estetla, Margarita and her family would return to her parental family in Tamazola, and Marcial would work for his father-in-law. Second, if Margarita for any reason decided to return to live with her parents, Marcial could not forcibly remove her. Such scenes had sometimes led to her mistreatment in the past. Finally, if Marcial violated any of these conditions, Margarita's father and the community officials of Tamazola had the right to arrest him and to reopen the suspended legal proceedings.[4]

The question we must ask is whether the emphasis on the wife's right of physical separation, backed by the surveillance and intervention of her parents, constitutes a mere quirk of a single case or is one instance of a wider cultural pattern in the region. For the Mixteca Alta the question is somewhat vexed. Although women left negligent or abusive husbands,[5] few examples explicitly corroborate the combined assertions of wifely separation rights and familial intervention rights to reclaim the daughter. When we turn to the Zapotec Valley and Villa Alta zones, however, we more readily find cultural conflicts and dialogues that promoted a certain latitude for female separation backed by a right of family elders to repossess a daughter subject to abuse. Juana Simona Paz of Coyotepeque (Zapotec Valley) admitted in 1799, for example, that she constantly rejected the efforts of her husband, Tomás, to drag her back to his pueblo. Tomás neglected Juana's economic needs, pursued an extramarital sexual liaison in his pueblo, and subjected Juana to beatings when she returned to his domain. In Coyotepeque Juana could work for herself and count on the backing of her parents, who supplied the occasional tortilla that staved off "begging." Life in Tomás's pueblo was different: "There he only wants to have me working."[6]

One even encounters, in Villa Alta, ritualized forms of repossession that signified divorce to Catholic priests. In a long, vehement letter to the viceroy in 1812, Padre Joseph Vicente María de Paz poured out his hatred, disgust, and fear of the insubordinate Indians of Yahuyê. Among the Indians' more contemptible practices was their reversal of betrothal and marriage arrangements. First the *novia*'s parents acted as hucksters haggling over competing brideprice offers from rival suitors and their families. Then they treated the marriage itself not as a sacrament but as a contingent and reversible transaction. "Having sold the daughters with the understanding that they were to live at the homes of the husbands' parents, in little time they stir up [the daughters] and return them to the [parents'] house on the pretext that they suffer maltreatment . . . which is a type of divorce. . . . They take [the daughters] by force from the side of the husband." If the parents repaid the brideprice to the former husband's family, the divorce was considered more final.[7]

The nuances of kidnap ritual draw out regional differences between Oaxaca and Morelos. To be sure, in both regions a wife might simply "steal herself" and seek refuge with family or friends. In such cases the woman herself took the spotlight as initiator of the action. This pattern was particularly evident in crisis moments of temporary flight to escape physical harm, allow passions to subside, or renegotiate a return to the marital home under altered conditions. But in cases of more indefinite separation or abandonment a woman sometimes had motive to arrange a different choreography. If a wife wished to avoid charges that she had chosen to abandon marriage and husband or if she wanted to give pause to a husband determined to track and seize her, she might prefer ritual kidnap to self-theft. In Morelos she might well arrange for an *amasio* to steal her. This kidnap was a drama of virility. It affirmed male-on-male rivalry between men who wished to possess the same woman, and it implied that possession of a woman was permanent unless one man robbed sexual property from another. In Oaxaca the same woman might arrange for her parents or family to execute the theft. This kidnap was a drama of familial ownership. It affirmed disputation and transaction among competing in-laws, and it implied that possession of a woman was subject to overlapping claims of family that rendered possession less than permanent or final.

Even in the absence of a kidnap ritual, a stronger sense of cultural normalcy seems to infuse the question of parental interference and repossession of married daughters in Oaxaca. In Yaeé (Villa Alta) in 1794, the Zapotec community's leaders found that warnings to mend ways and to live in peace had not sufficed to stop the discord between María Martín and her husband, Esteban de los Angeles, over Esteban's sexual liaison with a sister-in-law. The situation exposed María Martín to a near-wounding by rock and machete and a whipping in a subsequent confrontation. The community's leaders ordered María "that she go be with her father" until they could arrange a successful reconciliation. The delivery of María Martín to her father departed notably from the well-known colonial procedure of arranging protective custody of women by depositing them in a house of honor, a symbolically neutral site.[8]

In short, the practice of cultural argument framed the problem of female physical mobility and separation in marriage somewhat more evenly in Oaxaca than in Morelos. In both regions wives asserted a right to separate from abusive husbands and, conversely, to pressure negligent husbands to reverse their de facto abandonment of wives and children. But this female assertion was more beleaguered in Morelos—encumbered by masculine assertions of permanent sexual ownership that tended to limit female flight and in-law repossessions to temporary emergency measures and to place greater accent on robberies by sexual partners. In Oaxaca a stronger right of physical separation, backed by a stronger customary right of in-law surveillance and intervention, placed the husband's assertion of ownership on a somewhat softer cultural footing.

Let us turn to our second arena of evidence, the nuances of rhetoric by crossover allies who supported female positions in specific disputes. The Oaxaca incidents cited earlier include suggestive hints of a wider cultural affirmation of contingent right in male-female relations. Consider, for example, the comment of a male witness that Margarita Morales of Tamazola (Mixteca Alta) had cause to complain because her husband failed to provide "that reciprocal love that ought intercede between married persons." This is a language of crossover that goes beyond condemnation of a particularly unworthy or brutal patriarch inflicting excess on a victimized dependent who did not deserve punishment. It incorporates the condemnation within a more affirmative vision of reciprocal right and expectation in marriage. Consider, too, the reaction of the indigenous leaders of Yaeé (Villa Alta) when María Martín's rebuke of her husband's affair with his sister-in-law, María Rosa Velasco, unleashed marital discord and violence. In both Morelos and Oaxaca, discord and scandal might have forced a crossover intervention by community leaders to reconcile estranged wife and husband and thereby restore the necessary facade of community harmony. In Yaeé, however, moral responsibility attached not only to the indiscreet husband who had humiliated and hit his wife and not only to the evil *amasia* who had provoked trouble. "We also warned Joseph de los Angeles [the husband of the *amasia*, María Rosa] that he ought to go live in peace in tranquility with his wife without mistreating his wife

[and] without doing anything bad [to her]." In Morelos Joseph de los Angeles might have been warned simply to control the treacherous tendencies of a wife-turned-*amasia*. In Yaeé he was reminded of a positive duty to live in harmony and to avoid the discontents that might provoke a wife's restlessness.[9]

The language of male crossovers in Oaxaca suggests a somewhat wider cultural affirmation of mutuality and contingency of right in male-female relations. Even if husbands ideally ruled wives, families and communities required social peace to thrive. The ideology of balance implied that imperious or negligent husbands might well give wives legitimate cause to stray or to provoke trouble. The necessity of balance required that husbands accept, however grudgingly, a somewhat more even mutuality of right and power with wives, precisely because women were often outspoken and forceful, quick to defend their perceived rights. The reputation of Zapotec women, in particular, extended to Hispanic judges and their assistants. As one official put it in 1807 when discussing a lawsuit to force a male youth to fulfill an alleged marriage promise in Tlacochahuaya (Zapotec Valley), "The women, although they are Indians, are very zealous when it comes to defense of their rights." To achieve harmony under these circumstances required concessions to more contingent views of male gender right.[10]

Men's open recognition of female power to play leading or directing roles in masculine adult life serves as a third window exposing a somewhat distinctive configuration of gender and power in Oaxaca. Let us explore two dimensions of open cultural recognition of female power. On the one hand, the masculinization of subaltern politics proved somewhat more ambiguous — less one-sided — in Oaxaca. In Oaxaca as in Morelos the formal subaltern polity was constituted by the pueblo's citizen-patriarchs. Marriage signified passage into adulthood; adult men served as the *oficiales*, *pasados*, and *viejos* who formally guided community politics, assembly, and decision; the community's citizen-patriarchs served as the electors of pueblo authorities, the *topiles* who assisted in the implementation of community administration and justice, and the voices of assent in formal community assembly. The citizen-patriarchs derived credibility and political voice from their honorable standing as men among men.[11] In Oaxaca as in Morelos the language of political legitimacy conflated concepts of good and bad authority with concepts of good and bad fathers. A capricious community authority accused of abuse without cause was commonly discredited by reference to his excesses as a familial as well as a community patriarch. In Villa Alta, the Zapotec root term for "grandfather" (*sa gulé, sa gulá*; literally "old father") also signified village *cacique* or chief, the metaphorical grandfather of the pueblo (*be' ne' gúle*).[12]

In both regions this formal masculinization met with significant countervailing tendencies. In Oaxaca as in Morelos women garnered a reputation as fierce leaders and participants in the ad hoc mobilizations of emergency politics. At moments of collective crisis, women intervened forcefully and some-times led a gendered etiquette of revolt. The formal masculinization of sub-altern politics did not preclude informal seizures of political space and leader-ship by women who mounted ferocious defenses of community or familial right.[13]

In Oaxaca, however, the counterpoint to masculinization went beyond the interplay between formal political order normally constituted as a masculine domain and informal political practices that proved more receptive — espe-cially in emergencies — to feminine as well as masculine interventions. Even within the realm of formally recognized public power one detects ambiguous crosscurrents and partial acknowledgments of female power. The most glar-ing example of such ambiguities is the concept of female Indian *cacicas* (the feminine version of *caciques*, a term that denoted political leaders, bosses, or governors, presumably descended from leading lineages and sometimes asso-ciated with strongarm tactics of rule). In Morelos one is hard pressed to find examples of *cacicas* or analogous terms to denote female individuals publicly recognized as powerful, directing leaders. In Oaxaca the concept enjoyed greater currency and a sense of cultural normalcy despite the overall associa-tion of masculinity and political empowerment. For the Mixteca Alta and the Zapotec Valley zones, one encounters repeated reference to *cacicas*. The refer-ences seem to embrace powerful landowning women whose genealogy and in-heritance connected them to lines of indigenous rulers and notables but who did not necessarily hold formal political office or privilege, and powerful women considered either political rulers or notables in their own right or joint rulers alongside husbands and brothers. In short, notables traced politi-cal prerogative and property inheritance through female as well as male kin lines, and women laid claim to political and landed privilege in their own right. Significantly, *cacicas* did not lay claim to political clout and lands only in the absence of male heirs or upon the death of husbands. In Villa Alta the *caci-cazgo*, or *cacique* domain, was integrally tied to concepts of group or family rights in the *cacicazgo* and encouraged a language of brother-and-sister rule.[14]

Let us not exaggerate. The *cacica* phenomenon represented a complicating crosscurrent within the stream of cultural practice that generally merged po-litical rule and masculinity. The overwhelming majority of inherited *cacique* designations referred to males; the community's elected officials were men who ideally fulfilled fatherly roles; the electors were citizen-patriarchs consid-ered metaphorical sons of the community; and the *cacicas* who staked claims jointly or in competition with male counterparts might be considered junior partners or unusual cases by many villagers. Nonetheless, the *cacica* phenome-non pointed to a comparatively greater cultural recognition of female powers to play leading or directing roles in public life. At times this recognition could yield ironic twists or role reversals. In Yosondúa (Mixteca Alta) in 1760 the *cacica* Doña Angela Galicia was said, in a matter-of-fact context, to be the "*cacique* and head of the pueblo." Her husband, Benito Montoya, lacked the honorific "Don" and a claim to rulership. The Indians of Tepuxtepeque (Ayutla parish, in the Mixe area of southern Villa Alta) in 1768 worshiped Antonia Magdalena, an Indian "Virgin," on a sacred hilltop. The community and its leaders "consult her on everything." Significantly, the community's male leaders preceded their terms of office with a symbolic display of veneration. The newly elected officials marched up the hilltop with their *varas* (staffs of authority) to join in singing, sacrifice of animals, and other displays of homage.[15]

Masculine recognition of female powers to play leading roles in male destiny emerged not only in the realm of formal public power or politics but in more informal and familial contexts. On one level, of course, the forging of offstage powers of female control and resistance cannot be said to have distinguished Oaxaca from Morelos. What distinguished Oaxaca was the extra step of open cultural affirmation — by men as well as women. The female powers that might have elicited rather furtive, embarrassed, or joking acknowledgment from men in Morelos[16] drew a more matter-of-fact recognition, even manipulation, by men in Oaxaca. It was in Oaxaca that Antonio Flores of Ocotlán (Zapotec Valley), a married adult, stated without apparent embarrassment that he went to buy some *pulque* "by order of my godmother." It was in Oaxaca that Salvador Illescas's wife (unnamed in the document) took control of a negotiation to settle an assault charge: she increased her husband's offer by twenty pesos. It was in Oaxaca that Nicolás Matheo of Tepantlali (Villa Alta) complained that his wife and in-laws abused him and that his father-in-law threatened him — not with male-on-male violence but with female powers. Nicolás had better "be careful not to die or be killed by the witches [*brujas*] in the fields." Nicolás was later found dead, but the murder remained appropriately unsolved. It was in Oaxaca that male and female folk suspicion pinned the death of Juan Olivera of Tlaxiaco (Mixteca Alta) on his sexually jealous wife. As one male witness put it, "He suspects that in his house his wife killed him, but in reality he doesn't know anything."[17] The killings of Nicolás Matheo and Juan Olivera were but two drops in a persistent trickle of Oaxaca mystery murders that sometimes implicated female powers or avengers without hard proof.[18]

SPECIFICITIES: FEMALE POWER AND
FEMALE SUBORDINATION IN OAXACA (II)

We have argued that to compare Oaxaca with Morelos is to observe a blend of the familiar and the unfamiliar. The familiar struggle between absolute and contingent approaches to gender right in male-female relations unfolded in a somewhat more evenly matched cultural terrain. We have observed three manifestations of a distinctive configuration of gender and power. First, the actual content of gendered social conventions differed on some important issues. On the crucial question of physical mobility and separation in marriage, for example, we witnessed greater emphasis on a wife's right of separation backed by the heightened surveillance and intervention roles of her parents. Second, female views of mutuality and contingent right elicited a somewhat wider cultural affirmation. In particular the rhetoric of cultural crossover to support female grievance or to resolve male-female strife placed greater accent on a positive duty to achieve harmony or balance in all social relations, even those marked by hierarchy, deference, and prerogative. In this cultural logic, patriarchs who believed in the absolute right to demand deference and duty from wives, daughters, male juniors, and perhaps even *amasias* ought nonetheless to strike a peaceful social balance by acceding, in part, to the more contingent sense of mutuality preferred by subordinates. Third, men recognized more openly the powers of women to play occasional leading roles in masculine life and destiny. The *cacicas* and female religious leaders (whether venerated "virgins" or, more commonly, female *mayordomas* who cosponsored community religious celebrations) constituted a female counterpoint to the masculinization of politics. The female elders who ordered male juniors, controlled and bequeathed property in their own right, and presumed to intervene explicitly in social transactions fomented a certain porousness of masculine and feminine domains. The aggrieved women and supernatural specialists (*brujas*) who visited violence, retribution, and occasional mystery deaths upon men reminded all that the power to inflict harm and to wrench human destiny was not confined to men alone.

None of this implies an idealized vision of gender equality, let alone harmony, in indigenous Oaxaca. The overall structure of gender and power in subaltern life implied male dominance and female subordination in close relation to elder dominance and junior subordination. Young wives held comparatively greater rights of physical separation. But the right depended heavily on the interventions of parents, especially fathers, to reclaim daughters from abusive husbands and in-laws. Communities sometimes responded to gender conflicts and familial violence with a rhetoric of social peace that placed at least some of the onus on the man and proved close in spirit to female assertions of contingent right. But the choice to deploy or to withhold communal punishment and the rhetoric of mutuality was controlled by the community's metaphorical fathers and grandfathers. Women sometimes held publicly recognized power, and they sometimes inflicted harm on men. But the formal political domain remained predominantly masculine, and the violent assaults sufficiently injurious to call forth criminal proceedings remained, nine times out of ten, the work of male assailants. By contrast, three times out of ten the targets of recorded violence incidents were female, and in Oaxaca as in Morelos the more closely bonded the social relationship, the more likely the danger of violence for women compared with men.

In short, the specificities of Oaxaca point not to a subaltern life of gender equality and harmony in sharp contrast to Morelos, but to a distinctively configured terrain of gender contestation and hierarchy between men and women. Female remained subordinate to male, but the dialectic of female subordination and female power was culturally more visible — more forceful and explicit — in Oaxaca. Women and men still forged languages of argument over contingent and absolute gender right, but the content of gendered social convention, the accentuated tendency to affirm harmony as an overriding principle of life, and the fears of female power and retribution all contributed to a somewhat more evenly pitched battleground. The distinctions between late colonial Oaxaca and Morelos are more nuanced than crude; the comparatively greater foundations for female right in male-female relations do not imply an absence of female struggle or disadvantage.

We have thus far developed a feel for Oaxaca's subtly distinctive configuration of gender and power largely through qualitative analysis. Statistical analysis corroborates the sense of variation and shading within (or alongside) consistency. Let us recall some of the markers of consistency in violence incidents against women and female youth. In both Oaxaca and Morelos, sexual claims and contestations proved central yet less than subsumptive. Sexual claims accounted for a near-majority of cases (43.9 percent in Oaxaca and 48.4 percent in Morelos). Conflicts over nonsexual rights such as labor obligations, physical mobility, and verbal affronts, however, also proved important and accounted for about three-tenths of the incidents (28.8 percent in Oaxaca and 30.6 percent in Morelos). Both regions yielded similarly strong associations (Cramer's $V = .56$ in Oaxaca and .64 in Morelos; Yule's $Q = .92$ in Oaxaca and .97 in Morelos) between type of assailant/target bond and the gender of targets.[19]

If one probes further in the statistical materials, however, one also uncovers subtle variations aligned with those uncovered in the qualitative analysis. (See Table 10.1.) In both regions the overwhelming bulk of violent incidents against women and female youth involved gender-rooted disputes. In Oaxaca, however, women exhibited a somewhat greater capacity to intervene in social life in a manner that escaped nearly automatic redefinition in sexualized or gendered terms. Disputes leading to violence against female targets escaped definition as gender-rooted or sexual conflict about twice as often in Oaxaca as in Morelos. In both regions, specifically sexual claims and contestations proved important in violence against women and female youth and were comprised mainly of sexual assaults and *celos* disputes. In Morelos, however, the sexually charged cases of violence exhibited a more aggressive masculinity.

Outright sexual assault weighed more heavily, and among male *celos* cases imaginary incidents outnumbered plausible ones (the plausible to imaginary ratio was only 0.8 in both the restricted and the augmented case sets). In Oaxaca the imaginary betrayal incidents, although significant, played a more modest role (the plausible to imaginary ratio was 2.0 and 1.8 for the restricted and the augmented case sets, respectively).

In Oaxaca a man may have harbored suspicions that a woman who delayed while fetching water, who traded too often and enthusiastically in a micro-region's several *tianguis* days, or who greeted a bit too easily a male customer or bypasser was betraying him. But he was less likely to turn such suspicions into proof, in his own mind, for explicit accusation and justified violence. The small numbers in our *celos* samples caution, of course, against placing too much weight on the statistics alone. But the statistical hints prove consistent with the qualitative suggestions of a somewhat more even terrain of cultural assertion and dispute between women and men in Oaxaca. Indeed, one of the impressions left by a reading of female *celos* incidents in Oaxaca is that compared with their counterparts in Morelos, Oaxaca's women more readily affirmed an expanded right of sexual ownership in husbands — a right to contest a husband's sexual liaison with another woman even in the absence of the economic negligence and domestic violence that justified such contestations in Morelos.[20] In Oaxaca the contours of female right and assertion created a more explicit cultural dialectic between female power and female subordination.

IN SEARCH OF AN EXPLANATION:
ETHNOCULTURAL LEGACIES, DYNAMICS, AND MANHOODS

To discover a regional difference is not to explain it. The somewhat distinctive content of gendered social conventions, the wider cultural affirmation of contingent views of gender right in male-female relations, and the more open recognition of female powers in masculine life and destiny all imparted a particular texture to conflictual cultural dialogues over gender right among subaltern women and men in Oaxaca compared with Morelos. How might we account for this particularity?

In the search for an explanation we must set focused analysis of gender life and conflict within the wider context of regional experience as a whole. This widening of perspective does not, of course, guarantee definitive answers. But it does yield two lines of suggestive exploration: the particularities of indigenous culture in Oaxaca, and the emphatically ethnic dynamics of Oaxacan colonial experience.

Let us begin with indigenous culture. In the core Oaxacan districts under study the presence of Spaniards and *castas* who might have comprised a creole culture of influence was considerably more modest than in Morelos. This relative modesty of the colonial Hispanic presence comes through whether one looks at it as a question of statistical outcomes or as human choice and process. On the one hand, Spaniards and *castas* established only a light demographic presence in the region, especially outside the capital city of Antequera, and their appropriations of the indigenous land base also proved relatively slender. On the other hand, colonized communities reconstituted themselves as emphatically indigenous societies, webs of collective identity and destiny that held ethnic outsiders — including plebeian Spaniards and *castas* and indigenous visitors from other communities — at considerable sociopsychological distance. In the oral tradition of Morelos, a creole or mestizo *ranchero* figure could become the adopted son and hero of a rebellious peasant community and could become reconfigured as a person born into the Indian community and its struggles. This reconfiguration has marked the oral traditions in Anenecuilco concerning Francisco de Ayala, hero of the independence wars, and Emiliano Zapata, hero of the revolution.[21] This multiethnic and inclusionary redefinition of community was more alien to the oral traditions of Oaxaca. The rural presence of non-Indians remained more modest, and the polarized distinction between Indian and non-Indian and between different groups of Indians proved sharp and enduring.

This merely scratches the surface, however. Not only did indigenous cultural foundations project themselves more forcefully into the colonial lifeways of rural Oaxaca, but the indigenous cultural inheritance itself differed notably from that in Morelos. The indigenous peoples of Morelos were Nahuas, their regional world firmly planted in the geographical heartland of Nahua culture history and empire building. In the core districts of Oaxaca we have selected as our focus, the predominant indigenous cultures were Zapotec and Mixtec. Among the peoples who diversified the region's linguistic and cultural foundations, groups such as Mixe and Chinantec Indians (among others) proved culturally more important than Nahua émigrés. In other words, the Nahua cultural presence was rather spotty and selective. It was thicker on the coast than in the interior core of valley and mountain zones where most peoples lived and was confined largely to elite intrigues of marriage alliance, tributary extortion, and political and commercial maneuver.[22]

Significantly, the examples cited earlier to demonstrate Oaxaca's somewhat distinctive texture of gender right and struggle fall into clusters that suggest indigenous cultural specificity within the region. The bold women who forged a certain porousness of male and female domain, the treatment of community harmony and balance as overriding principles that eclipsed iron insistence on male gender right, and the in-law interventions that undermined patriarchal ownership by husbands — this combined triad of practices, notable for the way a certain leveling of the gender balance of power within generations depended on accentuation of elder authority between generations, derived mainly from Zapotec communities in the Zapotec Valley and Villa Alta. Examples of the female *cacica* phenomenon, by contrast, drew more evenly from both Mixtec and Zapotec life. Instances of strikingly open recognition of female supernatural power — masculine fear of avenging *brujas* or masculine submission to a living "Virgin" — drew on the Mixe zone of Villa Alta. The point here is not to suggest hard-and-fast, reified distinctions between Zapotec, Mixtec, and Mixe cultures. After all, these labels are loose ethnolinguistic umbrellas rather than indicators of political unity or translocal ethnic identification. Moreover, Oaxaca's long history of parallel cultural practices and concepts among several indigenous zones and of building some communities out of distinct ethnolinguistic parts warn against facile notions of absolute or quintessential difference between the region's indigenous cultures.[23] The main point is to underscore the indigenous sources of difference in gendered life between Morelos, a cultural world of Nahuas, and Oaxaca, a cultural world of Zapotecs, Mixtecs, Mixes, and other groups. Even within Oaxaca, one may discern subtle clusterings, an indigenous foundation for variation within consistency.

The particularities of indigenous cultures in late colonial Oaxaca — their comparative predominance in the region and their specificity compared to Nahuas of central Mexico — are important. But indigenous particularity cannot alone carry the burden of explanation. After all, Oaxaca's indigenous cultural inheritance was not fixed or transhistorical, but a living legacy. In the Spanish colonial era Oaxaca's native peoples selectively reconstituted — reinvented, altered, and redeployed — broad slices of their cultural inheritance to respond to challenges of power, opportunity, and devastation. This unfolding process of "resistant adaptation," moreover, did not exclude the possibility of selective redeployment of Hispanic cultural practice and discourse. Indian engagement of Catholic religion, Hispanic legal argument, and colonial commodity markets testify strongly to a redeployment of Hispanic as well as indigenous cultural resources.[24] Given this dynamic process of cultural selection, reconstitution, and redeployment, and given pervasive and sometimes violent gender tensions between indigenous women and men, reference to the indigenous cultural inheritance cannot by itself suffice as explanation. What other forces promoted a certain cultural will to tolerate assertive styles of female behavior, to accentuate a balance principle even in male-female relations and conflicts, and to reject a more aggressive brand of masculinity?

To answer this question we must turn to the second part of our suggested explanation: the emphatically ethnic dynamics of the colonial Oaxacan experience. Let us recall that in colonial Morelos, communities had proved somewhat receptive to multiethnic reconstitutions of Indian communities and to multiethnic networks of labor, marketing, and sociability in haciendas, village *tianguis* settings, and *ranchero* zones. Indeed, by the late colonial period Indians amounted to only about three-fifths of the regional population. This inclusionary strategy of struggle against the expansive sugar estate economy contrasted with that in our core districts of Oaxaca, where indigenous communities defended their land base and lifeways through a more sharply bounded, even polarized, sense of ethnocommunal group. In Oaxaca, where Indians still accounted for nineteen-twentieths of the population and where colonial expropriations focused more heavily on tributary and mercantile schemes than on outright land ownership, an exclusionary strategy of struggle had a certain logic. Outsiders (whether indigenous, *casta*, or Hispanic) were to be held at greater sociocultural distance, the better to blunt their ability to gain knowledge and collaborators that facilitated extortionary schemes.

This polarized drawing of distance seemed not only to depict the colonizing Other as a dangerous threat but also to condemn the Other's brand of aggressive, violent masculinity. Aggressively sexualized and violent self-assertions by men became the cultural markers of dangerous, perhaps perverted Others. An idealized principle of balance and mutuality became a cultural marker of the insider's indigenous community. A certain tolerance of assertive female styles, emphasis on peacemaking and mutual contingency even in male-female conflicts, and avoidance of aggressive male-on-male explosions became markers of cultural morality and self-definition. It was among Spaniards, other Indian communities, or deviants that one found an excess of the contrasting moral attributes: confinement of women to narrow ranges of permissible behavior, tyrannical enforcement of male right in male-female disputes, and confrontational masculinities that exploded in needless bloodletting. The gendered dynamics of ethnic legitimacy and ethnic foil, in short, supplied meaning and energy to idealized selection and reconstitution of indigenous cultural tradition and values. These sorts of formulations seem especially strong in the Zapotec materials.[25]

Let us scrutinize more closely such condemnations of aggressive, violent masculinity. In Ayoquesco (Zapotec Valley), Pedro Velasco and his son José had a reputation for a confrontational style of masculinity that blended drinking, insult, and violence: "They are the most perverse and provocative Indians in the Barrio of San Antonio." When Antonio Ximénez and two male companions saw José approach them rather drunk one August afternoon in 1809, they tried to shift directions to avoid a probable confrontation. José, however, had gotten close enough to pick a fight with Antonio: "What are you doing there, son of a whore, cursed be the whore who gave birth to you. . . . I'm a real man and fear nobody." The string of insults to Antonio's manhood continued until Antonio finally took the bait and responded in kind ("You're the one who's a son of a whore"). When the fight began, one of Antonio's companions quickly removed José's knife to prevent a disaster and ran to deliver it to and to get help from the community's Indian officials.[26]

The discourses of condemnation in the case are illuminating. Among the Indians of Ayoquesco a man had a right to protect his honor and standing as a man among men. But a quick readiness to provoke or join fights or to turn tension into tests of manhood was another matter. The confrontational masculinity of Pedro and José Velasco signified deviance from ethnic virtue and weakened their citizenship in the community. Avoidance of needless quarrel and confrontation and the ability to distinguish between times of confrontation and times of prudence were positive attributes that enhanced reputation. Francisco Alonso and his family, the exasperated neighbors of Pedro's family, moved to another residence several times to escape entanglement with men "who do not even respect the *viejos* of this pueblo." In this approving discourse, Francisco Alonso, like Antonio Ximénez and his companions, preferred to avoid gratuitous rancor and feuding. Pedro and José, by contrast, conducted themselves "with much *orgullo*." This confrontational pride or haughtiness led to one excess after another and caused the men to be excluded from invitations to serve the ethnic community. As one citizen-patriarch put it, because of Pedro's "audacious and provocative" character the community's male electors "have not wanted to give him any *oficio de república* [community political post]."[27] The sanction was serious. Failure to serve made a man a lesser citizen of the ethnic community.

In the case of Pedro and José, Indian condemnation of masculine swagger had focused on the internal Other, a deviant troublemaker with a bad reputation. In a region of militantly ethnic consciousness, however, the choicest targets were often external Others — Indians of other communities or representatives of the Spanish-*casta* world. Two Indians of Tabaá (Villa Alta) suffered an assault and robbery while drying chilies in 1792. The assailants, said the officials of Tabaá, were from Yateé, another Zapotec community. An elderly victim, unable to run away, perhaps lay dead or in agony in the field. But the violent reputation of Yateé's Indians intimidated those who might otherwise return to help one of their own: "The *hijos del pueblo* do not want to cross to the other side of the river because those of San Francisco de Yateé do not want to give up the bad customs they have."[28]

This was a discourse of ethnic character that distinguished among neighboring Zapotec communities. Such discourses about nearby pueblos formed an important part of oral traditions that constructed a sense of local group identity (indeed, the discourses will sound familiar to more contemporary historians and ethnographers of Zapotec areas of Oaxaca). Similar discourses could also apply to somewhat larger microzones. The Mixe Indians of southern Villa Alta, for example, had a particularly fierce reputation as robbers and killers who preyed on Zapotec as well as Spanish and mestizo travelers along the trade routes that linked Villa Alta and the Valley. The Ixtepeji Zapotecs to the north of Villa Alta—also a heavily traveled zone—acquired a similar ethnic reputation. The Mixteca Costa, the coastal "hot country" south of the Mixteca Alta, acquired a reputation for unusual ethnic chemistry and fierce bellicosity. The coastal Mixtecs who comprised the bulk of the area's indigenous population presumably descended from comparatively warlike native kingdoms and peoples, and the non-Indians of the area were presumably even more bellicose. The non-Indians, moreover, had unusual significance in the Mixteca Costa. They accounted for about a fourth of the microregion's population, a large proportion by the standards of Oaxaca's core districts. Also unusual for the region, the *castas* were heavily negroid and outnumbered Spaniards among the *rancheros* and supervisors, rural laborers and cowboys, and muleteers and peddlers who comprised the non-Indian group. Many of the *castas* descended from the African slaves brought to work cattle ranches and haciendas in the Zapotec Isthmus and the Costa Mixteca, and from the rebellious Afro-Mexican runaways who established and defended hideaway zones in the area.[29]

The attachment of disreputable character to ethnic Others set up a distinction between peaceable insider and bellicose outsider. Notwithstanding the overwhelmingly indigenous population of our three core districts, a sprinkle of merchants and peddlers; bureaucrats, priests, and militia soldiers; and artisans and independent small producers established a certain non-Indian presence (thickest in the Mixteca Alta, thinnest in Villa Alta) in rural life. The colonizing Other and his disorderly, aggressive brand of manhood was not simply a distant abstraction. The confrontational style of such men replaced respect with scandal, and their excess bravado endangered community order and harmony. One Sunday night in August 1789 Augustín Santiago, the Indian jailer (*alguacil*) of Tlacolula (Zapotec Valley) arrested a carpenter and a militiaman while making his usual evening inspection round (*ronda*) to check on community tranquility. The arrested men belonged to the *castizo* stratum of folk considered Spaniards (notwithstanding subtleties of phenotype) in local pueblo culture. The pair had insisted on late-night drinks at the home of a local *pulque* vendor, had mixed musical gaiety with declarations of manly valor, and ended up beating an Indian who had heard the music and wandered in. The next morning Manuel de la Cruz, the Indian *gobernador*, presided over a community assembly and ordered the men bound to the community pillory for public whipping and humiliation. When the miscreants objected that they were both militia soldiers and therefore immune from nonmilitary jurisdiction and punishment, the *gobernador* replied that this standard Spanish-*casta* ruse would not work. The volatile revelry and immunizing pretenses of their kind were too well known to fool Indians: "Well, many have used that pretext to free themselves of punishment . . . in order to come raise a ruckus and up-set the pueblo." The punishment would proceed as ordered.[30]

The discourses that assigned a sense of balance, or respect for community propriety and peace, to honorable Indian men and attributed a more uncon-trolled bellicosity to masculine Others need not be taken at sociological face value. In truth, the frequency and the internal dynamics of gender-rooted vio-lence in the Oaxaca materials testify to the volatile aspects of masculine rank, reputation, and prerogative in Indian life. A long string of episodes of male-on-male violence and epithet stirs memories of Morelos.[31] What distin-guished Oaxaca was neither the absence of gender-rooted outbursts by men nor statistically significant differences in the broad tripartite structure of mo-tivation (see Chapter 9). What imparted a distinctive cast was the intense in-terplay of ethnicity and manhood in the *cultural interpretation* of violence. In a region where ethnic militance and intercommunity suspicion ran strong—indeed, proved fundamental as a strategy of survival and well-being—Indi-ans often projected aggressive temperament onto the cultural Other. The blend of swagger, caprice, and intimidation that seemed to define a rather violent masculine honor and self-image among Spaniards and *castas* became a cultural foil against which to define indigenous virtue and self-image. Con-frontational masculinities, a readiness to escalate disputes into tests of man-hood, and the quick resort to homicidal violence were the disdained attributes of the Spanish-*casta* world or of disreputable Indian communities. The hon-orable men of one's own community balanced personal anger against com-munity necessity, avoided gratuitous confrontation, and struck back with vio-lence truly as a last resort.

As often happens, such discursive projections and self-identifications built on real social experiences, if only to exaggerate them into more quintessential, less ambiguous contrasts.[32] One may find examples of a peaceable manhood that avoided confrontational escalations. It is in Zapotec Oaxaca that one finds an alleged homicide settled by an agreement of the victim's relatives to accept the interpretation of the death as accidental, upon payment of a sum of money to care for the soul of the victim. The agreement, reached after the as-sailant had been confined several months, defused the standoff between the pueblos of the two men (Yalina and Zoogocho, in Villa Alta) and the atten-dant danger of a vengeance drama.[33] It was in Oaxaca, too, that we uncovered a lesser readiness by men to harden unverified *celos*, perhaps imaginary suspi-cions of sexual infidelity, into a proof that justified violence against women and female youth (see Table 10.1 above).

The ethnocultural dynamics of social life in Oaxaca had a profound impact on the balance of power evident in male-female struggles. In practical terms a militant insistence on prevention of meddling by ethnic outsiders encouraged the treatment of community harmony as an overriding principle of social life.

This implied—given the assertiveness and social networking of Oaxacan women—a search to resolve even domestic disputes in a manner that elicited sufficient assent to minimize outside intervention by in-laws, priests, or colonial officials. In symbolic terms the depiction of confrontational masculinity and violent temperament as attributes of evil Others could turn masculine avoidance of conflict and evenness of temperament into signals of virtue or good citizenship, not weakness or emasculation. This implied a certain cultural flexibility, a more elastic range of honorable masculine stances during the vicissitudes of male-female relations and familial life. None of this implies, of course, automatic cultural support for female positions in male-female disputes. Indigenous women in Oaxaca had to forge and enforce gendered rights and social conventions, if necessary by creating a ruckus or using physical force. But the cultural legacies and practices that indigenous peoples reconstituted under colonial conditions, the militantly ethnic dynamics of subaltern struggle and self-definition, converged into a somewhat stronger platform for female agency.

THE UNFAMILIAR CONFIGURATION OF THE FAMILIAR: CONCLUDING REFLECTIONS

Our interpretation of gender, power, and ethnicity in Oaxaca has blended the familiar and the unfamiliar. On the one hand, one encounters in Oaxaca striking memories of Morelos: the tensions between contingent and absolute visions of gender right in male-female relations, the paradox of sexual contestations as central yet less than subsumptive, the mobilization of stereotyped visions of male and female character flaws, the availability of crossover allies to men and women entangled in dispute, and the community political cultures that interpreted legitimate leaders as collective father-elders who looked after and imparted wise counsel to the community's metaphorical children. The strategies of female resistance and self-defense, too, call to mind the impressive repertoire of practical weapons first encountered in Morelos: the pluralization of patriarchal intervenors, the cultivation of female networks of conversation and alliance, the threats of institutional escalation via scandal or appeal to higher authorities, and the specter of supernatural retribution.

On the other hand, however, one also discovers social dynamics that inserted familiar phenomena into a more distinctive, unfamiliar configuration or context. The balance of gender power in Oaxaca placed gender struggle between women and men on a somewhat more even cultural footing. The content of gendered social conventions of the region contributed to a more culturally explicit dialectic of female power and female subordination, a somewhat more porous cultural boundary between male and female domains. The counterhegemonic brands of indigenous manhood salient in Oaxaca tainted confrontational masculinities. The violent distemper of Spanish-*casta* men and "bad" Indians met with cultural disdain or at least ambivalence. The reconstituted indigenous inheritance and the ethnic dynamics specific to the region illuminated the foundations for these more distinctive features of gendered life and power in subaltern Oaxaca.

From the point of view of narrative — the lifeblood of history — the blending of the familiar into the unfamiliar, of transregional phenomenon into specifically regional configuration, comes through in the distinction between story outline and story detail. The outlines of plot, imagery, and characters may inspire comfortable recognition, but suddenly an odd detail leaps out to command attention and unsettle the listener. On January 26, 1780, Cristóbal Miguel of Tutepetongo (Mixteca Alta) rose before dawn to leave for Tepeusila.[34] Three hours later another Indian traveler found him dead of stab wounds. That same day the Indian *alcaldes* learned the news and arrested Juan de la Cruz, an unmarried Indian youth about eighteen years old who lived in the pueblo with his father. The suspicion of Juan came rather easily. He had returned to Tutepetongo that day with cuts on his hand and had sent his bloody clothes for washing to his aunt Micaela. Juan claimed that he had cut himself because he slipped while cutting wood with a machete the previous afternoon, but the alibi proved transparent. Juan had pursued a sexual liaison with María Gertrudis, the wife of the now deceased Cristóbal. The discretion of Juan de la Cruz and María Gertrudis had apparently prevented Cristóbal Miguel from catching them together, but suspicion — perhaps fed by rumor or discreet information — had been sufficient, apparently, to yield an undercurrent of rivalry between the two men.

Juan sought to diminish his own responsibility for the fatal roadside encounter by transferring it to his sex rival and to his *amasia*. This he did by resorting to familiar cultural stereotypes — the wounded manhood and volatility of the betrayed husband, the evil treachery of the sexually unfaithful woman. In this discourse Cristóbal Miguel was a taunting aggressor eager to redeem his manhood by picking a fight. "Are you a man of courage?" he had asked at the start of the encounter. It would not be long before Cristóbal had drawn the reluctant Juan into the fatal fight. But the culpability of both men paled before that of María Gertrudis. In Juan's discourse she bore the ultimate responsibility of provoking the violent sexual rivalry. It was she — angry because "my husband doesn't pay attention to me, no food, no clothes, nothing for my children" — who had tempted the "boy" into a sexual connection and thereby drawn him into a deadly competition with her husband.

María Gertrudis, for her part, mobilized her own discursive tools of self-defense. She invoked a well-known cultural stereotype when the community leaders told her that they considered Juan the probable murderer. "If it turns out that he killed [my] husband," she exclaimed, "cursed be the father because he didn't marry him." Unmarried male youths — unburdened by familial responsibilities, unrecognized as adult citizen-patriarchs on the road to respectable status, and restless with sexual desire and with male junior status — were violent hotheads who caused trouble.

The outlines of plot, character, and scenery would have been familiar to a villager of Morelos. Two peasant men turn out to be sex rivals. One seeks to redeem his manhood by picking a fight with the thief of his sexual property. The place is an isolated spot where friends of the target could not intervene to stop the battle. The confrontation yields a twist of fate: the man who picks the fight had intended to intimidate or kill his rival, not to become the victim; the man who kills the would-be avenger had not wanted to be cornered into a kill-or-be-killed situation. The discourses of character mobilized by the survivors fit comfortably with cultural stereotype and experience. The husband is a man crazed by *celos* because he has lost his sexual property. The wife-*amasia* is a woman whose sexual treachery is at the root of violent self-destructiveness among men. The *amasio* is an unmarried male youth whose suffocation as a male junior builds an inner tension, a protest masculinity waiting to explode social convention and peace. The reader-listener of Morelos has heard or seen it all before.

Except for one detail. The oddity would have elicited special attention and comment and might even have seemed implausible, or it might have driven home the somewhat altered configuration of gender relations and conflicts in Oaxaca. When Juan de la Cruz sought to transfer moral responsibility for the killing to his *amasia* María Gertrudis, he did not merely invoke the transregional image of the sexually treacherous woman, the woman whose evil spawns fatal encounters among men. He took the further step of depicting the image of the bold and authoritative woman who plots out destiny — a woman so commanding that she specifically directs the murder conspiracy, provides the murder weapon, and bullies the unwilling male junior into compliance. "The Friday night before the murder . . . [María Gertrudis] told him, take this machete, and in the morning go kill my husband on the road. . . . He has to leave early for Tepeusila, since this my husband doesn't pay attention to me, no food, no clothes, nothing for my children. . . . To which he said how could he do such a crime: to which she said get going, get going and kill him, pressuring him hard to do it, and despite his resistance, and telling her he was afraid, compelled by her many arguments and forcefulness, [he] had to proceed with it."

In the Oaxacan version of a familiar story, the woman whose immorality spawns death becomes the directress who plots it. The truth or falsehood of Juan's effort to lessen his culpability does not, for our purposes, matter. What matters is that Juan drew on regional popular culture — the experience and lore of gender in Oaxaca — to construct culturally plausible mitigating circumstances. Juan's counterpart in Morelos would have resorted less readily to the image of the powerful female bully and conspirator. The woman's responsibility for murder would have remained a root cause, but an indirect one. The male sexual rival, eager to redeem his masculinity, would have taken on a more exclusive role as the active detonator of masculine death.

CHAPTER 11

The Plebeian Center

Struggling Women and Wayward

Patriarchs in Mexico City

BREAKING POINTS: TALES OF DESPERATION AND INVERSION

Don Joachim Villagrán, an imprisoned Mexico City tailor, vented his bitterness that December day in 1791.[1] Wives found it too easy to have barrio *alcaldes* (city judicial officers) jail their husbands on unproved charges of maltreatment. Such proceedings "open the door for women, who, desirous of
their liberty and dissolution, want to oppress their husbands."

There is a certain desperation in the words of Don Joachim — the sense of
a life spinning perilously out of control, the sense that women stood poised to
overturn the natural order of the sexes, that they even secured the collusion of
society's authorities. Significantly, this sense of a life on the edge of disaster
was not necessarily confined to the poorest subalterns. Don Joachim belonged
not to the ranks of the plebeian commoners who comprised the capital city's
laboring poor and lived only a few steps removed from a street life of utter
destitution. Don Joachim ranked, rather, among the city's "upper plebeian"
strata. The upper plebeians, like their less fortunate counterparts, survived by
their physical labor. For them, too, the sale of labor services or of cheap commodities made by the seller or by petty producers similar to the seller was the
hallmark of an urban livelihood. But the upper ranks of the plebeians blended
into the city's more middling strata. Advantages of social background or networks, occupational skill or education, property or business acumen, or patronage or good fortune allowed for a more decent standard of living and
a more convincing air of respectability. A prosperous plebeian man might
affix "Don" to his name, wear decent shoes, replace clothing before it shred-

ded into tatters, eat some wheat bread, hire an assistant or domestic servant, or even open up a small shop. Villagrán used the honorific "Don" and knew how to sign his name. His wife, Doña Josefa de Miranda, ran a small candle shop. Still, the economic immiseration that swept late colonial Mexico City squeezed the market for artisan services and cheap goods and could spell strain even for upper plebeian sectors. Doña Josefa complained that her husband the tailor failed to provide food and sustenance, that indigence had forced her to set up a candle shop to support the family and her mother-in-law, and that her husband had become a violent man who inflicted beatings. Don Joachim saw in his wife not a woman who sustained her family and defended her sense of right in marriage but a woman who dared to exercise a latitude of judgment and behavior improper in her sex. She drank too much, she tried to hit him when he criticized her, and she jailed him on false charges. Because the city's *alcaldes* lent credence to women's lies, "with one false complaint [the women] see themselves free, whether of the subordination to which they are obliged, or unrestrained to give themselves over to their wickedness." Even for a relatively advantaged and respectable man, moral order and control disintegrated.

Again and again in the case of Mexico City the strains of gendered life seem to have stretched social relations between plebeian men and women to the breaking point. A sense of desperation, rupture, and near-rupture looms close to the surface and breaks through repeatedly. In the case of Morelos the concept of contested patriarchal pacts seemed to capture well the conflictual dialogues over contingent and absolute gender right in the male-female relations of popular culture. The case of Oaxaca introduced significant variations on the theme. A modified notion of contested patriarchal pacts remained serviceable so long as it took into account the more evenly matched cultural terrain of male-female struggles in indigenous Oaxaca. For the case of plebeian life in Mexico City, too, an important modification is in order. In this instance one detects not only conflict over the practical, everyday meanings of gender right, but a profound testing of the necessity and continuity of gendered social pacts between men and women. One detects not only a contestation of patriarchal pacts, but a crisis of patriarchal pacts. The former refers to a contradictory and ambivalent process whereby gendered power relations between male and female are both accepted and contested; the latter refers to a desperation that transcends dialectics of complicity and resistance.

The sense of desperation affected both women and men. It unleashed graphic struggles to assert — or reassert — control over situations that seemed to defy control. Let us begin with a tale of female desperation. In April and May of 1792 María Antonia Tinoco, a mestiza twenty-seven years old, began to fear that her marriage with Josef Martines was sliding toward neglect and abuse.[2] Josef, a mestizo glovemaker who worked with his brother-in-law in the latter's small glove shop, had begun to adopt a fighting disposition at home and to stay away occasionally at night. These were signals that a significant sexual liaison was developing with another woman. In the lives of plebeian women the consequences that attended a husband's extramarital liaison — if it proved more than a fleeting, onetime encounter — were serious. A husband who began by proffering small gifts of money, meals, or clothing to an *amasia* could slide all too easily toward a begrudging stance vis-à-vis his wife and children and eventually might abandon his family obligations. In addition, the quarrels that ensued over his money and his whereabouts could easily turn the marital relationship toward beatings or other physical abuse.

One night when Josef stayed away, María Antonia sought solace and advice by sleeping with her sister. To her sister María Antonia confided not only her fears but the results of her spying forays. She thought she identified the root of her problem when she observed her husband talking and strolling with María Josefa Castañeda, a young woman only seventeen years old. María Josefa, an Indian of fairly respectable *cacique* lineage, worked in a chocolate shop with her older sister and mother and was readying herself to enter the Indian convent of Corpus Christi. The chocolate shop presumably brought her into contact with a variety of people, and it was normal for her to exchange greetings with customers and acquaintances of both sexes. Preparation for the nunnery — as María Antonia's sister observed — made it unlikely that the young woman would pursue a sexual connection with a married man, and indeed, the testimonies and proceedings failed to demonstrate consummation of the sexual undercurrent between potential *amasio* and *amasia*. Still, María Atonia had observed unmistakable signs of flirtatious encounter, and she knew where such beginnings could end — above all for a woman of humble means and status. Even her husband, who professed no sexual interest in a virginal youngster and future nun, and who asserted that he had continued to be a good husband "because all that he earns he places in [his wife's] hands," conceded that he once bought the young woman a meal. María Antonia elicited her brother-in-law's help. He advised Josef to stop the flirtation and to attend to his wife, but the advice had little effect. Finally, on the night of May 18, María Antonia and Josef fought bitterly over his intention to leave during night hours, and María Antonia was once more the abandoned wife. This time, however, her anxiety burst forth in a desperate attempt to destroy her husband's wanderings before it was too late.

In the early morning hours, around four o'clock, María Antonia convinced her sister and brother-in-law to help her spy on the chocolate shop where María Josefa worked and resided. Sure enough, the wayward Josef eventually showed up to knock at the *chocolatería* door after María Josefa's mother left for early Mass. When María Josefa opened the door and exchanged greetings, María Antonia and her sister had seen enough. They chased Josef away, seized and hit the struggling María Josefa (while Santiago Tinoco, the brother-in-law, prevented intervention by the young woman's older sister), labeled María Josefa "a homewrecking whore," and proceeded to drag their prisoner away — presumably to present her before a barrio *alcalde* on charges of adultery. First, however, the kidnapping party embarked on a detour intended to destroy María Josefa's sex. The women hauled her to an isolated clearing. There they beat her, and María Antonia's brother-in-law produced a bone with which to puncture and beat María Josefa's genitalia. The trio then dumped the wounded and humiliated victim at the *alcalde*'s door. María Josefa, too ashamed to complain about the attack, would not initiate proceedings against her assailants until she, too, was desperate. Only after a second beating and worsening pains that required medical examination and treatment of her wounded vagina and clitoris did she press charges of her own and open the way to a thorough airing of the conflict.

The assault on María Josefa was a graphic sign of the desperation that gnawed at the lives of plebeian women. Let us recall that María Antonia's own sister had observed that the nunnery candidate was unlikely to move beyond sexual undercurrent and passing flirtation and that the evidence failed to point to sexual consummation. But for a plebeian woman who lived only a few steps removed from destitution, when a husband began to stay out and to adopt a quarrelsome posture about his marital obligations, assuring conjectures were not enough. The beginnings of negligence, left unstopped, could spell ruin — poverty, physical abuse, or abandonment. One had to act boldly before life spun out of control.

As Don Joachim the tailor made clear, plebeian men, too, could experience a sense of gendered desperation — a powerlessness to impose order and control on relations of obligation and dependence with female kin and sexual partners. The conditions of Mexico City life seemed to configure a steady stream of independent — even defiant — female personalities. Consider, for example, the failed patriarchalism that framed the life of María Guadalupe Suárez.[3] The daughter of an impoverished Spanish weaver and an Indian mother, María Guadalupe had long lived in weak patriarchal settings. Her father proved too insolvent even to preserve appearances as an effective head of the family household. He had consented to have María Guadalupe, her sister, and her mother live separately as poor guests (*arrimadas* — in effect, domestic servants for a patron) in a more fortunate home. The two daughters developed strong personalities and did not submit easily to elders. María Guadalupe in particular had grown up accustomed to defying domestic authority. She disobeyed her mother; frustrated her female family's patron, José María Aguilar; and married a husband with whom she fought so forcefully that *he* resisted the authorities' efforts to reunite them. After she had been expelled by Aguilar, María Guadalupe lasted only two or three weeks as a guest-servant in the home of a shoemaker. For a half-year or so before her death she had gotten entangled in a rather rough sexual liaison with the leather currier José Bonifacio Martínez, alias "Chapín." María Guadalupe's strong sense of independent will came through in the relationship with her *amasio*. She tried to control when the relationship was "on" and "off" and to reside independently of her *amasio*. Chapín, in turn, tried from time to time to kidnap his *amasia*, evidently to set up a *casa chica* (literally a "little house" — that is, a quasi-marital household on the side) in which he could assert a more domineering control. This basic conflict yielded a relationship marked by beatings, loud confrontations, hiding, and fear of death. Finally, on the evening of April 17, 1797, Chapín caught up to his independent-minded *amasia*, allegedly after spying her with another man, and stabbed her before she could flee to safety.

The most amazing aspect of the case was not the *amasio*'s anger at an *amasia* who proved stubbornly resistant to personal domination. Remarkably, María Guadalupe's mother, father, and (separated/abandoned) husband all ended up pardoning the killer. Even María Guadalupe's mother conceded that her daughter had grown up defiant and provocative, beyond control. She had "always continued disobedient, coming and going to the street even though one tried to restrain her, since she never wanted to subordinate herself, and even on one occasion had the audacity to seize the declarant by the hair." Among the kin, only María Guadalupe's sister failed to pardon the homicide.

This was a saga of fragile control by would-be patriarchs and family elders, and of the ways such fragility induced deep angers toward female kin and sexual partners. The father figure is weak; at least one daughter grows up an alienated rebel servant; she captures the imagination and sympathy of her sister, and the enmity of her patrons and elders; and she proves unsuitably defiant as servant, daughter, wife, and *amasia*. Somehow the conditions of urban plebeian life seem to have conspired in the process — to have fostered a diverse and fluid network of potential employers, patrons, and social contacts that buttressed female physical mobility, temporary escapes from surveillance, and even temporary severings of bonds with patron and family elder and with husband and *amasio*. The end result was not only violence but an accumulating sediment of deep angers, the resentful sense that the target deserved the violence because she had long lived a life beyond control or redemption.

The capacity of Mexico City life to produce women of headstrong character could invert conventional propriety and call into question the very basis of male-female relationships. Consider, for example, the inversions and confusions that attended the life of Juana Guerrero, a young Spanish woman, only sixteen years old, who had married Anastasio Sandobal, an Indian *tocinero* (pork butcher) about twenty-five years old.[4] Anastasio faced difficulties establishing conventional dynamics of authority. Marital struggle called into question the premises of the social pact. The lines of gender and age worked at cross-purpose with those of ethnic descent; the housing arrangements and atmosphere constantly reinforced the crosscutting confusion (the couple rented a room in a house owned and run by more respectable Spanish "Doñas," who intervened in the domestic quarrels of the Indian guest); and Juana Guerrero's verbal deftness and assertiveness struck her husband as impudent. Not least of all, Juana was rather independent in her sexuality and had for a time taken up a sexual relationship with a *trigueño*—possibly an Indian, according to witnesses—named Francisco Zerón. All of this implied fragile lines of control and rank, even at the level of appearances. (*Trigueño*, literally "wheat colored," referred to a person of uncertain racial phenotype but who was too swarthy or olive-skinned to be considered white or *castizo*.)

One August evening in 1804 Anastasio failed to return home. Around nine o'clock Juana went to her husband's usual diversionary haunts to retrieve him. She tracked him without success for an hour or hour and a half, then returned home to find her husband seated at the doorstep, angered that his wife had been absent when he returned, and self-righteous because she had taken it upon herself to wander alone at night. When he asked for an explanation, Juana deftly inverted the accusation: "My soul [and] little son, to look for you." The quarreling that ensued—notwithstanding peacemaking interventions by the respectable Doñas of the house and brief moments of apparent reconciliation culminated in Anastasio wounding his wife by striking her on the head with a key. This was a relationship built on contradiction: a rather low-status Indian husband eager to assert his rights as a domestic patriarch coupled with an independent young Spanish wife friendly with a network of superior Spanish Doñas who ran the house and intervened in the lives of tenants. Within a year Juana had reestablished an open sexual liaison with Francisco Zerón, abandoned Anastasio, and physically resisted his effort to drag her back. Anastasio ended up killing Francisco. In the conjugal relations of city life, age, ethnicity, or property could more easily crosscut rank by gender, and a husband might find it particularly difficult to escape domestic dynamics that tagged him as a man feminized (*amujerado*) by a domineering wife.[5]

We have entered our journey into Mexico City with tales of desperation and role inversion: the desperation of women cognizant of the pressures that bore down on plebeian men, yet determined to block descent into economic ruin, physical abuse, and marital abandonment; the desperation of men cognizant of the city's penchant for producing uncontrolled and haughty women,[6] yet determined to block descent into a life stripped of patriarchal authority; the desperation of male and female lives perched precariously on the precipice of destitution. Forebodings of ruin haunted the hard struggle for plebeian survival. Plebeian life held enormous potential for mutual suspicion, anger, and rupture between male and female. Violence and intimidation could all too easily become a key arbiter and cement of gendered social bonds, a patterned stopgap response to a profound crisis of patriarchal pacts. Small wonder that this society produced the observation that women, "desirous of their liberty, and dissolution, want to oppress their husbands." Small wonder, too, that this society produced the observation that the plebeian man, humble by day, could turn into a tyrannical monster by night: "Even though he is humble with everyone, nonetheless with his poor wife he's all stings."[7]

Women poised to oppress men at every turn and men poised to sting women at every turn — these images, superficially in contradiction, were opposite sides of the single coin of desperation. The conditions of gendered life among plebeians seemed to transform the strains of contested patriarchal pacts into a crisis of their existence.

THE CONTEXTS OF SUBALTERN PATRIARCHAL CRISIS (I): FEMALE INITIATIVE

Let us explore the several contexts that could stretch strain into crisis. The viability of subaltern patriarchal pacts was called deeply into question by at least three conditions of urban plebeian life: the numerous uncontrolled pathways of female livelihood and initiative, the weakened economics of patriarchal control, and the opportunity for tactical convergence between female resistance and institutional repression.

Let us begin with the uncontrolled pathways of female livelihood and initiative. Women's work and economic adaptations, their heterogeneous networks of sociability and sociocultural affirmation, and their capacity for physical movement within and beyond barrios all opened arenas of female life and self-management beyond the horizons of personal control by subaltern elders and patriarchs. We have already discussed (see Chapter 2) the grim economics that polarized Mexico City in late colonial times into a society of fabulously wealthy oligarchs and sharply immiserated plebeians. We ought not to romanticize the precarious sustenance of plebeian women, therefore, when we observe their ability to develop income streams, work arenas, and economic management practices beyond effective vigilance by husbands, fathers, and *amasios*. In Mexico City plebeian women commonly worked outside their own homes as domestic servants, street sellers, and to a lesser extent, wage workers. About half the women and female youth officially recorded as employed in the census of 1811 worked as domestic servants.[8] As one might expect, domestic service in Mexico City could hardly be called a preferred option for plebeian women or youth. It exposed the servants to surveillance and mistreatment — including violence — by their employers/masters. Nonetheless, women's ability to float in and out of domestic service loosened the grip of husbands, fathers, and *amasios*.[9]

Comparatively preferable were those urban female livelihoods that allowed more independence. By the late eighteenth century, females held more diversified pathways into the wage labor force. In addition to traditional work such as cooking and waitressing in restaurants, they could seek jobs in factories and artisanal shops. Colonial policy in the late eighteenth century liberalized female entry into wage work for factories such as the *Real Fábrica de Zigarros* (Royal Cigar and Cigarette Factory) and into small-scale artisanal work such as shoe embroidery and repair. For policymakers the point was social engineering. A more robust employment of female plebeians presumably fit into a larger effort to mobilize women more effectively and to turn away from economic policies now viewed as archaic — overly restrictive and self-defeating. More liberal employment options for women also addressed fears that moral decay and prostitution, induced by unemployment and poverty, might undermine social order. For female laborers, even youths who had to turn in a portion of their wages to family elders, the new work arenas implied income streams and social contexts beyond direct vigilance and control by elders and patriarchs.[10]

More important than wage labor was the economic self-management that attended female street life and self-employment in petty business. Mexico City abounded with female street and market sellers. The street vendors mainly sold food and drink (street meals or specialties such as tortillas, cakes and sweets, tamales, *atole*, *pulque*, and chocolate). Self-employed females also served as producers, go-betweens, and vendors for cheap commodities such as clothes, cigarettes, fruit, candles, and flowers and provided services such as laundry, sewing, and herbal advice and remedies. The female vendors developed a streetwise independence and sometimes converted their homes, apartment rooms, and street stalls into informal diners, taverns, and shops — the latter to take in home work such as sewing and embroidery, laundry, cigarette rolling, or shoe repair. (Anyone familiar with the great cities of twentieth-century Latin America will recognize that the phenomenon of female street vending, petty shops, and self-employment continues to have large importance.) Whether moving along in the street, setting up regular stalls or squatting spots in the market or plaza, or managing petty businesses out of their rooms and homes, self-employed women developed a substantial network of social interactions, often with both sexes. These not only fell beyond the effective vigilance of husbands and *amasios*; they also added up to a certain independence rooted in daily experience.[11]

Indeed, subaltern women, like men, developed the street-hustling skills associated with living a hard life by one's wits — a life that leaves little margin for error but rewards those who quickly size up strangers and opportunities. Consider the complaint in 1797 of Pablo Tapia, a light-skinned mulatto weaver who worked in the Royal Tobacco Factory. A mature woman whom Pablo Tapia had never seen before approached him at a tavern (*pulquería*) and "began to treat him with familiarity, telling him, '*Chato* ["Pug Nose"], why don't you invite me for pulque?'" Thinking from her manner that she might be a go-between for a younger *amasia* or prostitute, Tapia spent two reales (a fourth of a peso, the equivalent of a day's food money in plebeian circles) on *pulque*, then consented to spend another two reales on drink. He again succumbed when she asked for two more reales, for which she would take him to her house, she said, to cook him a meal. The woman led Pablo Tapia by twist and turn to an alleyway, then told him to wait a minute until she returned. By this time Pablo Tapia understood that he was being hustled and objected loudly, but to no avail. Too tipsy from drink and possibly too disoriented by the urban maze through which he had been led, Pablo Tapia could not match wits or energy with his hustler. As barrio onlookers watched, the woman slapped him, threw rocks at him, and disappeared. The frustrated Tapia sat down on a doorstep and got himself into trouble by trying to pick a fight with the first barrio resident who passed by in the street.[12]

The ultimate symbolic subversion of personal vigilance and control of dependent women by patriarchs, however, was sexual. When women ran their own prostitution rings, economic and sexual escape from male supervision merged. We need not romanticize female-run prostitution houses. Poverty and domestic abuse might push a girl or a young woman into seeking refuge with an older woman who ran the business, deducted a charge for each male customer, and collected a fee for daily food. María Gertrudis Rojano, for example, a plebeian Spaniard only sixteen years old, fled from her aunts' maltreatment in 1808 and ended up laboring as a prostitute in the house of Manuela Castrejón Gonzales, a thirty-nine-year-old *castiza*. Manuela had her own hard-luck story: her abusive husband seemed perpetually in jail (at least once by her own petition); she had been forced to earn a living on her own; and her work as a laundress and as a runner (*corredora*) in community transactions brought only an irregular income. Taking in young female boarders placed the house's entire group of women and female youth on a sounder financial footing — even if the transformation of a respectable house of seamstresses, shoe embroiders, laundresses, and domestic servants by day into a house of prostitutes and male visitors by night scandalized some folk. María Gertrudis turned over a fourth of the payments for sex to her landlady and business manager, Manuela. In addition María Gertrudis owed Manuela a quarter of a peso (two reales) a day for meals. Since payments for sexual services ranged from one to four pesos, about two encounters a week sufficed to pay for commissions and food charges.[13]

What added force to the numerous pathways to female self-management and social independence was an economic precariousness that undercut clear social boundaries. The distinction between a female laborer, vendor, or business manager and an *ama de casa* (wife and housekeeper) enclosed in a domestic and familial web was fraught with ambiguity. Even when plebeian wives or common-law wives remained largely at home and had not set up notable home work services or shops, they might develop household management practices and social contacts that belied enclosure by the familial patriarch. In urban plebeian settings women at home often became house managers — petty versions of the middle-class *caseras* who ran apartment houses. The women took in male boarders, provided meals and cleaning services in return for money channeled into the household income stream, smoothed over social relations between boarders and family, and managed the household income fund. In addition, the mother/managers might demand a weekly allowance for the household fund not only from husbands but also from sons or daughters sent off to work or street selling. In short, the *ama de casa* became a household work and incomes manager and might even exert authority over the labor of sons. These practices not only blurred boundaries; they bred conflict. Claiming incomes from boarders and children enhanced a woman's economic means and social assertiveness and fed tension between female home managers and husbands who sought to establish checkpoints of control on family income streams. Taking in boarders nurtured the kind of cross gender contact and familiarity that bred sexual suspicion by husbands.[14]

Similarly distinctions could blur between an *amasia* possessed by an *amasio* and a prostitute whose bounded sales of sex implied a certain self possession. "Prostitute" was sometimes an exaggerated characterization for women who supplemented other means of support with occasional sexual visitations by two or three male clients or friends, and the *amasia* label did not necessarily imply that a woman refrained from commercial transaction of sexual services. To be sure, some *amasias* acted as "extra wives" in a long-term relationship of unequal reciprocities. In addition, many *amasios* tried to assert an exclusive and indefinite right of sexual possession. Often, however, the apparent stability and possessions of whole persons masked more bounded, transactional relations. The *amasio* might have to provide money or gifts at each sexual encounter. The *amasia* might coordinate several *amasios* at once, or she might establish a pattern of serial relationships, each heavily marked by material gift or money exchange upon sexual encounter. In short, the prostitute might be less a specialized seller of sex than a woman who incorporated occasional sexual sales within a larger strategy of self-management and survival, and the *amasia* might be less a possessed female dependent than a woman who incorporated sexual transactioning within a larger strategy of self-management and survival.[15]

The economic calculus that blurred distinctions between possessed *amasia* and independent vendor of sex came through in the words of Doña Guadalupe Barrera, a young Spanish woman about seventeen or eighteen years old in 1809. Doña Guadalupe had taken up a sexual relationship with Juan Bautista Peredo, an unmarried paralegal practitioner of more middle class means. Juan Bautista, she admitted, never promised marriage. But Guadalupe, who had been sent from Cuernavaca to live with her aunt in Mexico City six years earlier, and whose aunt had recently died, turned out to be a rather destitute Doña who got worn down having to support herself by sewing. Through the sexual relationship she "thought to have more rest" — economic support by an attentive *amasio*, perhaps followed by an evolution toward marriage. She found herself entangled instead in abusive dynamics and fear of violence. After two or three months she fled to the house of a female friend and spurned Juan Bautista's efforts to buy her back with promises of money.[16]

The movement of women in and out of domestic service and wage work, their lives of street selling and street hustling, their experiences of self-employment and self-managed business, and their movement in and out of sex work: these female paths to urban work and income streams, however much motivated by poverty or by abusive relationships and however incapable of lifting plebeian women and their children away from the economic precipice, weakened the grip of familial oversight by fathers, husbands, *amasios*, and their surrogates. A picture begins to form of the capacity of Mexico City — the largest urban metropolis in the Americas in late colonial times as in the late twentieth century — to produce relatively uncontrolled pathways of female livelihood, initiative, and sociability.[17]

Let us briefly add two elements to this picture of uncontrolled pathways. First, a considerable proportion of the city's women lived unattached to domestic patriarchs — as persons who had never married, as widows who had outlived their husbands, or as abandoned or separated women who might call themselves widows. According to Silvia Arrom's estimates, based on a sample of the 1811 census, among women twenty-five years or older about two-ninths were single and another three-ninths were widows. Only about four-ninths lived in church-sponsored or common-law unions with men. Although many single women might not head their own domestic units — they might live with parents or family elders or as boarders or domestic servants in other homes — women constituted nonetheless about a third of the city's household heads. In short, female-managed living arrangements, like female-managed wage and income streams, were not at all uncommon in Mexico City.[18]

Second, the city's plebeian cultural life and social networks were sufficiently heterogeneous and raucous to yield spectacles of female sensuality — open affirmations of desire that belied male control and broke down social enclosure of dangerous females and female temptations. Plebeian culture was filled with counterhegemonic raucousness, celebrations of the senses that defied elite social propriety and convention. For elites, who adapted and adopted a version of European Enlightenment culture that underscored elite reason, moderation, and refinement, the rowdy violations of taboo and propriety fed anxieties that an uncontrollable and dangerous rabble might plunge the city into chaos and violence. Women and female youth participated actively in the culture of plebeian scandal. The forum might be the street fiesta that satirized life and vented feeling through spicy songs, sexualized dance movements, and chants of female carnal desire; the bawdy entertainment spectacles of female comedians before mixed gender crowds in the city coliseum; the individual sensual flair expressed in the revealing clothing styles, smoking habits, and penchant for strutting culturally stereotyped as a mulatta sensibility; or the extension of mixed gender sociability from home and tavern to the bathhouses (*temascales*) prominent in Indian life cycle celebrations and family sociability. In all these varied ways the city seemed to spawn plebeian women who openly belied assumptions of vigilance and restriction by male patriarchs or sexual partners.[19] The point is not, of course, that most subaltern women partook of bawdy spectacle or carried themselves with a sauntering sensual flair. On the contrary, most plebeian women probably strove hard—and against misogynous assumptions—to assure themselves reputations of moral and sexual probity.[20] The point, rather, is the rich heterogeneity of cultural networks, celebrations, and personal styles within female plebeian life. In a city of numerous cultural backgrounds, social networks, and gathering spaces, some spectacles and some women publicly proclaimed a sensuality and a personal flair that broke even appearances of male control and female respect for propriety. In a city of numerous uncontrolled pathways of female livelihood and sociability, which aspiring patriarch was relaxed and secure in the knowledge that *his* female dependents would not be tempted or tainted by such networks or experiences or would not have the money or physical mobility to move in suspect circles and arenas?

The proliferation of uncontrolled pathways of female livelihood and initiative and sociability and self-management was in part an achievement by women, in part an adaptation to conditions of urban plebeian life. Either way, a certain structure of escape from direct patriarchal vigilance framed the social pacts among subalterns. Let us turn to two further conditions of life that called into question the viability of subaltern patriarchal pacts.

THE CONTEXTS OF PATRIARCHAL CRISIS (II):
THE FAILURE OF COUNTERVAILING FORCES

Subaltern women in Mexico City were not the only women to chart pathways of female initiative, livelihood, and escape from vigilance that weakened patriarchal control. What set the Mexico City of late colonial times apart from Morelos, Oaxaca, or smaller cities in Mexico? One part of the answer is obvious: the city's concentration of people and its specialized commodity and service markets, which outmatched in scale any other site in Mexico and thereby promoted greater variety and density of uncontrolled female pathways and livelihoods.

Another, equally important part of the answer is less obvious: the countervailing forces that theoretically might have contained the consequences of more independent female life management tended instead to crumble or backfire. That is, they tended to reinforce a loosening or delegitimation of pacts with familial or quasi-familial patriarchs. Let us examine briefly two key potential countervailing forces: gendered economics and institutional repression.

When women are more poorly remunerated for their work than men, the economic discrimination may end up buttressing male control. For all the pathways to income streams created directly by women's labor, services, or transactions beyond an unpaid familial arena, hard and poorly paid work by subaltern women may yield little income compared with hard and poorly paid work by subaltern men. The result is obvious to anyone who has experienced or observed the harsh realities of subaltern economic life: individual and household necessity and a gendered economy of work and remuneration yield enormous pressure on women to seek, accept, or persist in pacts — however contested, ambivalent, or even abusive — with male sexual partners and familial husband-patriarchs. The pressure is all the greater if women as mothers assume a personal commitment to the well-being of infants, children, or other relatives — that is, personal responsibility for the household economy of life and for multigenerational needs. For unmarried or abandoned women and for female youth contemplating the future, the pressure may encourage fantasies about finding a "good patriarch." The mythologized good patriarch will provide a solid economic foundation and good treatment, even if experience with most living men suggests otherwise.[21]

The specific dynamics of economic discrimination and dependence, of course, may vary considerably by sociocultural milieu. In village and peasant settings the economic dependence may be so embedded within wider sociocultural dynamics — so pervasively bound up with sexual divisions of labor and social rules of property and right — that to isolate measurable remuneration and income streams misses the point. A woman may need a man to gain effective access to land and the labor to work it; a man may need a woman to transform corn into tortillas and to provide children who will become a labor pool; and both may need to marry to gain the economic rights of gendered adulthood in their communities. Income streams in money as such or in easily convertible commodities may not dominate the economic calculus of patriarchal pacts. In predominantly plebeian settings such as cities and mining camps, however, even before an era of capitalist transformation of industry, work, and consumption relations, cash incomes may loom larger. The basics of life — food, drink, clothing, housing, candles, soap — might require money purchases. A woman who charts an independent path of female livelihood might purchase such commodities directly. But if a gendered economics of reward condemns her to poor remuneration compared with men of similar color-class standing, she and her children might find themselves driven to seek male income streams to escape a life of indigence and weariness.[22]

In short, a gendered economy of work and reward theoretically reestablishes female dependence on male partners and patriarchs and thereby serves as a countervailing force to more independent pathways of female livelihood and initiative. A man might bring to a woman problems of personal abuse and surveillance, but he might also represent a vital income stream for a household otherwise doomed to insecurity and indigence. The countervailing pressure, one would expect, increases as one moves down the economic ladder, and indeed the data of Mexico City suggest that middle and upper income women were more able to pursue a life trajectory that excluded marriage.[23]

In plebeian Mexico City in late colonial times, however, the countervailing effect proved fragile — not because economic discrimination proved absent but because plebeian underemployment and pauperization had reached such extreme levels. We need not repeat here our earlier sketch (see Chapter 2) of the economic polarization that afflicted the great city in late colonial times. For plebeians, estimated at four-fifths of the city population by contemporaries, the polarization implied a life haunted by depressed incomes and underemployment, heavy rural-to-urban migration, homelessness, malnutrition, and vulnerability to disease. Under these circumstances the economics of patriarchal pacts proved wobbly indeed. Plebeian laborers fortunate enough to find reasonably steady work as masons, carpenters, tailors, shoemakers, bakers, or cigar makers earned around three to six reales a day. But two reales a day was the standard calculation of plebeian food costs for one adult. Households survived by patching together multiple income streams, and the contributions of plebeian patriarchs — even those who found regular work and who had not been reduced to jobs such as human load carriers (*cargadores*) — were often minimal or irregular. Toward the close of the colonial period, when authorities rounded up male vagrants to draft them for military service or public works labor, a convenient method was to target for arrest the numerous men judged *desnudo* (literally, "naked," but meant to convey a person in clothing too threadbare or tattered to cover the body). Significantly, many of the *desnudos* were not unemployed.[24]

Gendered economics, in short, failed to yield a strong and consistent countervailing force binding poor women to poor men in contested patriarchal pacts. The extreme state of plebeian immiseration threw a precarious aura around even moderately successful plebeians and undermined the long-term credibility of male economic contributions.

The moral economy of masculine culture further diminished the binding effect. In Mexico City as in Morelos and Oaxaca the culture of popular manhood included affirmations of manly valor in vertical, familial, and horizontal contexts. In Mexico City (except in its Indian barrios) the pathways that ratified men's honor as citizen-patriarchs of subaltern communities were scarce compared with those in Morelos and Oaxaca. The culture of masculine sociability, challenge games, and spectacle carried all the more weight in horizontal affirmations of masculinity. Given the city's relative ability to hide off-stage lives and social contacts, moreover, men could channel substantial energy into sexual possession of *amasias* and common-law wives. These forms of masculine affirmation—the visible world of taverns, card games, and male sociability and the shadowy world of offstage sexual possession and power—depended on plebeian men's assertion of a right to retain substantial shares of their meager incomes for personal spending. Given the economic straits of plebeian households, such assertions could only exacerbate the air of crisis that surrounded patriarchal pacts among plebeians.[25]

If gendered economics represents one potential countervailing force that operated weakly and inconsistently in Mexico City, institutional repression represented another. Theoretically, in patriarchal social systems, when women chart uncontrolled pathways of female initiative, livelihood, and escape from patriarchal vigilance, institutional repression or cultural coercion might substitute, at least in part, for the loss of personal vigilance and control by patriarchs. Institutional or cultural sanction would set social constraints on women's behavior; define boundaries beyond which female independence becomes a deviance that sparks ostracism, isolation, or punishment; or place obstacles before the woman who seeks to sever patriarchal pacts.[26]

To some extent this countervailing effect did happen. In Mexico City as elsewhere, ecclesiastical divorce was rare, and criminal authorities considered it a primary duty to achieve a reconciliation of estranged wives to their husbands—even when wives thought their partners beyond redemption. In addition, just as a socially forceful widow might draw a certain stigma in peasant society, so it was with clusters of city women who lived in their own housing and developed social contacts with both genders. Female-managed houses drew attention and could fall under suspicion of prostitution, especially if the women included subalterns of less than middle class respectability. The female loners of such houses would need to guard their reputations carefully to avoid cultural or legal harassment. Finally, subaltern women in Mexico City, like their counterparts in Morelos and Oaxaca, experienced the ambivalent cross-fires induced by a repressive color-class order. Suffering in common among the women and men of plebeian families and friendship circles fostered a certain potential for sympathy and solidarity alongside the conflicts women experienced with the men in their lives. Poverty and institutional repression implied, moreover, that women did not lightly invite authorities to extort fines to punish subaltern men.[27]

Nonetheless, in plebeian Mexico City in late colonial times the countervailing effect of institutional repression on male-female relations was not only weak and irregular but profoundly contradictory. Indeed, one may even detect a tactical convergence of female resistance to abusive patriarchs and institutional repression of plebeians. Elites and state authorities in the late eighteenth century believed that a swelling plebeian population was subjecting Mexico City to social dissolution, an explosion of robbery and drunkenness; nakedness, street quarreling, and family crisis; sexual impropriety and moral decline; and violence and homicide. Literally and metaphysically the plebeians emptied foul excretions into the public life of the great capital city. Plebeians, in this line of thought, were responsible both for their own misery and for the city's social ills. The plebeian rabble's laziness, its disregard for propriety and self-restraint, and its attachment to a habitual drunkenness that unleashed excess and vice had subjected the city to moral disorder. In elite eyes, the plebeian penchant for drunkenness condensed into one symbol and root cause their many vices. As one alarmed reformer explained in 1777, "The people of low station are certainly seen lazy, audacious, criminal, but they are also seen assiduously drunk." In plebeian eyes, especially male plebeian eyes, the matter looked different. The city's taverns served not as a platform for drunkenness and dissipation but as a necessary and welcome gathering place folded into the rhythms and cares of daily life. The drinking spots provided a space for socializing and information exchange, economic and romantic transactions, songs and games, and bonding and venting. Occasionally this implied the risk of drunken excess and danger.[28]

The solution of the elite to the city's impending anarchy was institutional repression — a crackdown on plebeians through a strengthening of the apparatus of surveillance and control. The reforms began in earnest in the 1770s. The drinking hours, beverage types and serving quotas, and seating spaces of taverns came under strict regulation and inspection. Jails for men and women expanded to accommodate more vigorous arrests. Periodic roundups and arrests of drunks, street vagrants, and *desnudos* cleared the streets, at least temporarily, and channeled suitable targets into military and labor drafts. Most important for our purposes, the city built stronger mechanisms of state surveillance and intervention. The old system of policing, based on responses to complaints filed in one of five tribunals, was replaced in 1783 by a new grid of policing that divided the city into eight major districts (*cuarteles mayores*), each subdivided into four neighborhood districts (*cuarteles menores*). Each of

The Plebeian Center: Mexico City : 267

the thirty-two neighborhood districts had a chief magistrate and police officer (*alcalde de barrio*) to interrogate the suspicious, arrest presumed offenders and vagrants, and institute formal criminal proceedings against those who warranted it. The crackdown, backed by an expanded police force and judicial bureaucracy, should not be exaggerated. *Alcaldes* could not be everywhere at once; they often handled incidents, arrests, and sentencing informally; sentences tended toward the pragmatic rather than the draconian; and short-term detentions were more common than long-term confinement or draft labor. Nonetheless, the state's refortified apparatus amounted to more than paper reform. Before 1783 the policing system generated perhaps 1,000 arrests a year. By the 1790s the scale of arrests had multiplied by about ten. In 1798 alone perhaps one in eight persons among the urban poor suffered arrest.[29]

The best scholarship on the new conjuncture of policing depicts an effort at social control. An alarmed elite cracked down on a swelling plebeian sector whose members were viewed as criminal and violent fomenters of disorder. The interpretation is accurate but profoundly incomplete. Just as a new literature on gender and welfare systems in the United States and Europe has injected ambiguity into the vision of welfare interventions as social control of working class and immigrant life, so it is that gendered study of late colonial life injects ambiguity into the vision of a crackdown in Mexico City.[30] What is apparent when one reads the documents of barrio arrest, complaint, testimony, and detention is a certain tactical convergence between elite repression and female resistance. Whatever their disdain for elite pretense and repression and whatever their fear that state intervention might backfire by imposing fines or by forcing reconciliation with an embittered and vengeful husband, women sought to redeploy the new structure of policing for their own purposes. Precisely because patriarchal pacts in Mexico City were often strained to the breaking point, abused women saw in the new policing systems a potential opening for relief through state intervention. Whether the charge was chronic maltreatment (*mala vida*), adultery, assault leading to injury, or a combination thereof, women had their husbands, *amasios*, *novios*, and sex rivals jailed. Women constituted nearly two-thirds (63.8 percent) of the non-anonymous accusers in morality cases and better than a third (35.9 percent) in violence cases. The accusations mattered. Confinement, in a society where prisoners relied on female relatives for decent food; fines, in a society whose plebeians lived on the economic edge; and arrest, in a society whose delinquents and vagrants might become forced recruits for public works and the military, might pressure a wayward man to settle for an altered balance of power and right.[31]

It was this tactical convergence that informed the complaint by Don Joachim Villagrán, the imprisoned Mexico City tailor who introduced this chapter. The authorities, he claimed, indulged women's desire "to oppress their husbands." The institutional sanctions that subaltern men ought to have relied upon to check their wives' freedom of action had turned perverse: "With one false complaint [the women] see themselves free, whether of the subordination to which they are obliged, or unrestrained to give themselves over to their wickedness." It was this tactical convergence, too, that inspired the sarcasm of María de la Luz, a mulatta servant in the Convent of San Bernardo: "I told a nun that it was better to be the wife of a man and not of God because if [God] inflicted maltreatment one couldn't dispatch him to any presidio."[32]

The picture of tactical convergence requires qualification. We should not exaggerate subaltern women's ability or will to redeploy the state's policing apparatus. The case records include sobering sagas of women whose abuse continued for years before they aired their grievances before an *alcalde*. In addition, one needs to consider the problem of class advantage and disadvantage. The socioeconomic distribution of cases warns that not all women held equal advantages or faced uniform trade-offs when mobilizing *alcaldes* and courts to press morality charges such as maltreatment or adultery. A comparison of morality and violence cases demonstrates that in the absence of a specific recent incident of violent assault (that is, overlapping cases), commoners were moderately less likely than their upper plebeian and middling counterparts to make an accusation of sexual or family immorality. Nonetheless, it goes too far to suggest that in the absence of violent assault, redeployment of the police apparatus by women was mainly a domain or option of prosperous plebeian and middling sectors. The nonrandom associations were moderate rather than strong, the testimonies within specific cases blurred distinctions between violence and morality cases, and low plebeians still accounted for about half the accusers (49.3 percent) and the accused (56.0 percent) in the morality cases.[33]

The several social contexts that framed contestations of patriarchal pacts in plebeian Mexico City in late colonial times have now come into focus. We have argued that these contexts tended to stretch the everyday contestations and strains of patriarchal pacts into a crisis of existence and legitimacy. The city had a penchant for yielding numerous uncontrolled pathways of female livelihood, sociocultural networks, and initiatives, including initiatives that belied men's enclosure and ownership of women. The city's economic polarization and its masculine moral economy of diversion assured that few plebeian men could leverage women's economic disadvantages into sustained and convincing roles as indispensable family providers. The authorities' institutional crackdown, far from yielding a consistently promasculine social policy, opened newly accessible spaces for subaltern women to seek state intervention and intimidation of wayward patriarchs. These conditions yielded a certain fragility of expectations in the larger sense, a deep doubt about the continuity, necessity, or legitimacy of patriarchal pacts in subaltern life. As we saw at the outset of this chapter, a sense of impending doom infused hard and often contentious plebeian lives and yielded many a tale of desperation and violence.

SPECIFICITIES: THE SOCIAL CONVENTIONS AND CONFLICTS OF GENDER

The social conventions and conflicts of gender responded to the specific fragilities of plebeian life. Let us explore three arenas of plebeian adaptation and response: the culture of respectable consensual union, the dialectics of separation and ownership in persons, and the sexualization of gender conflict.

Let us begin with consensual unions. The fragile economic and institutional support of plebeian marriage brought knotty dilemmas to prospective sexual partners, especially women. On the one hand, the church and the state classified consensual sexual unions as vice rather than functional equivalents of marriage and cast special opprobrium on the woman whose sexual life strayed beyond marriage. In a city whose married men seemed tempted to consider wives and children a burden to be abandoned, either temporarily or permanently, this institutional stance granted even greater latitude for neglect by men in consensual unions. Institutional policy and male inconstancy both implied that it was important for young women to resist sexual contact until marriage. A woman who dared transact her virginity outside of marriage wasted a precious property. On the other hand, to refuse to contemplate sexual unions outside marriage could also prove problematic for many women. In addition to whatever issues of sexual desire and curiosity may have intervened, there was also the problem of indigence. For the poor, marriage fees and celebrations were no trifling matter. To postpone sexual union until marriage costs were first assembled could destroy potentially felicitous unions, subject a newly married couple to substantial debt, or invite parents to exert greater leverage over the marriage choices and adult destinies of youth. In the city, even in its Indian barrios, parents and community reciprocity grids played lesser, more irregular roles in the financing of subaltern weddings than in rural village settings.[34] Finally, even when a woman questioned a man's sincerity and intentions or when marriage clearly lay outside the prospective horizons of a relationship, a poor woman could not easily afford to rule out a sexual liaison. As we have seen, the occasional *amasio* or sexual liaison might become a significant element within a diverse package of female income streams and might even come to blur the distinction between *amasia* and prostitute. All of this implied that it was important for women to consider the possibility of sexual unions and understandings in the absence of formal marriage.

For plebeian men, marriage and sexual pacts posed lesser but still significant dilemmas. Marriage fees and celebrations imposed expenses difficult
to finance, and formal marriage implied potentially unwelcome economic,
social, and institutional obligations and entanglements. Yet sexual possession
of a woman outside marriage was hardly unencumbered in a city whose married women seemed to defy social enclosure and possession by husbands.
Amasias and common-law wives were even more capable of charting uncontrolled pathways of livelihood and social contact and asserting their own
visions of human obligation, self-governance, and separation rights in sexual
relationships. However much young men might resist formal marriage or seek
unencumbered sexual conquests and possessions, they might find such quests
elusive. Sexual possessions might require quasi-marital entanglements.

From these considerations and their social negotiation there emerged a
culture of respectable consensual union among persons too poor to marry.
The key point in determining social respectability and quasi-marital obligation outside formal marriage was intention and appearance rather than marriage itself. If a couple of limited means exchanged a promise to marry (*palabra de casamiento*), sealed the exchange with gifts, and proceeded openly to
pursue a "married life" (*vida maridable*), the pair could join the ranks of respectable conjugal unions. The man's gift was usually a material object—
a garment, a rosary, or a piece of cheap jewelry. A woman's gift might be
a similar object, or it might also be her bodily property, the virginity consumed in the act of sex. In short, among the poor the intention to marry
and to live as married could, if necessary, substitute for the sacrament of marriage. The records of plebeian life in Mexico City are filled with the stories of
persons who lived *vidas maridables* while remaining technically unmarried.
The culture of respectable consensual union, while not unknown in rural
Morelos or Oaxaca, proved especially commonplace and adaptive in plebeian
Mexico City.[35]

Some such lives yielded poignant stories. On May 1, 1797, the barrio *alcalde*
Don Francisco Rico picked up two Indians of the Belém neighborhood and
charged them with illicit sexual union (*incontinencia*). Macedonio de la Rosa
was a shoemaker about twenty-three years old, and María Guadalupe Romana was an avocado and fruit vendor about twenty years old. The two had
never been married and were therefore charged with incontinence rather than
adultery. Their sexual union was not particularly disreputable within plebeian
folk culture, did not disrupt established marriages, and might normally have
received the practical acceptance accorded the many *vidas maridables* that
drew little attention from barrio neighbors. But Macedonio had gotten into a
fight or two, wounded at least one man, and acquired some barrio enemies
who considered him a troublemaker. Under the circumstances, denunciation
of illicit sexual union served as a convenient tool of vengeance. Ironically,

however, the case brought to the fore the culture of respectable unions, sealed by marriage intention. Macedonio and María Guadalupe freely admitted that they had met a year earlier while María Guadalupe sold avocados in a city plaza, that Macedonio had courted and promised to marry her, and that they proceeded to have sex and live together. Significantly, Macedonio did not seek to discredit his common-law wife by claiming that she had been sexually impure before he met her. On the contrary, she had allowed him to take her virginity, and he remained committed to marrying her "because he owes her her honor." The main problem, the two agreed, was poverty. They barely made enough money to sustain themselves, and when María Guadalupe had fallen ill, Macedonio had had to spend on her cure the meager amount of money they had saved to finance an eventual marriage.[36]

The culture of respectable consensual union among persons too poor to marry represented a practical response to the dynamics of urban plebeian life, to the fragility of livelihoods and to the obstacles to gendered pacts sealed by formal marriage. It allowed for variation of economic condition and personal inclination and a measure of sociocultural tolerance. Well-off plebeians and middling sectors could continue to associate marriage and respectability closely in their own minds. Poorer plebeians for whom the bonds of intention seemed too fragile and tainted and for whom marriage represented a feasible eventual objective could try to save the necessary funds bit by bit, as Macedonio and María Guadalupe apparently did. Less ambivalent folk who lived on the economic edge and who perhaps welcomed freedom from the permanence of sacramental union might live for years as persons "married" on the basis of conjugal commitment, good-faith intentions, and social appearance.[37] Florentina Josefa Benita Rodríguez, a mestiza servant, and Pablo Trujano, a *castizo* mason, agreed in 1785 that they had lived a conjugal life for some fifteen years and had raised two children in a relationship sealed by the standard *palabra de casamiento*. For whatever reason, the two had parted ways for over a year, and Pablo developed a consensual union with María Guadalupe Aguila, a *castiza* widow to whom he had also declared an intention to marry. When interviewed by a church official, both women signified a certain indifference to marriage as such. Florentina said she still preferred to marry her old common-law husband but that the marriage decision did not matter all that much to her: "Well, then, [she] has found herself ready to continue working, if the said Pablo does not want to get married." María Guadalupe, Pablo's preferred choice, proved no less indifferent: "Let Pablo marry whomever he wants." María Guadalupe "leaves him free . . . also remaining so [herself]."[38]

If the culture of respectable consensual union widened spaces of plebeian conjugal dignity and self-affirmation, however, it also introduced specific dynamics of conflict. One detects two key axes of cultural argument. First, turns toward violence and coercion could transform consent (*voluntad*) into a euphemism or could at least steer relationships toward paradoxical blends of coercion and consent.[39] Second, issues of intention and obligation could become problematic rather than self-evident. Women and female youth argued that male suitors and seducers reneged on promises to marry. Some such remonstrances may be taken literally. That is, the *novia* had received an explicit marriage commitment; she expected her *novio* to fulfill it within a reasonable period; the *novio* seemed to back away from recognizing his promise; and financial considerations as such did not figure in the discourse of commitment. In other instances, however, a reading of the complaint at face value misses the point. Reading between the lines — and taking into account both the commonality of consensual union built on respectable intentions and the resolution of marriage promise disputes through financial settlements — it seems fair to say that for poverty-stricken women and female youth especially, a suitor often demonstrated bad faith not by failure to marry but by neglect. Economic assistance and social attentiveness made marriage promises and intentions more authentic, even if marriage itself was postponed. Men and male youth, for their part, commonly claimed that their erstwhile sexual partners had magnified consensual encounters into a courtship built on marriage promises. María Rosa de Mendoza, a mestiza "by appearance Indian," complained in 1760 that José Tomás Bautista, a *castizo* shoemaker "by appearance mestizo," had failed to fulfill his marriage promise despite his willingness to take her virginity (*violar su virginidad*). She demanded either marriage or financial compensation. José Tomás responded that she inflated a one-time, casual encounter that she had herself initiated. She had passed his workplace and "told me let's go cock-chasing [*correr gallo*, a metaphorical reference to a rooster-chasing game common in Carnival], that she had by now let go of proprieties." Juan said he had no money, went his version, but María replied that it did not matter.[40]

Individuals sometimes lied, of course, about their conversations, but cultural argument over intention and obligation could run deeper than simple truth and falsehood. The arguments also brought to the fore profoundly different interpretations of the symbolic and communicative meaning of action. At the extreme, one senses in female discourse a notion that a taking of virginity in a context of courting or seduction signified an implied obligation to marry — with or without explicit verbal promises and with or without a symbolic gift exchange. One Sunday evening in 1779 María Francisca Castillo, a sixteen-year-old who lived with her family in a comedy house, agreed to join Juan Antonio Gustinaza, a twenty-one-year-old tailor, on a stroll and picnic. The two youths agreed on the basic facts of the sexual encounter: María "lost her virginity to him" (in Juan's perspective, he "took her virginity"); the sexual union had been consensual rather than violent; and Juan had not verbalized a promise to marry. Nonetheless, the notion of implied promise — a culturally patterned interpretation of practical meanings signified by action and context — comes through in María's discourse. María, accompanied by her parents, marched to a judge, filed a complaint, and declared "that she was ready to get married since it was not right to remain mocked [*burlada*]." In María's discourse, moreover, Juan Antonio had been sufficiently cognizant of female cultural expectations to feel compelled to explain his reluctance to marry her. On the night of the picnic, when the two youths returned to María's house, "he turned her over to her mother telling her that he did not want to marry her because of [opposition by] those of his house."[41]

If a pregnancy ensued, female understandings of an implied marriage intention or obligation gained all the more urgency, even if the prospective mother had not been virginal. In 1777 Catarina María pressed her sexual partner Ignacio Cadena to fulfill his promise to marry. But Catarina did not press literal questions of verbal promises and female virginity very hard. She failed to contest Ignacio's claim that the couple had actually had a consensual relationship unmediated by an explicit marriage promise and that Catarina, far from a sexual innocent who lost her virginity to a seducer, mixed rather freely and easily with several men. It was Catarina's pregnancy — even in the absence of explicit promises or prior virginity — that created an urgent obligation. Let us recall that for women a marriage obligation, whether explicit or implied, could refer as readily to ongoing social and economic attentiveness as to sacramental union. This elasticity or double meaning implied that a financial settlement could serve to resolve argument. Although Catarina, for example, declared a readiness to marry Ignacio, she also declared a readiness to forgo the marriage provided that he "pay for the birth, or dower her." They agreed on a settlement of twelve pesos — about seven weeks of plebeian food money.[42]

Argument over intention and obligation in consensual unions also brought forth male visions of the symbolic and communicative meaning of action. At the extreme, the male vision held that since women tended toward moral and sexual treachery, one had to interpret social communication and obligation narrowly. Women's inferences of implied obligation — communicated through behavior, context, verbal intimation, and known cultural expectation — easily constituted malicious invention and embellishment. Moreover, women and female youth who consented to sex in the absence of an explicit verbal promise and gift exchange may not have been virginal anyway. Their veracity, therefore, was all the more suspect: "He doubts that the fetus is his," replied Ignacio Cadena to Catarina María's complaint.[43] In male argument, intention and obligation were clearest if four conditions prevailed simultaneously: (1) the *novia* or *amasia* had been a virgin (and had followed a sexually proper path with all other men), (2) she had agreed to a sexual relationship because of an explicit promise of marriage, (3) a pregnancy attributable to the *novio* or *amasio* had ensued, and (4) all such claims proved verifiable or uncontested.

Let us turn briefly to two additional arenas of gendered social convention and conflict that bore witness to the specifics of plebeian life. First, let us consider the dialectics of separation and ownership in persons. We have already observed that a common fear and complaint of women was that men might abandon them—sometimes literally, sometimes figuratively. The worst of both worlds for an indigent plebeian woman was for a man to continue to assert vigorously his permanent rights of possession in the woman—his right to a sexual monopoly, to sexual access on demand, to an accounting of her everyday movements and social contacts, to her domestic labors and her income streams, and to control over her children—while asserting his own right to take leave of his household bonds, presence, and obligations for days at a time. At bottom, separation and ownership constituted two sides of the coin of gendered property. To separate at will from an accounting to others signified ownership of the self. To prohibit separation by an Other who owed an accounting signified ownership of the Other.

In Mexico City the dialectics of separation and ownership reached a special intensity. Conjugal rupture, whether temporary or prolonged, seemed embedded in the fabric of social practice and expectation. As one might expect, conflicts often pitted masculine separation against feminine claims of ownership. But assertions of separation rights ran in the reverse direction as well. False certifications of husbands' deaths were not uncommon.[44] Husbands complained that wives asserted a right to abandon them   a kind of practical divorce—and women did not necessarily retreat from a decision to separate.

Consider, for example, the marital abandonments of Joaquina Francisca Ramos and Joaquín Rivera.[45] The two plebeian Spaniards married around 1777, when Joaquín was twenty-seven years old and Joaquina only fifteen. During the next twelve years Joaquina bore three live children, but by 1789 her marriage had also entered a crisis. Joaquín, who worked in the Royal Cigar and Cigarette Factory, had established a *casa chica* and fathered three additional children with an *amasia*, and Joaquina also complained of maltreatment in her marriage. That year she had Joaquín jailed. By this point Joaquina had concluded that her husband was beyond redemption, and she firmly resisted the authorities' efforts to achieve a reconciliation. When they released Joaquín after a week or two of imprisonment, Joaquina moved to dissolve her marriage on her own. Joaquina, now twenty-seven years old, fled into hiding, "maintaining herself [along] with the costs of her work, spinning candlewick [to support] herself, and her three children." Joaquín tracked her down and had her jailed for four months. When released in April 1790 under orders to reunite with her husband, Joaquina again resisted the pressure. She fled into hiding and moved from house to house, probably working as a domestic servant while plying her candlewick trade on the side. Eventually she moved to Chalco, a nearby rural district that served as Mexico City's maize granary. There Joaquina found refuge with an uncle who was also a pueblo priest, and she took up occasional sexual contact with an *amasio*.

Joaquina's de facto divorce held for about two years. On February 7, 1792, Joaquina returned to Mexico City to give birth to a child fathered by her *amasio*. She had established a reasonably independent life and had apparently achieved a modest prosperity. Joaquina managed to bring along two young female servants — perhaps to assist with the birth and postpartum domestic chores, to work in Joaquina's candlewick trade, or both. The return to Mexico City, however, exposed Joaquina to reprisal. By March 5 Joaquín had tracked down his wife and gotten her arrested. She fell ill in jail and within two weeks won release "on deposit" in an honorable house. Joaquín opposed her release for fear that she would flee once more, complained of the liberty with which she lived while theoretically "on deposit," and succeeded in having her jailed again in October. Joaquina fell ill once more — with rheumatism and gonorrhea — and Joaquín countered her petition for release by arguing that she should be sent to him for her cure. But Joaquina's opposition to a marital reunion remained unshakable: "She will not go with her husband, because he is not nor has been one, nor has he ever given her anything." Joaquina argued that given Joaquín's failure as a husband and her justified animosity and fear of violence, she ought to be granted a divorce. Over Joaquín's objection the *alcalde*, Don Antonio Mendes Prieto, granted Joaquina a permanent separation within the terms allowed by patriarchal ideology. Joaquina would be placed not with her husband but on deposit indefinitely in the house of Don Manuel Guerrero, a master brass artisan (*latonero*) who agreed to see that she would live honorably.

Joaquina Francisca Ramos's determination to achieve a de facto right of separation — her jailing of Joaquín, her extralegal flight from house to house in the city and finally to Chalco, her building of a new life based on her own income streams and networks of sociability and patronage, and her insistence that an indefinite on-deposit arrangement was superior to a forced marital reconciliation — constituted more than one individual's saga. In a city whose gendered pacts proved fragile and vulnerable to crisis, plebeian women struggled for the right to conclude that continuation of a pact was no longer worth its troubles and that a conjugal partner (whether a legal husband, a consensual partner in a *vida maridable*, or an *amasio*) had abdicated his rights of gendered possession. Again and again the documents of plebeian conjugal life bear witness to female efforts to forge a space or social convention of gender that tolerated de facto rights of separation, whether temporary or prolonged, that belied male ownership. We need not idealize, of course, sagas of female independence or separation. The process was often contentious and only partially successful, and it sometimes sparked violent vengeance. But not every husband resisted it as doggedly as Joaquín Rivera. One detects a measure of tolerance and resignation in the men who grudgingly let go of the effort to track and keep a resistant wife or *amasia*, a tacit acceptance in the employers, patrons, and house managers who did not inquire too strenuously about the reasons a woman found herself in need of work and housing.[46]

Let us turn, finally, to the sexualization of gender disputes. This, too, constituted a marker of and response to the precarious viability of patriarchal pacts in Mexico City. "Sexualization" here refers to the tendency to frame male-female conflicts, especially accusations and violence directed against female targets, as specifically sexual disputes. For example, a man who resents his woman's physical mobility, economic demands, income-earning initiatives, sociability networks, or conversational freedoms may escalate matters by accusing her of the ultimate female infraction: sexual looseness and betrayal. The escalation is, of course, self-serving since it invokes the classic female character flaw that anchored male legitimacy, control, and punishment (see Chapter 5). But to raise the specter of sexual immorality and betrayal need not always have implied self-conscious manipulation. The escalation may also have seemed a rather natural or self-evident inference — at least to men — in a social milieu where male-female pacts seemed haunted by imminent rupture or disintegration. Female sexual liberty or betrayal stood as the most potent cultural explanation of female deviance and insubordination.

Given the sexualization of gender disputes and accusations in Morelos, Oaxaca, and cultures beyond Mexico, it is especially important to clarify the terms of the argument.[47] The point of this chapter's argument on respectable consensual union, its argument on the dynamics of conjugal separation and ownership, and this book's larger argument on the question of many Mexicos, is not to draw an all-or-nothing contrast between quintessentially different regions. What matters is not purity of regional contrast but more subtle differences of configuration and relative weight of social phenomena recognizable across several regions. In Mexico City one observes a relatively more intense tendency to sexualize grievances against women and female youth. Among incidents of violence directed at female targets, sexual conflicts accounted for about four-sevenths (58.2 percent) of principal motives of dispute in Mexico City and about half and three-sevenths (48.4 percent and 43.9 percent) in Morelos and Oaxaca, respectively. The specific composition of sexualized dispute in Mexico City also bore witness to the fragility of male-female pacts. In all three regions, *celos* cases, in which an alleged sexual rival threatened a pact, and sexual assault cases, in which the violence focused on a taking of the female sexual body, accounted for the great majority of sexualized conflicts. But only in Mexico City did disputes about the "on" or "off" status of a preexisting sexual pact—even in the absence of an alleged sex rival or *amasio*—figure importantly as an independent category in its own right. In Mexico City the on-or-off clashes accounted for about a fourth (27.0 percent) of sexualized disputes leading to violence against women and female youth.[48] The sexualization of dispute, like the culture of respectable consensual union and the dialectics of separation and ownership in persons, bore witness to specificity: the wider fragility that framed contested patriarchal pacts in plebeian Mexico City.

MEMORIES OF MORELOS

We have argued in Part 3 of this book for the compatibility of transregional consistency and regional particularity within a world of many Mexicos. When we explored indigenous Oaxaca, we began with gendered experiences that elicited memories of Morelos, then proceeded to study the specific configurations or idiosyncrasies that set Oaxaca somewhat apart. Our journey into the plebeian world of Mexico City has proceeded in the reverse direction. We set out by exploring the aura of crisis and desperation that seemed to haunt gendered pacts and struggles, the specificities of urban life that drove contestation of ongoing pacts toward a crisis of pacts, and the social conventions and conflicts of gender that represented both an expression of and a response to the fragility of male-female pacts among the poor. We conclude our journey by returning to the theme of transregional resonance and consistency.

Somehow, the transitory and crisis-ridden atmosphere and the social conventions and conflicts of gender that attended the fragility of livelihoods and social pacts in plebeian Mexico City failed to preclude patterns of struggle and collaboration familiar in Morelos. It is less accurate to state that the contestations of patriarchal pacts familiar in Morelos and Oaxaca gave way to a crisis of their existence than to state that plebeian city life seemed to spawn both phenomena at once. It is as if plebeian life oscillated between contestations of the particular within a framework of expectations that affirmed the ongoing, necessary character of pacts between male and female, and ruptures of male control and livelihoods of female self-management so pervasive that all such expectations seemed at risk.

The sense of transregional consistency within or alongside regional variation emerges in myriad ways in Mexico City's documents of gendered life. The arsenal of female tactics and strategies often bore a striking resemblance to that uncovered in Morelos: women pluralized the relevant patriarchs in their lives; they established female networks of background conversation and assistance; they resorted to institutional escalation and to supernatural power when first-line tactics based on kin, friends, and informal advice and pressure failed; and they mobilized scandals if necessary to force a public resolution of once private or personal matters. The character flaws and stigmas that delegitimized the opposite gender at moments of conflict and that legitimated one's own orientation to gender right look much the same as those already encountered. The crossfires of gender and family and of color and class introduced in Mexico City the ambiguities, crossover alliances, and ambivalent zigzag movements between solidary and conflictual stances familiar elsewhere. The profoundly gendered understanding of legitimate and illegitimate political authority encouraged a political language of metaphorical fathers and irresponsible parasites in Mexico City as well as Morelos. Indeed, the city's most important colonial uprising—the famous corn riot of 1692—had followed a gendered etiquette for revolt.[49]

We need not explore in detail every facet of the resonance that tempers the contrast between Mexico City and Morelos. Let us focus briefly on three telling examples: the conflictual dialogue of contingent and absolute right evident in male-female relations, the modest weight of *descargas* and interior psychodramas in male-on-male violence, and the sheer familiarity of the narratives of gendered drama and conflict in subaltern life.

In Mexico City as in Morelos women emphasized the contingent character of gender right and obligation in disputes with men, who asserted a more absolute sense of innate patriarchal right. Female practice asserted a certain mutuality or reciprocity of obligation, however unequal the partners, on terms that entangled male claims of authority, service, and even sexual possession within the web of the conditional. As in Morelos, the tension between contingent and absolute orientations to gender right often sparked fierce conflict even when women refrained from challenging patriarchal first principles as such. Consider, for example, the complex tangle of disputes over sexual possession and freedoms, physical mobility, and economic obligation that tore at the marriage of María Olaya Piñeda, the *castiza* wife of Juan del Castillo, a Spanish carpenter.[50] In 1792 María petitioned for relief from her husband's chronic maltreatment and adultery. Juan had kept an *amasia*, María declared, during fourteen of their sixteen years of marriage. In María's view the liaison with Micaela Tapia had been the fundamental "cause of so much hitting, bad treatment, injurious words, hunger, nakedness, and troubles." One of the most dramatic charges by María was that Juan locked her up, as if María, the wife, were the semisecret *amasia*: "His uncontrolled wantonness has reached the point of taking me to live in the company of the said woman who is his *amasia*, locking me up in a room and treating her as his proper wife; well, all the neighborhood believes that I am not the wife but the opposite." In María's view Juan had effectively abandoned his marital obligations while continuing to assert an ironclad right of possession. His lockup prevented her from establishing her own networks of sociability, information, and conversation with neighbors; he granted her only one real of maintenance money a day (only about half a poor person's expected allotment) while channeling most of his income toward his *amasia*, now a wife by reputation, and his diversions; and he forced his wife to work as a domestic servant.

Juan did not deny his liaison with an *amasia* or that he had locked up his wife. He did not even deny that his economic support had faltered (although he claimed not to have provided regular sustenance to his *amasia*). But his explanation brought to the fore the ways a wife's contingent approach to female right and obligation in marriage might drive a husband to strong assertions of authority that overrode discourses of contingency and conditionality. María had gotten in the habit of abandoning him when displeased; he had had her imprisoned on runaway charges four times. Moreover, she had dared to find an *amasio* of her own, the master tailor José Salcedo. María's defiance of Juan's possession in her was unacceptable, regardless of Juan's long-standing *amasia* and economic negligence, and he had to reassert his rightful claims as a patriarch. "Although he has had his wife . . . locked up in a room, it was so that she wouldn't run away as she has done other times on account of illicit connection with Jose Salcedo." Significantly, María denied neither her physical flights and wanderings nor an earlier sexual liaison with José Salcedo. In her view such liberties emerged in relation to the negligence and abuse of a husband who failed to meet his obligations. If Juan's assumptions and reasoning fell squarely into the familiar mold of absolute patriarchal right unconditioned by contingencies, María's understanding of right fell squarely into the logic of contingent right shaped by human mutuality and obligation. Juan's maltreatment had driven her to assert, in justified defense of her own well-being, a greater right of control over her physical movements and whereabouts. Even her three-year sexual connection with José Salcedo, although terminated in 1789, had been understandable as a decision "brought about by [economic] necessity." The authorities eventually dragged the pair into an agreement to reconcile — after Juan languished in prison six months and María served three months on countercharges by her husband. We cannot know how long the reconciliation lasted before a struggle between contingent and absolute orientations to gender right in male-female relations reasserted itself. But we do know that conflictual dialogues along these lines suffused gender culture in plebeian Mexico City (as well as among more middling social strata) and that such struggles easily turned bitter or violent.[51]

Our second example of memories of Morelos refers us back to the surprisingly modest weight of *descargas* and interior psychodramas of masculine rage in male violence in general and male-on-male violence in particular. As we have seen for the case of Morelos, the cultural mythology of wounded manhoods exploding almost randomly in violence against the nearest available target played a rather modest role in male violence. The finding was counterintuitive precisely because elite stereotypes of the poor since colonial times, the construction of a quintessentially Mexican national culture and mythology in the twentieth century, and the ready availability of confirming anecdotes all run in the opposite direction. The counterintuitive finding invited us to scrutinize freshly the intersections of masculinity, power, and violence in everyday life in Morelos. Violence by men usually focused on tangibles rather than intangibles. Even in male-on-male violence, socially driven logics of masculinity — those driven by social relationships that molded one's effective claims to dignity, voice, and resources as a man among men — far outweighed more interior ventings of manhood or rage for no particular reason. Moreover, by avoiding one-on-one vengeance and escalation dramas in isolated spots and by developing a theater of playful masculine bravado amidst sociability, bonding, and friendly accompaniment, men found ways to steer conflicts and escalations away from violent climax while projecting self-legitimating enactments of masculine valor and rivalry.

Among our three regions, Mexico City — the metropolis of uprooted male plebeians and migrants subjected to color-class humiliation and patriarchal inadequacy, and the milieu that would yield the famed twentieth-century image of the excitable *pelado* who is both hapless and explosive — should be the one region that corresponds well with the image of *descarga* ventings. Here one should find the bursting forth of an interior masculine rage at unpredictable moments and for no particular reason, or more precisely, for interior reasons unconnected to the target or to the specific social relations between target and assailant. Yet here, too, the findings run in a counterintuitive direction that stirs memories of Morelos. (See Table 11.1.) Tangibles proved important, and *descarga* ventings were rather modest in male violence. Tangibles accounted for 60.4 percent of all cases with male assailants and 47.6 percent of male-on-male cases. *Descarga* ventings by strict definition amounted to only 6.0 percent and 4.8 percent, respectively. Moreover, among violence cases that may be interpreted as expressions of masculinity, those driven by a social logic far outweighed those plausibly driven by an interior logic (79.4 percent to 20.6 percent in all male assailant cases and 74.6 percent to 25.4 percent in male-on-male cases).

Our third example of the rich resonance between gendered life in Mexico City and Morelos refers to the sheer familiarity of the narratives of gender conflict in subaltern life. Notwithstanding the contrasting settings and the variations in gendered life explicated earlier, the story lines and characters of gendered drama could sound like authentic representations of life in Morelos. Consider, for example, the scenario that unfolded in 1792 when Don José

Gonzales Reina pinned an adultery charge on his wife of three years, Georja Gertrudis Orduña y Echevarría.[52] Don José, a gunsmith, was a reasonably prosperous and socially respectable plebeian. He was said by a friendly witness to have provided Georja three rather than two reales a day for sustenance, he could sign his name, and his racial category was more or less Spanish (notwithstanding a hint of partial mulatto ancestry). Despite her husband's solid economic standing, Georja, variously identified as Spanish and as a free *parda* (mulatta), lived an emphatically plebeian life. She earned an income by rolling cigarettes and cigars at home and by going out and about, like thousands of other female petty producers and vendors, to sell or deliver her product.

The larger battle pitted Don José's vision of female insubordination and treachery against Georja's vision of male negligence and irresponsibility. Don José complained bitterly that Georja "began to want to give the orders in my house, and to undertake visits that did not suit me, and now I've understood they are the *amasios* that she had before marriage." A friend of the couple said that, at bottom, they fought because Georja was often absent when Don José returned home from work to discover that "the meal is never ready." Witnesses saw Georja enjoy drinks, friendly banter, and occasional strolls in the company of men (or at least in mixed company), and Georja admitted at least one *amasio* connection to a neighbor. Georja had, in short, developed the habit of independence — she went out of her own accord on strolls or business; she neglected her duty to provide ready meals to a returning husband; and she undertook suspiciously direct conversations and contacts with male as well as female acquaintances. Perhaps most provocative of all, she responded to rebukes with sharp and humiliating rejoinders. When Don José returned one day to find Georja tying a broom with "Don Fernando," she refused to cower or repent, "and in front of him she threw the *gasto* [daily maintenance money] . . . that I used to bring her, and told me I should not return to her house, that she didn't want anything of mine." In another incident, when Don José resisted buying some quesadillas, Georja retorted "that he was a mulatto begotten with beans." Both incidents culminated with Don José striking Georja; in the second, Georja counterattacked and broke a vase on Don José's head.

Georja had her own complaints, of course. Her husband's economic provisions had been negligent. During their three years of marriage "he has not supplied her even one shirt . . . and in consequence she is short on maintenance." Her husband's jealousies had also been exaggerated. The male visitor to the house who inspired jealousy was actually a friend of Don José who originally visited at her husband's initiative. Her trips into street life were a necessary part of the tobacco trade that sustained her. Don José himself had been caught in a sexual liaison with one Francisca Berrospe. Finally, although Georja sometimes slept with a female neighbor rather than at home, "it is so that she not sleep alone in her room when her husband has left her, and so that he doesn't hit her [upon] catching her alone."

The story of the splitting apart of Georja and Don José bore the traces of city life — the cigarette trade, the daily *gasto* provisions, and the ready availability of mixed gender company in street life. Notwithstanding these idiosyncrasies, however, the story would have seemed familiar to many an ear in Morelos. The character of Georja, for example, might have seemed a composite of the Marías well known in Morelos. Georja's complaint of economic negligence, her irregular provision of meals, and her occasional sleepovers with a female friend stir memories of María Teresa of Texalpa, who left for her mother's house rather than provide food to an irresponsible husband. Her sharp tongue and symbolic affronts recall the taunts by María Gertrudis of Hacienda San Gaspar, who also minced no words and dared her husband to take back his alleged economic contribution. The travels, social contacts, and sexual ambiguities that attended an independent female livelihood bring to mind María Lucía of Oaxtepec and Totolapa, the petty trader who also ventured beyond the home soon after marriage, built up a network of social acquaintances, and got entangled in a web of male sexual jealousies.[53] Even some of the smaller details that enlivened the story of Georja and Don José would have sounded familiar.

First, consider the sequel. Don José claimed in a second incident later in 1792 that he caught Georja and her aunt speaking with an *amasio* and that the *amasio* drew a sword to kill him. Fortunately "the women neighbors came from the street, and the *casera* from my house," to chase the assailant away. The bold rush by women into moments of crisis and danger, the sense that men did foolish things if women left them to their own character flaws and excesses, and the assertion of female moral authority to block male excess and tragedy would have supplied the ring of truth to a listener of the story in Morelos.

Second, consider the detail supplied by one female witness. When she had earlier tried to convince Georja to cease her *amasio* connection, Georja "answered that she did not break the friendship so that Hermosillo [the *amasio*] would not kill her husband as he had proposed to do in case of a break of the illicit connection." The ambiguous blends of sexual coercion and consent, the process of female background conversation whereby a woman explained her social circumstances and justified apparently wayward behavior, and the drawing of sometimes skeptical female friends and acquaintances into a discreet complicity of knowledge were the kinds of details and asides that would have enriched a similar tale in Morelos.

Regional diversity in the world of many Mexicos presented blends of the familiar and the idiosyncratic, distinctive configurations built out of similar elements, patterns of overlap as well as difference. Notwithstanding the aura of crisis and desperation that seemed to doom the viability of patriarchal pacts in Mexico City, gendered life yielded tales of character and contestation reminiscent of Morelos. In a world where regional specificity failed to exclude transregional consistency, the story of the sundering apart of Georja and Don José would have traveled well.

CHAPTER 12

The Many Mexicos of
Every Mexican Region

Morelos Reconsidered

CULTURE, REGION, AND MICROREGION: PROLOGUE

We have argued, throughout Part 3 of this book, that a critical rethinking of regional diversity need not imply a straightforward substitution of one Mexico for many Mexicos. The point is not to suppress heterogeneity but to contextualize it. For the theme of gender and power, we have argued for a dialogue between transregional similarity and regional idiosyncrasy. This approach frames regional difference as partly a matter of the unique and idiosyncratic and partly a matter of distinctive shading and configuration among widely recognizable social dynamics. The net effect is to cut heterogeneity down to less fetishized dimensions. The contrapuntal play of similarity and difference, moreover, enables us to see more clearly the magnification of regional differences into full-blown, quintessential contrasts that obliterate transregional pattern and resonance. In this interpretive context, transregional consistency and regional variation escape treatment as mutually exclusive opposition. *Many* Mexicos meets many *Mexicos*.

We have already discussed in some detail (Chapter 9) the foundations of our approach in pluralized and conflictual theorizations of culture. On the one hand, cultural practice and discourse mobilize processes of conflict, mediation, and unity that constitute argument. We have explored the culture-as-argument dimension of social life at length in Part 2 of this book. On the other hand, cultural practice and discourse also mobilize processes of identifying self and group in relation to variant Others. The culture-as-variation dimension of social life has framed much of the discussion in Part 3 and will recast

285

the analysis of single regions in this chapter. Once one explores culture less as a unified and unifying body of values and understandings than as plural languages of argument and variation within shared social arenas, the mental grip of a mutually exclusive opposition between similarity and contrast weakens. The finding of transregional patterns of culture does not necessarily undermine a vision of culture as argument, and the finding of regional idiosyncrasies does not necessarily exclude patternings in common. In short, the comparative analysis of Mexican regional cultures of gender and power as a dialogue of transregional similarity and local difference becomes less paradoxical, less a leap into theoretical anarchy.

Although the theorization of culture as argument and variation solves some problems, however, it also opens up new ones. We have argued that the cultural language of the self, whether applied to an individual, a social group, or a regional or microregional world, implies a cultural language of the Other. Social solidarities and understandings have as their premise a discourse of variation. But the discourse of variation commonly focuses not only on cultural strangers beyond the self's social world but also on variance within or near the known world of the cultural insider. We have already seen, in the analysis of Morelos, culture as a language of variation and stereotype between the genders, between honorable and deviant individuals, and between superior and inferior versions of manhood and womanhood, within a given regional world. We have also seen, in our study of Oaxaca, culture as a language of variation and stereotype between a region's pueblos, microregions, and ethnic groups. Once we reflect seriously on the many Mexicos of every Mexican region, an important question arises. How do experiences and languages of difference within regions compare with experiences and languages of difference between regions?

Every region's peoples experienced and talked about cultural differences within and beyond the local worlds of everyday life. In this sense every region and microregion had its many Mexicos. Once we probe this aspect of social life, the ironic result may be to temper further the contrasts we might otherwise draw between regions. The eerie parallels in variation within and between regions and the eerie parallels in discourses about such variations meant that the many Mexicos of one region could elicit considerable recognition among the many peoples of another. The experience and language of heterogeneity itself did not necessarily exclude transregional parallel and resonance.

MORELOS RECONSIDERED: THE PARALLELS AND IRONIES OF MICROREGIONAL DIFFERENCE

Let us illustrate the point by returning to Morelos, the region to which we devoted our most detailed analysis. Let us recall that compared with Oaxaca,

Morelos had presented us with a geographically compact region characterized by considerable movement of peasants among the region's pueblos, haciendas, ranchos, and markets and by a social and racial mingling that diminished cultural distance between Indians and non-Indians. In addition, the statistical analysis of the Morelos violence incidents failed to yield significant variations by ethnic group or by microregion for our most important findings on gender and power: the leading role of gender-rooted dispute within the tripartite structure of major motivations; the comparatively strong connection between close social bonding and violence against specifically female targets; the socioracial normalcy of assailants and targets and the slight importance of loners; the role of sexuality as central yet less than subsuming in violence against females; and the preponderance of tangibles and socially driven logics in male violence.[1] Given the region's compact human geography, its history of socioracial movement and mingling, and the statistical findings, the decision to present data and analysis for the Morelos region as a whole rested on firm ground.

Nonetheless, as any student or resident of Morelos will attest, a basic microregional distinction has sometimes played a significant role in the region's history and its popular discourse. Notwithstanding the generally temperate climate and the relatively small distances and constant flow of people between points within the region, local history and lore encourage a certain contrast between the so-called *tierra fría* and the *tierra caliente*. The distinction coincides roughly with the transit from mountainous territory to foothills and basin along a line about 1,500 meters above sea level. In colonial times, the *tierra fría* zone of the temperate-to-cool sierras north and northeast of Cuernavaca remained a more decidedly Indian area whose pueblos exported people selectively and temporarily—seasonal laborers to the sugar estates south of the area and petty vendors to *tianguis* gatherings throughout the region. Community allegiance and residence remained important for most peasants, and the mountains facilitated escape and cover during times of confrontation with outsiders. It would be Tepoztlán, a village of the *tierra fría,* that presented an appealing facade of pueblo harmony and continuity to the anthropologist Robert Redfield in the 1920s. The larger and more heavily populated *tierra caliente* zone, dominated by the warmer, sugar-oriented basin south and southeast of Cuernavaca, witnessed a more intense history of hacienda-pueblo struggle over land; a more scattered distribution of populations among pueblos, hacienda estates, and interstitial *ranchero* zones of small independent proprietors; and a more pronounced racial mingling that blurred ethnoracial boundaries and imparted a certain African presence to the peasant population. In the twentieth century it would be land-starved Anenecuilco, a pueblo of the *tierra caliente,* that would elect Zapata its leader and come to symbolize the plight that drove peasants to become revolutionaries.[2]

Notwithstanding the consistency between the two zones on most of our major findings, the ethnic profiles in the violence records echoed the microregional distinction. (See Table 12.1.) The ethnic contrasts among assailants are relatively muted. Indians accounted for six-ninths (68.3 percent) of assailants in the *tierra fría* and five-ninths (55.2 percent) in the *tierra caliente*, a distinction too modest to prove statistically significant. Nonetheless, the weightier presence of *castas* and persons of African descent in the *tierra caliente* came through. *Castas* accounted for only an eighth (12.7 percent) of assailants in the *tierra fría* but for nearly two and a half eighths (29.5 percent) in the *tierra caliente*. Two-fifths (41.9 percent) of the *casta* assailants in the *tierra caliente* were explicitly identified as mulattoes, while none of their *tierra fría* counterparts were so identified. Among the targets of violence the ethnic distinctions come through more sharply. Indians accounted for nearly nine-tenths (87.5 percent) of the targets in the *tierra fría*, a figure reminiscent of Oaxacan ethnic proportions, but only five-ninths (55.4 percent) in the *tierra caliente*—a statistically significant contrast. The *casta* proportion for targets of violence was slight (7.1 percent) in the *tierra fría* but five times more substantial (37.0 percent) in the *tierra caliente*. Again, two-fifths (41.2 percent) of the *casta* group in the *tierra caliente* was explicitly identified as mulatto.

In short, although Indians accounted for majorities of assailants and targets in both microregions and although our major findings on gender, power, and violence hold up well in both areas, moderate contrasts in the ethnic profiles of the two zones indeed echoed the more Indian reputation of the *tierra fría* and its pueblos, and the more multiracial and African reputation of the *tierra caliente* and its mix of pueblos, haciendas, and ranchos. The variegated social and ethnic ambiances of the region lent potential support to microregional discourses of many Mexicos.

Two questions arise from such shadings. On matters of gender, power, and violence, did the peoples of Morelos construct a discourse of contrast out of such microregional distinctions? If so, did the language of contrast build on distinctions in social dynamics observable in the records of gender conflict and violence? After all, selective memory of real experience, magnified interpretation of authentic difference, may constitute a far more potent instrument of stereotyping than invention in the purist sense.

Let us begin with the discourse of difference. The discourse of microregional contrast and stereotype, although less than pervasive in the documents, comes through from time to time as a kind of background assumption about the character and cultural mores of the peoples who dominated the two zones. Totolapa, explained one official in 1802, was a "roguery mill" even though it was an ostensibly Indian pueblo of the *tierra fría*. The problem was that many non-Indians had invaded Totolapa, which had as a result gotten "tangled up with the *tierra caliente*."[3] Even to this day the discursive reputation of the *tierra caliente* is that of a district whose men are prone to confrontational brands of manhood—individualized acts of manly passion, swagger, and escalation that explode in violence. As one *tierra fría* informant told the anthropologist John Ingham (probably in the 1960s or 1970s), "There in the tierra caliente a man only thinks about getting a horse, saddle, and pistol. There they are more aggressive, they like to fight."[4]

In late colonial times especially, microregional stereotypes tended to be embedded within ethnoracial distinctions. The peoples of the *tierra caliente* were more mulatto, and ethnic stereotyping ascribed individual hotheadedness and antisocal violence to men and male youth of African descent. The stereotypes were not limited to colonial elites. A *tierra fría* Indian peddling his wares in the warm sugar country in 1806, said to have assumed that a dark mulatto he encountered was a probable thief and assailant, demanded, "What are you doing there, black one?" The episode had an aspect of self-fulfilling fear and prophecy, since the confrontation indeed escalated and ended in the murder of the Indian.[5]

Perhaps more revealing, in view of the racial blurring common in Morelos, was the way troublemakers were sometimes redefined as mulatto in the course of conflict. Various Indians of Xochitlán backed their *gobernador* against charges in 1789 that he had abused his authority and whipped Dionisio Náñez, who considered himself a *castizo*. In doing so they not only accused Dionisio of a sexual license and immorality that justified community punishment; they also declared—almost as a corollary of the argument—that he was a mulatto. In Cuautla Amilpas, José Silverio Barreto, an Indian tributary who charged his *gobernador* with abuse of power in 1805, found himself discredited by similar means: "There is still doubt about if he is [Indian] or mulatto, especially in view of a scandalous incontinence . . . and the absences of subordination and respect."[6]

The discursive stereotypes that applied to the *tierra fría* also blended microregional and ethnic labeling. Even in the mid-twentieth century—despite the decline in Nahuatl language use, the largely negative connotations of Indianness, and the rise of school, work, migration, and status patterns comparable to those in the more mestizo countryside—peoples in both the *tierra fría* and the *tierra caliente* considered the former the regional repository of Indianness. This presumably implied, among other characteristics, that the *tierra fría* folk held greater regard for community allegiance and peace and that the men avoided the kinds of highly individualized acts of passion, bravado, and violent explosion associated with manhood in the *tierra caliente*. Violence presumably took a less antisocial and individualized course. It stopped short of homicidal self-destruction, and it remained more fully bound up with collective pathways—the violence of community uprisings and intracommunity factionalism.[7] The women were presumably less harshly repressed—free to join with men, in the words of a colonial official in 1780, in the bouts of drinking whereby "they make themselves insolent."[8]

The answer to our first question is clear. On matters of gender, power, and violence, the peoples of Morelos did indeed construct a discourse of contrast and stereotype out of perceived microregional distinction. The discourse reached back to colonial times, and its mark on regional lore and oral tradition would extend well into the twentieth century. This discourse blended difference by microregion and by ethnicity, especially in colonial times, and one of its foci homed in on matters of masculine temperament: the individualized violence, sexual swagger, and vengeance dramas of men in the *tierra caliente* distinguished them from the conflict avoidance, reserve, and deference to community peace in the *tierra fría*. The discourse of microregion added another layer of connotation to the adjectives *fría* and *caliente*. The *tierra caliente* was not only a zone of hot climate but of hot temperament. The *tierra fría* was cool in both climate and temperament.

The parallels with discourses of human and ethnic variation in Oaxaca are striking. There we observed understandings of ethnic identity and variation that contrasted the peaceable men of harmony-seeking pueblos with the violent men of evil pueblos, and that distinguished the peaceable Indian men who refrained from exaggerated swagger, stubbornness, and repression of women from the violent Spaniards and *castas* who equated masculinity with bravado, intransigence in conflict, and tyranny over women. Even the "hot land" metaphor had a certain currency. The districts to the south of Oaxaca's interior mountain and valley zones descended to the hot Pacific coast. There a larger *casta* and African presence and a more evenly distributed blend of haciendas, ranchos, and pueblos fostered a distinctive ethnic and economic geography. In Oaxaca's version of the *tierra caliente*, as in Morelos's, "hot" referred to both climate and masculine temperament and invoked racial stereotypes that associated African descent and influence with antisocial explosiveness. In both regions, in short, microregional and ethnic sensibilities fed a gendered language of human contrast — more violently explosive men and more rigidly repressed women in one zone or ethnic group and more peaceable men and more assertive women in another.[9]

The language of contrast between neighboring regions and microregions introduces an irony to regional distinctions between Oaxaca and Morelos. As we have seen, notwithstanding the transregional patterns we uncovered, the evidence on the two regions suggested two important divergences in dynamics of gender, power, and violence. Violence incidents in Morelos tilted more sharply toward homicidal explosions, and male-female gender conflicts in Oaxaca seemed to unfold on a cultural platform somewhat more supportive of female assertions (notwithstanding patriarchal-elder hegemony in community life). Enlarged into stereotypes that obliterate countervailing points in common, these differences yield a familiar discourse of many Mexicos: Oaxaca's peaceable men, strong women, indigenous culture, and resilient communities stand apart from Morelos's rebellious men, subordinate women, syncretic culture, and desperate communities (locked in struggle to ward off internal factionalism and external land expropriations). The problem is that at least at the level of discourse, differences that serve to differentiate a Morelos from a Oaxaca also serve to distinguish one Morelos microregion from another.

The discursive parallels bring us, finally, to our second question. Notwithstanding the applicability of our major findings on gender, power, and violence to both microregions of Morelos, did the language of microregional contrast, even if exaggerated, build on authentic differences in social milieu or dynamics? Were the distinctions experiential as well as discursive?

Here it is instructive to pursue quantitative indexes of difference we observed between Morelos and Oaxaca. Let us consider, for example, the weight of homicide in everyday conflict and violence. Homicides accounted for about half (53.9 percent) the Morelos incidents but only a fourth (24.7 percent) of the Oaxaca incidents. The ratio of homicidal shares (2.2) seems to corroborate a greater explosiveness of individualized passion at moments of conflict in Morelos — a greater difficulty in deflecting or holding in check homicidal impulses in face-to-face disputes between individuals. Within Morelos, homicides accounted for about six-tenths (63.0 percent) of the *tierra caliente* incidents but only three-tenths (31.3 percent) of the *tierra fría* incidents. Surprisingly, the microregional contrast of homicidal shares within Morelos (a homicidal shares ratio of 2.0) mimics rather closely the contrast between Morelos and Oaxaca. (See Table 12.2.) The discourse of contrasting masculine temperament within Morelos not only built on and magnified distinctions in social experience evident in the documentary trails left by violence. In addition, the microregional distinction paralleled those that a historian might draw between the more mestizo version of rural Mexico evident in a Morelos and the more Indian version evident in a Oaxaca.

The parallels of microregional and regional contrast are more subtle when we compare the cultural platforms upon which male-female struggles unfolded. Let us begin by recalling patterns in common: In both Morelos and Oaxaca most criminal violence incidents against women and female youth were seriously injurious (homicides, major assaults requiring medical attention, and sexual assaults accounted for the overwhelming majority). The connection between closer social bonding and violence against specifically female targets was strong. The most life-threatening forms of violence directed against females came from their primary relations. Nonetheless, in some instances the statistical indexes of gender gaps in the social relations of violence in Morelos emerged somewhat more weakly in Oaxaca. The association between comparatively close social bonding and violence against female rather than male is strong but a bit diminished in Oaxaca. In addition the moderate gender gap in the likelihood of suffering homicidal rather than nonhomicidal violence nearly fades out in Oaxaca. For the case of Morelos, the gender gap in homicidal violence derived not from a lesser threat of homicide in cases of assault by primary relations but, rather, from a substantially lesser likelihood in cases of violence by nonprimary, especially secondary, relations. For the Oaxacan case the gender gap fades, in part because homicidal violence played a lesser role in the regional sample for both male and female targets (and therefore yielded lesser statistical effects on the case set as a whole), and in part because a gender gap in homicidal violence fails to appear in secondary relations cases. (See Table 12.3.)

These statistical indicators are consistent with our earlier, more qualitative line of reasoning about the cultural context of male-female power relations and conflicts in Oaxaca. They point to subtle regional shadings and differences, notwithstanding broad patterns in common, in the nexus of gender relations and social relations of power and violence. Oaxaca's women, compared with their Morelos counterparts, appear to have forged slightly more leading roles in confrontations involving secondary and tertiary social relations, and the severity of their injuries in such disputes was somewhat more parallel to the severity of injuries inflicted on men. Indeed, it is only in the case of assaults by primary relations that a modest and statistically significant gender gap favoring women appears; the sociocultural milieu in Oaxaca placed somewhat stronger obstacles against homicidal forms of violence in male-female conflicts.[10]

Once more, within Morelos the *tierra caliente* is to the *tierra fría* what Morelos is to Oaxaca. The association between closer social bonding and specifically female targets diminishes a bit when one moves from the *tierra caliente* to the *tierra fría*. The moderate gender gap in the frequency of homicidal rather than nonhomicidal violence tends to fade out in the *tierra fría*, and largely for the same reasons — the lesser role of homicide in the overall sample and the statistically tenuous gender gap in disputes among secondary relations. (Again, see Table 12.3.) Notwithstanding broad patterns in common, subtle microregional shadings in the cultural milieu that framed male-female conflict yielded statistical effects parallel to those evident in the comparison of Oaxaca and Morelos. As in the case of the explosiveness evident in homicidal violence, such shadings suggest an experiential basis for microregional languages of heterogeneity and stereotype — the magnification of modest or even tenuous distinctions into full-blown contrast and essentialism. One microregion's men are more volatile than another's; one microregion's women more assertive than another's.

The microregional shadings evident in Morelos — both as discourse and as social experience—suggest a necessary refinement of the idea of many Mexicos. The contrasts between a Morelos and a Oaxaca often are not between sui generis regional cultures but between configurations or emphases built out of a range of human behaviors and social dynamics well known to the peoples of *both* regions. As a language of variation that identifies the self in relation to the Other, cultural discourse may exaggerate such distinctions into full-blown, quintessential contrasts. Ironically, the many Mexicos of every region—the distinctions among neighboring regions and neighboring microregions—tempered the exotic or unfamiliar quality of more distant regions. Morelos had its language of Indian regions whose men were less inclined to escalate individual irritation and confrontation into homicidal violence. Oaxaca had its language of hot lands and peoples who injected more individualized bravado and violence into the very meaning of masculinity.

CONCLUDING REFLECTIONS: A *TIERRA CALIENTE* TALE OF MANHOOD AND POWER

Let us conclude with a classic story of manhood and power in a *tierra caliente* environment.[11] In February 1767 Feliciana María went to the sugar mill (*trapiche*) of Don Joseph Herrera to appeal for his intervention in a violent quarrel with her husband. Like many peasant wives, Feliciana integrated income-earning activities into her rhythms of work, in her case, cotton spinning or peddling brought in household income. Her husband, Joaquín Pastrana, was a boiler worker in the *trapiche* and a *casta* of uncertain racial ancestry. He labeled himself a *castizo* in legal documents, but he was also called a mulatto in a heated exchange with hacienda supervisors. Feliciana had come to the *trapiche* because Joaquín had gotten angry over two missing pounds of cotton that she had failed to turn over to him (it is unclear if she had not yet spun them, had lost them, or had traded them independently), and he had taken Feliciana to the *monte* and whipped her. Feliciana, far from accepting that this whipping constituted rightful punishment of a wife's negligence, and perhaps fearful of further violence, mobilized the hacienda's grand patriarch as a superior countervailing force. If he responded as a paternal protector of maltreated dependents, he might punish Joaquín and tip the domestic power balance of the couple. Don Joseph Herrera, sixty-two years old, was on the hacienda, perhaps because the harvest and grinding season was in full swing. He placed Joaquín and Feliciana in the hacienda's warehouse (*bodega*), tried in vain to achieve a reconciliation, then had Feliciana leave for a consultation with the priest who served the hacienda chapel and a nearby pueblo. Feliciana left for the consultation in the protective custody of the wife of the hacienda's majordomo. Meanwhile Don Joseph would see to it that Joaquín received his due. He ordered Joaquín tied up in the *bodega*, then had him whipped on the buttocks. Joaquín then promised not to fight with Feliciana over the cotton and was released. The ritual humiliation and restoration of order took place before other workers, who would presumably absorb the message and spread word of Joaquín's punishment.

The entire sequence conforms to *tierra caliente* scenarios with which we are already familiar. The racial categories are blurred, but there is a hint of African ancestry. Everyday life is organized around the rhythms of a sugar hacienda and the authority of its owner-master. A peasant patriarch expects to rule his wife's labor, and upon discovery of what he considered negligence or insubordination, is quick to respond with severe violence — a *monte* whipping, perhaps even a binding-and-whipping ritual that evoked parallels with institutional punishment of delinquents. The peasant wife appeals to the superior Spanish patriarch and landowner whom she knows equates superior color-class power with superior masculinity. The master-owner intervenes to strip the peasant husband of patriarchal pretense and, indeed, places the husband in a structurally female position by removing the man's wife, subjecting him to a humiliating public whipping on the buttocks, and coercing from him a promise not to exercise a husband's punishing authority in the matter again.

Even the denouement conforms to classic *tierra caliente* extremes of masculine dominance and degradation. Joaquín at first protested Don Joseph's intervention and whipping, but within a week the nexus of superior color-class power and vertical ranking of masculinities proved too daunting. "I made a complaint . . . for eight or twelve lashes he gave on his hacienda . . . which seemed to me to bring upon me dishonor and shame. . . . [But] having at present considered and reflected that the said punishment was fraternal correction as I am his servant and he my master for which reason at no moment can it bring contempt upon me, I withdraw . . . from the said complaint." Given the extremes of landed power and racial degradation in the sugar country, a laboring man might have to concede — at least outwardly — that no real honor was lost when a master punctured the manhood of his servant.

The *tierra caliente* clash of Joaquín, Feliciana, and Don Joseph was suffused with the trappings and dynamics of a Morelos. But it took place in sugar country far to the south, in the Cañada of Yosañahe, near Tlaxiaco, in the Mixteca Alta of Oaxaca. As every local knew, the Tlaxiaco and Teozacoalco valleys were warm and decently watered, veritably lush by the standards of the Mixteca Alta of Oaxaca.[12] Every region had its *tierra caliente*; every Mexico had its Other Mexico.

PART FOUR

Reflections

cial weapons deployed to contest them, and the specific social conventions whereby social peace might be grudgingly reestablished defined the substance of a life specific to Mexico. It was in corn-bound Mexico that struggles over a peasant woman's duty to provide food on demand implied struggle over the long and laborious grinding of soaked maize into fresh tortillas, a bread of the poor that failed to keep its freshness well. It was in colonized Mexico that an Indian woman who sought to deploy rival patriarchs or female allies to discipline an adulterous husband might find power in resorting to ethnoracial Others—a Spanish colonial judge whose contemptuousness of the manhood of "childlike" Indian men or whose interest in colonial extortion fed the will to hear a degraded woman's complaints, or a mulatta magical specialist whose African descent and livelihood placed her near the symbolic margins of the Spanish-mestizo-Indian social body and fed a cultural reputation for special supernatural powers. It was in Nahua Mexico that a daughter blocked in her choice of suitor but eager to preserve the possibility of reconciliation with her parental family might consent to an Indian-style ritual kidnapping by a male suitor and his kin and friends.[23] The theoretical usefulness of a framework culled from the particulars of Mexico does not imply a substantive lack of difference between Mexico and other societies. Mexico may yield paradigmatic knowledge without conceding its *mexicanidad*.

The impact question asks whether the social struggles over gender right we have studied in late colonial Mexico made any practical differences in the lives of subaltern women and men. After all, we have witnessed a great deal of violence and even homicide in our journey. Did women's efforts to assert a contingent orientation to gender right come to naught? Did the weapons they forged to assist or protect them turn out to be too unreliable or ineffective to shift the balance of gender power and gender right? Were instances of ameliorating or successful impact too sporadic and individualized to amount to much in a social sense?

The question of impact is particularly difficult because human history does not allow for controlled, laboratory-style manipulation of variables. The result is that we are drawn, in the absence of laboratory controls, to take a counterfactual leap of imagination: what might the balance of gender power and gender right have looked like in the absence of the female struggles, weapons, and strategies we have depicted? The counterfactual query resists a definitive, provable answer, but it illuminates the nature of the problem—that of teasing out the impact of struggles when the historical record binds everyday gender struggles and their impacts together simultaneously rather than separating them sequentially.

Two approaches offer clues to the impact of gender struggle on the balance of gender power. First, at a conceptual level, one might consider the significance of social conventions of gender—that is, the social practices of

CHAPTER 13

Conclusion

Power and Patriarchy
in Subaltern Life, Late
Colonial Times

MENTAL CHAINS

Time and time again our journey through the gendered maze of Mexican experience has brought us face to face with cultural mythology and stereotype. As we have seen, the stereotypes draw strength from the ways the construction of national identity — *lo mexicano* — hinged on a discourse of wounded manhood and its corollary, long-suffering womanhood. The Mexican woman, according to this corollary, is both profoundly violated and profoundly complicit in her violation.

The strength of gendered stereotype, however, runs deeper than a particular cultural construction, *lo mexicano*, in a particular historical conjuncture, the mid-twentieth century. Theorists have observed, from cross-cultural and comparative historical perspectives, that gender constitutes a near-universal touchstone in constructions of group identity, historical memory and origin myths, and socially legitimate power. In times of flux or transformation, moreover, the assertion of gender roles as a natural order to which society must return or through which society will recover its historic moorings imparts an apparently fixed quality to gender — the social interpretation of sexual difference. The cultural constructions tend to naturalize gender and to reassert proper gender roles as the basis of social order and well-being. Under the circumstances, entrenched cultural stereotypes are redeployed and the *plus ça change* refrain seems apt, albeit paradoxical and misleading.[1] Even if one retreats from universalizing theoretical statements, abundant scholarship demonstrates that gendered honor codes are widely diffused and culturally entrenched in Mediterranean and Latin American societies.[2] Under the circumstances one would be surprised if gendered stereotypes resonant with those we have encountered in this book were limited only to Mexico or only to the twentieth-century Mexico that constructed a myth of *lo mexicano*. The mental chains of stereotypes have been hardened by cultural imagery deployed and redeployed over long spans of time, beyond as well as within Mexico. We are all shackled to some degree; we are all potential prisoners.

In the Latin American context the Cuban experience demonstrates most graphically the entrenched, resilient quality of cultural constructions of gender. In the early years after the 1959 revolution the notion that patriarchal honor codes would disintegrate held sway. Presumably, the revolutionary struggles to construct both a new economic base and a new culture would create "new" men and women and more egalitarian familial and gender dynamics. The children born within the revolution would be the beneficiaries of the transformation. The 1969 film *Lucía* depicted a stifling prerevolutionary experience for women and a struggle to combat such legacies after 1959. This oppressive and contentious inheritance gave way, in the symbolic ending, to the optimistic vision of a carefree girl, a child of revolutionary times at play near purifying waters, free to develop her potential in the new scheme of things. The perception that gender and familial culture might change quickly and drastically was not limited to the intelligentsia or to filmmakers. In 1969, interviews of working class Cuban émigrés in Chicago revealed a striking motive for disillusion with the revolution. The revolution, complained the émigré men, had undermined family order and moral honor. Patriarchs no longer held authority in their homes, and daughters could escape traditional constraints on their sexual freedom. By the late 1970s and early 1980s the assumptions about the relative malleability of gender culture had given way to a more open-ended, problematic view that emphasized the resilience and adaptability of patriarchal mores even after a transition to socialism. Cuba and the Federation of Cuban Women underwent a politically contentious struggle to write a new family code and to prescribe revamped gender and family roles. The contentiousness of the process and the limits of the changes it induced underscored the durability of patriarchal social relations and honor codes across transformation in the mode of production. Theoretically, gender relations seemed less epiphenomenal or derivative, more structural or entrenched in their own right. The 1979 film *Retrato de Teresa* depicted a much more uncertain future for women than *Lucía*. Teresa's awakening—her emerging commitment to domestic gender equality and to a life of public as well as private involvement—ends up forcing her to separate from her husband, a person of revolutionary views and personal likability on most themes other than gender and sexuality. The symbolic conclusion has Teresa walk alone into an unknown and perhaps difficult destiny. Even in the context of a self-consciously revolutionary and egalitarian culture the durability and adaptability of gender stereotype seem to defy aggressive efforts at change. We are all shackled to some degree; we are all potential prisoners.[3]

Historians of women and of gender, in Latin America and beyond, have sought to break the mental chains, conscious and unconscious, forged out of resilient cultural imagery. This study is but one of many efforts in that direction.[4] The challenge is all the more daunting once we recognize that gendered stereotypes promote an idea of natural order and that gendered stereotyping is not limited to Mexicans. Again and again in this study our findings have pointed to the importance of framing stereotype not as a simple dichotomy between absolute truth and absolute falsehood, but as a problem of cultural exaggeration. Our findings transform The Truth inscribed in and magnified by stereotype into a truth whose magnification obliterates other truths — often more important ones. The result is to situate stereotyped truths within a new, less fetishized context and to bring to the fore findings obscured or suppressed by stereotype. These findings constitute our principal conclusions on power and patriarchy in subaltern life in late colonial times. As we shall see, to explore the implications and corollaries of each conclusion is to expose "secrets" out of the Mexican past.

THREE KEY FINDINGS: SECRETS OF THE MEXICAN PAST

Our first principal conclusion focuses on gender right and obligation in popular culture. *Among poor women and men in late colonial times, gender right was a bitterly contested arena of social power. Struggle between women and men exposed profound tension between a contingent or conditional model of gender right and power and a more absolute or innate framework.* Women generally contested not patriarchal first principles as such but their operational meaning in the practical workings of everyday life. As we have seen, the tension between these two approaches ran throughout women's several foundational roles vis-à-vis men, as wife-mothers, daughters, and *amasias*. Precisely because of such tensions, moreover, the figure of the independent female widow or loner could draw a special cultural stigma. Symbolically at least, the woman who escaped direct, personal patriarchal vigilance might subvert gender order and morality.

As we have also seen, the conflicts over gender right mattered. Disputes over gender turned readily toward violence. Gender-rooted dispute constituted by far the leading motivation in violence cases serious enough to spark criminal proceedings, even though gender-rooted violence is notoriously undercounted in most societies. The social weapons forged by women in such struggles were diverse and formidable. The pluralization of would-be patriarchs, the cultivation of a female network of allies and protectors, the threat of escalation via scandal or appeal to higher authorities, and the possibility of supernatural retribution were all matters taken seriously by men. The range of specific issues in play also proved impressive. The unresolved questions of practical life over which women and men tried uneasily and not always successfully to reach resolution ranged from labor and economics to physical mobility and punishment to sexuality and ownership of family dependents.

For heuristic purposes, let us illustrate this range of contestation by formulating literally the unresolved questions that might drive a wife and a husband toward bitter confrontation. Did a woman have an absolute duty to have tortillas, the end product of arduous female labor, ready for her husband on demand, or was this duty conditioned by her view of her husband's reliability as an economic provider? Might a woman tarry on her market, water-fetching, and church rounds without special permission from her husband? Was her latitude of semi-independent movement stretched if her husband proved irresponsible or unaccountable for his diversions and whereabouts? Did a woman have a duty to submit to physical punishment by her husband-patriarch as a private matter under his jurisdiction, or did she have a right to judge whether punishment was measured and proportionate? If she judged punishment unwarranted or excessive, did she have a right to transform it into a steadily more public matter via appeal to male and female kin, female friends, community elders, and priests and judges? Did a wife have an absolute duty to accept the sexual double standard — to tolerate her husband's infidelities and to avoid scrupulously any sexual liaisons of her own? Or did she have a right to evaluate whether her husband's liaisons led to economic negligence, physical abuse, or cultural humiliation and, if so, to contest his sexual freedom? Could she contest his freedom in part by seeking alliances — including sexually based alliances — with other men? Were the wife and her children the absolute property of the husband, if *he* chose not to abandon them, or might a woman assert her own right of separation if she found her husband negligent or abusive? None of these questions required a protofeminist challenge of patriarchal first principles as such. Each, however, represented a practical challenge to male authority in a popular culture torn between absolute and contingent approaches to gender right and authority.

The depth and seriousness of a struggle over legitimate gender right in male-female relations exposes several important secrets at odds with preconceived expectations. First, the absence of protofeminist thought or social movements does not imply an absence of serious struggle over basic premises of gender right and gender authority. For peasants and plebeians of late colonial Mexico the tension between absolute and contingent modeling of gender right was a deadly serious alternative to struggles over egalitarian gender right and status as such.

Second, our notions of female complicity in gender subordination must be revisited and rendered more complicated. It is all too easy to depict female complicity in rather flat and extreme terms. Before the historical awakening of feminist consciousness, presumably, women served, ironically and paradoxically, as culture carriers who accepted and passed on to children the hegemonic values of patriarchal civilization. The myth of complicity affects even outstanding feminist scholarship[5] and is especially strong in Mexico. The myth is not so much wrong as incomplete. The struggles over gender right analyzed in this book demonstrate that women's stances toward gender subordination involved a complex dialectic of practical complicity and practical resistance. For reasons of color and class as well as reasons of gender and family, women had cause to forge solidary stances with men and to accept the first principles of a patriarchal social order. But as we have seen, for reasons of practical self-protection and well-being women also had cause to forge a culture of resistance that entangled male authority and pretense in the realm of the conditional. The result was a complex interplay of assent and struggle — even in prefeminist or nonfeminist historical eras — that refines flat visions of female complicity.

A final secret exposed by popular contestation over gender right is the misleading yet commonplace assumption that a single code of honor/shame values provides a guide to traditional gender values and social relations among relatively Hispanized populations. This assumption, notwithstanding the achievements of a fine scholarly literature that demonstrates social fluidity and negotiation within honor/shame culture, is flawed on two counts.[6] First, the development of competing models of gender right and the ability of women and men to mobilize allies and institutions on their behalf demonstrate not only plural values within a culture of argument. They also demonstrate that the familiar honor/shame discourse of the scholarly literature was a less than overriding framework for conceptualizing gender, even within the relatively Hispanized popular cultures of Morelos and Mexico City. The practical discourse of absolute and contingent gender right is not easily subsumed within or reducible to the honor/shame discourse of proper masculinity and femininity. Second, our analysis of popular gender conventions demonstrates that to the extent that humble folk did indeed participate in the honor/shame complex of values, they adapted and redeployed its content in ways that diminished ratification of elite social status. As we have seen, popular notions of manly honor and affirmation in Morelos emphasized competence and courage in the face of adversity and challenge rather than the blend of personal and sexual command, household rule and provision, and respect for social rank and decorum that comprised an elite code of manly honor. Similarly, popular notions of feminine respectability might imply more flexible approaches to virginity than those of the hegemonic honor/shame complex. As we have seen, a plebeian culture of respectable consensual union might imply honorable status for the nonvirginal woman too poor to marry yet able to forge a conjugal relationship built on announced marital intention and marital-like obligation.

In short, the familiar honor/shame complex failed to constitute "the" foundation of gender culture and gendered contestation. At the level of popular culture the conflictual dialogue between contingent right, premised on the principle of mutuality, and absolute right, premised on the principle of obedience, probably constituted a more important foundation of gender culture. To the extent that the Hispanic honor/shame complex held importance, moreover, its diffusion up and down the social ladder implied a certain reworking of cultural values. The result was not one honor/shame code, manipulated by its various adherents and mainly useful to those with color-class privilege, but several overlapping yet distinct honor/shame codes in play at various levels of the color-class hierarchy.

Our second principal conclusion focuses on the relationship between gender culture and political culture. *Popular understandings of and arguments about legitimate and illegitimate authority rested on profoundly gendered foundations. The deep interplays between the politics of gender and the gendering of politics suffused popular culture.* They went far beyond restrictions of formal political voice to male citizen-patriarchs who served as electors and officeholders. As we have seen, the language of good and bad political authority echoed the language and experience of good fathers and irresponsible parasites in familial arenas of authority and conflict. Peasants (and probably plebeians) tended to extend and adapt familial experience of authority and legitimacy to suprafamilial settings rather than compartmentalize rigidly between public and private dynamics of legitimate authority and power. In peasant villages, understandings of political belonging, status, and etiquette deployed a familial idiom: commoners in need of protection were *hijos del pueblo* (sons/children of the pueblo); leaders who expected deference to their counsel were *viejos* (elders/patriarchs). Antagonists who complained about lack of deference by political inferiors or abuse of authority by political superiors referred to violations of "respect" (a codeword for rightful behavior between genders and generations within familial settings). In addition, rituals of family punishment and community punishment blurred distinctions between private and public violence. Punishing husbands, *amasios*, and fathers enlarged themselves into symbolic *alcaldes* and *gobernadores* binding their delinquent dependents to "stocks," and punished community delinquents, publicly shorn of clothing and whipped, were reduced to humiliated "children."

The gendering of politics came through even — or especially — in emergencies. As we have seen, at moments of crisis politics and community riot, subaltern women often rushed into public space and asserted their own versions of community citizenship, moral right, and political leadership. But as we have also seen, the necessity of emergency action did not simply loosen gendered social conventions. Crisis rechanneled convention, often, into what we have called a gendered etiquette of revolt. Women drew on their own gendered sensibilities of moral right — as outraged wives, mothers, and widows — to justify physical intimidation or attack against abusive or extortionary authorities. In doing so they also mobilized male proprietary sensibilities that further justified community riot. The physical ferocity and disrespect of the women dared male authorities to attack them, but if the authorities did so, the attack against female property and kin would enrage subaltern citizen-patriarchs who rioted to defend their women, their families, and their masculinity. The entire sequence — riotous subaltern women mobilized to defend gendered sensibilities of right, provoked male officials subjected to extreme disrespect by shameless females, and furious subaltern men who defended their violated female property — is inexplicable except as a theater of subaltern gender right mobilized in defense of community right. Again and again in subaltern life, understandings and assertions of legitimate political right — even the right to revolt — rested on a deeply gendered foundation.

The close interplay of gender culture and political culture draws out two secrets in the political history of Mexico. First, it draws out the contradictory culture of political argument that suffused peasant life. Peasant political culture was marked by a deep contradiction between egalitarian or democratic values that stressed reciprocities and likenesses among families and citizens who shared a rough similarity of economic condition and a readiness to subordinate individual interest to community well-being, and more hierarchical values that stressed obedience to constituted authority and legitimate differentiation of circumstances and privilege according to barrio or lineage, economic base, or political status. As we have seen, the scholarly literature, while cognizant of both currents within peasant political culture, has tended to segregate them as pertaining to different regional peasantries or ethnicities. Presumably, the community-minded villagers of Morelos follow a more egalitarian impulse, while the cacique-led rancheros of San Luís Potosí follow a more hierarchical path. The peasants of the more Indian south, with its base of landed communities, tilt toward more horizontal principles of reciprocity and community service, while the peasants of the more mestizo center-north, with its base of haciendas and ranchos, tilt toward more vertical principles of obedience and clientelism. The conceptual segregation is comfortable insofar as it permits us not only to respect but also to idealize oppressed subaltern heroes such as the peasant villagers of Morelos. But it may generate misleading conclusions or debates: one chooses between the idealization of Tepoztlán by

Robert Redfield or the sobering restudy of Tepoztlán by Oscar Lewis as if the two visions of the community are mutually exclusive.

Even within a Morelos, however, egalitarian and hierarchical political visions vied for hegemony among peasant villagers. Together these visions constituted the language of subaltern political factionalism and argument. The contradictions and mediations of peasant political culture, moreover, bore witness to the combined extension and adaptation of gendered conceptions of authority into public political space. The conflictual dialogue between egalitarian and hierarchical visions of political right and obedience resonated deeply with conflictual dialogues over conditional and innate premises of gender right. The political contradiction was mediated—imperfectly—through community *viejos* acting as wise metafathers of the community. Theoretically at least, the community *hijos* owed their esteemed *viejos* an iron respect. But the *viejos*, at least in theory, had gained great esteem precisely because they had served community needs as if bound by a more conditional, contingent relationship. When all worked well, the counsel of community fathers could steer their communities away from destructive internal parasitism, rebelliousness, or factionalism. A benevolent paternalism, exerted by grand community patriarchs who had earned the confidence of their community dependents in their wisdom and purpose, restored at least a facade of unity and well-being. (As we have also seen, all did not always work out so well in practice. The community elders might become tainted—viewed as selfish, egotistical, and parasitical in their own right—and their right and expectation of respect might crumble.)

The thick connections between gender culture and political culture not only illuminate the deeply contradictory foundations of peasant political life and the patriarchal mediations that fortified a sense of harmony and community good despite—or because of—such fractures. The connections also expose a second secret, a critical missing piece in the scholarly puzzle of paternalist impulses in Mexican political culture. Scholars have long been aware of the paternalist impulse in Mexico (and Spanish America more generally). In societies profoundly divided by color and class, elites characteristically sought legitimacy—in their own eyes as well as those of subordinates—by presenting themselves as paternal patrons who helped their unfortunate inferiors and clients and who tolerated some of the less serious foibles of childlike peoples. To build a paternalist political culture—a kind of veneer of paternal concern sustained by rituals of benevolence and intervention on behalf of dependents and clients—might at least soften social resentment and polarization. The huge gulf between rich and poor, the extortionary and windfall profit mechanisms of a colonial society, the evident readiness of subalterns to riot against abusive authorities, and the readiness of elites to repress troublemakers all rendered paternalist pretense somewhat hollow. It goes too far to argue that in practical experience elites and subalterns simply enacted and accepted paternal pretense at face value. Yet scholars have long known that it also goes too far to claim that subalterns proved altogether unreceptive to a paternalist political impulse — that is, to appeals for favor by authorities recast as metafathers and to assumptions that the rare good paternalist (if one could only find or mobilize him) exists somewhere and merits loyalty and legitimacy.[7]

The puzzle of paternalist political culture in Mexico is that it brings together apparently irreconcilable contradictions: elite pretense of paternal concern and intervention that belied abusiveness, social behaviors and outcomes that rendered such pretenses hollow for most subalterns in most specific cases, and a certain popular receptivity, nonetheless, to paternalist visions of loyalty, deference, and rightful authority. The third leg of this triad brings the mystery into sharpest relief. Why, if subalterns knew that most elites failed to live up to paternal pretense, did they nonetheless develop a partial receptivity to the premises of a paternalist political culture? The answers provided by earlier generations of scholars no longer suffice. In an earlier era scholars could invoke the social influence of the large landed estate to carry a large burden of explanation. Presumably, the seventeenth-century collapse of the heretofore vibrant colonial commercial economy induced the growth of haciendas that became largely self-sufficient worlds unto themselves. Organized around relations of colonial serfdom and debt peonage, these social worlds enabled estate owners to elevate themselves into the role of metaphorical fathers, capable of both cruel punishment and benevolent intervention, who induced both fear and appeal for favor in the estate's metaphorical children. The social psychology of the hacienda not only resonated with the church's emphasis on obedience to social and religious fathers once it moved past an early phase of missionary idealism. It also bequeathed an enormously important legacy that outlived colonial times. Given the enormous spatial expanse and social influence of the colonial hacienda system and its continuity and continued expansion after independence in 1821, the old social psychology of authority and politics would not suffer a severe battering until the Mexican Revolution had placed the entire Old Regime in jeopardy. Only in the Indian communities that had escaped being swallowed up by the hacienda system, presumably, could one find a substantially more egalitarian approach to authority that placed the accent on balance and community service.[8]

This interpretation was enormously influential in the mid-twentieth century, but its empirical and conceptual foundation unraveled on almost every front in the 1970s and 1980s. The notion of a seventeenth-century economic depression yielded to a picture of economic diversification marked by more bounded cycles of expansion and stagnation. The picture of a great collapse inducing an expansive and autarkic hacienda system yielded to a picture of sharp regional differentiation in hacienda expansion, and of landed entrepreneurial strategies that reduced only modest numbers of laborers and resident families to continuous residence and servile status on the estates. The bulk of labor on haciendas came from temporary infusions by peasants who lived in distinctive social worlds of their own much of the year. The most socially important owners of landed estates, moreover, followed life strategies that sharply circumscribed the patriarchal roles and preoccupations once associated with haciendas. A new literature brought to the fore an elite culture whose political economy rested on windfall profit mechanisms, diversified investment portfolios, and urban living. Even the notion of a spiritual conquest by a church that worked in tandem with the hacienda underwent significant revision. Indians and subalterns accepted, rejected, and redeployed colonial Catholicism in complex ways, and their version of Catholicism did not necessarily imply social obedience to church priests or other social fathers.[9]

The net result of these revisions has been to deepen the mystery of a partial popular receptivity — notwithstanding social conflicts, riots, and denunciations that bred a certain disillusion — to the premises of a paternalistic political culture. If most specific authorities and elites seemed more like parasites than benevolent paternalists, why might subalterns appeal for favors from authorities recast as metafathers? Why might their language of legitimacy suggest a commitment to an equation of good authority and paternal benevolence that ran deeper than cynical instrumentalism? Why might they persist in believing that the rare good patriarch existed out there, somewhere? Why might this partial receptivity exist notwithstanding the more egalitarian streak within peasant political culture? It is easy enough to see why political authorities and elites more generally sought to drape themselves in a paternalist cloak of political legitimacy. The defense of the viceroy stung by the 1692 corn riot, the most searing urban uprising of colonial times, sought to depict him not as a parasitical manipulator of the grain shortage and its attendant hoarding and high prices but as a benevolent and misunderstood metafather. Notwithstanding rumors to the contrary among the childlike rabble, he had done all he could to ease the grain shortage and had even spent his own funds to find and distribute grain. The colonial state, as William B. Taylor has shown, sought to respond to local riots by allowing them to burn out, then achieving a reconciliation by isolating for punishment a few key troublemakers and applying a forgiving paternal mercy to the rest of the rebels. Centuries later, in 1985, a *cacique* accused of political bossism defended himself by arguing that the term *patriarch* fit him better than *cacique*. He then explained that he "attended to people, even in their family matters; couples would come to see me when they had their internal conflicts and I would intervene to make peace in those homes." He was not the cutthroat tyrant connoted by *cacique*, but a man who looked after his dependents' well-being, even in the most personal or domestic contexts.[10]

The mystery resides not in explaining elite pretense but in understanding a partial popular receptivity to paternalist premises, however buffeted they were by more egalitarian and communal visions of legitimate authority and by a measure of cynicism rooted in practical experience. The earlier vision of an expansive, feudal-like hacienda buttressed by a patriarchal church that served landowner needs and owned many such estates itself no longer suffices. Neither can we assume, after a quarter-century of research demonstrating popular agency and ingenuity within the confines of oppressive social structures and situations, that subalterns merely succumbed to elite manipulation.[11] The secret that brings the problem into clearer focus, I would suggest, is the thick interplay of gender culture and political culture in subaltern life. Precisely because a contradictory popular culture promoted argument between more egalitarian and hierarchical visions of legitimate authority, and precisely because such contradictions were mediated through cultural constructions of wise community fathers (*viejos*) who had dedicated themselves to service and in whom the community children (*hijos*) vested high moral prestige, subalterns proved receptive to a vision that equated legitimate authority with a responsible brand of patriarchalism (paternalism). It was not the fault of subalterns, after all, if most specific elites behaved more as irresponsible parasites than as wise metafathers.[12]

This line of explanation, of course, is not mutually exclusive with those that emphasized the social worlds of the hacienda and the church. But it establishes a wide explanatory foundation for a demonstrable paternalist political impulse at the popular level even in the absence of a ubiquitous feudal-like hacienda. It also recasts the question of church influence in more dynamic terms that pay due respect to subaltern agency and wisdom rather than assuming a certain popular gullibility in the face of elite manipulation. Church theology stressed not only the principle of obedience to social superiors (elders, patriarchs, and rulers) but also the principle of reciprocity among unequals. Among humans, familial and metaphorical fathers were to use their authority moderately and wisely, with a sense of paternal obligation. In the supernatural realm the saints and holy images received social deference and service but were also to provide intercessions — punishment, mercy, and favor — that enhanced the well-being of their human children and servants. Not only was there an evident resonance between the reciprocity-among-unequals aspect of church teachings and contingent visions of legitimate authority. In addition, subalterns mobilized church fathers to impose such visions on irresponsible husbands and, occasionally, on civil authorities. From this point of view the special affinity of women for the church reflected not an innate or mysterious predisposition but an understandable social logic. From this point of view as well, popular appropriation of the village church site as a sacred symbol of moral authority — whatever the local sentiment about a specific parish priest or about the institutional church — made eminent sense in subaltern quests to assert contingent visions of political authority. The church bells called villagers together to riot against abusive tyrants who sought an absolute authority. The village church's patron saint inspired devotional celebrations that implied a certain obligation to reciprocate, a patronage of benevolent intercession by the venerated being. The annual round of church fiestas and duties served as a vehicle of community duty and reciprocity as well as community veneration. The social influence of the church and its version of apparently conditional and moderate patriarchalism derived not only from elite sponsorship and imposition but from subaltern incorporation — a process of selective adaptation, alteration, and redeployment.[13]

Our third major conclusion considers the problem of regional and ethnic diversity within Mexico. *The relations of gender and power evident in late colonial regions of Mexico belie essentialist reifications of the many Mexicos idea. The uniqueness of a region (or microregion) resided less in its character as an altogether different social world than in its singularity of synthesis: its blending of transregional patterning and local emphasis and idiosyncrasy into a distinctive regional package.* Comparative regional analysis contextualizes this interplay of diversity and commonality across Mexican regions. On the one hand, we noted distinctive configurations of gendered life in Morelos, Oaxaca, and Mexico City. The social conventions and strains of gendered life took on regionally specific twists or tonalities when we considered Morelos as a baseline against which to compare other regions. In indigenous Oaxaca, for example, one detected a somewhat more evenly matched dialectic of female power and female subordination; a wider cultural platform for contingent visions of female gender right, backed by a heightened accent on elder and parental authority; and an ethnically charged ambivalence about the confrontational and violent masculinities of the Other (whether colonizing or *casta* Others or rival Indians). In plebeian Mexico City in late colonial times one detected not only contested patriarchal pacts but a simultaneous crisis of their existence: a straining of pacts to the breaking point and a subversive stream of rather independent, headstrong female personalities who inverted gendered proprieties. In addition, one discerned social conventions particular to city life: tactical convergence, however fragile and contradictory, between desperate wives and the interventionism of the urban *alcalde* system; a culture of respectable consensual union marked by honorable intent and quasi-marital living by those too poor to marry formally; and a heightened female assertion of separation rights whose counterpoint was a heightened male tendency to sexualize gender conflicts regardless of the initial issue of contention.

On the other hand, these regional differences were best understood not as markers of sui generis social dynamics of gender and power but as unfamiliar configurations of rather familiar elements. The distinctive social dynamics of each region were well-known features of subaltern life — even if relatively less pronounced or predominant — in the other two regions. Both Oaxaca and Mexico City yielded striking memories of Morelos, stories of gendered life and conflict that would have elicited recognition among listeners in Morelos. Throughout the three regions a conflictual dialogue among the genders yielded a rather familiar interplay between contingent and absolute visions of gender right and a rather familiar string of specific issues in contention. In short, comparative regional analysis of gender and power in subaltern life yielded variation within consistency, consistency within variation.

The interplay of consistency and variation not only restores the Mexico in the many Mexicos thesis. It also brings to the fore an ironic secret obscured by quintessentialist visions of many Mexicos. On matters of gender, at least, the language of Mexican diversity was itself a language of social bonding and conflict that transcended specific regions and, indeed, imparted a certain cross-regional recognition. As we have seen, the theoretical basis for understanding this paradox resides in the idea that culture is not only a language of argument but a language of variation. The practical basis resides in the recognition that every region had its many Mexicos, its regional, microregional, and ethnic axes of consistency and variation. These axes were both experiential and discursive. Their effect was a certain parallelism in intraregional and cross-regional languages of presumed variation. Oaxaca's Indian communities had nearby markers of comparatively "hot" lands and peoples inclined toward confrontational masculinities and violent explosion. Morelos's sugar communities had nearby markers of "cool," classically Indian zones that placed greater accent on communal balance and harmony and on deflecting interpersonal escalation and violence. The existence of intraregional languages of zonal and ethnic variation and the exaggeration of such differences into discursive stereotypes or cultural foils serve to temper the cross-regional contrasts that we might otherwise draw. Cross-regional differences found their intraregional echo; local shading and particularity were stretched into more quintessentialist stereotypes. The ultimate irony of the many Mexicos discourse is that, probed deeply, it points not only to differences between regions (*many* Mexicos) but to language and experience in common (many *Mexicos*).

AN ADDITIONAL "SECRET" FOR EUROCENTRIC THEORISTS: MEXICO AS PARADIGMATIC?

A final "secret" exposed by the study of gender and power in Mexico is that it may well yield paradigmatic knowledge useful for understanding and theorizing gender struggle in a wide variety of societies and historical contexts — including the historical experience of the West. My hypothesis is that the conflictual dialogue between contingent and absolute visions of patriarchally organized gender right that we have analyzed in the Mexican context unlocks the mystery of gender struggle in many prefeminist or nonfeminist historical contexts — in Old Regime societies, if we are to use the conventional categories of European historical chronology.

Serious reflection on such a hypothesis requires first and foremost an inversion of entrenched predispositions about the sources of paradigmatic knowledge. Scholars who study so-called Third World societies are particularly well situated to observe the way that historically specific experiences of the West are rather easily — uncritically — transformed into universalizing or paradigmatic statements. Except in the realm of anthropology and the study of "primitives," perhaps, the case studies and experiences of the North Atlantic world or its antecedents in the ancient Mediterranean and Middle Eastern worlds lay a foundation for theory and paradigm in historical and social science knowledge. The case studies and experiences of the so-called Third World lay a foundation not for paradigmatic knowledge but for a knowledge of difference — the particulars that expose the limits or the underside of Western paradigms.

Scrutinized critically, of course, this construction of paradigmatic norm and particularistic deviation from the norm would appear to flow from a logic of power and resources rather than rigor. The intelligentsias of the advanced Western nations are the largest, the most well endowed, and the most widely published. For these intelligentsias the most accessible data and case studies — not to mention the formative personal and intellectual experiences — are understandably anchored mainly in their own societies. Such anchoring encourages, when non-Western experience is considered, an inscribing of ethnocentered preoccupation onto the exotic, deviant Other. In addition, the facts of global power and cultural influence during the last half-millennium have seemed to diffuse both Western intellectual training and Western models of social life throughout the globe.[14]

The point of these observations is not to engage in an all-too-easy moral denunciation of Western intellectual hubris and ethnocentrism. Such denunciations have happened and serve their purpose. For my purposes, however, a flat, accusatory discourse is diversionary and perhaps underestimates the deeper intellectual dilemma. Who, after all, can claim always to avoid a certain projection of locally known experience and preoccupation, however limited and particular, into a more universalizing or generalizing discursive plane? Who, in the interests of theoretical caution or purity, would favor the alternative of a particularism so extreme that it borders on the antiquarian? The important point, for our purposes, is neither to close the mind through an easy denunciation that invites defensiveness nor to pretend that interplay between the particular and the general is unavoidable or undesirable. The point, rather, is to notice the theoretical bias built into the power structure of contemporary intellectual life, the difficulty of defending that bias on strictly intellectual grounds, and the consequent importance of opening the mind to the possibility that we may draw paradigmatic knowledge from intellectually deviant, Third World case studies.

Such reflection provides a context for considering Mexico a source of knowledge useful not only to understand Mexico and its sister societies in Latin America, but useful as well for conceptual frameworks beyond Latin America. Indeed, perhaps because Latin America has so long been a region simultaneously Western and non-Western (in but not of the West, as Jorge Luís Borges once remarked of Argentina), and perhaps because its Western genealogy links it to Iberia, a region of Western Europe rarely invoked to supply classic paradigms, Latin America may provide especially useful paradigms for understanding the West.

Let us consider, then, the conceptual dilemma that confronts historians of gender and feminism in Europe's Old Regime societies and the ways that study of gender struggle in Mexico may contribute to its resolution. For our purposes, Old Regime societies may be defined as societies whose organizing (that is, hegemonic) principles of political order were premised conceptually on organic hierarchy and juridical segmentation. The chain of human life and moral order required an organic hierarchy: mutual collaboration and dependence in relations built on superiority and inferiority, ranging all the way from godhead and king through the major lords, princes, and figures of high authority (aristocracy and nobility) down the middling parts of the chain (gentry and masters) to subaltern peasant patriarchs and their wives, children, servants, and slaves. In this model of social organization the metaphor of familial patriarch readily ran up the chain of rule to higher authorities, the metaphor of kingship readily ran down the chain of rule to husband-fathers, and the patriarchal family ruled by a father-elder was the fundamental unit of social survival and collaboration. For most persons it was the unit through which property right and social claims were asserted and transmitted and through which one participated in a life-sustaining division of labor. The organic hierarchies of Old Regime societies were closely associated, too, with juridical segmentation. Different estates, towns and corporations, and social placements on the vertical chain of life implied distinctive bundles of juridical charter, privilege, obligation, and liability. All groups and statuses were in this sense special cases in their legal standing.[15]

Presumably, the Enlightenment and the French Revolution marked the contradictory and incomplete beginnings of a turn toward a new conceptual language of right, legal equality, and citizenship. Those parts of humanity still consigned to the organic hierarchy and juridical segmentation principles (women and children, unpropertied laborers and the poor, and exotic or subhuman Others such as the enslaved, the colonized, and the pagan) were still huge, but the language of right and equality provided a wedge with which to battle for a socially wider dismantling of traditional social practices and hierarchies. (Precisely for this reason the language of exclusion from political right could assume a rather hardened, contemptuous quality, and the public/private split might receive greater accent. The erosion of Old Regime premises was not at all automatic, but contradictory: it developed out of a struggle over who was fit to belong to the new scheme of things political, and why.) During and after the decisive historical turn, one may discern, for the case of gender, the rise of social movements pressing the rights and equality of women as such. In this period, too, one witnesses the rise of politically strong antislavery and working class movements. Before the turn, one discerns at most rather socially isolated outbreaks of feminist or protofeminist consciousness — by individual "women of genius" or by semiautonomous women, such as nuns or mystics, within quite constrained webs of social support. As Jean Franco and Gerda Lerner have brilliantly shown, for women such as Sor Juana Inés de la Cruz and Christine de Pizan the search for a female voice and a protofeminist language of right was marked by a certain social fragility or isolation.[16] The quest did not readily translate into or draw energy and protection from a protofeminist social movement. For most women and youths, patriarchal principles of family rule could not be questioned as such; the precondition of survival and well-being remained social collaboration within families ruled by patriarchs and elders.

The conceptual challenge presented by Old Regime settings is that of discerning a framework for theorizing gender conflicts in popular culture. One may readily conceptualize, for these societies, social tensions and struggles along lines of ethnicity (broadly defined to signify social relations of community membership and identity that sort humanity into distinct kinds of peoples, whether the sorting is done by religion, ethnolinguistic descent, social estate or lineage, racial descent, or some combination thereof) and along lines of class (broadly defined to signify social relations of property and work that divide humanity into antagonistic communities through a logic of economic benefit and exploitation). Indeed, the history of Old Regime societies is littered with religious-ethnic crusades, caste-like quarrels over social privilege, and peasant uprisings that render such tensions starkly visible. Struggle over gender right, however, presents a difficult conceptual dilemma. Battles between women and men were often discreet rather than socially visible and highly individualized rather than demonstrably patterned. Families were critical units of solidarity and survival and a fundamental metaphor of social rule; a language of equal rights that might crack the patriarchal scheme was not yet available; collective action or social movements to promote the rights of women as such had not yet taken root; and protofeminist women tended to fall into socially isolated categories such as "genius" or "deviant." In short, women awaited a feminist awakening and language of right to emancipate them from the era of gender subordination and female complicity. In this vision Engels's notion of a "world historical defeat" of the female sex — however much one might dispute the specific description, chronology, or theorization of it — finds a certain corroboration. Once patriarchy was created, it endured, notwithstanding socially isolated individuals who challenged it, until feminism arrived to overturn it.[17]

How, then, might we conceptualize struggles over gender right in prefeminist or nonfeminist social contexts such as those associated with Old Regime societies? One response, of course, is to reject the premise of the question. There is, after all, much truth in the picture presented above: in this argument, the conceptual dilemma is an intellectual artifice because the truth in the picture presented above is the overriding Truth of women's subordination before the era of feminism.

Yet, a vision of Old Regime history premised on an absence of social struggle over gender right is profoundly unsatisfying and incomplete. On the one hand, historical investigations demonstrate that households were social units of conflict and abuse as well as solidarity, and that gender right and female-male conflict comprised important axes of contention.[18] Our challenge is to elucidate the socially patterned language of right that may have suffused such conflicts, even though our own language of right — our intellectual imagination — descends so thoroughly from equality principles associated with Enlightenment thought and the political upheavals of capitalist industrialization. On the other hand, historical humility — if not the social history movement itself — cautions against the teleological temptation of assuming that humanity, or a large portion of it, endured a long Age of Complicity and Domination in relative silence and powerlessness, until a contemporary Age of Equal Right and Emancipation arrived to overturn it. The temptation to view *our* emancipatory movement as the first socially consequential contestation of hierarchical gender right is understandable, but it consigns pre-emancipatory objects of social domination to a kind of prehistoric status. It also slights a quarter-century of historical investigations that call into question visions of social domination that strip the dominated of their historical agency — their capacity not only to participate and endure but also to adapt, respond, resist, and assert in ways that contested elite prescriptions of social right.[19]

My hypothesis argues that gender struggle in Mexico in late colonial times offers paradigmatic knowledge useful for resolving this conceptual dilemma. In particular, the conflictual dialogue between contingent visions of gender right, whereby women and their allies sought to impose conditionality and reciprocity on specific social practices without challenging patriarchal first principles as such, and absolute visions of gender right, whereby men and their allies insisted on enforcement of innate rights regardless of how well or poorly, in female eyes, they fulfilled patriarchal obligation, may well describe the practical language and experience of argument on gender right in non-feminist or prefeminist historical settings. In popular culture this language of argument placed the accent on questions of mutuality and reciprocity. It captured the ambivalence induced by life and necessity in common, in a world where familial units of collaboration constituted a fundamental strategy of survival and where ethnic or class domination could weigh heavily on both genders. It left the door open, theoretically at least, to social collaboration and reconciliation, even in the aftermath of bitter conflict.

A corollary to this hypothesis suggests a dynamic interplay between the "female consciousness" of right and suffering constructed in this folk experience of gender struggle, and more specifically feminist consciousness. That is, feminist thinkers and political activists did not (and do not) invent sui generis visions of gender relations and gender right. Neither did they simply adapt and extend post-Enlightenment equality principles to the case of women. They also drew upon and adapted the gendered wisdoms and stereotypes of men and women built up in the background conversations and practical conflicts that suffused everyday life, even in thoroughly hegemonic patriarchal settings. It was on the battleground between contingent and absolute visions of right that women defined men as unworthy of their paternalist pretenses and their naturalized claims to innate authority. It was on the battleground between contingent and absolute visions of right that women defined themselves as beings who were both maltreated and worthy of social claims. In this sense, the protofeminist Sor Juana Inés de la Cruz — exceptional as she was in sheer intellectual brilliance and in her resort to a rationalist rather than mystical voice of female vindication — was not at all exceptional in her vision of marriage as a kind of consignment to hardship and abuse. Popular culture supplied the young Juana Ramírez plenty of legitimizing material for her aversion to marriage, her criticisms of men, and her view of conventual life as a potential escape.[20] In this sense, too, the Old Regime and its characteristic struggles over gender right did not simply die with the birth of feminist social movements but entered into dialogue with the creation and evolution of feminist politics and consciousness.[21]

The final secret of this study for Eurocentric theorists is that this book's introduction — the story of José Marcelino and María Teresa of Texalpa — is not only a story about Mexico. It is also a story about human history.

THREE HARD QUESTIONS

Books yield questions as well as conclusions. In my mind, three hard questions are especially pertinent and resist easy answers. Let us call them the

Boston question, the impact question, and the change-over-time question. We shall postpone the change-over-time question for the postscript but may share brief reflections on the others here.

The Boston question asks what distinguishes gender culture and struggle in popular culture in Mexico in late colonial times from gender culture and struggle in other historical societies. The question is compelling for two reasons. First, historical findings on family conflict elsewhere—Linda Gordon's splendid study of family life and violence in Boston circa 1880–1960 comes especially to mind—resonate with the contestations of gender right depicted for Mexico.[22] Second, we have suggested that Mexico's conflictual dialogues between contingent and absolute visions of gender right may yield paradigmatic knowledge useful for theorizing gender struggle beyond Mexico. How, then, might one understand the particularities of Mexico?

My response to the Boston question is twofold. First, a broad distinction ought to be drawn between those Old Regime societies where the politics of gender culture evinces a striking parallelism with the politics of authority more generally, and those societies where the formal organizing principles of authority in gender culture and political culture evince striking contradiction. In the United States—at least after the Civil War destroyed competing illiberal political premises in the Old South—the formal equality principle of the polis diverged strikingly from the principle of father-elder power in family politics. Even if one discerns familial arenas of power whose battles took shape as arguments between contingent and absolute visions of hierarchical gender right, that battleground existed alongside and in relation to battles to extend a socially accepted equality principle of political right to formerly excluded terrains (such as gender relations, race relations, and ethnic relations) and to formerly excluded people (such as women, blacks, and immigrants). By contrast, in late colonial Mexico a broad consistency marked the organizing principles of authority and struggle at various levels of society. The premise of social order and authority at both the family and the polity levels of society was an organic hierarchy that vested power in fathers and elders, both literally and metaphorically. In gender culture and in political culture more generally, the language and experience of argument—of conflicts and their mediations—hinged on the tension between more contingent and absolutist visions of right but rarely contested the first principles of hierarchically ordered right. To the extent that one discerns an egalitarian principle of political right, moreover, one discerns it as a subordinate leitmotif—at subaltern levels of peasant village politics rather than at the upper levels of the polity, and in conflictual dialogue with hierarchical political currents even at the level of peasant village politics.

Of course, one may discern contradictory hybrids or mediations that defy a neat contrast. In the United States, for example, the tensions between pater-

nalist and egalitarian principles of politics within the Old South and the efforts of city bosses to build political machines that recast political leaders as
father-patrons dispensing favor to loyal clients and dependents caution against
too seamless a view of a polis organized around an equality principle of right.
The larger point, however, remains. Even if one discerns striking resonance
between the gender struggles evident in late colonial Mexico and those evident in other historical societies, the total configuration of politics and authority within which such struggles took place and found their larger meaning
sets one historical society apart from another. Some societies evince more
consistency or parallelism than others in the organizing premises of authority
and struggle. Some societies evince sharper contradictions than others when
the politics of gender and familial authority are compared with the politics
of the polis.

The second part of a response to the Boston question argues from consideration of the limits of theory and abstraction. We have argued that a conflictual dialogue between contingent and absolute visions of gender right not only
illuminates patterns of conflict in Mexico but also yields a useful paradigm for
theorizing gender struggle in other nonfeminist or prefeminist historical settings. A theoretical framework, useful as it may be for understanding one or
more case studies, remains nonetheless an abstraction culled from the messy
historical particulars of life. The abstraction is useful, even powerful, if it captures a critical feature, pattern, or dynamic that illuminates or explains what
might otherwise be missed, or if it draws out the general within the particular.
One deploys the abstraction not out of arbitrary whim but with intellectual
conviction. But only if we reify the abstraction into a "thing" does it suggest a
lack of substantive difference or particularity between cases.

In late colonial Mexico and, say, early modern France one may discern
tension between contingent and absolutist orientations to gender right, and
the pattern may illuminate the politics of gender and the gendering of politics. But at a somewhat lower level of abstraction, important differences
would emerge. The range, categories, and relative weights of disputes leading
to injurious violence against women (sexual ownership, labor and economic
obligations, physical mobility, and verbal insolence, for instance) would yield
distinctive configurations of gender power and contentiousness; the social organization and cultural meanings of community life would translate into
quite distinctive theaters of female power and female subordination. (Even
within Mexico, one may recall, this level of analysis helped us to draw out regional distinctiveness, notwithstanding our effort to highlight cross-regional
consistencies.) Even if we were shocked to discover remarkable similarities at
more middling levels of abstraction, only by reifying abstraction into a thing
could we find gendered life in late colonial Mexico reducible to gendered life
in a region of early modern Europe. The specific issues in play, the specific so-

womanhood, manhood, and male-female relations that defined a range of behaviors and adaptations more or less accepted as normal or expected (conventional or *de costumbre*), whatever the ideals or pretenses of a patriarchal
culture. From this point of view one may interpret the slippage between patriarchal pretense and practical gender conventions as a marker of impact, a sign
of the conflictual negotiation of the practical rules of the patriarchal order.[24]
(Obviously, I refer here not to the inevitable slippage between ideal and practice that sparks little resentment and owes little to female agency, but to more
self-conscious, potentially resentful, concessions to the partial reality of female assertions.)

Second, at an empirical level one may take cognizance of the everyday
practices that suggest such slippage. The gap between idealized pretense and
practical acceptance—a kind of grudging resignation—comes through repeatedly in the testimonies of everyday life in almost every arena of patriarchal authority, even though the criminal violence records emphasize cases
where grudging resignation to the claims of the female Other broke down.
When men failed to flaunt their sexual prowess openly by taking established
amasias to village fairs but submitted to their wives' pressure to limit *amasia*
connections to fleeting, discreet contacts of little economic consequence;
when they reluctantly backed off from affirming continuous possession rights
in *amasias* who aggressively asserted independent self-ownership or in discontented young wife-servants reclaimed by their parents; when they engaged
in extra day labor under servile conditions in order to deflect the anger of
women who insisted on receiving a reliable household income allowance;
when they chose not to escalate household tension when women signified dis-
content with patriarchs through tardy or unreliable meal preparation; when
men discreetly tolerated a certain amount of unexplained tarrying in women's
water-fetching, *tianguis* trading, and church-going rounds; when they contained an angry impulse to severe violence out of fear of scandal, jailing, or supernatural retribution; when they submitted to such compromises to their
authority because they knew that such compromises were commonplace and
that many women—not just the notoriously headstrong—made such assertions and backed them up with social alliances (competing kin clusters, plural
patriarchs, female friend-and-ally webs, and supernatural consultants) that
rendered male intransigence foolish—in all these myriad ways, women's
struggles with men yielded an impact, however unequal the premises and outcomes, on the practical conventions of gendered life. These compromises, and
women's ability to pluralize patriarchs and thereby draw on male crossover allies in specific struggles, also yielded a half-acknowledged larger concession: a
partial legitimation of contingent approaches to patriarchal authority. In this
sense the conflictual dialogue between absolute and contingent approaches to

gender right turned out to be not only an argument between women and men but also an argument that ran through popular culture as a whole.

What is most important at an empirical level is that the sense of slippage between idealized pretense and practical compromise came through, in rather matter-of-fact ways, even in cases of extreme violence and conflict. Let us recall, in this context, José Marcelino of Texalpa. He originally told his wife, María Teresa, that his whereabouts and failure to work were none of her concern, ended up wounding her fatally because she challenged his authority with conditionality, yet slipped away to a nearby hacienda to work for two days' wages and thereby "remove his wife's anger." Let us recall, in this context, Francisco Gerónimo of Hacienda San Gaspar. He resented the taunting disrespect of his wife, María Gertrudis, and even killed her during one episode of scathing, yet had earlier responded more pliantly to an insulting rebuke with a Sunday outing of bathing, drink, and conviviality. Let us recall, in this context, José del Carmen Neria of Hacienda del Puente and Tesoyuca pueblo. He chose to overlook, in the interests of social peace, economic need, and marital reconciliation, the ambiguous complicity of his wife, Laureana Filomena, in her abduction by Dionicio José, and instead moved to Tesoyuca and forged a discourse that pinned complete responsibility for the adultery on Dionicio José.[25]

If one blends conceptual emphasis on the practical gender conventions of everyday life with empirical attention to the markers of reluctant, even resentful concessions to slippage between pretense and reality, one begins to define a convincing response to the impact question. A key impact of female struggles over contingent and absolute gender right was precisely the forging of gender conventions that implied greater practical acceptance of conditional dynamics of patriarchal authority and a concomitantly wider range of more or less acceptable female behaviors. This impact, which men resisted and which they had every reason either to hide or to trivialize in joking banter among men, was at best a half-acknowledged secret in subaltern life—too pervasive to be banished from consciousness altogether yet too delicate to be acknowledged openly. Relegated to female background talk and to occasional male banter, the impact of women's will on the practical dynamics of patriarchal rule was the ultimate secret within a secret history of gender.

CHAPTER 14

Postscript

The Problem of Ghosts

GHOSTS: THE EERIE SENSE OF CONTINUITY

Are the patterns of gender culture and political culture uncovered for late colonial Mexico best understood as particular to that historical conjuncture — subject to erosion or transformation in postcolonial times? Or are they best understood as entrenched and resilient — persistently reconstituted over the long sweep of Mexican history and civilization?

On one level, the eerie sense of continuity is personal. I went to Mexico in the mid-1980s to explore gender and power dynamics in subaltern life two centuries earlier. But as I read the criminal records and other documents of late colonial times, I also could not help but notice the apparent replays of history in contemporary lives. The culture of male bonding and rivalry that blends play, risk, and a ratification of masculine courage amidst life's adversities; the insistence by women, notwithstanding tension and danger, on embedding the innate gender rights and duties asserted by patriarchs within entangling webs of the conditional; the building of female background conversations, social alliances, and implied threats of vengeance as weapons of survival and struggle by women who also find themselves caught in ambivalent crossfires in their relations with men; the denunciation of authority that contrasts the parasitism of tyrants with the paternalism of protectors — the characters and language and the struggles and coping mechanisms sometimes seemed to have walked right out of the archives to assume, almost magically, a three-dimensional living form. Did the magic of this experience simply reflect the subjectivities and preoccupations of a particular colonial historian at a particular moment in time?

I think not. The mirrors of gendered past in the gendered present are too ubiquitous to be reduced to individual idiosyncrasy. An anthropologist visits Mexico repeatedly in the 1980s to explore women's lives, and she too experiences the magic. She meets a compelling woman who seems to have stepped forth from the colonial Inquisition records on sexual witchcraft studied by the same anthropologist.[1] Two scholarly generations earlier, in the mid-twentieth century, an anthropologist with a strong historical sensibility studies rural life in Morelos. Gender as an analytic category has not yet revamped anthropological and historical studies, and he stands squarely opposed to the kind of timelessness and romanticization that had infused earlier community studies. Yet the multidimensional ethnographies he bequeaths include striking parallels between gendered past and gendered present.[2]

The ethnographic mirrors of gendered history beckon at every turn, and their full exploration and analysis would divert us into another book, a full-scale journey to probe continuity and change in the nineteenth and twentieth centuries. For the more modest purposes of this postscript—presentation of paradoxical evidence suggesting both continuity and change in gendered social relations of power, and suggestion of a hypothesis that partly dissolves the paradox—we need only steal a few prolonged glances at the mirrors' magic. Let us recall that one of the principal findings of this study established the bitterly contested quality of patriarchal pacts among subaltern women and men and the ways such power struggles yielded tension between contingent, or conditional, orientations to gender right and more absolutist visions of innate right. In Morelos, the region we explored at length, this main finding and its various corollaries seem reproduced endlessly in the lives and characters of the people who fill the ethnographies of the mid- and late twentieth century. Esperanza de Martínez, formally depicted in rather submissive terms by Oscar Lewis, nonetheless dares to fight her husband Pedro over his extramarital sexual rights as he turns toward a more imperious and negligent style of household rule. Celsa, of San Antonio de Tepoztlán, successfully confronts and defeats the claim of permanent sexual possession by Enrique, a partner who sits ambiguously between the categories of common-law husband and *amasio* and whom Celsa views as negligent. The ethnographer Lola Romanucci-Ross discovers a world of women hardened by experience and background conversation: one expects from men a life of adversity, abuse, and struggles for control, even if the rare good patriarch exists out there, somewhere. The destiny of women is to entangle men's assertion of an absolute right of authority—and its legitimizing corollary, that women are by nature betrayers of moral and sexual order—within webs of contingency leading, if necessary, to women's practical right of separation. Oscar and Ruth Lewis discover a world of conjugal quarreling and violence over a range of gendered issues similar to those that inflamed late colonial households. Men's plausible and imaginary *celos*, women's interventions against the kinds of *amasia* relations that bring economic negligence or cultural humiliation, men's fury when a meal is not ready, women's insistence on negotiating a reliable *gasto*, men's quest to exercise strict vigilance over women's physical mobility and social outings, women's critique of men's diversionary dissipation and unannounced wanderings, men's insistence on an unquestioned right to administer physical punishment, women's insistence on evaluating proportionality and fairness in punishment — the full range of late colonial disputes, the accompanying tension between contingent and absolute visions of gender right, seem on display.[3]

Reading between the lines (or, if one prefers, against the grain) of Oscar Lewis's prefeminist ethnography, we discover that Esperanza de Martínez develops the social skills and networks to cope with poverty and with the tensions and abuses of her conjugal life, and that Pedro Martínez is resentful and fearful that her contacts and coping mechanisms may harm him. Listening to the voices, one hears familiar echoes of absolute and contingent gender right and their associated gender stereotypes. As a husband and as a local judge hearing marital disputes, Pedro remarks, "If the man gives in and isn't free even to get drunk, that's bad. If the man lets his wife raise a hand to him, that's bad. When a man gives in, the woman expands like a leafy green plant. One must know the ways of the women." As a father-elder instructing youth, especially sons, Pedro displays a similar orientation. "They have to work for me. That is why I have sons. . . . As long as they are in my house, as long as they are not of age, my children have to obey me, to submit, and they may not question their parents' actions."

As a wife and mother Esperanza leans toward more contingent views of gender right. The quality of mutuality serves to strengthen or erode patriarchal right. It serves to narrow or widen the range of female and youth right. Pedro has become tyrannical, in a sense nonrelational, in his stance toward his wife and children. "He scolds for everything and rarely says an affectionate word, not even to his children. When they were little he would hug them and say nice things to them, but not now anymore. . . . He takes care of them, yes, the way he takes care of his mule, so they can keep on working." Understandably, the result of such tyranny is a trail of conflict that may push a son to withdraw his labor and obedient demeanor: "Felipe was on strike and wasn't speaking to his *papá*." A similar trail of struggle may also lead a wife to go on strike. When Pedro becomes abusive in Esperanza's eyes, he not only loses his right to the etiquettes of verbal deference — she refuses to talk. He also loses his sexual rights in Esperanza — "I don't let him touch me" — despite the threats unleashed by her withdrawal.[4]

In short, even as they pay lip service to patriarchal ideals and appearances, the women of the Morelos ethnographies tend "to regard the completely submissive wife more as a fool than an ideal." The appearances and etiquettes of patriarchal rule are partly belied by the negotiation — often tense and sometimes bitter and violent — of the practical gender conventions that gain social acceptance, or at least acquiescence. As in late colonial times, the result of this conflictual negotiation is a wider range of social characters and conventions than that suggested by the formal first principles of patriarchal rule to which virtually everyone more or less subscribes. Doña Zeferina of Hueyapan, a strong woman who outlives three husbands, seems to heed a common female proverb in Morelos: "When we give in, the men impose." Disappointed by her quality of life with her first husband, she issues him an ultimatum — at the age of twenty-two, five years after the marriage ceremony. She refuses henceforth to wake up early to grind his tortillas. For years he relies on a sister to prepare his tortillas. As she outlives husbands and takes on the role of ruling family elder, Doña Zeferina acquires a servant in historically familiar fashion. Juana, her daughter-in-law, puts in long hours preparing tortillas on the *comal*, washing clothes in the company of other women on large boulders in a nearby stream, caring for young children, and preparing the evening *temascal* (adobe steam bath) under her mother-in-law's direction. Men, for their part, see subaltern masculinity as a kind of condemnation to struggle against evil and adversity — including the evils and adversities posed by women — and ratify their competence in a social theater of masculine bonding and wordplay reminiscent of late colonial times. The men, too, have their legitimizing proverb. "When the man relaxes, the women take over." [5]

Even some of the social weapons evident in twentieth-century Morelos seem to draw on a long historical genealogy. The husband or *amasio* who fears that his partner's network of female allies and consultants includes a specialist in supernatural vengeance, or who knows that if he goes too far his wife will leave with her children for the house of a relative or friend; the judge who feels weighed down by women who insist on escalating domestic complaints and violence to a higher institutional level, notwithstanding the institutional bias in favor of patriarchal authority and conjugal reconciliation; and the father who discovers that his daughter has established a pluralized web of patriarchs, kin clusters, and residence options, thereby limiting the authority of any one elder or patriarch, all would have felt at home in the documentary tales of gender conflict in late colonial times. [6]

The twentieth-century ethnography of Morelos seems filled with living ghosts, reconstituted versions of the social characters, languages, and weapons of gender right and justification we encountered two centuries earlier. A close reading of ethnographic data on the social conventions and strains of gendered life in subaltern Mexico City and Oaxaca would take us too far afield but would also resonate strikingly with our late colonial materials. [7]

Similarly, the language of political praise, denunciation, and self-justification evident in the world of Mexico's institutionalized revolution evokes memories of the thick interplays of gender culture and political culture found in late colonial times. The language of political praise and legitimacy sometimes evokes the familiar symbolism of the good patriarch who intervenes personally to look after the well-being of his clients and dependents. We have already heard the self-serving justification of a *cacique* who proclaimed, in 1985, that critiques of his *caciquismo* were misplaced. "I'm a *patriarch* not a *cacique*," went the newspaper headline that summarized his position. More revealing is the folklore and symbolism that accrued to President Lázaro Cárdenas, the architect of institutionalized revolutionary rule and Mexico's most revered president. Cárdenas made a point of visiting village after village—by horseback, if necessary—not only during the presidential campaign but during his term in office (1934–40). Once he arrived, he sat in audience to hear the peasant supplicants who streamed in. They offered flowers or other tokens to seal a personal reciprocity and deference with their president, and they told him of their families' practical needs and troubles. Cárdenas listened and responded. Out of such meetings there developed, presumably, a presidential "good patriarch" whose esteem—like that of successful village elders—rested upon a personal reputation for service, attentiveness, and if need be, direct interventions that helped community *hijos*. A city joke that arose about Cárdenas summed up his remarkable attentiveness to the symbolism of a rural politics that equated legitimacy with personal interest by an intervening patriarch.

> One morning while dispatching business in the capital his secretary laid a list of urgent matters, and a telegram, before him. The list said: *Bank reserves dangerously low.* "Tell the Treasurer," said Cárdenas. *Agricultural production falling.* "Tell the Minister of Agriculture." *Railways bankrupt.* "Tell the Minister of Communications." *Serious message from Washington.* "Tell Foreign Affairs." Then he opened the telegram, which read: "My corn dried, my burro died, my sow was stolen, my baby is sick. Signed, Pedro Juan, village of Huitzlipituzco."
>
> "Order the presidential train at once," said Cárdenas. "I am leaving for Huitzlipituzco."[8]

It would be misleading, of course, to resort to a reductionism that excludes more tangible material pacts—Cárdenas, after all, distributed land at a dizzying pace unmatched before and since his presidency. It would also be inaccurate to exclude from the political legitimacy equation a host of variables extraneous to the image of the good patriarch. Among these, the images of the revolution as redeemer of national pride and sovereignty and as engine of social and economic development have been particularly important. It remains to be seen whether the increasingly technocratic turn of the state (in the 1980s and 1990s) in an era of revitalized free market ideology may effectively inject an expertise-competence factor into the political legitimacy equation.[9] But in 1985 I was reminded of the continuing appeal of the image of the good patriarch when listening to a political speech by a beer factory worker collecting contributions on the subway. After presenting a rather militant, hard-line discourse on exploitation of the workers by the factory bosses and on the corruption of state authorities who refused to consider the workers' demands, he concluded with a startlingly weak appeal to President Miguel de la Madrid for personal favor and mercy. Presumably a good president would, upon learning of the workers' plight, intervene personally to protect them from harm. To a historian listening to the discourse, the hope — even among subalterns with a hard-bitten consciousness of injustice and suffering at the hands of irresponsible authorities — that the good patriarch existed out there, somewhere, perhaps even at the apex of authority, seemed uncannily colonial. Three years later, during the first presidential campaign of Cuauhtémoc Cárdenas, the left-leaning candidate who had broken with the PRI (the dominant Party of the Institutional Revolution), some two thousand individuals handed the candidate letters and notes. Many captured not only disillusion with the hegemonic party and the desperation of subaltern life but also the hunger that a good patriarch existed out there, somewhere. "I am a peasant woman 95 years old alone and a widow," explained one supplicant. "Señor ingeniero I want to ask you for help because I am sick in my eyes that is all and señor ingeniero forgive the bother and I live here at Venito Juárez at calle revolución." Many drew explicit links with Lázaro Cárdenas, father of the candidate and the Mexican people alike. "Your father was our *tata* [father-protector] and we still think of him that way because he has not died, he sends you to see how we his hijos are so that you can see if his rule is being followed. . . . He ordered lands with their respective credits for the peasant[;] we don't have lands and surely no credits." [10]

The flip side of political legitimacy is, of course, political denunciation. Here, too, one discovers an interplay between the notions of legitimate and illegitimate authority evident in gender culture and political culture. On the one hand, at the national level the most commonplace denunciation of the ruling group heard in Mexico has focused on its extreme parasitism: the personal corruption that fattens rulers whose style of authority is so absolute and autocratic that no excess — however arbitrary, destructive, or untempered by obligation — lies beyond reach. This denunciation of parasitism resonates strikingly with the language of denunciation we explored in a colonial context (see Chapter 8).[11] On the other hand, students of women's involvement in village political mobilization in Morelos in the 1980s have found that the women injected a gendered and morally charged sensibility about authority that drew parallels between bad authority in the family ("gender culture") and in the polity ("political culture"). Men's deficiencies and dissipation as political leaders went in tandem with their deficiencies and dissipation as husband-fathers. For the women activists, the dissipation in individual drinking and diversion that family patriarchs claimed as an absolute right led them to neglect their obligations and to engage in destructive violence against women and one another. Exactly the same sorts of *egoísmo* (egotistical individualism) fed the dissipatory behavior of men as political leaders and rendered local politics ineffectual except as a device for personal enrichment. To save their families and their communities, and the men from themselves, the women would have to press their own sensibility about moral order and legitimate authority into public political spaces. The women, in short, rejected a rigid demarcation between the effort to establish a contingent vision of authority — one defined by mutuality, a set of obligations whose fulfillment conditioned rights and permissible behavior — in familial politics and in subaltern politics at large. Denunciations of dissipatory egotism and autocracy could target both the parasitic family patriarch and the parasitic village patriarch.[12]

Politics as praise and politics as denunciation are opposite sides of the same coin. In the twentieth century, is the coin of legitimate authority a historical alloy — the product of long, dense fusions between the politics of gender and the gendering of politics since colonial times? Once again, as in our review of contested patriarchal pacts, living ghosts impart an eerie sense of continuity. The archives seem to tell of the world we have not yet lost.

THE RECONSTITUTION OF OLD DYNAMICS
IN NEW SOCIAL CONTEXTS (I)

The paradoxical character of the change-over-time question may now come squarely in view. On the one hand, the specific life histories and ethnographies of subaltern life in the twentieth century seem to present continuities of patriarchal power, gender struggle, and associated cultural argument over right, and continuities in the gendering of political culture, that seem to belie historical fluidity and transformation. On the other hand, Mexico has experienced dramatic upheaval and social transformation, especially in the twentieth century, and the gendered dimension of these processes has been important.

Already in the nineteenth century the emergence of Liberal anticlerical politics during the Reforma and French Intervention era (1855–72) yielded important new stirrings — efforts to reform civil law, including family law, and to establish public schooling for girls and boys. These were stirrings mainly at the level of ideas — not many schools were built and changes in family law were modest and largely postponed — within a battle to reconceptualize politics and society in a Mexican "nation." The ideas, moreover, drew on late colonial antecedents: notions that wider employment opportunities and better education might mobilize women more effectively for a more efficient, orderly, and enlightened patriarchal society. But the political battles of mid-century were followed, during the Porfirian era (1876–1910), by a spurt in economic growth and modernization that boosted urban service and educational sectors. Together these changes laid a modest groundwork for change — a certain widening of public roles for women as workers, educators, and professionals, an emerging constituency for a middle class feminist movement in the early twentieth century.[13]

It was in the twentieth century, however, that upheaval and transformation ran sufficiently deep and wide to create an expectation of major change in gender dynamics. The revolution itself (the war years of 1910–19) was a thoroughly gendered upheaval. The foundational stories explaining the revolutionary awakening of Zapata and Villa as youths captured the charged blendings of color-class power with ranked masculinities and femininities in the Old Regime. The tears of a father when a sugar estate usurped village lands and the rape of a sister by a landowner sent Zapata and Villa, respectively, on their paths to a revolutionary destiny. The ballads (*corridos*) of revolutionary culture linked a vision of subaltern emancipation with a vision of liberated manhood accompanied by devoted womanhood. Valiant revolutionary men would wreck the old equations of color-class inferiority and humiliated manhoods. The processes of war, privation, and struggle for a new social destiny would also unleash a reinvigorated solidarity of women with their subaltern patriarchs, encoded in the popular image of the *soldadera* — the female camp follower who accompanies her man, finds his food and grinds his corn, serves him sexually, and if fate and loss decree, becomes a ferocious soldier herself driven by devotion to a fallen patriarch. In popular culture, in short, ideas of revolutionary upheaval and emancipation were integrally linked to ideas of gender upheaval and transformation.[14]

In addition, the revolution's emergencies and its social questioning injected a certain fluidity and open polemicism into the politics of women's social roles. Some women took up soldiering on a continuing basis, won a certain fame and legitimacy as "colonels" who led men in battle, and developed habits of command and independence that did not mesh easily with patriarchal decorum. A first-wave feminist movement, moreover, began to crystallize in middle-class urban politics by the eve of the revolution, established an alliance with the victorious Constitutionalist revolutionaries, and for a time in the 1920s received special encouragement from Felipe Carrillo Puerto, the radical socialist governor of Yucatán. A certain political space, however fragile and subject to closure by the revolution's patriarchs, had begun to open up and to call into question the desirability of traditionalist views on legal personhood, suffrage, divorce, and the sexual double standard.[15]

Once the revolution moved beyond the rather chaotic politics of personal rule, rivalry, and spoils in the 1920s and early 1930s and achieved greater political definition and institutionalization, moreover, it did indeed sponsor a major overhauling of rural life that placed old-style power relations and values on the defensive. The revolutionary state consolidated an enduring political base and a capacity for constitutional continuity during the populist presidency of Lázaro Cárdenas (1934–40). As the left-leaning architect of a new political order, Cárdenas distributed nearly 50 million acres of land — twice as much as the combined total of the revolutionary presidents who preceded him — and in many regions effectively destroyed the Old Regime's landowning class. In addition, Cárdenas promoted an extensive socialist education program to supersede traditional Catholic and hacienda schooling in the countryside. Between 1935 and 1940 the number of rural primary schools shot up by over half, from 7,729 to 11,974, and the schools experimented with a socialist curriculum. In short, Cárdenas placed the high patriarchs of rural political culture — the *hacendados* and the church fathers — on the defensive and promoted discourses that linked legitimate authority with communal well-being and egalitarianism. The tearing away of the old moorings implicated gender, even if indirectly. The socialist education curriculum, for example, tread warily on gender equality. It backed away from sexual education, in view of protests that demonstrated the volatility of the subject, and avoided suggestion that the new education aimed to overturn society's sexual division of labor. (A similar ambivalence or wariness was evident in the politics of women's suffrage. Cárdenas promised to support women's right to vote but backed away from pressing the matter hard in the Chamber of Deputies as the 1940 presidential elections approached. A gradualist process ensued and postponed women's vote at the presidential level until 1958.) But the new policy insisted on coeducation rather than consignment of girls to the home or to segregated classrooms. It deployed a language of equal rights in discussions of male and female, and it promoted a discourse of progress that framed hierarchical rural values as both unjust and archaic. The assault on landed wealth and the church, the insistence on the relevance of an integrated education for girls, and the discourse of social equality unsettled conventional articulations of gender culture, political culture, and traditionalist morality in the countryside.[16]

Perhaps most important, even when the revolutionary state veered sharply toward conservative politics in the 1940s and 1950s, it oversaw a profound, long-term transformation of everyday life bound to unsettle the inherited dynamics of contested patriarchal pacts. The state promoted a political economy of industrialization sufficiently successful to yield a "Mexican miracle." As the manufacturing sector and a modern administrative and service sector (including teaching, health, and legal professions; clerking and secretarial work; sales and accounting positions; and middle and upper level bureaucracy and management) loomed ever larger in Mexican pathways to economic well-being and prosperity, and as these expansions were accompanied by a rural population boom and worsening terms of trade for small rural producers, migration to the cities turned into a powerful, self-sustaining spiral. One moved to the cities to find better education or social connections and with them the good life in the form of a decent working class or service sector job. Or more realistically, for most subalterns, one moved to the cities to meld into the lower status service and informal economy sectors that provisioned the large urban populations and to build a better life for one's children. By the 1980s the population of Mexico was two-thirds urban, Mexico City was the world's largest urban metropolis (20–25 million inhabitants), and even small provincial cities like Cuernavaca amassed populations surpassing a quarter million.

The implications for subaltern patriarchal dynamics were important. The migration and education tracks and the declining sufficiency of peasant-based income streams meant that the economic destiny of rural youths was not as firmly anchored in decisions over property by peasant patriarchs. The transformations in education and work implied that young women contemplated female labor markets and income streams far more diversified than the domestic service and street selling tracks. The ideology of state-led modernization and progress fostered, in the mid-twentieth century, a vision of *lo mexicano* that defined subaltern machismo as both quintessential and pathological, a version of masculinity inherited from a wounding Mexican past, yet in need of exposure and renunciation if Mexico were to transcend the drag on its future. By the 1970s and 1980s the dynamics of urban politics, education, and social movements had nurtured a second-wave feminist movement that won significant cultural visibility and institutional tolerance, and grassroots movements that pressed women's needs and rights more explicitly. The politics and culture of Mexico once more began to include a debate about extending the equality principle to women.[17]

The twentieth century, in short, constituted times of revolution in a double sense. Mexico experienced the colossal, violent political energy directed at exploding the Old Regime and charting a new destiny. This was the dramatic Revolution of historic fame. It also experienced the more subtle and continuous revampings of personal pathways, decisions, and obstacles that fed into a more urban and modernized structure of the acceptable and the desirable, the feasible and the impossible. This was the silent revolution that has unfolded in many parts of Latin America. Both upheavals were thoroughly gendered. They introduced new fluidity and rupture to the daily practices of gendered life, and they introduced new debate on the future of subaltern manhood, womanhood, and male-female relations.

How are we to reconcile or explain the paradox of ghostlike continuity in gendered life alongside dramatic change implicating gendered life? The response I propose here — in schematic form, in the spirit of provoking debate, reflection, and research—asks us to consider the ways vast changes may reconstitute old dynamics within new contexts. The effect of this new contextualization is that even traditional or familiar social dynamics may take on distinct social meanings, functions, and consequences. Continuity ends up representing not so much a flat projection of past into present—a kind of inertia of inherited legacy and habit—but a more generative process, a recreation or redeployment of the historically familiar in response to the changing imperatives and conditions of life. In this scheme a simple contrast between change and continuity yields to more subtle and interactive blendings. Reconstituted continuity becomes embedded within social change, implications of social change become embedded within tales of continuity.

My more specific hypothesis argues that the doubled revolution of the twentieth century—the loud and violent Revolution and the more silent, long-term transformation of everyday life—cut away at the Old Regime's moorings of patriarchal power in rural subaltern life and that the result of this fluidity and erosion was to transform the meanings of similar acts of gender struggle and repression in everyday life. The same quarrels and acts of violence that once expressed prerogative and tension within a living regime of patriarchal gender power—a regime reasonably well adapted to other institutions of power in an ongoing society and accompanied by social expectations that the current regime would reproduce itself far into the future—now represented the desperate stopgaps, rearguard actions, and breakups of a patriarchal regime under siege. To put it another way, the localized crisis of existence that haunted patriarchal pacts in Mexico City in late colonial times now turned into a more generalized crisis. The erosion of patriarchal power in rural subaltern life injected a sharper intensity, a more salient social subversiveness, into historically old quarrels over gender right. The implication of specific quarrels reverberated more widely for patriarchal authority in society at large. For the patriarch unwilling or unable to adapt to the changing tide or to let go of his authority in relative silence, the impulse to domestic violence as an ultimate stopgap might prove all the more irresistible. Over time the same act of quarrel over gender right, the same act of violence to reestablish domestic authority, had received a somewhat distinctive social implication.

We have already pointed to the general forces that cut away at the old patriarchal moorings. The Mexican Revolution, although thoroughly patriarchal in its vision of a liberated subaltern manhood, also placed expectations of social deference on the defensive and generated new experiences of right and possibility. The subversive effects of wartime mobilization, of attacks on Old Regime institutions and classes, of experimentation with new languages and programs of right and equality, and of new social movements, political clients, and pressure groups in dialogue and conflict with the state, although not mainly directed at questions of gender, nonetheless introduced a new fluidity and uncertainty affecting gender. As Heather Fowler-Salamini and Mary Kay Vaughan have observed, the revolution was both a "patriarchal event" in the cultural imagery it unleashed and a subversion of patriarchal habit and expectation in the social spaces and emergencies it created.[18] As we have also seen, the silent, long-term revolution in the structure of daily life options and survival strategies was probably even more important than the explicit politics of revolutionary upheaval and state construction. As Mexico went, during the course of the twentieth century, from a society two-thirds rural to a society two-thirds urban, as its new political economy of growth and industrialization transformed family survival strategies, and as hegemonic cultural discourse seized upon subaltern machismo as the symbol of a Mexican pathological inheritance, a form of masculinity to be transcended, new spaces and possibilities opened for women. A new social configuration defined rural life. For young women in the countryside, schooling and school-based contacts with other youth, migration to a city, and labor outside the home and outside domestic service offered pathways of escape from a traditional destiny—as the young daughter whose marital future is transacted by family elders and as the young wife-servant whose labor belongs both to husband and mother-in-law. For aging patriarchs in the countryside the declining sufficiency of peasant property to provide for a family, the declining cultural appeal of rural life, and the alternate pathways to a youthful livelihood in cities implied a loosening grip on the decisions of youths, a slow crumbling of respectful deference to the rule and wisdom of elders.

These general trends, however plausible and important as forces eroding patriarchal authority in rural subaltern life, do not by themselves suffice to explain what changed and why. They mainly tell us about a changing structure of possibility. Just as important, for our purposes, is an examination of the ways Mexican women moved within and pushed this changing structure of possibility. Women actively conjoined the changing technological and social horizons of twentieth-century life with old gender struggles and problems, thereby forging new social conventions of gender that responded to their needs and set old ways on the defensive. Let us recall that patriarchal slippage in the practical negotiation of gender conventions represented, in our portrait of late colonial times, an important gateway to the impact question. Here the issue is not so much the slippage between absolutist and contingent approaches to patriarchal right within a world of more or less accepted gender conventions as it is transformation of the gender conventions themselves. In this brief postscript we cannot take up a systematic analysis of the entire range of changing social conventions.[19] But we can explore several telling examples: the transition from stone grinding to mill grinding in women's tortilla work; the movement of female youth from a predominantly patrilocal/domestic pathway of residence, work, and schooling to a grid of multiple pathways of residence, work, and schooling; and the rise of male youth trajectories in work and politics that eroded the influence of elders.

The transition from stone grinding to mill grinding of *nixtamal* (maize soaked in lime and water) to produce the wet corn flour (*masa*) for tortillas marked an enormous change in the social conventions of gender in rural Mexico.[20] Although steam-driven mills were in use in cities and on some technologically advanced haciendas and plantations in the last ten or fifteen years of Porfirian rule (1876–1910), the transition from the *metate* to the *molino* (mill) unleashed tensions and anxiety in the village-based countryside. The resistance complicated adoption of the *molino* technology, which spread unevenly in rural Mexico between the 1920s and the 1950s. Part of the problem, of course, was economic. Switching from women's unpaid grinding labor to mill payments was not a casual economic decision for peasant families and patriarchs. In Tepoztlán, Morelos, for example, the *molino* technology was widespread by the 1940s; but *molino* expenses represented a larger item in peasant family budgets than any cost except food, and the *molino* money exceeded outlays for meat, rice, bread, milk, or coffee. Among poor peasants, families who had adopted the *molino* practice sometimes reverted back to the *metate* to save money.

The obstacles to adoption of the *molino*, however, went beyond the problem of expense. As a cultural symbol the *metate* signified women's duty, subordination, and competence in the sexual division of labor. As social practice, the *metate* bound women physically to their households. *Metate* technology implied three to six arduous hours of food preparation labor—at least half of it the back-straining work of grinding—just to get the day off to a proper start. (Size of family, degree of labor assistance and number of household *metates*, and seasonal variation in consumption could affect, of course, the number of daily hours of labor. For poor women who could not count on a full-time *molendera* servant, three to six hours defines a normal range of daily start-up work.) During the planting and the harvesting seasons the women awoke in the very early morning (in some instances as early as two o'clock, often by four o'clock) to prepare fresh tortillas for the men working the *milpas*. The initial shelling and lime soaking that transformed dry corn into *nixtamal*, the exhausting grinding of the *nixtamal* into *masa*, the patting of *masa* into fresh tortillas cooked on a hot *comal*—the basic daily start-up tired the women, bound them to their households for long stretches of time, and constricted opportunities to venture away except for brief outings or essential household duties such as fetching water, purchasing small amounts of food, delivering tortillas to men in the fields, or washing clothes. At the heart of the process was enslavement to the *metate*. One female informant in Morelos recalled that her mother-in-law foisted the corn-grinding work onto her: "It was I who got stuck with one of the hardest jobs in a household." Another recalled female life before the *molinos* in more specific terms: "We had backs of iron."[21] For women to send children to the *molino* with buckets of *nixtamal* rather than grind the *masa* themselves implied, both practically and symbolically, an important transformation.

The change did not come, however, without a fight and a compromise that rendered it partial. The first mill established in Tepoztlán in 1925 met with too much resistance to succeed; the outsider who built it left the pueblo within two years. Women appeared to react cautiously at first — the expense had to be considered, as did the possibility of diminished status as socially competent, morally responsible women. But the prospect of the *molino* replacing *metate* work provoked particularly intense resistance by peasant men, who not only argued that mill-ground *nixtamal* yielded poor-tasting tortillas but also that release of wives from *metate* labor would increase the kind of unsupervised time that led to sexual mischief and betrayal. (The latter fear had also been voiced by peasant men in late Porfirian experiments with the *molinos*.) Nonetheless by 1927 a group of village women launched a drive to establish a successful *molino*, and — in the words of a male informant — "the revolution of the women against the authority of the men" triumphed over the opposition. By 1942 four *molinos* operated in Tepoztlán, and a new social convention of gender was emerging in the Morelos region. This new social convention included a symbolic compromise. In families that could afford it, the women had the *molinos* perform the main grinding, but the women also did a bit of regrinding on the *metate* to improve texture and taste. As symbol and practice, this was a mixed *molino*-and-*metate* system. As one woman remarked, "There is always some grinding that has to be done." Nonetheless, women had succeeded, despite men's objections and suspicions, in shifting the main grinding work to the *molinos* and in making the *molino* fees a high priority in the family budget.[22]

A similar process and shift in gender conventions was evident in many rural regions and received special support from the Cárdenas administration in the late 1930s. From Morelos to Chiapas, the Cárdenas administration organized rural unions, proved sympathetic to petitions for *molinos*, and helped provide the gasoline or electric generators to power mills. During the Cárdenas years the number of *molinos* jumped from less than one thousand to nearly six thousand.[23]

The transition from the *metate* to the *molino* (or, more precisely, to a mixed *molino*-and-*metate* practice) represented a profound shift in the specific social conventions of gender. Precisely for this reason it sparked struggles between women and men and fears that patriarchal control and morality might crumble. As we have seen, however, it goes too far to suggest that women undertook this struggle without allies (or only in alliance with *molino* entrepreneurs, who stood to benefit from a new approach to *nixtamal* grinding). The bumpy, incomplete transition toward the *molino* offers us an important example of the way Mexican women in the twentieth century conjoined old hardships and struggles—men's insistence on fresh tortillas on demand and its enslaving consequences for women's work and physical movements—with a changing field of technological, political, and ideological possibility. Not only did the *molino* represent an alternate technical means of transforming *nixtamal* into *masa*. It also demonstrated the ways the politics of revolution and the ideology of progress could foster ambivalence and splits among men that undercut unity and stubbornness in struggles over specific gender conventions of the Old Regime. As we have seen, the Cárdenas administration saw in the *molinos* and in electric generators an opportunity to foster progress—to provide benefits that improved the quality of rural life and, in the process, to build rural political clienteles and integrate villages into the revolutionary nation-state. Within the villages the power of the ideology of progress and its accompanying politics of revolution eventually bred the factionalism and uncertainty that wears down resistance. By the late 1930s, women's interest in the *molino* could merge with male drives for progress that placed *molino* opponents in a more defensive, reactionary position. In the process cultural argument over the *metate* versus the *molino* had taken on a complex, crosscutting quality. It had become in part an argument between subaltern women and men over family food, economics, and morality and in part an argument about progress and future directions that ran through popular culture as a whole.

The male opponents of switching to the *molino* method of grinding *nixtamal* were right to fear a wider unsettling effect on the social relations and conventions of gender. But the spin-off effects did not necessarily coincide with those envisioned by the men. The evidence seems to point not to a surge in unsupervised female leisure time and sexual freedom but to a reallocation of female labor and to a subtle opening of decision-making space to youths on questions of marriage and residence.

On the one hand, lessening enslavement to the *metate* implied that women could reallocate labor time toward earning additional income for their families. Some of these activities represented an amplification of traditional female pursuits. In Morelos, for example, the incorporation of *molino* and sewing machine technology into household practice meant that women could devote greater time to tending fruit and vegetable gardens, raising chickens and pigs, sewing and knitting clothes, and peddling produce, animals, clothes, food, and other products in urban markets such as Cuernavaca. Some activities represented more of a departure into new forms of female wage labor. In Michoacán in the 1960s, for example, village women streamed into the strawberry packing plants in Zamora despite criticism by male villagers. A teasing *corrido* composed by two men in Quiringuicharo explicitly drew the connection between the wage labor of female destemming workers and the decline of domestic *metate* labor and symbolism: "They go to the cooling plant / to the destemming of the strawberry / but they go because / they're afraid of the *metate*."[24]

In addition to fostering reallocations of female labor toward old and new female income-earning pursuits, the decline of the *metate* contributed subtly toward a widening of marriage and residence options by youths. As long as subaltern women were enslaved to long and arduous hours at the *metate*, those who were too poor to hire a *molendera* could ameliorate or escape their condition mainly by acquiring young resident daughters-in-law to be trained in the duties of household service. The apprenticeship of the newly acquired servant would last for at least several years, until the new couple could establish a more independent residence within or beyond the family housing compound. The *metate*, in short, gave mothers incentive to press elder sons to marry young and to insist as well that the young couples follow the patrilocal residence patterns that provided labor assistance to female family elders. The connection struck Oscar Lewis when he studied the Pedro Martínez family economy and household dynamics in the late 1940s. "Had it not been for the mill," he noted, "Esperanza [de Martínez] would have long before insisted that Felipe, the eldest son, marry and bring home a daughter-in-law." None of Esperanza's sons provided their mother a resident daughter-in-law and household servant during her lifetime. The main economic value of sons to the home was the labor they could provide to the family patriarch or the weekly expense money they could contribute to the family budget.[25]

As mothers experienced declining incentives to press for customary marriage ages and residence arrangements by sons and acquired reasons of their own to believe in progress, the erosion of elder commitment to tradition could subtly open decision-making space for daughters. Indeed, mothers might envision their daughters' marital futures in terms explicitly different from the mothers' own life destinies. As Catalina, a Morelos villager who eventually moved to Cuernavaca, put it in the 1980s, "I'd married at seventeen and had six babies in nine years. . . . [A]fter I got married I was so busy with the children and doing what my husband wanted. . . . No, I didn't want Gloria to marry young as I had. I wanted her to have time for herself." For the mothers in Cuernavaca, many of them rural migrants, studied by Sarah LeVine and Clara Sunderland Correa in the 1980s, "time for herself" meant that a daughter acquired the education and independent employment experience that might enable her to support herself—to separate from an abusive husband or to survive abandonment by a negligent one. In earlier times, the mothers observed, their own parents considered female education a waste and focused parental pressure and energy mainly on steering young daughters toward a reasonably successful marriage.[26]

We have discussed the transition from *metate* to *molino* in some detail not only because it was important in its own right but also because it serves to illustrate several crucial themes: the contentiousness of shifts in major social conventions of gender; the importance of women's agency and aspirations within such processes; the strategic undermining of patriarchal tradition or opposition when women managed to conjoin long-standing grievances or desires with a rapidly shifting landscape of technology, politics, and culture; and the ripple effect whereby a transformation of one major social convention of gender yielded unsettling spin-offs in other areas of gendered life and power dynamics.

For our purposes we need not enter into similar detail regarding the other two major shifts we identified in the social conventions of gender. Suffice it to say that the ethnographic evidence of the mid- to late twentieth century leaves little doubt that these shifts have happened and that they had a corrosive effect on the patriarchal power dynamics of rural life. On the one hand, the patrilocal/domestic pathway of residence, work, and schooling that once constituted a rather hegemonic social convention of gender gave way to a grid of multiple pathways. Under the Old Regime a young woman's work and education unfolded as movement along a predominantly domestic and patrilocal pathway. In the home and under the supervision of a mother or mother-in-law, or as a domestic servant, a subaltern girl or young wife was trained in her role within the gendered division of labor and was constricted in her independent physical mobility. The interest of mothers-in-law in enforcing a patrilocal residence pattern that brought young wives into a servant role fit well with the pattern and also meant that family patriarchs could infuse their networks of dependents with youthful females and domestic workers even after their own daughters married or moved away. The results reinforced patriarchal authority and training. A young wife faced an imposing intergenerational triad of authority: the ruling family patriarch (her father-in-law), her immediate supervisor in labor and physical movements (her mother-in-law), and a patriarch in the making (her husband).

Among the poor a rural woman might outlive the patrilocal/domestic track and reach a semiautonomous position as a matriarch—a widow or family elder—with a measure of power and respect. But relatively few could step outside the patrilocal/domestic track at a young age—could aspire to a convent or other pathway of residence and work distant from father, husband, or *amasio*—without giving up cultural respectability and economic sustenance.

The evidence of the twentieth century suggests not that the patrilocal/domestic pathway disappeared but that it became reconfigured as one destiny within a grid of destinies and detours. We have already seen in the discussion of spin-offs of the transition from *metate* to *molino* that women's potential labor and income earning paths diversified and began to include reallocations of time and entry into newer forms of female wage labor as well as secretarial, teaching, and service positions. We saw, too, that the new context of female life cycle needs and available social and technical strategies subtly shifted mothers' attitudes regarding the necessity of resident daughters-in-law and the perils of too early a marriage by daughters. A heightened emphasis on formal schooling rather than domestic training came to be seen by parents as necessary and desirable to prepare a daughter for adulthood.[27] New forms of schooling and work, in turn, implied that young females escaped the direct vigilance of family elders and patriarchs for longer stretches of time and incorporated a circuit of travel, life experience, and detours that might include larger towns and cities and derail the plans and transactions of father-patriarchs.

The decline of patrilocal custom from hegemonic destiny into one among several trajectories of work, residence, and education was captured in the matter-of-fact language of Celia of San Antonio de Tepoztlán. "There are those wives who want to live with their mothers-in-law. Others prefer to live with their husbands in their own houses if they can afford it and still others continue living with their own mothers and bring their husbands into their houses." In these times, Celia noted with some exaggeration, a young woman even "has a choice of living alone if she wants, and no one bothers her." Just as important as the decline from hegemonic pathway to option within a grid of pathways was the shortening of patrilocal residence into a transitional expedient rather than a work-and-training experience that might last for years. In the mid-twentieth century Oscar Lewis observed that even when young couples followed patrilocal custom, they moved to set up independent households more quickly. One consequence was that young wives asserted their authority and desires more readily, and young husbands could not as easily mobilize immediate support by elders in the husbands' attempts to control or train wives.[28]

The third major shift we identified in social conventions of gender was the rise of male youth trajectories in work and politics that eroded elder influence. Put another way, the twentieth century witnessed a widening split in rural life between the symbolic deference or respect owed to fathers and elders, and the tangible power that real and metaphorical fathers wielded over younger men's behavior and life decisions in familial and community contexts. In the Old Regime, respect for elders was marked by a tighter unity of cultural symbolism with powers to sanction behavior. To be sure, generational tension and even open confrontations sometimes marred such authority and tainted the prestige of specific elders deemed parasites or tyrants inclined to excess. But the metaphorical language of good and bad authority also seemed to equate legitimate moral order with responsible exercise of power by wise paternal elders over appreciative youths in a generational pact of reciprocity and service among unequals. The cultural language of argument, in short, testified to the vital connection between the symbolism of father-elder superiority and the tangible decision-making powers of elders over youths. By the mid- to late twentieth century this sense of connection weakened. The cultural value of the symbolism acquired a certain hollow ring. The counsel and preoccupations of elder men, however much respected in theory and cultural etiquette, proved more irrelevant to the futures of young men.

The increasing ability of male youths to pursue life decisions outside the pathways of authority and property marked out by village patriarchs was captured, in familial context, in the resigned comment of a peasant father in Santa María (Morelos) when he was asked (ca. 1960) by the *novio* of his eloped daughter to consent to the customary formal marriage agreement among the youths' families. He shrugged off the importance in contemporary times of a familial alliance and patching up of appearances arranged after the fact. "I don't want any friends," he explained when he rejected formal transaction of male friendship and female exchange. "A father is not worth anything any more. Nowadays only the children arrange things. So go on arranging things yourselves." [29]

Of course the lament by elders that youths no longer listen obediently is a recurring refrain in history. But the ethnographic and migratory evidence does indeed point to the elders' loosening grip, at once personal, familial, and political. The authority of the familial father no longer received cultural echo and backing by the authority of the metaphorical village father. Consider Pedro Martínez's lament that young men were no longer interested in politics, at least not the politics of village need and destiny that had preoccupied local elders and earned them leading roles in local life. "The new generation in my village has opened its eyes to other things but not to politics. When one talks about what is good for the *municipio* or for them, the young people don't come around to listen. Only the old ones do. Nowadays we even shout through a microphone to the young people, but they pay no attention to it. Even the cooperative work parties are falling into disuse." The elders might receive polite respect in face-to-face encounters, but they seemed headed toward an indifference to their counsel and direction. This indifference was far more subversive than open disrespect. [30]

The transition from the *metate* to the *molino* in women's food production; the movement from a hegemonic patrilocal/domestic track to a grid of multiple tracks in female youths' residence, work, and schooling; and the development of male youth trajectories less receptive and less vulnerable to counsel by peasant and village metafathers were facilitated not only by the initiatives and agency of women and youths, but also by a dramatically shifting terrain of technology, politics, and culture. This shifting terrain not only implied new potential alliances and political spaces that cracked open previous structures of gendered authority; it also bred a powerful discourse of progress. The sense that rural folk needed to discover and incorporate the world of progress into their own worlds if they or their children were to advance to a better life imparted a certain ambivalence even to the views of patriarchs determined to exercise an unbroken dominance of wives, *amasias*, and children. Life had to change anyway. The power of the rural discourse of progress informed the wondrous words of José Arcadio Buendía, the fictional patriarch of Gabriel García Márquez's Macondo. "Incredible things are happening in the world," he exclaimed. "Right there, across the river, there are all kinds of magical equipment, while we go on living like donkeys."[31]

The wonders of progress were captured, too, in the ambivalence of Pedro Martínez's life history. Consider each of our three examples of shifting gender conventions. First, the male villagers of Tepoztlán had generally resisted the initial *molino* experiments, saw their defeat as "the revolution of the women against the authority of the men," and worried that leisure might lead to female independence and treachery. Pedro Martínez certainly agreed that women had to be steered away from independent time or pleasures and that it was better to tie them to drudgery. But the *molino* also represented progress. Whatever his initial inclinations, after the new social convention of food production had taken hold, Pedro Martínez reconstructed his memory of the early years on terms that aligned him unambivalently with the forces of progress. In *his* family, at least, things had been different. He had urged Esperanza to break with her stubborn traditionalism — "she was not progressive, not industrious" — and try out the new machine. Second, the transition to a grid of female residence, work, and schooling options circumscribed the effective authority and surveillance powers exercised by patriarch-fathers over their daughters, and this infuriated Pedro Martínez. Yet the redemptive powers of education and progress proved so strong that Pedro worked for several years as a servile peon — a life condition he found detestable and humiliating, a throwback to prerevolutionary suffering — so that his daughter Conchita could travel to a decent school and become a teacher. (Later, when Conchita got into trouble at school and a *novio* came to Tepoztlán to ask for her, Pedro beat Conchita hard, and she attempted suicide by ingesting malaria medicine and phosphorous from match tips. Another round of violence, fury, and eventual reconciliation also erupted when Conchita's first teaching job resulted in her impregnation by a village school principal.) Third, the declining grip of elders over youths troubled Pedro Martínez, who had adopted a domineering style over his sons and their labor and who ended up isolated in his old age. He found himself eating meals on his own — "buying my *tortillas* in the plaza, and eating my dinners in a little *fonda*" — and unable to count on regular expense money from the sons he had alienated. Yet the same domineering patriarch also proclaimed proudly that he had advanced his family by educating his sons, even at the cost of poverty and abandonment in old age.

"Your sons are illiterate while none of mine are," he told one critic. "Your sons help you and you can buy things but . . . what you have is nothing. You'll see how your sons will end up." Pedro Martínez, partly because of his own commitment to progress, had undermined his position as an aging peasant patriarch, and he knew it. "The truth is, my sons are not peasants any more. They don't even know where my cornfield is now!"[32]

THE RECONSTITUTION OF OLD DYNAMICS IN NEW SOCIAL CONTEXTS (II)

The paradox of deep continuities in gendered life and argument in times of transformation that injected rupture and fluidity into gendered life and argument begins to dissolve. As we have seen, the moorings that had supported regimes of patriarchal power in rural popular culture did indeed suffer attack and atrophy. The social conventions of gender that had once organized patriarchal power and that had structured a terrain of gender struggle gave way to new social conventions of gender. For the sake of argument we have focused on shifting social conventions within rural life. Yet it is important to observe that a focus on rural life alone understates the shifts in popular culture. As Mexico has moved toward a predominantly urban society, as subaltern women have gained prominence and experience in urban social movements, and as these experiences have promoted dialogues with activist youth, feminists, and intellectuals (in addition to sometimes contentious husbands and sexual partners), the political and cultural landscape of gendered claim and argument has undermined traditionalist expectations and social conventions even more sharply. It may now be possible to speak of a partial transition from cultural argument about mutuality among unequals, an argument about the absolute or contingent qualities of gender right within a vertically ordered world that divides male and female into distinct spheres and roles, toward cultural argument about mutuality among equals or near-equals, an argument about equity of right and duty among partner-companions in a world where male and female spheres and roles might overlap considerably.[33]

As the foundations of patriarchal power and confidence corroded, the same act of gender struggle and repression might take on a somewhat distinctive social meaning. What once expressed cultural prerogative and argument within a living regime of patriarchal power—one expected to extend indefinitely into the future and buttressed by metaphorical echoes in the realm of formal politics—might now express a desperate, compensatory attempt to shore up or reassert authority within a patriarchal regime under siege. The vignettes and assertions that at first sight suggest the "fixity" of gendered life might represent instead an effort to reinvent or reconstitute fixity against an irresistible tide of change.[34] When a Pedro Martínez asserted an absolutist vision of patriarchal authority against the more conditional or contingent views asserted by his wife and children, and when a Pedro Martínez enforced such views by administering a beating, did he represent a living ghost who reincarnated the men and arguments of late colonial times? Or did he represent the desperate lashing out of a patriarch-elder swept along to cultural isolation, a death by social criticism and irrelevance?

We need not pose the question in quite such stark, mutually exclusive terms. On the one hand, social context redefines and reconstitutes the meaning of the traditional and the familiar. Vast social changes that undermine or threaten earlier regimes of power and order may lead persons — precisely to roll back, advance, or otherwise cope with transformations of power — to redeploy old dynamics of quarrel, claim, repression, and power. This reconstitution takes place on a new terrain of social meaning, function, and consequence. On the other hand, however distinctive the wider context that defines social meanings, in the face-to-face human relations and confrontations that often comprise cultural argument between women and men the immediate human meanings of old social acts, claims, and quarrels may bear strong resemblance to the immediate meanings of similar acts in other eras. The arguments about contingent and absolute right, the tactics of alliance and escalation, the presence of intimidation and violence, and the legitimizing and delegitimizing stereotypes of woman and man as human types might draw participants into dramas of reenactment whose most basic, immediate meanings seem strikingly continuous with earlier times, even if the participants were also aware of wider social changes that jeopardized the continuity of traditional authority.

In the gendered life histories of the Morelos villagers whom we have met in this chapter — a Pedro Martínez or an Esperanza or a Conchita, a Celsa or a Doña Zeferina or her daughter-in-law Juana — a flat conceptual contrast between change and continuity in gendered life and quarrel seems profoundly misplaced. We must turn instead to a more subtle, interactive conceptualization. Reconstituted continuity becomes embedded within a changing regime of gendered power; implications of change become embedded within apparent traditional practice.[35]

The ghosts of the late colonial past are both illusionary and real. The macroanalyst steps back to see the illusion of the continuity thesis; the microanalyst steps forward to see its authenticity. The long view captures the changing field or context of gendered drama; the close-up view scrutinizes the inner meaning of human struggles for control. The person of doubled vision will integrate both truths, both perspectives, within a vision of change and reconstitution.

Let us conclude our journey with the cultural mythologies that encode historical experience. The grip of historical ghost and memory is strong in Mexico, and it mingles with mythological archetypes through which Mexican intellectuals constructed a sense of Mexican manhood, womanhood, and nationality in the twentieth century. One reason our journey in this book matters and may provoke controversy is precisely that it taps into cultural mythologies at the heart of Mexican reflections on the meaning of *mexicanidad*.

Among the mythological archetypes of the Mexican woman, the two most widely diffused and celebrated in intellectual writings by men are the figure of the violated woman who is also a traitor, and therefore unworthy of trust or protection, and the figure of the devoted mother-servant who provides ceaseless loyalty and service, forgiveness and understanding. The violated traitor-woman is the historically rooted figure of La Malinche or Malintzin, the indigenous woman who played a strong role in the Spanish conquest as a diplomatic go-between and translator and as Cortés's consort. Given the coercive dynamics of the Spanish conquest and Malintzin's language skills, she probably had no alternative to sexual possession by a Spaniard and to service as an intermediary of some sort. Given the pre-Hispanic dynamics of indigenous politics and exchange of women and her personal subjection to interethnic exchange and enslavement before the arrival of Cortés, she had no reason to adhere to Aztec/Mexica interests and plenty of reason to take on a role in the conquest era more active and engaged than mere acquiescence to coercive pressure. In short, in the cultural mythology that encodes an archetype of woman, La Malinche has served as a powerful symbol conjoining the themes of woman's violation and woman's treachery into the image of woman's deserved violation. The other common representation of the violated traitor is La Chingada, "The Fucked One," a conversion of the historically rooted mythology of La Malinche into a more universal Mexican archetype beyond specific historical moments or individuals.[36]

The archetype that encodes the total devotion of a mother-servant has also taken two common forms. The sacred representation is the desexed figure of La Virgen de Guadalupe, the Indian Virgin Mary who appeared miraculously in early colonial times to symbolize the Virgin's specific protection of and devotion to Mexico's indigenous and mestizo peoples. La Virgen captures the notion that the perfect woman is a sacred creature whose attributes lie beyond human reach. She is desexed yet generative, deserving of service yet understanding of human foibles. No woman in real life, with the possible exception of a mythologized and long-suffering mother who has abandoned a sexual existence, can begin to approximate the sacred image of La Virgen. The profane, more sexualized representation of female devotion is the image of the revolutionary *soldadera*—the female camp follower who accompanied the revolutionary armies. Totally devoted notwithstanding the hardship of war or the abusiveness of her man, the *soldadera* provides food and provisions, labor and sex, and if necessary, protection in the form of spying or fighting.[37]

These female archetypes encode a male-stream vision of womanhood and gender experience in Mexican history and civilization. Only recently have they undergone a project of reclaiming and reinterpretation by feminist intellectuals in Mexico and the Mexican diaspora.[38] As with the Mesoamerican god who transforms readily into multiple specific forms, these representations in some ways merge or, more precisely, depict distinct aspects and dimensions of a single being: Mexican Woman. As Roger Bartra put it, "This archetype of the Mexican woman is the duality Malintzin-Guadalupe. It is Chingadalupe."[39] Inside every devoted, forgiving, long-suffering mother or *soldadera* there dwells the latent Malinche or Chingada. Chingadalupe prevails precisely because women cannot live up to the ideal prescribed for them and are prone to immoral treachery. The Malinche/Chingada archetype encodes what men ought to expect if they fail to control their women; the Virgen/*soldadera* archetype encodes an idealized womanhood of devoted suffering that few real women can match.

These female archetypes, however, are not the only such encodings of gender experience and expectation in Mexico. Less celebrated in the formal cultural writings of male intellectuals but truer to the spirit of this historical study and its findings is the figure of La Llorona, the "Weeping Woman." The story of this haunted female ghost spirit takes several forms and continues to evolve, but the background event that sparks La Llorona's suffering is normally an act of betrayal that sparks anger. Often it is the adultery by a mate of similar color-class standing (although occasionally a betrayal by a social superior). Almost always La Llorona has responded to her troubles with the most chilling and destructive act available to a woman — the killing of her children. Overcome with grief and pain, La Llorona becomes a powerful, dangerous, weeping monster-spirit who cannot rest and who haunts the night in search of her lost children.[40]

The La Llorona legend is a tale told by mothers and grandmothers to their children in Mexico and the greater Mexican diaspora. A version of it is found in historical documents of central Mexico as early as the sixteenth century; Chicana schoolgirls in Watsonville, California, recounted it with relish in 1991 while schoolboys fidgeted. It is La Llorona—not La Malinche or La Chingada, not La Virgen or *la soldadera*—who is the most favored female archetype in the female-headed oral traditions of Mexican popular culture.[41]

The tale of La Llorona is chilling and scary. At one level, of course, it is simply a fine night fright and admonition story, told with the occasional playful touch: "Psst . . . don't go out! La Llorona might get you!" But its roots run deep and wide in Mexican time and space; its meanings seem to tap the cultural imagination. Among the multiple meanings of La Llorona is not only a metaphor about the historical orphanhood of the Mexican people (the children sought by the grief-stricken mother), but also a warning about the dangerous consequences of betrayal and, most especially, the betrayal of a mother or a wife. The betrayed woman may turn out to harbor a secret desire for a horrible revenge; she may acquire supernatural powers and form that destroy the tranquility of the living; she may suddenly rush up to seize the wayward person who ventures out at night alone.

Yet what La Llorona seeks — and this, too, is part of the message — is not permanent estrangement from her kin and the world of the living, but rebirth and redemption, reconciliation within a new cycle of life. La Llorona seeks a world without betrayals, a world with a distinct balance or reciprocity, even a distinct balance of gendered power. La Llorona characteristically searches for her lost children near bodies of water or during the rains. The life-giving waters of the Mexican gods (the "female" Chalchihuitlicue and the "male" Tlaloc) herald fertilization and rebirth, the start of a renewed round of life. It is in the places and seasons of water, of rebirth and renewal, that La Llorona dares to hope that estrangement will give way to unity, that affliction will give way to reconciliation.[42]

The dream of reconciliation remains elusive. In selecting La Llorona as a preferred female archetype, Mexican women express a truth, at once historical and contemporary, of life and struggle in the vast bottoms of the Mexican color-class pyramid. For what became painfully evident to me in the subways and bars and markets, in the home life and street life and work life, in the Mexico of the 1980s was the truth of that encoding. La Llorona — dangerous yet weeping, powerful yet betrayed, restless and vengeful yet desirous of reconciliation — still haunts the Mexican night.

Tables

TABLE 2.1 Racial Population Estimates in Late Colonial Times: Morelos, Oaxaca, and Mexico City

Region	Year(s)	Indians Percent	Castas/ Blacks Percent	Whites Percent	Regional Population (Total No.)
Morelos	1800–1803	62.5	29.8[a]	7.7	89,839
Oaxaca					
Study area	1793	95.1	1.2	3.7	165,965
Intendancy	1793	88.3	5.3	6.3	411,336
Mexico City	1803	24.1	26.6[b]	49.3	ca. 137,000

Sources: For Morelos, AGN, Tributos, vol. 43, exp. 9, año 1805, fols. 271–93 (cf. Gerhard 1972: 93, 97, 104, 294), with supplementation by sources listed in note below; for Oaxaca, AGN, Historia, vol. 523, año 1793, esp. fol. 94r (cf. Reina 1988a, 187–92; AGN, Tributos, vol. 43, exp. 9, año 1805); for Mexico City, Humboldt 1811, vol. 2, bk. 3, chap 8, 81–88, esp. 82 (cf. vol. 4, note C, 291–98; AGN, Historia, vol. 72, exp. 24).

Notes: The Morelos estimate, the most tedious to construct, relied on the following applications. The population of the Morelos region was defined as the sum of the following districts: Cuautla Amilpas, Cuernavaca, the Morelos portion of Chalco y Tlayacapa (i.e., the Tlayacapa zone), and Tetela. The ratio of mulatto tributaries to total black/mulatto families in Cuautla Amilpas (2.24, based on AGN, Padrones, vol. 8, año 1791, fols. 3–264, as modified by growth rates given in Gerhard 1972, 93) was applied to Cuernavaca; the ratio of black/mulatto population to other castas for Cuernavaca was considered midway (1.04) between the poles of Cuautla Amilpas (1.77) and the Morelos portion of Chalco (.30); the Morelos portion of Chalco was considered 24.2 percent of the Chalco district (based on data in AGN, Tierras, vol. 1518, exp. 1 [año 1770], fols. 28–33); the ratio of blacks/mulattos to other castas (.30) that prevailed for the Morelos portion of Chalco was applied to Tetela; where "other castas"/"españoles" were combined into one category, they were disaggregated by applying the proportions from Cuautla Amilpas (39.8 percent españoles; from AGN, Padrones, vol. 8, año 1791, fols. 3–264). To convert family totals into individuals for non-Indians (for which individual figures were not always available in the 1800–1803 censuses used), the multiplier for black/mulatto in Tetela was that derived from the Morelos portion of Chalco (3.68, based on the 1800 census); the multiplier for "other castas"/"españoles" in all four Morelos districts, 1800–1803, was that derived from Cuautla Amilpas ratio in 1791 (3.42; from AGN, Padrones, vol. 8, fols. 3–264). It is noteworthy that the differential multipliers used to convert families into total populations do not change the ethnoracial proportions much. For families, the shares are 58.3 percent Indian, 33.9 percent castas/blacks (22.0 percent blacks/mulattos; 11.9 percent mestizos/other castas), and 7.8 percent whites/españoles.

The study zones for Oaxaca were the Mixteca Alta, defined as the Teposcolula and Nochistlán districts; the south-central Zapotec Valley, excluding Antequera and the Etla Valley, defined as districts of Mitla y Tlacolula, Zimátlan, half of Cuatro Villas, and half of Corregimiento; and the Villa Alta district within the Sierra Zapoteca. For further discussion, see Chapter 2, n. 45. For all districts, the figures given for priests, monks, and nuns were added to the español/white figures.

[a] Within this group, the mulatto/black estimate is 18.2 percent, and the mestizo/other castas estimate is 11.6 percent.

[b] Within this group, the mulatto/black estimate is 7.3 percent, and the mestizo/other castas estimate is 19.3 percent.

TABLE 3.1 Deviance Markers in Violence Cases: Late Colonial Morelos

Marker	No.	Percent	N (total valid cases)
ASSAILANTS			
Loners rather than family-attached	40[a]	27.6[b]	145
Previous arrest	28	19.3[c]	145
Previous arrest for violence	8	5.5	145
TARGETS			
Loners rather than family-attached	23	17.0	135
CIRCUMSTANCES			
Late-night hours	15[d]	12.7	118
Isolated spot	25[e]	14.3[e]	175
Assailant-target relation: strangers	32	16.2	198

Sources: PDBO, Morelos, Powviol.out, pp. 97, 70; Powviol3.out, p. 70; Powviol2.out, p. 46 (cf. p. 27); Powviol1.out, pp. 14, 26. For regional loner and family-attached calculation for n. a below, AGN, Tributos, vol. 43, exp. 9, fol. 267r.

[a]Among the 105 family-attached individuals, 93 (88.6 percent) were married, and the remainder were dependent minors.

[b]For the Morelos tributary adult population as a whole, the loner share is estimated at 22.8 percent (for the male-only tributary adult population, the estimate is 23.7 percent).

Estimates of family-attached and loners percentages are based on the 1800–1803 censuses for Chalco de Morelos (calculated as a 24.2 percent share of Chalco totals, in accord with the ratio explained in Table 2.1), Cuautla Amilpas, and Cuernavaca districts. Loners were people recorded in the *viudas y solteras* and *viudos y solteros* columns. Family-attached persons were those recorded in the columns designated *casados con sus iguales* (multiplied by two), *casados sin edad* (multiplied by two), *casados con otras castas*, and *mujeres de casados con otras castas*. The following columns were ambiguous on family-attached versus loner status and hence did not enter the calculation: *caciques, gobernadores, reservados, ausentes,* and *próximos a tributar*. The *niños y niñas* column was deleted because it emphasizes children younger than the youth and adults in the assailant population.

[c]If one excludes individuals subjected previously only to harassment arrests for vagrancy or drunkenness, the figure drops to 16.6 percent.

[d]Late-night hours are between about 10:00 P.M. and the next morning's wake-up. The majority of incidents (54.2 percent) took place during morning and afternoon hours. Evening after dusk but before late night accounted for the balance (33.1 percent).

[e]An additional ten incidents (5.7 percent) were cases where the degree of isolation was ambiguous. Nearly half the incidents (45.7 percent) took place in indoor settings, whether public gatherings in bars, homes, the workplace, and the like, or more "private" domestic settings; outdoor settings near people or homes in villages, estates, and rancho settlements accounted for another third (34.3 percent).

TABLE 3.2 Drinking and Violence: Late Colonial Morelos

Importance of Drinking	Assailants		Targets	
	No.[a]	Percent	No.[b]	Percent
Unimportant	111	64.9	131	78.2
Ambiguous	22	13.1	17	10.3
Important	35	20.8	17	10.3
Distributions				
Homicidal cases				
Drinking important				
or ambiguous	41	43.6	28	31.8
Drinking unimportant	53	56.4	60	68.2
Nonhomicidal cases				
Drinking important				
or ambiguous	16	21.6	6	7.8
Drinking unimportant	58	78.4	71	92.2
Odds ratio				
Odds that case is				
homicidal when				
drinking matters[c]	2.8:1		5.5:1	

Sources: PDBO, Morelos, Powvioli.out, p. 27; Morhom2, pt. 1, pp. 9, 10.
[a] $N = 168$ total valid cases.
[b] $N = 165$ total valid cases.
[c] Chi-square significance was .0047 for assailants, .0003 for targets.

T A B L E 3.3 Sociocultural Profiles of Assailants and Targets: Late Colonial Morelos

	Assailants[a]			Targets[b]		
Ethnicity	No.	Percent	Regional Population Percent	No.	Percent	Regional Population Percent
Indians	91	55.5	62.5	94	65.3	62.5
Castas	44	26.8[c]	29.8	39	27.1[d]	29.8
Whites	29	17.7	7.7	11	7.6	7.7

			Cumulative			Cumulative
Class/Status	No.	Percent	Percent	No.	Percent	Percent
DISAGGREGATED SHARES						
Totally destitute	1	0.6	0.6			
Low peasant	81	48.2	48.8	76	46.6	46.6
High peasant	18	10.7	59.5	12	7.4	54.0
Low peasant/ plebeian	8	4.8	64.3	14	8.6	62.6
High peasant/ plebeian	1	0.6	64.9	7	4.3	66.9
Low plebeian	32	19.0	83.9	37	22.7	89.6
High plebeian	12	7.1	91.1	9	5.5	95.1
Privileged	15	8.9	100.0	8	4.9	100.0
AGGREGATED SUBTOTALS BY PEASANT/PLEBEIAN[e]						
Peasants (restricted)	99	62.3		88	62.0	
Peasants (amplified)	108	64.3		109	66.9	
Plebeians (restricted)	44	27.7		46	32.4	
Plebeians (amplified)	53	31.5		67	41.1	
AGGREGATED SUBTOTALS BY LOW/MIDDLING/HIGH						
Low: commoners/ *macehuales*	122	72.6		127	77.9	
Middling: upper peasants/plebeians	31	18.5		28	17.2	
High: privileged/elite	15	8.9		8	4.9	

Sources: PDBO, Morelos, Powviol3.out, pp. 66, 96; Powviol2.out, pp. 20, 45; Table 2.1 above.

Note: This table defines class position according to the household viewpoint rather than individual viewpoint variables as defined in the PDBO Codebook.

TABLE 3.3 (*continued*)

[a]For the assailant group, $n = 164$ valid cases for ethnic profile, $n = 168$ valid cases for class/status profile.

[b]For the target group, $n = 144$ valid cases for ethnic profile, $n = 163$ valid cases for class/status profile.

[c]The disaggregation of this category yields the following breakdown: "near-whites" (*castizos, moriscos,* etc.) = 5.5 percent; mestizos = 11.0 percent; mulattoes = 8.5 percent; other *castas* not specifically identified by preceding categories = 1.8 percent.

[d]The disaggregation of this category yields the following breakdown: "near-whites" = 4.2 percent; mestizos = 3.5 percent; mulattoes = 9.7 percent; other *castas* = 9.7 percent.

[e]The restricted model deletes overlapping peasant/plebeian categories and calculates percentage shares from the remaining group; the amplified model includes overlapping categories and calculates percentage shares accordingly. The overlapping peasant/plebeian categories include only those mixed cases for which one could not identify with confidence a predominantly peasant or predominantly plebeian household economy. Other mixed cases were assigned according to the predominant pattern of household economy.

TABLE 3.4 Sex and Age Distribution of Assailants and Targets:
Late Colonial Morelos

Gender	No.	Percent	Assailants[a] Percent Excluding Mixed	No.	Percent	Targets[b] Percent Excluding Mixed
Male	166	89.7	92.2	121	65.4	66.5
Female	14	7.6	7.8	61	33.0	33.5
Mixed[c]	5	2.7		3	1.6	

Age (years)	No.	Percent	Cumulative Percent	No.	Percent	Cumulative Percent
Under 15	1	0.9	0.9	6	9.8	9.8
15 to 24	32	27.8	28.7	12	19.7	29.5
25 to 34	49	42.6	71.3	21	34.4	63.9
35 to 44	24	20.9	92.2	9	14.8	78.7
Above 44	9	7.8	100.0	13	21.3	100.0

Median age	Assailants: 26.00		Targets: 30.00	
Mean age		29.66		31.84
Standard deviation		9.45		14.22

Sources: PDBO, Morelos, Powviol3.out, pp. 65, 98, 102; Powviol2.out, pp. 20, 47, 51; cf. Powviol1.out, pp. 14, 20.

Note: The number of valid cases for gender was slightly less than 206 for technical reasons related to eliminating double counting in cases involving multiple assailants and/or targets. If one analyzes the data by incident rather than by individual, the differences are negligible.

The large number of missing values (70 for assailants, 124 for targets) limits the range of implication to be drawn from the age data, and the absence of comparable age group studies for regional populations of late colonial Mexico makes comparison with age groups in the general population unfeasible. What may be seen here is the degree of age spread among those whose ages were given and recorded and, in particular, the wider spread (evident in the standard deviation figures) in the target group. On the complexity and methodology of age group analysis in colonial Mexico, see Cook and Borah 1971–79, 1:201–99.

[a] For assailant group, $n = 185$ valid cases for gender profile, $n = 115$ valid cases for age profile.
[b] For target group, $n = 185$ valid cases for gender profile, $n = 61$ valid cases for age profile.
[c] Refers to mixed-gender bands of assailants or targets.

TABLE 3.5 Disaggregated Motives of Violent Dispute:
Late Colonial Morelos

Short Description	No.[a]	Percent	Cumulative Percent
01. Male-female dispute over patriarchal right/obligation	47	24.1	24.1
02. Male-male dispute over claims in female (sex rivals, in-laws, etc.)	26	13.3	37.4
03. Female-female dispute over claims in male	1	.5	37.9
04. Assertions of masculinity by restricted definition: direct questioning of masculine honor or valor (excluding nos. 01, 02)	17	8.7	46.7
05. Assertions of masculinity by amplified definition: male bonding/honor frames interaction, but not in explicit dispute	22	11.3	57.9
06. Female defense of relatives/friends (excluding nos. 01, 03)	5	2.6	60.5
07. Female defense of feminine reputation, honor (excluding nos. 01, 03, 06)	1	0.5	61.0
08. Property/class dispute: issues of money/property/labor/debt/robbery	41	21.0	82.1
09. *Descarga* ventings by narrow definition: release of rage on easy or available target	0	0.0	82.1
10. Culturally casual or inexplicable: assailant is provoked, but the provocation seems inexplicable or trivial within the cultural milieu	3	1.5	83.6
11. No apparent motive: total drunkenness, accidental, etc. (excluding no. 09)	12	6.2	89.7
12. Other (excluding nos. 01–11, 13–14)	17	8.7	98.5
13. Female substitute for male target	3	1.5	100.0
14. Explicit ethnic hatred/confrontation[b]			
99. Unknown/missing value	11		

Source: PDBO, Morelos, Powviol.out, p. 29; Mormv1a.lis, pp. 5–6.

[a]N = 195 total valid cases (i.e., excluding 11 missing value cases listed as item 99 above).

[b]This category of motive was one I did not have to create until the coding of the Oaxaca materials and was therefore inapplicable in the Morelos case set.

Tables : 353

TABLE 3.6 Major Motives of Violent Dispute: Late Colonial Morelos

Motivation of Dispute	Restricted Model		Amplified Model		Midway Point
	No.[a]	Percent	No.[b]	Percent[b]	Percent[b]
Gender-rooted	97	49.7	122	62.6	56.2
Property/class	41	21.0	53	27.2	24.1
Descarga ventings	15	7.7	40	20.5	14.1
Other/miscellaneous	42	21.5	12	8.7	—

Definitions	Conceptual	Operational
GENDER-ROOTED		
Restricted model	Disputes in which a person's assertions/reponses directly focused on claims of gender right, masculinity, or femininity	Items 01–04, 06, 07 from Table 3.5
Amplified model	Same as restricted model	Same as restricted model, plus items 05, 13
PROPERTY/CLASS		
Restricted model	Disputes over money, property, debt, theft or over work or tributary claims in color-class relations of superiors/subordinates	Item 08 from Table 3.5
Amplified model	Same as restricted model	Same as restricted model, plus cases where item 08 is listed as a secondary motive
DESCARGA VENTINGS		
Restricted model	Ventings of anger/frustration on an available target in contexts that suggest casual violence bearing little specific motive or connection to the target	Items 09, 10, 11 from Table 3.5
Amplified model	Same as restricted model	Same as restricted model, plus items 05, 13[c]

TABLE 3.6 (*continued*)

Source: Adapted from PDBO, Morelos, Powviol.out, pp. 29–30.

[a]$N = 195$ total valid cases.

[b]Because the amplified models of major categories use generous criteria that create overlapping and ambiguous cases assigned to more than one category, the case numbers exceed 195 and the percentages exceed 100. The same logic applies to the percentages in the midway point column.

[c]In the amplified model of *descargas*, casual violence in gendered contexts of male bonding that lack confrontations over masculine honor as such (item 05 in Table 3.5) is treated as if it represents casual ventings without specific motivation. This is the case even though some of the cases are clearly not *descarga* (e.g., men defending relatives as part of their masculine and familial duty) and even though the violence occurs in contexts of heavily gendered behavior. Item 13 (from Table 3.5) plays a similar crossover role in the amplified model.

TABLE 3.7 Gender-Rooted Violence (Restricted Model) by Gender of Targets: Late Colonial Morelos

Distributions[a]	Male Targets		Female Targets	
	No.	Percent	No.	Percent
Gender-rooted	42	32.3	52	86.7
Not gender-rooted	88	67.7	8	13.3

ODDS RATIO [b]

Odds that case is gender-rooted
  when target is female, compared to
  odds if target is male   13.6:1

Source: PDBO, Morelos, Newhyp01.lis, p. 39.

[a]$N = 190$ total valid cases.

[b]Chi-square significance was .0000; Phi, .51; Lambda with gender-rooted violence dependent, .47; Yule's Q, .86.

TABLE 3.8 Major Motives of Male-on-Male Violent Dispute:
Late Colonial Morelos

Motivation of Dispute	Restricted Model No.[a]	Restricted Model Percent	Amplified Model No.[b]	Amplified Model Percent[b]	Midway Point Percent[b]
Gender-rooted	37	34.3	59	54.6	44.5
Property/class	27	25.0	33	30.6	27.8
Descarga ventings	13	12.0	35	32.4	22.2
Other/miscellaneous	31	28.7	9	8.3	—

Sources: Adapted from PDBO, Morelos, Mormv1a.lis, pp. 30–31; for male-on-male amplified property/class share, Powpat data entry for Case IDs 2, 73, 123, 124, 125, 153, 184, 194, 195, 224, 230, 246.
Note: For definitions of major motive categories, see Table 3.6.
[a] N = 108 total valid cases.
[b] Because the amplified models of major categories use generous criteria that create overlapping and ambiguous cases assigned to more than one category, the case numbers exceed 108 and the percentages exceed 100. The same logic applies to the percentages in the midway point column.

TABLE 3.9 Family Status of Female Targets of Violence:
Late Colonial Morelos

Family Status	Female Targets of Violence No.[a]	Female Targets of Violence Percent	Tributary Adult Population Percent (all)	Tributary Adult Population Percent (females only)
Family-attached	48[b]	84.2	77.2	78.1
Loners	9[c]	15.8	22.8	21.9

Source: PDBO, Morelos, Newhypol.sup, p. 160.
Note: Estimates of family-attached and loners percentages for the Morelos region follow the procedures and use the source specified in Table 3.1 above.
[a] N = 57 total valid cases (i.e., 5 missing values).
[b] Among these 48 cases, 37 (64.9 percent of all valid cases) were married individuals; the remaining 11 (19.3 percent of all valid cases) were dependent minors.
[c] Among these 9 cases, 7 (12.3 percent of all valid cases) were widows and may therefore have lived with children and been "family-attached" in the broader sense (notwithstanding the apparent absence of supervising patriarchs or familial elders).

TABLE 3.10 Assailant/Target Relationships: Late Colonial Morelos

Assailant/Target Relationship	Female Targets		All Targets	
	No.[a]	Percent	No.[b]	Percent
PRIMARY	38	63.3	57	28.8
01. Spouse (legal or common-law)	20	33.3	21	10.6
02. Sex partner or concubine (excluding 01)	11	18.3	12	6.1
03. Kin (excluding 01, 02; including fictive kin, in-laws)	6	10.0	15	7.6
04. *Novios* (sweetheart/betrothed)	1	1.7	1	0.5
05. Very close friend (quasi-familial)	0	0.0	8	4.0
SECONDARY	19	31.7	109	55.1
06. Sex rival	1	1.7	10	5.1
07. Friend, known acquaintance	18	30.0	99	50.0
TERTIARY	3	5.0	32	16.2
08. Strangers	3	5.0	32	16.2

Sources: PDBO, Morelos, Newhypo1.sup, p. 160 (cf. Powhypo2, pp. 22–23); Powviol1.out, p. 26.
[a] N = 60 total valid cases.
[b] N = 198 total valid cases.

TABLE 3.11 Assailant/Target Relationships by Gender of Targets: Late Colonial Morelos

Relationship[a]	Male Targets		Female Targets	
	No.	Percent	No.	Percent
Inner primary	2	1.5	32	53.3
Outer primary	17	12.8	6	10.0
Secondary	88	66.2	19	31.7
Tertiary	26	19.5	3	5.0

ODDS RATIOS:[b]

Odds that relationship is X if female
target, compared to odds if male

X = Primary	10.4:1
X = Inner primary[c]	20+:1
X = Outer primary[d]	1:1.3
X = Secondary[e]	1:4.2
X = Tertiary[f]	1:4.6

Source: PDBO, Morelos, Morofvil.lis, p. 24.

[a] N = 193 total valid cases.

[b] For refined model, Chi-square significance was .000; Cramer's V, .64; Lambda with target's gender dependent, .50; Yule's Q on inner primary odds ratio, .90+. Listing the inner primary odds ratio as 20+ compensates for a deceptively high actual figure (74.9; Yule's Q, .97); see Chapter 3, n. 39, for additional explanation.

[c] Spouses, sex partners/concubines, or *novios*

[d] Other kin (including fictive kin and in-laws) and very close (quasi-familial) friends

[e] Friends, acquaintances, or sex rivals

[f] Strangers (unknown to each other before incident)

TABLE 4.1 Motives of Violence against Female Targets:
Late Colonial Morelos

Motive of Dispute	Restricted Case Set[a]		Expanded Case Set[b]		Midway Percent
	No.	Percent	No.	Percent	
RESTRICTED MODEL[c]					
Sexual claims[d]	30	48.4	46	49.5	49.0
Nonsexual gender claims[e]	19	30.6	31	33.3	32.0
Total female insubordination	2	3.2	2	2.2	2.7
Attacked to dishonor a man	3	4.8	5	5.4	5.1
Nongendered altercations and miscellaneous	8	12.9	9	9.7	11.3
AMPLIFIED MODEL[f]					
Sexual claims	35	56.5	56	60.2	58.4
Nonsexual gender claims[g]	25	40.3	36	38.7	39.5
Total female insubordination	2	3.2	2	2.2	2.7
Attacked to dishonor a man	3	4.8	5	5.4	5.1
Nongendered altercations and miscellaneous	8	12.9	9	9.7	11.3

Sources: Adapted from PDBO, Morelos, Powvioli.out, p. 33; Powmorei.sys, p. 34.

[a]The restricted case set is limited to the incidents of violence against female targets that led to criminal proceedings ($n = 62$ total valid cases).

[b]The expanded case set adds to the restricted case set incidents that *could* have led to criminal violence proceedings ($n = 93$ total valid cases). This case set was useful for consistency checks against the restricted case set.

[c]The restricted model of motives lists cases by prime motive rather than the sum of prime and near-prime motives.

[d]For a breakdown by type of sexual conflict, see Table 4.2.

[e]Within this category the leading disputes were over physical mobility or abuse (15.6 percent midway share) and labor or economic obligations (8.1 percent midway share). The remainder (8.4 percent) was made up of verbal affronts, attacks on female defense of relatives, and miscellaneous gender claims. The amplified model yields similar results.

[f]The amplified model of motives includes both prime and near-prime motives for classification of a given incident. It therefore allows for overlapping and proxy motive cases and leads to percentages adding up to more than 100.

[g]Within this category the leading disputes were over physical mobility or abuse (21.6 percent midway share) followed by labor or economic obligations (10.8 percent) and verbal affronts (8.6 percent).

TABLE 4.2 Sexual Disputes in Violence against Female Targets:
Late Colonial Morelos

| Type of Sexual Dispute | Restricted Case Set[a] | | Expanded Case Set[b] | | Midway |
	No.	Percent	No.	Percent	Percent
Sexual assault[c]	14	40.0	18	32.1	36.1
Celos: all cases[d]	17	48.6	34	60.7	54.7
Male *celos*	12	34.3	18	32.1	33.2
Female *celos*	8	22.9	19	33.9	28.4
Male *celos* as percentage of celos		70.5		52.9	61.7
Female *celos* as percentage of *celos*		47.1		55.9	51.5
Other/miscellaneous[e]	4	11.4	4	7.1	9.3

Sources: Adapted from PDBO, Morelos, Powviol1.out, pp. 36–37; Powmore1.sys, pp. 37–38.

[a]The restricted case set is limited to the incidents of sexual or sexually motivated violence against female targets that led to criminal proceedings ($n = 35$ total valid cases).

[b]The expanded case set adds to the restricted set incidents that could have led to criminal violence proceedings. This case set was useful to check consistency ($n = 56$ total valid cases).

[c]The numbers given exclude two cases where sexual assault took place "after the fact," as a kind of epilogue to attacks made initially for other reasons (e.g., assault to commit robbery). The percentage figures would not diverge significantly if these cases had been included.

[d]Because of overlapping male and female *celos* cases, the total number of *celos* cases is 17 rather than 20 for the restricted set and 34 rather than 37 for the augmented set. For the same reason, male *celos* as percentage of all *celos* and female *celos* as percentage of all *celos* add up to more than 100.

[e]This category includes three cases of kidnapping with an eye on eventual sexual conquest or marriage and one case of violence against a class inferior for alleged illicit sex.

TABLE 4.3 Plausible and Imaginary *Celos* by Gender of Accuser:
Late Colonial Morelos

Quality of Accusation[a]	Male *Celos*		Female *Celos*	
	No.	Percent	No.	Percent
Plausible	7	41.2	15	83.3
Imaginary	10	58.8	3	16.7

ODDS RATIO: [b]

Odds of plausibility if female
  celos, compared to odds if
    male *celos*   7.1:1

Source: Adapted from PDBO, Morelos, Powmore1.sys, pp. 37–38.
[a] $N = 35$ total valid cases.
[b] Chi-square significance, .026; Phi, .44; Lambda with accuser's gender dependent, .41; Yule's Q, .75.

TABLE 7.1 Male Assailants and Violent Dispute, Major Motives:
Late Colonial Morelos

Motivation of Dispute	Restricted Model		Amplified Model[a]		Midway Point
	No.	Percent	No.	Percent	Percent
MALE ASSAILANT CASES[b]					
Gender-rooted	90	52.9	115	67.6	60.3
Property/class	29	17.1	39	22.9	20.0
Descarga ventings	14	8.2	39	22.9	15.6
Other/miscellanenous	37	21.8	12	7.1	—
MALE-ON-MALE CASES[c]					
Gender-rooted	37	34.3	59	54.6	44.5
Property/class	27	25.0	33	30.6	27.8
Descarga ventings	13	12.0	35	32.4	22.2
Other/miscellaneous	31	28.7	9	8.3	—

Sources: PDBO, Morelos, Mormv1a.lis, pp. 5–6, 30–31; Table 3.6 above; Powpat data entry outputs for Variables 10, 22, 46 (for amplified property/class frequencies).

Note: For definitions of major motive categories, see Table 3.6.

[a] Because the amplified models of major categories use generous criteria that create overlapping and ambiguous cases assigned to more than one category, the case numbers exceed 108 and the percentages exceed 100. The same logic applies to the percentages in the "midway point" column.

In the amplified model of *descargas*, casual violence in gendered contexts of male bonding that lack confrontations over masculine honor as such (item 05 in Table 3.5) is treated as if it represents casual ventings without specific motivation. This is the case even though some of the cases are clearly not *descarga* (e.g., men defending relatives as part of their masculine and familial duty) and even though the violence occurs in contexts of heavily gendered behavior. Item 13 (from Table 3.5) plays a similar crossover role.

[b] $N = 170$ total valid cases.

[c] $N = 108$ total valid cases.

TABLE 7.2 Social Expressions of Masculinity: Late Colonial Morelos

Social Contexts/Motives	No.	Percent of All Cases	Percent of Masculinity Cases
MALE ASSAILANT CASES [a]			
Male-female relations [b]	76	44.7	66.1
Male honor [c]	17	10.0	14.8
Background bonding/honor [d]	22	12.9	19.1
Total: cumulative social expression of masculinity	115	67.6	100.0
MALE-ON-MALE CASES [e]			
Male-female relations [b]	23	21.3	39.0
Male honor [c]	14	13.0	23.7
Background bonding/honor [d]	22	20.4	37.3
Total: cumulative social expression of masculinity	59	54.6	100.0

Source: Adapted from PDBO, Morelos, Mormv1a.lis, pp. 5–6, 30–31.

[a] N = 170 valid cases.

[b] Male-female relations refer to disputes directly connected to male claims in or social relations with specific women or female youth.

[c] Male honor refers to disputes over masculine honor, valor, or status as such in male-centered social contexts. It excludes manhood challenges linked to specific male-female relations.

[d] Background bonding/honor refers to conflicts in which a background of masculine social bonding or honor frames the context of interaction, but in which masculine honor or valor as such is not the explicit issue in dispute.

[e] N = 108 valid cases.

TABLE 7.3 "Tangibles" and "Intangibles" in Male Violence:
Preliminary Model, Late Colonial Morelos

	Male Assailant Cases[a]		Male-on-Male Cases[b]	
	No.	Percent	No.	Percent
"TANGIBLES"				
Gender-rooted, linked to				
male-female rights/claims	76	44.7	23	21.3
Property/class disputes	29	17.1	27	25.0
Total	105	61.8	50	46.3
"INTANGIBLES"				
Restricted Model				
Descarga ventings	14	8.2	13	12.0
Male-centered honor	17	10.0	14	13.0
Total	31	18.2	27	25.0
Amplified Model				
Restricted model total	31	18.2	27	25.0
Indirect/amplified model				
cases of honor-*descarga*[c]	22	12.9	22	20.4
Total	53	31.2	49	45.4

Source: Adapted from Tables 7.1 and 7.2.
[a] $N = 170$ total valid cases.
[b] $N = 108$ total valid cases.
[c] These cases are the "background bonding/honor" cases of Table 7.2 that may arguably be considered additional (and overlapping) honor-*descarga* episodes if one uses elastic criteria.

TABLE 7.4 "Social" and "Interior" Logics of Violent Masculinity:
Preliminary Model, Late Colonial Morelos

Contexts/Motives	No.	Percent of All Cases	Percent of Masculinity Cases
MALE ASSAILANT CASES [a]			
Male-female relations	76	44.7	58.9
Male honor	17	10.0	13.2
Background bonding/honor	22	12.9	17.1
Invisible rage plausible [b]	14	8.2	10.9
Subtotals			
Driven by "social" logic [c]	98	57.6	76.0
Driven by "interior" logic [d]	31	18.2	24.0
Total: cumulative expression of violent masculinity	129	75.9	100.0
MALE-ON-MALE CASES [e]			
Male-female relations	23	21.3	31.9
Male honor	14	13.0	19.4
Background bonding/honor	22	20.4	30.6
Invisible rage plausible [b]	13	12.0	18.1
Subtotals			
Driven by "social" logic [c]	45	41.7	62.5
Driven by "interior" logic [c]	27	25.0	37.5
Total: cumulative expression of violent masculinity	72	66.7	100.0

Source: Adapted from Tables 7.1–7.3.
Note: Because inclusion of the invisible rage plausible group increases the total number of violent masculinity cases, the percent of masculinity figures given here are distinct from those in Table 7.2.
[a] $N = 170$ valid cases.
[b] Invisible rage plausible cases refer to *descarga* ventings. For the sake of argument, these are interpreted as a bursting forth of "interior" masculine rage.
[c] Cases driven by a "social" logic of violent masculinity are male-female relations and background bonding/honor cases.
[d] Cases driven by an "interior" logic of violent masculinity are male honor and invisible rage plausible cases.
[e] $N = 108$ valid cases.

TABLE 7.5 Homicidal Violence, Secondary Relations, and Gender: Late Colonial Morelos

Violence Inflicted by Secondary Relation	Male Targets		Female Targets	
	No.	Percent	No.	Percent
ASSAILANTS[a]				
Homicidal	55	62.5	2	10.5
Nonhomicidal	33	37.5	17	89.5
ODDS RATIO[b]				
Odds that violence by secondary relation is homicidal, male targets compared with female targets		14.2:1		

Source: PDBO, Morelos, Morofvi1.lis, pp. 80, 19, 121–22, 82.

Note: Although the risk of homicidal violence by secondary relations assailants contrasted sharply for male versus female targets, the gender gap did not hold for primary relations. Within the violence case set, primary relations were no less associated than nonprimary relations with risk for homicidal rather than nonhomicidal violence ($n = 198$; Chi-square significance, .45); slightly more women than men (19 and 15, respectively) were killed by primary relations; and among primary relations cases, tests for statistically significant associations of homicide by gender of the target proved negative ($n = 57$; Chi-square, .07) — even though the one-sided distribution of rapes almost automatically diminished the percentage of murders for women compared with men.

[a] $N = 107$ total valid cases.

[b] Chi-square significance was .0001; Phi, .40; Lambda with homicidal violence dependent, .30; Yule's Q, .87.

TABLE 7.6 "Tangibles" and "Social" Logics in Violent Masculinity:
Modified Modeling, Late Colonial Morelos

	No.	Percent of All Cases	Percent of Masculinity Cases
MALE ASSAILANT CASES [a]			
"Tangible" claims			
Original model (restricted)	105	61.8	
Modified model (amplified)	144	84.7	
Midway share	—	73.3	
"Socially" driven logic of masculinity			
Original model (restricted)	98	57.6	76.0
Modified model (amplified)	115	67.6	89.1
Midway share	—	62.6	82.6
MALE-ON-MALE MASES [b]			
"Tangible" claims			
Original model (restricted)	50	46.3	
Modified model (amplified)	86	79.6	
Midway share	—	63.0	
"Socially" driven logic of masculinity			
Original model (restricted)	45	41.7	62.5
Modified model (amplified)	59	54.6	81.9
Midway share	—	48.2	72.2

Sources: Adapted from Tables 7.3 and 7.4.

Notes. The original restricted models are defined and computed in Tables 7.3 and 7.4 above. The amplified models include male honor and background bonding/honor cases within "tangibles" and include male honor cases within "socially" driven logics of masculinity. The restricted and amplified models may be interpreted respectively as minimum and maximum thresholds of plausibility.

[a] $N = 170$ total valid cases; masculinity cases, $n = 129$.

[b] $N = 108$ total valid cases; masculinity cases, $n = 72$.

TABLE 7.7 Elusive Associations Regarding Homicidal Violence and Sociocultural Groups: Late Colonial Morelos

Questions about Nonrandom Associations	Findings	Statistical Summaries Chi-square Significance	Phi	Yule's Q
Were plebeian assailants more or less associated with homicidal violence than peasant assailants?	Moderately more associated	.000	.30	.61
Were plebeian targets also more associated with homicidal violence?	Modestly if at all: borderline statistics	.043[a]	.19	.38
Were non-Indian assailants more or less associated with homicidal violence than Indian assailants?	Modestly more if at all: weak correlations	.022	.18	.36
Were non-Indian targets more associated with homicidal violence?	Modestly more if at all: weak correlations	.026	.19	.39

Source: PDBO, Morelos, Morhom2, part 1, pp. 3, 6, 4, 7.

[a]This is borderline significance if one uses the standard .05 threshold of significance in Chi-square tests of nonrandom association.

TABLE 9.1 Net Criminal Case Sets for Statistical Analysis:
Late Colonial Morelos, Oaxaca, and Mexico City

Regional Case Set[a]	No.	Percent Homicide	Percent Homicide or Serious Injury[b]
Morelos: violence	206	53.9	85.0
Oaxaca: violence	251	24.7	78.1
Mexico City: violence	156	39.7	71.8
Mexico City: violence and sexual/family morality	251[c]		
Triregional total: violence only	613	38.3	78.8
Triregional total: violence/morality	708		

Sources: PDBO, Tri-regional, Folder1a; Morelos, Powviol1.out, pp. 14, 48; Oaxaca, Oaxviol2.lis, pp. 19, 56; Mexico City, Mexviol2.lis, pp. 17, 54; Mxmoral3.lis, p. 3.

Note: For the violence case sets, sampling error margins ($\pm$ x percent) using conservative criteria—a 95 percent confidence level and a P* = .50 distribution—run as follows for Morelos, Oaxaca, Mexico City, respectively: 6.8 percent, 6.2 percent, and 7.8 percent. (For the triregional set as a whole, the calculation is 4.0 percent.) If one uses the gender distribution of the target population for P* (roughly a two-thirds/one-third split, rather than a half/half split), the error margins are 6.4 percent, 5.6 percent, and 7.6 percent (3.7 percent triregional). For insight on the statistics of populations and samples, see Mueller et al, 1977, 383–411. For further information on case sets and statistical procedures, see the Appendix.

[a] As net case sets, these exclude family or sexual morality cases in the gross Morelos and Oaxaca sets. Such cases proved too few for regional statistical analysis (although they remained useful from a qualitative point of view). The only morality cases that survived pruning for these two regions were those that met the criteria given in note c for overlap as violence cases.

[b] This group is defined as homicides, major assaults (i.e, producing injuries that warrant medical attention), sexual assaults, and kidnappings.

[c] This total includes 108 family or sexual morality cases, but 13 of these were overlapping cases included in the net violence case set. To avoid double counting, the net total is 251, not 264. To qualify as a violence case, a morality proceeding had to focus with at least equal emphasis on a specific recent incident of violent assault rather than limiting charges of violence to complaints of old assaults or chronic violence embedded within a larger discourse about immoral maltreatment (*mala vida*).

TABLE 9.2 Sociocultural Profiles of Assailants and Targets:
Late Colonial Morelos, Oaxaca, and Mexico City

	Assailants			Targets		
	No.	Percent	Regional Population Percent	No.	Percent	Regional Population Percent
ETHNIC PROFILE[a]						
Morelos						
Indians	91	55.5	62.5	94	65.3	62.5
Castas	44	26.8	29.8	39	27.1	29.8
Whites	29	17.7	7.7	11	7.6	7.7
Oaxaca						
Indians	149	77.6	95.1	176	88.9	95.1
Castas	27	14.1	1.2	14	7.1	1.2
Whites	16	8.3	3.7	8	4.0	3.7
Mexico City						
Indians	35	27.6	24.1	35	33.7	24.1
Castas	27	21.3	26.6	24	23.1	26.6
Whites	65	51.2	49.3	45	43.3	49.3
CLASS STATUS PROFILE[b]						
BY PEASANT/PLEBEIAN[c]						
Morelos						
Peasants (restricted)	99	62.3		88	62.0	
Peasants (amplified)	108	64.3		109	66.9	
Plebeians (restricted)	44	27.7		46	32.4	
Plebeians (amplified)	53	31.5		67	41.1	
Oaxaca						
Peasants (restricted)	145	73.2		157	76.6	
Peasants (amplified)	157	79.3		169	82.4	
Plebeians (restricted)	32	16.2		28	13.7	
Plebeians (amplified)	44	22.2		40	19.5	
Mexico City						
Peasants	1	0.8		1	0.8	
Plebeians	121	90.9		108	91.5	
CLASS/STATUS PROFILE						
BY LOW/MIDDLING/HIGH[d]						
Morelos						
Low	122	72.6		127	77.9	
Middling	31	18.5		28	17.2	
High	15	8.9		8	4.9	

TABLE 9.2 (*continued*)

	Assailants			Targets		
	No.	Percent	Regional Population Percent	No.	Percent	Regional Population Percent
Oaxaca						
Low	147	74.2		165	80.5	
Middling	42	21.2		32	15.6	
High	9	4.5		8	3.9	
Mexico City						
Low	99	74.4		92	78.0	
Middling	23	17.3		17	14.4	
High	11	8.3		9	7.6	
AGE/SEX PROFILE [e]						
Morelos						
Mean age	29.7			31.8		
Standard deviation	9.5			14.2		
Oaxaca						
Mean age	32.1			30.1		
Standard deviation	11.7			10.9		
Mexico City						
Mean age	26.5			26.3		
Standard deviation	8.9			9.3		
Morelos: male/female		92.2/7.8			66.5/33.5	
Oaxaca: male/female		92.6/7.4			70.5/29.5	
Mexico City: male/female		87.3/12.7			63.0/37.0	

Sources: For Morelos, Tables 3.3, 3.4 above; for Oaxaca and Mexico City, PDBO, Oaxaca, Oaxviol5.lis, pp. 15, 18, 59, 13; Oaxviol4.lis, pp. 21, 23, 60, 20; Mexico City, Mexviol5.lis, pp. 14, 16, 57, 13; Mexviol4.lis, pp. 18, 20–21, 58, 18; for regional ethnic percentage estimates, Table 2.1 above.

[a] For ethnic profiles of Morelos, Oaxaca, and Mexico City, respectively, total valid cases n = 164, 192, and 127 for assailants; 144, 198, and 104 for targets.

[b] For class/status profiles of Morelos, Oaxaca, and Mexico City, respectively, total valid cases n = 168, 198, and 33 for assailants; 163, 205, and 118 for targets.

[c] The amplified model of peasants/plebeians includes overlapping categories and calculates percentage shares accordingly; the restricted model deletes these cases. Overlapping cases include only those mixed cases for which one could not identify with confidence a predominantly peasant or predominantly plebeian household economy.

[d] "Low" refers to commoners/*macehuales*; "middling" refers to upper peasants/plebeians; "high" refers to privileged/elite.

[e] For age profiles of Morelos, Oaxaca, and Mexico City, respectively, total valid cases n = 115, 96, and 97 for assailants; 61, 81, and 69 for targets. The large number of missing values indicates that caution is warranted. For sex profiles of the three regions, n = 180, 215, and 150 for assailants; 182, 220, and 138 for targets. (These figures are smaller than the number of incidents because technical adjusments were made to eliminate mixed gender groups and double counting in incidents of more than one assailant or target. As a practical matter, the results are virtually identical without the adjustments.)

TABLE 9.3 Major Motives of Violent Dispute: Late Colonial Morelos, Oaxaca, and Mexico City

Motivation of Dispute	Morelos [a] Percent	Oaxaca [b] Percent	Mexico City [c] Percent
Gender-rooted	49.7	46.7	57.6
Property/class	21.0	26.8	14.6
Descarga ventings [d]	7.7	7.7	5.3

Sources: PDBO, Morelos, Powviol1.out, pp. 29–30; Oaxaca, Oaxviol2.lis, p. 34; Mexico City, Mexviol2.lis, pp. 31–32.

Note: The figures given here correspond to the restricted model explained in Table 3.6 above. The amplified and midway point models, also explained in Table 3.6 above, fail to yield different comparative results.

[a] $N = 195$ total valid cases.

[b] $N = 246$ total valid cases.

[c] $N = 151$ total valid cases.

[d] The amplified modeling of *descarga*, used for statistical testing of regional variation, yields the following shares: 20.5 percent, 22.4 percent, and 21.9 percent for Morelos, Oaxaca, and Mexico City, respectively.

TABLE 9.4 Assailant/Target Relationships and Gender of Target: Comparative Regional Measures of Association in Late Colonial Times

Region [a]	Statistical Summary of Nonrandom Association (Female Target = Closer Relation More Probable; Male Target = Looser Relation More Probable)			
	Chi-Square Significance	Cramer's V	Lambda [b]	Yule's Q [c]
Morelos	.000	.64	.50	.97
Oaxaca	.000	.56	.41	.92
Mexico City	.000	.60	.50	.92

Sources: PDBO, Tri-regional, Morofvi1.lis, p. 24; Oaxofvi1.lis, p. 24; Mexofvi1.lis, p. 24.

Note: This table is based on the refined spectrum of assailant/target relations (inner primary, outer primary, secondary, tertiary) explained in Table 3.11 above.

[a] For Morelos, Oaxaca, and Mexico City, respectively, $n = 193$, 239, and 144 total valid cases.

[b] The Lambda measure is with target's gender as dependent variable.

[c] The Yule's Q measure is based on the following odds ratio: the odds that a female target was assailed by an inner primary relation compared with the odds that a male target was assailed by an inner primary relation. For the odds ratio based on primary relations as a whole, Yule's Q is .82, .72, and .78 for Morelos, Oaxaca, and Mexico City, respectively.

TABLE 9.5 Major Motives of Violent Dispute: Intraregional Comparison, Late Colonial Oaxaca

Motivation of Dispute	Mixteca Alta[a] Percent	Zapotec Valley[b] Percent	Villa Alta[c] Percent
Gender-rooted	48.1	45.6	45.9
Property/class	23.1	22.1	36.5
Descarga ventings[d]	8.7	10.8	2.9

Sources: Adapted from PDBO, Intra-regional, Oaxreg1.lis, pp. 41–43; Oaxreg3.lis, pp. 7, 42.

Note: The figures given here correspond to the restricted model explained in Table 3.6 above. The amplified and midway point models, also explained in Table 3.6 above, accord with these comparative results.

[a]$N = 104$ total valid cases.

[b]$N = 74$ total valid cases.

[c]$N = 68$ total valid cases.

[d]The amplified modeling of *descarga*, used for statistical testing of intraregional variation, yields the following shares: 26.9 percent, 23.5 percent, and 14.9 percent for the Mixteca Alta, Zapotec Valley, and Villa Alta zones, respectively.

TABLE 10.1 Regional Variation in Violence against Female Targets:
Late Colonial Morelos and Oaxaca

Violence against Female Targets	Restricted Case Set		Expanded Case Set	
	Morelos	Oaxaca	Morelos	Oaxaca
Among all cases, percent not gender-rooted	8.1	15.2	6.5	14.4
Among sexual cases, percent sexual assault[a]	43.2	17.1	34.5	23.5
Among all *celos* cases,[b] ratio of plausible to imaginary	1.8	3.3	1.8	2.5
Among male *celos* cases, ratio of plausible to imaginary	.8	2.0	.8	1.8

Sources: Adapted from PDBO, Morelos, Powviol.out, pp. 33, 36; Powmore1.sys, pp. 34, 37; Oaxaca, Oaxviol2.lis, pp. 37, 41; Addoaxl.lis, pp. 37, 40.

Note: Total valid cases for all cases against female targets, sexual cases, *celos* cases, and male *celos* cases, respectively, are as follows: Morelos restricted n = 62, 37, 17, 10.5; Oaxaca restricted n = 66, 35, 26, 15; Morelos expanded n = 93, 58, 34, 16.5; Oaxaca expanded n = 97, 51, 35, 22. For definitions of restricted and expanded case sets, see Table 4.1 above.

[a] Figures given include incidents where sexually motivated violence or sexual assaults were present as "secondary" or after-the-fact features of the incident. The practical effect expands slightly the number of cases classified as sexual conflict or sexual assault but does not change the comparative findings.

[b] *Celos* cases refer overwhelmingly to male or female jealousy in connection with a third-person sexual or conjugal partner (whether "imagined" or "real"). The category includes, however, a very slight number of cases in which the *celos* dispute focused on a woman's right to continue or stop an already established sexual relationship, in the absence of allegations about an additional sexual partner. These instances of dispute over a woman's right to reclaim sexual ownership of herself are classified .5 male/.5 female *celos*, and are considered plausible rather than imaginary.

TABLE 11.1 "Tangibles" and "Social" Logics of Masculinity in Violence: Late Colonial Mexico City

"Tangibles" and "Intangibles"[c]	Male Assailant Cases[a]		Male-on-Male Cases[b]	
	Percent	Morelos Figure	Percent	Morelos Figure
Gender-rooted, linked to male-female rights/claims	44.8	44.7	23.8	21.3
Property/class disputes	15.7	17.1	23.8	25.0
Descarga ventings	6.0	8.2	4.8	12.0
Male-centered honor	10.4	10.0	13.1	13.0
Subtotals				
"Tangibles"	60.4	61.8	47.6	46.3
"Intangibles"	16.4	18.2	17.9	25.0

Social Contexts of Masculinity[d]	Percent of All Cases	Percent of Masculinity Cases	Percent of All Cases	Percent of Masculinity Cases
Male-female relations	44.8	56.1	23.8	33.9
Male honor	10.4	13.1	13.1	18.6
Background bonding/honor	18.7	23.4	28.6	40.7
Invisible rage plausible	6.0	7.5	4.8	6.8
Subtotals				
Driven by "social" logic	63.4	79.4	52.4	74.6
Driven by "interior" logic	16.4	20.6	17.9	25.4

Sources: PDBO, Tri-regional, Mexmv1a.lis, pp. 5–6, 30–31; for the Morelos comparison figures, Table 7.3 above.

[a] *N* = 134 total valid cases.

[b] *N* = 84 total valid cases.

[c] The models of "tangibles" and "intangibles" used here correspond to the restricted criteria defined and presented in Tables 7.2 and 7.3 above. If one used amplified modeling procedures described in Tables 7.3 and 7.6, the amplified "intangibles" would amount to 35.1 percent and 46.4 percent for male assailant and male-on-male cases, respectively. The amplified "tangibles" would amount to 89.6 percent and 89.3 percent for male assailant and male-on-male cases, respectively. The amplified percentages add up to more than 100 because amplified modeling draws on overlapping and ambiguous cases.

[d] The cases expressive of masculinity are 107 for male assailant cases and 59 for male-on-male cases (79.9 percent and 70.2 percent of all male assailant and male-on male cases, respectively).

The definitions of "social" and "interior" logics of masculinity expressed in violence correspond to the criteria defined in Table 7.4 above. Cases driven by a "social" logic are male-female relations and male background bonding/honor. Cases driven by an "interior" logic are male honor and invisible rage plausible. Invisible rage plausible cases refer to *descarga* ventings, interpreted, for the sake of argument, as a bursting forth of interior masculine rage.

TABLE 12.1 Ethnoracial Profiles in Morelos Microregions:
Late Colonial Assailants and Targets

			Ethnoracial identification (percentages)	
			African-Related Descent	
			Among	Among
	Indian	Castas	All	Castas
ASSAILANTS [a]				
Tierra fría	68.3	12.7	0.0	0.0
Tierra caliente	55.2	29.5	12.4	41.9
TARGETS [b]				
Tierra fría	87.5	7.1	0.0	0.0
Tierra caliente	55.4	37.0	15.2	41.2

Source: PDBO, Intra-regional, Morreg1.lis, pp. 11–16.

Note: Testing for statistically significant nonrandom association of Indians by microregions yielded the following: among assailants, the Indian variation by microregion was not statistically significant (Chi-square significance level: .13); among targets, the variation was significant (Chi-square significance level: .00; Phi correlation was a moderate .33).

[a] For assailants identified by race, $n = 168$ total valid cases divided as follows: 63 tierra fría (37.5 percent), 105 tierra caliente (62.5 percent).

[b] For targets identified by race, $n = 148$ total valid cases divided as follows: 56 tierra fría (37.8 percent), 92 tierra caliente (62.2 percent).

TABLE 12.2 The Parallels of Regional and Microregional Comparison:
Homicidal Violence in Late Colonial Morelos and Oaxaca

	Homicidal Shares within Criminal Violence Incidents	
	Homicide as	
	Percent of	Ratio of Shares by
Region/Microregion [a]	Incidents	Region/Microregion
Morelos	53.9	
Oaxaca	24.7	
Regional ratio		2.2:1
Morelos tierra caliente	63.0	
Morelos tierra fría	31.3	
Microregional ratio		2.0:1

Sources: PDBO, Tri-regional, Interreg1.lis, Version "A," p. 1; Intra-regional, Morreg1.lis, pp. 5, 51.

Note: The microregional contrast in homicidal shares yields a Chi-square significance at the .00 level, a moderate Phi correlation of .30, and a moderate to strong Yule's Q measure of .58.

[a] For Morelos, Oaxaca, tierra caliente, and tierra fría, respectively, $n = 206, 251, 127,$ and 67 total valid cases. The microregional total for Morelos is slightly short of the regional total because of the exclusion of 12 ambiguous cases.

TABLE 12.3 The Parallels of Regional and Microregional Comparison: Gender and Violence, Late Colonial Morelos and Oaxaca

	Regions		Microregions (Morelos)	
Nonrandom Associations[a]	Morelos	Oaxaca	*Tierra Caliente*	*Tierra Fría*
1. Between closeness of social bond and gender of target				
Statistically significant?	yes	yes	yes	yes
If yes, correlation measure	.64	.56	.71	.55
2. Between homicidal violence and gender of target				
Statistically significant?	yes	"yes"[b]	yes	no
If yes, correlation measure	.27	.17	.26	
3. Between homicidal violence and gender of target, in secondary relations cases				
Statistically significant?	yes	no	yes[c]	no
If yes, correlation measure	.40		.42	
4. Between homicidal violence and gender of target, in primary relations cases				
Statistically significant?	no	yes	no	yes[d]
If yes, correlation measure		.30		.39

Sources: PDBO, Tri-regional, Morofvi1.lis, pp. 24, 80, 82; Oaxofvi1.lis, pp. 24, 80, 82; Oaxtst1.lis, p. 26; Morelos, Morhom2, part 1, p. 5; Intra-regional, Morreg4.lis, pp. 26, 82 (cf. 85), 84; Morreg3.lis, pp. 26, 82, 84.

[a]For Morelos, Oaxaca, *tierra caliente*, and *tierra fría*, respectively, $n = 206, 251, 127$, and 67 total valid cases.

For item 1, the direction of the association is closeness of social bond (i.e., primary relations between assailant and target) with female targets, distance of social bond (secondary and tertiary relations) with male targets; the linear correlation measure is Cramer's V. For items 2–3, for the Morelos region and the *tierra caliente* microregion the direction of the association is homicidal violence with male targets; the linear correlation measure is Phi. For item 4, for the Oaxaca region and the *tierra fría* microregion, the direction and correlation measures are as in items 2–3. For all cases, statistical significance is defined at the .05 Chi-square significance level.

[b]The "yes" response here is partly a statistical reflection of the large number of cases in the test; the correlation measure is extremely weak (.17, below a cut-off level of .20).

[c]The existence of a cross-tabulation cell with MEF < 5 means that these results should be viewed with caution. But the direction of the association and the results of the comparative analysis are confirmed by tests that combine secondary and tertiary relations into a "nonprimary relations" cell that supersedes the MEF problem and yields a similar correlation (.40).

[d]Small numbers and cross-tabulation cells with MEF < 5 mean that these results should be viewed with caution.

Appendix
A Note on Quantitative Methods

This book is not based primarily on statistical methods and analyses, even though I have found some quantitative assessment useful within a mainly qualitative approach. Most of what one needs to know about the quantitative aspects of the work and the case sets is in the text itself, especially in Chapter 9, which provides a triregional overview, and in Chapter 3, which dissects a single region and its case set in more detail and discusses questions of typicality in the social dynamics discerned in the criminal records.

Here, however, it will be useful to provide additional technical details about case sets and procedures. First, procedures to construct case sets were pragmatic and reflected the historian's hope that record survival was more or less random. I should acknowledge that the case sets available to a historian of gender and violence in late colonial Mexico will not satisfy a statistician or social scientist concerned with laboratory- or surveylike procedures to guarantee randomness. Not only are recorded criminal violence cases themselves but one slice within a larger field of violence. In addition, technical differences between regional case sets possibly affect randomness, or at least comparability. For Morelos, for example, for reasons of jurisdictional history as well as the salience of homicide cases and the proximity of the region, criminal violence records seemed to be forwarded rather routinely to the supervisory judges of the Marquesado and the Audiencia in Mexico City, and I was able to lean heavily on the run of records in the criminal section of the Archivo General de la Nación (AGN). I reviewed relevant cases in all 740 volumes (the first 307 are catalogued; the rest required a check of each volume). The filing of cases at the AGN was much spottier for Oaxaca and Mexico City and required supplementation at the regional repositories listed in the Bibliography. For Mexico City the Archivo Judicial del Tribunal Superior de Justicia del Distrito Federal was helpful, and I read alternating *legajos* (case bundles) within the Penales section (*legajos* 3, 5, 7, 9). For Oaxaca I read all the relevant cases in the archives listed in the Bibliography but cross-checked between BNAH and CROT to avoid double counting. Given the vagaries of record keeping and survival and the different strategies required to construct case sets, I was somewhat surprised by the degree of consistency (notwithstanding variations) that emerged between regional case sets and by the resonance of qualitative and quantitative findings.

Second, I systematically developed procedures to check against quantitative findings that might have dubious value or at least outstrip the reliability of the data. (1) I reviewed statistical findings and printouts in relation to qualitative expectations and tried to understand any discrepancies that appeared rather than assign, a priori, higher truth value to one approach or the other. (2) I limited statistical procedures to fairly elementary SPSS exercises: simple descriptive statistics to establish basic data profiles; Chi-square testing for nonrandom variation within cross-tabulation sets (the significance levels provided in tables and endnotes are "Yates corrected" levels); and in cases of nonrandom association, simple association measures such as Phi/Cramer's V, supplemented by odds ratios/Yule's Q and, when illuminating, PRE measures such as Lambda. Readers should know that because of mathematical properties associated with uneven distribution of populations within a variable (for example, uneven distribution of men and women within a cross-tabulation by gender), the Phi/Cramer's V linear correlations tend toward weak or understated measures. The Yule's Q measures compensate by focusing on key odds ratios or probability relations within a cross-tabulation. As a courtesy to readers, I normally provide both measures in the tables and endnotes. (3) To check against unwarranted conclusions or assumptions that built in unexpected biases, I normally did redundant statistical testing that used slightly revised assumptions. For example, I ran frequency tests counting violent incidents by assailant, by target, and by relational incident, and I constructed multiple versions of primary-to-stranger social relations spectra. Again, if discrepancies appeared in the results, I tried to get to the bottom of them rather than assign, a priori, higher truth value to one assumption over another. (4) Finally, to avoid truth claims based solely on conservative definitions that tended to exclude cases of ambiguity and/or overlap from a classification category (say, *descarga* ventings) or based solely on elastic definitions that tended to include cases of ambiguity and/or overlap, I normally constructed restricted and amplified models of the same tests. This double modeling provided lower and upper thresholds of plausibility and built in a caution against treating constructed figures as precise truth. As a courtesy to readers, I have often displayed both models in the tables and used their midway points as shorthand in the narrative discussions.

For overall orientation to statistical reasoning, I found R. Johnson 1984 helpful. For interpretation of odds ratios and other measures of correlation, see Reynolds 1977, esp. 35–44.

The codebook, data entries, and statistical tests, organized as electronic and hard copy files within the Powpat Data Base and Outputs (PDBO) collection cited in the notes, will be deposited and available at the Memorial Library of the University of Wisconsin at Madison three years after publication of this book. In the meantime the files may by consulted at the Department of History.

Notes

ABBREVIATIONS USED IN THE NOTES

AE	*American Ethnologist*
AEO	Archivo General del Estado de Oaxaca
AGN	Archivo General de la Nación
AGNCr	AGN, Ramo Criminal
AHC	Archivo Histórico de la Ciudad de México
AHR	*American Historical Review*
AJT	Archivo Judicial del Tribunal Superior de Justicia del Distrito Federal
ATOVA	Archivo del Tribunal Superior de Oaxaca, Juzgado de Villa Alta
BNAH	Biblioteca Nacional de Antropología e Historia: Archivo de Microfilm, Serie Oaxaca
BNM	Biblioteca Nacional de México: Colección LaFragua
CONDUMEX	Centro de Estudios de Historia de México CONDUMEX
CROT	Centro Regional del Instituto Nacional de Antropología e Historia, Oaxaca: Microfilm del Archivo del Juzgado de Teposcolula
JAH	*Journal of American History*
JFH	*Journal of Family History*
JTWS	*Journal of Third World Societies*
PDBO	Powpat Data Base and Outputs (codebook, data entries, and statistical tests and outputs, in electronic and hard copy files, constructed for this project)

CHAPTER ONE

1. The episode described in the following pages is drawn from AGNCr, vol. 46, exp. 3, Texalpa 1806, fols. 89–125, esp. 95v–98v, 101v–103v, 106r–111v, 120v. The quotations that follow are on fols. 97r, 97v (*trastornado* and *consentidor* quotes), 96r, 98r ("considering" and "anger" quotes), 106r. I surmised the youth of María Teresa from José Marcelino's age (about twenty-five years), the couple's apparent childlessness, and a tone in the documents suggesting the kind of in-law relationships associated with young couples. Quotations from criminal documents in this book will normally be taken from the verbatim or near-verbatim (rather than formulaic) portions of witness testimonies and declarations.

2. This is not to say that José Marcelino and María Teresa held no claims to *milpas* (loosely "cornfields," but more broadly, agricultural fields that supported a combination of maize and other crops such as beans and squash in the maize-based agricultural system) or to land-use rights of their own. But they belonged to that stratum of peasants whose meager resource base implied considerable dependence on day work for others. On internal differentiation in Morelos and for the broad context of sharpening competition over land and water rights between hacienda owners, *rancheros* (small-scale independent proprietors), and villagers, see Rodríguez Lazcano 1984, 102–5; C. E. Martin 1985, 71–192 passim; cf. C. E. Martin 1982, 1984; Gruzinski 1989b, 105–72; Tutino 1986, 142–45. See also AGNCr, vol. 277, exp. 9, Zahuatlán (Xonacatepec) 1793, fols. 198–222, esp. 199v, and more generally vol. 277, exps. 9–12; vol. 205, exp. 9, Ystaquaque 1769, fol. 412r (cf. vol. 205, exp. 7); vol. 277, exp. 3, Xochitlán 1789, fols. 55r, 63r; vol. 228, exp. 26, Atlatlauca 1807, fol. 355v.

3. Texalpa lay about two kilometers east of Atlacomulco. See Barrett 1970, map on 27; cf. AGNCr, vol. 46, exp. 3, Texalpa 1806, fol. 98r; C. E. Martin 1985, map on 36–37.

4. The gendered pattern of umbilical cord burials, quite diffuse in central Mexico, reached back to the pre-Hispanic era and in some regions persisted into the twentieth century. Actual burial sites varied by locale and time period, but the key distinction was between burial within or away from the house. See Hellbom 1967, 154, 156–157; González Montes and Iracheta Cenegorta 1987, 129.

5. For a superb overview of women's daily tortilla work, see Bauer 1990; for additional detail, see also Chapter 14 below.

6. José Marcelino did not produce a niece, father, or other witness to corroborate the story of his niece's warning, even though the story, if true, should easily have yielded such witnesses, and corroborating testimony would have made José Marcelino's actions more excusable as a spontaneous response to his wife's provocation.

7. Colonial Spanish criminal proceedings generally relied on formal complaint by an aggrieved party and often privileged reconciliation between offender and victim as the desired outcome, even in cases when a preliminary period of prison and punishment was also considered appropriate. Micaela María's formal pardon and desistance was therefore important if José Marcelino were eventually to win a royal pardon and early release.

8. This added claim was probably meant to underscore that Micaela María granted the pardon as an act of free will rather than in submission to coercion or pressure. As such, it constitutes the kind of revealing slip that undermines the intended point.

9. In fact Andrés Francisco, a former *gobernador* listed as seventy years old, played this role for José Marcelino and also testified to his good character. See the matter-of-fact testimony in AGNCr, vol. 46, exp. 3, Texalpa 1806, fol. 97v. The other elders who testified on José Marcelino's behalf were listed as seventy-five and eighty-five years old (fols. 109r–111v).

10. My notes do not definitively confirm that Micaela María was a widow. The absence of a father pressing the criminal complaint against José Marcelino, however, makes it extremely likely that Micaela María was either a widow or abandoned.

11. The most stimulating recent work on harmony ideology in a context of social and legal disputation is the Oaxaca research of Nader (1989, 1990). For historical studies emphasizing the ways peasant villagers forged a sense of cohesion to blunt external and internal threats, see Taylor 1979; Stern 1983; cf. Wolf 1957, 1986.

12. The wheels of royal justice and mercy did not, however, turn rapidly. A final royal pardon and disposition of the case did not occur until February 9, 1809.

13. Later we shall explore the literature on these themes in detail: see esp. Chapter 2; cf. Chapters 3, 7, 13. Although we shall have many occasions to explore the limits of female complicity, the phenomenon is sufficiently real to have drawn the attention of prominent feminists: see, e.g., de Beauvoir 1952 (cf. B. Miller 1983, 21–22); Castellanos 1973, esp. 14, 23–25; G. Lerner 1986, esp. 217–18, 234, 249–50.

14. My emphasis on the practical meanings and uses of cultural principles—their embeddedness in everyday life, necessity, and conflict—derives mainly from the archival research process itself. But I have learned much, too, from the approaches to culture developed in Bourdieu 1977; Mintz and Price 1976; Sabean 1984.

15. See, e.g., Rosaldo 1974; Ortner 1974; Rubin 1975; Hartmann 1979 (cf. Sargent 1981); T. Kaplan 1982. For a critical retrospective, see Rosaldo 1980. Other important statements implicitly accepted the public/private split insofar as they sought to valorize and politicize the female domestic sphere by arguing that the dynamics of childbirth, mothering, and familial bonding and individualization constituted the foundation of social behavior and dominance in all arenas, public and private: see, e.g., Chodorow 1978; M. O'Brien 1981; cf. Janeway 1980. All these pioneering works wanted, in some ultimate sense, to problematize

and overcome the public/private split or the intellectual and political uses to which it had been put. For that very reason, however, the early language of critique necessarily remained bound, in a kind of mirror image effect, to the dichotomy.

16. For a particularly vitriolic attack, see Elton 1984, esp. 39; cf. Elton 1991, 117–18; Hamerow 1987, 201–2. For the broader context of turbulence and fragmentation in the historical profession, see Novick 1988, esp. 463–64, 607–11; Stern 1993, esp. 6–7, 17 n. 3.

17. See Foucault 1965, 1977, 1978–86 (vol. 1), 1980, 1984. Admittedly, vols. 2 and 3 of the 1978–86 work, *The History of Sexuality*, in some ways run counter to this characterization. For perceptive orientation to Foucault, see Rabinow 1984; P. O'Brien 1989.

18. See, e.g., Gailey 1987; G. Lerner 1986; J. W. Scott 1988; cf. Rosaldo 1980. An emerging cluster of works on gender and welfare states provides a particularly rich example of such rethinking. See, e.g., Gordon 1988, 1990; *AHR* 1990.

CHAPTER TWO

1. Celebrated novels in this tradition span at least a half-century and range from one-dimensional denunciations in the language of social realism (e.g., Icaza 1953 [1936]) to more complex portraits that mix denunciation and empathy in the language of magical realism (e.g., García Márquez 1976 [1975]). A classic Mexican example is Fuentes 1964. For context and critique and for the imagery of women in literature, see Franco 1989; González Echevarría 1985; B. Miller 1983. Allende 1986 [1982] marks the emergence of a genre of more woman-centered treatments of the theme of patriarchalism; cf. Mastretta 1985; Boullosa 1987.

2. The quintessentials of a culture become all the more noticeable and absorbing if they are perceived as in danger of disappearing or as an obstacle to progress that must disappear. In the nineteenth century this phenomenon was obvious in the literature of civilization versus barbarism: see, e.g., da Cunha 1944 [1902]. In the early to mid-twentieth century a similar sense applied to the traditions of the old agrarian regime and fostered fascination by critics and apologists alike. For a splendid interpretation of Gilberto Freyre's work and the Brazilian myth of "racial democracy" along these lines, see Viotti da Costa 1985, 234–46.

3. See Freyre 1943 [1933]; Paz 1959 [1950]; Chevalier 1963 [1952]; Wolf 1959.

4. A perceptive mid-twentieth-century effort to account for the blend of professed paternalism and calculated exploitation in colonial Spanish governance was Morse 1954. For an introduction to the Black Legend and feudalism-capitalism controversies, see Keen 1985; Stern 1988b.

5. On Spanish political philosophy a good starting point remains Morse 1954, 1964. For amplification, see Góngora 1951; Phelan 1967 (cf. 1978). The centrality of patriarchalism in political philosophy is a subject that spills beyond the Iberian world to encompass the Western and biblical political traditions as a whole. For the breadth and variations of patriarchalism in Western political thought, see Schochet 1975; Elshtain 1982; Shaw 1987; cf. G. Lerner 1986, 207–10. In early modern English law the murder of one's husband or master was considered a form of treason (Beattie 1986, 79 n. 10, 100).

6. The preoccupation with a male psychology of dominance/emasculation was especially prominent in Mexico; see Paz 1959 [1950]; for further discussion, see Chapter 7 below.

7. This insight is basic to deconstructionist scholarship and links the analysis of simultaneous awareness and suppression in discourse to questions of power. One need not subscribe to deconstructionism, however, to appreciate the importance of the insight (consider, for example, Hegel's dictum that all choice is also a negation). Moreover, the screening out of competing or alternative perceptions may be welcomed as a precondition

of knowledge; the omitted or negated perception is damaging only if what is suppressed turns out to be germane. (See, e.g., Stern 1988a, 893–94.) Nonetheless, only if one asks what is suppressed or negated can one decide consciously if the heretofore unacknowledged underside of a formulation turns out to have been germane to the original formulation and to an analysis of power in discourse.

8. See the works cited in nn. 1, 3 above. For recent studies of Mexico that make valuable contributions to our understanding of the politics of manhood by the wielders of power yet fall prey to similar limitations, see O'Malley 1986; Friedrich 1986.

9. Examples of literature in each arena of contribution are in nn. 10–24 below, but it is important to note that many specific works contributed simultaneously to the several arenas of contribution delineated below. (Two works that cut across these areas of contribution but that came into my hands too late in the drafting of this chapter for systematic incorporation and source citation below are Gonzalbo Aizpuru 1991 and Seminario de Historia de las Mentalidades 1991.) One should not assume a rigid divide, therefore, between works cited in different notes. The citations in nn. 10–24 will emphasize Mexico but will also include influential examples from other regions. For fine overviews of the state of research in Latin American women's history at different moments in time, written by the field's outstanding pioneer, see Lavrin 1978a, 1978b, 1987, 1989a, 1989b. Cf. Knaster 1976; Pescatello 1976; Navarro 1979, esp. 120; Stoner 1987; Arrom 1991.

10. On dowry and inheritance rights, see Lavrin and Couturier 1979; Couturier 1985; Kellogg 1984, 1986; Metcalf 1986. On convents and female-specific institutions and education, see Soeiro 1978; Muriel 1946, 1963, 1974 (cf. 1982); Gonzalbo Aizpuru 1987a, 1987b; Arenal 1983. On civil and ecclesiastical law, prescriptive codes, and the evolution of patriarchal ideology, see Arrom 1985a, 1985b; Rípodas Ardanaz 1977; Nizza da Silva 1984, 1989; Socolow 1980; Lavrin 1989a, 1989c; Gonzalbo Aizpuru 1987a, 1987b; Carner 1987; Ramos Escandón 1987a.

11. The corpus of historical works exploring women's subordinate yet active social participation is by now quite large. For examples of work on women's economic roles and their importance in the social organization of rich and poor households, see Burkett 1978; Villanueva 1985; Couturier 1978; Arrom 1985b; Nash 1980; Guy 1981; Keremitsis 1984; Mallon 1987; Stolcke 1984. Cf. Bourque and Warren 1981. On collective acts such as riots, rituals, and political revolts, see Taylor 1979 (which resonates interestingly with T. Kaplan 1982); Cherpak 1978; Silverblatt 1987; Rascón 1979; Soto 1979. For broad overviews of women's participation in the long sweep of history, see *fem* 1979, 1983; Muriel 1982; Ramos Escandón 1987b; Tuñón Pablos 1987; Silverblatt 1987.

On gender and color-class imperatives, see the astute observations of Mallon 1987, esp. 379, 401–2; cf. González Montes and Iracheta Cenegorta 1987; González de la Rocha 1988a, 1988b; Arizpe 1986, 59; Schutte 1988–89, 68–75, 78–81; Polémica 1980. For a broad discussion, see Kelly 1984, 51–64. Burkett (1978, cf. 1975; contrast Silverblatt 1980, 1987) at one time argued for a dynamic interplay between gender and color-class ideologies that opened a space for Indian women's social advancement rather than imposing a doubled burden of discrimination. The hypothesis exaggerated women's advantages relative to men; underestimated the cost to women, in personal and sexual domination, of "social climbing"; and left aside the equally strong evidence of social climbing by a small minority of Indian males. Burkett 1979 is a self-critical retrospective.

12. Particularly interesting in this regard is Tutino 1983; cf. Bourque and Warren 1981, 115–23; Taylor 1979, 154–56.

13. The most illuminating works on honor/shame values in a Latin American context are Martínez-Alier (now Stolcke) 1974; Gutiérrez 1985 (cf. 1980, 1984, 1991); Fox 1973; cf. Twinam 1989; Socolow 1980; McCaa 1984. Seed 1988b (cf. 1985, 1988a) contributes significant material but should be used with caution since she conflates specific institutional

efforts by the state to strengthen parental authority with the direction of social change in civil society. In addition, her depiction of ecclesiastical doctrine and of the church's actual impact on marriage decisions are in some respects misleading: see the apt comments of Lavrin 1989a: 6, 17–18, 40–41 n. 45.

Perhaps the most compelling presentation of Latin American honor/shame codes in action is the ingenious novella by García Márquez (1981).

The honor/shame literature for Latin America was inspired by an important body of work on honor/shame values in the Mediterranean world. See Peristiany 1966; Schneider 1971; Pitt-Rivers 1971 [1954], 1977; cf. Collier 1989, 203, 213–14. My presentation of the honor/shame complex refers to the refined version of the code that reflected luster on the colonial elite and that sets the context for paradigmatic presentations of the code in the Latin American scholarship cited above. My critique of the culture concept that informs uses of the honor/shame complex in the scholarly literature refers to the Latin American literature and does not necessarily apply to the Mediterranean literature. The Mediterranean literature is subtly different: the ethnographic literature on honor/shame values for the Mediterranean generally focused on plebeian social strata—peasants, pastoralists, plebeian villagers—for paradigmatic explication of the codes, viewed elite behavior as deviations from a plebeian norm, and generally explored the shifting meaning of honor according to social rank and context. See esp. Pitt-Rivers 1966, 39, 23, 64–72; Caro Baroja 1966, 119–22; Bourdieu 1966.

14. The connection between an impossible standard of perfection and the expectation that living women were inherently suspect—too frail, morally, to live up to the standards of female goodness and therefore inclined to evil, betrayal, and wrongdoings unless strictly monitored—accounts for the paradox that church ideologies could simultaneously propagate an ideal of mutuality in male-female relations and misogynistic denunciations of women as evildoers. For a revealing discourse simultaneously praising a female ideal while proclaiming that few living women could really meet such standards of perfection, see León 1583, chap. 1; cf. Perry 1985, esp. 138, 139, 152–55, 157; Boxer 1975, 97–112; and the provocative theoretical discussion of de Lauretis 1984, esp. 5–6.

15. In addition, a fine home or villa staffed by servants might allow for discreet forms of sexual liaison that preserved outer proprieties. Finally, the combined effect of subaltern women's vulnerability to coercive sex and to violence by male superiors, and subaltern men's social inferiority vis à vis wealthy men, perhaps deflected the intensity and coerciveness of predatory sexual pressure targeted at women of leading families.

16. There is a lively debate on the relative importance of race and class in colonial society and on their interplay as "social race." For fine works exploring social race, see R. D. Anderson 1988; Seed 1982. For a fairly recent cycle of debate, see Chance and Taylor 1977, 1979; McCaa et al. 1979; McCaa and Schwartz 1983; Seed 1983; Seed with Rust 1983; cf. Chance 1978. New works that break out of the paradigms set by these debates include Chambers 1992; Cope 1994. This is not the place to attempt a full explication and resolution of the debate. For our purposes, two key points stand out: almost all researchers agree that at the upper levels of society, elites were white and that the persons of color who managed to break into the upper reaches of society could be and often were culturally redefined as white.

17. On racial ideology and the resentments directed at social climbers, see Stern 1982, chap. 7. For purchase of legal certificates of whiteness and elite fears of racial infiltration, see Andrews 1985.

18. See Tutino 1983.

19. The building of power groups and the economic diversification common in elite entrepreneurship meant that family and kinship alliances were fundamental to elite political economy. In this context values that prescribed deference to the family patriarch-elder and

that fostered a mystique of female virginity facilitated efforts of family leaders to control the marriage choices of daughters and thereby pursue a political economy of kinship and marriage alliance. At the same time the role of family and lineage in cultural definitions of honorable elite manhood gave an incentive to young Spanish immigrant men to marry into honorable creole families, thereby acquiring the trappings of family honor while infusing new wealth and capital into distinguished families. For insight and discussion regarding family alliances and business, see Kicza 1983; *JFH* 1985; Ladd 1976; Brading 1971; cf. Tutino 1983; and for postcolonial times, Lomnitz and Pérez L. 1987. On power groups in colonial society, see Stern 1982, chap. 4.

20. This is quite apparent if one analyzes the social and class composition of the samples studied by Martínez-Alier 1974; Seed 1988b. The statistical comparison of morality and violence cases for Mexico City in Chapter 11 below and the social composition of the marital litigants in Arrom 1985b are consistent with this pattern.

21. For a sampling of this literature, see Lavrin 1989d; Ortega Noriega 1986a; Seminario de Historia de las Mentalidades 1982; cf. Lavrin 1987, 110; Kuznesof and Oppenheimer 1985, 224; Arrom 1985b. The sense of space for individual maneuver is further underscored by research on eighteenth- and nineteenth-century ideology that condemned traditional gender mores as backward and favored limited openings, under male tutelage and the better to perform female roles, of new education and employment opportunities. See Arrom 1985b; Ramos Escandón 1987a; Kish 1983.

22. This is an especially well developed theme for Mexico and has sparked an outstanding study by Franco (1989) of women's search for a voice of their own. Other notable studies of such nonconformists include Alberro 1982, 1987a; Seminario de Historia de las Mentalidades 1987; Behar 1987, 1989; Chambers 1989; *fem* 1983; González Marmolejo et al. 1982; Macías 1982; Ortega Noriega 1986a; Rascón 1979; Tuñón 1987.

23. See M. Douglas 1966 (cf. 1970) and Foucault's insistence that the knowledge, discourses, and institutions of deviance are integral to study of the "power of normalization" (1977, 308, for quote; cf. 1978–86, vol. 1).

24. Especially illuminating within this framework is Lavrin 1989a, 1989d; cf. the more general interpretation of baroque culture in I. A. Leonard 1959; Paz 1982; and the sources in n. 21 above.

25. Some clarification is in order here. In their sophisticated studies, Martínez-Alier (1974) and Gutiérrez (1985, 1980, 1984) devote considerable attention to tension between competing normative value systems and to the individual maneuvers and social transformations linked to such tensions. But the competition of values lies outside the realm of the honor/shame tradition itself, which is presented as a system of values that enjoyed a wide consensus in the Hispanized sectors of civil society before the advent of major historical change. Instead the tensions in values are linked either to the transition to capitalist values (i.e., status based on individual achievement in a society based on the free contract principle, rather than status based on ascription from birth in a society founded on a hierarchical principle linked to biological descent) or to the competing institutional stances by church and state on the specific question of freedom to choose one's marriage partner. Excluded from this picture is neither individual manipulation of honor concepts commanding wide assent nor differences between church and state also subject to manipulation nor even a sense of grand transition from one normative system to another. Excluded, rather, is the notion that the traditional codes of gender right, obligation, and honor associated with the honor/shame complex may themselves have been contested and multiple. (For a frank retrospective remark that makes a partial concession in this direction, see Stolcke 1989, xv.)

At a theoretical level the treatment of the honor/shame complex as a culture — a worldview and body of values agreed upon and manipulated by all — relies on a rather seamless and consensual culture concept increasingly questionable in view of recent scholarship criticizing the universality of meaning systems in a given culture and underscoring the power dynamics *within* culture. See Hunt 1989; Walters 1980; Sabean 1984, esp. 28–30, 95, 195; cf. the sharp revision of the once idealized image of the Russian *mir* in Hoch 1986. Sabean's notion of culture as a "language of argument" about the issues that arise in shared situations captures nicely the new approach to culture. A profound challenge to the epistemological foundations of the earlier culture concept is Bourdieu's "theory of practice," much of which was developed out of his studies of honor culture among the Kabyle (1977, 1966).

26. There has long been recognition, of course, that Indians might have pursued a distinctive cultural code regarding gender and sexuality. A classic synthetic statement is Wolf 1959, 202–56 passim; more recent works that implicitly contrast the gender code of Indians and that of Hispanized society include Gruzinski 1987 (cf. 1988); Gutiérrez 1991; Ortega Noriega 1986b. For outstanding studies that somewhat dissolve these distinctions and limitations, see Behar 1987, 1989. In these works women who sought to compensate magically for their powerlessness within the social body could invoke the assistance and remedies of female magical specialists from the socially and ethnically degraded margins of the respectable social body. One might interpret this either as a dialectical play between insider and deviant, in a multiethnic world, who collaborated in desperate or compensatory acts at the fringes of an accepted code of behavior, or as evidence of an alternative world of gender values and practices in female popular culture — evidence, that is, of a competing gender culture within the social body. Behar appears to lean toward the latter view.

27. See Gutiérrez 1985, 84–86, 95–96; Martínez-Alier 1974, 124; cf. Tutino 1983, 378–81; Pescatello 1976, 147, 154, 169.

28. For Mexico specifically, see Soto 1979; Rascón 1979; Macías 1982. For other cases, see Navarro 1981, 1982, 1988; *JTWS* 1981; Chaney 1979. It is important to note that by the 1990s the "postponement" began to dissolve; one could discern the beginnings of historical efforts to study the deep interplays of gender culture and political culture along the lines suggested here. For a pioneering example, see Guy 1991; cf. O'Malley 1986 and the second part of n. 29 below.

29. Many of these studies, like this book, seek to open the door to these questions by examining the politics of family relations and violence. For Mexico, see Arrom 1985b, chap. 5; Behar 1987, 1989; Boyer 1989; González Montes and Iracheta Cenegorta 1987; Lavrin 1989c. For comparison elsewhere in Latin America, see Flores Galindo and Chocano 1984; Nizza da Silva 1989. See also the comments of Lavrin 1987, 110.

The larger picture is the movement in feminist scholarship to merge the history of gender and the history of politics and states into a unified framework of analysis. For important programmatic statements, see J. W. Scott 1988; G. Lerner 1986; Radku 1986; Gailey 1987; cf. Silverblatt 1988. For fine case studies that engage the theoretical issues at stake from a variety of world regions including Latin America, see Brown 1990; Gordon 1988; Guy 1991; Koonz 1987; MacLean 1989; O'Malley 1986.

30. This concept of patriarchy is sufficiently specific to make *patriarchy* a potential subset, in theory, within a larger theoretical category such as *gender subordination* or *male supremacy*. It organically integrates gender subordination in society as a whole and father-elder dominance in families in particular. This sort of specificity is needed if we are to discern historical change between distinct systems of gender subordination or if we are to analyze theoretically the varied articulations between household organization and wider gender patterns in society. My thinking on these matters has been influenced and enriched by Gordon 1988, esp. vi–vii; Mallon 1987. See also Meillassoux 1977 and the provocative study of Stacey 1983.

31. This approach to ranking within gender groups and the play between multiple masculinities and femininities within a society where color-class axes of hierarchy come into

relation with gender axes of hierarchy differs from early feminist theory that emphasized more exclusively the alliance of men as a group in subordinating women as a group. For a recent theoretical discussion of multiple and hierarchical masculinities and femininities, see Connell 1987, esp. 109–11, 183–90; cf. Gordon 1988, 254–55; Tomes 1978. For a pointed early critique of the tendency to overlook rankings within the genders, see A. Y. Davis 1981, esp. 5–19, 23, 172–201.

32. The empirical bases for the specific patterns mentioned above will emerge in the course of this book. For the present, suffice it to note that close observers of peasantries in modern Mexico and in other regions have also found an interlocked age and sex principle fundamental to understanding family and community power dynamics. See, e.g., Lewis 1951, 51–53, 73–79, 210, 281–82, 325, 411–12, 419–20; cf. Pitt-Rivers 1977, 77–83; Hoch 1986.

33. For a highly illuminating theoretical approach to understanding culture within a framework of practice rather than cognitive maps explicated by informants to anthropological interviewers, see Bourdieu 1977; cf. Connell 1987 for the specific case of gender.

34. This is not to deny, of course, that a treasure trove of sensitive analysis of gender may emerge from a study of this evangelical context and the institutional discourses it produced. For the possibilities and limitations, see, e.g., Seminario de Historia de las Mentalidades 1980 (cf. 1982, 1987); Gruzinski 1988, 1989a; Burkhart 1989; Clendinnen 1982b; Krippner-Martínez 1989, 1990.

35. For the conjoining of economic immiseration and boom into a single process, see, aside from the specific regional sources cited in nn. 41, 44, and 54 below, Van Young 1986; cf. Coatsworth 1982; Florescano 1969, 1971; Garner 1985, esp. 299–300, 321 n. 51; Humboldt 1811, vol. 1, bk. 2, chap. 6, 184–86; chap. 7, 223–35; Ladd 1976, 1988; Lynch 1973, 295–302; Tutino 1986, pt. 1.

36. This logic of colonial political economy is a complex theoretical problem essential to understanding the apparent paradoxes of colonial economic life. For monographic treatments where the logic of conjoined immiseration and prosperity come through starkly, see Góngora 1974; Florescano 1969; Larson 1988 (cf. 1980). For a more theoretical discussion, see Stern 1988b.

37. For crime and crackdown on the plebeians, see Scardaville 1977, 1980; Haslip 1980; Viqueira Albán 1987. On agrarian reform proposals by Friars Antonio de San Miguel and Manuel Abad y Queipo of the bishopric of Michoacán, see Florescano 1971, 480–87; Brading 1991, 530, 567–73. The concern with family and racial order may be gleaned from Arrom 1985b; Gutiérrez 1991; Seed 1988b; cf. Andrews 1985. On the heightened presence and role of militias, see Archer 1977; Brading 1971, 156–58, 274–78, 284–91; Pastor 1987, 197–98. On fear of provoking wider uprisings, see Taylor 1979, 120. Fine guides to elite tensions and popular insurrection — a topic with a vast historiography — include Lynch 1973, chap. 9; Tutino 1986, pt. 1; Hamnett 1986, 1971; Priestley 1916, esp. 135–233; cf. Katz 1988b: esp. chaps. 1–7, 17–18, for long-term and comparative perspectives.

38. For example, economic immiseration may sharpen tensions over household allowances, income streams, and income pooling. For vivid examples of the importance of these issues among the poor of contemporary Mexico, see Benería and Roldán 1987, 109–63; González de la Rocha 1988b, 1988a. For criminological and sociological perspectives on the role of access to resources in family stress and violence, see, e.g., Gelles 1974, 119–30, 137; Gelles 1987; Goode 1975; and the cautionary discussion in Gordon 1988, 173–74, 285–88.

39. The two alternatives are not, of course, mutually exclusive. For the notion that a sense of flux may provoke efforts to reassert "fixity," I am indebted to the insightful discussion in J. W. Scott 1986, 1067–68, 1072–74.

40. For fine recent treatments of the regionalism question, see Joseph 1991; Van Young 1992a, 1992b; cf. Altman and Lockhart 1976, esp. 3–28. The "many Mexicos" phrase was coined by Simpson (1941). Of course, for topics that have produced a plethora of superb re-

gional studies, it is more feasible to write a grand narrative that ties together regional social histories and is therefore not limited to an elitist level of analysis. For Mexico the most notable example of such an opportunity is the social and political history of the Mexican Revolution itself: see, e.g., Knight 1986; Katz 1981. The related question of peasant agrarian movements is another example: see, e.g., Katz 1988b; Tutino 1986.

41. The description of Morelos that follows is based mainly on the ample secondary literature (inevitably filtered and amplified by my own archival and direct observations). For the purposes of my study I have defined "Morelos" as the region comprised of the following four *alcaldía mayor* districts: Cuautla Amilpas, Cuernavaca, the Tlayacapa-Totolapa jurisdiction within Chalco, and Tetela del Volcán. For basic background on these districts, see Gerhard 1972; on the logic of treating Morelos as an ecological and historical region, notwithstanding its failure to gain jurisdictional status as such until the nineteenth century, see Barrett 1976.

The best succinct interpretation of late colonial Morelos is C. E. Martin 1982, which resonates beautifully with Sotelo Inclán 1943; cf. Hernández Chávez 1991. These works are supplemented by the following fine studies: Crespo 1984 (esp. the essays by Maldonado J., C. E. Martin, Rodríguez Lazcano, Von Wobeser, Scharrer Tamm, Huerta, Von Mentz); C. E. Martin 1985; Von Mentz 1988; Warman 1976, 20–52, 71; Lewis 1951, xxiii–xxv, 3–11, 20–22, 26–30, 48, 81–89, 114, 226–30, 253–58; Riley 1973; Barrett 1970; García Martínez 1969; Haskett 1987, 1988, 1991a, 1991b; Hassig 1985, 61, 200; Von Wobeser 1983; Crespo and Frey 1982; Carrasco 1982; Gruzinski 1989b, 105–72. See also Brading 1971, 116; Hamnett 1986, 71–72, 143, 157–59, 163–64, 174, 229 n. 40. For comparison of Morelos with the history of communities in nearby regions of central Mexico, see Gibson 1964; Lockhart 1992; cf. Cline 1986; García Martínez 1987; Tutino 1986.

42. This aspect of the *tierra fría* adaptation comes through especially vividly in Lewis 1951, xxiii–xxv, 3–11, 20–22, 26–30, 48, 81–89, 114, 226–30, 253–58; cf. de la Peña 1980, 28–29, 57. On the interest of sugar haciendas in integrating *tierra caliente* and *tierra fría*, see Warman 1976, 47–49.

43. For interethnic blurring in Morelos, the following archival sources have been quite useful: AGNCr, vol. 38, exp. 2, Tesoyuca 1809, fols. 39r, 58v (multiple ethnic labels/same person); vol. 47, exp. 7, Hda. del Puente (interethnic networks: girls collecting *leña*); exp. 13, Hda. Miacatlán 1815 (networks); vol. 48, exp. 5, Hda. del Puente 1816 (networks); vol. 202, exp. 5, Achichipico 1802, fols. 395–400 (multiethnic peasantry and petty commodity production); vol. 212, exp. 16, Cuautla Amilpas 1800, fol. 247r (Indians and mulattoes riot together); vol. 215, exp. 11, Yautepec 1775, fol. 311v (mulatto who understands Nahuatl); vol. 253, exps. 2/3, Tepoztlán 1768, fols. 23r, 27r, 33v (multiple ethnic labels/same person); exp. 8, Tepoztlán 1802, fols. 231v–232r (multiple ethnic labels/same person; multiracial labor network); vol. 254, exp. 3, Zamatitlán 1803 (networks); exp. 6, Yautepec 1792, fols. 138r–146v (racial composition of witness network); vol. 262, exp. 3, Xuchitepec 1772, fols. 74r, 86v (same man, married to mulatta, variously identified as "Indian," "mulatto"); exp. 4, Xochitepec 1816, fols. 108v, 112r (interracial *novios*). Also illuminating are C. E. Martin 1982, 1985, esp. 174–75; Rodríguez Lazcano 1984, 97–99; Sotelo Inclán 1943, 101–4, 114–16, 122–23, 138–46, 229 n. 1; Hernández Chávez 1991, 27–39.

44. The description of Oaxaca that follows draws mainly on the extensive secondary literature (amplified by my own research and observations) and focuses on the three core subregions defined more precisely in n. 45 below. The best succinct analyses are Reina 1988a; Romero Frizzi 1988. Pioneering studies that bear on the region as a whole are Carmagnani 1982, 1988; Hamnett 1971; Taylor 1979. For further background, see Humboldt 1811, vol. 3, bk. 4, chap. 10, 72–79; Hamnett 1986, 143, 145–49, 162, 168–71; Pastor et al. 1979 (but cf. Garner 1985, 322–23); and Reina 1988b for long-term perspective. For the Mixteca Alta specifically, see Romero Frizzi 1985 (cf. 1979, 1983); Pastor 1987; Spores 1967, 1984. On

the Zapotec Valley, see Taylor 1972; Whitecotton 1977; cf. Dennis 1987. For Villa Alta, Chance 1989 (cf. 1985) is fundamental. For background on the capital city of Antequera, see Chance 1978; Chance and Taylor 1977.

45. The three subregions I have defined as constituting the core region of Oaxaca for purposes of this study are the following: (1) the Mixteca Alta, comprised of the *alcaldías mayores* of Teposcolula and Nochistlán; (2) the Villa Alta *alcaldía mayor* district, a major portion of the Sierra Zapoteca; and (3) the south-central portion of the Zapotec Valley. The *alcaldía mayor* designations of the latter are far more complicated because of a complex institutional and jurisdictional history that turned the relevant *alcaldía mayor* districts into archipelagos of nonadjoining lands (see Gerhard 1972; García Martínez 1969) and because I have excluded the northern Etla arm of the valley region. (I did so because the Etla valley zone was the most fertile area and attracted the most intense penetration by non-Indians in agriculture; its inclusion would have diluted the contrasts established for comparative regional purposes.) Therefore, for purposes of this study, the Zapotec Valley subregion includes the *alcaldías mayores* of Zimatlán (excluding its coastal fragment); Mitla y Tlacolula (sometimes named Teotitlán del Valle, after its *cabecera*); the southern portion of Cuatro Villas (excluding the Etla valley section); and the southern valley portions of the Corregimiento de Antequera provinces (i.e., excluding coastal Colotepec and northern fragments of Sosola and Ixtlán). These subregions fall within the larger subregions defined as Valle, Sierra Norte, and Mixteca by Reina (1988a, 187–92) and are designed to heighten the contrast with Morelos. The three major subregions accounted for 76.2 percent of the entire Oaxaca intendancy population in 1793; each of my somewhat smaller core subregions was roughly equal to the others in total population.

46. By far the most profound analysis of ethnic reconstitution is Carmagnani 1988, whose approach resonates strongly with Farriss 1984. For a different interpretation and findings from the Valley of Mexico, see Lockhart 1992. For comparison with Andes, see Burga 1988. Carmagnani's vision of the dynamics of ethnicity and political officeholding, stated succinctly in his 1982 essay, is different from that of Chance 1989. My archival research lends support to Carmagnani's stronger emphasis on internal differentiation and social ranking among Indians, and the relationship between such internal hierarchies and the dynamics of officeholding and elections.

47. See esp. Taylor 1974; cf. 1972, 1979.

48. The doctoral dissertation research of Jeremy Baskes of the University of Chicago history department may well yield, however, revisionist findings on the presumably coercive aspects of the *repartimiento de mercancías* (personal communications by Baskes to author).

49. This less well known aspect of life in colonial Morelos comes through repeatedly in the archival documents. For examples, see AGN, Alcaldes Mayores, vol. 10, Cuernavaca 1749, fols. 40–48; AGNCr, vol. 44, exp. 14, Agueguecingo 1792; vol. 222, exp. 10, Tlayacapa 1779, fol. 72; AGN, Historia, vol. 132, exp. 26, Cuernavaca ca. 1793; vol. 157, exp. 13, Cuernavaca [1790s], fol. 146r.

50. Among the subregions of Morelos, Cuautla Amilpas stands closest to multiethnic reconstructions, and Chalco de Morelos/Tetela del Volcán stand closest to more exclusionary constructions of Indian ethnicity. Still, it is important to remember that these comments qualify rather than undermine the contrast. A vivid example of multiethnic constructions of community in emphatically Indian *pueblitos* is the study of Anenecuilco by Sotelo Inclán. In the 1799 *padrón*, the count of household adult heads and spouses of the *pueblo de naturales* of Anenecuilco is listed as 89.1 percent Indian (49 of 55 *casados/casadas, viudos/viudas*, adult *solteros/solteras*), but when amplified by a list of *Agregados a dicho Pueblo*, Anenecuilco's Indian proportion drops to 82.3 percent (51 of 62 adults). Even more important are the practical social alignments in specific contexts of identity and struggle. In Anenecuilco's 1807 conflict with the Mayorazgo de Salgado estate, the Indian village of

Anenecuilco presented four mestizo witnesses from Mapaztlán who paid rent to the Indians rather than to the hacienda for the lands on which they resided; the witnesses explicitly recognized the Indians as owners of the land. (The hacienda presented five witnesses, also land tenants, but their testimony was more lukewarm. Although they paid rent to the Mayorazgo de Salgado, they said they did not know who really owned the land. The implication was that their payments reflected coercion, not recognized land ownership.) In an 1808 conflict with Hacienda Mapaztlán, the Indians presented ten such witnesses, among them four whites (*españoles*), one *castizo*, two mulattoes, two mestizos, and only one Indian. Finally, during the War of Independence mobilization in Cuautla, Anenecuilco treated the local leader, the white Mapaztlán *ranchero* Don Francisco Ayala, as one of their own *hijos del pueblo* and constructed an oral tradition attributing his birthplace to Indian Anenecuilco. Sotelo Inclán recognized the parallelism with Emiliano Zapata. See, for all the above, Sotelo Inclán 1943: 101–4, 114–18, 122–23, 138–46, 169–90, 229 n. 1.

51. This problem of internal factionalism and charges of abuse against indigenous authorities is sometimes overlooked or minimized in overall interpretations of village life. But numerous specific instances pervade the archival documentation and may be gleaned from works whose main emphases lie elsewhere (Taylor 1979; cf. Chance 1989). For analysis that devotes more explicit attention to the problem, see Haskett 1991a (cf. Pastor 1987; Romero Frizzi 1985).

52. Less prominent cultural foundations may be provisionally defined as "bricolage-and-broker" cultures of slaves and racially mixed *castas* forging new cultural resources out of a diverse repertoire of remembered and newly invented knowledge drawn from diverse cultural roots. For a fuller and more theoretical treatment of this kind of cultural innovation, see the pioneering interpretation of African American cultural construction in Mintz and Price 1976. For Afro-Mexican cultural constructions more specifically, see Palmer 1976.

53. For a sensitive general statement of the common Indian/mestizo contrast and its connection to a sense that an Indian ethos placed emphasis on community and household harmony while a mestizo ethos emphasized individual dominance and power, see Wolf 1959, 214–42. For specific historical and ethnographic works that illustrate the relative weight (notwithstanding ambiguity) of gender complementarity, women's self-confidence and visibility, and a related community harmony ethos, in discussions of the indigenous Mesoamerican South, see Clendinnen 1982b; Elmendorf 1976; Mathews 1985 (cf. 1982); Nader 1989, 328–29 (but cf. 1990); Taylor 1979, esp. 155–56; Chiñas 1992. On female *cacicas* specifically in Oaxaca, see Heijmerink 1973, 290; Romero Frizzi 1985, 90; Spores 1967, 10–13, 132–54 passim; Taylor 1972, 45, 38; Whitecotton 1977, 155–56; cf., for Central America, Sherman 1979, 304. The discourse of indigenous gender complementarity spills beyond Mesoamerica: see, e.g., Isbell 1976. It can also lead to partial dissent from a view of Nahua cultures as patriarchal: see, e.g., Clendinnen 1991.

54. Aside from archival sources, my understanding of colonial Mexico City derives especially from the following: Arrom 1985b; Cope 1994, which is very pertinent and illuminating notwithstanding the midcolonial focus; Humboldt 1811, esp. vol. 1, bk. 2, chap. 7; vol. 2, bk. 3, chap. 8; Morales 1976; Scardaville 1977, 1980; Viqueira Albán 1987; see also Cooper 1965; Gibson 1964, 368–402; González Angulo Aguirre 1983; Haslip 1980 (cf. 1984); Lira 1983; López Monjardín 1985. For economic context in a society where agrarian crisis had a direct impact on city life, Florescano 1969 and Van Young 1986 are exceedingly useful; for a long-term view, see also Tutino 1986.

55. Humboldt 1811, vol. 2, bk. 3, chap. 8, 82, for population figures and quote. The ethnic proportions of 1803 were virtually identical to those of the 1790 census, even though the city's population had increased substantially in the intervening period. See BNM, vol. 117, año 1790, "Estado General de la Población."

56. Villarroel 1788, cited in Viqueira Albán 1987, 132 n. 1; cf. the remarkably similar esti-

mate by Arrom (1985b, 7–8), who uses live-in servants as a measure of elite and middling social rank.

57. Morales 1976, 375, 385–89, 400; cf. Arrom 1985b, 7–8.

58. See Humboldt 1811, vol. 1, bk. 2, chap. 6, 184; chap. 7, 223–29, 234–35.

59. I owe my understanding of the vertical ordering of space to the wonderfully vivid depiction of street life by Viqueira Albán 1987, 21, 133–38, and to the observations of Cope 1994 (the latter supplemented by personal communication).

60. On the Indian *parcialidades* of Tenochtitlán and Tlatelolco, the movement of people within the old Spanish section of the city, and the distinction between the Indian sections' more central urban districts and their more outlying satellites, see Lira 1983, esp. 31–42.

61. For dynamics of race and class in a relatively whitened regional capital in Indian Mexico, see Chance 1978; cf. Chance and Taylor 1977; R. D. Anderson 1988. For a superb portrait of middling respectability and aspiration in the whitened city of Arequipa, Peru, see Chambers 1992.

62. For the one-fifth estimate, see n. 56 above.

63. I believe, in any event, that for the gender struggles and conventions of daily life that are the focus of this book the last half-century of colonial rule would be too short a period for a revealing study of change over time, from both statistical and qualitative viewpoints. I will take up the change-over-time question briefly, within a much longer time span, in the postscript (Chapter 14). On the unsettling implications of women's history and gender study for historical periodization, see the classic essays reprinted in Kelly 1984, 1–18, 19–50.

64. The problems of summary, stylization, and institutional mediation come to the fore notably when one adopts a comparative perspective on criminal procedure in early modern times. For a superb interpretive account of the stylized pardon pleas by assailants in French homicide cases, see N. Z. Davis 1987; for the dependence of historians on formal indictments rather than verbatim witness testimony in research on England, see Beattie 1986, 19–22, esp. 22–23. For a description of criminal trial records in colonial Mexican homicide and assault cases, see Taylor 1979, 76–77.

CHAPTER THREE

1. Lewis 1964. For a fascinating study of Oscar Lewis that sets the *Pedro Martínez* biography in the context of Lewis's lifetime trajectory, work methods, and intellectual temperament, see Rigdon 1988. "Pedro Martínez" and his relatives were given fictitious names to protect their identities.

2. For the historical ethnography of Tepoztlán, see Lewis 1951; cf. Rigdon 1988, 27–45, 85 n. 10, 137–39, 185–218, 235–42. I mention Ruth Lewis specifically because she assumed major responsibility for editing and shaping raw interview materials into a powerful narrative; for a telling example of how important their collaboration was on the *Pedro Martínez* biography, see Rigdon 1988, 85 n. 10. As Rigdon 1988 makes clear, one of Oscar Lewis's talents was to develop a collaborative work method that drew in diverse people and talents. My own view of the corpus of Lewis's work, based on direct readings as well as Rigdon 1988, is that Lewis's best work came out of his early research cycle in Mexico. These works (1951, 1959, 1964, cf. 1944) blended ethnographic skill, teamwork, and direct fieldwork by Lewis. The Sánchez family biography (Lewis 1961; cf. 1969) is powerful reading as literature but marks the transition to emphasis on dramatic individuals more removed from the sense of time, place, and community that pervaded Lewis's earlier cycle of research. In addition it marked a transition to the culture of poverty imbroglio. These transitions culminated in Lewis's far less illuminating, profoundly more questionable publications on Puerto Rico (see esp. 1966).

3. This comes through strongly in Lewis 1964, esp. 6–53 passim, 218–46 passim; cf. Lewis 1951, 322, 327–28, 334–36.

4. See Lewis 1964, 56, 59; cf. 397–98. I am grateful to Eileen Findlay for drawing my attention to this passage.

5. Lewis 1964, 92; cf. the depictions of sexual assault by Zapatistas and anti-Zapatista troops in Tirado 1991, 74; Romanucci-Ross 1986, 18, 211.

6. Lewis 1964, 395–96; cf. 397–98. *Hija* literally means daughter, but as a colloquialism it may be used more broadly to signify social rank and a certain affect between speaker and listener.

7. Lewis 1964, 398.

8. The problem of whether criminal records and behavior illustrate mainly individual deviance and pathology or whether they might illuminate broader cultural patterning among populations that are in many ways sociologically normal has marked the evolution of the criminological and family violence literatures themselves. In an early era of criminological theory and study, analysis focused on problems of individual pathology. By the mid-to late twentieth century, studies that looked for the sociological networks and the cultural patterning that yielded criminal behavior emphasized concepts of subculture, protest masculinity, and the like. (This evolution, of course, is complicated by the necessity of taking into account the existence of some individuals, however few in proportional terms, who are so unquestionably pathological and idiosyncratic that their acts resist socioculturally normalized analysis.) For examples, orientation, and discussion, see esp. Wolfgang 1958, 1967; Wolfgang and Ferracuti 1967; Smart 1976; Messerschmidt 1986 (cf. 1993). See also Chesney-Lind 1986; Clinard and Abbot 1973; del Olmo 1981; Klein 1976; E. B. Leonard 1982; López-Rey 1970; Rico 1981; Schwendinger and Schwendinger 1983.

For the family violence literature and its contribution to the sociologically normalized study of violence, see esp. Dutton 1988; Gelles 1974, 1983, 1987; Gelles and Cornell 1983; Finkelhor et al. 1983; Levinson 1989; Steinmetz and Straus 1975; Straus et al. 1980. For specifically feminist critical appraisals of this literature, see Breines and Gordon 1983; Dobash and Dobash 1979; Gordon 1986; Kurz 1989; Russell 1975, 1982; Yllö and Bograd 1988. For a sampling of the use of criminal records in European social history to illustrate the wider sociocultural milieu and social relations, see Gatrell et al. 1980; Ruggiero 1975, 1979, 1985; Hay et al. 1975; Beattie 1986; Sharpe 1982, 1984, 1985; Stone 1983; Tomes 1978. For cultural interpretation of homicide in African scholarship, the starting point is Bohannan 1960c.

9. For the construction of net case sets and the exclusion of morality cases from the Morelos group, see Chapter 2 and the Appendix. The gross number of incidents for Morelos was 252.

10. PDBO, Morelos, Powviol1.out, p. 27; Powviol3.out, pp. 70, 65. The widespread availability of machetes and knives in the Morelos region may have contributed to the severity of wounds in many instances; these weapons were used in about half (50.3 percent) the incidents. For figures on weapons, $n = 181$ total valid cases. For assailant figures, $n = 185$ total valid cases. (The total figures for assailants and targets sometimes add up to less than 206 not only because of missing values but also because of measures taken to avoid double counting in cases when an assailant attacked, for example, more than one target in organically joined incidents, and vice versa. As a practical matter, the number of such incidents is small, the statistics turn out to be consistent whether such duplication is allowed or not, and I always check both sets of outputs for consistency. When citing data about assailants or targets, I almost always draw on databases designed to correct for the potential double-counting problem.) The percentages of male (89.7 percent) and female (7.6 percent) offenders do not add up to 100 percent because a few mixed-gender assailant groups create missing values (2.7 percent). If one excludes the mixed-gender groups, the percentages are 92.2 percent male and 7.8 percent female.

11. This is a conservative estimate because the count of unmarried individuals (*solteros, solteras, doncellas*) living as adults or household-head equivalents, and widows/widowers, gives an inflated number of loners. In practice many of these people lived with children and had dense relationships with relatives and/or lovers (*amasios, amasias*), and these relationships make it misleading to consider all such individuals loners rather than family-attached.

12. PDBO, Morelos, Newhypo1.lis, p. 29 (Chi-square significance, .31); cf. p. 33. Loners were also no more likely to commit *descarga* violence; ibid., p. 83; cf. Mormv1a.lis, p. 55. A battery of tests designed to see if loner status was statistically correlated with differences in severity of violence also proved negative.

13. See MacAndrew and Edgerton 1969; Menéndez 1988; Gelles 1974, 111–17, esp. 114; cf. Taylor 1979, 28–72, 92, 96.

14. See PDBO, Morelos, Newhypo1.lis, pp. 46–49.

15. These sorts of gender dynamics in male-on-female and male-on-male violence are pervasive in the materials discussed in detail below in Chapters 4 and 7.

16. See esp. Wolfgang and Ferracuti 1967; Messerschmidt 1986.

17. See the family violence literature and feminist critiques cited in n. 8 above.

18. See esp. Smart 1976; cf. E. B. Leonard 1982.

19. The mestizo/Indian contrast is discussed in Chapter 2 above. The plebeian/peasant contrast is related because the go-betweens, urban migrants, and sellers of nonagricultural services (i.e., artisans, shop laborers, miners, peddlers and muleteers, and the like) who comprise the plebeian sector are presumably more often mestizos or poor whites than Indians, while the Indians are more often peasants. (For an example of the relationship between the mestizo/Indian and plebeian/peasant contrasts, see Wolf 1959, 216–56 passim.) In addition, the literature on self-destructive and sexually charged expressions of male dominance focuses on the *pelado*, the pauperized plebeian migrant in the mestizo milieu of the large cities, as the purest expression of this social phenomenon. See Chapter 7 below; cf. Paz 1959; for brilliant critiques and analysis, see Bartra 1987; Monsiváis 1981, 1988.

20. See PDBO, Morelos, Newhypo1.lis, pp. 18, 24; cf. Mormv1a.lis, pp. 25–26. Once one disaggregates the category of gender-rooted violence, some subtle distinctions come into play. The only statistically significant associations are those between homicidal versus nonhomicidal violence, and Indian versus non-Indian ethnicity. But the strength of the associations is quite weak. (For assailants, the Chi-square is significant at .02 level, but Phi is only .18. For victims, the figures are .04 and .18, respectively.) See Morhom2, pt. 1, pp. 4, 7.

21. See PDBO, Morelos, Newhypo1.lis, pp. 17, 23; cf. Mormv1a.lis, pp. 23–24. The main statistically significant association is that plebeian assailants tended moderately more often than peasants (Chi-square significance, .0003; Phi correlation, .30; odds ratio, 4.1) to be charged with homicidal rather than nonhomicidal violence. See PDBO, Morelos, Morhom2, pt. 1, pp. 3, 6. It is possible that plebeian assailants were a bit more shielded than peasants from prosecution for nonhomicidal violence.

22. PDBO, Morelos, Powviol3.out, p. 69; Powviol2.out, p. 23. It is worth noting, however, that most of those who could not sign their names apparently did not require a Spanish translator. This group apparently comprised 64.7 percent of assailants and 64.2 percent of targets. The problem with such figures, however, is the possibility that the lack of interpreters is overstated due to carelessness on this point in the documentation. These figures are primarily useful, therefore, for comparisons between regions, and the most reliable language data for single regions is that on ability to sign names. Finally, it is worth noting that the pool of known cases shrinks sharply in the case of violence targets because numerous homicides create missing values in the target group. (For assailants, total valid $n = 133$, while for targets of violence, total valid $n = 81$.)

23. See PDBO, Morelos, Newhypo1.lis, pp. 19, 25 (cf. 22, 28); Mormv1a.lis, pp. 27–28; Newhypo5, pt. 1, p. 36.

24. It is possible, of course, that the narrow representation of targets under the age of fifteen is connected with the etiology of family violence. Cross-cultural studies suggest that adults, especially wives, tend to suffer the most physically injurious and debilitating family violence. See Levinson 1989, 81–82. The problem is that since the cross-cultural studies rely on records that may partly screen violence against younger children, this finding may be somewhat overstated.

25. These findings on assailants' gender are consistent with international work on the gender of assailants in homicide cases. See, e.g., Wolfgang 1958, 1967; Wolfgang and Ferracuti 1967; cf. Clinard and Abbot 1973; Levinson 1989; Bohannan 1960a. For historical consistency, see Beattie 1986, 83 (table).

26. This is the image that comes through in the classics by Sotelo Inclán 1943; Womack 1968; cf. C. E. Martin 1982.

27. For a detailed discussion on the imagery of *descarga* ventings, see Chapter 7 below; cf. the discussion of contemporary Brazilian violence in Linger 1990; the historical study of Renaissance Italy in Ruggiero 1979, 179; and the "subculture of violence" and "protest masculinity" ideas in Wolfgang and Ferracuti 1967; Messerschmidt 1986. For colonial elites' views that degraded folk — plebeians and Indians — killed for no good reason, see Chapter 7, n. 10, below. For a thoughtful analysis of the related problem of "fighting words," in Mexican context, see C. E. Martin 1990; Taylor 1979, 81–83.

28. For intelligent comment on the psychological dimension and the obstacles it poses for the analysis of motivation, see Wolfgang 1958, 185–99; Wolfgang and Ferracuti 1967, 209–10; Bohannan 1960b, 25–27 (cf. 1960a, 250–52); Taylor 1979, 91–93. On the advantages of crimes of passion rather than rational calculation an illuminating discussion resonant with the Mexican materials is Ruggiero 1979, 171–82.

29. Examples of the screening consequences of this kind of personal and institutional obfuscation are pervasive in the criminological literature. For example, some 95 percent of homicides are attributable to crimes of passion rather than premeditation. This dichotomy makes the category of passion so large that it obscures more than it reveals. See Wolfgang and Ferracuti 1967, 140–41; cf. Wolfgang 1967, 27, 272–75. In the Philadelphia police blotters of 1948–52 used in Wolfgang's classic study of homicide, "trivial altercations" alone accounted for better than a third of the homicides, and when "domestic quarrels" were added, these categories accounted for half the cases. The weight of these sorts of institutional glosses in the total picture was not at all unusual. See Wolfgang 1958, 190, 196–99. In Taylor's pioneering and perceptive study of colonial Mexico, extreme caution about the motivation issue led him to limit his quantitative tracking to self-ascribed motives by offenders. In his Central Mexico regions, the largest categories of self-ascribed motives are alcohol (26.7 percent) and *riñas* (the equivalent of trivial altercations; 18.7 percent). When self-defense in contexts of *riñas* and accidental killings (4.6 percent) are taken into account, the screening effect by assailants affects fully half the sample. See Taylor 1979, 94.

30. This is the larger point of the subculture of violence and family violence studies that moved away from the earlier criminological focus on interior psychology and pathology. See esp. Wolfgang and Ferracuti 1967, esp. 209–10; Gelles 1974, esp. 155. In his classic Philadelphia study, Wolfgang (1958, 187) made a useful distinction between motive and intent. The latter "refers to the actor's ability to comprehend the nature of his act. . . Intent is the resolve to commit an act, whereas motive is the inducement which stimulates a person to commit it." In this scheme, intent raises the more profound and vexing issues of interior psyche, while motive refers to the culturally recognizable, on some level understandable, issues that animate conflict, escalation, and violence.

31. The shift in perspective becomes obvious not only in self-defense cases but also in disputes precipitated by the victim. On the latter, see Wolfgang 1958, 252, 258; cf. Smart 1976, 17.

32. One of the most persuasive demonstrations of the importance and feasibility of this

sort of contextual social analysis for the specific issue of gender-rooted violence is Dobash and Dobash 1979 (cf. 1983). In the process, their study does a great deal to demystify myths of casual violence as well as related myths of deviance and psychopathology. From a different perspective the various works of Gelles (1974, 1983, 1987; Gelles and Cornell 1983) effectively undermine the same myths.

33. Wolfgang and Ferracuti 1967, 209; cf. Bohannan 1960b, 26–27; Beattie 1986, 102.

34. The results are as follows (total valid $n = 170$). For gender-rooted violence, restricted model = 52.9 percent; amplified model = 67.6 percent; midway model = 60.3 percent. For property/class violence, restricted = 17.1 percent; amplified = 22.9 percent; midway = 20.0 percent. For *descarga* ventings violence, restricted = 8.2 percent; amplified = 22.9 percent; midway = 15.6 percent. These figures are derived from PDBO, Morelos, Mormv1a.lis, pp. 5–6, and for calculation of the amplified property/class category, Morelos Powpat data entry outputs for variables 46 and 10 (case IDs 2, 73, 123, 124, 125, 153, 184, 194, 195, 224, 230, 246).

35. See PDBO, Morelos, Newhyp05, pt. 1, p. 6 (cf. pp. 5, 8–9); Mormv1a.lis, p. 66.

36. The resentment of such independent women is abundantly clear in the Lewis ethnographies (1951, 1964, 1959). The association with women's age comes through in an intriguing way in Mexican homicide statistics in the mid-twentieth century: see Bustamante and Bravo 1957. For historical examples in the 1760–1821 period, see Chapter 5 below.

37. See PDBO, Morelos, Powhyp01, p. 11. The results of the cross-tabulation by gender are important because they confirm the conclusions drawn from the frequency distributions within the comparatively small pool of female assailants through a Chi-square test involving a much larger pool ($n = 145$) of valid cases.

38. In truth, I prepared five different refined models to analyze which of them captured the gender contrast most strongly and to discern what the effect of different assumptions might be. These changes in assumptions included checking, for example, what might happen if one distinguished between "unofficial" and "official" primary relations, or if one constructed a primary-secondary-tertiary spectrum that ran parallel with a bonded-to-enemy spectrum. The result of the five-way refined model testing was that the distinctions turned out to have little statistical importance compared with the general contrast corroborated by *all* the refined model types. (The strength of correlation measure Cramer's V ranged in these models from .50 to .64.) To spare space and tediousness I refer here only to the refined model (identified as Ofvicre5 in the computer files and printouts) that best captured the contrast. See PDBO, Morelos, Morofvi1.lis, pp. 22–26.

39. The odds ratio is technically 74.9, but this is misleading since the odds ratio has no mathematical cap (it can range from 0 to infinity). Moreover, since cases of extremely tight associations can yield extremely small numbers of actual counts notwithstanding high numbers of expected values in a contingency table, slight changes in actual counts can yield strong changes in the odds ratio once the odds ratio is already quite strong. In this instance, for example, given the scarcity of inner primary relations with male victims, if the pool of total cases were augmented by an extra two cases of inner primary cases with male instead of female targets, the odds ratio would drop by half, to 37.4. A measure of association that compensates for the deceptive aspect of this mathematical characteristic of the odds ratio [o]is Yule's Q ($[o - 1] \div [o + 1]$), which has a finite range between 0 and 1 and reaches a very high 0.9 level of association when the odds ratio reaches 19 (and a 0.95 level when it reaches 39). In the refined model under discussion here, Yule's Q is 0.97, but even if one halved the odds ratio to 37.4, Yule's Q would fall only slightly, to 0.95. The larger point, therefore, is not to take the 74.9 multiple literally but to note that once an odds ratio soars toward 20 or higher, it points to extremely strong probability contrasts.

40. Only two of the sixty-two cases in the Morelos set of violence against women involved female-on-female violence. PDBO, Morelos, Powhyp03.out, p. 5.

41. The problem of underreporting of domestic violence is well known in the family violence literature: see the sources cited in n. 8 above. For the suggestion that even homicide was underreported in domestic violence cases in a region of colonial Mexico, see MacLeod 1989; cf. Wolfgang 1958, 284–89. MacLeod's suggestion was confirmed, in my experience, by the Mexico City maltreatment (*mala vida*) cases discussed in Chapter 11 below; by my Addpat data files in PDBO (a database of violence against females that did not lead to criminal cases for the core data set, even though the violence could have justified criminal proceedings); and by "mystery cases" I encountered in the Oaxaca records, especially the ATOVA files from Villa Alta.

42. This must be qualified once one takes age into account. If one takes unreported violence against youth (say, dependent or unmarried minors approximately fourteen to nineteen years of age) and younger children of both sexes into account, the data may turn out not to understate the gender contrast. It is seriously doubtful that the data overstate the contrast, however, if one restricts the definition of violence to incidents serious enough to produce plausible criminal proceedings rather than adopting a definition so elastic that it includes acts ranging from mild slaps and shoves, to assaults leading to serious wounds requiring medical attention, to homicide. For a critique of the elastic definition that prevails in some sociological literature on family violence, see Yllö and Bograd 1988.

43. $N = 62$ total valid cases. See PDBO, Morelos, Morofvi1.lis, pp. 122, 120, 124; Newhypo5, pt. 1, p. 12 (cf. p. 11; Newhypo5, pt. 2, pp. 87, 86).

44. Students of the discourse and sociology of rape will recognize certain parallels: while discourses often focus attention on the "deviance" of rape targets or upon the terror of sexual violence by vicious strangers, rape most often targets "normal" women or female youth and most often occurs between people who know each other. These parallels suggest that the well-known contrast between the discourse and sociology of rape is, at least in the Mexican case, a subset of a contrast applicable to all severely injurious violence — including but not limited to rape — against women and female youth. For an introduction to the (often highly polemical) literature illustrating the contrast between the discourse and the sociology of rape, see Brownmiller 1975; A. Y. Davis 1981, 172–201; Smart 1976, 93–95; Russell 1975, 1982, 1984. Among the thirteen Morelos sexual assaults, five were by primary relations and six by secondary relations. See PDBO, Morelos, Morofvi1.lis, p. 18; Morofvi2.lis, p. 18.

45. In this discourse, too, "good" husbands learned to restrain their *descarga* fits to explosions that were less than seriously injurious. This notion underlies the apparent contradictions in the following discursive sequence: "There were times when I beat my wife, it's true. . . . But I did not make a slave of my wife. . . . The rights I gave her were: not to be treated badly, not to be beaten" (excerpts from a longer discourse by Pedro Martínez in Lewis 1964, 397–98). Even if Lewis rearranged materials for readability, the sequence illuminates the notion that husbands who restrained their *descarga* violence did not truly mistreat or beat their wives.

46. Lewis 1964, 398.

47. For this calculation, $n = 130$ valid cases (excluded missing values = 9). See PDBO, Morelos, Newhypo1.lis, p. 84; cf. Mormv1a.lis, pp. 7–8; Powvio1.out, p. 29. Statistical tests of the association between *descarga* incidents (by amplified definition, since restricted definitions yield small numbers for both male and female targets) and male rather than female targets confirm the intuitive sense given by these numbers: *descarga* was moderately more associated with a world of male-on-male violence. For tests according to the gender of the targets, the Chi-square significance level was .0019, the linear correlation coefficient Phi was .24, and the actual probability of *descarga* violence for male targets amounted to 1.31 of random probability, while the ratio for females was only 0.32. See PDBO, Morelos, Newhypo1.lis, pp. 84, 90; Mortst1.lis, pp. 7, 9.

48. Research in *mala vida* cases and construction of an augmented database (known in

PDBO as the Addpat files) of violence against women that *could* have justified criminal proceedings but did not, for one reason or another, lead to criminal proceedings incorporated in the core statistical case set corroborates that such incidents occurred. Cf. Boyer 1982, 1989; Arrom 1976; Arrom 1985b, 206–58.

49. Even a woman who fought with her husband and feared his violence might think that his domestic ill temper and violent inclinations were a result of problems in his relations with men outside the domestic arena. See, e.g., AGNCr, vol. 47, exp. 8, Xoxocotla 1804, fol. 242v; cf. n. 50 below.

50. See, for example, the discourse of Esperanza de Martínez when trying to pull her sons into family reconciliation despite their father's ill temper and violence (Lewis 1964, 374). The larger issue, of course, is the way that solidarities of color, class, and family could place women in a crossfire of conflict and solidarity with their men, thereby encouraging discourses that might in some way excuse or explain their abuses. For further discussion of such crossfires and the ambivalence they encouraged, see Chapters 6 and 8 below; cf. Polémica 1980. For a chilling examination of women's receptivity to reconciliation efforts and men's promises of improved behavior after battering, especially in early stages of the battering syndrome, see Walker 1983.

51. This is evident throughout the archival documents and will become clearer in Chapter 4. The point also comes through in the elopement patterns discussed in the honor/shame literature: see esp. Martínez-Alier 1974; Gutiérrez 1980, 1984, 1985; Seed 1988b.

52. For a vivid contemporary example of this cruel dilemma, see González de la Rocha 1988a (cf. 1988b).

53. The description that follows is drawn from Lewis 1964, 269–70, 306–9, 332–36, 353–62, 395–98, 404, 488–89; Lewis 1959, 33–38.

54. The problem was further compounded because Esperanza had developed a drinking problem after the death of her newborn daughter Sara in 1939. In effect she ended up — like Pedro — setting aside some money for personal or discretionary spending that diminished the family allowance.

55. In Pedro Martínez's version of the events, the rope undertaking was a mere act of charity for a poverty-stricken widow with whom he had no sexual liaison. Relatives and neighbors had stirred up rumors and trouble. His rather benign version of events is belied, however, by the voices of Esperanza and their son Felipe, by his rather volcanic escalation when challenged, and by the traumatic impact of the episode on the family.

56. Lewis 1964, 307. On fears of women's magic and the taming of men, see Lewis 1951, 324–25, 281–82, 294–95; Lewis 1964, 500; cf. Behar 1987, 1989, 1993.

57. One must remember that families often constitute ambivalent arenas that blend solidarity as well as conflict. This ambivalence may be seen in parent-child as well as husband-wife relations. The same Pedro Martínez who beat his daughter Conchita severely for school expulsion and sexual improprieties and who at one point drove her to attempt suicide also financed her schooling by giving up independent agricultural work for peon labor for three years. This was all the more remarkable because servile field labor in the prerevolution years constituted a vivid and humiliating boyhood memory associated with beatings and symbolic emasculation. See Lewis 1964, 249–58, 339, 342–44, 471–72; Lewis 1959, 30, 49–51; Oscar Lewis to Carolina Luján, Dec. 12, 1962, in Rigdon 1988, 237. The same Esperanza who refused to recast the conflict with Eulalia as a *descarga* episode mobilized the discourse of Pedro's temporary — and therefore tolerable — *descarga* fits when trying to convince her children to return home. See Lewis 1964, 374.

58. See esp. Lewis 1964, 395–98, for the idealized retrospective that deals forthrightly with the fact that domestic violence "happened" without once mentioning specific disputes or conflicts, let alone the Eulalia episode.

59. Lewis 1964, 398, 356, for quotes.

1. The account of the first María is drawn from AGNCr, vol. 262, exp. 11, Hda. San Gaspar 1803, fols. 160–201, esp. 161r–166v, 169r–171r, 176v, 182r, 187r–193r, 200r–v. Quotations are on fols. 163r ("filthy," from María Gertrudis's own testimony, and "skirts"; cf. 166v, 170r, 176v); 166v ("contented" and "two of them"); 170r ("go to shit"; cf. 176v). María Gertrudis Martínez was about twenty-five years old, and her husband Francisco Gerónimo was about thirty years old.

2. María Francisca was a twenty-one-year old monolingual Nahuatl speaker, unlike the bilingual María Gertrudis and Francisco Gerónimo, and her willingness to work as a *molendera* places her family among the lower peasant strata of Hacienda San Gaspar.

3. See C. E. Martin 1985, 143; cf. Gibson 1964, 251–52.

4. The account of the second María is drawn from AGNCr, vol. 253, exp. 5, Oaxtepec 1817, fols. 138–60, esp. 139r, 141r–145v, 148v–149v, 151r–155r. Quotations are on fols. 151v ("wounded" and "himself sought out death"); 154v ("persecuted" and "Devil"); 145r ("not side by side").

5. The evidence does not allow one to infer reliably whether María Teresa of Texalpa could claim a measure of success in her life with José Marcelino.

6. This statement is based on a common pattern in other cases when women contested male sexual freedom rather than specific information regarding Esquicio Ponciano's wife. This pattern will be elucidated with appropriate reference citations later in this chapter.

7. It is very important not to project backward to early modern history the contemporary assumption that rape is an act nearly universally condemned in society. In early modern Europe as well as colonial Latin America, whether rape transgressed patriarchal boundaries and proprieties depended on the social circumstances surrounding the act. The color-class standing of assailants and targets, their kin relationship or the absence thereof, and their respective ages, marital status, and moral standing all contributed to defining in practice whether a rape drew cultural and legal treatment as a serious criminal transgression of sexual property and social propriety or was handled as a more humdrum matter. On Europe, see, e.g., Ruggiero 1985; Rossiaud 1978. For the complexities of legal and cultural treatment of rape in colonial Latin America, see BNM, vol. 971, Echebarria y Ojeda 1791, 38–39, 48–49; Burkett 1975; Giraud 1987. The ongoing researches of Carmen Castañeda on Guadalajara have also done much to illuminate our knowledge.

8. The classic Cuban film of female awakening, *Retrato de Teresa* (Portrait of Teresa), captures the image nicely. When the female hero Teresa dared to contest her husband's prerogatives and in particular his sexual infidelity, Teresa's mother reminded her that it was unwise to question the double standard: "Woman will always be woman and man will always be man. . . . That's something even Fidel can't change!" (*La mujer siempre será mujer y el hombre siempre será hombre. . . . ¡Eso no lo puede cambiar ni Fidel!*)

9. See AGNCr, vol. 253, exp. 10, Tepoztlán 1765, fol. 344r.

10. See AGNCr, vol. 47, exp. 13, Hda. Miacatlán 1815, esp. fols. 417v–419r (418v for quote; emphasis added), 420r–422v.

11. AGNCr, vol. 44, exp. 12, Hda. de Dolores 1808, fols. 303–42 (324v for quote). José María Jaymes was variously identified as a *castizo* and a mestizo (see fols. 310v, 324r, 340r). The women were not racially identified, but their network of relatives and acquaintances suggests that they may have been mulattas (see fols. 308v, 310r). For an example of abandonment in a more Indian and village-oriented context, cf. AGNCr, vol. 47, exp. 9, Tetecala 1814, fol. 313.

12. AGNCr, vol. 44, exp. 12, Hda. de Dolores 1808, fol. 309r for quote. The identification of women with their children comes through in the documentation in a variety of ways. When women abandoned men, they normally took the children with them. When women

spoke of children, they sometimes used the singular first person possessive rather than the plural first person. The links of mothering, identity, and female self-legitimation are extremely powerful culturally and historically in Latin America and have come through vividly in twentieth-century ethnographic and political studies. See, e.g., the ethnographic insights in Bunster and Chaney 1985 (informants' response to mother-infant photo); Benería and Roldán 1987, 142, 150; cf., on politics, Chaney 1979; Navarro 1988; J. Martin 1990.

13. For examples in a wide variety of ethnic and residential contexts, see AGNCr, vol. 215, exp. 4, Mapaztlán 1810, fols. 110v, 120v, 126r; vol. 263, exp. 20, Yautepec 1809, fols. 327–31; vol. 253, exp. 10, Tepoztlán 1765, fol. 301r; vol. 537, exp. 6, Cuautla Amilpas 1806, fols. 2v–3r; vol. 254, exp. 4, Huispalca (Tlaltizapán) 1809, fol. 95r; vol. 214, exp. 12, Cuautla Amilpas 1779, fol. 216v; vol. 174, exp. 7, Cuautla Amilpas 1802, fol. 242r; vol. 45, exp. 16, Hda. Atlacomulco 1820, fol. 423v.

14. AGNCr, vol. 2, exp. 15, Tlayacapan 1786, fol. 344v.

15. AGNCr, vol. 277, exp. 5, Tepalcingo 1807, fols. 96v–126r, esp. 99v–100r, 104r.

16. AGNCr, vol. 1, exp. 21, Tlayacapan 1809, fols. 405–15, 418–22 (413v for quote).

17. See, e.g., AGNCr, vol. 38, exp. 16, Hda. San Gaspar 1809, fol. 325v; vol. 46, exp. 14, Tetelpa 1816, fol. 350v; vol. 174, exp. 3, Cuautla Amilpas 1801, fols. 47r–48r.

18. AGNCr, vol. 174, exp. 3 (cf. exps. 4, 5, 1; and Matrimonios, vol. 18, exp. 2), Cuautla Amilpas 1801, fols. 47r–48r.

19. Figures are adapted from PDBO, Morelos, Powvioli.out, pp. 33–39; Powmore1.sys, pp. 34–42. Figures are midway points between those derived from the restricted set ($n = 62$ total valid cases) and the augmented set ($n = 93$ total valid cases).

20. Of course women also appeared in other gendered roles vis-à-vis aspiring patriarchs — as sisters, nieces, and mothers-in-law, for example. But as we shall discuss below, these may be viewed as variations or blends of three fundamental roles: wife (or wife-mother), *amasia*, and daughter.

21. See AGNCr, vol. 254, exp. 3, Zamatitlán 1803, fol. 42r–v (and note the matter-of-fact quality of the assertion); cf. vol. 214, exp. 12, Cuautla Amilpas 1779, fol. 216v.

22. See, e.g., AGNCr, vol. 39, exp. 25, Tlaquiltenango 1762, fols. 437–54, esp. 447v, 452v, 453v; vol. 50, exp. 26, Xoxocotla 1799, fols. 415–98, esp. 423r–434r, 442r; vol. 253, exp. 10, Tepoztlán 1765, fol. 301; vol. 254, exp. 1, Yautepec 1806, fols. 11v–12r; vol. 3, exp. 8, Tlayacapa 1793, fol. 78v; and for a *novio-novia* variation on this theme, vol. 54, exp. 16, Hda. Atlacomulco 1820, esp. fols. 417r–424v.

23. AGNCr, vol. 47, exp. 4, Hda. Chiconguaque 1813, fols. 106–85, esp. fols. 110v–112r (111r–v for quotes), 118r.

24. See ibid., esp. fols. 123r–v, 131v–137r (132v for quote), 167v–172v, 184r–185r.

25. AGNCr, vol. 3, exp. 8, Tlayacapan 1793, fols. 77–97 (quotes are on 89r, 86r), esp. 83r, 85r–92r; cf. vol. 47, exp. 8, Xoxocotla 1804, fols. 233–99, esp. 241v–244r, 269r–272r.

26. AGNCr, vol. 253, exp. 10, Tepoztlán 1765, fol. 301r–v for the petition and quote; cf. the experience of Andrea Antonia, a mulatta, in AGNCr, vol. 214, exp. 12, Cuautla Amilpas 1779, esp. fols. 216r–217r.

27. For young girls — two Indians and a poor white — sent to the *monte* by their mothers to collect wood, and indications that customarily girls walked together for company and presumed protection, see AGNCr, vol. 47, exp. 7, Hda. del Puente 1818, fols. 192–232. (The sad irony in this instance is that the practice comes to our attention because the girls were attacked and one of them was raped.) On woodcutting and charcoal making as male domains and on charcoal making as a very low status male occupation, see AGNCr, vol. 44, exp. 7, Chamilpa 1804, fols. 139–94; AGN, Historia, vol. 212, exp. 20, Totolapa 1787, fols. 10r, 7v. In 1985 one could still see poor men going to wooded hillsides to cut and collect firewood in Tepoztlán. Cf. Lewis 1951, 128, 163–65.

28. For extension of such gender roles into the etiquettes of *fandangos* and entertain-

ment, see, e.g., AGNCr, vol. 46, exp. 2, Cuernavaca 1807, fols. 33–88 passim, and esp. 38r; vol. 356, exp. s.n., Atotonilco 1799, esp. fols. 23r–26r. For a boy ten years old helping out in the *milpa*, see AGNCr, vol. 50, exp. 26, Xoxocotla 1799, fol. 446r. In the extreme the training of girls to take on more adult responsibilities could transform a female youth into the tyrannized domestic servant of a widower, father, or uncle. Cf. the picture of children, labor, and life cycle stages in Lewis 1951. For a discussion of the history and sources concerning childhood in Mexico, see Lavrin 1991.

29. On Nahua housing compounds and domestic living arrangements in central Mexico and Morelos, see Haskett 1988, 47–48; Lockhart 1992, 59–66; Cline 1986, 97–98, 52, 78; AGNCr, vol. 222, exp. 10, Tlayacapa 1779, fol. 72r. The most revealing ethnographic discussion of the implications of such living arrangements for family authority (in a context of twentieth-century erosion of the pattern) is in Lewis 1951, 59–61, 323–24, 347–50 (see also 178–80).

30. This relationship was not always adversarial, since the quality of in-law relations might vary considerably and since a mother-in-law might also view her role as one of teaching her son the legitimate boundaries of marital behavior. For a case of a woman hit by her own son when she defended her daughter-in-law from his abusive treatment, see AGNCr, vol. 278, exp. 7, Xalostoque 1796, esp. fols. 243r, 245r. For a sharply contrasting case, in which a fourteen-year-old Indian wife who fled her husband agreed to reunite with him only if he agreed that they would no longer live with his family, see AGNCr, vol. 274, exp. 13, Tepetlixpa 1797, esp. fols. 208v, 213v–214r.

31. For a particularly vivid example, see AGNCr, vol. 228, exp. 1, San Miguel (de Tlayacapa), fols. 1r, 2v, 3v. Cf., in this context, the role of relatives in the stories of María Teresa of Texalpa (Chapter 1), María Gertrudis of Hacienda San Gaspar (Chapter 4), and the crossfire incidents related in Chapter 6 below. The continuing presence of women's parental families — parents, siblings, aunts and uncles, and the like — in the lives and disputes of daughters convinces me that Taylor's speculation (1979, 107–8) about the "isolation" of wives upon marriage to husbands of different barrios or villages is overstated.

32. See the discussion of the statistical data on sexual assaults, many by relatives, and on violence against women by outer primary relations in Chapter 3 above.

33. For a particularly telling example marked by ambivalence anchored in different evaluations of a stepfather and a mother by the daughter, see AGN, Matrimonios, vol. 3, exp. 17, Tetecala 1796, fol. 102r.

34. AGNCr, vol. 47, exp. 2, Santa María 1819, fol. 18v.

35. See the complaint in 1777 of Don Manuel de Gamboa, a priest whose relations with the Indians of Tepoztlán were particularly embattled, that Indian male youths with pretenses of future marriage sank into "moral corruption by living . . . in concubinage with the *novias* for three or four years" (AGNCr, vol. 203, exp. 4, Tepoztlán 1777, fol. 110r).

36. De Curiel 1905, 8–9, as quoted and translated in Ingham 1986, 24.

37. For banditry and theft of women, see AGNCr, vol. 212, exp. 7, Cuautla Amilpas 1810, fol. 117r. For a woman invoking the metaphor of abduction to describe a sexual runaway episode that blended coercion and consent ambiguously, see, AGNCr, vol. 38, exp. 2, Tesoyuca 1809, fol. 59v.

38. AGNCr, vol. 3, exp. 9, Atlatlaucan 1778, esp. fols. 99r–100v (99r for quotes). It is important to note that in other *rapto* episodes the reality of forcible abduction made the question of female consent more ambiguous. The distinction between a consensual or prearranged theft against the will of parents and a kidnapping that rode roughshod over the will of the *novia* as well as that of her parents could prove tenuous. See, e.g., AGNCr, vol. 15, exp. 6, Tepoztlán 1783, fols. 85–87, for an incident in which the kidnapped wife-to-be was deposited with the local agent (*teniente*) of the priest to proceed toward marriage in an orderly manner compatible with ecclesiastical law but then fled her legal seclusion (*depósito*),

thereby calling into question the degree to which the *rapto* was forced or consensual in the first place. Cf. coercive pressure and ambiguity in AGNCr, vol. 45, exp. 16, Hda. Atlacomulco 1820, fols. 415–26.

39. For a perceptive discussion of patterns of resistance, legitimation, and delegitimation embedded in the small and often invisible acts of women in daily gendered life, see Janeway 1980.

40. These subtleties are most evident, of course, in twentieth-century life histories rich in ethnographic detail. See esp. Lewis 1959, 1964. But there is no reason to believe that the subtle shadings of behavior and response evident in ethnographic work represented a new phenomenon. For a compelling example of the insights available when ethnographic sensibilities are brought to bear, with care, on historical research, see Price 1990.

41. AGNCr, vol. 3, exp. 4, Tlayacapan 1783, fols. 57–61 (58r for quote). For other examples of women exercising physical force, cf. female resistance to dragging in the story of María Teresa of Texalpa in Chapter 1 above; and see AGNCr, vol. 213, exp. 1, Mapaztlán 1806, fols. 1v, 8r, 16r; vol. 3, exp. 8, Tlayacapan 1793, fols. 83r, 85–92, esp. 89r; and the discussions of women's forcefulness in Chapters 6 and 8 below.

42. See n. 30 above and the qualification contained therein; cf. AGNCr, vol. 272, exp. 19, Texcalpan 1784, esp. fol. 273.

43. See AGN, Inquisición, vol. 1127, fols. 360, 364, 365, 367–71, 378 (360r for quote); cf. AGNCr, vol. 44, exp. 12, Hda. de Dolores 1808, fols. 303–42; vol. 47, exp. 4, Hda. Chiconguaque 1813, fols. 106–85.

44. For an introduction to the colonial legal system, its authorities and brokers, and the particularities of Morelos's Marquesado jurisdiction, the following sources are quite useful: Borah 1983; García Martínez 1969; MacLachlan 1974; Taylor 1984; cf. Haslip 1980; Scardaville 1977.

45. The legal preference for reconciliation implying a return of wife to husband and the lesser legal credibility granted to testimony by persons of inferior social rank are pervasive in the archival documentation. For a particularly vivid and bitter example of an Indian wife pressured to reconcile with her husband despite a serious threat of homicide, see AGN, vol. 2, exp. 15, Tlayacapan 1786, fols. 339–47. Perceptive analysis of the legal standing of women may be found in Arrom 1985b. For discussion of the color-class imperatives that might render women ambivalent about intervention by legal authorities in women's gender struggles, see Chapter 6 below.

46. For examples in a variety of spatial, social, and ethnic contexts, see AGNCr, vol. 175, exp. 10, Mapaztlán 1806, fol. 252r; vol. 204, Mazatepec 1804, fols. 49r, 56r; vol. 254, exp. 6, Yautepec 1792, fols. 142v–143r, 172r–v (cf. 175r–177v); vol. 254, exp. 10, Tlaltizapán 1765, fol. 262r; vol. 278, exp. 4, Yecapixtla 1805, fol. 168v; vol. 278, exp. 6, Xalostoque 1796, fols. 195r–v, 200r, 204v, 236v–237v (cf. exp. 7, fols. 239–61); vol. 692, exp. 1, Xochiapa 1781, fols. 5r, 5v. See also the story of María Gertrudis Martínez at the beginning of this chapter.

47. See AGNCr, vol. 278, exps. 6–7, Xalostoque 1796, fols. 194–261.

48. AGNCr, vol. 277, exp. 2, Atlacahualoya 1789, fols. 33v–34r (34r for quote), 41v–42r. For other examples where a woman's female relatives were the principal targets of male frustration and anger, see AGNCr, vol. 277, exp. 5, Atlacahualoya 1789 [untitled *expediente* concerning the petition of Sebastián Peres, attached to the *expediente* entitled "Causa criminal . . . contra el reo José Antonio Terrón . . ."], fol. 127r; vol. 262, exp. 15, Cuernavaca 1802, fol. 218v; cf. vol. 44, exp. 12, Hda. de Dolores 1808, fols. 303–42.

49. For the five examples cited, see AGNCr, vol. 38, exp. 16, Hda. San Gaspar 1809, fols. 316r–331r passim; vol. 203, exp. 7, Cuernavaca 1801, fols. 326v–331v; vol. 214, exp. 12, Cuautla Amilpas 1779, fols. 216v, 220r; vol. 254, exp. 3, Zamatitlán 1803, fols. 34v, 36r–v, 40v, 41r–43v; vol. 2, exp. 15, Tlayacapa 1786, fols. 339–47.

For some readers the culture of background conversation, friendship, and alliance among females may prompt questions about potential lesbian sexual dynamics or undercurrents. Such issues did not arise, however, in documentation of sexual conflicts between men and women or of female-female alliances and seem irrelevant to the relationships discussed here. This was the case even though suggestion of "deviant sexuality," such as adultery and prostitution, was used to discredit women, and even though idiosyncratic gender presentation, such as cross-dressing by females in bandit gangs, occasionally left traces in the criminal documentation. A certain degree of cross-cultural and historical caution is advisable. Even in the Inquisition records, which are more likely to provide evidence of female sexual "deviance" beyond adultery or prostitution, the main such issue seems to have been not lesbian sex or eroticism as conventionally understood but a female autoeroticism connected with mysticism. See Franco 1989.

50. A term like *comadre* or *compadre* might also be used more casually to signify a friendly rather than hostile disposition, to defuse an escalating quarrel, or to acknowledge a transitory sense of bonding. These more casual uses seem more prevalent among men than women in contemporary folk culture.

51. For a pioneering study of conflictual and hegemonic constructions of community and their connections to male gender claims, see Mallon 1994a, chap. 3, from which I have benefited enormously. The larger point is that the very meaning and practice of community does not preclude a reality of internal hierarchy, differentiation and fragmentation, and struggle to impose meaning and practice. On the contrary, the meaning and practice of community arises out of the way such splits are compromised, suppressed, deflected, or otherwise dealt with. For an example in the context of the literature on so-called closed corporate communities, see Stern 1983.

52. See AGNCr, vol. 254, exp. 6, Yautepec 1792, fol. 175r.

53. We shall explore the metaphorical language of appeals to male political authority in more detail in Chapter 8.

54. A longer initial draft of this chapter yielded thirteen anecdotal cases of female intervenors cited in the text. Among them the breakdown was as follows: (1) mother or surrogate mother (six cases): four mothers, one mother-in-law, one aunt; (2) horizontal kin/friend/*comadre* (five cases): two friends, one *comadre*, one cousin, one neighbor; (3) ambiguous (two cases): one mistress who was only four years older than her servant, one intervention by female bystanders at a party, probably older than the beneficiary but in a context suggesting a diffuse sense of solidarity rather than a motherly role.

55. For male resentment and fear of gossip (*chismes*), a strong sense that men were especially deviant and treacherous if they broke discretion by participating in local gossip mongering (*chismología*), and a sense that talkers (*chismosos/-as*, *soplones*) placed individuals and communities at risk, see AGNCr, vol. 47, exp. 13, Hda. Miacatlán 1815, fols. 417v–419r, 420r–422v; vol. 90, exp. 27, Atlautla 1767, fols. 403–13; vol. 254, exp. 10, Tlaltizapán 1765, fol. 258r; vol. 277, exp. 2, Atlacahualoya 1789, fols. 37r–39v.

56. AGNCr, vol. 253, exp. 8, Tepoztlán 1802, fol. 233v.

57. For examples of women airing discreet knowledge publicly at selected moments, see AGNCr, vol. 277, exp. 3, Xochitlán 1789, fols. 54–72, esp. 61r, 55v, 63r; vol. 215, exp. 1, Tetela del Volcán 1812, fols. 7v, 4r; cf. vol. 90, exp. 27, Atlautla 1767, fol. 406r.

58. On María Lucía and Esquicio Ponciano's wife, see above; on the threat of *se dice*, see AGNCr, vol. 253, exp. 8, Tepoztlán 1802, fols. 231v, 234r (cf. the citations in n. 55 above).

59. See, e.g., AGNCr, vol. 254, exp. 6, Yautepec 1792, fols. 133–221; cf. exp. 4, Huispalca 1809, fols. 62–106.

60. AGNCr, vol. 214, exp. 12, Cuautla Amilpas 1779, fol. 216v; vol. 90, exp. 27, Atlautla 1767, fol. 406r (quote). See above for the cases of Esquicio Ponciano's wife and Pasquala María; AGNCr, vol. 215, exp. 4, Mapaztlán 1810, fol. 105r (quote).

61. We were first introduced to the idea of an oscillation between public and private han-

dling of gendered strife in the story of María Teresa of Texalpa that opened this book. For an example of an adulterous liaison generally tolerated by a village over a twelve-year period, except when it caused disruptive scandals that broke up the facade of social peace, see AGNCr, vol. 3, exp. 8, Tlayacapa 1793, fols. 77–97. For a certain tolerance of individual idiosyncrasy, including that of females who crossed conventional gender boundaries, the nicknames bestowed on individuals who formed part of the local social fabric offer useful clues. See, e.g., the cases of "Gertrudis la Torera" (Gertrudis the Bullfighter), a widow who had been a barber-surgeon in Tlayacapa for fifteen years by 1820, and the female curer on Hacienda de Guadalupe in 1794 known as "La Zapatera" (The Shoemaker). AGNCr, vol. 142, exp. 8, Tlayacapa 1820, fols. 217r, 217v; vol. 213, exp. 12, Tehuixtla ca. 1794, fol. 318r. On nicknames in cultural context, see the astute observations of Pitt-Rivers 1971, 160–69.

62. See the following superb studies, from which I have learned a great deal: Alberro 1982, 1986, 1987a, 1987b; Behar 1987, 1989; Franco 1989; cf. Aguirre Beltrán 1955; Chambers 1989; Palmer 1976, 154–66. For context and background to Inquisition activity and its regional distribution, see Alberro 1981; cf. Greenleaf 1969. In my own scrutiny of Inquisition records at the AGN (admittedly less systematic than my scrutiny of criminal records), it was obvious that Morelos was not among the regions that provided a thick set of cases for study.

63. For an extremely perceptive discussion of colonial and Nahua religious culture, see Gruzinski 1989b (cf. 1988), which is itself inspired by the pioneering tour de force by López Austin 1980.

64. These aspects come through especially strongly in Franco 1989; Chambers 1989.

65. AGNCr, vol. 262, exp. 32, Ocotepec/Ahuatepec/Amatepec 1808, fol. 373r; vol. 372, exp. s.n. [concerns "Ponciano el tocinero"], Cuautla Amilpas 1803, fol. 14r; vol. 254, exp. 3, Zamatitlán 1803, fols. 40v, 43r (kerchief quote); vol. 142, exp. 8, Tlayacapa 1820, fols. 217r, 217v; vol. 213, exp. 12, Tehuixtla ca. 1794, fol. 318r; vol. 38, exp. 16, Hda. San Gaspar 1809, fol. 326r; vol. 47, exp. 8, Xoxocotla 1804, fol. 243v (cf. 269v, 270r); vol. 214, exp. 11, Ocuituco 1786, fols. 206–13 (209v for quote regarding mother and son).

66. See Lewis 1951, 199, 281–82, 294–95, 324–25 (cf. Behar 1993, 1987, 1989).

CHAPTER FIVE

1. My approach to culture is inspired by Sabean 1984, esp. 28–30, 95, 195; cf. Hunt 1989; Sabean 1990; Medick and Sabean 1984.

2. Janeway 1980 provides an illuminating discussion of the importance of the legitimacy question in highly gendered, personal relationships.

3. I frankly admit that my intuition has been influenced not only by the cumulative effect of archival immersion but also by a feel for twentieth-century ethnographies of Morelos: see Lewis 1951, 1964; Romanucci-Ross 1986; Foley 1986, 1990; Ingham 1986; Friedlander 1975; J. Martin 1990; Tirado 1991; LeVine with Correa 1993; see also Fromm and Maccoby 1970. For additional context, see de la Peña 1980; Warman 1976, 1980. For an overview of Morelos-based ethnographies, see Lomnitz-Adler 1984. I am aware of the "ethnographic present" problem and would not argue for a shallow, one-dimensional view of continuity (see Chapter 14). But ethnographic sensibilities sometimes assist historical intuition: see, e.g., Price 1990.

4. The literature on hegemony is enormous, but I have been especially influenced by Gramsci's original formulations (printed in Gramsci 1971, 206–76), by subsequent treatment during the 1970s boom of work on slavery and antislavery (Genovese 1969, 1974; D. B. Davis 1975), and by Mallon's new work (1994a, 1994b) on peasant and nation in postcolonial Mexico and Peru. For important recent debate and extensions of the concept, see the

divergent treatments of hegemony in J. C. Scott 1985 (cf. 1990); Mouffe and Laclau 1985; and the journal *Subaltern Studies*. See also the strikingly original vision of peasant intellectuals in Feierman 1990 and the concepts of "hegemonic masculinity" and "emphasized femininity" in Connell 1987.

5. See Perry 1985 (cf. 1990, 1980) for a particularly discerning treatment within an Iberian context. See Young 1989 for the flip side of the same coin: iconization of the exceptionally heroic and virtuous virgin-martyr. The larger issue, of course, is the image of Woman in Western thought as flawed and dangerous Other (see de Beauvoir 1952).

6. For Western and biblical lore, de Beauvoir remains the classic starting point. Cf. pioneering recent works by G. Lerner (1986) and M. O'Brien (1981), from whom the notion of "male-stream" thought is borrowed, and the honor/shame literature cited in Chapter 2, n. 13 above. For notions of personhood, excess, and depravity in indigenous Mesoamerican culture history, see the insightful works of Clendinnen 1985, 1991; López Austin 1980, 1982; Gruzinski 1982, 1987, 1988.

7. On Catholic culture and teachings relevant to gender imagery and morality, see esp. Lavrin 1989a, 1989c; León 1583; Vives 1523; Benítez 1985; Boxer 1975; Burkhart 1989; Gutiérrez 1991; Paz 1982; Seed 1988b.

8. See, in addition to nn. 5–6 above, Morse 1954, 1964; Phelan 1967.

9. Note the resonance of such views with folk characterizations in contemporary ethnographics of Morelos. See esp. Lewis 1951, 1964; Romanucci-Ross 1986; Ingham 1986; cf. the somewhat less helpful Fromm and Maccoby 1970.

10. The María Teresa and María Lucía episodes are presented in the opening sections of Chapters 1 and 4, respectively.

11. AGNCr, vol. 263, exp. 20, Yautepec 1809, fols. 327–31 (328r, 328v for quotes). The conspiracy charge eludes definitive corroboration, but its plausibility — as important as its truth for our purposes — was sufficient to induce an investigation.

12. AGNCr, vol. 278, exp. 7, Xalostoque 1796, fols. 243r, cf. 245r.

13. AGNCr, vol. 38, exp. 16, Hda. San Gaspar 1809, fols. 321r, 330r.

14. Ibid., fols. 305–36, esp. the testimonies on 316r–326r, 329r–331r. The quotes are from fols. 321r, 317v, 322v, respectively.

15. It is well known that higher male mortality rates and male abandonment of women implied a certain population of mature female loners even among previously married women. See the loner statistics for Morelos in Table 3.9; cf. the data for Mexico City in Arrom 1985b, 129–34. On migration in Morelos, see Chapter 2 above; cf. de la Peña 1980. Long ago Oscar Lewis (1951, 321–22, 420) recognized that historical patterns of male migration in Morelos implied prolonged absences from the domestic site of male authority and thereby yielded a certain tension point within the structure of patriarchal authority. On the psychological aspects of sons living under the rule of widows in a patriarchal culture, see Ruggiero 1985, 207 n. 46; cf. Slater 1968. (The latter work raises suggestive questions but requires caution since Slater slides over the problems inherent in psychoanalytic readings of historical time-spaces distinct from our own.)

16. AGN, Historia, vol. 212, exp. 20, Totolapa 1787, fol. 11v (cf. 10r, 11v).

17. AGNCr, vol. 50, exp. 26, Xoxocotla 1799, fol. 466r.

18. On the misuses of the psychology of pathology, see the critiques of the literature of Mexican national character and culture by Bartra 1987; Monsiváis 1979, 1980, 1981, 1988; cf. O. Lewis's conflicts with Carolina Luján over Pedro Martínez, in Rigdon 1988, 235–42, esp. 235–37.

19. See M. Douglas 1966, 1970; cf. the treatments of deviance, power, and social norming in Foucault 1965, 1977, 1978–86, vol. 1, and the problem of mature females in historical studies of witchcraft (see Silverblatt 1987 for discussion in a Latin American context).

20. See AGNCr, vol. 537, exps. 6–7, Cuautla Amilpas 1806.

1. Cf. Stansell (1986, 79), who recounts the murder of a wife by a working class husband in New York City in 1853 after a quarrel about money matters. The man's neighbors saw him talking to his wife's corpse, "calling her name and asked if she didn't love him and he her." I am grateful to Stephanie McCurry for drawing my attention to this episode. On the historical development of middle class ideals of love and companionate marriage, a provocative interpretation is Stone 1977. The family violence literature of the 1970s and 1980s shows that the middle class ideal may be understood as an important social myth that does not preclude considerable violence and battering dynamics among respectable social strata: see Chapter 3, n. 8, above.

2. AGNCr, vol. 47, exp. 4, Hda. Chiconguaque 1813, fol. 111 (quote); vol. 3, exp. 8, Tlayacapan 1793, fols. 77–97, esp. 89r, 86r; and the conclusion of Chapter 3 above for Pedro Martínez.

3. AGNCr, vol. 3, exp. 4, Tlayacapa 1783, fol. 58r; cf. vol. 44, exp. 10, Yecapixtla 1816, esp. fols. 281v–282r.

4. The evidence on these points was presented in Chapters 3 and 4; on loner figures, see Table 3.9.

5. For ethnic figures, see Table 2.1. For ethnicity and elite political economy in Morelos, see Chapter 2 above. On overlapping power groups in colonial life more generally, see Stern 1982, chap. 4; cf. Ladd 1976.

6. For quotes, AGNCr, vol. 205, exp. 5, Cuernavaca 1763, fol. 255r; vol. 262, exp. 19, Hda. Temisco 1811, fol. 238v (cf. 235–256 passim, esp. 236r–237v); cf. vol. 47, exp. 15, Cuernavaca 1810, fols. 443–574, esp. 444r–457r. The owner of Hacienda Temisco was Gabriel de Yermo, a merchant-landowner who had invested some 200,000 pesos to modernize his Cuernavaca sugar holdings, moved in high peninsular circles in Mexico City politics and finance, and led the preemptive *gachupín* coup against Viceroy Iturrigaray in 1808. See Brading 1971, 116; Warman 1976, 89–90; Hamnett 1971, 121.

7. It is worth noting, too, that even among those who turned against the insurgents or remained indifferent, upheaval and danger promoted consciousness of group interest and well-being. On the independence wars in the Morelos region, see, among published sources, the following: Hamnett 1986, 71–72, 143, 239 n. 49, 157–59, 163–64, 174; C. E. Martin 1985, 189–95; Sotelo Inclán 1943, 138–46, 229 n. 1; Warman 1976, 89–90. Tutino's fine study of agrarian history (1986, 139–51, 188–92, 212) echoes the traditional interpretation, influenced by Lucas Alamán, that the villages of Mexico's central highlands responded to the insurgents in lukewarm to indifferent terms. Significantly, however, his analysis turns more cautious and modulated for the specific case of Morelos (see 188–92, esp. 191 n. 17). Among unpublished criminal sources that illuminate a more synergistic interplay between insurgent forces and Morelos peasants than is sometimes acknowledged, see AGNCr, vol. 38, exp. 11, Ahuatepec 1812, fols. 243r, 264r–v; vol. 47, exp. 15, Cuernavaca 1810, fols. 443–574; vol. 91, exp. 7, Tlayacapa 1818, fol. 92r; vol. 141, exp. 13, Tlayacapa 1817, fols. 367r–368v (esp. 367v); vol. 157, exp. 1, Tlayacapa 1811, fols. 1–68; vol. 159, exp. 2, Tlayacapa 1810, fols. 66r, 68r; vol. 214, exp. 17, Huepalcala 1817, fol. 376r; vol. 215, exp. 1, Tetela del Volcán 1812, fol. 9r; vol. 262, exp. 19, Hda. Temisco 1811, fols. 235–56; vol. 537, exp. 10, Cuautla Amilpas 1811, fols. 1r, 9r. The AGN, Infidencias documents, and Eric Van Young's forthcoming book on this period will no doubt further refine the picture.

8. Domingo de Vitoria to Sr. Intendente Dn. Bernardo Bonavía, Cuernavaca, Mar. 11, 1790, AGN, Padrones, vol. 98, fol. 7r; AGNCr, vol. 141, exp. 13, Tlayacapa 1817, fol. 367v.

9. For a discussion, see Chapter 2 above. For *repartimiento* practices in Morelos, see AGN, Alcaldes Mayores, vol. 10, fols. 40–48; Historia, vol. 132, exp. 26 [1793–94]; AGNCr, vol. 2, exp. 9, Totolapa 1802, fols. 178–193 passim.

10. AGNCr, vol. 254, exp. 6, Yautepec 1792, fols. 135r–148r, 172r–v (quote). The archival documents abound with such complaints. See, e.g., AGNCr, vol. 1, exp. 11, Tlayacapa 1784, fols. 140v, 173r–185r; vol. 2, exp. 9, Totolapa 1802, fols. 182v–183v (cf. 179r–180r); vol. 3, exp. 8, Tlayacapa 1793, fol. 78v; vol. 38, exp. 3, San Andrés Acacuyoacán (sujeto de Yautepec) 1770, fols. 84–93; exp. 4, Yautepec 1769, fols. 94–101; vol. 44, exp. 14, Agüeguecingo 1792, fols. 381–91; vol. 48, exp. 13, Xonacate 1796, fols. 337–42; exp. 14, Xalostoque 1796, fols. 343–66; vol. 90, exp. 15, Tlayacapa 1764, fols. 287r–288r, 289v; vol. 91, exp. 7, Tlayacapa 1818, fol. 92r; AGN, Historia, vol. 157, exp. 13 [1794], esp. fol. 146r; cf. Haskett 1987, 224.

11. The problem of village political culture and factionalism will be examined in greater depth in Chapter 8. For examples of the pressures and opportunities that pressed village notables and "upper peasants" to join multiracial power groups, the success of such pressures and enticements in some (but not all) instances, and the partly related problem of factionalism, see AGNCr, vol. 254, exp. 10, Tlaltizapán 1765, fols. 256–84, esp. 261r, 270v; vol. 39, exp. 21, Tepoztlán 1769, fols. 408–15; vol. 38, exp. 17, Amacusaque 1817, fols. 337–431; see also C. E. Martin 1985, 155–92; C. E. Martin 1984, 87–88; Haskett 1991a (cf. 1987, 1988, 1991b; and Stern 1982, chap. 4).

12. AGNCr, vol. 262, exp. 3, Xochitepec 1772, fols. 69–106, esp. 70r–74r, 86v, 88r (see 88r, 74r for quotes). The colloquial *esclabonía* might in theory be taken to refer either to the whole lot of slaves or to the slave women in particular, but context and the use of *maltratándolas* (not *maltratándolos*) make clear that the reference is to slave women specifically.

13. AGNCr, vol. 2, exp. 9, Totolapa 1802, fols. 172–98, esp. 173r–176r, 179r–183v (174v for quote). For additional blendings of gender and color-class grievance, see, e.g., AGNCr, vol. 262, exp. 30 (cf. exp. 23), Tepoztlán 1792, fols. 323–31; vol. 263, exp. 9, Ayacapixtla 1792, fols. 120–24; vol. 174, exp. 1 (cf. exp. 3), Cuautla Amilpas 1805, fols. 1–24. For evidence that priests, although sometimes mobilized as sympathetic authorities who might alleviate women's gender oppressions, were also members of local power groups capable of sexual abuse and color-class repression, see AGN, Inquisición, vol. 1086, exp. 14 [Cuautla Amilpas district, 1760s], fols. 298–319; vol. 1313, exp. 5 [Cuernavaca and Chalco districts, 1790s], fols. 1–16; AGNCr, vol. 204, exp. 17, Xonacatepec 1818, fols. 384–92. For a thoughtful discussion of priests and district power balances in late colonial Mexico, see Taylor 1984 (to be amplified in Taylor's forthcoming book on priests and brokers); for a useful macrolevel review of church-state politics, see Farriss 1968.

14. The dependence of peasant men on women for food was a theme introduced in the story of María Teresa of Texalpa that opened this book. For an Indian who thought it plausible to argue that he initiated a sexual liaison with an *amasia* because his wife had abandoned him "and he had no one who could make him a tortilla," see AGNCr, vol. 47, exp. 8, Xoxocotla 1804, fol. 270v. For an important European study that carefully considers the practical significance of material life for family and household relations, see Sabean 1990.

15. For evidence that among the poor in village culture claims to marginal *monte* lands considered community property were important, and that claims to less marginal lands considered to belong to an individual or family by right of custom or inheritance had as their precondition membership in a community that exerted a higher jurisdictional claim, required fulfillment of tributary or service obligations of citizenship, and guarded against rustling and theft by intruders, see AGNCr, vol. 3, exp. 7, Tlalnepantla 1783, fols. 72–76, esp. 73r; vol. 253, exp. 11, Yautepec 1796, fols. 357–420, esp. 361r; vol. 262, exp. 18, Ixtla 1772, fols. 232–34; vol. 263, exp. 10, Xocotitla 1803, fols. 125–29; cf. vol. 1, exp. 4, Tlayacapa 1750, fols. 30–56. For banditry and theft, particularly in the Cuautla district, and their impact on peasant communities and haciendas, see AGNCr, vols. 212–13.

The problem of uneven land-labor ratios and the seasonality of work rhythms will be familiar to any student of peasant agriculture. Reasonably well-off peasants might fill out their labor supply by calling upon relatives, mobilizing reciprocities with other peasants, or hiring temporary help; land-poor peasants might offer their labor on a field in exchange for a share of the harvest, thereby filling out their effective possession of land, or they might work as temporary day laborers to enlarge their stream of income or goods in kind. (For ethnographic perspective from Morelos, see esp. Lewis 1951, 1964; Warman 1976 [cf. 1980]; de la Peña 1980.) All of this implied a web of small reciprocities and mutual dependencies and a kind of cultural proximity, even in cases of internal economic differentiation among peasants. For families going out together to harvest a *milpa*, see AGNCr, vol. 253, exp. 8, Tepoztlán 1802, fols. 231–32; for a pioneering exploration of the importance of such reciprocities and linkages, even in rural proletarian contexts, see Mintz 1974.

16. See AGNCr, vol. 253, exp. 8, Tepoztlán 1802, esp. fol. 232r, for a depiction of male and female presence at the corn harvest that is so matter-of-fact that it is impossible to discern if female collaboration also included help in harvesting the corn. For ethnographic evidence that this happened in at least some villages in the twentieth century, see Lewis 1951, 49, 98. For a subtle discussion in a Peruvian peasant context of how formal ideology renders such participation less visible by conflating agricultural work with more specific tasks restricted to males only (but performed by only a minority of males), see Bourque and Warren 1981; cf. the discussion of women, war, and military combat in Enloe 1983; Macdonald et al. 1987.

17. On the religious cargo or fiesta system, see n. 18 below. For *cofradías* as a kind of community bank, see AGNCr, vol. 203, exp. 1, Xalostoque 1795, fols. 1r–v, 3r, 36r–37v; cf. vol. 175, exp. 14, Tetelzingo 1778, fol. 515v. For perceptive remarks on their sociopsychological appeal in the nearby Valley of Mexico, see Gibson 1964, 127–32.

18. For a woman as a recognized *mayordoma* of a religious fiesta obligation for which a man could also serve as *mayordomo*, see AGNCr, vol. 277, exp. 2, Atlacahualoya 1789, fols. 33r, 41v. For a woman adopting, during her husband's absence, the public powers of her *gobernador* husband to mobilize village *alcaldes* to deal with a violence incident, see AGNCr, vol. 50, exp. 26, Xoxocotla 1799, fols. 427r, 436v, 438r. See also Mathews 1985. Based on work in the Valley of Oaxaca, Mathews argues that when the religious domain of the civil-religious cargo system had more importance, women's roles and prestige in sponsoring fiestas were publicly recognized. In effect, the sponsorship (*mayordomía*) of a cargo was assumed by household, and women as well as men were recognized as *mayordomas* and *mayordomos*. An earlier view of the cargo system assumed that only men served as *mayordomos* and represented the household in the public sphere. Even if the argument turns out to require refinement or not to apply fully to Morelos, it opens a larger "horizon of the possible" that makes the evidence of female *mayordomas* in Morelos less anomalous. (For suggestive evidence regarding Morelos, see Ingham 1986, 92–93; de la Peña 1980, 277, 265–67.) Scholarship on the civil-religious cargo system and the related topic of the closed corporate community has a long genealogy and generated significant revisions in the 1980s. For an introduction and orientation, see, aside from Mathews 1985, Wolf 1957, 1986; Carrasco 1961; Stern 1983; Chance and Taylor 1985; Rus and Wasserstrom 1980.

19. See, e.g., AGNCr, vol. 228, exp. 1, San Miguel de Tlayacapa 1766, fols. 1r, 2v, 3v; cf. the discussions of María Gertrudis Martínez and María del Carmen in Chapter 4 above.

20. The thickest clusters of women whose resources allowed for such a path would be expected in cities with substantial middling strata. See the apt discussion in Arrom 1985b, 134–45.

21. For a poignant example of an impoverished young woman caught in repeated cycles of domestic service, physical or sexual maltreatment, flight, and return to domestic service in a new house, see AGNCr, vol. 45, exp. 11, Cuernavaca 1808, fols. 303–32 passim; for the vulnerability of widows to community pressures and elders, see vol. 253, exp. 11, Yautepec 1796, fols. 359r–361r.

22. See, e.g., AGNCr, vol. 263, exp. 25, Ayacapixtla 1798, fols. 359–62, esp. 360r; vol. 228,

exp. 26, Atlatlauca (Tlayacapa) 1807, fol. 355r; vol. 38, exp. 2, Tesoyuca 1809, esp. fol. 56; cf. vol. 45, exp. 17, Mazatepec 1820, fol. 439v; and n. 23 below.

23. See AGNCr, vol. 2, exp. 7, Totolapa 1801, fols. 144–51, 222–27, 242–75, esp. 145r–v, 249r–251r (250r for quote), 255r–256r (255v for quote). (It is worth noting that Spanish law technically distinguished between rape as *estupro*, the deflowering of an "honest" virgin, and rape as *violación*, a more inclusive category that included among its subsets sexual assault on nonvirginal women and seductions accompanied by false promises of marriage.) For comparison with the standard male line of defense in rape cases, see vol. 205, exp. 7, Rancho de Ystaquaque 1768, fols. 374–409, esp. 400r, 377r–378v.

24. See, e.g., AGNCr, vol. 228, exp. 26, Atlatlauca (Tlayacapa) 1807, fols. 355r, 356r; vol. 215, exp. 4, Mapaztlán 1810, fols. 105r–v, 118v. These cases also underscore that as a practical matter by the time a wife targeted a female enemy as a cause of misfortune, tension and violence over the matter had already developed in her relationship with her husband.

25. On this aspect of "dueling," see Bourdieu 1966, esp. 194, 197; cf. Ruggiero 1979, 74.

26. See AGNCr, vol. 38, exp. 2, Tesoyuca 1809, fols. 31–83, esp. 45r, 42v–43r, for José del Carmen's stance on wife and *amasio*. On the ambiguities of Laureana Filomena's role and initiative in the early stages of her abduction and the eventual turn of the relation to outright bullying and intimidation by an abductor she rejected, see fols. 59v, 45r–v.

27. The notion that deviance defines the norm is diffuse and inspired superb studies by M. Douglas (1966, 1970) and Foucault (1965, 1977, 1978–86, vol. 1).

28. See, e.g., AGNCr, vol. 253, exp. 10, Tepoztlán 1765, for an aunt who pushed an *amasia* to break off a sexual relationship; cf. the ire directed by an *amasio* at his *amasia*'s aunt, in vol. 2, exp. 15, Tlayacapa 1786, fols. 339–47.

29. See, e.g., AGNCr, vol. 263, exp. 8, Ocotepeque 1798, esp. fols. 65r, 69r–v, 73v, 93r; vol. 35, exp. 21, Xoxocotla, esp. fols. 445r, 475r, 438v; vol. 253, exp. 3, Tepoztlán 1802, esp. fols. 92r, 97r.

30. AGNCr, vol. 2, exp. 9, Totolapa 1802, fol. 194v. For similar characterization of subalterns as criminal and occasional use of such stereotypes by legal defenders who played on a kind of paternal racism to argue for light sentences of offenders innately prone to excess, see vol. 38, exp. 5, Tepoztlán 1765, fol. 111r–v; vol. 44, exp. 4, Hda. San Gabriel 1799, fol. 72r–v; vol. 44, exp. 7, Chamilpa 1804, fols. 160v–161r; vol. 90, exp. 15, San Joseph (sujeto a Tlayacapa) 1764, fols. 290v–291r.

31. See AGNCr, vol. 50, exp. 26, Xoxocotla 1799, fols. 415–98 (425r–v for quotes; cf. 433r, 445r).

32. Ibid., fol. 429v, for the testimony of Ysidro Vicente's mother on these points; cf. 441r for Ysidro Vicente's admission that his father had whipped him and that his mother had tracked him down at a tavern.

33. For examples of extreme zigzags as well as moderate intimidation-and-reconciliation tactics by both husbands and wives, see AGNCr, vol. 215, exps. 1–2, Tetela del Volcán 1812, fols. 7v, 22r; vol. 222, exp. 6, Totolapa 1801, fol. 57r; vol. 228, exp. 26, Atlatlauca 1807, fols. 354–58; vol. 254, exp. 6, Yautepec 1792, fol. 172r–v; vol. 262, exp. 3, Xochitepec 1772, esp. fols. 70r–71v, 72v.

34. The tension climaxed in early November, when the rainy season ended and the cycle of irrigated winter maize agriculture began and when Gaspar Melchor's responsibilities focused on the distribution of water among peasant claimants. Indeed, Gaspar Melchor claimed that the intensity of this work made it difficult for him to follow closely the machinations of the village power group. The hint resonates with the knowledge that in the hot country, water rights often sparked considerable contention — not only between villages and haciendas but also within an internally differentiated peasant sector. See AGNCr, vol. 50, exp. 26, Xoxocotla 1799, fols. 424r, 431v (cf. Gibson 1964, 316, on winter maize cycles).

35. For the specific points mentioned and the fear of vengeance built around the son's adultery, see AGNCr, vol. 50, exp. 26, Xoxocotla 1799, fols. 431v, 436v, 423v (quote), 429r.

36. Ibid., fols, 428v–429r.

37. The language of familial defense by Gaspar Melchor illustrated that a contingent view of the gender rights of junior patriarchs, mediated by a fusion of elder and patriarchal power, was fully compatible with classic claims of a more absolute patriarchal dominion over wives. Angered at the rough physical treatment of his wife, Angela María, Gaspar Melchor scolded an *alcalde* by asking "what right did he have to lay violent hands on a married woman and to have treated her like a whore in public" (ibid., fol. 423r). Angela María belonged absolutely to Gaspar Melchor. To treat her roughly intervened in this dominion and symbolically denigrated the worthiness of her patriarch as a custodian of male gender right who supervised the behavior and moral honor of his women.

38. See ibid., fols. 423r–424r, 426r, 427r, 428r, 429r, 430r, 431v–432r.

39. See AGNCr, vol. 47, exp. 8, Xoxocotla 1804, esp. fol. 242r–v (cf. 270v). For a detailed example of the vulnerability of an isolated female loner-servant to economic and sexual suffering, see AGNCr, vol. 45, exp. 11, Cuernavaca 1808, fols. 303r–313v.

40. AGNCr, vol. 46, exp. 13, Alpuyeca 1804, fol. 274r–v (quote), 298r–v.

41. The cultural value placed on secrets and knowledge of discreet information comes through in distinct ways in ethnographic and testimonial literature. See Menchú 1984 for a political context; Lewis 1951, 1964; Romanucci-Ross 1986 for daily life contexts. At a more theoretical level, the offstage dimensions of peasant life have been brought forcefully to the fore in the context of state/village and elite/peasant relations in the work of J. C. Scott (esp. 1990).

42. AGNCr, vol. 222, exp. 10, Tlayacapan 1779, fol. 72v.

43. A zealous inspector of public order and morality could seize on extramarital sexual liaisons, public bathing, drinking and *fandangos*, walking with weapons, vagrancy, and violation of night curfews to serve such a purpose. See AGN, Acordada, vol. 29, exp. 23 [1777], fol. 248.

44. AGNCr, vol. 254, exp. 10, Tlaltizapán 1765, fols. 257r–258r (258r for quote), 261r (cf. 258v–266v, 271r–v).

45. On the Atlacahualoya affair and for background on Don Nicolás Ycazbalceta, his two sugar haciendas (the other was the equally productive Santa Clara Montefalco), and agrarian conflict in the Xonacatepec district, see AGNCr, vol. 277, exp. 2, Atlacahualoya 1789, fols. 28–52; C. E. Martin 1985, 104, 108, 133, 137, 144, 146, 149, 152–53 (tables 6.13, 6.14), 169–71, 195. On the comparative scale of Hacienda Tenango's production, see Humboldt 1811, vol. 3, bk. 4, chap. 10, 1–8 (esp. 8), 13. On the sugar vortex of the late eighteenth century and its effect on sugar prices and production beyond French Haiti, Schwartz 1985 is quite revealing; cf. C. E. Martin 1982.

46. For comparison with other riots and colonial efforts to defuse confrontations, see Taylor 1979, 113–51, 168–70.

47. AGNCr, vol. 277, exp. 2, Atlacahualoya 1789, fols. 38v, 39v for quotes (cf. 37r–v).

48. The rape and incest statements are presented in a matter-of-fact tone that suggests that no one contested the truth of the charges. See ibid., fols. 37r–v, 38v. In addition, it would have made little sense to deliver a denunciation that could not be backed up with credible witnesses, since rape and incest proceedings were especially dependent on credible verification by someone other than the victim and since accusation without proof simply invited ostracism.

49. See ibid., esp. fols. 33r–34r (33r for quote), 41r–42r; cf., on the custom of asking for the *mayordomía*, de la Peña 1980, 264–65.

50. One of the most notable historical studies of colonial peasant women's forceful participation in the defense of their communities is Taylor 1979, 113–51 passim, 154–56; cf. T.

Kaplan 1982. Notable examples from more recent times in Latin America include women's prominence in so-called new urban social movements: see Massolo 1992; cf. Monsiváis 1987; Alvarez 1990. There is a sense in this literature that women's defense of family and community merge into acts of collective violence or mobilization, but there is little discussion of family defenses apart from wider collective action. For more individualized actions, see n. 51 below.

51. AGNCr, vol. 223, exp. 23, Tlalnepantla 1805, fols. 383r–388v; vol. 253, exp. 2/3, Tepoztlán 1768, fols. 23r, 27r; vol. 253, exp. 1, Amatlán 1769, fol. 5r; vol. 214, exp. 12, Cuautla Amilpas 1779, fols. 215r, 218v; vol. 203, exp. 1, Xalostoque 1795, fols. 1r–2r.

52. AGNCr, vol. 47, exp. 13, Hda. Miacatlán 1815, fols. 418v–419r; vol. 47, exp. 3, Tlaltizapán 1815, fols. 54v–60v, esp. 55r (quote).

53. AGNCr, vol. 91, exp. 15, Tlayacapan 1805, fols. 335–36 (336r for quote).

CHAPTER SEVEN

1. Buñuel 1982, 201. My summary falls between a paraphrase and a verbatim transcription of Buñuel's account. I have not wanted to stray too far from Buñuel, but I have also wanted to avoid a long quote that might weaken the effect of Buñuel's concluding quote.

2. AGNCr, vol. 142, exp. 4, Tlayacapan 1805, fol. 82v (for similar accounts and quotations by other witnesses, see 81v, 88r, 89r, 90r). Cf. AGNCr, vol. 45, exp. 1, Tlaltizapán 1806, esp. fol. 19v.

3. I have relied heavily on the astoundingly incisive and witty Bartra 1987 (cf. 1986, 71–83); Monsiváis 1988, esp. 77–96, 103–17; and O'Malley 1986; cf. Bartra 1993 for a discussion of Mexican political culture in a "post-national" context. For a dynamic on-the-ground view of changing masculinities in Mexican working class culture, see Gutmann 1994 (to be amplified in Gutmann forthcoming). On women's search for a voice amidst construction of Mexican national culture in male voice, see Franco 1989. On nations as "imagined communities," see B. Anderson 1983.

4. Buñuel 1982, 202, 201, 205. As with the "killed for asking" story, I have told the story without quotes (except for those within the story), although I have followed Buñuel's language fairly closely.

5. See Ramos 1934, Monsiváis 1988, 77–96 (on Cantínflas); Paz 1959, esp. 54, 57, 64–66. For Paz's ideas stretched to dubious historical propositions, see Goldwert 1983; cf. 1980, 1982.

6. One detects the preoccupation with the interior maladies and psychology of Mexican men in a variety of cultural corners: in popular song commemorating the revolution and its heroes, in the state's hero cults and film industry, and in the sometimes discordant dialogues between the ethnographer Oscar Lewis, the Erich Fromm group of psychologist-ethnographers, and the Asociación Psicoanalítica Mexicana in the Mexico City of the 1950s. See O'Malley 1986; Lamas 1978; Monsiváis 1988, esp. 103–17; Rigdon 1988, 64, 71 n. 36, 222, 234, 294, 48–71 passim, 229–70 passim. Cf. Lewis 1951; Fromm and Maccoby 1970; Maccoby 1970; Romanucci-Ross (based originally on fieldwork with Fromm's group) 1986; González Pineda 1961; Ramírez 1959; Ingham 1986 (orig. fieldwork in 1965–66).

7. Contestation over multiple visions marked the effort to define the meaning of Mexican national experience and the Mexican Revolution between the 1920s and the 1950s. In this sense culture was as contested and ambiguous an arena as the politics of the revolutionary state and its public policy and could not be separated from it. For outstandingly original and theoretically engaged exploration along these lines, see Joseph and Nugent 1994b, 1994a. Even as a kind of celebratory lament of male outrage and machismo came to embody the heart of lo mexicano and thereby became a dominant cultural paradigm, femi-

nist groups and female artists presented distinctive visions of culture and politics. For perspective, see *fem* 1983; Macías 1982; cf. Rascón 1979; Soto 1979; Tuñón 1987; Franco 1989. See also n. 8 below.

8. One notes the tension from the beginning: in the pessimistic "novel of the Revolution," Azuela's *The Underdogs* (*Los de abajo*) (1915), and in Reed's more optimistic memoir (1914). Cf. Katz 1985. On the movement toward a depiction of Pancho Villa in terms that emphasized his gender — his masculinity, interior character, and personal leadership — while stripping the legend of other social content, see Monsiváis 1988, 104–5; cf. O'Malley 1986, 87–112, 143–44.

9. On a theoretical level, cf. the concept of "hegemonic masculinity" in Connell 1987. For the specifically Mexican sources of this interpretation, see n. 3 above and Paz 1959. For other Latin American examples of struggle over legitimate masculinity, see Besse 1989; Lancaster 1992.

10. AGNCr, vol. 44, exp. 4, Hda. San Gabriel 1799, fol. 72v; cf. vol. 2, exp. 9, Totolapan 1802, fols. 194v–195r; vol. 44, exp. 7, Chamilpa 1804, fols. 158r–v, 160v; vol. 38, exp. 5, Tepoztlán 1765, fol. 111r–v.

11. It should be apparent that this refers to the restricted model of *descargas*, the nearly pure outbursts of apparently inexplicable violence. The amplified *descarga* category includes ventings more susceptible to social analysis (the background cases of male honor and bonding mentioned above).

12. For tests of *descarga* associations with distinctions of peasant/plebeian, Indian/non-Indian, and commoner/middling strata, all of which proved negative, $n = 141, 155, 149$ total valid cases, respectively. For the association of explicit masculine honor-bonding conflicts with non-Indians and implicit honor-bonding with Indians, $n = 37$, Chi-square significance was borderline (.046), Phi was moderate (.38), and the odds ratio (odds of implicit rather than explicit for Indians, compared with odds for non-Indians) was also moderate (2.4). Association tests were adapted from data in PDBO, Morelos, Mormv1a.lis, pp. 9–10, 13–14, 17–18 (adjusted by removal of female assailants identified in Morelos, Data Entry Outputs).

13. Recent work that is both historically sensitive and theoretically engaged has argued for close connections between gender and power. The more specific theoretical implication is the connection between masculinity and power in its varied manifestations. See Connell 1987; Messerschmidt 1993; cf. J. W. Scott 1986, 1988; G. Lerner 1986; and de Beauvoir 1952, still useful and brimming with insight.

14. For a highly illuminating example of interplay between social reputation and interpretation of violent outbursts and accidents, see AGNCr, vol. 253, exp. 6, Yautepec 1816, fols. 161–226, esp. 170r, 217v, 193r–194r, 200r–213v, 223v–225v; cf. the depictions of drinking in Taylor 1979, 42.

15. On social inequality as an obstacle to duels, see Bourdieu 1966, esp. 194, 197; Ruggiero 1979, 74. On duels as outmoded, see BNM, vol. 971; Echebarria y Ojeda 1791, 36–37. On colonial Enlightenment culture and self-conscious distancing by elites from popular excesses of violence, impulse, and sensuality, see Viqueira Albán 1987.

16. AGNCr, vol. 48, exp. 12, San Diego Atliguayan 1775, fol. 331v. On institutional practice of female deposit, see Muriel 1974.

17. See AGNCr, vol. 141, exp. 13, Tlayacapan 1817, fols. 359–75, esp. 360r–v (360v for quotes), 364v, 367r; cf. vol. 91, exp. 7, Tlayacapan 1818, fol. 92r.

18. AGNCr, vol. 274, exp. 21, Totolapa 1795, fol. 285r (for context, see fols. 275–91; on Ortíz's probable ownership of a hacienda, see fols. 277v–278v). For theoretically astute treatment of the feminization of other men as a means to assert masculinity, in a context of sexual practice rather than punishment, see Lancaster 1992, esp. 235–78.

19. I have relied on the insight of Clendinnen 1982a on this point.

20. See Chapter 8 below for a discussion of the deep interplays between gender culture and political culture evident in acts of whipping.

21. AGNCr, vol. 692, exp. 2, Tetelpan 1780, fol. 4r. The slur is taken from Manuel Antonio's testimony and cannot be confirmed because of the isolated circumstances of the incident. For our purposes what matters most is the cultural plausibility of the incident — its factual ring rather than its factual occurrence.

22. For a particularly striking example in a northern community of colonial Mexico, see C. E. Martin 1990, 317 (this and Taylor 1979, 81–83, are the best studies of male fighting words and insult in colonial Mexico).

23. See, e.g., AGNCr, vol. 91, exp. 13, Totolapa 1803, fol. 311r; vol. 228, exp. 15, Tepetlixpa 1803, fol. 258r; vol. 262, exp. 30, Tepoztlán 1792, fols. 323–31.

24. See AGN, Clero Regular y Secular, vol. 76, exp. 4, fol. 154r–v. The sparse documentary record makes it difficult to evaluate veracity, but for our purposes the appeal to known social experience to support the truth claims of the petition is more important.

25. For examples of these weapons of the powerful, see, in addition to the cases cited in nn. 24 and 26, AGNCr, vol. 174, exp. 1, Cuautla Amilpas 1805, fols. 1v–2r (cf. 10r–v, 17r–20r, 24r); vol. 263, exp. 25, Ayacapixtla 1798, fols. 359–62 (note the relative immunity of Francisco Ramírez compared with his *amasia* Dominga Salgado); vol. 223, exp. 6, Tlayacapa 1766, fols. 80–86, esp. 81r–v, 84v–85r; AGN, Matrimonios, vol. 36, exp. 71, Hacienda Mapaztlán 1773, fols. 186–219.

26. AGNCr, vol. 175, exp. 3 (cf. exp. 2), Cuautla Amilpas 1779, fol. 180r.

27. AGNCr, vol. 174, exp. 8, Yecapixtla 1799, esp. fols. 270v (quote); 270v–272v, 280v (ethnic identities and employment of assailants); 271r, 272r (utterance of a *desvergüenza*); 269r–274v, 282v–283r (conflicting testimonies regarding robbery, but an overall sense that robbery was not the point of the attack); 272r (retreat after serious head wound); cf. the dynamics of masculine "fun" and gang rape in vol. 278, exp. 5, Xonacatepec 1806, fols. 171–193, esp. 182, 181r, 175v.

28. See Chapter 2 above and the especially pertinent C. E. Martin 1982, 1985.

29. A century after the colonial period a peasant drew on this aspect of popular culture to advise Emiliano Zapata why he had been elected to lead Anenecuilco's struggle for land. "We'll back you. We just want a man with pants on" (Sotelo Inclán 1943, 175–76, as cited in Womack 1968, 9).

30. AGNCr, vol. 141, exp. 13, Tlayacapan 1817, fols. 359–75, esp. fol. 360r (quote of José Francisco); vol. 274, exp. 21, Totolapa 1795, fols. 278v–280r; vol. 692, exp. 2, Tetelpan 1780, fols. 2r–v, 3v–4r; AGN, Clero Regular y Secular, vol. 76, exp. 4, fol. 154; cf. AGNCr, vol. 278, exp. 5, Xonacatepec 1806, fols. 171–93; vol. 223, exp. 6, Tlayacapa 1766, fols. 80–86, esp. 84v–85r.

31. This formulation owes much to Connell 1987. See also the explorations of "protest masculinity" and masculinized subcultures of violence in Wolfgang and Ferracuti 1967; Messerschmidt 1986 (cf. 1993). On hegemony and counterhegemony as a more general issue in historical theory, see Chapter 5, n. 4; for application and critique in a Mexican context, see Joseph and Nugent 1994a.

32. See AGNCr, vol. 264, exp. 3, Tepoztlán 1791, fols. 156–207, esp. 157r–162r, 186r–v, 188r; for an inversion example without rape, see vol. 142, exp. 6, Atlatlauca 1802, esp. fols. 168r, 169v; for further context on political factionalism in Tepoztlán, see vol. 262, exps. 23, 30, fols. 267–70, 323–31.

33. For insight on the paradox of a masculine gender consciousness that seeks not only to possess the woman Other but to find legitimacy from the relationship with her, see Janeway 1980; de Beauvoir 1952. For woman-centered novels that weaken Latin American patriarchs by underscoring their failure to achieve this deeper power of possession, see Allende 1986; Mastretta 1985.

34. Although strong words were reasonably common in disputes leading to violence against women and although male assailants had an interest in demonstrating that women had provoked an uncontrollable rage, it is striking that female verbal affronts figured as prime or near-prime causes of dispute in only about one-tenth of the violence cases directed at female targets. (For the restricted case set [$n = 62$], the figure is 11.3 percent; for the expanded case set [$n = 93$], the figure is 8.6 percent. PDBO, Morelos Powvioli.out, pp. 33–34, variables MVW1–4; Powmore1.sys, pp. 34–35, variables MVW1–4.) That is, even when women voiced strong words, they might be sparing in the kind of direct (rather than oblique or lateral) attacks on manhood that might "justify" male violence. For a vivid anecdotal example of such ambiguity, see the case of María Gertrudis Martínez in the introduction to Chapter 4 above.

35. For perceptive treatment of the role of "space" in the development of women's consciousness, see Evans 1979; cf. Evans and Boyte 1986.

36. In *tierra fría* villages such as Tepoztlán and Tlayacapan, Indian bullfighting had entered the annual cycle of community festivals. See AGNCr, vol. 45, exp. 11, Cuernavaca/Ocotepec/Tepoztlán 1808, fol. 323r; vol. 91, exp. 7, Tlayacapa 1818, fol. 92v; Ingham 1986, 147; Haskett 1991a, 18, 221 n. 36.

37. My interpretation of cockfights and Indian bullfights has been greatly assisted by ethnographic and comparative reading (in addition to my own experience). On bullfighting spectacles and metaphors in Tlayacapa and more generally, see Ingham 1986, 126, 135, 146–51, to whose interpretation of masculinity and femininity I am heavily indebted; cf. Gallo S. 1983, 63–72, 114–15, 142, 144; Pitt-Rivers 1971, 89–91; C. B. Douglas 1984. Some of the most perceptive treatments of the significance of bulls and bullfighting in rural settings and popular culture come from the Andes: see Arguedas 1968; Anrup 1990, 207–29. For the flavor of bullfighting and cockfighting in the Mexican provinces in the early nineteenth century, albeit in cases of fighting events organized as large spectacles including attendance by elites, see Calderón de la Barca 1982, 169–70, 215–17, 291–94 (letters numbered 16, 21, 28); cf., for colonial institutional background, Sarabia Viejo 1972. On cockfighting, see not only the well-known classic by Geertz (1973, 412–53) and the critique by Roseberry (1989) but also the comparative ethnographic material and interpretations of masculinity in Dundes 1994a.

38. Calderón de la Barca 1982, 215 (letter of June 15, 1840).

39. On late colonial tensions over spectacles that encouraged popular rowdiness, and an effort to promote an elite culture distinct from such spectacles, see Viqueira Albán 1987. For a hint that the illegitimacy of subaltern cockfights meant that provincial elites who openly attended them were socially tarnished or diminished, see AGNCr, vol. 91, exp. 7, Tlayacapa 1818, fol. 92v.

40. On male conviviality and drink in village contexts, see Taylor 1979, 58–60, 62, 66–67. For specific examples in hacienda and village contexts, see AGNCr, vol. 39, exp. 18, Cuernavaca 1818, fols. 313–38; vol. 44, exp. 3, Hda. Chiconguaque 1805, fols. 46–52; vol. 44, exp. 4, Hda. San Gabriel 1799, fols. 53–97; vol. 47, exp. 4, Hda. Chiconguaque 1813, fols. 106–85 (esp. 111r, 119v); vol. 48, exp. 5, Hda. del Puente 1816, fols. 35–76 (esp. 42r, 43r); vol. 48, exp. 10, Cuentepec 1815, fols. 140–96; vol. 159, exps. 1–3, Tlayacapa 1810, fols. 1–161 (esp. 46r, 49v–50r); vol. 175, exp. 10, Mapaztlán 1806, fols. 243–84; vol. 262, exp. 10, Hda. San Gabriel 1817, fols. 148–59, esp. 151v, 154v, 158r; vol. 264, exp. 2, Mazatepec 1806, fols. 141–55; vol. 274, exp. 24, Tlayacapa 1774, fols. 301–7.

41. The patterns discussed in the preceding paragraphs are distilled from the sources cited in n. 40 above. On the wordplay of *albures*, see also Colín Sánchez 1987, 228–30, 222; Ingham 1986, 144–45; Paz 1959, 35. The manuscript sources indicate, however, that *albures* referred both to wordplay and to a card game. The homology is revealing: both were forms

of competitive play. See also the discussion of "fighting words" in Taylor 1979, 81–83; C. E. Martin 1990.

42. See, e.g., AGNCr, vol. 274, exp. 4, Tlayacapa 1774, fols. 302, 305v, 306v.

43. This statement is based on the examples cited in n. 40 above rather than the more selective examples cited below in this paragraph.

44. AGNCr, vol. 44, exp. 4, Hda. San Gabriel 1799, fols. 53–97; vol. 48, exp. 10, Cuentepec 1815, fols. 144r–163r (includes citations of *parense carajos*); vol. 39, exp. 18, Cuernavaca 1818, fols. 313–38 (316v for "step outside" quote, cf. 318v); vol. 48, exp. 5, Hda. del Puente 1816, fols. 35–76 (42r for "spurt blood" quote); vol. 159, exp. 1, Tlayacapa 1810, fols. 45v, 46r, 48r ("determined provocations" phrases, altered into first person and present tense from verbatim versions in third person and past tense); and for friends who quarreled violently without jeopardizing friendship, vol. 38, exp. 1, Guichilaque 1809, fols. 4v–5r, 14v–15v; vol. 44, exp. 3, Hda. Chiconguaque 1805, fols. 46–52; cf. vol. 39, exp. 18, Cuernavaca 1818, fol. 317r; vol. 44, exp. 4, Hda. San Gabriel 1799, fols. 53–97.

45. AGNCr, vol. 537, exp. 1, Hda. Casasano 1803, fol. 7v.

46. I am aware that for some readers, homosocial bonding activities spiced by sexual innuendo may suggest latent fears of homosexuality, or even homoeroticism: see, e.g., Dundes 1994b. My own view is more cautious. Questions of homosexuality did not arise in the records I studied (they may be more evident in Inquisition records than in criminal records). In Latin American cultural contexts, moreover, men may be stigmatized as feminized or passive men rather than for heterosexual or homosexual acts as such. The active or aggressive partner in a homosexual act may suffer no cultural stigma. For important cautionary discussions, see Lancaster 1992; Paz 1959; Alonso and Koreck 1993; note also the dispute between Oscar Lewis and his collaborator Carolina Luján reproduced in Rigdon 1988, 236–40.

47. For a pioneering treatment of the materiality of manhood, at once theoretical and in a Latin American ethnographic context, see Lancaster 1992; suggestive, in the colonial Mexican context, is C. E. Martin 1990.

48. AGNCr, vol. 1, exp. 21, Tlayacapan 1809, fol. 413v; vol. 277, exp. 2, Atlacahualoya 1789, fols. 33r, 41v–42r; vol. 3, exp. 1, Atlatlauca 1783, fol. 6r; vol. 2, exp. 7, Totolapa 1801, fol. 223v.

49. Cf. the sense of cultural variation and argument and individual choice evident in pioneering studies of popular masculinity in Mexico and Nicaragua: Gutmann 1994; Lancaster 1992.

50. For the overall structure of motivation, see Chapter 3 above; on *descarga* and honor-bonding findings, see n. 12 above.

51. For examples suggesting the particular importance accorded to "respect" in Indian village culture and suggesting that communal, generational, and familial pathways of masculine respectability resonated strongly, see AGNCr, vol. 39, exp. 21, Tepoztlán 1769, fol. 408v; vol. 39, exp. 22, Temimiltzinco 1766, fol. 416v; vol. 277, exp. 3, Xochitlán 1789, fols. 54–72, esp. 55r–v, 59v, 61r–v, 62v–63r; vol. 263, exp. 8, Ocotepeque 1798, fols. 65r–v, 69r–v, 73r–74r, 93r; vol. 35, exp. 21, Xoxocotla 1806, fols. 429v, 438r–v, 474r–475r, 508r–510r.

52. The standard socioethnic imagery associated black descent with troublemakers who hounded women or female youth. For an example, see AGNCr, vol. 215, exp. 8, Llanos de Tlayecac 1806, fols. 243r–246v.

53. AGNCr, vol. 253, exp. 3, Tepoztlán 1802, esp. fols. 90r–v, 92r (quote), 100r; vol. 263, exp. 8, Ocotepeque 1798, esp. fols. 93r (quote), 69r, 73v; for an inverted instance of generational tension, in which a rather imperious uncle ended up killing his insubordinate nephew, see vol. 35, exp. 21, Xoxocotla 1806, esp. fols. 426r–438v, 474r–475r, 508r–510r.

54. See García Márquez 1981.

55. This judgment has emerged cumulatively from archival immersion in hundreds of

cases. For examples of the ways that personal violation of manhood, reputation, or family seemed to demand and justify retribution, and the ways that escalating dynamics that transmuted property conflicts into manhood conflicts proved especially dangerous, see AGNCr, vol. 44, exp. 1, Tetecala 1807, fols. 2–18, esp. 5r–v; vol. 44, exp. 7, Chamilpa 1804, fols. 144v, 146v (cf. 158r, 160r–161v); vol. 46, exp. 1, Xiutepec 1820, fols. 1–32; vol. 46, exp. 2, Cuernavaca 1807, fols. 37v, 63r, 74; vol. 202, exp. 4, Miacatlán 1798, esp. fols. 337r, 339r–v, 342r, 354r; vol. 212, exp. 19, Mapaztlán 1803, fols. 393–404; vol. 215, exp. 11, Yautepec 1775, esp. fols. 307r–v, 310v, 311v; vol. 277, exp. 1, Xonacatepec 1805, fols. 1–27, esp. 4v–6r.

56. The best evidence for the role of companionship is the matter-of-fact statement, told in passing, that assumes that companions who joined a man in arenas of informal play and bonding helped out in moments of trouble. See, e.g., AGNCr, vol. 39, exp. 18, Cuernavaca 1818, fol. 317r; cf. vol. 48, exp. 5, Hda. del Puente 1816, fols. 35–76; vol. 48, exp. 10, Cuentepec 1815, fol. 153r; vol. 274, exp. 24, Tlayacapa 1774, fol. 302r–v; and n. 57 below.

57. AGNCr, vol. 215, exp. 11, Yautepec 1775, fol. 307v, for quote; 304r, 318r for the Tlayacapa connection; 310r for ambiguities about the *milpa* possessions; 297r (exp. 10), 302r, 304r, for various identifications as mestizo and mulatto.

58. In this case, however, accident intervened and ruined the theater of aggressive retreat. The rocks thrown by Augustín Ruíz either missed altogether or hit Antonio de la Cruz on the arms, legs, or body — all but one, that is. One rock smashed Antonio de la Cruz in the head; he died a half hour later, and his assailant was subjected to criminal proceedings. See AGNCr, vol. 215, exp. 11, Yautepec 1775, esp. fols. 305v (wounds and their location), 307v (death), 308r ("Let him be" quote; confrontation with Espinoza), 310v ("tongue" quote), 322r–v, 324r–v; cf. exp. 10, Yautepec 1802, fols. 296r–297r.

59. AGNCr, vol. 47, exp. 13, Hda. Miacatlán 1815, fols. 415–39, esp. 417v–419r, 420r–422v, 438r–439v; cf. vol. 38, exp. 2, Tesoyuca 1809, fol. 45r; cf. the shrewd observations of Lancaster 1992, 197, on honor, avoidance, and the military draft in Nicaragua in the late 1980s.

60. See, e.g., AGNCr, vol. 38, exp. 16, Hda. San Gaspar 1809, fols. 320v–321r; vol. 254, exp. 3, Zamatitlán 1803, fol. 39v; cf. vol. 175, exp. 11, Cuautla Amilpas 1787, fol. 307v; vol. 47, exp. 4, Hda. Chiconguaque 1813, fols. 111r–v, 116v.

61. For a particularly vivid example, see AGNCr, vol. 38, exp. 2, Tesoyuca 1809, fols. 31–83, esp. 45r, 42v, 36r, 56r.

62. I do not dispute that the tale told in García Márquez 1981 — the complicity of a community in a homicide dictated by the code of honor despite the reluctance of the avengers — can happen in Latin America. Indeed, the novella is based on a 1951 event García Márquez observed as a provincial journalist in Colombia. See Apuleyo Mendoza and García Márquez 1983, 27–28. (For a 1993 incident in Mexican/U.S. border culture that could provide similar material for a future novelist, see M. Brenner 1993.) Nonetheless, I hope the previous discussion has demonstrated the way the novella's vision is overdetermined if taken to refer to the dictates of cultural response that preclude maneuver short of outright homicide or permanent flight.

63. AGNCr, vol. 142, exp. 4, Tlayacapan 1805, fol. 93r; cf. the astute comments on gaucho "violence for show" in Chasteen 1990.

CHAPTER EIGHT

1. The account of the Jiménez de Cisneros affair in 1763–64 is based on AGNCr, vol. 205, exps. 1–5, Cuernavaca 1763–64, fols. 1–288 (fol. 278r for quote); vol. 39, exp. 24, Cuernavaca 1764, fols. 425–36.

2. On conditions in Morelos in 1762–63, see, in addition to n. 1 above, C. E. Martin 1985,

161; AGNCr, vol. 39, exp. 25, Tlaquiltenango 1762, fols. 447r, 443v; vol. 90, exp. 15, Tlayacapa 1764, fol. 291r. On windfall profit mechanisms and grain scarcity in colonial Mexico and the corn riot of 1692, see Florescano 1969, esp. 103, 107, 186–88, 196 (cf. Larson 1980); Cope 1994, chap. 7; Don Carlos de Sigüenza y Góngora to Admiral Pez, Mexico City, Aug. 30, 1692, in I. A. Leonard 1929, 210–77, esp. 237, 243.

3. Later that month a crowd of armed men invaded the house of his widow, Doña María Juana Palomeque, threatened to kill her, and seized her late husband's personal servant Sánchez. AGNCr, vol. 205, exp. 4, Cuernavaca 1764, fol. 224r; exp. 5, Cuernavaca 1764, fols. 251–71; vol. 39, exp. 24, Cuernavaca 1764, fols. 425–36.

4. For the quotations and similar praise by other pueblos, see AGNCr, vol. 205, exp. 5, Cuernavaca 1764, fols. 251r, 255r, 257r, 258r–v, 259r, 261r, 263r, 265r, 266r–v, 268v.

5. The description that follows is drawn from AGNCr, vol. 1, exp. 11, Tlayacapan 1784, fols. 132–86, esp. fols. 134v, 139–42 (140v–141r for *semillero*), 153–57, 170r–171r, 173r–185r (173r for "loss of life" quote).

6. See ibid., fols. 179r, 173r, 173v, for the quotes in this paragraph.

7. See ibid., fols. 139v, 141r.

8. On this point, see esp. ibid., fol. 140v.

9. Warman 1988, 330. The reference is to the relations between Zapatista army leaders and commoner troops and between the army and peasant civilians. The Zapatista movement of Morelos and Indian communities of the Mexican south have inspired some of the strongest images of community cohesion and/or egalitarianism. See, e.g., Sotelo Inclán 1943; Warman 1976; Taylor 1972, 1979; Carmagnani 1988; cf. Farriss 1984; Warman 1980; Wolf 1959, 212–28.

10. Falcón 1988, 446. The reference is to a *cacique* client of Saturnino Cedillo, the chief *cacique* of San Luís Potosí during the 1920s and 1930s. The image of a peasantry bound to vertical lines of community power embodied in *cacique* bosses is quite strongly developed for center-north and center-west communities. On the *caciquismo* phenomenon, see Brading 1980, Friedrich 1986. A case where the communal and *cacique* images merge is in the history of Yucatán in the Mexican Revolution. The problem is introduced in Joseph 1988, a superb history of the revolution in Yucatán, and will no doubt be illuminated further in a forthcoming book on Yucatán by Gilbert Joseph and Allen Wells.

11. Katz 1988a, 13 (cf. 17).

12. For the regional and ethnic contrasts, see nn. 9–11 above; for the famous study and restudy of Tepoztlán, see Redfield 1930; Lewis 1951; cf. Lomnitz Adler 1982; Rigdon 1988, 28–33, 40–44, 48, 203–6, 207–8, 212–14. Joseph and Nugent 1994a is a landmark rethinking of popular politics, from bottom up and top down, that encourages transcendence of many such dichotomies.

13. Lockhart 1992, esp. 15–28, 436–40; cf. García Martínez 1987; Carmagnani 1988. Note, however, that Lockhart does not take modular organization to imply egalitarianism (94–140).

14. AGNCr, vol. 3, exp. 7, Tlalnepantla 1787, fol. 73r (*monte* quotes); vol. 1, exp. 4, Tlayacapan 1750, fols. 30–56 (rustlers); vol. 2, exp. 9, Totolapan 1802, esp. fols. 173r–176v, 179r–183v (semiclandestine network); vol. 39, exp. 25, Tlaquiltenango 1762, fol. 448r–v (protection of *comunero*); vol. 253, exp. 11, Yautepec 1796, fol. 361r (communal precondition of land); vol. 90, exp. 26, Totolapa 1801, fol. 400v (drinking custom quote).

15. AGNCr, vol. 262, exp. 30, Tepoztlán 1792, fol. 324v. Instances of disobedience and factionalism in the face of vertical power and prerogative, and complaints by notables of lack of respect, run throughout the criminal records of late colonial Morelos. For examples, see AGNCr, vol. 3, exp. 7, Tlalnepantla 1787, esp. fol. 75v; vol. 39, exp. 21, Tepoztlán 1769, fol. 408v; exp. 22, Temimiltzinco 1766, fol. 416v; vol. 90, exp 26, Totolapa 1801, esp. fols.

400r–401v; vol. 223, exp. 23, Tlalnepantla 1805, fol. 383; vol. 226, exp. 11, Quantempa 1810, fols. 462–501; vol. 274, exp. 10, Tlayacapa 1782, fols. 168v–169v.

16. On vertical aspects of political life in Morelos in pre-Hispanic and colonial times as reflected in the machinery of elections and the sociology of officeholding, see Haskett 1991a, esp. 31, 54, 200–201; cf. Carmagnani 1982. For ranking among constituent parts of the political whole, cautionary contrast between indigenous understandings and the colonial *cabecera-sujeto* concept, and pervasive descent ranking, see Lockhart 1992, chaps. 2, 4; Carmagnani 1988; García Martínez 1987; Rounds 1979.

17. See nn. 15, 23, 26, for examples.

18. AGNCr, vol. 277, exp. 2, Atlacahualoya 1789, fol. 39r, for quote (taken from a rebel *gobernador* in a land struggle that included discrediting the older power group; see the discussion of Atlacahualoya in Chapter 6 above); Mallon 1994a, chap. 3; cf. 1994b. The rather ironic "democratic patriarchy" term was coined by Stacey (1983, 116) to capture family policy — a "radical redistribution of patriarchy" — in revolutionary China.

19. On widows' lands, see AGNCr, vol. 253, exp. 11, Yautepec 1796, fols. 359v, 361r, 369r (cf. Chapter 5 above). On women and ad hoc politics, see below; cf. Taylor 1979, 113–51 passim. On male resistance to extensions of conditional right to family and gender relations, see Chapters 1 and 4 above.

20. AGNCr, vol. 90, exp. 26, Totolapa 1801, fol. 400r; vol. 253, exp. 1, Amatlán 1769, fol. 5r.

21. That age alone did not suffice to establish credentials as an esteemed *viejo* comes through in the testimony of a seventy-five-year-old Tepoztlán Indian that he had heard that the *viejos* had become angry with the current *gobernador*. See AGNCr, vol. 203, exp. 2, Tepoztlán 1769, fol. 72v (cf. 63r–v); cf. vol. 254, exp. 4, Huispalca 1809, fols. 64r, 75r.

Readers should be aware that my view of service and esteem represents a partial dissent from Chance and Taylor 1985, an important and perceptive revision of the scholarship on the civil-religious cargo system in Mesoamerica. I am partly persuaded by their suggestion that a rather reified classic version of the cargo system found in anthropological and ethnohistorical writings — especially the fusion of the civil and religious service roles into a neat ladder of alternating service domains as one climbed the prestige ladder — represented a postcolonial development. But I think the case is somewhat overstated: the same persons and families did, even in late colonial times, garner esteemed *viejo* status through establishing a record of service in both domains. In short, Chance and Taylor's historicization of form does not necessarily preclude a certain continuity of substance.

22. A powerful rendition of the theory as embedded in local oral tradition and documentation spanning several centuries of peasant struggle in Morelos is Sotelo Inclán 1943; cf. Womack 1968, 3–9. For the theory in action, see nn. 23–25 below. For further illumination of elder roles in theory and practice, see the analysis of "harmony ideology" in Nader 1990.

23. AGNCr, vol. 204, exp. 14, Miacatlán 1775, fols. 361–65 (361v for "satisfaction" and "tears" quotes); vol. 90, exp. 26, Totolapa 1801, fols. 399–402; vol. 91, exp. 13, Totolapa 1803, fols. 309–12; vol. 226, exp. 11, Quantempa 1810, fols. 462–501 (480r for "despotic" and *hijos* quotes).

24. See AGNCr, vol. 35, exp. 21, Xoxocotla 1806, fols. 426r–437v, esp. 429v; vol. 262, exp. 25, Xochitlán 1792, fols. 278–82, esp. 281.

25. This interpretation of the blurred distinction between *oficial, pasado,* and *viejo* emerges from the language of the manuscript sources as well as the illuminating study by Haskett 1991a. (I should acknowledge, however, that Haskett argues for little distinction in political function and practice among *oficiales, pasados,* and *viejos,* while my interpretation sees distinction marked by overlap and blurring.)

26. See AGNCr, vol. 203, exp. 2, Tepoztlán 1769, fols. 61–88 (63v for quote, cf. 74v); vol. 39, exp. 21, Tepoztlán 1769, fols. 408–15.

27. My sense of the ways that brokers, like the state itself, paradoxically concentrate and mediate contradictions has been influenced by research conversations with Florencia E. Mallon (cf. 1994a) and by Karen Spalding's work on brokers in the Andes (see 1970, 1973, 1984); see also Haskett 1991a.

28. AGNCr, vol. 692, exp. 2, Tetelpan 1780, fol. 1r (cf. 2r–v).

29. AGNCr, vol. 254, exp. 4, Huispalca 1809, fols. 62–106, esp. fols. 63r–64v (64r for quote), 74r–78r (75r, 76v, for *viejos* in the mind; 75r, 77v, for "beseeching" and respect), 92r, 95r.

30. On the analytical significance of women's extension into public political arenas of moral sensibilities they forged in familial and quasi-familial contexts, see T. Kaplan 1982; Navarro 1988; Deutsch 1991. Cf. the discussion of women and riot in colonial Mexico in Taylor 1979 and of women and politics in contemporary Mexico in Massolo 1992; J. Martin 1990.

31. AGNCr, vol. 263, exp. 8, Ocotepeque 1798, fol. 80v; vol. 1, exp. 11, Tlayacapan 1784, fols. 173v, 174r; cf. vol. 45, exp. 17, Mazatepec 1820, fol. 435r.

32. Taylor 1979, 116.

33. AGNCr, vol. 175, exp. 14, Tetelzingo 1778, fols. 507–17, esp. 509r (quotes).

34. For other examples of women's prominence in community violence and tumult, see, aside from the cases cited in nn. 35–36 below, AGNCr, vol. 262, exps. 32–33, Octepec/Ahuatepec 1808, fols. 359r–360r, 362r, 366v–367r, 371v, 385r; vol. 277, exp. 2, Atlacahualoya 1789, fols. 36r–37r, 40r; vol. 202, exp. 5, Achichipico 1802, fols. 385–433, esp. 389v–390r. The latter case is an unusually clear example of the screening process that buries a specifically female presence in the documentary record. The tumult focused initially on the wrath provoked by a visiting priest who sequestered Indian girls for schooling and on the fierce opposition of Indian mothers to the taking of their daughters. As the documentary file proceeds, however, these specificities of gender drop out of the ongoing language of the record and are displaced by masculinized generic categories (e.g., words such as *indios* or *hijos* displace *indias* or *hijas*).

35. AGNCr, vol. 277, exps. 9–12, Zahuatlán 1793, fols. 198–304, esp. 199r–200v, 205r–206v, 222r, 226r–227v (227r for quotes), 242r–246v, 273r–v.

36. The account of the Tepoztlán rebellion has been gleaned from AGNCr, vol. 312, exp. 2, Tepoztlán 1777, esp. fols. 9r–18v, 26r–32v, 35v–38v, 40r–41r, 46r, 73r–74v, 101r–v; vol. 263, exp. 19, Tepoztlán 1777, esp. fol. 325r; vol. 203, exp. 4, Tepoztlán 1777, esp. fols. 110r–111r, 116r–121v. Hereinafter, notes on the Tlayacapan affair will serve only to identify quotations.

37. AGNCr, vol. 312, exp. 2, Tepoztlán 1797, fols. 101r, 28v, 14r, 29r.

38. Ibid., fol. 15v.

39. Ibid., fol. 18v.

40. Ibid., fol. 73r.

41. AGNCr, vol. 203, exp. 4, Tepoztlán 1777, fol. 120v.

42. As noted earlier (Chapter 2), I have drawn theoretical inspiration for a culture-as-practical-argument view from the works of Sabean 1984, esp. 28–30, 95, 195, and Bourdieu 1977. I wish to acknowledge that at one point (95), Sabean's language is close to mine: "Culture is a series of arguments among people about the common things of their everyday lives." For an introduction to recent rethinking of culture concepts in history, see Hunt 1989, especially the trenchant essay by Desan.

43. See Lewis 1959, 28, 30; 1964, 332, 494, cf. 333.

44. On flogging in a variety of contexts, see, in addition to nn. 45–46 below, AGNCr, vol. 2, exp. 15, Tlayacapan 1786, fols. 340r, 345r; vol. 47, exp. 8, Xoxocotla 1804, fol. 271v; vol. 48, exp. 13, Xonacate 1796, fol. 341v; vol. 44, exp. 6, Tetelilla 1800, fol. 112r; vol. 215, exp. 2, Tetela

del Volcán 1812, fols. 22r, 38r; vol. 254, exp. 6, Yautepec 1792, fols. 177r–v; vol. 263, exp. 10, Xocotitla 1803, fols. 125–29; vol. 266, exp. 18, Yxtla 1772, fol. 233v; vol. 272, exp. 19, Texcalpa 1784, fols. 272v, 273v; vol. 278, exp. 4, Yecapixtla 1805, fols. 166r, 166v.

45. AGNCr, vol. 277, exp. 3, Xochitlán 1789, fols. 55r, 59v (cf. 62v), for quotes. The child parallel borrows from the insight of Clendinnen 1982a, esp. 41–46 (for wider context, see Clendinnen 1987).

46. AGNCr, vol. 278, exp. 7, Xalostoque 1796, fols. 242r, 240r, 242v, 244r; cf. vol. 46, exp. 14, Tetelpa 1816, fols. 342–95; vol. 50, exp. 26, Xoxocotla 1799, fols. 429v, 441r; vol. 203, exp. 8, Guaxomulco 1798, fols. 367r–368r, 377r, 380v; and n. 48 below.

47. It is worth noting that I found repeated instances of the phenomenon for Oaxaca as well as Morelos; this underscored the importance of moving beyond mental assignment of such cases to bizarre individual pathology.

48. AGNCr, vol. 274, exp. 13, Tepetlixpa 1797, fols. 206–16, esp. 213v, 208v; cf. fusion of kin and official roles, this time in reaction to the murder of a goddaughter, in vol. 215, exp. 2, Tetela del Volcán 1812, fols. 224, 38r.

49. Cf. Lockhart 1992, 440.

50. AGNCr, vol. 253, exp. 1, Amatlán 1769, fol. 5r; vol. 90, exp. 26, Totolapa 1801, fol. 400r.

51. See AGNCr, vol. 213, exp. 14, Cuautla Amilpas 1805, fols. 365r–368r (365r, 368r for "intrepid," "undeniable"), 402v–403v (402v for "insurgent"), 409r.

52. On restraint of inner potentials for destruction and dissipation in Nahua culture, the most illuminating discussions are Clendinnen 1985, 1991; see also López Austin 1980. Lockhart 1968, 1972 may be interpreted to suggest the great efforts of conquistadors to construct quickly, at least among themselves, a sense of place, seniority, and order that almost seems fictional in view of extensive civil war and social turbulence; cf. Stern 1992, 8–11. On the efforts of Spanish American colonizers to build Iberian social linkage and normalcy in transatlantic contexts, see Altman 1989; cf., for a dramatically ill-fated case, Cook and Cook 1991. For interpretations of baroque culture as suppression of an exuberance released in controlled or subterranean contexts, see I. A. Leonard 1959; Paz 1982. On stereotypes of blacks and mulattoes, one of the most vivid examples comes from the criminal case we have just discussed. José Silverio was such a flagrant and sexually licentious troublemaker, said the *fiscal* who summed up the case, that "it is even doubted if he is of this *calidad* [Indian], or mulatto" (AGNCr, vol. 213, exp. 14, Cuautla Amilpas 1805, fol. 409r). For further discussion of racial stereotyping, see Chapter 12 below.

CHAPTER NINE

1. See Simpson 1941, 10, for quote. Note that the "many Mexicos" idea that framed the book forcefully at the beginning and end (xii–xiii, 3–10, 323) often slips out of view in the synthetic history of the whole that constitutes the main body of the text. I wish to thank an anonymous reader for stressing differences between Simpson's original treatment of "many Mexicos" and the regionalism that came to prevail later.

2. For an outstanding analysis of a century of changes in the U.S. historical profession, see Novick 1988; for Latin American and African perspectives on the last quarter-century and a partial critique of Novick, see Stern 1993.

3. The two paragraphs that follow are based, in addition to my own observations, on the following: For excellent overviews and critiques of the turn toward regionalism, see Joseph 1991; Vanderwood 1987; Fowler-Salamini 1993; cf. Van Young 1983, 1992a. For historical writing in Mexico more generally since the mid-twentieth century, see Florescano 1991. For the outstanding Mexican advocate of microhistory, see González y González 1968, 1971, 1973. On local intellectuals, the state, and history, see Mallon 1993; cf. the theorization of

culture and "localist ideology" in Lomnitz-Adler 1991. On Tlatelolco, political disillusion, and historical writing, see Joseph and Nugent 1994b, 5–12, esp. 8; Florescano 1991, 73–77, esp. 74.

4. See Joseph 1991, esp. 3–4; Van Young 1983, 33–34, 26, 40; Vanderwood 1987; cf. Fowler-Salamini 1993. Recent methodological approaches emphasize historicity over essentialism and conceptualize regions "as processual spaces whose internal architecture and direction are subject to constant negotiation by actors both within and without" (Van Young 1992a, 27). This framework meshes well with the approach advocated in this book and in n. 5 below.

5. On unique local synthesis of trends or patterns that reverberate more widely, the comments of Lewis (1951, xxi–xxvii) and the theoretical discussion of regional culture and power by Lomnitz-Adler (1991) are instructive.

6. De Beauvoir 1952; for gendered language of Othering and self-legitimation in a Mexican context, see Chapter 5 above.

7. The pioneering classic in ethnic and imperial contexts is Said 1978. For gender, the classic is de Beauvoir 1952. For illuminating recent work on these themes, see, e.g., AE 1989; Bernal 1987; Domínguez 1989; Said 1993; Sider 1987. For female deviant Others in early modern Spain, see Perry 1985, 1990.

8. PDBO, Tri-regional, Mormv1a.lis, p. 66 (cf. 62–63); Oaxmv1a.lis, p. 86 (cf. 81–82); Mexmv1a.lis, p. 66 (cf. 62–63).

9. The comparative spread of the Oaxaca materials derives from the organization of the provincial court records I was able to consult in Oaxaca, particularly at the ATOVA and CROT archives. For the Mexico City cases, especially those at the AJT, the thickness of preserved records increased as one proceeded forward in time (perhaps in part as the result of an increased crackdown on plebeians), and my sampling choices emphasized the 1790s. For the Morelos cases I leaned heavily on the AGN records filed with the supervisory judges of the Marquesado and the Audiencia. These also thickened as one proceeded forward in time, and placed a greater accent on homicidal cases. The vagaries of institutional level, documentary loss and preservation, and sampling opportunities make all the more remarkable the interregional consistencies in the structure of major motivation, and the sense that important patterns of change in gender relations and interpersonal violence are best discerned not within the 1760–1821 period but over a longer time frame.

10. For Oaxaca and Mexico City, respectively, deviance markers were as follows: assailants previously arrested, 10.4 percent and 28.2 percent (the latter a reflection of institutional crackdown on plebeians in Mexico City, where the police arrested, often on harassment charges such as drunkenness, vagrancy, and public disorder, more than one-eighth [12.9 percent] of the plebeians in 1798 alone); assailants previously arrested for violence, 3.1 percent and 11.5 percent; assailants who were loners rather than family-attached, 15.3 percent (regional loner estimate was 32.6 percent) and 33.9 percent (regional loner estimate was 30.9 percent); targets who were loners, 12.4 percent and 16.0 percent; drinking by assailant considered important, 20.6 percent and 24.2 percent; drinking by target considered important, 12.4 percent and 16.0 percent; "late night" confrontation, 7.6 percent and 4.3 percent; isolated spot as setting for violence, 11.8 percent and 0.0 percent (the latter a reflection of urban setting); stranger relation between assailant and target, 11.2 percent and 14.3 percent. (For further discussion and definition of deviance markers, see Chapter 3 above.) Sources: PDBO, Oaxaca, Oaxviol5.lis, p. 19; Oaxviol4.lis, p. 24; Oaxviol2.lis, pp. 19, 31; Mexico City, Mexviol5.lis, p. 17; Mexviol4.lis, p. 21; Mexviol2.lis, pp. 17, 28, 29; AGN, Tributos, vol. 43, exp. 9, fols. 276v, 277v; Scardaville 1977, 25. For the failure of loner and drinking markers to yield statistically significant associations with gender-rooted violence, see PDBO, Oaxaca, Oxnwhyp1.lis, pp. 18–19, 37–38; Mexico City, Mxnwhyp1.lis, pp. 18–19, 37–38. (The only qualification is that drinking by targets did yield a statistically significant

association for Mexico City, but the relationship was inverse and the Phi correlation [.23] was weak. See PDBO, Tri-regional, Mextst1.lis, p. 5.)

11. PDBO, Oaxaca, Oxnwhyp2.lis, pp. 6–8, 12–14; Mexico City, Mxnwhyp1.lis, pp. 6–8, 12–14.

12. The process of coding itself encouraged expectations of contrast. For example, I discovered, upon turning to Oaxaca, that I had to add a new category of motivation: disputes rooted in explicitly ethnic hatred. In Oaxaca such motivations could not as easily be subsumed by other motivations. Another example was that the Oaxaca profiles included a few individuals who required a Spanish-language interpreter yet could sign their names.

13. See PDBO, Tri-regional, Intereg1.lis (corrected version), p. 21, for the Chi-square test ($n = 556$); cf. pp. 17, 19. The Chi-square significance level was .07, and Cramer's V amounted to an anemic .09.

14. Triregional nonrandom association tests also proved negative, and even biregional tests ranged from negative to weak results. See PDBO, Tri-regional, Intereg1.lis (both corrected and uncorrected versions), p. 22. For three-way comparison, $n = 183$; for Morelos/Oaxaca, $n = 128$; for Oaxaca/Mexico City, $n = 121$.

15. The internal variety of Oaxaca's microregions is reviewed in fuller detail in Chapter 2 above. For brief examples that illuminate the microregional characteristics mentioned, see Romero Frizzi 1985; Taylor 1988, 230–31; Mathews 1985 (cf. 1982); Stephen 1992; Nader 1990; Chance 1989. On women and on ethnic militance in the Isthmus Zapotec zone, see Chiñas 1992; H. B. Campbell 1990.

16. For a modestly greater tilt toward non-Indians and plebeians in the Mixteca Alta profiles, see PDBO, Intra-regional, Oaxreg1.lis, esp. pp. 14–17.

17. PDBO, Intra-regional, Oaxreg3.lis, p. 7; cf. Oaxreg1.lis, pp. 41, 43.

18. On the proportion of homicides in the overall case set, see Table 9.1. The possibility that the difference in proportion is due to idiosyncrasies of record keeping and sampling arises because my Oaxaca and Mexico City research tapped into at least some records that were not sent on to viceregal courts for review, while the Morelos records relied predominantly on cases sent to the Marquesado judge and/or the *audiencias* for review. We shall see in the comparison below and in the microregional reconsideration of Morelos (Chapter 12), however, that sampling bias does not fully account for the difference.

For calculation of comparative murder rates, I used the following method: Over the sixty-two-year period 1760–1821, the Morelos sample generated 111 homicides, and the Oaxaca sample 62 homicides. The estimated Morelos population (for 1800–1803) was 89,838, and the estimate for the three Oaxaca districts (in 1793) was 165,965. I calculated the respective ratio as follows: For Morelos, the annual sample rate per 100,000 = (111/62)/ (89,839/100,000) = 1.99. For Oaxaca, the annual sample rate = (62/62)/(165,965/100,000) = .60. The ratio, therefore, is 1.99/.60 = 3.3. Even if one assumes that the effect of unsolved deaths (I found quite a few in Oaxaca, especially in Villa Alta) and the apparently thick run of Morelos homicides encountered in the *audiencia* records of the AGN led to serious underestimation of the annual sample rate for Oaxaca, the "double or more" estimate seems fair and conservative.

Readers should remember that for purposes of this study "Oaxaca" refers to the three core zones under study, not to the entire intendancy or region. Inclusion of the coastal isthmus zone would, for example, probably change the ratio notably.

One may construct a guess of murder rates per 100,000 population as follows: Data from the Mixteca Alta suggests an order of magnitude of approximately 10 per 100,000 in late colonial times. (This is based on figures of 5–6 homicides a year for Teposcolula in the period 1816–18, as recorded in the "Relación de Reos" documents in BNAH, Oax. I, Rollos 1–2; for a similar estimate, cf. Taylor 1979, 74, who suggested 12 per 100,000.) If the Zapotec and Villa Alta rates were more or less consistent and the comparative regional ratio given above is reasonably accurate, a quite conservative projection for Morelos would be roughly 20 per 100,000. Given the quality of the data, however, one must stress that such figures are at best crude guesstimates. For Mexico City my best guesstimate yields a figure of about 11 per 100,000 in the 1770s (based on data reported in AGN, Padrones, vol. 52, fols. 345v–346r).

CHAPTER TEN

1. See CROT, rollo 17, leg. 50, exp. 17, Cuquila 1775, esp. fols. 1r–7v (2v for quote), 13r–14v.

2. For examples designed to show a spread of microregions and contested gender issues, see, aside from nn. 1 and 3, the following: for the Mixteca Alta, CROT, rollo 17, leg. 50, exp. 10, San Miguel Tisahá 1768; rollo 16, leg. 49, exp. 44, Yodzondúa 1776; for the Zapotec Valley, AEO, Real Intendencia II, leg. 1, exp. 6, Ayoquezco 1787; leg. 1, exp. 25, Santa Cruz Nisila 1787 (second exp. within exp. beginning "La justicia del pueblo de la Asunción Ocotlán da declaración"); leg. 13, exp. 38, Zaachila 1811; for Villa Alta, ATOVA, leg. 7, exp. s.n. re: Antonio Rafael, Yoeche 1806; leg. 7, exp. s.n. re: María Dolores, Tabaá 1806; leg. 7, exp. s.n. re: Felipe de Arce, Solaga 1805.

3. CROT, rollo 16, leg. 48, exp. 28, Quilitongo 1805, fol. 2r; rollo 18, leg. 51, exp. 7, San Juan Copala 1770, fol. 8v.

4. The case summarized above is drawn from BNAH, Oaxaca I, rollo 51, exp. re: Marcial Lopez, Sta. Catarina Estetla 1784, fols. 1r–5v, 12r–19v, 22v–28v, 32r (1v, 4v, 3r, 16r–v for quotes).

5. See, e.g., CROT, rollo 16, leg. 48, exp. 28, Quilitongo 1805, esp. fol. 1v.

6. AEO, Real Intendencia I, leg. 11, exp. 8, Coyotepeque 1799, fol. 1v; cf. Real Intendencia II, leg. 13, exp. 31, Tlalixtac 1810, esp. fols. 1v–2r.

7. AGN, Indios, vol. 88, Paz to Viceroy, Yahuyuê, Mar. 16 1812, fols. 301v–302r (301v for quote); cf. Whitecotton 1977, 140. For a Zapotec Valley case suggesting that Paz's complaints of parental bargaining and reversal of marriage agreements were not simple fabrications, see AEO, Real Intendencia I, leg. 2, exp. 30 (mistakenly labeled exp. 52 in AEO's printed catalogue; re: Anastacio García), Tlacochahuaya 1792. See also the suggestive (but probably apocryphal) complaint of wife-robbery by her uncle in ATOVA, Criminal, leg. 7, exp. s.n. re: María Dolores, Tabaá (Villa Alta) 1806; and the more contemporary ethnographic discussion in Avendaño de Durand 1982, 90–91.

8. ATOVA, Criminal, leg. 6, exp. s.n. re: Esteban de los Angeles, Yaeé 1794, fol. 1v, for quote. On the *depósito* custom and female institutional confinement more generally, see Muriel 1974. For a suggestive Zapotec Valley example of a community kidnap of a woman abused while on deposit in a house of honor, see AEO, Obispado, leg. 1, exp. 5, Zoquitlán 1754–55.

9. BNAH, Oaxaca I, rollo 51, exp. s.n. re: Marcial Lopez, Sta. Catarina Estetla 1784, fol. 26v; ATOVA, Criminal, leg. 6, exp. s.n. re: Esteban de los Angeles, Yaeé 1794, fol. 1v.

10. AEO, Real Intendencia II, leg. 28, exp. 10, Tlacochahuaya 1807, fol. 2r (quote). The importance of harmony ideology in the culture history of Oaxaca and the implications for gender come through in the superb ethnographic study by Nader 1990 (cf. 1989).

11. These themes are discussed for Morelos in Chapters 7 and 8 above. For Oaxaca the most insightful discussions of community political and electoral structures are Carmagnani 1982, 1988; but for a dissenting point of view and additional evidence, cf. Chance 1989; AEO, Alcaldías Mayores, leg. 27, exp. 22, San Pedro Apóstol (Ocotlán) 1781, fols. 1v–6r passim. For a sense that an honorific culture required that men attend to their reputation as men if they wished to function effectively in public or community life, see AEO, Alcaldías

Mayores, leg. 37, exp. 30, Ocotlán 1785; ATOVA, Criminal, leg. 7, exp. s.n. re: Fernando Hernández, Talea 1796, fol. 9v; cf. Whitecotton 1977, 95.

12. See Chance 1989, 125, 204 n. 16, 194 n. 60, on *cacique* as "grandfather"; cf. de la Fuente 1949a, esp. 191–97; de la Fuente 1949b, 165, 163, 212. For a sampling of suggestive evidence on the metaphors and interplays of gender culture and political culture, see the following: for the Mixteca Alta, Pastor 1981, chap. 3, p. 49 (cf. Carmagnani 1988, 199); AEO, Real Intendencia II, leg. 27, exp. 67, San Sebastian Río Dulce 1806, esp. fols. 4r–5v; CROT, rollo 16, leg. 47, exp. 27, Quilitongo 1799, esp. fol. 2r; for the Zapotec Valley, AEO, Real Intendencia II, leg. 41, exp. 8, Sta. Cruz Amilpas [1790?], fol. 1r–v; leg. 29, exp. 42 (cf. exp. 51), Ocotlán 1817, fol. 1r; leg. 33, exp. 3, Sta. Cruz Papalutla/San Juan Bautista Teitipaque (Zimatlán) 1788–90, esp. fol. 1v; for Villa Alta, ATOVA, Criminal, leg. 5, exp. s.n. re: fiscales de Tabaá, Tabaá 1769, esp. fols. 1r–2v; leg. 5, exp. s.n. re: assault between Indians of San Miguel and San Pedro, Caxonos 1781, esp. fol. 3v; leg. 7, exp. s.n. re: Juan Antonio de los Angeles, Yaeé 1796, fols. 5v, 6v.

13. For Morelos, see Chapter 8 above. For Oaxaca the starting point is the pioneering study by Taylor 1979, 113–51, esp. 116, 155. For a sampling of specific cases that resonate with the analysis of Morelos, see, for the Zapotec Valley, AGN, Epidemias, vol. 15, exp. 2, Teotitlán del Valle 1796, esp. fols. 7r, 38v, 39v, 41v–42r, 46r–v (cf. exps. 7–9, esp. exp. 9, fol. 25r); vol. 314, exp. re: riot in Ocotlán, Ocotlán 1784, fol. 139r; for the Mixteca Alta, AGNCr, vol. 306, exps. 1–3, Teozacualco 1774, esp. fols. 2v–3r, 32r–v, 34v, 39r, 40r, 44r–45v, 47v, 48v; CROT, rollo 2, leg. 14, exp. 11, Achiutla 1785, esp. fol. 7r; for Villa Alta, vol. 644, exp. s.n. re: alboroto, Solaga 1806, esp. fols. 2v–3r, 9r; AGN, Indios, vol. 88, Yahuyuê 1811–12, Paz to Viceroy, Mar. 16, 1812, esp. fols. 296v, 309v, 310v.

14. For evidence from all three microregions of Oaxaca, see the following: for the Mixteca Alta, Heijmerink 1973, 290; Romero Frizzi 1985, 90; CROT, rollo 18, leg. 51, exp. 51, Yosondúa 1760, fol. 11r; cf. Spores 1967, 10–11, 145–50, 152–54; Spores 1984, 203–4; Taylor 1972, 38; for the Zapotec Valley, AEO, Alcaldías Mayores, leg. 24, exp. 33, Tlacochahuaya 1738–83, fol. 1r; Real Intendencia I, leg. 10, exp. 24, Zaachila 1792, fol. 1r; cf. leg. 5, exp. 14, Ixtlahuaca (technically in the northern part of the valley, outside our study zone) 1792, fol. 1r; Taylor 1972, 38; Whitecotton 1977, 155–56; for Villa Alta, Chance 1989, 128–31. These materials bear comparison with the findings of Sherman 1979 for Central America and with the important ethnographic revision by Mathews 1985 (cf. 1982) of gender and *mayordomías* in the Oaxaca Valley region.

15. See CROT, rollo 18, leg. 51, exp. 51, Yosondúa 1760, esp. fols. 8r–9r, 11r (quote); AEO, Obisbado, leg. 2, exp. 5, Ayutla/Tepuxtepeque 1768, esp. fols. 1v–2r (1v for quote), 3r–v. Antonia Magdalena was married to a member of the community who served in the important but symbolically lesser post of community *fiscal de iglesia* (community enforcer of church rules). On sacred spots such as hilltops and ethnic identity, see Carmagnani 1988.

16. For an example of joking acknowledgment drawn from regional lore in Morelos in the mid-twentieth century, see Fromm and Maccoby 1970, 150 n. 2.

17. See AEO, Alcaldías Mayores, leg. 37, exp. 30, Ocotlán 1785, fol. 1r ("godmother"); ATOVA, Criminal, leg. 6, exp. s.n. re: Salvador Illescas, Paraje Beloag Yagsache (Villa Alta) 1796, fol. 13r; leg. 5, exp. s.n. re: Nicolás Matheo, Tepantlali 1781, fol. 2r ("witches"); CROT, rollo 16, leg. 49, exp. 22, Tlaxiaco 1799, fol. 8v ("wife killed"; cf. 5r–v, 9r–v, 10v).

18. The mystery deaths phenomenon came up repeatedly in my research in all three microregions, involved both male and female victims, and blurred distinctions between accidental death, violent assault, supernatural bewitching, and suicide. In Villa Alta in particular some of the dead were said to have hanged themselves and to lack bruises indicating a struggle. For the flavor of these cases, see the examples cited in n. 17 above, and CROT, rollo 18, leg. 51, exp. 8, Achutla (Mixteca Alta) 1768; AEO, leg. 35, exp. 9, Mixtepeque (Valle)

1775; ATOVA, Criminal, leg. 5, exp. s.n. re: unexplained death, Tlahuytoltepec (Villa Alta) 1778.

19. See Chapter 9 above, esp. Table 9.4.

20. See, e.g., CROT, rollo 16, leg. 49, exp. 51, Yanhuitlán 1796; rollo 2, leg. 25, exp. 30, Coyotepeque 1800; ATOVA, Criminal, leg. 7, exp. s.n. re: Lorenzo Santiago, Analco 1798, esp. fols. 1r–2v; leg. 6, exp. s.n. re: Esteban de los Angeles, Yaeé 1794.

21. See Sotelo Inclán 1943, 229 n. 1, 138–46, for Ayala, and passim for Zapata.

22. For background and references on the colonial Hispanic presence, indigenous culture, and regional life more generally, see Chapter 2 above.

23. On divergent and parallel evolutions among the Zapotec and Mixtec peoples of Oaxaca over the millennia, see Flannery and Marcus 1983. While the book's overarching framework is "divergent evolution," specific essays and content also demonstrate contact, influence, and parallel evolutions (see esp. 3, 217–26, 355–60).

24. On ethnic reconstitution in Oaxaca, see Carmagnani 1988. For theorized discussion of "resistant adaptation," see Stern 1987a, 9–13. On redeployment of the Hispanic, see Stern 1992, 15–23.

25. Contemporary Oaxacan ethnographies informed by a sense of history have done much to illuminate ethnic Othering, especially among Zapotecs, and the related themes of community "harmony," peaceability, and violence. The most searching discussion is Nader (1990; cf. 1989, 1964), who interprets harmony ideology as a legacy of colonial Christian ideology and of community responses to external threats. On community ideologies of violence and antiviolence, see Paddock 1975; cf. Nader 1990, 8, 219–20, 275, and the excellent critique of Paddock by Dennis 1987, 127–31. That ideologies of harmony represent an idealization and a resource used in conflicts and their resolution comes through in all the works cited above as well as Parnell 1988.

26. See AEO, Real Intendencia II, leg. 11, exp. 25, Ayoquesco 1809, fols. 4r–10r (8v, 7v, for quotes).

27. The quotes are from ibid., fols. 8v ("exasperated," viejos), 7v (orgullo; cf. 6r, 8r), 6v (oficio de república).

28. ATOVA, Criminal, leg. 6, exp. s.n. re: Marcial Morales, Tabaá/Yaeé 1792, fol. 1v.

29. For discourses of contrast among Zapotec communities in the twentieth century, see Nader 1964; Nader 1989, esp. 333, 334, 336; Nader 1990; Parsons 1936, 365–85 passim. For historically rooted discourses of contrast with Mixes and Ixtepeji Zapotecs, see ATOVA, Criminal, leg. 5, exp. s.n. re: Antonio Pedro, Ayutla 1765, fol. 32v; AEO, Real Intendencia II, leg. 34, exp. 16, Ixtepeji 1807, fol. 1r. See also ATOVA, Criminal, leg. 5, exp. s.n. re: Nicolás Pascual, Tepuxtepeque 1761; leg. 5, exp. s.n. re: Francisco Esteban, Villa Alta 1762. For historic tensions between Mixes and Zapotecs, see Chance 1989, 73 (cf. Parsons 1936, 365–66). On the Mixtecan "hot country," see, for historical background and contemporary ethnography, Flanet 1977, esp. 26–27, 37, 134–39, 169–70; Reina 1988a, 189 (entries for "Costa" districts); Tibón 1981. On the neighboring Zapotec Isthmus region, its Afro-Mexican dimension, and its reputation for rebelliousness, see Brockington 1989; Reina 1988a, 190; H. B. Campbell 1990.

30. BNAH, Oaxaca I, rollo 51, exp. s.n. re: Manuel de la Cruz, Tlacolula 1789, fol. 4v, for quote; cf. rollo 15, exp. s.n. re: Cavo de Chalcatongo, Chalcatongo 1774; AGN, Acordada, vol. 28, exp. 1, Coixtlahuaca 1805.

31. For a small sampling involving Indian men, see the following: for the Mixteca Alta, CROT, rollo 18, leg. 51, exp. 34, Quilitongo 1798, esp. fol. 2v; rollo 17, leg. 50, exp. 20, Añuma/Yucucata 1765, esp. fols. 4r, 8r; rollo 2, leg. 13, exp. 7, Tejupa 1786, esp. fols. 7v, 9v–10v; for the Zapotec Valley, BNAH, Oaxaca I, rollo 52, exp. s.n. re: José Ventura, Zaachila 1808, esp. fols. 6v, 7v, 12v; AEO, Real Intendencia II, leg. 12, exp. 6, Mextepeque 1809,

esp. fols. 4r, 16r, 18r; leg. 8, exp. 13, Ejutla 1804, esp. fols. 5v–7r; for Villa Alta, ATOVA, Criminal, leg. 7, exp. s.n. re: Juan Jiménez, Santo Domingo Roayaga 1806, fol. 1v; leg. 6, exp. s.n. re: Agustín Francisco, Solaga 1786, esp. fols. 6r, 7r; leg. 6, exp. s.n. re: Juan José Velasco, Tanatze 1795, esp. fols. 1, 4.

32. Cf. Barthes's analysis of myth as purification of the real (1972, 109), as cited in O'Malley 1986, 5.

33. ATOVA, Criminal, leg. 5, exp. s.n. re: Juan Mendosa, Sogacho 1764, fols. 10r, 11r, 12r.

34. The murder story that follows is drawn from CROT, rollo 18, leg. 51, exp. 1, Tutepetongo 1780, esp. fols. 1r–5v, 9r–v, 12r, 22r–24r. Quotes are on fols. 24r ("man of courage"), 23v ("no food, no clothes"), 9v ("cursed be").

CHAPTER ELEVEN

1. AJT, Penales, leg. 7, exp. 10, Mexico City 1791, fol. 7r–v, for quote.

2. See AJT, Penales, leg. 7, exp. 59, Mexico City 1792, esp. fols. 1r–18r (16v, 5v for quotes), 28v–29v, 32v, 33v, 34v; cf. 29v–30r, 40v–44r.

3. See AGNCr, vol. 116, exps. 11, 12, 13, Mexico City 1797, esp. fols. 222r–229v, 233r–237r (233v for quote), 242v–243v, 248–256v.

4. See AGNCr, vol. 625, exp. s.n. re: Anastasio Sandobal, Mexico City 1804, esp. fols. 4r–6v (5v for quote); exp. s.n. re: Francisco Seron, Mexico City 1805, esp. fols. 2r–v, 6r–24v.

5. For an extreme example, see AGNCr, vol. 667, exp. 1, Mexico City 1771, esp. fols. 1r–13r (fol. 5r for *amujerado*), 23r–28v, 31r–41v, 50r–53v, 59v–62r.

6. It is suggestive to compare the sense of dangerously independent and uncontrolled women in late colonial Mexico City with the materials on early modern Seville explored by Perry (1990; cf. 1985; 1980, 212–34).

7. AJT, Penales, leg. 7, exp. 38, Mexico City 1791, fol. 5r.

8. This is based on the census sample analysis by Arrom 1985b, 158–62.

9. On the vicissitudes of domestic service and patriarchal control, see AGNCr, vol. 89, exp. 9, Mexico City 1810, fols. 299r, 304r; AJT, Penales, leg. 3, exp. 17, Mexico City 1765, fols. 1r–4r; cf. Arrom 1985b, 160, 186.

10. On wage work and the mobilization of women, see Arrom 1985b, 14–52 (esp. 26–32), 159–64, 193–95; Deans-Smith 1992, esp. 210–11; AJT, Penales, leg. 7, exp. 57, Mexico City 1792, fols. 1r, 3r; AGN, Reales Cédulas Originales, vol. 178, exp. 11, 16-II-1800; AGN, Bandos, vol. 16, 30-XII-1792, fol. 236; vol. 20, 22-IV-1799, Bando no. 21.

11. The images of female street vendors and self-employed women emerge in a large variety of contemporary documents. For an overview, see Arrom 1985b, 157–60, 162, 166–70, 180; cf. Kicza 1983, chap. 5; Deans-Smith 1992, 12–13.

12. AJT, Penales, leg. 9, exp. 3, Mexico City 1797, esp. fols. 1r, 2r–3v, 6r–v (6v for quote), 7v, 10r.

13. See AGNCr, vol. 89, exp. 1, Mexico City 1808/1809, esp. fols. 3r–v, 12r–17r. The materials actually involve two sequential accusations roughly a year apart, and in the second incident the female networks investigated actually implicated two houses accused of nighttime prostitution.

Lesbianism and female polygamy—the latter facilitated by migration to Mexico City and accompanying pretenses that first husbands were dead or nonexistent—represented an even greater subversion of symbolic sexual control by men. For examples of both, see AGN, Inquisición, vol. 1203, exp. 16, Mexico City 1780, fols. 122–25; vol. 1275, exp. 16, Mexico City 1788, fols. 1–110; vol. 1257, exp. 2, Mexico City 1784, fols. 1–131. On the whole, such practices were either rarer or less visible than prostitution, and they were less tolerated.

Male clients as well as the church and the state could ambivalently accept prostitution as a kind of necessary evil, to be held within moderate or semidiscreet bounds rather than eliminated entirely; cf. Perry 1985.

14. On boarders, the economics and conflicts of family household allowances, and sexual suspicions, see AGNCr, vol. 86, exp. 4, Mexico City 1811, fols. 60r–66r, esp. 62r–v (sexual jealousies); vol. 89, exp. 9, Mexico City 1810, fols. 295r–v, 299r, 303r (sons and obligations to mothers and fathers); vol. 393, exp. s.n. re: María de la Encarnación, Mexico City 1795, fol. 1r (mother's complaint that son fails to provide allowance); cf. Arrom 1985b, 182 (daughters and family allowances); AGNCr, vol. 364, exp. 1, Mexico City 1803 (bonding potential of male boarder and female *casera*).

15. For materials suggestive of the ambiguous range of extramarital sexual dynamics, see AJT, Penales, leg. 7, exp. 48, Mexico City, 1792, esp. fol. 4r–v; exp. 35, Mexico City 1791, esp. fols. 1v, 2r; exp. 49, Mexico City 1792, esp. fols. 1v, 6v; AGN, Presidios y Cárceles, vol. 15, exp. 8, Mexico City 1789, fol. 55r–v; Historia, vol. 479, exp. 8, Mexico City, 1797, esp. fol. 3v; AGNCr, vol. 211, exp. 8, Mexico City 1795, fols. 332r–333v, 394r–v; and nn. 13, 14 above.

16. AGN, Historia, vol. 147, exp. 1, esp. fols. 23r–v (23v for quote), 25r–26v, 14v–18r, 5r–6v.

17. Let us underscore the caveat: *uncontrolled* is a contextual or relative term. It refers not to an absolute absence of social constraint or control but to pathways uncontrolled or weakly controlled by familial patriarchs and sexual partners in a society where surveillance and control were exercised in direct face-to-face relations.

18. Arrom 1985b, 111–13, 116, 121, 130, 133.

19. On plebeian cultural practices that included a sensuality and raucousness offensive to elites eager to draw cultural distance from and to crack down on plebeian excess, the best source is is Viqueira Albán 1987, 132–241 (esp. 163–66); cf. 15–16, 266–69, 274–80. On the crackdown, see also Scardaville 1977, 1980; Haslip 1980, 1984. On early nineteenth-century fears of "dangerous classes," see Di Tella 1973; Arrom 1988. For archival sources that further illuminate a "counterhegemonic" sensuality and raucousness among plebeians, see AGN, Inquisición, vol. 1162, exp. 32, Mexico City 1772, fol. 382; vol. 1168, exp. 19, Mexico City 1771, fols. 244–45; AHC, Festividades Religiosas, vol. 1066, exp. 5, Mexico City 1822, fols. 1r, 2r; AHC, Policía, vol. 3621, exp. 5, Mexico City 1793, fols. 1–4; vol. 3627, exp. 43, Mexico City 1788, fols. 21r–26v; vol. 3630, exp. 183, Mexico City 1814, fols. 1r–v, 31v–36v; AJT, Penales, leg. 7, exp. 28, Mexico City 1791, esp. fols. 1r 4r; AGN, Bandos, vol. 11, 15-III-1779, fol. 9; Historia, vol. 477, exp. 7, Mexico City 1796–97, esp. fol. 3r.

20. Denunciations by plebeians and upper plebeians of other subaltern folk inclined to immorality or excess or to slander of the moral reputation of the denouncer are rather common in the historical documentation cited in n. 19 above; see also AGNCr, vol. 365, exp. 3, Mexico City 1793, fol. 1r; AGN, Historia, vol. 479, exp. 9, Mexico City 1797, esp. fol. 41.

21. The foregoing comments are theoretical, but they reverberate strongly not only with economic modeling of incentive and opportunity cost but with ethnographic studies of female life attentive to gendered economics and female poverty. On the relatively disadvantaged income prospects of women consigned largely to domestic work and the "informal economy," see Benería and Roldán 1987; Bunster and Chaney 1985; cf. the discussion of multiple incomes, economic crisis, and household economic strategies in González de la Rocha 1988b and the attachment of "good" female waged work in factories to relatively brief phases in the life cycle, as analyzed in Fernández-Kelly 1983. For debate on the effect of gendered economics on women's endurance of abusive male partners, and contrasting dynamics for women of somewhat different means, see the exchange between González de la Rocha, Chant, and de Barbieri, in Gabayet et al. 1988, 181–234. For motherhood as a source of legitimacy and joy in otherwise difficult lives, see Benería and Roldán 1987; Bunster and

Chaney 1985; fantasies about good patriarchs, notwithstanding contrary experiences with specific men, come through in Fernández-Kelly 1983.

22. The insertion of economic dependence within a sociocultural grid of family and generational right in peasant village settings emerges strongly not only in the documents of Morelos and Oaxaca but in innovative work by European historians: see esp. Medick and Sabean 1984; Sabean 1990; Hoch 1986. On purchase in Mexico City of consumer goods that might, in other social contexts, have been provided through household production, see Arrom 1985b, 155–56.

23. See Arrom 1985b, 134–49.

24. On plebeian life and polarized economics in late colonial Mexico City, the following published sources are illuminating: Viqueira Albán 1987; Morales 1976; Humboldt 1811, vol. 1, bk. 2, chaps. 6, 8, 184–86, 223–35; Arrom 1985b; González Angulo Aguirre 1983; Scardaville 1977, 1980; see also Cooper 1965; Florescano 1969; Haslip 1980; Lira 1983; López Monjardín 1985; Moreno Toscano 1978; Seminario de Historia Urbana 1974–76. My vision of plebeian work and income needs and the vulnerability of *desnudos* and vagrants to roundups has been illuminated by manuscript sources too numerous to cite in full. For particularly useful data on roundups during the pressure of the Independence War, see AGNCr, vol. 86, exp. 16, Mexico City 1812, esp. fols. 414r–416r (cf. fols. 424r–427v, 447r–448v, 449r–451v, 460r–461v). For viceregal commentary on plebeian states of undress (*desnudez*) and their liability to labor draft, see AGN, Bandos, vol. 20, 22-V-1799, fol. 112r. The four-fifths plebeian estimate is from Villarroel 1788, as cited in Viqueira Albán 1987, 132 n. 1.

25. The culture of masculine diversion comes through repeatedly in the documents charging criminal violence or transgressions against familial or sexual morality. Resentment of men's claims to discretionary spending on diversion comes through strongly in the chronic maltreatment (*mala vida*) cases ($n = 25$). Sexual infidelities and jealousies (64 percent), economic negligence and dissipation (84 percent), and physical abuse or cruelty (76 percent) dominated women's complaints and were usually seen as a package of related abuses. See PDBO, Mexico City, Mxmoral2.lis, pp. 40–42. These findings are largely consistent with Arrom's findings (1985b, 234) on "lower class" complaints. The main exception is that sexuality figures less strongly in her "lower class group." Arrom's finding on this point, however, is consistent with my own cross-tabulations demonstrating that when one considers all morality cases rather than *mala vida* cases only, plebeians were indeed less likely than middle class and elite figures to complain about sexual infractions only. (See PDBO, Mexico City, Mxmorax1.lis, p. 18; Chi-square significance = .0001; Cramer's V = .47; $n = 83$ valid cases.) When sexual infractions were entangled with other charges of abuse or violence, the poor were more disposed to press charges.

26. Among the most illuminating work I have read on "deviant" women and institutional responses, for the case of Mexico, is Franco 1989; see also Seminario de Historia de las Mentalidades 1987. On the usefulness of convents and seclusion houses (*recogimientos*) as social enclosures of women who might otherwise strain the social fabric, see Soeiro 1978; cf. Muriel 1974.

27. On ecclesiastical divorce, see Arrom 1976 (cf. 1985b, chap. 5). The duty to reconcile estranged spouses emerged again and again in the archival documents themselves and was consistent with legal guidelines: see Echebarria y Ojeda 1791, 15–16, 58–59; cf. Scardaville 1977, 181–82; Haslip 1980, 133–41. For a particularly vivid case, see AJT, Penales, leg. 9, exp. 19, Mexico City 1797. On the suspicions that attended female-managed housing, see n. 13 above and AGNCr, vol. 84, exps. 13/14, Mexico City 1809, fols. 203–33. Evidence of the crossfire effect emerges in the twists and turns whereby women first supported then withdrew support of incarceration of male kin, and in women's occasional tendency to focus

special blame on the "other woman," thereby easing familial reconciliation. For revealing examples of crossfire and ambivalence, see AJT, Penales, leg. 9, exp. 2, Mexico City 1797, fol. 4r–v; leg. 3, exp. 4, Mexico City 1762, fols. 1r–6v; AGNCr, vol. 86, exp. 4, Mexico City 1811, case no. 3 of 21, fols. 60r–66r; vol. 569, exp. s.n. re: José Gama, Mexico City 1805, esp. fols. 1r–v, 19r; vol. 365, exp. 1, Mexico City 1789, fols. 8r, 19r–21r.

28. The quote is from AGN, Padrones, vol. 52., Mexico City 1770s, fol. 347v; see also fols. 342r–355r, 295–303 bis.; AHC, Policía, vol. 3627, exp. 43, año 1788, esp. fols. 21r–26v; vol. 3630, exp. 183, año 1814, esp. fols. 31v–36v; Scardaville 1977, 1980; Viqueira Albán 1987.

29. See Scardaville 1977, 1980; Haslip 1980, 1984; cf. MacLachlan 1974; Viqueira Albán 1987; for arrest figures, see Scardaville 1977, 30 n. 29, 33, 64, 274.

30. This is my principal critique of otherwise superb studies by Viqueira Albán (1987) and Scardaville (1977, 1980). On new approaches to welfare, see Gordon 1988, 1990; *AHR* 1990.

31. For the statistics cited, see PDBO, Mexico City, Mxmoral3.lis, p. 14; Mxviol2.lis, p. 22. The AJT Penales manuscripts are filled with women's efforts to redeploy the state's revamped policing system; cf. the first-rate discussions of *mala vida* complaints in Boyer 1989; Arrom 1985b, 206–58.

32. AGN, Inquisición, vol. 1167, exp. 2, año 1778, fol. 25r.

33. For nonrandom associations by accusers, for violence and morality cases, $n = 185$ total valid cases; Chi-square significance = .000; Cramer's V = .29. For low plebeian shares in morality cases, $n = 67$ non-anonymous accusers; $n = 150$ accused. PDBO, Mexico City, Almxcit2.lis, p. 9; Almxcit3.lis, p. 10.

34. This difference is quite apparent in the matter-of-fact way that couples referred to the individual difficulty of the *novio* or the *novio novia* couple in assembling the resources to mount a wedding. The causes of the contrast are probably several. First, plebeian families could ill afford to finance weddings, and more of the requisite goods to be consumed probably required purchase. Second, extended kin grids were more easily ruptured or were at least a less continuous presence and source of economic support in Mexico City, which also received a large influx of migrants in the late eighteenth century. Third, plebeian families in Mexico City enjoyed less communal backing in financing major projects such as weddings. In this regard it is intriguing to note that the city's Indian sections (*parcialidades*), San Juan Tenochtitlán and Santiago Tlatelolco, maintained a certain corporate functionality well into the nineteenth century and that the city's Indians also had a higher marriage rate than whites (*españoles*). See Lira 1983; Arrom 1985b, 134–35.

35. For examples of *vidas maridables*, many of them sealed by *palabras de casamiento*, see, in addition to the cases cited in nn. 36 and 38 below, AGNCr, vol. 86, exp. 16, Mexico City 1812, fols. 398r–399v, 403r–407v; exp. 3bis, Mexico City 1811, fols. 46–52, esp. 52r; vol. 73, exp. 1, Mexico City 1806, fol. 3r–v; AGN, Clero Regular y Secular, vol. 203, exp. 10, Mexico City 1783, fols. 284–306; vol. 145, exp. 7, Mexico City 1784, esp. fols. 206r–207v, 210r; AGNCr, vol. 365, exp. 3, Mexico City 1793, fols. 1r–2r. On the *palabra de casamiento* as formal concept and ritual practice, see Lavrin 1989a: 4–6; Lavrin 1989c: 61.

36. AJT, Penales, leg. 9, exp. 15, Mexico City 1797, fol. 2v, for quote.

37. See, e.g., AGN, Clero Regular y Secular, vol. 145, exp. 7, Mexico City 1784, esp. fols. 207r, 210r; AGNCr, vol. 86, exp. 3bis, Mexico City 1811, fol. 52r; exp. 16, Mexico City 1812, fol. 405.

38. AGN, Clero Regular y Secular, vol. 81, exp. 6, Mexico City 1785, fols. 354r–358r (356r, 357r for quotes); cf. AGNCr, vol. 85, exps. 13/13bis, Mexico City 1808, fol. 482r.

39. See, e.g., AJT, Penales, leg. 7, exp. 62, Mexico City 1792; AGN, Clero Regular y Secular, vol. 145, exp. 9, Mexico City 1784; vol. 81, exp. 6, Mexico City 1787.

40. AGN, Matrimonios, vol. 25, exp. 50, Mexico City 1760, fol. 265v, for quote. The AGN

Matrimonios documents are filled with disputes about marriage promises and obligations. For a selection illuminating various facets of the phenomenon, see vol. 30, exp. 50; vol. 47, exp. 72; vol. 54, exp. 74; vol. 55, exp. 33; cf. AGN, Clero Regular y Secular, vol. 81, exp. 6, fols. 337r–353r; vol. 138, exp. 8, fols. 255r–260v.

41. AGNCr, vol. 715, exp. s.n. re: Juan Antonio Gustinza, Mexico City 1779, fols. 2r, 2v, 1r, for quotes.

42. AGN, Matrimonios, vol. 47, exp. 72, Mexico City 1777, fols. 300–302 (300v, for quote).

43. Ibid., fol. 300v; cf. AGN, Matrimonios, vol. 25, exp. 50, Mexico City 1760, fols. 269v, 265r; AJT, Penales, leg. 3, exp. 7, Mexico City 1763, fol. 2r–v.

44. False certifications of husbands' deaths are exposed repeatedly in the AGN Inquisición records; cf. AGN, Clero Regular y Secular, vol. 57, exp. 2, Mexico City 1796, fol. 149r; AJT, Penales, leg. 7, exp. 26, Mexico City 1791, fols. 1r, 4v; and n. 13 above.

45. See AJT, Penales, leg. 7, exp. 46, Mexico City 1792, esp. fols. 1r–2v, 8r–10r, 12r–14r, 17v, 19r–22r, 23v–24v, 25v–26r, 28v (9r, 24v, for quotes).

46. For additional examples of female separations and their attendant disputes and social conventions, see AJT, Penales, leg. 3, exp. 5, Mexico City 1763, esp. fol. 4r; leg. 7, exp. 13, Mexico City 1791; leg. 7, exp. 26, Mexico City 1791; leg. 7, exp. 49 (cf. exp. 79), Mexico City 1792, esp. fols. 6v–7v, 14r; leg. 7, exp. 51, Mexico City 1792, esp. fols. 1r–v, 7r–8r; leg. 9, exp. 17, Mexico City 1797, esp. fols. 1r–3v, 7v; AGN, Inquisición, vol. 1292, exp. 11, Mexico City 1788, fols. 87r–88v, 91r–v; AGN, Matrimonios, vol. 58, exp. 3, Mexico City 1783, fols. 36r–38r; AGN, Clero Regular y Secular, vol. 76, exp. 4, Mexico City 1784, fol. 203r–v; AGNCr, vol. 86, exp. 4, Mexico City 1811, case no. 4 within exp.: Contra José María Salinas, fol. 6v; case no. 18, Contra Luis López y otros, fol. 136v; AGNCr, vol. 118, exp. 13, Mexico City 1807, esp. fols. 475–81.

47. See the acute observations of Smart 1976, 19–24, 132–34.

48. The triregional figures for sexualization of dispute are based on the restricted case sets of violence against female targets; total valid cases, $n = 55, 62, 66$ for Mexico City, Morelos, and Oaxaca, respectively. The percentage shares for the augmented case set are virtually the same: 57.7 percent, 49.5 percent, and 44.3 percent for the three regions, respectively; $n = 78, 93, 97$. For the role of on-off disputes in the composition of celos, the figure cited is midway between the restricted and the augmented case set shares (24.3 percent and 19.6 percent, respectively; $n = 37, 54$). For Morelos the midway share is only 2.2 percent ($n = 37, 58$); for Oaxaca, the share is only 9.6 percent ($n = 35, 51$). For all figures, see PDBO, Mexico City, Mexviol2.lis, pp. 35, 39; Addmex1.lis, pp. 36, 39; Morelos, Powvioh.out, pp. 33, 36; Addupd1.lis, pp. 20, 24; Oaxaca, Oaxviol2.lis, pp. 37, 41; Addoax1.lis, pp. 37, 40.

49. The resonance with patterns from Morelos emerges from hundreds of dossier bundles (expedientes) too tedious to list here but is evident in the cases explicated earlier and later in this chapter; on the 1692 corn riot and the gendered etiquette of revolt, see I. A. Leonard 1929, appendix; Cope 1994.

50. See AJT, Penales, leg. 7, exp. 49 (cf. exp. 79), Mexico City 1792, esp. fols. 1r–3r, 7r–v, 13v–14r, 18r (1r–v, 7v, 14r, for quotes).

51. For illuminating examples, see AJT, Penales, leg. 7, exp. 5, Mexico City 1791; exp. 38, Mexico City 1791; leg. 63, Mexico City 1792; leg. 67, Mexico City 1792; leg. 9, exp. 13, Mexico City 1797; AGN, Matrimonios, vol. 29, exp. 121, Mexico City 1801, esp. fols. 415v–416v; AGN, Civil, vol. 1773, exp. 5, Mexico City 1760.

52. See AJT, Penales, leg. 7, exp. 56, D. José Gonzales contra Georja Gertrudis Echevarría, esp. fols. 1r–v, 2v, 3r, 5r–8r, 11r–12r, 13r–17r. Quotes, in order of appearance, are from fols. 1r, 6v, 1v, 5r, 7v, 8r, 13v, 14v. For hints of mulatto traces in Don José's ancestry, note the switch in Georja's identification (española to parda), her epithet in an argument ("mulatto begotten with beans"), and a mulatta neighbor and friend (see fols. 17r, 5r, 14r–v).

53. The three Marías of Morelos mentioned in this paragraph are those who introduced Chapters 1 and 4, respectively.

CHAPTER TWELVE

1. The regional analysis by ethnic group was presented in Chapter 3 above; for parallel tests by microregion, see PDBO, Intra-regional, Morreg1.lis, esp. pp. 23–24, 28–29, 45–46; Lastpow1.lis, p. 12; Lastpow3.lis, p. 12.

2. The *tierra fría*/*tierra caliente* distinction is discussed succinctly and in relation to *tierra templada* characterizations often subsumed within the more basic distinction in C. E. Martin 1985, 4–5; see also de la Peña 1980; Ingham 1986; Warman 1976; and for more implicit treatment, Friedlander 1975; Fromm and Maccoby 1970; Romanucci-Ross 1986. For the harmonious veneer in Tepoztlán, see Redfield 1930; cf. Lewis 1951. On Anenecuilco and Zapata, the classic works are Sotelo Inclán 1943; Womack 1968.

3. AGNCr, vol. 2, exp. 9, Totolapa 1802, fol. 194v.

4. Ingham 1986, 12.

5. AGNCr, vol. 215, exp. 9, Llanos de Tlayecac 1806, fol. 258v, for quote.

6. See AGNCr, vol. 277, exp. 3, Xochitlán 1789, fols. 55r, 64r (cf. 57r); vol. 213, exp. 14, Cuautla Amilpas 1805, fol. 409r (quote); cf. the cultural symbolism applied to African-related men in a highland Maya region far removed from elite discourses in central Mexico, in Blaffer 1972.

7. See Ingham 1986, 12–13; cf. Friedlander 1975; Lewis 1951. For images of ethnic contrast in dynamics of personal enmity and violence, see Wolf and Hansen 1972, 71–99, esp. 94–99; cf. Paz 1959; Nader 1990.

8. AGNCr, vol. 223, exp. 19, Suchitlán 1780, fol. 324r.

9. For discussion and sources, see Chapter 10 above. To avoid misunderstandings we should note that microregional difference was but one of several axes in local discourses of variation. As we already noted in Chapter 10 and as is also true for Morelos (see Lewis 1951, 49, 54, 98–99, cf. 281–82), regional peoples have also constructed languages of difference that contrasted the character and social mores of nearby pueblos more properly viewed as neighbors *within* a microregion. To pursue this point, however, would take us afield and would merely underscore the argument that local languages of difference may resonate with more well known regional languages of difference.

10. For primary relations test of likelihood of homicidal violence by gender of target in Oaxaca, Chi-square significance was .02, Phi was .30, Yule's Q was .58. PDBO, Tri-regional, Oaxofvii.lis, p. 82.

11. See CROT, rollo 18, leg. 51, exp. 30, Yosoñahe 1767, fols. 1r–7r (7r for quote).

12. On sugar *trapiches* in the Mixteca Alta and Baja in the eighteenth century, and Don Joseph Herrera's role as a leading producer, see Pastor 1987, 235–37; for ecological considerations, see also Cook and Borah 1968, 5–8.

CHAPTER THIRTEEN

1. An influential version of this argument has been made quite forcefully by Joan Wallach Scott (1986, esp. 1070–74; reprinted and amplified in J. W. Scott 1988) but has been nourished by wider streams of feminist scholarship during the 1970s and 1980s. For a sampling of this evolving literature, see Rosaldo and Lamphere 1974 (esp. the essays by Rosaldo, Ortner, Sacks, and Bamberger); Reiter 1975 (esp. the essay by Rubin); Kelly 1984, 51–64;

Rosaldo 1980; M. O'Brien 1981; Elshtain 1982; G. Lerner 1986; Gailey 1987; Silverblatt 1988; Sacks 1989. For an astute discussion of the consequences of gendered stereotypes of peasant women in Mexico, see Arizpe 1977, esp. 25.

2. See, e.g., Peristiany 1966; Pitt-Rivers 1971, 1977; Martínez-Alier [now Stolcke] 1974; Perry 1985; Gutiérrez 1985, 1991; Lavrin 1989d (esp. the essay by Twinam); Chambers 1992; cf. García Márquez 1981.

3. *Lucía* and *Retrato de Teresa* are available in U.S. university collections, including Learning Support Services at the University of Wisconsin. On the Cuban émigrés, see Fox 1973. For further context and for an introduction to struggles over the family code and gender roles in the 1970s, see Purcell 1973; King 1979; Randall 1979, 1992 (esp. 121–53). For a wider sense of disillusion with assumptions that egalitarian transformations of gender relations might flow from revolutionary upheavals to transform political economy, see Sargent 1981; Randall 1992.

4. These scholarly currents have been reviewed and referenced in detail in Chapter 2 above. It must be acknowledged here that although the task of writing a gendered history of politics and political culture was initially postponed for understandable reasons explicated in Chapter 2, by the 1990s a number of fine historical writings have begun to map out a more engendered political history. See, e.g., Deutsch 1991; Guy 1991 (esp. 209, for a particularly sharp statement of implications); F. Miller 1991; O'Malley 1986; cf. Seminar on Feminism 1990.

5. See, e.g., G. Lerner 1986, 217–21, 226, 234; T. Kaplan 1982; Castellanos 1973, 14; cf. Segovia 1979, 7–8. Obviously I use "myth" in the anthropological sense rather than as "falsehood" contrasted with "truth."

6. The honor/shame literature is discussed and referenced in detail in Chapter 2 above.

7. The blend of elite paternal pretense vis-à-vis social inferiors akin to children in their foibles, and an angry popular perception that specific elites profiteered rather than lived up to paternal obligation and pretense, came through with great clarity in Don Carlos Sigüenza y Góngora's account of the 1692 corn riot in Mexico City (reprinted in I. A. Leonard 1929, appendix). For the fuller context and a reexamination of the riot, see Cope 1994; cf. Israel 1975. On elite windfall profit mechanisms and grain shortages, see Florescano 1969.

8. For particularly influential and perceptive works in this tradition, see Chevalier 1963; Wolf 1959, esp. 202–32; cf., for the demographic and economic underpinnings, Borah 1951; Zavala 1944; and for church matters, Ricard 1966.

9. On landed estates, seventeenth-century economic diversification, and elite political economy, some of the most important revisionist works were published in the 1970s: see Bakewell 1971; Taylor 1972, 1974; Florescano 1969; Van Young 1981; Ladd 1976; cf. Van Young 1983. For indigenous response to and redeployments of colonial Catholicism, a revisionist literature crystallized in the 1980s: see Klor de Alva 1982; Clendinnen 1982a, 1987; Gruzinski 1988, 1989b; cf. Burkhart 1989; Krippner-Martínez 1990.

10. See n. 7 above for defense of the viceroy and the wider context. On the colonial state and riots, see Taylor 1979; cf. Coatsworth 1982. For the *cacique* who defended himself as a patriarch, see Soy 1985.

11. For a review and contextualization of this literature for Africa and Latin America and its relationship to wider trends in the historical profession, see Cooper et al. 1993.

12. For a provocative Russian comparison, cf. Hoch 1986; Kolchin 1987, 307.

13. The resonance of church theology with notions of reciprocity among unequals in familial contexts was underscored in oral commentary by Pilar Gonzalbo Aizpuru at the conference "Familia y vida privada: América, siglos XVI a XIX" held in Mexico City by El Colegio de México/Universidad Nacional Autónoma de México in May 1993; cf. Lavrin 1989a: esp. 17, 41 n. 48; Perry 1990, 60–62. Whether church teachings went so far as to trans-

late reciprocity into contingent authority, however, is another matter. For the wider context of religious teachings and practice regarding women, see Gonzalbo Aizpuru 1987a; cf. Benítez 1985.

14. I have learned a great deal about these issues from a collaborative project with African and Latin American colleagues: see Cooper et al. 1993. For the classic analysis of ethnocentered inscribing of preoccupations onto the exotic Other, see Said 1978; cf. 1993.

15. I am aware, of course, that reference to Old Regime societies as a whole constructs a binary distinction that breaks down if one explores historical change and particularity within Old Regime contexts, especially differences evident in late Old Regime societies whose monarchs and/or propertied classes overrode practices and ideas of legitimate rule associated with more customary, anterior versions of Old Regime rule. Nonetheless, I consider the distinction heuristically and theoretically useful within the context of Western history for the purpose of exploring the question of gender right and contestation in non-feminist historical contexts. To avoid equation of a particular historical society with a theorized category in the spirit of a historical sociology of societies, I use the term *Old Regime* rather than *ancien régime* deliberately. Among the more illuminating discussions of the chain of life as an organic hierarchy between the mutually dependent, and of the role of gender or family in the modeling of sociopolitical order more generally, are the following: Bloch 1961; Desan 1990, 3–4 esp. n. 3; Elshtain 1982; Hahn 1984; G. Lerner 1986; Morse 1954, 1964; Schochet 1975; Shanley 1982; Shaw 1987; cf. Bouton 1993, esp. 167–68; Hanley 1989; Landes 1988; Plumb 1985, 32; J. W. Scott 1986; Stone 1977. On the family as a fundamental unit of survival, among the most illuminating works are Sabean 1990; Hoch 1986.

16. See Franco 1989, G. Lerner 1993; cf. Arenal 1983. For the "women of genius" idea, see G. Lerner 1993, esp. 16–17; Peden 1987, introduction.

17. I would argue that such assumptions, particularly the idea of a decisive world historical defeat, help explain the strong interest in origins scholarship. For superb recent scholarship in this tradition, see G. Lerner 1986; Gailey 1987; cf. Silverblatt 1988; Engels 1972. A Third World twist on such notions is the idea that Western colonization brought about the Great Fall for women in native cultures. See, e.g., Leacock 1981; cf. Etienne and Leacock 1980.

18. Among the most perceptive and revealing works for Europe are N. Z. Davis 1987; Sabean 1990. For Mexico, Arrom 1985b is fundamental.

19. For an introduction to such trends in historical scholarship, with special emphasis on Africa and Latin America, see Stern 1993; cf. Novick 1988; *JAH* 1989.

20. For Sor Juana's views on men, women, and marriage, see Peden 1987; on her unusually rationalist voice, see Franco 1989; for additional feminist reevaluations, see Merrim 1991. It is provocative to compare Sor Juana's life and its interpretation by Paz 1982 with the *mujer esquiva* theme in Spanish Golden Age theater: see McKendrick 1983. On the problem of Sor Juana's exceptionalism, see the astute comments of Monsiváis 1980, 101; cf. Tuñón 1987, 67–71; BNM, vol. 422, Siglo XIX, "Versos de la solterita."

21. The notion of interplay between strictly feminist consciousness and forms of female consciousness directed at establishing contingent authority and mutuality in collaborations between women and men of similar color-class standing while avoiding the question of gender equality itself is offered as a hypothesis to spark future research. In truth, little formal historical scholarship has explored such interplay (but see F. Miller 1991, 218–37), although evidence of it is not difficult to find in testimonial literature and contemporary self-studies of feminists and grassroots women's groups in Latin America. For a vivid Mexican example of the tensions that might emerge out of this interplay, see Polémica 1980. For more positive possibilities and dynamics, also in a Mexican context, see Massolo 1992; cf. Monsiváis 1987; and for tension and promise beyond Mexico, see Alvarez 1990; F. Miller 1991, 218–37. The sort of interplay suggested here and especially evident in grassroots women's organizations in various parts of the Americas in the 1980s belies the rather nar-

row vision of feminism presented and critiqued in Fox-Genovese 1991; for a pertinent discussion of multiple feminisms within the historical experience of the West, see Offen 1988.

22. See Gordon 1988; Stansell 1986; Tomes 1978 for U.S. and British studies that resonate with the Mexican materials. I am grateful to Nell Painter for formulating the problem of resonance as the Boston question. (Linda Gordon's 1988 book inspired the phrase.)

23. In early modern France, to take one example, the particulars would have contrasted. Struggles over the daily bread would have taken a different twist; tension would more often have been directed outward, at issues of provisioning and pricing by merchants and authorities, rather than at issues of domestic labor. See Bouton 1993; cf. S. Kaplan 1976. In domestic struggles over food preparation that might have developed, moreover, the classic Mexican problems of tortilla freshness, distances from home to *milpa*, and reliance on domestic grinding of wet corn into flour suitable for tortillas would not have intervened. Similarly, the mobilization of rival patriarchs or female allies against an adulterous or abusive husband would not have involved ethnoracial or colonizing Others deemed to hold special powers — although fault lines between Catholic and Protestant allegiance and the ritual role of rural youth-abbeys in disciplining married adults might have proved important intervening forces in conjugal quarrels and gender mores. See N. Z. Davis 1975, 65–187, esp. 91–123, 180–84; see also Desan 1990, 165–216, for cross-cutting considerations in the significance of Catholicism and Protestantism for women. For evidence that female maneuver and male-female conflict would not have been unusual within a French world of patriarchal pacts, see N. Z. Davis 1983, 1987. For an instructive review and critique of scholarship on ritual punishment (charivari, "rough music") of misbehaving wives and husbands for the case of England, see Hammerton 1991.

24. Cf. the interpretation of Stansell 1986, 80–81, for the case of New York City in the nineteenth century.

25. The stories of José Marcelino and Francisco Gerónimo are presented in detail in the openings of Chapters 1 and 4 above. On José del Carmen Neria, see the brief mention in Chapter 6 above and AGNCr, vol. 38, exp. 2, Tesoyuca 1809, fols. 31–83, esp. 45r–v, 42v–43r, 59v.

CHAPTER FOURTEEN

1. See Behar 1993, esp. 3, a brilliant life history that resonates not only with Behar 1987, 1989, but also with the women studied in this book.

2. I refer, of course, to Lewis 1951, 1964, whose foil was Redfield 1930. For context on Lewis and on ethnography in the Morelos region, see Rigdon 1988; Lomnitz-Adler 1984.

3. On Esperanza de Martínez, see Lewis 1964, 356–57 (cf. 306–9, 335–36; and Chapter 3 above). On Celsa, see Tirado 1991, 38–39. On women hardened by experience, see Romanucci-Ross 1986, esp. 56. On the Lewises' world of conjugal quarrel, see Lewis 1951, 319–52 (esp. 319–20, 324–29), 498–500. For the role of Ruth Lewis as collaborator and silent coauthor, see Rigdon 1988. For manhood, womanhood, and gender relations, see also Ingham 1986; Fromm and Maccoby 1970 (which is revealing, if one treats its psychological modeling and jargon with great caution); Foley 1986, 1990.

4. For the preceding two paragraphs, Lewis 1964, 307–8 (fears of Esperanza's contacts, cf. 61–62); 275, 335 (quotes of Pedro); 353, 356 (quotes of Esperanza).

5. Lewis 1951, 320 (submissive wife quote, female and male proverb quotes); Friedlander 1975, esp. 35–36, 4, 7–26 (Doña Zeferina, Juana); Ingham 1986, esp. 139–60 (subaltern masculinity).

6. See Lewis 1951, 199, 281, 294–95, 324–25, 402, 405 (fear of vengeance; cf. Lewis 1964, 307–8; Behar 1993); Tirado 1991, 41 (woman leaving for friend's house); Lewis 1964, 274–75

(judge burdened by institutional escalation; cf. Nader 1989, 1990); Lewis 1964 (daughters changing residence within pluralized network of kin and patriarchs). See also Romanucci-Ross 1986 for amplification on many of these points.

7. For me the resonances are especially striking, in the Mexico City case, in Benería and Roldán 1987; see also Lewis 1959. For Oaxaca, particularly illuminating is Nader 1990; see also Greenberg 1989.

8. Soy 1985 (newspaper headline); A. Brenner 1971, 148–49 (photos of Cárdenas on horseback, Cárdenas receiving petition of male peasant who brought flowers), 91 (city joke about Cárdenas's political style and priorities).

9. Among the most perceptive observers of the cultural and political exhaustion of the revolutionary state's older legitimacy platform are Roger Bartra (1987, 1993) and Carlos Monsiváis (1987, 1988). See also n. 10 below.

10. Gilly 1989, 151, 224, for quotes. For a facsimile reproduction of the widow's note, see the inside cover. As with our earlier discussion of the image of Lázaro Cárdenas, it is important to avoid reductionism. The full array of letters also brought to the fore specific needs, proposals, and ideas that cannot simply be reduced to the hunger for a good presidential patriarch. It is worth noting, too, that the notorious "computer breakdown" during the 1988 election tally and the voting pattern itself convinced many Mexicans and foreign observers that Cárdenas actually won the vote. The contrasting result in the 1994 election may indeed signify a more salient expertise-competence factor in the dynamics of political legitimacy.

11. The denunciation of a parasitism founded in irresponsible authority and a consequent corruption and failure of the revolution is familiar to almost any visitor of Mexico who bothers to talk with Mexicans. The discourse has a long genealogy that reaches back to the revolution itself: see Azuela 1915 for its prominence in the classic early novel of the revolution; cf. Cosío Villegas 1947, esp. 33–34, 39–40, 43–45, for an early reflection by one of Mexico's most distinguished historians.

12. See Foley 1986, 1990, cf. J. Martin 1990 and, for Oaxaca, Greenberg 1989, 230–34.

13. For orientation to these themes, see García Peña 1994a, 1994b; Arrom 1985a, 1985b; Ramos Escandón 1987b (esp. the essay by Ramos Escandón); Macías 1982. For pioneering research and reflection on the long-term significance of the Reforma and French Intervention era, see Mallon 1994a.

14. For the foundational story about Zapata, see Sotelo Inclán 1943, 170, 172, 232 n. 1; cf. Lewis 1964, 87; Womack 1968, 6. On Villa, see Guzmán 1968, 9–17; cf. Reed 1914, 122; Pinchon 1933, 69–72. For further analysis of both cases, see O'Malley 1986, 41–70, esp. 61, 87–112, esp. 88, 102. For insight on the blending of color-class humiliation and gendered humiliation in the Old Regime, see also Lewis 1964, 17–18, 74–75; Lewis 1951, 93–94; Lewis 1959, 30; Rueda Smithers 1984, 231. For subaltern emancipation as newly liberated manhood accompanied by devoted womanhood, see Deutsch 1991, 264 esp. n. 10; Herrera-Sobek 1990; Katz 1985, 47; O'Malley 1986, esp. 46, 60–61, 88, 102, 113–45, 171 n. 61; Franco 1989, esp. 102–28, 148–52; Macías 1982, esp. 158; see also Heau 1984; Salas 1990.

15. For pioneering studies, see Macías 1982; Soto 1979; Salas 1990, esp. 36–101; cf. Rascón 1979; Cano 1988; Pérez 1988; Foley 1990, 461. For a superb overarching analysis of the revolution, two of the best works are Katz 1981 and Knight 1986. On the revolution in Yucatán and Felipe Carrillo Puerto, see Joseph 1988.

16. The significance of Cárdenas as the architect of the institutionalized revolutionary state and as an aggressive distributor of land is rather well known; for a good overview and long-term perspective, see Hamilton 1982; Hansen 1971; P. Smith 1979. On a crumbling of social deference that antedated Cárdenas, see the perceptive comments of Knight 1986, 2:519–22. For the cultural struggles and implications of the Cardenista period in the countryside, a highly original and insightful study is Becker 1994. On socialist education policy

in particular, see Sotelo Inclán 1982, esp. 262–65; V. Lerner 1979, esp. 98, 127 (statistics on schools); Guevara Niebla 1985, esp. 130–32; and for background, Vaughan 1982. On women's suffrage and Cárdenas, see Macías 1982, 138–45; Tuñón 1987.

17. For early dissection of the Mexican miracle and its conservative political economy, see Hansen 1971. For a closer look at the economics of agriculture and rural life, see Warman 1976; Sanderson 1986. On the urbanization of Mexican society, women's lives in urban contexts, and the scale of small provincial cities, see Benería and Roldán 1987; Gabayet et al. 1988; LeVine with Correa 1993. On the construction of subaltern machismo as both quintessentially *mexicano* and pathological, see the enormously perceptive works of Bartra 1987; Monsiváis 1988; and the classic essay on *lo mexicano* by Paz 1959 (cf. Ramos 1934; Bermúdez 1955; Ramírez 1959; González Pineda 1961; Alegría 1974). On Mexico's second-wave feminist movement, the prominence of women in urban social movements, and the emergence of a female voice in literature, see Bartra et al. 1983; Franco 1989, 175–87; Massolo 1992; Monsiváis 1987, 91–103; Steele 1992. To set Mexico's twentieth-century history of feminism and women's movements in a broad Latin American context, extremely helpful works are F. Miller 1991; Seminar on Feminism 1990.

18. See esp. the introduction in Fowler-Salamini and Vaughan 1994, a ground-breaking study of gender and women in Mexico since the mid-nineteenth century.

19. A systematic discussion is probably elusive, in any event, until a fuller corpus of specific research investigations is available. But see Fowler-Salamini and Vaughan 1994 (which appeared too late for systematic incorporation in the drafting of this chapter) for a very important contribution in this direction that will no doubt inspire additional research.

20. My overview of the transition and the specific data cited are based on the following sources and rely heavily on the Morelos experience: Bauer 1990 (the outstanding interpretive synthesis); Lewis 1951, 99, 107–8, 184, 198, 323; Lewis 1959, 25; Lewis 1964, lv–lvi, 55, 93, 111, 224, 258, 260, 417, 469; Friedlander 1975, 4, 7–11, 35–36, 49, 62, 63, 67; Tirado 1991, 34, 69, 98, 11, 108; Foley 1990, 478 n. 34; Foley 1986, 97–99. On the economics and labor issues regarding the *molinos* themselves and the ways men secured the best wage labor positions in what had once been "women's work," see Keremitsis 1984.

21. Tirado 1991, 34; Foley 1986, 98, for quotes.

22. For men's resistance in general and the Tepoztlán story in particular, see Bauer 1990, esp. 15–16; Lewis 1944, 303–4; Lewis 1951, 108 (includes "the revolution" quote; cf. 327); Lewis 1959, 25; Lewis 1964, lv–lvi, 258; Tirado 1991, 69, 98 ("always some grinding" quote).

23. On the Cárdenas administration and the *molinos*, see Bauer 1990, 16; Keremitsis 1984, 297–98.

24. On reallocations of female labor, see Lewis 1951, 99, 323; Lewis 1944, 299, 303–4. For the *corrido* regarding the *fresera* workers, see Mummert 1994, appendix 1. The Spanish version is as follows: *Van a la congeladora / al despate de la fresa / pero se van porque / le tienen miedo al metate.*

25. See Lewis 1964, 469, for quote.

26. See LeVine with Correa 1993, 73 (quote), 64, 78, 125, 199; cf. Foley 1990, 477.

27. Significantly, this shift of emphasis may be found not only in relatively mestizo or "progressive" regions such as Morelos but also in Oaxacan communities that present a more "traditionalist" or indigenous face to the external world. See Stephen 1992.

28. Tirado 1991, 113, 22 (cf. 34), for quotes by Celia; Lewis 1951, 323–24, 79 (cf. Lewis 1964, 499, 505, 398), for the more transitory, fragile quality of patrilocal arrangements.

29. Lewis 1964, 409 (cf. xxiii).

30. Ibid., 454, for quote; cf. 445–46. For the declining grip of elders in the southern and heavily indigenous region of Chiapas, see Cancian 1965, 130–32 (incl. n. 3), 187–94. For a beautifully historicized account of the generational, internal, and local-national dynamics, see Rus 1994.

31. García Márquez 1967, 15 (my translation).

32. Lewis 1964, 258, 451, 445, 446, for quotes of Pedro Martínez. On Conchita's schooling and Martínez's temporary return to servile labor, see Lewis 1959, 49–50; Lewis 1964, esp. 339–40, 470–72.

33. Particularly valuable and pioneering in this regard is Massolo 1992. Cf. Monsiváis 1987; LeVine with Correa 1993; Foley 1986, 1990; and for the wider Latin American context, F. Miller 1991; Seminar on Feminism 1990.

34. I owe a debt to J. W. Scott 1986, esp. 1068, 1072, 1073–74, both for the "fixity" term, and for insight on the ways that gendered fixity may become salient precisely at moments of political rupture or cataclysm.

35. It is important to note, in this regard, that the weakening of the patriarchal Old Regime implied neither the end of gender subordination nor the end of patriarchal pacts in subaltern life. To discuss and document such a transition at length would take us too far afield in this postscript, but a brief reflection may be warranted here. I think it useful to speak broadly of a transition in the system of female subordination — from a patriarchal system of gender subordination, as analyzed in our study of late colonial times, to a competitive system of gender subordination, increasingly common in societies of the late twentieth century. In the latter system the patriarchal familial cell no longer serves effectively as a metaphorical foundation of social authority, and the social conventions of gender no longer yield as clear and psychologically fixed a division of labor among the sexes. But notwithstanding competition between the sexes in public roles and increased leakage of women outside classic forms of patriarchal vigilance, social discrimination — backed by misogyny or androcentric bias — yields a gendered differentiation of wages and incomes, skills and social voice, and everyday rights and duties. The process ranks and segments male and female more informally and yields an ironic contradiction: discriminatory life prospects and outcomes provide personal incentives to girls and women to consider patriarchal pacts as a life strategy, despite the overall weakening of the patriarchal system of authority. I hope to revisit this theme in a later venue. For debate that illuminates many of these issues, see González de la Rocha 1988a; Chant 1988; de Barbieri 1988. For a sensitive account from Peru of the ways that a young woman with apparent new social options could feel trapped, see Orlove 1988.

36. On La Malinche and La Chingada in the construction of national identity, the most culturally influential essay was Paz 1959. For recent analysis and critiques of principal female archetypes, see esp. Soto 1986; Leal 1983; Bartra 1987, 205–24; Tuñón Pablos 1987, 13, 37–47, 67–71. On La Malinche specifically and for a recent reclaiming and recasting by feminists, see the illuminating study by Cypess 1991; cf. Alarcón 1983; Phillips 1983; Franco 1989, xviii–xix, 6, 101, 131–46; and n. 38 below.

37. On La Virgen in a wider context, see the sources on principal female archetypes cited in n. 36 above. On the Virgen cult in Mexico, the classic — and perceptive — short account of an earlier scholarly era is Wolf 1958; cf. Turner 1974, 98–155, esp. 105–6, 151–52; Lafaye 1976; Paz 1976; and the sympathetic de la Maza 1953. For a splendidly historicized and subtle reinterpretation, see Taylor 1987. On the Virgen cult within the wider cross-cultural context of mother worship, see the studies in Preston 1982 (note esp. the essay by E. Campbell). On la soldadera, see E. Salas 1990; Herrera Sobek 1990; cf. n. 14 above and the studies of female archetype in twentieth-century literature and song by Clark 1980; Lamas 1978; Monsiváis 1979.

38. The outstanding woman-centered recasting of the soldadera image is Poniatowska 1969; see also Salas 1990. For powerful and poetic examples of Chicana reclaiming of female goddesses and archetypes, see Anzaldúa 1987, esp. 27–34, 41–51; cf. Alarcón 1983; Cypess 1991. I have borrowed the "male-stream" term from M. O'Brien 1981, 12.

39. R. Bartra 1987, 222.

40. My presentation of La Llorona borrows heavily from Limón 1986, a brilliant interpretation of La Llorona as "contestative" discourse and performance, and I wish to acknowledge the intellectual debt. If my presentation has any originality, it resides not in ideas of female-headed oral tradition, collective orphanhood, betrayal-and-vengeance dynamics, and redeeming waters, but in the implicit dialogue established between this encoding of history and the historical experience presented in this book. This dialogue, I think, extends Limón's argument.

I wish to acknowledge, too, the multivalent aspects of archetypes and the ways that the La Llorona tale, as appropriated in male-stream thought and use, may emphasize woman as suffering, sinful, and/or repentant. For interpretation along these lines, see Soto 1986; cf. Marroquí 1887; Ingham 1986, 110–12.

For further information on sixteenth-century antecedents, see González Obregón 1944, 1:17–20; cf. Tuñón Pablos 1987, 31–32; Lewis 1951, 256–57; Ingham 1986, 111–12.

41. I am grateful to Professor Gaea Leinhardt for sharing her observation of the La Llorona recounting in a California school.

42. The metamorphosing quality of many Mesoamerican gods, including the water deities, meant that sexual androgyny, gender twinning, and multiple representational forms were common attributes of the sacred. This makes it somewhat misleading to consider each sacred representation as a clearly separate deity of fixed male or female attribute. For this reason I have placed quote marks around "female" and "male," even though Chalchihuitlicue and Tlaloc are normally considered female and male, respectively. For perceptive discussion of transformation of form and androgyny among Mesoamerican gods, see Clendinnen 1991, 167–69; for further context, see López Austin 1980; Gruzinski 1989b.

Bibliography

ARCHIVAL SOURCES

The research core of this book, although supplemented by vast readings of published sources, relies mainly on manuscript documents in archival repositories. Even a cursory skim of the endnotes to Parts 2 and 3 will provide an indication of how indebted I am to the organizers and custodians of Mexico's vast array of archives. I owe much to Mexicans' keen sense of history and historical preservation and to their graciousness with foreign as well as Mexican historical researchers.

For most historians of colonial Mexico the richest and most varied archival repository is the Archivo General de la Nación (AGN). This proved true in my case as well, and I relied heavily on a thorough scouring of the entire Ramo Criminal (both the catalogued and uncatalogued sections, which together yielded 740 volumes of criminal records). These I supplemented with substantial research in complementary sections or *ramos*. The AGN criminal records were especially thick and helpful for late colonial violence records from the Morelos region (for complicated reasons of jurisdiction, appeal, and remnant Marquesado del Valle rights), but were somewhat spottier for Mexico City and Oaxaca violence cases. The entire complement of AGN *ramos*, however, proved important for my understanding of all three regions. The AGN *ramos* I researched included the following: Acordada, Alcaldes Mayores, Bandos y Ordenanzas, Cárceles y Presidios, Civil, Clero Regular y Secular, Criminal, Epidemias, Historia, Hospital de Jesús, Indios, Inquisición, Intendencias, Matrimonios, Ordenanzas, Padrones, Presidios y Cárceles, Reales Cédulas Originales, and Tierras. Other *ramos* received more cursory looks.

In addition to the AGN, I researched the documentation of eight complementary repositories in Mexico City and Oaxaca: Archivo General del Estado de Oaxaca (AEO); Archivo Histórico de la Ciudad de México (AHC); Archivo Judicial del Tribunal Superior de Justicia del Distrito Federal (AJT); Archivo del Tribunal Superior de Oaxaca, Juzgado de Villa Alta (ATOVA); Biblioteca Nacional de Antropología e Historia: Archivo de Microfilm, Serie Oaxaca (BNAH); Biblioteca Nacional de México: Colección LaFragua (BNM); Centro de Estudios de Historia de México CONDUMEX (for Index to AGN, Civil; CONDUMEX); Centro Regional del Instituto Nacional de Antropología e Historia, Oaxaca: Microfilm del Archivo del Juzgado de Teposcolula (CROT).

Aside from the AGN, the AEO, AJT, ATOVA, BNAH, and CROT collections were particularly useful for complementary criminal violence and morality records. In some instances (i.e., BNAH and CROT), the criminal records were microfilm copies. I cross-checked these documents against those I found in other depositories to assure against double counting during computer coding and statistical testing.

The specific archival documents cited as supporting evidence are identified in the endnotes by archival identifying marks or numbers, place and date of the start of an incident or situation leading to historical record keeping, and, in cases (i.e., the ATOVA and AJT collections) where the identifying marks and place-date are insufficient to specify the exact document or document packet (*expediente*), by summary title of document.

The methodological aspects of my use of criminal records, quantitative analysis, and noncriminal records for supplementary research, context, and consistency checks against criminal violence records are thoroughly discussed in the text (especially Chapters 2 and 3) and in the Appendix.

My ideas and information, although formulated mainly through archival immersion, have also benefited from extensive readings in published sources. I have defined relevance broadly in my readings in printed sources. These have included readings in Mexican history, in the history of other regions (including Europe and the United States as well as other Latin American and Third World regions), and in fields of theoretical interest or relevance (e.g., criminology, family violence sociology, feminist theoretical critiques and social analysis, theoretically engaged historical analyses of women or gender in history, and the like). To save space, these sources are cited in the endnotes using standard social science citation procedure. The full bibliographic citations appear below.

REFERENCES CITED

Abelove, Henry, Michèle Aina Barale, and David M. Halperin, eds. 1993. *The Lesbian and Gay Reader.* New York: Routledge.

AE. 1989. *American Ethnologist* 16, no. 4 (Nov.).

Aguirre Beltrán, Gonzalo. 1955. *Medicina y magia: El proceso de aculturación y el curanderismo en México.* Mexico City: Instituto Nacional Indigenista.

AHR. 1990. *American Historical Review* 95, no. 4 (Oct.). Thematic focus on women and welfare politics.

Alarcón, Norma. 1983. "Chicana's Feminist Literature: A Re-vision through Malintzin/or Malintzin: Putting Flesh Back on the Object." In Moraga and Anzaldúa 1983, 182–90.

Alberro, Solange. 1981. *La actividad del Santo Oficio de la Inquisición en Nueva España, 1571–1700.* Mexico City: Instituto Nacional de Antropología e Historia.

———. 1982. "La sexualidad manipulada en Nueva España: Modalidades de recuperación y de adaptación frente a los Tribunales Eclesiásticos." In Seminario de Historia de las Mentalidades 1982, 238–57.

———. 1986. "La licencia vestida de santidad: Teresa de Jesús, falsa beata del siglo XVII." In Ortega Noriega 1986a, 219–38.

———. 1987a. "Herejes, brujas y beatas: Mujeres ante el Tribunal del Santo Oficio de la Inquisición en la Nueva España." In Ramos Escandón 1987b, 79–94.

———. 1987b. "El matrimonio, la sexualidad y la unidad doméstica entre los criptos judíos de la Nueva España, 1640–1650." In Seminario de Historia de las Mentalidades 1987, 103–45.

Alegría, Juana Armanda. 1974. *Psicología de las mexicanas.* Mexico City: Editorial Samo.

Allende, Isabel. 1986. *The House of the Spirits.* 1982. Translated by Magda Bogin. New York: Bantam.

Alonso, Ana María, and María Teresa Koreck. 1993. "Silences: 'Hispanics,' AIDS, and Sexual Practices." In Abelove et al. 1993, 110–26.

Altman, Ida. 1989. *Emigrants and Society: Extremadura and America in the Sixteenth Century.* Berkeley: University of California Press.

Altman, Ida, and James Lockhart, eds. 1976. *Provinces of Early Mexico: Variety of Spanish American Regional Evolution.* Los Angeles: UCLA Latin American Center.

Alvarez, Sonia E. 1990. *Engendering Democracy in Brazil: Women's Movements in Transition Politics.* Princeton: Princeton University Press.

Anderson, Benedict. 1983. *Imagined Communities: Reflections on the Origins and Spread of Nationalism.* London: Verso.

Anderson, Rodney D. 1988. "Race and Social Stratification: A Comparison of Working-Class Spaniards, Indians, and Castas in Guadalajara, Mexico, in 1821." *Hispanic American Research Review* 68, no. 2 (May): 209–44.

Andrews, George Reid. 1985. "Spanish American Independence: A Structural Analysis." *Latin American Perspectives* 12, no. 1 (Winter): 105–32.

Anrup, Roland. 1990. *El taita y el toro: En torno a la configuración patriarcal del régimen hacendario cuzqueño.* Stockholm: University of Stockholm, Latin American Studies Institute.

Anzaldúa, Gloria. 1987. *Borderlands/La Frontera: The New Mestiza.* San Francisco: Spinsters/Aunt Lute.

Apuleyo Mendoza, Plinio, and García Márquez, Gabriel. 1983. *The Fragrance of Guava.* Translated by Ann Wright. London: Verso.

Archer, Christon I. 1977. *The Army in Bourbon Mexico, 1760–1810.* Albuquerque: University of New Mexico Press.

Arenal, Electa. 1983. "The Convent as Catalyst for Autonomy: Two Hispanic Nuns of the Seventeenth Century." In B. Miller 1983, 147–83.

Arguedas, José María. 1968. *Yawar fiesta.* 2nd ed. Santiago: Editorial Universitaria.

Arizpe, Lourdes. 1977. "Campesinas, capitalismo y cultura." *fem* 3 (Apr.–June): 25–31.

———. 1986. "Las mujeres campesinas y la crisis agraria en América Latina." *Nueva Antropología* 8, no. 30 (Nov.): 57–66.

Arrom, Silvia M. 1976. *La mujer mexicana ante el divorcio eclesiástico (1800–1857).* Mexico City: Secretaría de Educación Pública.

———. 1985a. "Changes in Mexican Family Law in the Nineteenth Century: The Civil Codes of 1870 and 1884." *Journal of Family History* 10, no. 3 (Fall): 305–17.

———. 1985b. *The Women of Mexico City, 1790–1857.* Stanford: Stanford University Press.

———. 1988 "Popular Politics in Mexico City: The Parián Riot, 1828." *Hispanic American Historical Review* 68, no. 2 (May): 245–68.

———. 1991. "Perspectivas sobre historia de la familia en México." In Gonzalbo Aizpuru 1991, 389–99.

Avendaño de Durand, Carmen Cordero. 1982. *Supervivencia: De un derecho consuetudinario en el valle de Tlacolula.* Oaxaca: Fondo Nacional Para Actividades Sociales.

Azuela, Mariano. 1915. *The Underdogs.* Translated by E. Munguía, Jr. Reprint, New York: New American Library, 1962.

Bakewell, Peter J. 1971. *Silver Mining and Society in Colonial Mexico: Zacatecas, 1546–1700.* Cambridge: Cambridge University Press.

Bamberger, Joan. 1974. "The Myth of Matriarchy: Why Men Rule in Primitive Society." In Rosaldo and Lamphere 1974, 263–80.

Barrett, Ward. 1970. *The Sugar Hacienda of the Marqueses del Valle.* Minneapolis: University of Minnesota Press.

———. 1976. "Morelos and Its Sugar Industry in the Late Eighteenth Century." In Altman and Lockhart 1976, 155–76.

Barthes, Roland. 1972. *Mythologies.* Translated by Annette Lavers. New York: Hill and Wang.

Bartra, Eli, María Brumm, Chela Cervantes, Bea Faith, Lucero González, Dominique Guillemet, Berta Hiriart, and Angeles Necoecha. 1983. *La Revuelta: Reflexiones, testimonios y reportajes de mujeres en México, 1975–1983.* Mexico City: Martín Casilla.

Bartra, Roger. 1986. *La democracia ausente.* 2nd ed. Mexico City: Grijalbo.

———. 1987. *La jaula de la melancolía: Identidad y metamorfosis del mexicano.* Mexico City: Grijalbo.

———. 1993. *Oficio mexicano.* Mexico City: Grijalbo.

Bauer, Arnold. 1990. "Millers and Grinders: Technology and Household Economy in Meso-America." *Agricultural History* 64, no. 1 (Winter): 1–17.

Beattie, J. M. 1986. *Crime and the Courts in England, 1660–1800.* Princeton: Princeton University Press.

Becker, Marjorie. 1994. *Setting the Virgin on Fire: Lázaro Cárdenas, Michoacán Peasants, and the Redemption of the Mexican Revolution.* Berkeley: University of California Press.

Behar, Ruth. 1987. "Sex and Sin, Witchcraft and the Devil in Late-Colonial Mexico." *American Ethnologist* 14, no. 1 (Feb.): 34–54.

———. 1989. "Sexual Witchcraft, Colonialism, and Women's Powers: Views from the Mexican Inquisition." In Lavrin 1989d, 178–206.

———. 1993. *Translated Woman: Crossing the Border with Esperanza's Story.* Boston: Beacon Press.

Benería, Lourdes, and Martha Roldán. 1987. *The Crossroads of Class and Gender: Industrial Homework, Subcontracting, and Household Dynamics in Mexico City.* Chicago: University of Chicago Press.

Benítez, Fernando. 1985. *Los demonios en el convento: Sexo y religion en la Nueva España.* Mexico City: Ediciones Era.

Bermúdez, María Elvira. 1955. *La vida familiar del mexicano.* Mexico City: Antigua Librería Robredo.

Bernal, Martin. 1987. *Black Athena: The Afroasiatic Roots of Classical Civilization.* Vol. 1. New Brunswick, N.J.: Rutgers University Press.

Besse, Susan K. 1989. "Crimes of Passion: The Campaign against Wife Killing in Brazil, 1910–1940." *Journal of Social History* 22, no. 4: 653–66.

Blaffer, Sarah C. 1972. *The Black-man of Zinacantan: A Central American Legend.* Austin: University of Texas Press.

Bloch, Marc. 1961. *Feudal Society.* 2 vols. Translated by L. A. Manyon. Chicago: University of Chicago Press.

Bohannan, Paul. 1960a. "Patterns of Murder and Suicide." In Bohannan 1960c, 230–66.

———. 1960b. "Theories of Homicide and Suicide." In Bohannan 1960c, 3–29.

———, ed. 1960c. *African Homicide and Suicide.* Princeton: Princeton University Press.

Borah, Woodrow. 1951. *New Spain's Century of Depression.* Berkeley: University of California Press.

———. 1983. *Justice by Insurance: The General Indian Court of Colonial Mexico and the Legal Aides of the Half-Real.* Berkeley: University of California Press.

Boullosa, Carmen. 1987. *Mejor desaparece.* Mexico City: Océano.

Bourdieu, Pierre. 1966. "The Sentiment of Honour in Kabyle Society." In Peristiany 1966, 191–241.

———. 1977. *Outline of a Theory of Practice.* Translated by Richard Nice. Cambridge: Cambridge University Press.

Bourque, Susan C., and Kay Barbara Warren. 1981. *Women of the Andes: Patriarchy and Social Change in Two Peruvian Towns.* Ann Arbor: University of Michigan Press.

Bouton, Cynthia A. 1993. *The Flour War: Gender, Class, and Community in Late Ancien Régime French Society.* University Park: Pennsylvania State University Press.

Boxer, C. R. 1975. *Mary and Misogyny: Women in Iberian Expansion Overseas, 1415–1815: Some Facts, Fancies, and Personalities.* London: Duckworth.

Boyer, Richard. 1982. "Escribiendo la historia de la religión y mentalidades en Nueva España." In Seminario de Historia de las Mentalidades 1982, 119–37.

———. 1989. "Women, La Mala Vida, and the Politics of Marriage." In Lavrin 1989d, 252–86.

Brading, D. A. 1971. *Miners and Merchants in Bourbon Mexico, 1763–1810.* Cambridge: Cambridge University Press.

———. 1991. *The First America: The Spanish Monarchy, Creole Patriots, and the Liberal State, 1492–1867.* New York: Cambridge University Press.

———, ed. 1980. *Caudillo and Peasant in the Mexican Revolution.* New York: Cambridge University Press.

Brannon, Jeffrey T., and Gilbert M. Joseph, eds. 1991. *Land, Labor, and Capital in Modern Yucatán: Essays in Regional History and Political Economy.* Tuscaloosa: University of Alabama Press.

Breines, Wini, and Linda Gordon. 1983. "The New Scholarship on Family Violence." *Signs* 8, no. 3 (Spring): 490–531.

Brenner, Anita. 1971. *The Wind That Swept Mexico: The History of the Mexican Revolution of 1910–1942.* 2nd ed. Austin: University of Texas Press.

Brenner, Marie. 1993. "Letter from Brownsville: Murder on the Border." *New Yorker,* Sept. 13, 52–75.

Brockington, Lolita Gutiérrez. 1989. *The Leverage of Labor: Managing the Cortéz Haciendas in Tehuantepec, 1588–1688.* Durham: Duke University Press.

Brown, Kathleen Mary. 1990. "Gender and the Genesis of a Race and Class System in Virginia, 1630–1750." Ph.D. diss. University of Wisconsin, Madison.

Brownmiller, Susan. 1975. *Against Our Will: Men, Women, and Rape.* New York: Simon and Schuster.

Bunster, Ximena, and Elsa M. Chaney. 1985. *Sellers and Servants: Working Women in Lima, Peru.* New York: Praeger.

Buñuel, Luis. 1982. *Mi último suspiro (memorias).* Mexico City: Plaza and Janes.

Burga, Manuel. 1988. *Nacimiento de una utopía: Muerte y resurrección de los incas.* Lima: Instituto de Apoyo Agrario.

Burkett, Elinor C. 1975. "Early Colonial Peru: The Urban Female Experience." Ph.D. diss. University of Pittsburgh.

———. 1978. "Indian Women and White Society: The Case of Sixteenth-Century Peru." In Lavrin 1978c, 101–28.

———. 1979. "In Dubious Sisterhood: Class and Sex in Spanish Colonial South America." In *LAP* 1979, 17–25.

Burkhart, Louise M. 1989. *The Slippery Earth: Nahua-Christian Moral Dialogue in Sixteenth-Century Mexico.* Tucson: University of Arizona Press.

Bustamante, Miguel E., and Miguel Angel Bravo B. 1957. "Epidemiología del homicidio en México." *Higiene* 9:21–33.

Calderón de la Barca, Frances. 1982. *Life in Mexico.* 1842. Reprint, Berkeley: University of California Press.

Campbell, Ena. 1982. "The Virgin of Guadalupe and the Female Self-Image: A Mexican Case History." In Preston 1982, 5–24.

Campbell, Howard Blaine. 1990. "Zapotec Ethnic Politics and the Politics of Culture in Juchitán, Oaxaca, 1350–1990." Ph.D. diss. University of Wisconsin, Madison.

Cancian, Frank. 1965. *Economics and Prestige in a Maya Community: The Religious Cargo System in Zinacantan.* Stanford: Stanford University Press.

Cano, Gabriela. 1988. "El coronel Robles: Una combatiente zapatista." *fem* 64 (Apr.): 22–24.

Carmagnani, Marcello. 1982. "Local Governments and Ethnic Government in Oaxaca." In Spalding 1982, 107–24.

———. 1988. *El regreso de los dioses: El proceso de reconstitución de la identidad étnica en Oaxaca, siglos xvii y xviii.* Mexico City: Fondo de Cultura Económica.

Carner, Françoise. 1987. "Estereotipos femeninos en el siglo XIX." In Ramos Escandón 1987b, 95–109.

Caro Baroja, Julio. 1966. "Honour and Shame: A Historical Account of Several Conflicts." In Peristiany 1966, 79–137.

Carrasco, Pedro. 1961. "The Civil-Religious Hierarchy in Mesoamerican Communities: Pre-Spanish Background and Colonial Development." *American Anthropologist* 63:483–97.

————. 1982a. "Estratificación social indígena en Morelos durante el siglo XVI." In Carrasco 1982b, 102–17.

Carrasco, Pedro, ed. 1982b. *Estratificación social en la Mesoamérica prehispánica.* 2nd ed. Mexico City: Instituto Nacional de Antropología e Historia.

Castellanos, Rosario. 1973. *Mujer que sabe latín.* Mexico City: Secretaría de Educación.

Chambers, Sarah C. 1989. "Witches, Mystics, and the Devil: The 'Magical' Mediation of Gender Relations in Colonial Mexico." Seminar Paper. University of Wisconsin, Madison.

————. 1992. "The Many Shades of the White City: Urban Culture and Society in Arequipa, Peru, 1780–1854." Ph.D. diss. University of Wisconsin, Madison.

Chance, John K. 1978. *Race and Class in Colonial Oaxaca.* Stanford: Stanford University Press.

————. 1985. "Social Stratification and the Civil Cargo System among the Rincón Zapotecs of Oaxaca: The Late Colonial Period." In *Iberian Colonies, New World Societies: Essays in Memory of Charles Gibson,* edited by Richard L. Garner and William B. Taylor, 143–59. Corrected ed. Privately printed.

————. 1989. *Conquest of the Sierra: Spaniards and Indians in Colonial Oaxaca.* Norman: University of Oklahoma Press.

Chance, John K., and William B. Taylor. 1977. "Estate and Class in a Colonial City: Oaxaca in 1792." *Comparative Studies in Society and History* 19:454–87.

————. 1979. "Estate *and* Class: A Reply." *Comparative Studies in Society and History* 21:434–42.

————. 1985. "Cofradías and Cargos: An Historical Perspective on the Mesoamerican Civil-Religious Hierarchy." *American Ethnologist* 12, no. 1 (Feb.): 1–26.

Chaney, Elsa. 1979. *Supermadre: Women in Politics in Latin America.* Austin: University of Texas Press.

Chant, Sylvia. 1988. "Mitos y realidades de la formación de las familias encabezadas por mujeres: El caso de Querétaro, México." In Gabayet et al. 1988, 181–203.

Chasteen, John Charles. 1990. "Violence for Show: Knife Dueling on a Nineteenth-Century Cattle Frontier." In L. L. Johnson 1990, 47–64.

Cherpak, Evelyn. 1978. "The Participation of Women in the Independence Movement in Gran Colombia, 1780–1830." In Lavrin 1978c, 219–34.

Chesney-Lind, Meda. 1986. "Women and Crime: The Female Offender." *Signs* 12, no. 1 (Autumn): 78–96.

Chevalier, François. 1963. *Land and Society in Colonial Mexico: The Great Hacienda.* 1952. Translated by Helen Katel. Berkeley: University of California Press.

Chiñas, Beverly. 1992. *The Isthmus Zapotecs: A Matrifocal Culture of Mexico.* 2nd ed. Fort Worth: Harcourt Brace Jovanovich College Pub.

Chodorow, Nancy. 1978. *The Reproduction of Mothering: Psychoanalysis and the Sociology of Gender.* Berkeley: University of California Press.

Clark, Stella T. 1980. "Camila o La Pintada: Tipo y mito de la mujer mexicana." In Guerra-Cunningham 1980, 243–51.

Clendinnen, Inga. 1982a. "Disciplining the Indians: Franciscan Ideology and Missionary Violence in Sixteenth-Century Yucatan." *Past and Present* 94 (Feb.): 27–48.

————. 1982b. "Yucatec Maya Women and the Spanish Conquest: Role and Ritual in Historical Reconstruction." *Journal of Social History* 15, no. 3: 427–42.

————. 1985. "The Cost of Courage in Aztec Society." *Past and Present* 107 (May): 44–89.

————. 1987. *Ambivalent Conquests: Maya and Spaniard in Yucatan, 1517–1570.* Cambridge: Cambridge University Press.

————. 1991. *Aztecs: An Interpretation.* Cambridge: Cambridge University Press.

Clinard, Marshall B., and Daniel Abbott. 1973. *Crime in Developing Countries: A Comparative Perspective*. New York: John Wiley and Sons.

Cline, S. L. 1986. *Colonial Culhuacan, 1580–1600: A Social History of an Aztec Town*. Albuquerque: University of New Mexico Press.

Coatsworth, John H. 1982. "The Limits of Colonial Absolutism: The State in Eighteenth-Century Mexico." In Spalding 1982, 25–51.

Colín Sánchez, Guillermo. 1987. *Así habla la delincuencia*. Mexico City: Editorial Porrúa.

Collier, George A. 1989. "The Impact of Second Republic Labor Reforms in Spain." In Starr and Collier 1989, 201–22.

Collier, George A., Renato I. Rosaldo, and John D. Wirth, eds. 1982. *The Inca and Aztec States, 1400–1800: Anthropology and History*. New York: Academic Press.

Connell, R. W. 1987. *Gender and Power: Society, the Person, and Sexual Politics*. Stanford: Stanford University Press.

Conniff, Michael, ed. 1982. *Latin American Populism in Comparative Perspective*. Albuquerque: University of New Mexico Press.

Cook, Alexandra Parma, and Noble David Cook. 1991. *Good Faith and Truthful Ignorance: A Case of Transatlantic Bigamy*. Durham: Duke University Press.

Cook, Sherburne F., and Woodrow Borah. 1968. *The Population of the Mixteca Alta, 1520–1960*. Berkeley: University of California Press.

———. 1971–79. *Essays in Population History*. 3 vols. Berkeley: University of California Press.

Cooper, Donald B. 1965. *Epidemic Disease in Mexico City, 1761–1813: An Administrative, Social, and Medical Study*. Austin: University of Texas Press.

Cooper, Frederick, Allen F. Isaacman, Florencia E. Mallon, William Roseberry, and Steve J. Stern. 1993. *Confronting Historical Paradigms: Peasants, Labor, and the Capitalist World System in Africa and Latin America*. Madison: University of Wisconsin Press.

Cope, R. Douglas. 1994. *The Limits of Racial Domination: Plebeian Society in Colonial Mexico City, 1660–1720*. Madison: University of Wisconsin Press.

Cosío Villegas, Daniel. 1947. "La crisis de México." *Cuadernos Americanos* 32 (Mar.–Apr.): 29–51.

Couturier, Edith. 1978. "Women in a Noble Family: The Mexican Counts of Regla, 1750–1830." In Lavrin 1978c, 129–49.

———. 1985. "Women and the Family in Eighteenth-Century Mexico: Law and Practice." *Journal of Family History* 10, no. 3 (Fall): 294–304.

Crespo, Horacio, ed. 1984. *Morelos: Cinco siglos de historia regional*. Cuernavaca: Universidad Autónoma del Estado de Morelos.

Crespo, Horacio, and Herbert Frey. 1982. "La diferenciación social del campesinado como problema de la teoría y de la historia, hipótesis generales para el caso de Morelos, México." *Revista Mexicana de Sociología* 44, no. 1 (Jan.–Mar.): 285–313.

Crites, Laura, ed. 1976. *The Female Offender*. Lexington, Mass.: D. C. Heath.

Cypess, Sandra Messinger. 1991. *La Malinche in Mexican Literature: From History to Myth*. Austin: University of Texas Press.

da Cunha, Euclides. 1944. *Rebellion in the Backlands*. Translated by Samuel Putnam. 1902. Reprint, Chicago: University of Chicago Press.

Davis, Angela Y. 1981. *Women, Race, and Class*. New York: Random House.

Davis, David Brion. 1975. *The Problem of Slavery in the Age of Revolution, 1770–1823*. Ithaca: Cornell University Press.

Davis, Natalie Zemon. 1975. *Society and Culture in Early Modern France*. Stanford: Stanford University Press.

———. 1983. *The Return of Martin Guerre*. Cambridge, Mass.: Harvard University Press.

———. 1987. *Fiction in the Archives: Pardon Tales and Their Tellers in Sixteenth-Century France.* Stanford: Stanford University Press.

Deans-Smith, Susan. 1992. *Bureaucrats, Planters, and Workers: The Making of the Tobacco Monopoly in Bourbon Mexico.* Austin: University of Texas Press.

de Barbieri, M. Teresita. 1988. "Las mujeres y la reproducción social: Comentarios." In Gabayet et al. 1988, 229–34.

de Beauvoir, Simone. 1952. *The Second Sex.* Translated by H. M. Parshley. New York: Knopf.

de la Fuente, Julio. 1949a. "Documentos para la etnografía e historia zapoteca." *Anales del Instituto Nacional de Antropología e Historia* 3:175–97.

———. 1949b. *Yalalag: Una villa zapoteca serrana.* Reprint, Mexico City: Instituto Nacional Indigenista, 1977.

de la Maza, Francisco. 1953. *El guadalupanismo mexicano.* Mexico City: Fondo de Cultura Económica.

de la Peña, Guillermo. 1980. *Herederos de promesas: Agricultura, política y ritual en los Altos de Morelos.* Mexico City: Casa Chata.

de Lauretis, Teresa. 1984. *Alice Doesn't: Feminism, Semiotics, Cinema.* Bloomington: Indiana University Press.

Dennis, Philip A. 1987. *Intervillage Conflict in Oaxaca.* New Brunswick, N.J.: Rutgers University Press.

de Olmo, Rosa. 1981. *América Latina y su criminología.* Mexico City: Siglo XXI.

Desan, Suzanne. 1989. "Crowds, Community, and Ritual in the Work of E. P. Thomson and Natalie Davis." In Hunt 1989, 47–71.

———. 1990. *Reclaiming the Sacred: Lay Religion and Popular Politics in Revolutionary France.* Ithaca: Cornell University Press.

Deutsch, Sandra McGee. 1991. "Gender and Sociopolitical Change in Twentieth-Century Latin America." *Hispanic American Historical Review* 71, no. 2 (May): 259–306.

Di Tella, Torcuato S. 1973. "The Dangerous Classes in Early Nineteenth-Century Mexico." *Journal of Latin American Studies* 5, no. 1 (May): 79–105.

Dobash, R. Emerson, and Russell Dobash. 1979. *Violence against Wives: A Case against the Patriarchy.* New York: Free Press.

———. 1983. "Do We Need New Methods for Studying Wife Abuse?" In Finkelhor et al. 1983, 261–76.

Domínguez, Virginia R. 1989. *People as Subject, People as Object: Selfhood and Peoplehood in Contemporary Israel.* Madison: University of Wisconsin Press.

Douglas, Carrie B. 1984. "Toro muerto, vaca es: An Interpretation of the Spanish Bullfight." *American Ethnologist* 11, no. 2 (May): 242–58.

Douglas, Mary. 1966. *Purity and Danger: An Analysis of Concepts of Pollution and Taboo.* London: Routledge and Kegan Paul.

———. 1970. *Natural Symbols: Explorations in Cosmology.* New York: Pantheon.

Dundes, Alan, ed. 1994a. *The Cockfight: A Casebook.* Madison: University of Wisconsin Press.

———. 1994b. "Gallus as Phallus: A Psychoanalytic Cross-Cultural Consideration of the Cockfight as Fowl Play." In Dundes 1994a, 241–82.

Dutton, Donald G. 1988. *The Domestic Assault of Women: Psychological and Criminal Justice Perspectives.* Boston: Allyn and Bacon.

Echebarria y Ojeda, Don Pedro Antonio. 1791. *Manual alfabético de delitos y penas según las leyes y pragmáticas de España.* Madrid: Imprenta Real.

Eckstein, Susan, ed. 1988. *Power and Popular Protest: Latin American Social Movements.* Berkeley: University of California Press.

Elmendorf, Mary. 1976. *Nine Mayan Women: A Village Faces Change*. New York: John Wiley and Sons.

Elshtain, Jean Bethke, ed. 1982. *The Family in Political Thought*. Amherst: University of Massachusetts Press.

Elton, G. R. 1984. "Happy Families." *New York Review of Books*, June 14, 39–42.

———. 1991. *Return to Essentials: Some Reflections on the Present State of Historical Study*. New York: Cambridge University Press.

Engels, Frederick. 1972. *The Origin of the Family, Private Property, and the State*. New York: International Pub.

Enloe, Cynthia. 1983. *Does Khaki Become You? The Militarisation of Women's Lives*. London: Pluto.

Etienne, Maria, and Eleanor Leacock, eds. 1980. *Women and Colonization: Anthropological Perspectives*. New York: Praeger.

Evans, Sara M. 1979. *Personal Politics: The Roots of Women's Liberation in the Civil Rights Movement and the New Left*. New York: Knopf.

Evans, Sara M., and Harry C. Boyte, eds. 1986. *Free Spaces: The Sources of Democratic Change in America*. New York: Harper and Row.

Falcón, Romana. 1988. "Charisma, Tradition, and Caciquismo: Revolution in San Luís Potosí." In Katz 1988b, 417–47.

Farriss, Nancy. 1968. *Crown and Clergy in Colonial Mexico, 1759–1821: The Crisis of Ecclesiastical Privilege*. London: Athlone.

———. 1984. *Maya Society under Colonial Rule: The Collective Enterprise of Survival*. Princeton: Princeton University Press.

Feierman, Steven. 1990. *Peasant Intellectuals: Anthropology and History*. Madison: University of Wisconsin Press.

fem. 1979. *fem* 11 (Nov.–Dec.). Special issue, "La mujer en la historia de México."

———. 1983. *fem* 30 (Oct.–Nov.). Special issue, "Feminismo en México: Antecedentes."

Fernández-Kelly, María Patricia. 1983. *For We Are Sold, I and My People: Women and Industry in Mexico's Frontier*. Albany: SUNY Press.

Finkelhor, David, Richard J. Gelles, Gerald T. Hotaling, and Murray A. Straus, eds. 1983. *The Dark Side of Families: Current Family Violence Research*. Beverly Hills: Sage.

Flanet, Véronique. 1977. *Viviré si Dios quiere: Un estudio de la violencia en la mixteca de la costa*. Mexico City: Instituto Nacional Indigenista.

Flannery, Kent V., and Joyce Marcus, eds. 1983. *The Cloud People: Divergent Evolution of the Zapotec and Mixtec Civilizations*. New York: Academic Press.

Florescano, Enrique. 1969. *Precios del maíz y crisis agrícolas en México, 1708–1810*. Mexico City: El Colegio de México.

———. 1971. "El problema agrario en los últimos años del virreinato, 1800–1821." *Historia mexicana* 20, no. 4 (Apr.–June): 477–510.

———. 1991. *El nuevo pasado mexicano*. Mexico City: Cal y Arena.

Flores Galindo, Alberto, and Magdalena Chocano. 1984. "Las cargas del sacramento." *Revista andina* 2, no. 2 (Dec.): 403–23.

Foley, Michael W. 1986. "The Languages of Contention: Political Language, Moral Judgment, and Peasant Mobilization in Contemporary Mexico." Ph.D. diss. University of California, Davis.

———. 1990. "Organizing, Ideology, and Moral Suasion: Political Discourse and Action in a Mexican Town." *Comparative Studies in Society and History* 32: 455–87.

Forster, Robert, and Orest Ranum, eds. 1978. *Deviants and the Abandoned in French Society: Selections from the "Annales, Economies, Sociétés, Civilisations," Vol. 4*. Translated by Elborg Forster and Patricia M. Ranum. Baltimore: Johns Hopkins University Press.

Foucault, Michel. 1965. *Madness and Civilization: A History of Insanity in the Age of Reason.* Translated by Richard Howard. New York: Pantheon.

———. 1977. *Discipline and Punish: The Birth of the Prison.* Translated by Alan Sheridan. New York: Pantheon.

———. 1978–86. *The History of Sexuality.* 3 vols. Translated by Robert Hurley. New York: Pantheon.

———. 1980. *Power/Knowledge: Selected Interviews and Other Writings, 1972–1977.* Edited by Colin Gordon. New York: Pantheon.

———. 1984. *The Foucault Reader.* Edited by Paul Rabinow. New York: Pantheon.

Fowler-Salamini, Heather. 1993. "The Boom in Regional Studies of the Mexican Revolution: Where Is It Leading?" *Latin American Research Review* 28, no. 2:175–90.

Fowler-Salamini, Heather, and Mary Kay Vaughan, eds. 1994. *Women of the Mexican Countryside, 1850–1990: Creating Spaces, Shaping Transition.* Tucson: University of Arizona Press.

Fox, Geoffrey E. 1973. "Honor, Shame, and Women's Liberation in Cuba: Views of Working-Class Emigré Men." In Pescatello 1973, 273–90.

Fox-Genovese, Elizabeth. 1991. *Feminism without Illusions: A Critique of Individualism.* Chapel Hill: University of North Carolina Press.

Franco, Jean. 1989. *Plotting Women: Gender and Representation in Mexico.* New York: Columbia University Press.

Freyre, Gilberto. 1943. *Casa-grande e senzala.* 2 vols. 1933. 4th ed. Rio de Janeiro: J. Olympio.

Friedlander, Judith. 1975. *Being Indian in Hueyapan: A Study of Forced Identity in Contemporary Mexico.* New York: St. Martin's Press.

Friedrich, Paul. 1986. *The Princes of Naranja: An Essay in Anthrohistorical Method.* Austin: University of Texas Press.

Fromm, Erich, and Maccoby, Michael. 1970. *Social Character in a Mexican Village: A Sociopsychoanalytic Study.* Englewood Cliffs, N.J.: Prentice-Hall.

Fuentes, Carlos. 1964. *The Death of Artemio Cruz.* Translated by Sam Hileman. New York: Farrar, Straus and Giroux.

Gabayet, Luisa, Patricia García, Mercedes González de la Rocha, Silvia Lailson, and Agustín Escobar, eds. 1988. *Mujeres y sociedad: Salario, hogar y acción social en el occidente de México.* Guadalajara: El Colegio de Jalisco.

Gailey, Christine Ward. 1987. *Kinship to Kingship: Gender Hierarchy and State Formation in the Tongan Islands.* Austin: University of Texas Press.

Gallo S., Joaquín. 1983. *Tepoztlán: Vida y color.* 4th ed. Mexico City: Editorial Libros de México.

García Márquez, Gabriel. 1967. *Cien años de soledad.* Buenos Aires: Editorial Sudamericana.

———. 1976. *The Autumn of the Patriarch.* 1975. Translated by Gregory Rabassa. New York: Harper and Row.

———. 1981. *Crónica de una muerte anunciada.* Bogotá: Editorial La Oveja Negra.

García Martínez, Bernardo. 1969. *El Marquesado del Valle: Tres siglos de régimen señorial en Nueva España.* Mexico City: El Colegio de México.

———. 1987. *Los pueblos de la sierra: El poder y el espacio entre los indios del norte de Puebla hasta 1700.* Mexico City: El Colegio de México.

García Peña, Ana Lidia. 1994a. "El matrimonio y el divorcio en México, 1859–1940." Proyecto de Tesis, Universidad Nacional Autónoma de México.

———. 1994b. "Problemas metodológicos de las mujeres: La historiografía dedicada al siglo XIX mexicano." *Avances de Investigación y Docencia.* Programa Universitario de Estudios de Género. Mexico City: UNAM.

Garner, Richard L. 1985. "Price Trends in Eighteenth-Century Mexico." *Hispanic American Historical Review* 65, no. 2 (May): 279–325.

Gatrell, V. A. C., Bruce Lenment, and Geoffrey Parker, eds. 1980. *Crime and the Law: The Social History of Crime in Western Europe since 1500.* London: Europa.

Geertz, Clifford. 1973. *The Interpretation of Culture.* New York: Basic Books.

Gelles, Richard J. 1974. *The Violent House: A Study of Physical Aggression between Husbands and Wives.* Beverly Hills: Sage.

———. 1983. "An Exchange/Social Control Theory." In Finkelhor et al. 1983, 151–65.

———. 1987. *Family Violence.* 2nd ed. Beverly Hills: Sage.

Gelles, Richard J., and Claire Pedrick Cornell, eds. 1983. *International Perspectives on Family Violence.* Lexington, Mass.: D. C. Heath.

Genovese, Eugene D. 1969. *The World the Slaveholders Made: Two Essays in Interpretation.* New York: Pantheon.

———. 1974. *Roll, Jordan, Roll: The World the Slaves Made.* New York: Pantheon.

Gerhard, Peter. 1972. *A Guide to the Historical Geography of New Spain.* Cambridge: Cambridge University Press.

Gibson, Charles. 1964. *The Aztecs under Spanish Rule.* Stanford: Stanford University Press.

Gilly, Adolfo, ed. 1989. *Cartas a Cuauhtémoc Cárdenas.* Mexico City: Era.

Giraud, François. 1987. "La reacción social ante la violación: Del discurso a la práctica, Nueva España, Siglo XVIII." In Seminario de Historia de las Mentalidades 1987, 295–352.

Goldwert, Marvin. 1980. *History as Neurosis: Paternalism and Machismo in Spanish America.* Lanham, Md.: University Press of America.

———. 1982. *Psychic Conflict in Spanish America: Six Essays on the Psychohistory of the Region.* Lanham, Md.: University Press of America.

———. 1983. *Machismo and Conquest: The Case of Mexico.* Lanham, Md.: University Press of America.

Góngora, Mario. 1951. *El estado en el derecho indiano: Época de fundación, 1492–1570.* Santiago de Chile: Universidad de Chile.

———. 1974. *Origen de los inquilinos de Chile central.* 2nd ed. Santiago de Chile: Instituto de Capacitación e Investigación en Reform Agraria.

Gonzalbo Aizpuru, Pilar. 1987a. *Las mujeres en la Nueva España: Educación y vida cotidiana.* Mexico City: El Colegio de México.

———. 1987b. "Tradición y ruptura en la educación femenina del siglo XVI." In Ramos Escandón 1987b, 33–59.

———, ed. 1991. *Familias novohispanas: Siglos XVI al XIX.* Sponsored by Seminario de Historia de la Familia. Mexico City: El Colegio de México.

González Angulo Aguirre, Jorge. 1983. *Artesanado y ciudad a finales del siglo XVIII.* Mexico City: Fondo de Cultura Económica.

González de la Rocha, Mercedes. 1988a. "De por qué las mujeres aguantan golpes y cuernos: Un análisis de hogares sin varón en Guadalajara." In Gabayet et al. 1988, 205–27.

———. 1988b. "Economic Crisis, Domestic Reorganization, and Women's Work in Guadalajara, Mexico." *Bulletin of Latin American Research* 7, no. 2: 207–23.

González Echevarría, Roberto. 1985. *The Voice of the Masters: Writing and Authority in Modern Latin American Literature.* Austin: University of Texas Press.

González Marmolejo, Jorge René, Dolores Enciso, Ana María Atondo R., María Elena Cortés J., José Abel Ramos Soriano, and Solange Alberro. 1982. "Algunos grupos desviantes en México colonial." In Seminario de Historia de las Mentalidades 1982, 258–305.

González Montes, Soledad, and Pilar Iracheta Cenegorta. 1987. "La violencia en la vida de las mujeres campesinas: El distrito de Tenango, 1880–1910." In Ramos Escandón 1987b, 111–41.

González Obregón, Luís. 1944. *Las calles de México.* 2 vols. 6th ed. Mexico City: Ediciones Botas.

González Pineda, Francisco. 1961. *El Mexicano: Psicología de su destructividad.* Mexico City: Editorial Pax-México, S.A.

González y González, Luis. 1968. *Pueblo en vilo: Microhistoria de San José de Gracia.* Mexico City: El Colegio de México.

———. 1971. "Microhistoria para Multiméxico." *Historia mexicana* 21, no. 2 (Oct.–Dec.): 225–41.

———. 1973. *Invitación a la microhistoria.* Mexico City: Sepsetentas.

Goode, William J. 1975. "Force and Violence in the Family." In Steinmetz and Straus 1975, 25–43.

Gordon, Linda. 1986. "Family Violence, Feminism, and Social Control." *Feminist Studies* 12, no. 3 (Fall): 453–78.

———. 1988. *Heroes of Their Own Lives: The Politics and History of Family Violence.* New York: Viking.

———, ed. 1990. *Women, the State, and Welfare.* Madison: University of Wisconsin Press.

Gramsci, Antonio. 1971. "State and Civil Society." In *Selections from the Prison Notebooks,* by Antonio Gramsci, 206–76. Edited by Quintin Hoare and Geoffrey Nowell Smith. New York: International Pub.

Greenberg, James B. 1989. *Blood Ties: Life and Violence in Rural Mexico.* Tucson: University of Arizona Press.

Greenleaf, Richard. 1969. *The Mexican Inquisition of the Sixteenth Century.* Albuquerque: University of New Mexico Press.

Gruzinski, Serge. 1982. "La 'conquista de los cuerpos.'" In Seminario de Historia de las Mentalidades 1982, 177–206.

———. 1987. "Confesión, alianza y sexualidad entre los indios de Nueva España: Introducción al estudio de los Confesionarios en lenguas indígenas." In Seminario de Historia de las Mentalidades 1987, 169–215.

———. 1988. *La colonisation de l'imaginaire: Sociétés indigènes et occidentalisation dans le Mexique espagnol, XVIᵉ–XVIIIᵉ siècle.* Paris: Gallimard.

———. 1989a. "Individualization and Acculturation: Confession among the Nahuas of Mexico from the Sixteenth to the Eighteenth Century." In Lavrin 1989d, 96–117.

———. 1989b. *Man-Gods in the Mexican Highlands: Indian Power and Colonial Society, 1520–1800.* Translated by Eileen Corrigan. Stanford: Stanford University Press.

Guerra-Cunningham, Lucía, ed. 1980. *Mujer y sociedad en América Latina.* Mexico City: Editorial del Pacífico.

Guevara Niebla, Gilberto, ed. 1985. *La educación socialista en México, 1934–1945.* Mexico City: Secretaría de Educación Pública.

Gutiérrez, Ramón A. 1980. "Marriage, Sex, and the Family: Social Change in Colonial New Mexico, 1690–1846." Ph.D. diss. University of Wisconsin, Madison.

———. 1984. "From Honor to Love: Transformations of the Meaning of Sexuality in Colonial New Mexico." In R. Smith 1984, 237–63.

———. 1985. "Honor Ideology, Marriage Negotiation, and Class-Gender Domination in New Mexico, 1690–1846." *Latin American Perspectives* 12, no. 1 (Winter): 81–104.

———. 1991. *When Jesus Came, the Corn Mothers Went Away: Marriage, Sexuality, and Power in New Mexico, 1500–1846.* Stanford: Stanford University Press.

Gutmann, Matthew C. 1994. "Machismo and Lo Mexicano: An Ethnohistorical Appraisal." Paper presented at Latin American Studies Association, Atlanta, Mar. 10–12.

————. Forthcoming. "The Meanings of Macho: Changing Male Identities in Mexico City." Ph.D. diss. University of California, Berkeley.

Guy, Donna J. 1981. "Women, Peonage, and Industrialization: Argentina, 1810–1914." *Latin American Research Review* 16, no. 3: 65–89.

————. 1991. *Sex and Danger in Buenos Aires: Prostitution, Family, and Nation in Argentina*. Lincoln: University of Nebraska Press.

Guzmán, Martín Luis. 1968. *Memorias de Pancho Villa*. 11th ed. (rev.). Mexico City: Compañía General de Ediciones.

Hahn, Steven. 1984. "Honor and Patriarchy in the Old South." *American Quarterly* 36, no. 1 (Spring): 145–53.

Hamerow, Theodore S. 1987. *Reflections on History and Historians*. Madison: University of Wisconsin Press.

Hamilton, Nora. 1982. *The Limits of State Autonomy: Post-Revolutionary Mexico*. Princeton: Princeton University Press.

Hammerton, A. James. 1991. "The Targets of 'Rough Music': Respectability and Domestic Violence in Victorian England." *Gender and History* 3, no. 1 (Spring): 23–44.

Hamnett, Brian R. 1971. *Politics and Trade in Southern Mexico, 1750–1821*. Cambridge: Cambridge University Press.

————. 1986. *Roots of Insurgency: Mexican Regions, 1750–1824*. Cambridge: Cambridge University Press.

Hanley, Sarah. 1989. "Engendering the State: Family Formation and State Building in Early Modern France." *French Historical Studies* 16 (Spring): 4–27.

Hansen, Roger D. 1971. *The Politics of Mexican Development*. Baltimore: Johns Hopkins University Press.

Hartmann, Heidi I. 1979. "The Unhappy Marriage of Marxism and Feminism: Towards a More Progressive Union." *Capital and Class* 8 (Summer): 1–33.

Hartz, Louis, with Kenneth D. McRae, Richard M. Morse, Richard N. Rosecrance, and Leonard M. Thompson. 1964. *The Founding of New Societies*. New York: Harcourt, Brace, and World.

Haskett, Robert S. 1987. "Indian Town Government in Colonial Cuernavaca: Persistence, Adaptation, and Change." *Hispanic American Historical Review* 67, no. 2 (May): 204–31.

————. 1988. "Living in Two Worlds: Cultural Continuity and Change among Cuernavaca's Colonial Indigenous Ruling Elite." *Ethnohistory* 35, no. 1 (Winter): 34–59.

————. 1991a. *Indigenous Rulers: An Ethnohistory of Town Government in Colonial Cuernavaca*. Albuquerque: University of New Mexico Press.

————. 1991b. "'Our Suffering with the Taxco Tribute': Involuntary Mine Labor and Indigenous Tribute in Central New Spain." *Hispanic American Historical Review* 71, no. 3 (Aug.): 447–75.

Haslip, Gabriel James. 1980. "Crime and the Administration of Justice in Colonial Mexico City, 1696–1810." Ph.D. diss. Columbia University.

————. 1984. "Criminal Justice and the Poor in Late Colonial Mexico City." In Spores and Hassig 1984, 107–26.

Hassig, Ross. 1985. *Trade, Tribute, and Transportation: The Sixteenth-Century Political Economy of the Valley of Mexico*. Norman: University of Oklahoma Press.

Hawes, Joseph M., and N. Ray Hiner, eds. 1991. *Children in Historical Perspectives: An International Handbook and Research Guide*. Westport, Conn.: Greenwood.

Hay, Douglas, Peter Linebaugh, John G. Rule, E. P. Thompson, and Cal Winslow. 1975. *Albion's Fatal Tree: Crime and Society in Eighteenth-Century England*. New York: Pantheon.

Heau, Catherine. 1984. "Trova popular e identidad cultural en Morelos." In Crespo 1984, 261–73.

Heijmerink, J. J. M. 1973. "La tenencia de la tierra en las comunidades indígenas en el estado de Oaxaca, el caso de Santo Tomás Ocotepec en la región de la Mixteca Alta." *Revista Mexicana de Sociología* 35, no. 2 (Apr.–June): 289–99.

Hellbom, Anna-Britta. 1967. *La participación cultural de las mujeres Indias y Mestizas en el México precortesiano y postrevolucionario.* Stockholm: Ethnographical Museum.

Hernández Chávez, Alicia. 1991. *Anenecuilco: Memoria y vida de un pueblo.* Mexico City: El Colegio de México.

Herrera-Sobek, María. 1990. *The Mexican Corrido: A Feminist Analysis.* Bloomington: Indiana University Press.

Hoch, Steven L. 1986. *Serfdom and Social Control in Russia: Petrovskoe, a Village in Tambov.* Chicago: University of Chicago Press.

Huerta, María Teresa. 1984. "Formación del grupo de hacendados azucareros morelenses, 1780–1840." In Crespo 1984, 149–63.

Humboldt, Alexander von. 1811. *Political Essay on the Kingdom of New Spain.* 4 vols. Reprint, New York: AMS Press, 1986.

Hunt, Lynn, ed. 1989. *The New Cultural History.* Berkeley: University of California Press.

Icaza, Jorge. 1953. *Huasipungo: Novela.* 2nd ed. Buenos Aires: Editorial Losada.

Ingham, John M. 1986. *Mary, Michael, and Lucifer: Folk Catholicism in Central Mexico.* Austin: University of Texas Press.

Isbell, Billie Jean. 1976. "La otra mitad esencial: Un estudio de complementariedad sexual andina." *Estudios Andinos* 5, no. 1 (1976): 37–55.

Israel, J. I. 1975. *Race, Class, and Politics in Colonial Mexico, 1610–1670.* London: Oxford University Press.

Jacobsen, Nils, and Hans-Jürgen Puhle, eds. 1986. *The Economies of Mexico and Peru during the Late Colonial Period, 1760–1810.* Berlin: Colloquium.

JAH. 1989. "A Round Table: What Has Changed and Not Changed in American Historical Practice?" *Journal of American History* 76 (Sept.): 393–488.

Janeway, Elizabeth. 1980. *Powers of the Weak.* New York: Knopf.

JFH. 1985. *Journal of Family History* 10, no. 3 (Fall). Special issue, "The Latin American Family in the Nineteenth Century."

Johnson, Lyman L., ed. 1990. *The Problem of Order in Changing Societies: Essays on Crime and Policing in Argentina and Uruguay, 1750–1940.* Albuquerque: University of New Mexico Press.

Johnson, Robert. 1984. *Elementary Statistics.* 4th ed. Boston: Duxbury.

Joseph, Gilbert M. 1988. *Revolution from Without: Yucatan, Mexico, and the United States, 1880–1924.* 2nd ed. Durham: Duke University Press.

———. 1991. "The New Regional Historiography at Mexico's Periphery." In Brannon and Joseph 1991, 1–9.

Joseph, Gilbert M., and Daniel Nugent, eds. 1994a. *Everyday Forms of State Formation: Revolution and the Negotiation of Rule in Modern Mexico.* Durham: Duke University Press.

———. 1994b. "Popular Culture and State Formation in Revolutionary Mexico." In Joseph and Nugent 1994a, 3–23.

JTWS. 1981. *Journal of Third World Societies* 15 (Mar.). Special issue, "Women and Politics in Twentieth-Century Latin America."

Kaplan, Steven. 1976. *Bread, Politics, and Political Economy in the Reign of Louis XV.* 2 vols. The Hague: Martinus Nijhoff.

Kaplan, Temma. 1982. "Female Consciousness and Collective Action: The Case of Barcelona, 1910–1918." *Signs* 7, no. 3 (Spring): 545–66.

Katz, Friedrich. 1981. *The Secret War in Mexico: Europe, the United States, and the Mexican Revolution.* Chicago: University of Chicago Press.

———. 1985. "No queremos cucaracha, queremos revolución." *Nexos* 92 (Aug.): 47–49.

———. 1988a. "Introduction: Rural Revolts in Mexico." In Katz 1988b, 4–17.

———, ed. 1988b. *Riot, Rebellion, and Revolution: Rural Social Conflict in Mexico.* Princeton: Princeton University Press.

Keen, Benjamin. 1985. "Main Currents in United States Writings on Colonial Spanish America." *Hispanic American Historical Review* 65, no. 4 (Nov.): 657–82.

Kellogg, Susan. 1984. "Aztec Women in Early Colonial Courts: Structure and Strategy in a Legal Context." In Spores and Hassig 1984, 25–38.

———. 1986. "Aztec Inheritance in Sixteenth-Century Mexico City: Colonial Patterns, Prehispanic Influences." *Ethnohistory* 33, no. 3 (Summer): 313–30.

Kelly, Joan. 1984. *Women, History, and Theory: The Essays of Joan Kelly.* Chicago: University of Chicago Press.

Keremitsis, Dawn. 1984. "Del metate al molino: La mujer mexicana de 1910 a 1940." *Historia mexicana* 33, no. 2 (Oct.–Dec.): 285–302.

Kicza, John E. 1983. *Colonial Entrepreneurs: Families and Business in Bourbon Mexico City.* Albuquerque: University of New Mexico Press.

King, Marjorie. 1979. "Cuba's Attack on Women's Second Shift." In *LAP* 1979, 118–31.

Kish, Kathleen. 1983. "A School for Wives: Women in Eighteenth-Century Spanish Theater." In B. Miller 1983, 184–200.

Klein, Dorie. 1976. "The Etiology of Female Crime: A Review of the Literature." In Crites 1976, 5–31.

Klor de Alva, Jorge. 1982. "Spiritual Conflict and Accommodation in New Spain: Toward a Typology of Aztec Responses to Christianity." In Collier et al. 1982, 345–66.

Knaster, Meri. 1976. "Women in Latin America: The State of Research, 1975." *Latin American Research Review* 11, no. 1: 3–74.

Knight, Alan. 1986. *The Mexican Revolution.* 2 vols. New York: Cambridge University Press.

Kolchin, Peter. 1987. *Unfree Labor: American Slavery and Russian Serfdom.* Cambridge, Mass.: Harvard University Press.

Koonz, Claudia. 1987. *Mothers in the Fatherland: Women, the Family, and Nazi Politics.* New York: St. Martin's.

Krippner-Martínez, James. 1989. "Male Dominance among the Nahua: Traces of Gender Hierarchy in the Writings of Bernardino de Sahagún." Seminar paper. University of Wisconsin, Madison.

———. 1990. "The Politics of Conquest: An Interpretation of the Relación de Michoacán." *Americas* 47, no. 2 (Oct.): 177–98.

Kurz, Demie. 1989. "Social Science Perspectives on Wife Abuse: Current Debates and Future Directions." *Gender and Society* 3, no. 4 (Dec.): 489–505.

Kuznesof, Elizabeth, and Robert Oppenheimer. 1985. "The Family and Society in Nineteenth-Century Latin America: An Historical Introduction." *Journal of Family History* 10, no. 3 (Fall): 215–33.

Ladd, Doris. 1976. *The Mexican Nobility at Independence, 1780–1826.* Austin: University of Texas Press.

———. 1988. *The Making of a Strike: Mexican Silver Workers' Struggles in Real del Monte, 1766–1775.* Lincoln: University of Nebraska Press.

Lafaye, Jacques. 1976. *Quetzalcóatl and Guadalupe: The Formation of Mexican National Consciousness, 1531–1813.* Translated by Benjamin Keen. Chicago: University of Chicago Press.

Lamas, Marta. 1978. "De abandonada a leona: La imagen de la mujer en la canción ranchera." *fem* 6 (Jan.–Mar.): 20–28.

Lancaster, Roger N. 1992. *Life Is Hard: Machismo, Danger, and the Intimacy of Power in Nicaragua*. Berkeley: University of California Press.

Landes, Joan B. 1988. *Women and the Public Sphere in the Age of the French Revolution*. Ithaca: Cornell University Press.

LAP. 1979. *Women in Latin America: An Anthology from Latin American Perspectives*. Riverside, Calif.: Latin American Perspectives.

Larson, Brooke. 1980. "Rural Rhythms of Class Conflict in Eighteenth-Century Cochabamba." *Hispanic American Historical Review* 60, no. 3 (Aug.): 407–30.

————. 1988. *Colonialism and Agrarian Transformation in Bolivia: Cochabamba, 1550–1900*. Princeton: Princeton University Press.

Lavrin, Asunción. 1978a. "In Search of the Colonial Woman in Mexico: The Seventeenth and Eighteenth Centuries." In Lavrin 1978c, 3–22.

————. 1978b. "Some Final Considerations on Trends and Issues in Latin American Women's History." In Lavrin 1978c, 302–32.

————. 1987. "Women, the Family, and Social Change in Latin America." *World Affairs* 150, no. 2 (Fall): 109–28.

————. 1989a. "Introduction: The Scenario, the Actors, and the Issues." In Lavrin 1989d, 1–43.

————. 1989b. "El segundo sexo en México: Experiencia, estudio e introspección, 1983–1987." *Mexican Studies/Estudios Mexicanos* 5, no. 2 (Summer): 297–312.

————. 1989c. "Sexuality in Colonial Mexico: A Church Dilemma." In Lavrin 1989d, 47–95.

————. 1991. "Mexico." In Hawes and Hiner 1991, 421–45.

————, ed. 1978c. *Latin American Women: Historical Perspectives*. Westport, Conn.: Greenwood.

————. 1989d. *Sexuality and Marriage in Colonial Latin America*. Lincoln: University of Nebraska Press.

Lavrin, Asunción, and Edith Couturier. 1979. "Dowries and Wills: A View of Women's Socioeconomic Role in Colonial Guadalajara and Puebla, 1640–1790." *Hispanic American Historical Review* 59, no. 2 (May): 280–304.

Leacock, Eleanor Burke. 1981. *Myths of Male Dominance: Collected Articles on Women Cross-Culturally*. New York: Monthly Review.

Leal, Luís. 1983. "Female Archetypes in Mexican Literature." In B. Miller 1983, 227–42.

León, Fray Luis de. 1583. *La perfecta casada*. Reprint, Mexico City: Editorial Concepto, 1981.

Leonard, Eileen B. 1982. *Women, Crime, and Society: A Critique of Theoretical Criminology*. New York: Longman.

Leonard, Irving A. 1929. *Don Carlos de Sigüenza y Góngora, a Mexican Savant of the Seventeenth Century*. Berkeley: University of California Press.

————. 1959. *Baroque Times in Old Mexico*. Ann Arbor: University of Michigan Press.

Lerner, Gerda. 1986. *The Creation of Patriarchy*. New York: Oxford University Press.

————. 1993. *The Creation of Feminist Consciousness: From the Middle Ages to Eighteen-Seventy*. New York: Oxford University Press.

Lerner, Victoria. 1979. *La educación socialista*. Mexico City: El Colegio de México, 1979.

LeVine, Sarah, with Clara Sunderland Correa. 1993. *Dolor y Alegría: Women and Social Change in Urban Mexico*. Madison: University of Wisconsin Press.

Levinson, David. 1989. *Family Violence in Cross-Cultural Perspective*. Newbury Park, Calif.: Sage.

Lewis, Oscar. 1944. "Social and Economic Changes in a Mexican Village: Tepoztlán, 1926–1944." *América Indigena* 4, no. 4 (Oct.): 281–314.

———. 1951. *Life in a Mexican Village: Tepoztlán Restudied*. Urbana: University of Illinois Press.

———. 1959. *Five Families: Mexican Case Studies in the Culture of Poverty*. New York: Basic Books.

———. 1961. *The Children of Sánchez: Autobiography of a Mexican Family*. New York: Random House.

———. 1964. *Pedro Martínez: A Mexican Peasant and His Family*. New York: Random House.

———. 1966. *La Vida: A Puerto Rican Family in the Culture of Poverty — San Juan and New York*. New York: Random House.

———. 1969. *A Death in the Sánchez Family*. New York: Random House.

Limón, José E. 1986. "La Llorona, the Third Legend of Greater Mexico: Cultural Symbols, Women, and the Political Unconscious." *Renato Rosaldo Lecture Series Monograph* 2 (Spring): 59–93.

Linger, Daniel T. 1990. "Essential Outlines of Crime and Madness: Man-Fights in São Luís." *Cultural Anthropology* 5, no. 1 (Feb.): 62–77.

Lira, Andrés. 1983. *Comunidades indígenas frente a la ciudad de México: Tenochtitlán y Tlatelolco, sus pueblos y barrios, 1812–1919*. Mexico City and Zamora: El Colegio de México y El Colegio de Michoacán.

Lockhart, James. 1968. *Spanish Peru, 1532–1560*. Madison: University of Wisconsin Press.

———. 1972. *The Men of Cajamarca: A Social and Biographical Study of the First Conquerors of Peru*. Austin: University of Texas Press.

———. 1992. *The Nahuas after the Conquest: A Social and Cultural History of the Indians of Central Mexico, Sixteenth through Eighteenth Centuries*. Stanford: Stanford University Press.

Lomnitz, Larissa, and Marisol Pérez Lizaur. 1987. *A Mexican Elite Family, 1820–1980: Kinship, Class, and Culture*. Princeton: Princeton University Press.

Lomnitz-Adler, Claudio. 1982. *Evolución de una sociedad rural*. Mexico City: SEP/Fondo de Cultura Económica.

———. 1984. "La antropología de campo en Morelos, 1930–1983." In Crespo 1984, 395–418.

———. 1991. "Concepts for the Study of Regional Culture." *American Ethnologist* 18, no. 2 (May): 195–214.

López Austin, Alfredo. 1980. *Cuerpo humano e ideología: Las concepciones de los antiguos nahuas*. México: Universidad Nacional Autónoma de México.

———. 1982. "La sexualidad entre los antiguos nahuas." In Seminario de Historia de las Mentalidades 1982, 141–76.

López Monjardín, Adriana. 1985. *Hacia la ciudad capital: México, 1790–1870*. Mexico City: Instituto Nacional de Antropología e Historia.

López-Rey, Manuel. 1970. *Crime: An Analytical Appraisal*. New York: Praeger.

Lynch, John. 1973. *The Spanish American Revolutions, 1808–1826*. New York: Norton.

MacAndrew, Craig, and Robert B. Edgerton. 1969. *Drunken Comportment: A Social Explanation*. Chicago: Aldine.

McCaa, Robert. 1984. "Calidad, Clase, and Marriage in Colonial Mexico: The Case of Parral, 1778–1790." *Hispanic American Historical Review* 64, no. 3 (Aug.): 477–501.

McCaa, Robert, and Stuart B. Schwartz. 1983. "Measuring Marriage Patterns: Percentages, Cohen's Kappa, and Log-Linear Models." *Comparative Studies in Society and History* 25:711–20.

McCaa, Robert, Stuart B. Schwartz, and Arturo Grubessich. 1979. "Race and Class in Colonial Latin America: A Critique." *Comparative Studies in Society and History* 21:421–33.

Maccoby, Michael. 1970. *Social Change and Social Character in Mexico and the United States*. Cuernavaca: Centro Intercultural de Documentación.

Macdonald, Sharon, Pat Holden, and Shirley Ardener, eds. 1987. *Images of Women in Peace and War: Cross-Cultural and Historical Perspectives*. Madison: University of Wisconsin Press.

Macías, Anna. 1982. *Against All Odds: The Feminist Movement in Mexico to 1940*. Westport, Conn.: Greenwood.

McKendrick, Melveena. 1983. "Women against Wedlock: The Reluctant Brides of Golden Age Drama." In B. Miller 1983, 115–46.

MacLachlan, Colin M. 1974. *Criminal Justice in Eighteenth-Century Mexico: A Study of the Tribunal of the Acordada*. Berkeley: University of California Press.

MacLean, Nancy K. 1989. "Behind the Mask of Chivalry: Gender, Race, and Class in the Making of the Ku Klux Klan of the 1920s in Georgia." Ph.D. diss. University of Wisconsin, Madison.

MacLeod, Murdo J. 1989. "Death in Western Colonial Mexico: Its Place in Village and Peasant Life." In Szuchman 1989, 57–73.

Maldonado J., Druzo. 1984. "Producción agrícola en el Morelos prehispánico." In Crespo 1984, 49–72.

Mallon, Florencia E. 1987. "Patriarchy in the Transition to Capitalism: Central Peru, 1830–1950." *Feminist Studies* 13, no. 2 (Summer): 379–407.

————. 1993. "Those Who Keep the Archive Mold the Citizen, If They Live Long Enough." Paper presented at conference, "The State and the Construction of Citizenship," University of California, San Diego, Oct.

————. 1994a. *Peasant and Nation: The Making of Postcolonial Mexico and Peru*. Berkeley: University of California Press.

————. 1994b. "Reflections on the Ruins: Everyday Forms of State Formation in Nineteenth-Century Mexico." In Joseph and Nugent 1994a, 69–106.

Marroquí, José M. 1887. *La llorona: Cuento histórico mexicano*. [Mexico City] (?): Imprenta de I. Cumplido.

Martin, Cheryl English. 1982. "Haciendas and Villages in Late Colonial Morelos." *Hispanic American Historical Review* 62, no. 3 (Aug.): 407–27.

————. 1984. "Historia social del Morelos colonial." In Crespo 1984, 81–93.

————. 1985. *Rural Society in Colonial Morelos*. Albuquerque: University of New Mexico Press.

————. 1990. "Popular Speech and Social Order in Northern Mexico, 1650–1830." *Comparative Studies in Society and History* 32:305–24.

Martin, Joann. 1990. "Motherhood and Power: The Production of a Women's Culture of Politics in a Mexican Community." *American Ethnologist* 17, no. 3 (Aug.): 470–90.

Martínez-Alier, Verena. 1974. *Marriage, Class, and Colour in Nineteenth-Century Cuba: A Study of Racial Attitudes and Sexual Values in a Slave Society*. London: Cambridge University Press.

————. 1989. *Marriage, Class and Colour in Nineteenth-Century Cuba: A Study of Racial Attitudes and Sexual Values in a Slave Society*. 2nd ed. Ann Arbor: University of Michigan Press.

Massolo, Alejandra. 1992. *Por amor y coraje: Mujeres en movimientos urbanos de la ciudad de México*. Mexico City: El Colegio de México.

Mastretta, Angeles. 1985. *Arráncame la vida*. Mexico City: Océano.

Mathews, Holly F. 1982. "Sexual Status in Oaxaca, Mexico: An Analysis of the Relationship between Extradomestic Participation and Ideological Constructs of Gender." Ph.D. diss. Duke University.

————. 1985. "'We Are Mayordomo': A Reinterpretation of Women's Roles in the Mexican Cargo System." *American Ethnologist* 12, no. 2 (May): 285–301.

Medick, Hans, and David W. Sabean, eds. 1984. *Interest and Emotion: Essays on the Study of Family and Kinship*. New York: Cambridge University Press and Fondation de la Maison des Sciences de l'Homme.

Meillassoux, Claude. 1977. *Mujeres, graneros y capitales: Economía doméstica y capitalismo*. Mexico City: Siglo XXI.

Menchú, Rigoberta. 1984. *I . . . Rigoberta Menchú: An Indian Woman in Guatemala*. New York: Verso.

Menéndez, Eduardo L. 1988. "Alcoholismo, grupos étnicos mexicanos y los padecimientos denominados 'tradicionales.'" *Nueva Antropología* 10, no. 34 (Nov.): 55–81.

Merrim, Stephanie, ed. 1991. *Feminist Perspectives on Sor Juana Inés de la Cruz*. Detroit: Wayne State University Press.

Messerschmidt, James W. 1986. *Capitalism, Patriarchy, and Crime: Towards a Socialist Feminist Criminology*. Totowa, N.J.: Rowman and Littlefield.

————. 1993. *Masculinities and Crime: Critique and Reconceptualization of Theory*. Lanham, Md.: Rowman and Littlefield.

Metcalf, Alida C. 1986. "Fathers and Sons: The Politics of Inheritance in a Colonial Brazilian Township." *Hispanic American Historical Review* 66, no. 3 (Aug.): 455–84.

Miller, Beth, ed. 1983. *Women in Hispanic Literature: Icons and Fallen Idols*. Berkeley: University of California Press.

Miller, Francesca. 1991. *Latin American Women and the Search for Social Justice*. Hanover, N.H.: University of New England Press.

Mintz, Sidney W. 1974. "The Rural Proletariat and the Problem of Rural Proletarian Consciousness." *Journal of Peasant Studies* 1, no. 3 (Apr.): 291–325.

Mintz, Sidney W., and Richard Price. 1976. *An Anthropological Approach to the Afro-American Past: A Caribbean Perspective*. Philadelphia: Institute for the Study of Human Issues.

Monsiváis, Carlos. 1979. "Sexismo en la literatura mexicana." In Urrutia 1979, 102–25.

————. 1980. "La mujer en la cultura mexicana." In Guerra-Cunningham 1980, 101–17.

————. 1981. "¿Pero hubo alguna vez once mil machos?" *fem* 18 (Apr.–May): 9–20.

————. 1987. *Entrada libre: Crónicas de una sociedad que se organiza*. Mexico City: Ediciones Era.

————. 1988. *Escenas de pudor y liviandad*. Mexico City: Grijalbo.

Moraga, Cherríe, and Gloria Anzaldúa, eds. 1983. *This Bridge Called My Back: Writings by Radical Women of Color*. 2nd ed. New York: Kitchen Table Press.

Morales, María Dolores. 1976. "Estructura urbana y distribución de la propiedad en la ciudad de México en 1813." *Historia mexicana* 25, no. 3 (Jan.–Mar.): 363–402.

Moreno Toscano, Alejandra, ed. 1978. *Cuidad de México: Ensayo de construcción de una historia*. Mexico City: Instituto Nacional de Antropología e Historia.

Morse, Richard M. 1954. "Toward a Theory of Spanish American Government." *Journal of the History of Ideas* 15, no. 1 (Jan.): 71–93.

————. 1964. "The Heritage of Latin America." In Hartz et al. 1964, 123–77.

Mouffe, Chantal, and Ernesto Laclau. 1985. *Hegemony and Socialist Strategy: Towards a Radical Democratic Politics*. London: Verso.

Mueller, John H., Karl F. Schuessler, and Herbert L. Costner. 1977. *Statistical Reasoning in Sociology*. 3rd ed. Boston: Houghton Mifflin.

Mummert, Gail. 1994. "From Metate to Despate: Rural Mexican Women's Salaried Labor and the Redefinition of Gendered Spaces and Roles." In Fowler-Salamini and Vaughan 1994, 192–209.

Muriel, Josefina. 1946. *Conventos de monjas en la Nueva España.* 2 vols. Mexico City: Editorial Santiago.

———. 1963. *Las indias caciques de Corpus Christi.* Mexico City: Universidad Nacional Autónoma de México.

———. 1974. *Los recogimientos de mujeres: Respuesta a una problemática social novohispana.* Mexico City: Universidad Nacional Autónoma de México.

———. 1982. *Cultura femenina novohispana.* Mexico City: Universidad Nacional Autónoma de México.

Nader, Laura. 1964. *Talea and Juquila: A Comparison of Zapotec Social Organization.* Berkeley: University of California Press.

———. 1989. "The Crown, the Colonists, and the Course of Zapotec Village Law." In Starr and Collier 1989, 320–44.

———. 1990. *Harmony Ideology: Justice and Control in a Zapotec Mountain Village.* Stanford: Stanford University Press.

Nash, June. 1980. "Aztec Women: The Transition from Status to Class in Empire and Colony." In Etienne and Leacock 1980, 134–48.

Navarro, Marysa. 1979. "Research on Latin American Women." *Signs* 5, no. 1 (Autumn): 111–20.

———. 1981. *Evita.* Buenos Aires: Ed. Corregidor.

———. 1982. "Evita's Charismatic Leadership." In Conniff 1982, 47–66.

———. 1988. "The Personal Is Political: Las Madres de Plaza de Mayo." In Eckstein 1988, 241–58.

Nizza da Silva, Maria Beatriz. 1984. *Sistema de casamiento no Brasil colonial.* São Paulo: T. A. Queiroz.

———. 1989. "Divorce in Colonial Brazil: The Case of São Paulo." In Lavrin 1989d, 313–40.

Novick, Peter. 1988. *That Noble Dream: The 'Objectivity Question' and the American Historical Profession.* New York: Cambridge University Press.

O'Brien, Mary. 1981. *The Politics of Reproduction.* Boston: Routledge and Kegan Paul.

O'Brien, Patricia. 1989. "Michel Foucault's History of Culture." In Hunt 1989, 25–46.

Offen, Karen. 1988. "Defining Feminism: A Comparative Historical Approach." *Signs* 14, no. 1 (Autumn): 119–57.

O'Malley, Ilene V. 1986. *The Myth of the Revolution: Hero Cults and the Institutionalization of the Mexican State, 1920–1940.* Westport, Conn.: Greenwood.

Orlove, Benjamin S. 1988. "A Stranger in Her Father's House: Juanita's Suicide." In Weil 1988, 161–201.

Ortega Noriega, Sergio, ed. 1986a. *De la santidad a la perversión, o de porqué no se cumplía la ley de Dios en la sociedad novohispana.* Mexico City: Grijalbo.

———. 1986b. "Teología novohispana sobre el matrimonio y comportamientos sexuales, 1519–1570." In Ortega Noriega 1986a, 19–47.

Ortner, Sherry B. 1974. "Is Female to Male as Nature Is to Culture?" In Rosaldo and Lamphere 1974, 67–87.

Paddock, John. 1975. "Studies on Antiviolent and 'Normal' Communities." *Aggressive Behavior* 1, no. 3: 217–33.

Palmer, Colin A. 1976. *Slaves of the White God: Blacks in Mexico, 1570–1650.* Cambridge: Harvard University Press.

Parnell, Philip C. 1988. *Escalating Disputes: Social Participation and Change in the Oaxacan Highlands.* Tucson: University of Arizona Press.

Parsons, Elsie Clews. 1936. *Mitla, Town of the Souls . . . .* Chicago: University of Chicago Press.

Pastor, Rodolfo. 1981. "Campesinos y reformas: La mixteca, 1748–1856." Ph.D. diss. El Colegio de México.

———. 1987. *Campesinos y reformas: La mixteca, 1700–1856*. Mexico City: El Colegio de México.

Pastor, Rodolfo, Lief Adleson, Erika Berra, Flor Hurtado, Josefina MacGregor, and Guillermo Zermeño. 1979. *Fluctuaciones económicas en Oaxaca durante el siglo XVIII*. Mexico City: El Colegio de México.

Paz, Octavio. 1959. *El laberinto de la soledad*. 1950. 2nd rev. ed., Mexico City: Fondo de Cultura Económica.

———. 1976. "Foreword: The Flight of Quetzalcóatl and the Quest for Legitimacy." In Lafaye 1976, ix–xxii.

———. 1982. *Sor Juana Inés de la Cruz, o, las trampas de la fé*. Barcelona: Seix Barral.

Peden, Margaret Sayers, ed. and trans. 1987. *A Woman of Genius: The Intellectual Autobiography of Sor Juana Inés de la Cruz*. 2nd ed. Salisbury: Lime Rock Press.

Pérez, Emma Marie. 1988. "Through Her Love and Sweetness: Women, Revolution, and Reform in Yucatán, 1910–1918." Ph.D. diss. University of California, Los Angeles.

Peristiany, J. G., ed. 1966. *Honour and Shame: The Values of Mediterranean Society*. Chicago: University of Chicago Press.

Perry, Mary Elizabeth. 1980. *Crime and Society in Early Modern Seville*. Hanover, N.H.: University Press of New England.

———. 1985. "Deviant Insiders: Legalized Prostitutes and a Consciousness of Women in Early Modern Seville." *Comparative Studies in Society and History* 27:138–58.

———. 1990. *Gender and Disorder in Early Modern Seville*. Princeton: Princeton University Press.

Pescatello, Ann M., ed. 1973. *Female and Male in Latin America: Essays*. Pittsburgh: University of Pittsburgh Press.

———. 1976. *Power and Pawn: The Female in Iberian Families, Societies, and Cultures*. Westport, Conn.: Greenwood.

Phelan, John Leddy. 1967. *The Kingdom of Quito in the Seventeenth Century: Bureaucratic Politics in the Spanish Empire*. Madison: University of Wisconsin Press.

———. 1978. *The People and the King: The Comunero Revolution in Colombia, 1781*. Madison: University of Wisconsin Press.

Phillips, Rachel. 1983. "Marina/Malinche." In B. Miller 1983, 97–114.

Pinchon, Edgcumb. 1933. *Viva Villa! A Recovery of the Real Pancho Villa . . . .* New York: Harcourt, Brace, Jovanovich.

Pitt-Rivers, Julian. 1966. "Honour and Social Status." In Peristiany 1966, 19–77.

———. 1971. *The People of the Sierra*. 1954. 2nd ed. Chicago: University of Chicago Press.

———. 1977. *The Fate of Shechem, or the Politics of Sex: Essays in the Anthropology of the Mediterranean*. Cambridge: Cambridge University Press.

Plumb, J. H. 1985. "Spreading the News." *New York Review of Books*, Jan. 17, pp. 26, 31–32.

Polémica. 1980. "Polémica: El caso de las mujeres y la Laguna." *fem* 13 (Mar.–Apr.): 85–87.

Poniatowska, Elena. 1969. *Hasta no verte, Jesús mio*. Mexico City: Ediciones Era.

Preston, James J., ed. 1982. *Mother Worship: Themes and Variations*. Chapel Hill: University of North Carolina Press.

Price, Richard. 1990. *Alabi's World*. Baltimore: Johns Hopkins University Press.

Priestley, Herbert Ingram. 1916. *José de Gálvez, Visitor-General of New Spain, 1765–1771*. Berkeley: University of California Press.

Purcell, Susan Kaufman. 1973. "Modernizing Women for a Modern Society: The Cuban Case." In Pescatello 1973, 257–71.

Rabinow, Paul. 1984. Introduction to Foucault 1984, 3–29.

Radku, Verena. 1986. "Hacia una historiografía de la mujer." *Nueva Antropología* 8, no. 30 (Nov.): 77–94.

Ramírez, Santiago. 1959. *El mexicano: Psicología de sus motivaciones*. 2nd ed. Mexico City: Editorial Pax-México.

Ramos, Samuel. 1934. *El perfil del hombre y la cultura en México*. Mexico City: Imprenta Mundial.

Ramos Escandón, Carmen. 1987a. "Señoritas porfirianas: Mujer e ideología en el México progresista, 1880–1910." In Ramos Escandón 1987b, 143–61.

———, ed. 1987b. *Presencia y transparencia: La mujer en la historia de México*. Mexico City: El Colegio de México.

Randall, Margaret. 1979. "'We Need a Government of Men and Women . . . !' Notes on the Second National Congress . . . ." In *LAP* 1979, 132–38.

———. 1992. *Gathering Rage: The Failure of Twentieth-Century Revolutions to Develop a Feminist Agenda*. New York: Monthly Review Press.

Rascón, María Antonieta. 1979. "La mujer y la lucha social." In Urrutia 1979, 139–74.

Redfield, Robert. 1930. *Tepoztlán, a Mexican Village*. Chicago: University of Chicago Press.

Reed, John. 1914. *Insurgent Mexico*. Reprint, New York: International Pub., 1969.

Reina, Leticia. 1988a. "De las reformas borbónicas a las leyes de Reforma." In Reina 1988b, 1:181–268.

———, ed. 1988b. *Historia de la cuestión agraria mexicana: Estado de Oaxaca*. 2 vols. Mexico City: Juan Pablos Editor et al.

Reiter, Rayna R., ed. 1975. *Toward an Anthropology of Women*. New York: Monthly Review Press.

Reynolds, H. T. 1977. *The Analysis of Cross-Classifications*. New York: Free Press.

Ricard, Robert. 1966. *The Spiritual Conquest of Mexico: An Essay on the Apostolate and the Evangelizing Methods of the Mendicant Orders in New Spain, 1523–1572*. Translated by Lesley Byrd Simpson. Berkeley: University of California Press.

Rico, José M. 1981. *Crimen y justicia en América Latina*. 2nd rev. ed. Mexico City: Siglo XXI.

Rigdon, Susan M. 1988. *The Culture Facade: Art, Science, and Politics in the Work of Oscar Lewis*. Urbana: University of Illinois Press.

Riley, G. Michael. 1973. *Fernando Cortés and the Marquesado in Morelos, 1522–1547*. Albuquerque: University of New Mexico Press.

Rípodas Ardanaz, Daisy. 1977. *El matrimonio en Indias: Realidad social y regulación jurídica*. Buenos Aires: Fundación para la Educación, la Ciencia y la Cultura.

Rodríguez Lazcano, Catalina. 1984. "Los pueblos del área de Cuautla en el siglo XVIII." In Crespo 1984, 95–105.

Romanucci-Ross, Lola. 1986. *Conflict, Violence, and Morality in a Mexican Village*. Rev. ed. Chicago: University of Chicago Press.

Romero Frizzi, María de los Angeles. 1979. "Los intereses españoles en la mixteca, siglo XVII." *Historia mexicana* 29, no. 2 (Oct.–Dec.): 241–51.

———. 1983. "Evolución económica de la Mixteca Alta, siglo XVII." *Historia mexicana* 32, no. 4 (Apr.–June): 496–523.

———. 1985. "Economía y vida de los españoles en la Mixteca Alta, 1519–1720." Ph.D. diss. Universidad Iberoamericana, México.

———. 1988. "Epoca colonial, 1519–1785." In Reina 1988b, 1:107–79.

Rosaldo, Michelle Zimbalist. 1974. "Women, Culture, and Society: A Theoretical Overview." In Rosaldo and Lamphere 1974, 17–42.

———. 1980. "The Use and Abuse of Anthropology: Reflections on Feminism and Cross-Cultural Understanding." *Signs* 5, no. 3 (Spring): 389–417.

Rosaldo, Michelle Zimbalist, and Louise Lamphere, eds. 1974. *Women, Culture, and Society.* Stanford: Stanford University Press.

Roseberry, William. 1989. *Anthropologies and Histories: Essays in Culture, History, and Political Economy.* New Brunswick, N.J.: Rutgers University Press.

Rossiaud, Jacques. 1978. "Prostitution, Youth, and Society in the Towns of Southeastern France in the Fifteenth Century." In Forster and Ranum 1978, 1–46.

Rounds, J. 1979. "Lineage, Class, and Power in the Aztec State." *American Ethnologist* 6, no. 1 (Feb.): 73–86.

Rubin, Gayle. 1975. "The Traffic in Women: Notes on the 'Political Economy' of Sex." In Reiter 1975, 157–210.

Rueda Smithers, Salvador. 1984. "La dinámica interna del zapatismo: Consideración para el estudio de la cotidianeidad campesina en el área zapatista." In Crespo 1984, 224–49.

Ruggiero, Guido. 1975. "Sexual Criminality in the Early Renaissance: Venice, 1338–1358." *Journal of Social History* 8, no. 4: 18–37.

———. 1979. *Violence in Early Renaissance Venice.* New Brunswick, N.J.: Rutgers University Press.

———. 1985. *The Boundaries of Eros: Sex Crime and Sexuality in Renaissance Venice.* New York: Oxford University Press.

Rus, Jan. 1994. "The 'Comunidad Revolucionaria Institucional': The Subversion of Native Government in Highland Chiapas, 1936–1968." In Joseph and Nugent 1994a, 265–300.

Rus, Jan, and Wasserstrom, Robert. 1980. "Civil-Religious Hierarchies in Central Chiapas: A Critical Perspective." *American Ethnologist* 7, no. 3 (Aug.): 466–78.

Russell, Diana. 1975. *The Politics of Rape: The Victim's Perspective.* New York: Stein and Day.

———. 1982. *Rape in Marriage.* New York: Macmillan.

———. 1984. *Sexual Exploitation: Rape, Child Sexual Abuse, and Workplace Harassment.* Beverly Hills: Sage.

Sabean, David Warren. 1984. *Power in the Blood: Popular Culture and Village Discourse in Early Modern Germany.* London: Cambridge University Press.

———. 1990. *Property, Production, and Family in Neckarhausen, 1700–1870.* New York: Cambridge University Press.

Sacks, Karen Brodkin. 1974. "Engels Revisited: Women, the Organization of Production, and Private Property." In Rosaldo and Lamphere 1974, 207–22.

———. 1989. "Toward a Unified Theory of Class, Race, and Gender." *American Ethnologist* 16, no. 3 (Aug.): 534–50.

Said, Edward. 1978. *Orientalism.* New York: Pantheon.

———. 1993. *Culture and Imperialism.* New York: Knopf.

Salas, Elizabeth. 1990. *Soldaderas in the Mexican Military: Myth and History.* Austin: University of Texas Press.

Sanderson, Steven. 1986. *The Transformation of Mexican Agriculture: International Structure and the Politics of Rural Change.* Princeton: Princeton University Press.

Sarabia Viejo, María. 1972. *El juego de gallos en Nueva España.* Seville: Escuela de Estudios Hispanoamericanos de Sevilla.

Sargent, Lydia, ed. 1981. *Women and Revolution: A Discussion of the Unhappy Marriage of Marxism and Feminism.* Boston: South End Press.

Scardaville, Michael C. 1977. "Crime and the Urban Poor: Mexico City in the Late Colonial Period." Ph.D. diss. University of Florida.

———. 1980. "Alcohol Abuse and Tavern Reform in Late Colonial Mexico." *Hispanic American Historical Review* 60, no. 4 (Nov.): 643–71.

Scharrer Tamm, Beatriz. 1984. "La tecnología en la industria azucarera: La molienda." In Crespo 1984, 115–27.

Schneider, Jane. 1971. "Of Vigilance and Virgins: Honor, Shame, and Access to Resources in Mediterranean Societies." *Ethnology* 10, no. 1 (Jan.): 1–24.

Schochet, Gordon J. 1975. *Patriarchalism in Political Thought: The Authoritarian Family and Political Speculation and Attitudes, Especially in Seventeenth-Century England.* Oxford: Basil Blackwell.

Schutte, Ofelia. 1988–89. "Philosophy and Feminism in Latin America: Perspectives on Gender Identity and Culture." *Philosophical Forum* 20, no. 1–2 (Fall–Winter): 62–84.

Schwartz, Stuart B. 1985. *Sugar Plantations in the Formation of Brazilian Society: Bahia, 1550–1835.* New York: Cambridge University Press.

Schwendinger, Julia R., and Herman Schwendinger. 1983. *Rape and Inequality.* Beverly Hills: Sage.

Scott, James C. 1985. *Weapons of the Weak: Everyday Forms of Peasant Resistance.* New Haven: Yale University Press.

———. 1990. *Domination and the Arts of Resistance: Hidden Transcripts.* New Haven: Yale University Press.

Scott, Joan Wallach. 1986. "Gender: A Useful Category of Historical Analysis." *American Historical Review* 91, no. 5 (Dec.): 1053–75.

———. 1988. *Gender and the Politics of History.* New York: Columbia University Press.

Seed, Patricia. 1982. "Social Dimensions of Race: Mexico City, 1753." *Hispanic American Historical Review* 62, no. 4 (Nov.): 569–606.

———. 1983. "Across the Pages with Estate and Class." *Comparative Studies in Society and History* 25:721–24.

———. 1985. "The Church and the Patriarchal Family: Marriage Conflicts in Sixteenth- and Seventeenth-Century New Spain." *Journal of Family History* 10, no. 3 (Fall): 284–93.

———. 1988a. "Marriage Promises and the Value of a Woman's Testimony in Colonial Mexico." *Signs* 13, no. 2 (Winter): 253–76.

———. 1988b. *To Love, Honor, and Obey in Colonial Mexico: Conflicts over Marriage Choice, 1574–1821.* Stanford: Stanford University Press.

———, with P. Rust. 1983. "Estate and Class in Colonial Oaxaca Revisited." *Comparative Studies in Society and History* 25:703–10.

Segovia, Tomás. 1979. "Carta prólogo a Elena Urrutia." In Urrutia 1979, 7–43.

Seminario de Historia Urbana. 1974–76. *Investigaciones sobre la historia de la Ciudad de México.* 2 vols. Mexico City: Instituto Nacional de Antropología e Historia.

Seminario de Historia de las Mentalidades. 1980. *Seis ensayos sobre el discurso colonial relativo a la comunidad doméstica.* Mexico City: Instituto Nacional de Antropología e Historia.

———. 1982. *Familia y sexualidad en Nueva España.* Mexico City: Fondo de Cultura Económica.

———. 1987. *El placer de pecar y el afán de normar.* Mexico City: Joaquín Mortiz/Instituto Nacional de Antropología e Historia.

———. 1991. *Familia y poder en Nueva España.* Mexico City: Instituto Nacional de Antropología e Historia.

Seminar on Feminism and Culture in Latin America. 1990. *Women, Culture, and Politics in Latin America.* Berkeley: University of California Press.

Shanley, Mary Lyndon. 1982. "Marriage Contract and Social Contract in Seventeenth-Century English Political Thought." In Elshtain 1982, 80–95.

Sharpe, J. A. 1982. "The History of Crime in Late Medieval and Early Modern England: A Review of the Field." *Social History* 7, no. 2 (May): 187–203.

———. 1984. *Crime in Early Modern England, 1550–1750.* New York: Longman.

———. 1985. "'Last Dying Speeches': Religion, Ideology, and Public Execution in Seventeenth-Century England." *Past and Present* 107 (May): 144–67.

Shaw, Brent D. 1987. "The Family in Late Antiquity: The Experience of Augustine." *Past and Present* 115 (May): 3–51.

Sherman, William L. 1979. *Forced Native Labor in Sixteenth-Century Central America.* Lincoln: University of Nebraska Press.

Sider, Gerald. 1987. "When Parrots Learn to Talk, and Why They Can't: Domination, Deception, and Self-Deception in Indian-White Relations." *Comparative Studies in Society and History* 29:3–23.

Silverblatt, Irene. 1980. "'The Universe has turned inside out. . . . There is no justice for us here': Andean Women under Spanish Rule." In Etienne and Leacock 1980, 149–85.

———. 1987. *Moon, Sun, and Witches: Gender Ideologies and Class in Inca and Colonial Peru.* Princeton: Princeton University Press.

———. 1988. "Women in States." *Annual Review of Anthropology* 17:427–60.

Simpson, Lesley Byrd. 1941. *Many Mexicos.* New York: G. P. Putnam's Sons.

Slater, Philip Elliot. 1968. *The Glory of Hera: Greek Mythology and the Greek Family.* Boston: Beacon Press.

Smart, Carol. 1976. *Women, Crime, and Criminology: A Feminist Critique.* London: Routledge and Kegan Paul.

Smith, Peter H. 1979. *Labyrinths of Power: Political Recruitment in Twentieth-Century Mexico.* Princeton: Princeton University Press.

Smith, Raymond T., ed. 1984. *Kinship Ideology and Practice in Latin America.* Chapel Hill: University of North Carolina Press.

Socolow, Susan M. 1980. "Women and Crime: Buenos Aires, 1757–97." *Journal of Latin American Studies* 12, no. 1 (May): 39–54.

Soeiro, Susan A. 1978. "The Feminine Orders in Colonial Bahia, Brazil: Economic, Social, and Demographic Implications, 1677–1800." In Lavrin 1978c, 173–97.

Solana, Fernando, Raúl Cardiel Reyes, and Raúl Bolaños. 1982. *Historia de la educación pública en México.* 2 vols. Mexico City: Fondo de Cultura Económica.

Sotelo Inclán, Jesús. 1943. *Raíz y razón de Zapata.* Mexico City: Editorial Etnos.

———. 1982. "La educación socialista." In Solana et al. 1982, 1:234–326.

Soto, Shirlene Ann. 1979. *The Mexican Woman: A Study of Her Participation in the Revolution, 1910–1940.* Palo Alto: R&E Research Associates.

———. 1986. "Tres modelos culturales: La Virgen de Guadalupe, la Malinche y la Llorona." *fem* 48 (Oct.–Nov.): 13–16.

Soy. 1985. "Soy *patriarca* no cacique, dice Leobardo Reynoso." *La Jornada,* June 16, 1, 4.

Spalding, Karen. 1970. "Social Climbers: Changing Patterns of Mobility among the Indians of Colonial Peru." *Hispanic American Historical Review* 50, no. 4 (Nov.): 645–64.

———. 1973. "*Kurakas* and Commerce: A Chapter in the Evolution of Andean Society." *Hispanic American Historical Review* 53, no. 4 (Nov.): 581–99.

———. 1984. *Huarochirí: An Andean Society under Inca and Spanish Rule.* Stanford: Stanford University Press.

———, ed. 1982. *Essays in the Political, Economic, and Social History of Colonial Latin America.* Newark, Del.: Latin American Studies Program.

Spores, Ronald. 1967. *The Mixtec Kings and Their People.* Norman: University of Oklahoma Press.

———. 1984. *The Mixtecs in Ancient and Colonial Times.* Norman: University of Oklahoma Press.

Spores, Ronald, and Ross Hassig, eds. 1984. *Five Centuries of Law and Politics in Central Mexico.* Nashville: Vanderbilt University Press.

Stacey, Judith. 1983. *Patriarchy and Socialist Revolution in China.* Berkeley: University of California Press.

Stansell, Christine. 1986. *City of Women: Sex and Class in New York, 1789–1860.* New York: Knopf.

Starr, June, and Jane F. Collier, eds. 1989. *History and Power in the Study of Law: New Directions in Legal Anthropology.* Ithaca: Cornell University Press.

Steele, Cynthia. 1992. *Politics, Gender, and the Mexican Novel, 1968–1988: Beyond the Pyramid.* Austin: University of Texas Press.

Steinmetz, Suzanne, and Murray A. Straus, eds. 1975. *Violence in the Family.* New York: Dodd, Mead.

Stephen, Lynn. 1992. *Zapotec Women.* Austin: University of Texas Press.

Stern, Steve J. 1982. *Peru's Indian Peoples and the Challenge of Spanish Conquest: Huamanga to 1640.* Madison: University of Wisconsin Press.

————. 1983. "The Struggle for Solidarity: Class, Culture, and Community in Highland Indian America." *Radical History Review* 27:21–45.

————. 1987a. "New Approaches to the Study of Peasant Rebellion and Consciousness: Implications of the Andean Experience." In Stern 1987b, 3–25.

————. 1988a. "'Ever More Solitary.'" *American Historical Review* 93, no. 4 (Oct.): 886–97.

————. 1988b. "Feudalism, Capitalism, and the World-System in the Perspective of Latin America and the Caribbean." *American Historical Review* 93, no. 4 (Oct.): 829–72.

————. 1992. "Paradigms of Conquest: History, Historiography, and Politics." *Journal of Latin American Studies* 24 (Quincent. supplement): 1–34.

————. 1993. "Africa, Latin America, and the Splintering of Historical Knowledge: From Fragmentation to Reverberation." In Cooper et al. 1993, 3–20.

————, ed. 1987b. *Resistance, Rebellion, and Consciousness in the Andean Peasant World, Eighteenth to Twentieth Centuries.* Madison: University of Wisconsin Press.

Stolcke, Verena. 1984. "The Exploitation of Family Morality: Labor Systems and Family Structure in São Paulo, 1850–1979." In R. Smith 1984, 264–96.

————. 1989. "Introduction to the Second Edition." In Martínez-Alier 1989, xi–xix.

Stone, Lawrence. 1977. *The Family, Sex, and Marriage in England, 1500–1800.* New York: Harper and Row.

————. 1983. "Interpersonal Violence in English Society, 1300–1980." *Past and Present* 101 (Nov.): 22–33.

Stoner, K. Lynn. 1987. "Directions in Latin American Women's History, 1977–1984." *Latin American Research Review* 22, no. 2: 101–34.

Straus, Murray A., Richard Gelles, and Suzanne Steinmetz. 1980. *Behind Closed Doors: Violence in the American Family.* Garden City, N.Y.: Anchor.

Szuchman, Mark D., ed. 1989. *The Middle Period in Latin America: Values and Attitudes in the Seventeenth to Nineteenth Centuries.* Boulder: Lynne Rienner.

Taylor, William B. 1972. *Landlord and Peasant in Colonial Oaxaca.* Stanford: Stanford University Press.

————. 1974. "Landed Society in New Spain: A View from the South." *Hispanic American Historical Review* 54, no. 3 (Aug.): 387–413.

————. 1979. *Drinking, Homicide, and Rebellion in Colonial Mexican Villages.* Stanford: Stanford University Press.

————. 1984. "Conflict and Balance in District Politics: Tecali and the Sierra Norte de Puebla in the Eighteenth Century." In Spores and Hassig 1984, 87–106.

————. 1987. "The Virgin of Guadalupe in New Spain: An Inquiry into the Social History of Marian Devotion." *American Ethnologist* 14, no. 1 (Feb.): 9–33.

————. 1988. "Banditry and Insurrection: Rural Unrest in Central Jalisco, 1790–1816." In Katz 1988b, 205–46.

Tibón, Gutierre. 1981. *Pinotepa nacional: Mixtecos, negros y triques*. 3rd ed. Mexico City: Editorial Posada.

Tirado, Thomás C. 1991. *Celsa's World: Conversations with a Mexican Peasant Woman*. Tempe: Center for Latin American Studies, Arizona State University.

Tomes, Nancy. 1978. "A 'Torrent of Abuse': Crimes of Violence between Working-Class Men and Women in London, 1840–1875." *Journal of Social History* 11, no. 3: 328–45.

Tuñón, Enriqueta. 1987. "La lucha política de la mujer mexicana por el derecho al sufragio y sus repercusiones." In Ramos Escandón 1987b, 181–89.

Tuñón Pablos, Julia. 1987. *Mujeres en México: Una historia olvidada*. Mexico City: Planeta.

Turner, Victor. 1974. *Dramas, Fields, and Metaphors: Symbolic Action in Human Society*. Ithaca: Cornell University Press.

Tutino, John. 1983. "Power, Class, and Family: Men and Women in the Mexican Elite, 1750–1810." *Americas* 39, no. 3 (Jan.): 359–81.

———. 1986. *From Insurrection to Revolution in Mexico: Social Bases of Agrarian Violence, 1750–1940*. Princeton: Princeton University Press.

Twinam, Ann. 1989. "Honor, Sexuality, and Illegitimacy in Colonial Spanish America." In Lavrin 1989d, 118–55.

Urrutia, Elena, ed. 1979. *Imagen y realidad de la mujer*. Mexico City: Sepdiana.

Vanderwood, Paul. 1987. "Building Blocks but Yet No Building: Regional History and the Mexican Revolution." *Mexican Studies/Estudios Mexicanos* 3, no. 2 (Summer): 421–32.

Van Young, Eric. 1981. *Hacienda and Market in Eighteenth-Century Mexico: The Rural Economy of the Guadalajara Region, 1675–1820*. Berkeley: University of California Press.

———. 1983. "Mexican Rural History since Chevalier: The Historiography of the Colonial Hacienda." *Latin American Research Review* 18, no. 3: 5–61.

———. 1986. "The Age of Paradox: Mexican Agriculture at the End of the Colonial Period, 1750–1810." In Jacobsen and Puhle 1986, 64–90.

———. 1992a. "Introduction: Are Regions Good to Think?" In Van Young 1992b, 1–36.

———, ed. 1992b. *Mexico's Regions: Comparative History and Development*. La Jolla: University of California Center for U.S.–Mexican Studies.

Vaughan, Mary Kay. 1982. *The State, Education, and Social Classes in Mexico, 1880–1928*. DeKalb: Northern Illinois University Press.

Villanueva, Margaret A. 1985. "From Calpixqui to Corregidor: Appropriation of Women's Cotton Textile Production in Early Colonial Mexico." *Latin American Perspectives* 12, no. 1 (Winter): 17–40.

Viotta da Costa, Emilia. 1985. *The Brazilian Empire: Myths and Histories*. Chicago: University of Chicago Press.

Viqueira Albán, Juan Pedro. 1987. *¿Relajados o reprimidos? Diversiones públicas y vida social en la ciudad de México durante el Siglo de las Luces*. Mexico City: Fondo de Cultura Económica.

Vives, Juan Luis. 1523. *Formación de la mujer cristiana*. In *Obras completas*, translated by Lorenzo Riber. 2 vols. Madrid: M. Aguilar, 1947–48, 1:985–1352.

Von Mentz, Brígida. 1984. "La región morelense en la primera mitad del siglo XIX: Fuentes e hipótesis de trabajo." In Crespo 1984, 131–47.

———. 1988. *Pueblos de indios, mulatos y mestizos, 1770–1870: Los campesinos y las transformaciones protoindustriales en el poniente de Morelos*. Mexico City: Casa Chata.

Von Wobeser, Gisela. 1983. "El uso del agua en la región de Cuernavaca: Cuautla durante la época colonial." *Historia mexicana* 32, no. 4 (Apr.–June): 467–95.

———. 1984. "Las haciendas azucareras de Cuernavaca y Cuautla en la época colonial." In Crespo 1984, 107–13.

Walker, Lenore E. 1983. "The Battered Woman Syndrome Study." In Finkelhor et al. 1983, 31–48.

Walters, Ronald G. 1980. "Signs of the Times: Clifford Geertz and Historians." *Social Research* 47, no. 3 (Autumn): 537–56.

Warman, Arturo. 1976. . . . *Y venimos a contradecir: Los campesinos de Morelos y el estado nacional.* Mexico City: Casa Chata.

———. 1980. *Ensayos sobre el campesinado en México.* Mexico City: Nueva Imagen.

———. 1988. "The Political Project of Zapatismo." In Katz 1988b, 321–37.

Weil, Connie, ed. 1988. *Lucha: The Struggles of Latin American Women.* Minneapolis: Prisma Institute, Minnesota Latin American Series.

Whitecotton, Joseph W. 1977. *The Zapotecs: Princes, Priests, and Peasants.* Norman: University of Oklahoma Press.

Wolf, Eric R. 1957. "Closed Corporate Peasant Communities in Mesoamerica and Central Java." *Southwestern Journal of Anthropology* 13, no. 1 (Spring): 1–18.

———. 1958. "The Virgin of Guadalupe: A Mexican National Symbol." *Journal of American Folklore* 71:34–39.

———. 1959. *Sons of the Shaking Earth: The People of Mexico and Guatemala—Their Land, History, and Culture.* Chicago: University of Chicago Press.

———. 1986. "The Vicissitudes of the Closed Corporate Peasant Community." *American Ethnologist* 13, no. 2 (May): 325–29.

Wolf, Eric, and Hansen, Edward C. 1972. *The Human Condition in Latin America.* New York: Oxford University Press.

Wolfgang, Marvin. 1958. *Patterns in Criminal Homicide.* Philadelphia: University of Pennsylvania Press.

———, ed. 1967. *Studies in Homicide.* New York: Harper and Row.

Wolfgang, Marvin, and Franco Ferracuti. 1967. *The Subculture of Violence: Towards an Integrated Theory in Criminology.* London: Tavistock.

Womack, John, Jr. 1968. *Zapata and the Mexican Revolution.* New York: Vintage.

Ylló, Kersti, and Michele Bograd, eds. 1988. *Feminist Perspectives on Wife Abuse.* Beverly Hills: Sage.

Young, Kathleen Z. 1989. "The Imperishable Virginity of Saint Maria Goretti." *Gender and Society* 3, no. 4 (Dec.): 474–82.

Zavala, Silvio. 1944. "Orígenes coloniales del peonaje en México." *El Trimestre Económico* 10, no. 4 (Jan.–Mar.): 711–48.

Index

Abila, Gregorio, 90
Acosta, Don Manuel Vicente, 207, 208
Adultery, 140, 210, 254, 271. See also
   Amasias
Afecto, defined, 99
African slaves, 246
Afro-Mexicans. *See* Blacks; Mulattoes
Agata, 68–69
Agriculture: labor sources, 28, 130, 306,
   407–8 (n. 15); *tlacolol*, 68; green revolu-
   tion, 218. *See also* Haciendas; Peasants;
   Rancheros
Aguila, María Guadalupe, 272
Aguilar, José María, 255
Alberro, Solange, 109
Albures, 155; defined, 174, 414–15 (n. 41)
Alcahueta, defined, 104
Alcahuete, 175
Alcaldes, 253, 268, 269; defined, 100, 252
Alcaldes mayores, 189, 190, 191; defined, 31
Alcohol use, 267; and violence, 50–51,
   173–74, 349
Alles, María Nicolasa, 165
Alteptel, 196; defined, 195
Ama de casa, defined, 261
Amasias, 86, 95, 170; defined, 82; marital
   conflicts over, 82, 133–34, 318; contested
   gender rights and obligations, 87–91, 96,
   97, 121, 127; violence against, 88–89; legal
   vulnerability, 101; compared to prosti-
   tutes, 261–62
Ana Salinas, 122–23
Anastacio José, 133
Andrea Antonia, 104, 108
Andrea María, 82, 104–5
Andrés Antonio, 98–99, 192, 193–94
Anenecuilco, 287, 390–91 (n. 50)
Angela Galicia, Doña, 237–38
Angela María (of Totolapa), 133
Angela María (of Xoxocotla) 140, 410
   (n. 37)
Annales school, 218
Antequera, 29, 31
Anthropology, 310
Antonia Magdalena, 238, 424 (n. 15)
Antonio de la Cruz, 185–86

Antonio Flores, 238
Antonio Sosa, 81, 186
Aparicio Antonio, 155, 175
Aristotle, 8
Arrom, Silvia, 262
Ascarte, Don Miguel, 164
Atlacahualoya, 144–47
Atole, defined, 122
Audiencia, defined, 89
Augustina María, 137–38, 140
Augustín Mariano, 102–3, 116, 117, 211
Augustín Santiago, 246
Ayala, Don Francisco de, 242, 390–91
   (n. 50)

Baltasar, 229–30
Barrera, Doña Guadalupe, 262
Barreto, José Silverio, 212, 289, 420 (n. 52)
Bartolomé Baptista, 108
Bartra, Roger, 152, 343
Bautista, José Tomás, 273
Bautista, Onofre, 151–52, 187–88
Beauvoir, Simone de, 220
Behar, Ruth, 109
Benita Rodríguez, Florentina Josefa, 272
Berrospe, Francisca, 282
Bilbao, Guillermo, 164–65, 169
Black Legend, 12
Blacks, 28; stereotyping of, 213, 289, 290,
   415 (n. 52)
Borges, Jorge Luís, 311
"Boston question," 315–16
Bourdieu, Pierre, 118
Brideprice, 207, 234
Brujas, 243; defined, 239
Bucareli, Viceroy, 208
Bullfighting, 172, 414 (n. 36)
Buñuel, Luis, 151, 153, 155, 174, 187, 411 (n. 1)
Burlar, defined, 166
Bustamante, Bachiller Don Juan, 102–3

Cabeceras, 33, 166, 196, 197; defined, 25
Cacicas, 237–38, 239, 243; defined, 34
Cacique, 306, 417 (n. 10); defined, 237
Caciquismo, 324; defined, 194–95
Cadena, Ignacio, 274

Federation of Cuban Women, 298
Feliciana María, 293, 294
Felipe de Santiago, Don, 145, 146
Female alliances, 103–7, 121, 125, 278, 402–3
(n. 49). *See also* Crossover alliances
Female weapons, 98, 110–11; pluralization
of patriarchs, 99–103, 105–6, 107, 125,
209, 278; mobilization of alliances,
103–7, 121, 125, 278, 402–3 (n. 49); magic,
108, 109–10; scandal, 108–9, 142–43, 279
Femininity, 14–15, 16–17, 301–2; archetypes
of, 20–21, 340–42. See also *Amasias*;
Children; Daughters; Daughters-in-law;
Mothers; Mothers-in-law; *Novias*; Par-
ents; Widows; Wives
Feminism, 8–9, 52, 301, 343, 433–34 (n. 21);
of colonial-era women, 80, 312–13, 314;
revolutionary-era first wave, 327; second
wave, 329
Ferrer, Vicente, 141–42
Fiscal, defined, 89
Fiscal de iglesia, defined, 198
Foucault, Michel, 8, 17–18
Fowler-Salamini, Heather, 331
France, 316, 434 (n. 23)
Francisca María, 90
Francisco Alonso, 245
Francisco Doroteo, 88–89, 125
Francisco Gerónimo, 70–72, 75, 77, 319, 399
(n. 1)
Francisco Xavier, 103, 146–47
Franco, Jean, 109, 312
Free market ideology, 324–25
French Intervention, 326
French Revolution, 311
Freud, Sigmund, 55

Gachupines, 127–28; defined, 127
Gamboa, Don Manuel de, 206–7, 208–9,
401 (n. 35)
García, Juan, 140
García del Barrio, Don Francisco, 205
García Márquez, Gabriel, 184, 339, 416
(n. 62); *Chronicle of a Death Foretold*,
184, 185, 187, 416 (n. 62)
Gaspar Melchor, 138, 139, 140, 409 (n. 34),
410 (n. 37)
Gender relations. *See* Crossover alliances;
Domestic violence; Families; Female
alliances; Female weapons; Femininity;
Gender-rooted disputes; Honor/shame

codes; Marriage; Masculinity; Patriarchy; Sex; Sexual assault; "Sexualization" of gender disputes; Violence
Gender-rooted disputes, 52–53; proportion
of violent incidents, 55, 57, 58–59, 67–68,
78, 156, 158–59, 223, 225, 299–300, 355;
cause of violence against women, 57, 58,
59, 66–68, 78; cause of male-male vio-
lence, 58, 59, 156–59, 177–78; regional
comparisons, 222, 223, 224, 225, 226, 227,
240, 287
Gente de razón, 166; defined, 145
Gertrudis, 108
Gil, Don Martín, 165
Gobernadores, 145; defined, 4
Gonzales Reina, Don José, 281–83, 284
Gordon, Linda, 315
Gossip, 107, 143, 144, 147, 148
Grain shortages, 189–90
"Gran Chichimeca," 217
Guadalupe, María Torivia, 71
Guaracha, Nicolás, 207
Guerrero, Don Manuel, 276
Guerrero, Juana, 256–57
Gustinaza, Juan Antonio, 273–74
Gutiérrez, Anastasio Antonio, 212

Hacendados, 22
Hacienda Cuahuixtla, 206
Haciendas: land struggles with villages,
24–25, 31; sugar estates, 24–25, 55, 127–
28; labor migration to, 28; paternalism
of, 305–6
Hacienda San Gaspar, 70
Hacienda Santa Ana Tenango, 144–46, 147
Hacienda Temisco, 406 (n. 6)
Hechicería, defined, 109
Heresy, 109
Herrera, Don Joseph, 293–94
Hija, defined, 393 (n. 6)
Hijos del pueblo, 191, 199, 202, 307; defined,
302
Hilario José, 94
Hipólito Graciano, 133
Hispanic culture. *See* Spanish culture
Home ownership, 35–36
Homicide, 366; proportion of violence
cases, 49–50, 62–63, 226, 291, 422–23
(n. 18); alcohol influence and, 51; socio-
cultural status and, 54, 183, 368; motiva-
tions, 55, 57, 395 (nn. 29, 30); crimes of

Parents, 93–94, 239
Party of the Institutional Revolution (PRI), 325
Pasados, 21, 210; defined, 201
Pasquala María, 103, 108
Pasqual de la Trinidad, 89
Pastrana, Joaquín, 293–94
Patriarchs, pluralization of, 99–103, 105–6, 107, 125, 209, 278
Patriarchy: familial, 6–7, 11–12, 20, 21, 126, 211, 264, 266, 311, 312, 410 (n. 37); right of punishment, 7, 77, 210–11, 294, 302; political, 12, 19, 20–21, 197, 199, 202, 304–5, 306–7, 311, 324–25; gender roles in, 12–13, 19; defined, 21–22, 387 (n. 30); cultural backgrounds, 33, 37; protection of women from violence, 60–61, 62, 63, 65; unattached women's escape from, 65–66, 117–18, 120–22, 131–32, 299; and sexual rights, 78–79; contestation of patriarchal pacts, 97–98, 110–11, 112–14, 177, 253, 269–70, 278, 283–84, 313–14, 321, 322–23; church influence and, 114, 308; "democratic patriarchy," 197–98, 418 (n. 18); vertical male rankings, 198; female complicity in, 301; feminism and, 313; erosion of authority of, 318–19, 330, 331, 333, 336, 340–41, 437 (n. 35); Mexican Revolution and, 330–31
Patrilocal residence, 335, 338
Paz, Juana Simona, 233–34
Paz, Octavio, 153–54, 155; *Labyrinth of Solitude*, 153–54
Peasants, 394 (n. 19); conflicts with haciendas, 22, 25, 28–29, 32, 127; economic conditions, 23, 32, 34, 130, 332; in Morelos, 25, 28, 32, 286–87; agricultural labor, 28, 31, 130, 306, 407–8 (n. 15); in Oaxaca, 31, 32, 33; and gender-rooted violence, 49, 52, 53, 55; political culture, 139, 194–97, 198–99, 236, 302, 303–4; and gossip, 142, 144; and masculine honor and violence, 154, 156, 160, 161, 180–81, 182, 183; social hierarchies among, 166–67; and colonial officials, 191; dependence on women for food, 407 (n. 14)
Pedro Luís, 145, 146–47
Pedro Marcos, 208
Pelados, 281; defined, 154
Peredo, Juan Bautista, 262
Pérez, Don Matías, 146

Physical mobility, 83, 85, 86–87, 92, 232, 235, 239
Piñeda, María Olaya, 279–80
Pizan, Christine de, 312
Plácido, Lucas, 88
Placiencia, Luciana Francisca, 84
Plebeians: economic conditions, 23, 34–36, 252–53, 264–66; institutional repression of, 23, 36, 266, 267–68, 269; popular culture, 35, 36–37, 262–63; employment, 35, 252, 265; Mexico City population, 35, 265; ethnic composition, 35, 394 (n. 19); and gender-rooted violence, 49, 52, 53, 55, 224, 258; and masculine honor and violence, 154, 156, 160, 161, 180–81, 182, 183, 281; contestation of patriarchal pacts, 224, 253, 255, 257–58, 268–70, 275, 276–78; women's employment, 258–62; sexual unions and marriage, 270–75, 302, 429 (n. 34)
Police repression, 267–68
Politics: patriarchalism, 12, 19, 20–21, 197, 199, 202, 304–5, 306–7, 311, 324–25; role of gender culture in, 19–20, 21, 203–4, 209–13, 302–3, 304, 307, 315–16, 323–24; women's role in, 19–20, 197–98, 204–9, 236–38, 239, 303, 325; peasant community structures, 139, 194–97, 198–99, 236, 302, 303–4; and subaltern masculinity, 171–72; supervision by *viejos*, 199–203, 209, 210, 302, 304, 307; corruption in, 325–26, 435 (n. 11); feminism in, 327. *See also* Rebellions
Polygamy, 115; female, 426–27 (n. 13)
Ponciano, Eugenio Esquicio, 72–73, 74, 75–77, 88, 107, 108, 115–16
Porras, María Josefa de, 129
Pregnancy, 274–75
Priests, 128, 130, 234. *See also* Catholic Church
Property/class disputes: provocation of violence, 49, 55, 57–58, 67, 156, 158–59; regional comparisons, 222, 223, 224, 225
Prostitution, 260, 261, 266, 426–27 (n. 13)
Psychology, 120–21
Public/private demarcation, 7–9, 382–83 (n. 15)
Public schools, 326, 328
Pulque, defined, 31
Punishment, 7, 77, 102–3, 162, 210–11, 294, 302

Quevedo, María Antonia, 100
Quitería, Simona, 104, 118, 119

Race: racial subjugation, 15–16; racial
stereotyping, 213; population compo-
sition, 347; "social race," 385 (n. 16).
See also Ethnicity
Rafael Hilario, Don, 72–73
Ramírez, Ana la, 104, 108
Ramírez, Máxima Micaela, 116
Ramos, Joaquina Francisca, 275–76
Ramos, Samuel, 154; *Profile of Man and
Culture in Mexico*, 153
Rancheros, 34, 242, 303; defined, 22
Rape, 165, 166, 230–31, 397 (n. 44), 399
(n. 7), 409 (n. 23), 410 (n. 48). *See also*
Sexual assault
Rapto, 95, 234, 317, 401–2 (n. 38); defined,
94
Raya, defined, 71
Rebellions, 306; women's role in, 205, 208,
237, 279, 303
Redfield, Robert, 195, 287, 303–4
Reforma, 326
Regional diversity, 23–24, 195, 217–21, 278,
285–86, 308–9; violence comparisons,
221–27
Rendón, Guillermo Desiderio, 107
Repartidores de tierras, 145
Repartimiento de mercanías, 128; defined,
31
Respeto, falta de, 182, 198, 212–13; defined,
196
Retrato de Teresa (film), 298–99, 399 (n. 8)
Rico, Don Francisco, 271
Riñas, 155, 162
Rita Desideria, 211
Rivera, Joaquín, 275, 276, 277
Rivera, Josef Timoteo, 122–23
Roa, Gregorio, 81, 186
Rodríguez, Juana, 149
Rodríguez, María Manuela, 107
Rojano, María Gertrudis, 260
Rojas, María Teresa de, 170
Romana, María Guadalupe, 271–72
Romanucci-Ross, Lola, 321
Royal Cigar and Cigarette Factory, 259
Ruíz, Augustín, 185–86, 416 (n. 58)

Salcedo, José, 280
Salvador Antonio, 146

Sandobal, Anastasio, 256–57
San Luís Potosí, 195, 303
Santa María, Don Nicolás de, 192, 193
Santo Tomás Miacatlán, 199–200
Scandal, 108–9, 142–43, 279
Semillero, defined, 192
Serna, José Eusebio, 175
Sewing machine technology, 334
Sex: honor/shame complex and, 14–15;
extramarital unions, 75–76, 82, 140, 270–
75; sexual possession, 76, 78–79, 84; con-
flicts over, leading to violence, 76–77,
78–82, 84–85, 223, 240, 277–78, 360
Sexual assault, 49–50, 63, 79, 164–65, 241,
397 (n. 44). *See also* Rape
"Sexualization" of gender disputes, 277–78
Simpson, Lesley Byrd: *Many Mexicos*, 217
Siqueiros, David Alfaro, 153
Smallpox epidemic (1762), 189
Social history movement, 8, 217–18
"Social race," 385 (n. 16)
Soldadera, 342–43; defined, 327
Soltera, 118, 122; defined, 90
Sons, 91–92, 210, 211, 322
Soplón, 144; defined, 143
Spanish colonialism: economic system,
22–23, 31, 128; in explanation of mascu-
line violence, 154; political organization,
196–97; criminal proceedings, 382 (n. 7);
rape law, 409 (n. 23)
Spanish culture: honor/shame complex,
18, 34, 301, 302; patriarchalism in, 33, 34;
regional variations, 37, 195; interaction
with Indian cultures, 115, 213, 241–42,
243
Suárez, María Guadalupe, 255–56
Subdelegados, defined, 31
Sugar haciendas, 24–25, 55, 127–28
Sujeto villages, 28, 33, 196, 197; defined, 25

Tapia, María Antonia de, 79, 90–91
Tapia, Micaela, 279
Tapia, Pablo, 260
Taylor, William B., 205, 306
Temascales, defined, 263
Teozacoalco Valley, 294
Tepeatlaco, Paulino Antonio, 163
Tepoxpisca, María, 207
Tepoztlán: Lewis study of, 45–46, 303–4;
political power struggles, 169, 201–2;
women-led revolt in, 206–9; Redfield

The historical arguments and conceptual sweep of Stern's book will inform not only students of Mexico and Latin America but also students of gender in the West and other world regions. Stern's interpretation both undermines and transcends previous perceptions of a single Latin American gender culture, including the notions of male rage and female complicity.

Jeff Miller

STEVE J. STERN is professor of

history and director of the Latin American and Iberian studies program at the University of Wisconsin–Madison. His books include *Peru's Indian Peoples and the Challenge of Spanish Conquest: Huamanga to 1640* and *Resistance, Rebellion, and Consciousness in the Andean Peasant World, 18th to 20th Centuries.*

THE UNIVERSITY OF NORTH CAROLINA PRESS

Post Office Box 2288
Chapel Hill, NC 27515-2288